MAGNETO-OPTICAL RECORDING MATERIALS

IEEE Press
445 Hoes Lane, P.O. Box 1331
Piscataway, NJ 08855-1331

Books of Related Interest from the IEEE Press . . .

FERROMAGNETISM, An IEEE Classic Reissue
Richard M. Bozorth
1994   Hardcover   992 pp   IEEE Order No. PC3814   ISBN 0-7803-1032-2

MAGNETIC RECORDING TECHNOLOGY, Second Edition
C. Denis Mee and Eric D. Daniel
1996   Hardcover   750 pp   IEEE Order No. PC5659   ISBN 0-07-041276-6

MAGNETIC STORAGE HANDBOOK, Second Edition
C. Denis Mee and Eric D. Daniel
1996   Hardcover   752 pp   IEEE Order No. PC5688   ISBN 0-07-041275-8

MAGNETIC RECORDING: The First 100 Years
Edited by Eric D. Daniel, C. Denis Mee, and Mark H. Clark
1999   Softcover   360 pp   IEEE Order No. PP5396   ISBN 0-7803-4709-9

MAGNETO-OPTICAL RECORDING MATERIALS

Edited by

Richard J. Gambino
State University of New York at Stony Brook

Takao Suzuki
Toyota Technological Institute, Nagoya, Japan

IEEE Magnetics Society, *Sponsor*

IEEE
PRESS

The Institute of Electrical and Electronics Engineers, Inc., New York

This book and other books may be purchased at a discount
from the publisher when ordered in bulk quantities. Contact:

IEEE Press Marketing
Attn: Special Sales
Piscataway, NJ 08855-1331
Fax: (732) 981-9334

For more information about IEEE Press products, visit the
IEEE Press Home Page: http://www.ieee.org/organizations/pubs/press

Printed in the United States of America

10   9   8   7   6   5   4   3   2   1

ISBN 0-7803-1009-8
IEEE Order Number: PC3582

Library of Congress Cataloging-in-Publication Data

Magneto-optical recording materials / edited by Richard J. Gambino,
  Takao Suzuki.
       p.   cm.
    Includes bibliographical references.
    ISBN 0-7803-1009-8
    1. Computer storage devices—Materials.   2. Magnetooptical
devices—Materials.   3. Thin films, Multilayered.   I. Gambino,
Richard J., 1935–   . II. Suzuki, T. (Takao)
  TK7895.M4M34   1999
  621.39'76—dc21   99-27335
                                                           CIP

CONTENTS

Chapter 3   New MO Recording Media Based on Pt/Co and Pd/Co Multilayers and Pt-Co Alloys   58
Peter F. Carcia, Takao Suzuki

Chapter 4   Garnet Media   105
Takao Suzuki

Chapter 6   Domain Dynamics and Recording Physics in Magneto-Optical Recording Media   194
Dieter Mergel

Chapter 9   Magnetically Induced Superresolution   350
Masahiko Kaneko

PREFACE

Digital data storage is one of the most rapidly evolving fields of technology. It is also extremely broad in scope. We have endeavored to narrowly focus this book on magneto-optical storage technology. We have further placed an emphasis on materials for magneto-optical storage media materials defined broadly to include multilayered thin films, exchange coupled layers, practical materials used in current products, and materials of possible interest but of no present practical application. The physics of magneto-optical recording has been included because an understanding of this subject is essential to make intelligent use of the materials properties discussed in other chapters. Similarly, the design and construction of magneto-optical disk storage systems have been discussed in sufficient depth that materials issues are clearly defined.

The subject matter of this book has not been addressed in any previous text. Certainly magnetic recording in a broader scope has been covered by several excellent volumes. The works of Mee and Daniel are widely read in this field. There are also excellent texts on the physic of magneto-optical recording and on the physic of magneto-optical phenomena. The emphasis of our book on magneto-optical materials fills a need, and significantly augments the existing literature.

The book is a reference book, which can also be used as a textbook for a graduate level course or for a short course for professionals in the field of magnetic recording. We assume the reader has an undergraduate level education in engineering or physical science. The book is thus intended for working engineers and scientists in the digital data storage field as well as graduate students and advanced undergraduates. Students will benefit most from the early chapters, and specialists in the field may be more interested in the later chapters.

The field of magneto-optical data storage is very dynamic so it is difficult to project into the future. Various techniques including magnetically induced superresolution (MSR) and magnetic field modulation techniques have been successfully applied to magneto-optical recording to achieve high density. At the same time, optical storage seems to be moving toward the DVD format because of its large volumetric density. Although the materials of choice for DVD media are currently phase change type compounds, there has been much activity in industry on the use of magneto-optical recording materials for this application, because MSR and MFM can be successfully applied in this case. At the same time, there is interest in the magnetic recording field in thermally assisted magnetic recording to achieve higher density using very high coercivity media with conventional recording head materials such as Permalloy. Therefore, some aspects of magneto-optical recording may find their way into magnetic hard disk technology. Hence, this book should be of value to workers in magnetic recording technology, in general.

Professor Richard J. Gambino, State University of New York at Stony Brook
Professor Takao Suzuki, Toyota Technological Institute

ACKNOWLEDGMENTS

This book required the cooperation of many people all over the world. We want to thank all the authors who contributed to this work. We especially want to thank Mrs. Trees Ackermann for her able editorial assistance. Her help was essential for the successful completion of this project. We also thank Ms. Linda Matarazzo of the IEEE Press for her guidance. Lastly, we wish to thank our families for their patience and forbearance while this book was being written and edited.

Professor Richard J. Gambino, State University of New York at Stony Brook
Professor Takao Suzuki, Toyota Technological Institute

LIST OF CONTRIBUTORS

Masanori Abe
Tokyo Institute of Technology
Department of Physical Electronics
2-12-1 Ookayama, Meguro-ku
Tokyo 152, Japan

Peter F. Carcia
DuPont Central Research and
Development
Experimental Station
P.O. Box 80356
Wilmington, Delaware 19880-0356 USA

Richard J. Gambino
State University of New York
at Stony Brook
Laboratory of Magnetic-Optic Materials
Materials Science and Engineering
Stony Brook, New York 11794-2275 USA

S. Igarashi
Sony Corporation
Data Media Department
Recording Media and Energy Company
3-4-1, Sakuragi, Tagajo
Miyagi 985, Japan

Masahilo Kaneko
Sony Corporation
Corporate Research Laboratories
6-7-35 Kitashinagawa, Shinagawaku
Tokyo 141, Japan

Dieter Mergel
Universität GH Essen
Fachbereich 7, Physik
AG Dünnschichttechnologie
D-45117 Essen, Germany

Y. Nakane
Sony Corporation
Data Media Department
Recording Media and Energy Company
3-4-1, Sakuragi, Tagajo
Miyagi 985, Japan

Jun Saito
Nikon Corporation
New Business Development Department
1-6-3, Nishi-Ohi, Shinagawa
Tokyo 140, Japan

James C. Suits
Los Gatos Computing
16130 Kennedy Road
Los Gatos, CA 95032

Takao Suzuki
Toyota Technological Institute
Information Storage
Materials Laboratory
2-12-1 Hisakata, Tenpaku-ku
Nagoya, 468-8511, Japan

Shigeru Tsunashima
Nagoya University
Department of Electronics
Furo-Cyo, Chikusu-ku
Nagoya 464-01, Japan

H. Yoshimura
Sony Corporation
Data Media Department
Recording Media and Energy Company
3-4-1, Sakuragi, Tagajo
Miyagi 985, Japan

INTRODUCTION

Takao Suzuki

1.1 INTRODUCTION

Today, electronic information is pervasive: text, digital audio and video, graphics, telecommunication and so on, and various information-storage technologies have been developed in the past decade. Among them, optical storage is rather a newcomer, though its unique features and advantages in the storage industry have been known for a long time. With significant developments in the laser and semiconductor industries, optical storage technology has already successfully emerged into the consumer market and more recently into the computer-based data storage market as well.

The 120 mm, prerecorded compact disc (CD), having the standard format specified in the Red Book[1] and the rewritable $5\frac{1}{4}''$ and $3.5''$ size magneto-optical (M-O) technologies are noteworthy. While it took more than seven years for the CD market to take off, it is now a very prosperous industry, with over 500 million disks produced in 1996 vs. 200 million in 1993. For computer-based data storage and multifunctional purposes, the first generation of the ISO[2] standard $5\frac{1}{4}''$ M-O drive (325 MB × 2/ double-sided) was introduced in 1988 and the $3.5''$ drive (128 MB) in 1991. Since then, progress has been remarkable in capacity and data transfer rate as well as cost performance, and the so-called 2X (650 MB × $2/5\frac{1}{4}''$ double-sided disk) and 3X (1 GB × $2/5\frac{1}{4}''$ double-sided disk) drives are now in the market. Also, a remarkable product called the MiniDisc ($2.5''$), which was the first recordable optical system for both the consumer and the data market, has made a breakthrough in the technology utilizing data compression and direct overwrite schemes. Furthermore, archival storage has become, for legal reasons, a more necessary requirement of various financial, medical, and telecommunication industries as well as government agencies, where terabytes of storage (10^{12} bytes) are not atypical. In this application area, various types of write-once/read-many (WORM) optical libraries have been developed, where their permanent form of storage is being well accepted in the marketplace.

Many types of optical storage media have been intensively studied for various applications. Figure 1.1 illustrates some examples. Except for the magneto-optical recording medium, the optical contrast (signal) results from the reflectivity difference between the written and unwritten marks. For magneto-optical recording media, a

---

[1]The physical standards for CD Audio were originally published in a red binder and have become known as the Red Book. Subsequent standards have been called the Yellow Book for CD-Read-only Memory (CD-ROM), the Green Book, Orange Book, etc. (see Table 1.1, and also Chapt. 11).

[2]ISO stands for International Standards Organization. The file format for the CD-ROM is defined in Standard ISO 9660.

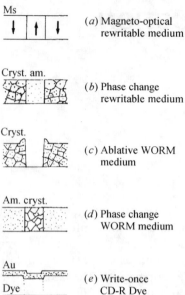

Figure 1.1 Various types of optical media: (*a*) and (*b*) are rewritable media, (*c*) through (*e*) are the writable media.

change in polarization direction due to the magnetization direction is the source of the contrast.

Key features of optical storage technology are removability and high capacity on a disk. The removability is important because it allows access to multifunctional applications with compatibility from drive to drive. It also allows us to transport huge amounts of information by hand. For example, one can carry the information equivalent to a 40,000-page document (2 ft high) in an optical 5¼ ″ disk. Capacity is important because it translates to low cost/MB and to space-efficient storage. The latter is important especially for places such as Japan where land/office prices are anomalously high. Consider, for instance, an insurance company that desperately needs to rid itself of paper claim forms—but needs access to customers' records instantly. Scanning these original documents and storing them on magnetic hard disk drives would be too costly, while tape systems would not have enough speed to randomly retrieve hundreds of thousands of images in a timely manner. Optical storage provides the best solution for this dilemma. Figure 1.2 shows the progress of optical disk storage technology under 12″ size. The increase in capacity is more than 50% per year in the past six years.

While optical storage is an attractive storage technology, magnetic hard disk recording is the dominant technology for information storage. Its growth rate in density has been almost 30% per year for the past 40 years. In the past couple of years, the increase is close to 60% and is expected to continue on the increased capacity rate well into the foreseeable future. Driven by such an ongoing increase in storage densities of magnetic recording, and confronted by upcoming multimedia applications which demand more user data capacity, substantial efforts have been focused on the improvement of storage density (and data transfer rate) in optical storage systems as well.

By no means is the solution for increasing the capacity simple since such an increase must be decided by such factors as backward compatibility. This feature is important to removable media because the customer expects new products to be com-

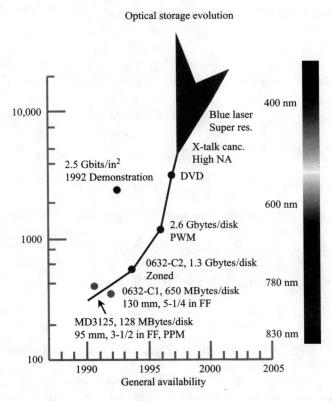

Figure 1.2 Evolution of optical storage technology. The acronyms are explained in the text.

patible with their previous investments in data stored on older generation media. Another key factor is cost. The sale price ($/MB) must be significantly lower compared to other prior generations of optical storage products and alternative storage systems (e.g., removable hard disk drives).

To increase the capacity in optical storage media, many solutions are possible:

Shorter wavelengths [1],

$$1.5(670\,\text{nm}) \sim 3.8\text{X}(428\,\text{nm})$$

Magnetically induced super resolution (MSR) [2, 3] (see Chapter 9)

$$\geq 2\text{X}$$

Pulse width modulation (PWM)

$$1.5 \sim 2\text{X}$$

Volumetric recording [4] (multilayer)

$$\geq 2X$$

Land/groove recording with crosstalk cancellation

$$2X$$

Partial response channels

$$> 1.3$$

Banding of data (zoned)

$$1.5X$$

Higher numerical aperture [5, 6, 7] (high NA)

$$> 1.2$$

High leverage items for improving capacity, apart from creative approaches such as magnetically induced super resolution (MSR), are "short wavelength" and "high NA," which can reduce the diffraction limited spot size.

The use of a shorter wavelength laser for optical recording has already been demonstrated by several groups. Blue wavelength recording with a frequency doubling laser (429 nm) [15] has already been shown to increase the density up to 2.5 Gbit/in^2 with a data rate of a few MB/s [1]. Another example is the work reported using a green laser, which demonstrated a carrier-to-noise ratio (CNR) of 45 dB at 0.4 μm mark size at a track pitch 0.9 μm [8]. For the short wavelength recording, media must exhibit high polar Kerr activity in the magneto-optical case. In the so called phase change, media information is stored by creating amorphous spots in a polycrystalline film by melting and quenching a small region by laser heating. A high reflectivity change between the amorphous and crystalline phases in the phase change is needed for short wavelength recording in the phase change scheme. (The name "phase change" has been commonly used as an erasable optical medium in which the reflectivity change between crystalline and amorphous phases is used as the source for signal. A typical medium is GeTeSb.) In going to a shorter wavelength, on the other hand, the efficiency of the detector becomes degraded and thus an increase of the optical power incident on the detectors is necessary to keep up the same read signal level in order to maintain the same media-noise-limited performance. This requires desensitization of the media, leading to a higher read power or to a higher amount of light reflected by the polarization beam splitter to the detector channel [1]. The increase in writing power speeds up degradation of the medium, thus shortening media lifetime.

One example of using a high NA method was demonstrated using a solid immersion lens (NA = 1.1) optics [6]. A spot size as small as 600 nm was achieved at λ = 830 nm, resulting in a performance of CNR = 50 dB at 1 Mhz with TbFeCo disks. A recent experiment showed a further reduction of a spot size at 830 nm.

The so called volumetric scheme approach is not new; however, it has been proven to be a favorable candidate for high-capacity recording using CD-ROM [4].

Mark-edge recording (PWM) is the scheme already used in some write-once optical and 3X magneto-optical recording drives [9]. Since the information can be stored at the edge of a written mark, the density can be nearly doubled as compared to conventional pit position recording (PPM). However, the issue with this approach is to precisely place the edge of written marks, regardless of variations in writing conditions, without causing high jitter in readout signal. In addition, the mark edge has to be extremely stable after writing and with extensive reads as this contributes to the jitter (= noise) as well. Causes for such a shift may come from the nonuniformity in thermal magnetic and optical properties. Furthermore, the repetition of read/write processes may lead to additional edge shift, the physical scale of which is as small as 100 Å. For determining the disk structure for green/blue recording in conjunction with PWM recording, such issues become serious.

For high-density recording, the choice of substrates is also important. Birefringence plays a role in the focusing servo [20], which is of critical importance when a track pitch becomes smaller. The land/groove shape[3] (depth, width, smoothness) influences noise and crosstalk levels. Without addressing these substrate issues, one cannot consider achieving high-capacity optical storage media. It is a critical consideration in the performance of an optical disk.

1.2 REWRITABLE OPTICAL RECORDING MEDIA

In this section, magneto-optical and phase-change recording media, which are most commonly used in the currently available drives, are discussed.

1.2.1 Magneto-Optical Recording Media

The magneto-optical recording media used in the "ISO standard 1X" and 2X are amorphous REFeCo films (RE = Tb, Gd, and Dy). These media exhibit high perpendicular magnetic anisotropy ($> 10^6$ erg/cc), high hysteresis loop squareness and high coercivity, in addition to a relatively low Curie point (250 $\sim$ 300°C). The amorphous rare earth transition metal alloys are ferrimagnets so some compositions show compensation points where the net magnetization is zero because of cancellation of the rare earth and transition metal magnetization. Also, the compensation point can be adjusted by the amounts of RE as well as Fe and Co, thus leading to various dependences of saturation magnetization [42] (Fig. 1.3). While the polar Kerr activity of these REFeCo films is relatively low (0.3°) at 780 $\sim$ 830 nm (wavelength of lasers used in most of the current drives), compared to other crystalline materials, these amorphous films have been accepted as the most suitable storage media. Figure 1.4 and Table 1.1 and Table 1.2 illustrate the evolution of the media for 1X, 2X, and 3X [10, 42]. Since the first ISO MO drive came to the market in 1988, the capacity has tripled in six years with 4X capacities expected in 1997. The advantage of using such amorphous materials may be summarized as follows:

[3]In a magneto-optical disk, tracks are defined by pregrooves. The region between neighboring grooves is the so-called land. Data may be written either in the grooves or on the land, or on both.

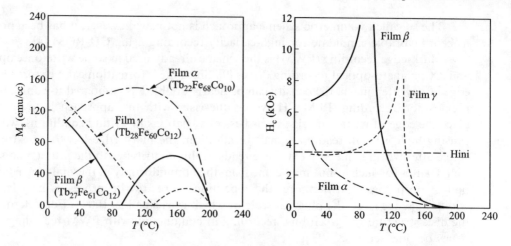

Figure 1.3 Temperature dependences of magnetic properties of so-called 1X (film α), 2X (film β) and 3X (film γ) media [9], [10], [42].

TABLE 1.1   Evolution of Optical Storage Industry ($5''$ and $5\frac{1}{4}''$ disks)

Name	Year	Described Format	Standard
Compact disc	1982	Compact disc digital audio	Red book IEC-908
CD-ROM	1986	Compact disc read-only memory	Yellow Book ISO 10149
130 mm MO	1988	$5\frac{1}{4}''$ Rewritable MO disc	ISO/IEC 10089
CD-R	1989	Compact disc write once	Orange Book
MiniDisc	1990	$2.5''$ MiniDisc system	Rainbow Book
130 mm PC	1990	$5\frac{1}{4}''$ IGB rewritable phase-change drive	
90 mm MO	1991	$3.5''$ Rewritable MO disk	ISO/IEC 10090
130 mm MO	1991	$5\frac{1}{4}''$ 1.3 GB MO (2X)	
130 mm PC	1993	$5\frac{1}{4}''$ 1.5 GB rewritable/1.4 GB WORM phase-change drive	
130 mm MO (3X)	1994	$5\frac{1}{4}''$ rewritable MO	

TABLE 1.2   130-mm ISO-MO vs. 120-mm CD

	ISO/IEC 10089 1X (1988)	ISO/IEC 13549 2X (1991)	ISO DIS 13841 3X (1994)	Red Book 1984
Capacity (double-sided)	2×325 MB	2×650 MB	2×1 GB	650 MB
Data density (MByte/cm^2)	4	8	12	8
Wavelength (mm)	780	780	780	780
Track pitch (μm)	1.6	1.39	1.34	1.8
Compatibility		backwards	backwards	backwards

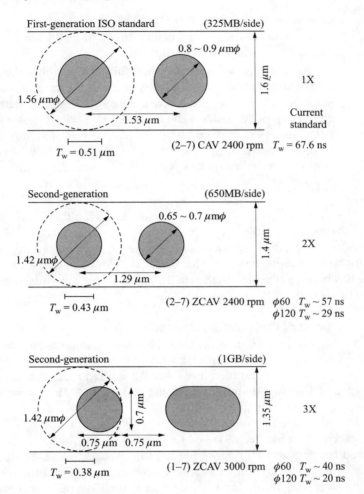

Figure 1.4 Description of the first generation (1X) and second generation (2X and 3X) MO media [42]. The track pitch is indicated by the distance between the parallel lines. The method of rotation and rate of rotation rpm are also shown. The constant angular velocity (CAV) or zoned (ZCAV) methods are used for MO disks as opposed to the constant linear velocity (CLV) used for CD-Audio. The transition width, T_w, is given both in μm and in ns for a given rate of revolution and track diameter in mm.

1. Because of the amorphous state where no crystalline grains are present, and since the material can be considered uniform on a scale of about 100 Å or so, media-noise and write-noise resulting from both magnetically and optically inhomogeneous local regions are very small (less than a few dB). On the other hand, crystalline films were found to exhibit higher media- and write noise (close to 10 dBm or more) due to grain to grain variations in reflectivity and other defects [11].

2. Because of the ferrimagnetic nature where two sublattices are present, the magnetic properties, such as magnetization, anisotropy, coercivity, can be almost continuously varied by changing the atomic fraction of rare earth

element (R = Tb, Gd, and Dy). This is an important characteristic used in tuning the recording performance to writing and reading conditions, which cannot be matched by crystalline films.

3. The significant development in film fabrication technologies has made it possible to control film quality for materials of choice. The advantage inherent in amorphous REFeCo film fabrication by sputtering is that films of large area can be deposited under well-controlled conditions, leading to high yield and better cost performance. Also, noteworthy is that no annealing after film deposition nor heating of substrates during deposition is required. In contrast, all of the crystalline materials considered as media require substrate heating or annealing.

The disadvantage, on the other hand, is associated with the potential structural instability of the metastable state of the amorphous phase. Also, because of the strong chemical activity of rare-earth elements, there is always a concern regarding corrosion. However, various types of protective layers have been developed so that media life greater than 50 years has been assured for the current magneto-optical storage media supplied to the market.

(a) Shorter Wavelength Approach

As long as a laser beam is the means for writing and reading, the spot size on a disk is the decisive factor for determining storage capacity. The diffraction limited spot size is given by $0.56\lambda/NA$, and therefore a smaller written mark can be obtained by increasing NA and by using a shorter wavelength. In this section, we discuss the approach toward shorter wavelength recording.

After the introduction of low power visible laser diodes (670 nm) to the market in 1988, much effort has been focused on laser technology achieving higher power, longer life, and better cost performance needed for optical storage. To achieve shorter wavelengths, frequency doubling lasers have been pursued. One promising approach uses a non-linear crystal resonator ($KNbO_3$) with high overall conversion efficiency from electrical input to the diode laser to blue output (10%) [15] for developing more than 40 mW of 428 nm radiation (Fig. 1.5).

The magnetic-optical (MO) readout signal is proportional to the effective polar Kerr rotation angle θ_{eff} and is given by

$$\theta_{eff} = (\theta_K^2 + \varepsilon_K^2)^{1/2} \tag{1.1}$$

where θ_K and ε_K are the polar Kerr angle and ellipticity, respectively. Therefore, it is desirable to have a high rotation angle θ_{eff} and a high reflectivity R at shorter wavelengths. However, as demonstrated in Figure 1.6, the current RFeCo media exhibit a decrease of the polar Kerr activity with decreasing wavelength from 780 to 500 nm [16]. The addition of light rare earth elements such as Nd and Pr has been reported to enhance the Kerr activity at wavelengths around 500 nm [12], [13], but this is accompanied by a degradation of the magnetic properties such as coercivity and perpendicular magnetic anisotropy field [14]. Nevertheless, much effort has been made to optimize the disk structure of TbFeCo at a short wavelength, and recent work has reported high mark carrier-to-noise ratio (CNR) more than 62 dB at 488 nm on a flat substrate [17].

(a)

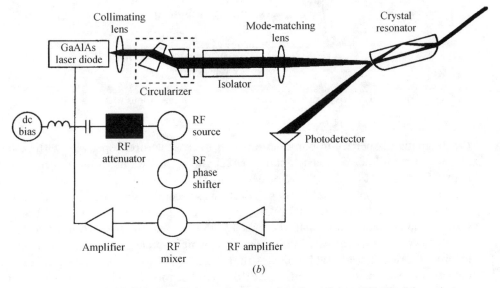

(b)

Figure 1.5 (a) Blue laser using a frequency doubling scheme [15]. (b) Schematic description of frequency doubling laser.

Beside REFeCo media, there are several other candidates, namely, multilayers of cobalt and platinum (denoted as (Co/Pt)) [18], [19], [21], rare earth-iron garnets such as $(BiDy)_3(FeGa)_5O_{12}$ [11] and manganese bismuth MnBi [25], [26].

Multilayers of (Co/Pt) $\times$ N (N: layer numbers) are of considerable interest. They exhibit strong perpendicular magnetic anisotropy ($> 10^6$ erg/cc), high coercivity (> 1 kOe) and most importantly high Kerr rotation and ellipticity at blue wavelengths (Fig. 1.6). Typical thicknesses of Co and Pt are $3 \sim 5$ Å and $8 \sim 12$ Å, respectively and N is in the range of 10 to 30. Voluminous research had been performed to understand

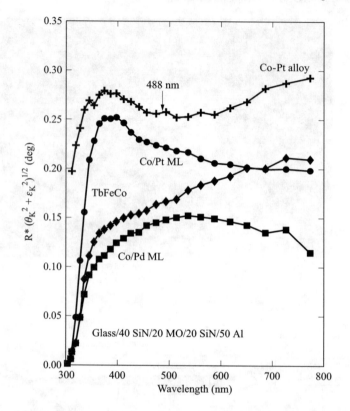

Figure 1.6 Kerr signal as a function of wavelength for various MO materials [16].

the magnetic properties in conjunction with microstructure, especially with respect to interfacial properties between each layer [22] and to relate this to the recording performance [16], [17], [19], [27]. CNR of 64dB at 488 nm for a large mark size in a (Co/Pt) multilayer made onto a flat glass substrate was recently reported [16]. One drawback with this system, however, is its relatively high Curie point ($\approx 400°C$) and thus a high saturation magnetization which requires a high bias field to write. High Curie temperatures also require a high-writing laser power, which accelerates the degradation of the medium. A recent study [66] indicates that the degradation takes place near or at local defects under accelerated conditions. Effort had been made to lower the Curie point by adding other elements [23], [24].

Another potential candidate is bismuth (Bi) substituted garnet films. Figure 1.7 shows the expected signal as a function of wavelength for garnet (thickness d), together with (Co/Pt) and TbFeCo [28]. The expected MO signal is far larger than those of (Co/Pt) and TbFeCo at blue wavelengths. One serious disadvantage is that grains and other defects are the source of high media-and write noise in the readout signal.

In an attempt to minimize such noise, intensive effort has been made to optimize the crystallization condition from the (as-deposited) amorphous state. The work utilizing the in-situ crystallization showed CNR of 58 dB at 488 nm for a large mark size onto a grooved $Gd_3Ga_5O_{12}$ (GGG) disk [11]. Another approach to minimize grain size is rapid thermal annealing with a high ramp rate ($100°C/s$ up to $650°C$) [29]. This

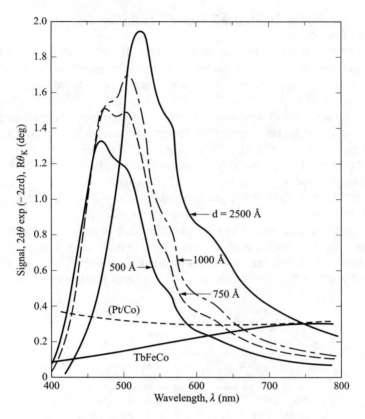

Figure 1.7 Readout signal for garnet film with thickness d, together with (Co/Pt) and TbFeCo [28].

technique yields a grain size of about 100 Å, much smaller than those obtained through oven annealing or in-situ crystallization.

The drawback with Bi-garnet is the necessity of high temperature crystallization ($\cong 650°C$). This limits the choice of substrate materials, which may prevent the manufacture of low-cost media.

Other crystalline materials such as MnBi [25], [26] and PtMnSb [30] have been the subject of many studies. MnBi was the first material that demonstrated Curie point writing [37]. MnBi is known to possess two phases, the low temperature (ltp) and the high temperature (htp) phases. The ltp has a higher Kerr rotation than the htp. Its Curie temperature, however, is close to the temperature at which decomposition takes place, resulting in a relatively small latitude for the recording power. The htp is formed on rapid quenching from a temperature above 630 K. The reduced Curie point results in improved write sensitivity for the htp at the expense of read signal. Further, this htp is unstable to thermal cycling during the read/write process and gradually reverts to the ltp. Attempts have been made to stabilize the htp by alloying with Cu, Ti, Rh, Ru, and Al [25], [38]. Though recent work claimed an effect of Al on the phase stability [25], no conclusive evidence was ever produced. So far, the write performance is still not so attractive, largely because of the high media noise arising from the decomposition of the htp to ltp and from grains [26].

(b) Magnetically Induced Super Resolution (MSR) Approach

A written mark with size smaller than the diffraction limit determined by the numerical aperture of the objective lens and the wavelength of the laser cannot be detected in conventional optics. The magnetically induced super resolution (MSR), which was proposed in 1991 [31], [32] and in 1993 [33] is the scheme that makes it possible for such small written marks to be detected by masking a portion inside a spot by cleverly utilizing the temperature distribution due to laser irradiation of the magnetic film. [Fig. 1.8(a) and (b) [31], [32] and Fig. 1.9 [33] for Front Aperture Detection (FAD), Rear Aperture Detection (RAD) and Center Aperture Detection (CAD) methods, respectively.] Also, reported is a new MSR scheme utilizing a magneto-static coupling between the layers [34]. All those approaches successfully demonstrated higher density in recording than in the non-MSR case. The CAD approach, where the readout layer has in-plane magnetization at room temperature and then becomes vertically magnetized at a higher temperature achieved by a certain read power, seems to have good potentiality. This scheme has a simple disk structure where no external magnet is required and has high crosstalk cancellation ($\cong -30$dB at 0.765 µm) [33]. Using mag-

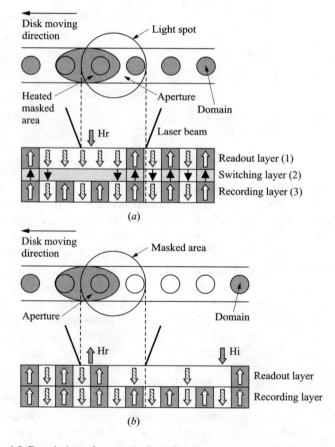

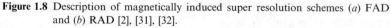

Figure 1.8 Description of magnetically induced super resolution schemes (a) FAD and (b) RAD [2], [31], [32].

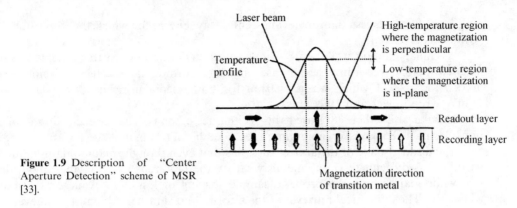

Figure 1.9 Description of "Center Aperture Detection" scheme of MSR [33].

netic field modulation, 2.2 Gbit/in^2 at 680 nm, 0.6 μm mark length was demonstrated with this scheme [35]. Also, recent work [36] using both MSR [double aperture detection (DAD)] and land/groove recording $\lambda = 680$ nm and with 0.6 μm track pitch, demonstrated a similar density.

(c) Direct Overwrite (DOW) [39]

Direct overwrite (DOW) is another crucial issue for optical storage. It is crucial for a high data transfer rate. Direct over-write in magneto-optical recording can be accomplished by either field modulation [40] or light intensity modulation [41]. For a phase-change rewritable medium, single beam over-write is possible, as discussed later. Until now, only field modulation MO systems, such as employed on MiniDisc or MD-data have been introduced into products although media DOW solutions appear promising. The combination of field modulation with MSR and PWM has been proposed [42] using a high field-sensitive MO-medium [43], which can in principle lead to 10X capacity at blue recording with high numerical aperture optics.

(d) Solid Immersion Lens Near Field Optical Approach

In optical recording, the areal density is by any means governed by the size of the focused laser spot, which is limited by the laws of diffraction to be about $\lambda/2$ NA, where λ is the wavelength of laser and NA the numerical aperture of the focusing lens. Since a typical value of NA is 0.5 for actual devices, the diffraction limited spot size would be determined by the wavelength λ. However, this limit can be circumvented by using near-field optical techniques. Near-field optics is based on the idea to image through a pinhole that is smaller than the diffraction-limited spot size. If the pinhole is placed very close to the object, the pinhole size essentially determines the definition of the spot size. The first demonstration of this idea was made in 1984 by Pohl et al. [85] using an extremely narrow aperture of a quartz rod covered by metal film and a resolving power of $\lambda/20$ was achieved. Betzig et al. [86] also demonstrated the high potentiality of obtaining a smaller spot size than the diffraction limited one through near-field optics. They observed the domain written marks down to about 60 nm in Co/Pt multilayer films using Ar laser ($\lambda = 510$ nm for writing), close to $\lambda/9$. They used an optical fiber probe which was covered with a film. The distance between the tip of the fiber and the multilayer film was less than the evanescent decay length, for which the resolution 30–50 nm was achieved.

A similar method was used by Imura et al. [87] who applied this scheme to both magneto-optical recording and phase change recording media. They could record marks, the size of which was 60–80 nm for both media using a 785 nm laser with 15 mW write power and 10 μs pulse width.

Hosaka and others [88] used this technique for phase change recording applications. Using a 785 nm laser, a minimum recorded bit of 60 nm in diameter was achieved.

The disadvantage of the above work was that even though small domains could be written, it is difficult to simultaneously satisfy the requirement of having a high data rate while maintaining the probe-to-sample spacing of less than evanescent distance which is λ. The dynamical retrieval of the information is rather difficult to achieve, that is, the data rate may not be high enough for real applications.

Kino et al. [89], [90] showed a different method in near-field optics using a solid immersion lens (SIL). The principle of the solid immersion lens near-field optics is that by focusing light inside a high index of refraction lens, where the speed of light is slower, hence the wavelength is reduced by a factor of n, where n is the refractive index of the lens. The resolution is expected to improve by a factor n. In its near-field mode of operation, this microscope uses the evanescent fields just outside the flat bottom surface of the SIL for near-field imaging in air.

Terris and the coworkers [91], [92] have developed this technique for testing real magneto-optical recording disks at high data rates. They used a supersphere SIL which leads to a spot size smaller by a factor of n^2. Using 830 nm laser beam, a 360 nm optical spot size was obtained at the exit surface of the SIL and is transferred across a small air gap to the surface of a spinning magneto-optical disk, where the sub-wavelength gap between the SIL and the medium surface was maintained at media velocity of 1.25 m/s by incorporating the lens into an air-bearing slider. Reading and writing of data were achieved at a density of 3.8×10^8 bits/cm^2 with a data rate of 3.3×10^6 bits/s. A recent study using magnetic force microscopy showed the density larger than 2×10^9 marks/in^2 at $\lambda = 780$ nm [94]. Different from the disk structure mentioned above, Ichimura et al. [93] proposed an alternative approach to use near-field optics. A SIL of a truncated hemisphere was used, which was placed close to the substrate surface whose refractive index was the same as the SIL. The beam was focused to the bottom of the substrate. In this case, an effective NA is limited to 1, which is a disadvantage. The major advantage with this scheme is that the air gap can be as large as 100 μm if the spherical aberrations are properly taken into account. It follows that the system can be tolerant for dust, as opposed to the method by Terris et al.

A recent announcement of a high-density drive beyond 20 Gbits/in^2 by an industry laboratory indicates the strong interest for this SIL near-field optics application, which could provide potentially advantageous points over hard disk drives as well.

(e) Domain Expansion Technique

A novel technique has been developed, in which a recorded mark whose size is less than the diffraction limit of a given wavelength is expanded only at the time of reading it. This technique, called "domain expansion technique" can be realized in the medium consisting of two layers with different Hc values. A domain with a size less than the diffraction limited size can be read by amplifying the size only at the time of reading. This process can be realized by applying the magnetic field along the direction for expanding the domain in the readout layer. Figure 1.10 illustrates the correlation between the magnetic field applied and the signal. Figure 1.11 shows the domain expansion process for the readout. The signal amplification can be made through domain expansion by applying a magnetic field Hr, the direction of which is to expand the domain in the GdFeCo readout layer. The clock of the alternating magnetic field is synchronized with one two times faster than the recording clock. In Figure 1.11(*a*), there is no domain in the readout layer because the external field (Hs) is applied to shrink the domains in the recording layer. In Figure 1.11(*b*), when the magnetic field becomes zero, the domain (A) in the recording layer makes the copy domain in the readout layer. In Figure 1.11(*c*), the external field (He) in the expanding direction enlarges the domain to a size which is about the same as the diffraction limited one. In this way, the readout signal can be amplified. In Figure 1.11(*d*), the size of the expanded domain in the read-out layer shrinks to the initial size because the external

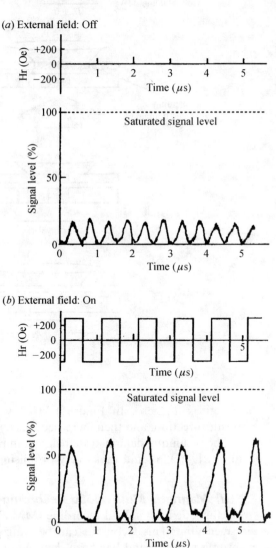

Figure 1.10 (*a*) Readout waveform of 0.3 μm domain without an external field (Hr = 0 Oe). (*b*) Readout waveform of expanded domain with an external field (Hr = ± 260 Oe).

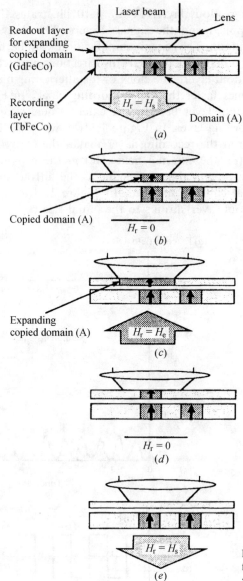

Figure 1.11 The domain expansion processes for the medium having GdFeCo (readout) and TbFe Co (recording).

field returns to zero. In Figure 1.11(e), when the external field is switched to the opposite direction, and then increased, the copied domain will shrink to finally collapse.

The technique demonstrated signal amplification for domains as small as 0.08 μm diameter [94], [95], and looks very promising for future high-density recording.

(f) Magnetic Multivalued Recording

Magnetic multivalued recording (MMV) has been recently proposed for high-density recording. This technique can be realized using a quadri-valued magneto-optical recording medium and has been demonstrated in a system with an exchange coupled

TbFeCo/PtCo bilayer structure. By switching the external field on four levels, four coupled magnetization states are independently formed, as shown in Figure 1.12 [97]. These magnetization states can be distinguished through the differences among their total sum of Kerr rotation angles as output signal levels. The basic performance of the MMV recording has been discussed. For practical use, the recording sensitivity is a serious issue still to be overcome.

1.2.2 Phase-Change Media

Phase-change optical storage technology has been developing at a rapid pace. Already various types of erasable phase-change drives are on the market. They can perform single-beam direct overwrite, and have high read/erase cyclability ($> 10^6$) with low error rate: Furthermore, media life seems no longer to be a serious issue (Fig. 1.13) [51].

The concept of phase-change optical storage is more than 20 years old [44]. Phase-change media have two stable phases. The detection of written marks in optical storage is based on the reflectivity difference between the amorphous and the crystalline phases. The difference must be high enough to give rise to a high contrast, or high signal in reading. Normally, a written spot is amorphous in the matrix of crystalline phase (Fig. 1.14). In order to be amorphous after the laser beam is moved away, the quenching speed must be higher than the so-called critical quenching speed [45] ($> 10^{10}$ C/s). Among many candidates satisfying this condition, GeTe [46], Sb_2Te_3 [47] and compositions along the pseudo-binary GeTe-Sb_2Te_3 tie line such as $Ge_2Sb_2Te_5$, $GeSb_2Te_4$, and $GeSb_4Te_7$ are noteworthy. Another group of materials, which has a lower reflectivity in the crystalline than in the amorphous phase is In_3SbTe_2 [48], compositions along the InSb-GaSb tie line [49], and InSeTl [50]. The criterion to choose fast crystallization media is that the composition is at or near single-phase stoichiometry in the phase diagram. For the current phase-change media, GeTeSb is the medium with demonstrated high performance in optical storage [51]. Figure 1.15 shows an example which is a quadrilayer medium structure, designed for high quenching and for high performance [51].

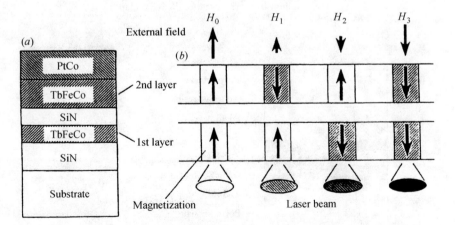

Figure 1.12 External field response of magnetization state on the MMV MO medium [97].

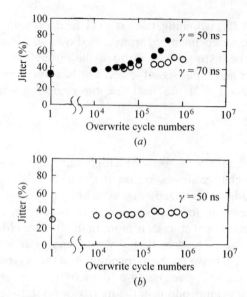

(a)

(b)

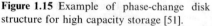

Figure 1.13 Media lifetime test [51]. The signal random (2-7) RLLC. (a) Inner track (6.2 m/s) and (b) outer track (11.3 m/s).

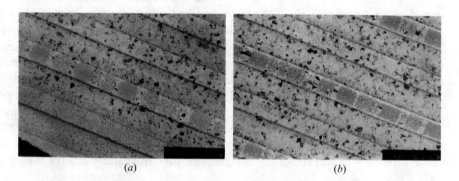

(a)   (b)

Figure 1.14 Written mark in a phase-change GeTeSb medium (a) as-written initial state and (b) after 10^6 read/write cycle times [51]. Notice that even after the 1 million overwrite cycling, the marks still remain.

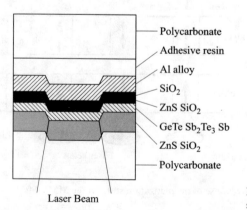

Polycarbonate
Adhesive resin
Al alloy
SiO_2
$ZnS\ SiO_2$
$GeTe\ Sb_2Te_3\ Sb$
$ZnS\ SiO_2$
Polycarbonate

Laser Beam

Figure 1.15 Example of phase-change disk structure for high capacity storage [51].

One of the attractive features of phase change is the capability of direct overwrite using a single-beam scheme, as illustrated in Figure 1.16. There are three power levels of a laser: *write power*, *erase power*, and *read power*. The temperature corresponding to the write power must be high enough to melt the crystalline phase, but for better medium life it should not be too high. The erase power level should be chosen so that the temperature is just high enough to crystallize the amorphous written marks. The read power level should be as low as possible to keep marks from degrading, but must be high enough to give good CNR. Figure 1.14(*b*) shows the erased mark beside an amorphous written mark. The erased mark has undergone 10^6 cycles for PWM recording. There is no sign indicating degradation of the marks as well as of the neighboring regions.

Much work has been done on writing at short wavelengths (680 nm) with high numerical aperture, PWM, direct overwrite, land/groove recording, crosstalk cancellation, modified constant angular velocity method (MCAV), channel/coding, and so on. Recent work, for example, demonstrated 1 GB density per side of a 3.5″ disk, where NA is 0.6, λ is 690 nm, PWM, and ZCAV (zoned constant angular velocity) are essential for digital video application.

Before leaving this section, it should be noted that there has been a growing activity of applying phase-change media for rewritable CD (CD-E) and for small form factor disk drives. Recent work for CD-E using In-Ag-Te-Sb showed high CNR and high modulation at a CD linear speed ($\approx$1 m/s) [82], and a doubling of the CD speed [83]. The application for CD-E is, therefore, very promising. Flat type 2.5″ disk drive (prototype, 15 mm height), which has 160 MB capacity, 1 MB/s data rate, and overwrite capability, has been developed using a phase-change medium [84]. This is a good example to demonstrate the strength of phase-change media where no magnet is necessary for direct overwrite.

1.3 RECORDABLE WRITE-ONCE MEDIA

Storing information in an archival form is required for most legal documents. The amount of documents to be stored has been growing rapidly where terabytes of information is not uncommon. Further, multifunctional applications are favorably accepted

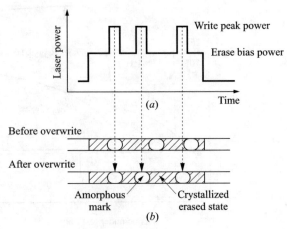

Figure 1.16 Single-beam direct overwrite using three levels of power. (*a*) Laser power levels. (*b*) Written marks before and after DOW.

in today's environment [56] where both rewritable and write-once storage capabilities are required. WORM is the recording scheme where the stored information is retrieved for many times (more than 10^6 times). WORM storage today involves the widest variety of materials and recording mechanisms. The formation of recorded marks in an active layer is generally due to an irreversible thermal response such as the vaporization, deformation, and compositional or structural changes. They may be called: *ablative* [58], *phase change* [75], *alloying* [78~81] and *deformation* [73].

1.3.1 Ablative Type

Materials for ablative type WORM have been widely investigated [58~65]. Among them, Te is ideal since the element has high optical absorption, low melting point, boiling point and low thermal diffusivity. However, Te itself is unstable in air and converts to TeO_2 very quickly. The stability of Te against oxidation can be considerably enhanced by the addition of Se [57]. This is shown in Figure 1.17. Voluminous work on the ablative mechanism [58~65] occurred in the late 70s and early 80s. Since then, there has been much improvement toward the achievement of clean hole openings by small amounts of various additives [64], [65]. The mechanism of hole opening is associated with variations of surface tension over the area irradiated by a laser beam, in that a minimum in surface tension is at the hottest point of the molten spot. A shear stress pulls material away from the center of the melt toward the edge, forming a rim.

Since an ablative mechanism is based on the material flow away from the substrate, Te-alloy active films are usually deposited on underlayers which play a role in improving write sensitivity [62], [64], [65].

The current ablative WORM disks available in the market are 1X and 2X for the 5 ¼ form-factor (PPM), and 7 GB for 12″ size (PWM). One example of written marks in such a 12″ WORM disk is shown in Figure 1.18 [63]. The life of ablative type WORM is very attractive; the claim is more than 100 years in a normal environment, presumably limited by the formation of a physical hole. Because of this uniqueness, this type of media has been well accepted in library files for many applications, including financial and insurance institutions, hospitals, and government agencies. The extendibility of ablative media for higher density recording (PWM) has already been demonstrated [63] and further improvement is likely by optimizing media structure [64].

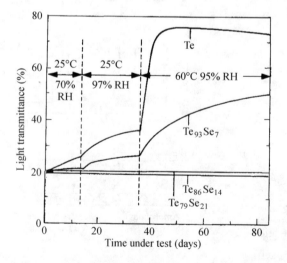

Figure 1.17 Dependence of light transmittance on composition of Te-Se films during life test at the specific condition [57].

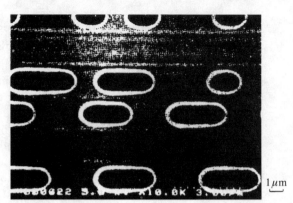

Figure 1.18 SEM image of WORM written marks [63].

1.3.2 Writable CD-R

Dyes for optical recording have been known for years [67], but just recently so-called recordable CD (CD-R) has attracted much attention [68], [69]. This technology possesses great potential for emerging into data storage.

Typical materials for CD-R are the phthalocyanine dyes that have excellent light stability [73]. Figure 1.19(a) illustrates the formula for such a dye used for CD-R [73]. Here the X groups are in the β position and each n is independently selected from 0, 1, and 2 such that at least one of the X groups is selected from the formulas given in Figure 1.19(b).

CD-R disk has the following features [70]:

1. It has a high reflectivity ($\geq 70\%$), a high modulation ($\geq 60\%$), low jitter (< 30 ns for 3T) at 786 nm and thus has compatibility with the current compact disc standard, specified in the Red Book [71].

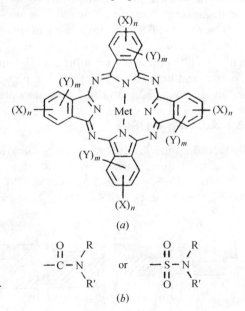

Figure 1.19 Example of chemical formula of CD-dye [73].

2. Written marks are in the groove regions, the reflection of which decreases.
3. The information area of a blank disk has a wobbled pregroove, which is for tracking, and timing purposes.
4. The media cost in volume can be made very low because of spin coat fabrication, as compared to other optical media.

The writing mechanism of CD-R is believed to be a combination of possible deformations (as shown in Fig. 1.20 [69]), namely a bump at the interface between dye and polycarbonate substrate, a pit at the dye/Au interface, and/or a bubble at the dye/Au interface. They are all related to the softening of polycarbonate substrate at 170°C and with a transition of the dye at 265°C.

Current CD-R capacity is 600 MB. Effort is under way to extend the application of such organic dyes to shorter wavelengths [72] for the next generation higher capacity data storage. Since the optical constants of organic dyes are a strong function of wavelength, the type of organic dye may have to be changed from one wavelength to another to optimize the writing condition at each wavelength. Therefore, backward incompatibility is a concern at present.

Another type of CD-R material, AgO_x sputtered film, was also reported [74]. Reflectivity of more than 70% was reported at wavelengths from 760 to 800 nm, and thus it is considered potentially useful.

1.3.3 Phase-Change WORM

The principle of phase-change recording is based on the strong temperature dependence of the crystallization rate. For use as an optical recording medium, a phase-change material needs to have a low rate of crystallization at around room temperature so that the medium can be kept for many years without transforming to the crystalline state. It is also necessary that the rate increase significantly at elevated temperatures so that during the writing process the local region heated by a laser beam can complete the crystallization process in a few nanoseconds.

The alloys of Sb-Sn have been extensively studied for this purpose, and are the materials of choice for phase-change recording. The Sb-Sn alloy media with additives such as In [75] and Se [76] exhibit good writing sensitivity, high CNR, wide wavelength response, and high resolution [77]. The phase-change WORM media have been already used in the 5¼″, 12″, and 14″ product optical disks.

1.3.4 Alloying WORM

The recording mechanism of this type of write-once medium is based on the reflectivity enhancement due to the alloying effect in a local heated region. Examples of alloy WORM are $Sb_2Se_3/Bi_2Te_3/Sb_2Se_3$ [78], [79], [80] and $GeSbTe/BiTe$ [81]. In the writing process, the region heated by a laser beam will undergo alloying, leading to the loss of

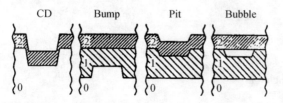

Figure 1.20 Proposed mechanism of writing mechanism in CD-R [69].

the sharp interfaces and in turn giving rise to a different reflectivity. This type of WORM has the advantage of maximizing writing sensitivity and CNR by tuning the medium structure to a given wavelength.

TABLE 1.3 Table of Acronyms

CAD	Center aperture detection
CD	Compact disc
CD-E	Compact disc erasable
CD-ROM	Compact disc read-only memory
CNR	Carrier-to-noise ratio
DAD	Double aperture detection
DOW	Direct overwrite
DVD	Digital versatile disc
FAD	Front aperture detection
GB	Gigabyte
GGG	$Gd_3Ga_5O_{12}$
ISO	International Standard Organization
MB	Megabyte
MCAV	Modified constant angular velocity
MMV	Magnetic multivalued (recording)
MSR	Magnetically induced super resolution
NA	Numerical aperture
PPM	Pit position modulation
PWM	Pulse width modulation
RAD	Rear aperture detection
SIL	Solid immersion lends
WORM	Write-once read-many
ZCAV	Zoned constant angular velocity
1X, 2X, 3X, 4X	1, 2, 3, 4 times the capacity compared with that of the first-generation drive

REFERENCES

[1] J. E. Hurst, Jr and W. J. Kozlovsky, *Japan. J. Appl. Phys.*, vol. 32-11B, p. 5301, 1993.

[2] K. Aratani, A. Fukumoto, M. Ohta, M. Kaneko, and K. Watanabe, *Proceedings of SPIE, 1499 Optical Data Storage Topical Meeting*, p. 209, Colorado Springs, 1991.

[3] Y. Murakami, N. Iketani, J. Nakajima, A. Takahashi, K. Ohta, and T. Ishizuka, *J. Mag. Soc. Japan*, vol. 17-S1, p. 201, 1993.

[4] K. Rubin, H. Rosen, T. Strand, W. Imano, and W. Tang, presented at Optical Data Storage Topical Meeting, WA3-1, Dana Point, CA, 1994.

[5] S. M. Mansfield and G. S. Kino, *Appl. Phys. Lett.*, vol. 57, p. 2615, 1990.

[6] B. D. Terris, H. J. Mamin, and D. Rugar, *Proceedings of Magneto-Optical Recording International Symposium*, 1994, *J. Magn. Soc. Japan*, vol. 19, S1, 409, 1995.

[7] E. Betzig, J. K. Trantman, R. Wolfe, E. M. Gyorgy, P. L. Finn, M. H. Kryder, and C.-H. Chang, *Appl. Phys. Lett.*, vol. 61, p. 142, 1992.

[8] M. Kaneko, Y. Sabi, I. Ichimura, and S. Hashimoto, *IEEE MAG*-29, p. 3766, 1993.

[9] T. Maeda, H. Tsuchinaga, H. Ide, A. Saito, T. Toda, F. Kugiya, M. Ojima, S. Mita, and K. Shigemasu, *Japan J. Appl. Phys.*, vol. 32-11B, p. 5335, 1993; H. Ide, T. Toda, F. Kirino, T.

Maeda, F. Kugiya, S. Mita, and K. Shigematsu, *Japan J. Appl. Phys.* vol. 32-11B, p. 5342, 1993.

[10] J. A. Th. Verhoeven and Q. van Vlimmeren, J. *One to One*, 48, July/August 1994.

[11] K. Shono, S. Kuroda, and S. Ogawa, *IEEE MAG*-27, p. 5130, 1991.

[12] R. J. Gambino and T. R. McGuire, *J. Appl. Phys.*, vol. 57, p. 3906, 1985.

[13] T. Suzuki and T. Katayama, *IEEE MAG*-22, p. 1230, 1986.

[14] T. Suzuki, C.-J. Lin and A. E. Bell, *IEEE MAG*-24, p. 2452, 1989.

[15] W. Kozlovsky, W Lenth, E. E. Latta, A. Moser, and G. L. Bona, *Appl. Phys. Lett.*, vol. 56, p. 2291, 1990.

[16] D. Weller, J. Hurst, H. Notarys, H. Brandle, R. F. C. Farrow, R. Marks, and G. Harp, *J. Mag. Soc. Japan*, vol. 17-S1, p. 72, 1993.

[17] J. Hurst, D. Weller, and H. Notarys, *J. Mag. Soc. Japan*, vol. 17-S1, p. 299, 1993.

[18] W. B. Zeper, F. Greidanus and P. F. Carcia, *IEEE MAG*-25, p. 3764, 1989.

[19] S. Hashimoto, Y. Ochiai, and K. Aso, *Japan J. Appl. Phys.*, vol. 28, p. L1824, 1989.

[20] S. Sugaya and M. Mansuripur, *Appl. Opt.*, vol. 33, p. 5073, 1994.

[21] P. Carcia, Proceedings of the International Symposium "Physics Magnetic Materials," 240, *World Sci. Publ.*, 1987.

[22] Z. G. Li and P. F. Carcia, *J. Appl. Phys.*, vol. 71, p. 842, 1992.

[23] S. Hashimoto, *J. Appl. Phys.*, vol. 75, p. 438, 1994.

[24] T. Suzuki, S. Iwata, H. Brandle, and D. Weller, *J. Magn. Soc. Japan*, vol. 19, Supplement 51, pp. 219–220, 1995.

[25] Y. J. Wang, C. P. Luo, L. C. Kong, X. S. Qi, D. Huang, and Y. Chen, *J. Mag. Soc. Japan*, vol. 17-S1, p. 294, 1993.

[26] M. Nakada and M. Okada, presented at *MORIS'94*, 27B-03, Tokyo, September 1994.

[27] W. Zeper, A. Jongenelis, B. Jacobs, H. van Kesteren, and P. F. Carcia, *IEE MAG*-28, p. 2503, 1992.

[28] T. Suzuki, *J. Appl. Phys.*, vol. 69, p. 4756, 1991.

[29] T. Suzuki, F. Sequeda, H. Do, T. C. Huang, and G. Gorman, *J. Appl. Phys.*, vol. 67, p. 4435, 1990.

[30] M. Takahashi, H. Shoji, Y. Hozumi, and T. Wakiyama, *J. Magn. Mater.*, vol. 30, p. 67, 1994.

[31] A. Fukumoto, S. Yoshimura, T. Udagawa, K. Aratani, M. Ohta, and M. Kaneko, *Proc. Data Storage Topical Mtg.*, TuB4, Colorado Springs, 1991.

[32] M. Ohta, A. Fukumoto, K. Aratani, M. Kaneko, and K. Watanabe, *J. Mag. Soc. Japan*, vol. 15, Supplement S1, p. 319, 1991.

[33] Y. Murakami, N. Iketani, J. Nakajima, A. Takahashi, K. Ohta, and T. Ishikawa, *J. Magn. Soc. Japan*, vol. 17 Supplement S1, p. 201, 1993.

[34] Y. Murakami, presented at "*Workshop on magneto-optical Recording Materials*," Los Alamos, June 1994.

[35] T. Kawano, H. Ito, H. Yoshida, and Y Kobayashi, presented at *MORIS'94*, 29Q-04, Tokyo, September 1994.

[36] M. Birukawa, Y. Fukamichi, N. Miyatake, and T. Kawabata, presented at *Optical Memory Symposium*, Mo-C4, July 1994.

[37] H. J. Williams, R. C. Sherwood, F. G. Foster, and E. M. Kelly, *J. Appl. Phys.*, vol. 28, p. 1181, 1957.

[38] K. Chida, B. Tsujiya, A. Katsui, and K. Egashira, *IEEE MAG*-13, p. 982, 1979.

[39] H. Hartman, J. Braat, and B. Jacobs, *IEEE MAG*-20, p. 1013, 1984.

[40] T. Nakao, M. Ojima, Y. Miyamura, S. Okamine, H. Sukeda, N. Ohta, and Y. Takeuchi, *Japan J. Appl. Phys.*, vol. 26-4, p. 149, 1987.

[41] J. Saito, N. Sato, H. Matsumoto, and H. Akasaka, *Japan J. Appl. Phys.*, vol. 26-4, p. 155, 1987.

[42] N. Ohta, *Japan J. Appl. Phys.* vol. 32-11B, p. 5185, 1993.

[43] S. Ohnuki, K. Shimazaki, N. Ohta, O. Inagoya, and A. Sukeda, *J. Magn. Soc. Japan*, vol. 17-S1, p. 205, 1993.

[44] S. R. Ovshinsky, *J. Non-Cryst. Solids*, vol. 2, p. 99, 1970; R. J. von Gutfeld and P. Chaudhari, *J. Appl. Phys.*, vol. 43, p. 4688, 1972.

[45] K. A. Rubin, R. W. Barton, M. Chen, V. B. Jipson, and D. Rugar, *Appl. Phys. Lett.*, vol. 50, p. 1448, 1987.

[46] M. Chen, K. A. Rubin, and R. Barton, *Appl. Phys. Lett.*, vol. 49, p. 1255, 1986.

[47] N. Yamada, E. Ohno, N. Akahira, K. Nishiuchi, K. Nagata, and M. Takao, *Japan J. Appl. Phys.*, vol. 26, p. 61, 1987.

[48] Y. Maeda, H. Andoh, I. Ikuta, and H. Minemura, *J. Appl. Phys.*, vol. 64, p. 1715, 1988.

[49] K. A. Rubin and M. Chen, *Thin Solid Films*, vol. 181, p. 129, 1989.

[50] T. Nishida, M. Terao, Y. Miyauchi, S. Horigome, T. Kaku, and N. Ohta, *Appl. Phys. Lett.*, vol. 50, p. 667, 1987.

[51] T. Ohta, K. Inoue, T. Akiyama, and K. Yoshida, *SPIE*, vol. 1663, p. 436, 1992.

[52] H. Kobori, H. Hasegawa, and T. Sugaya, presented at *Optical Data Storage Topical Meeting*, 67, Dana Point, CA, 1994.

[53] K. A. Rubin, *J. Magn. Soc. Japan*, vol. 15, Supplement S1, p. 127, 1991.

[54] M. Kubo, S. Harada, H. Takeshima, T. Kobayashi, T. Ohmori and Y. Kobayashi, *Japan J. Appl. Phys.*, vol. 32, Supplement 11B, p. 5329, 1993.

[55] M. Terada, K. Furuya, T. Okamura, I Morimoto, and M. Nakao, *Japan J. Appl. Phys.*, vol. 32, Supplement 11B, p. 5219, 1993.

[56] E. Engler, *Proceedings of Magneto-Optical Recording International Symposium* 1994, *J. Magn. Soc. Japan*, vol. 1, 1995.

[57] M. Terao, S. Horigome, K. Shigematsu, Y. Miyauchi, and M. Nakazawa, *SPIE Proceedings*, vol. 382, p. 276, 1983.

[58] M. Terao, K. Shigematsu, M. Ojima, Y. Taniguchi, S. Horigome, and S. Yonezawa, *J. Appl. Phys.*, vol. 50, p. 6881, 1979.

[59] P. Kivits, R. DeBont, B. Jacobs, and P. Zalm, *Thin Solid Films*, vol. 87, p. 215, 1982.

[60] G. M. Blom, *J. Appl. Phys.*, vol. 54, p. 6175, 1983.

[61] M. Chen, V. Marrello, and U. G. Gerber, *Appl. Phys. Lett.*, vol. 41, p. 894, 1982.

[62] C. R. Davis, W. Y. Lee, M. Chen, and H. Ito, *SPIE*, vol. 420, p. 260, 1983.

[63] H. Watanabe, E. Koyama, T. Nunomura, T. Taii, M. Miura, A. Gothoh, T. Nishida, S. Horigome, and N. Ohta, *SPIE*, vol. 1499, p. 21, 1991.

[64] M. Horie, T. Tamura, M. Ohgaki, H. Yoshida, Y. Kisaka, and Y. Kobayashi, *J. Appl. Phys.*, vol. 75, p. 2680, 1994.

[65] N. Nobukuni, M. Takashima, T. Ohno, and M. Horie, *J. Appl. Phys.*, vol. 78, p. 6980, 1995.

[66] S. Sumi, Y. Teragaki, Y. Kusumoto, K. Torazawa, S. Tsunashima, and S. Uchiyama, *J. Mag. Soc. Japan*, vol. 17-S1, p. 151, 1993.

[67] J. E. Kuder, J. Imaga, *Sci.*, vol. 32, p. 51, 1988.

[68] E. Hamada, Y. Shin, and T. Ishiguro, *SPIE*, vol. 1978, p. 80, 1989.

[69] A. H. M. Holtslag, E. F. McCord, and G. H. W. Buning, *Japan J. Appl. Phys.*, vol. 31, p. 484, 1992.

[70] A. Inoue, J. G. F. Kablau, J. P. J. Heemskerk, K. Ogawa, and H. Yamauchi, *International Symposium of Optical Memory Proceedings*, p. 120, 1993.

[71] Compact Disc System, "*Red Book*," Standard from SONY and Philips.

[72] A. Inoue and E. Muramatsu, presented at *Optical Data Storage Topical Meeting*, MA-3, Dana Point, CA, 1994.

[73] For example, refer to "*European Patent Application*" (#0519395A1), June 16, 1992.

[74] J. Tominaga, S. Haratani, K. Uchiyama, and S. Takayama, *Japan J. Appl. Phys.*, vol. 31, p. 2757, 1992.

[75] For example, refer to K-C. Pan, Y-S. Tyan, and D. R. Preuss, "*United States Patent* #4,960,680," October 2, 1990.

[76] T. Nishida, H. Sugiyama, and S. Horigome, presented at *Optical Data Storage Topical Meeting*, TuC4, Dana Point, CA, 1994.

[77] K-C. Pan, Y-S. Tyan, F. Vazan, and D. R. Preuss, *United States Patent* #4,981,772, January 1, 1991 and #5,077,181, December 31, 1991.

[78] K. Watanabe, Y. Nakane, T. Yanada, and S. Miyaoka, *J. Appl. Phys.*, vol. 56, p. 3024, 1984.

[79] Y. Nakane, N. Sato, H. Makino, and S. Miyaoka, *SPIE*, vol. 529, p. 76, 1985.

[80] K. Watanabe, T. Oyama, Y. Aoki, N. Sato, and S. Miyaoka, *SPIE*, vol. 382, p. 191, 1983.

[81] M. Matsubara, H. Ohkawa, T. Yoshimura, and S. Koyahara, *Japan J. Appl. Phys.*, vol. 32, Supplement 11B, p. 5234, 1993.

[82] T. Handa, J. Tominaga, S. Haratani, and S. Takayama, *Japan J. Appl. Phys.*, vol. 32, Supplement 11B, p. 5226, 1993.

[83] H. Iwasaki, M. Harigaya, O. Nonomiya, Y. Kageyama, M. Takahashi, K. Yamada, H. Deguchi, and Y. Ide, *Japan J. Appl. Phys.*, 32, Supplement 11B, p. 5241, 1993.

[84] H. Minemuru, Y. Sato, N. Tsuboi, T. Suguita, T. Fushimi, S. Yasukawa, H. Andoh, N. Muto, F. Kugiya, and T. Tsunoda, *Japan J. Appl. Phys.*, vol. 32, Supplement 11B, p. 5365, 1993.

[85] D. W. Pohl, W. Denk, and M. Lenz, *Appl. Phys. Lett.*, vol. 44, no. 7, pp. 651–653, 1984.

[86] E. Betzig, J. K. Trautman, R. Wolfe, E. M. Gyorgy, P. L. Finn, M. H. Kryder, and C.-H. Chang, *Appl. Phys. Lett.*, vol. 61, no. 2, pp. 1432–1444, 1992.

[87] R. Imura, T. Shintani, K. Nakamura, and S. Hosaka, *Proceedings of the Third Symposium on Physics of Magnetic Materials*, ISPMM, 1995, Seoul, Korea. pp. 511–514.

[88] S. Hosaka, T. Shintani, M. Miyamoto, A. Hirotsnume, M. Terao, M. Yoshida, K.Fujita, and S. Kammer, *Japan J. Appl. Phys.*, vol. 35, pp. 443–447, 1996.

[89] S. M. Mansfield and G. S. Kino, *Appl. Phys. Lett.*, vol. 57, no. 24, pp. 2615–2616, 1990.

[90] M. Born and E. Wolf, *Principle of Optics*, Oxford: Pergamon, 1980, p. 253.

[91] B. D. Terris, H. J. Mamin, D. Ruger, W. R. Studenmund, and G. S. Kino, *Appl. Phys. Lett.*, vol. 65, p. 388, 1994.

[92] B. D. Terris, H. J. Mamin, and D. Ruger, *Appl. Phys. Lett.*, vol. 68, no. 2, pp. 141–143, 1996.

[93] I. Ichimura, K. Osato, F. Maeda, H. Owa, H. Ooki, and G. S. Kino, *Proc. SPIE*, vol. 2514, pp. 176–1181, 1995.

[94] P. Glijer, T. Suzuki, and B. Terris, *J. Magn. Soc. Japan*, vol. 20, Supplement S1, pp. 297–302, 1996.

[95] H. Awano, S. Ohnuki, H. Shirai, and N. Ohta, *Appl. Phys. Lett.*, vol. 68, no. 27, pp. 4257–4259, 1996.

[96] H. Awano, S. Ohnuki, H. Shirai, N. Ohta, A. Yamguchi, S. Sumi, and K. Torazawa, presented at Intermag'97, New Orleans, April 1997, paper #EC-01.

[97] K. Shimazaki, N. Ohta, M. Yoshihiro, N. Nagai, S. Imai, and H. Takao, *J. Magn. Soc. Japan*, vol. 20, Supplement S1, pp. 67–72, 1996.

Chapter 2

RARE EARTH–TRANSITION METAL AMORPHOUS ALLOY MEDIA

Richard J. Gambino

2.1 INTRODUCTION

2.1.1 History

Amorphous rare earth-transition metal alloys are the only commercially used magneto-optical storage medium. The development of these materials for this application by Chaudhari, Cuomo, and Gambino [1] is an interesting case study of a fundamental discovery leading to technological innovation. The history of these materials can be traced to early work on rare earth-transition metal intermetallic compounds [2]. Compounds like $GdCo_5$ were studied in the early 1960s in an effort to find better magnetic materials, in particular permanent magnets. The heavy rare earth elements like gadolinium and terbium have high magnetic moments but low Curie temperatures. It was thought that by exchange coupling the rare earths to a magnetic transition metal like cobalt it would be possible to take advantage of the high moments of the heavy rare earth metals at room temperature. It was found, however, that the heavy rare earths (Gd to Lu) always couple antiferromagnetically to the transition metal moments and thus the net magnetization is the difference, not the sum, of the sublattice magnetizations. The light rare earths couple ferromagnetically so they are used in permanent magnets though they have relatively small magnetic moments. A typical example is $SmCo_5$, which was until recently the permanent magnet material with the highest energy product.

In a separate development also in the late 1960s, two groups became interested in metastable phases prepared by rapid thermal quenching. Duwez and coworkers at California Institute of Technology used liquid quenching to extend the range of solid solutions in metallic alloys [3]. Mader and Nowick at IBM Research studied vapor quenching; that is, they codeposited elements onto cold substrates [4]. Both of these groups showed that in certain alloy systems and in certain composition ranges within those systems, they obtained amorphous products. Both groups also showed that some of the amorphous alloys they produced are magnetic [5]. Mader and Nowick used electron diffraction to show that Co-Au films are amorphous and at the same time used Lorentz microscopy to show that the films have magnetic domains confirming that they are ferromagnetic [4], [6]. It was emphasized in this work and in the work on liquid quenched amorphous magnetic alloys that these amorphous magnetic materials are very isotropic. In fact one of the advantages of amorphous magnetic materials cited in the patent literature at that time is the fact that amorphous materials are expected to be isotropic, almost by definition. The properties of evaporated Gd-Fe films were studied by Orehotsky who reported that the magnetization as a function of composition passes through a minimum [7]. The magnetization of each composition studied was measured as a function of temperature at a fixed field so no information was obtained on magnetic anisotropy of the Gd-Fe films.

At about the same time, there was intense interest in new materials for magnetic bubble domain devices [8], [9]. A bubble material must have an anisotropy field, H_k, greater than its demagnetizing field, $4\pi M_s$. Materials with low saturation magnetization like the ferrimagnetic garnets were being studied for this reason. It was known that certain cuts from flux grown bulk single crystals of magnetic garnets had enough perpendicular anisotropy to support magnetic bubbles [10]. Gambino and Ruf prepared small single crystals of GdCo$_5$ which was known to also be a ferrimagnet with a low M_s and showed that polished sections have domain patterns like that of a thick magnetic bubble material [11]. Gambino and Cuomo tried to grow c-axis (easy magnetic axis) epitaxial films of the hexagonal phase GdCo$_5$ as a magnetic bubble material [12]. They sputter deposited films onto various single crystal substrates held at elevated temperatures during deposition. They obtained mainly Gd$_2$Co$_{17}$ films with in-plane magnetic easy axis. They did one experiment with the substrates maintained water cooled and found by X-ray diffraction analysis that the product film was amorphous even though it was deposited on a single crystal mica substrate. They also showed that the film was magnetic but no detailed magnetic measurements were made on it. At that time the work on epitaxial growth was abandoned. Gambino worked on amorphous semiconductors, and Cuomo worked on the sputter deposition of garnet films.

At a later date, Cuomo and Gambino, at the suggestion of P. Chaudhari, decided to try to induce magnetic anisotropy in the amorphous magnetic Gd-Co films using stress anisotropy. Stress in epitaxial garnet films was being used at that time to induce perpendicular anisotropy in these cubic ferrimagnets [13]. The experiment planned for the amorphous materials was to deposit films on a number of different substrate materials with different thermal expansion coefficients at elevated substrate temperature so as to use the thermal expansion mismatch between the film and the substrate to induce a stress anisotropy. This method had been used to study the effect of biaxial stress on the Curie temperature of crystalline gadolinium [14]. A control experiment was done first with the substrates water cooled so no thermal expansion induced anisotropy was expected. Films were prepared in two thickness ranges, 400 Å for electron microscopy studies and Lorentz microscopy and thick films of about 3000 Å for magnetization measurements and Bitter pattern observations. Evidence of perpendicular anisotropy was obtained in both sets of films in the "control" experiments. The domain patterns observed were stripe domains, clear evidence that the material has perpendicular anisotropy (Fig. 2.1). The composition dependence of the saturation magnetization of a series of amorphous Gd-Co alloys is shown in Figure 2.2. These initial observations suggested that the anisotropy is growth induced rather than stress induced [15].

A series of experiments was undertaken by Chaudhari, Cuomo and Gambino to investigate the anisotropy mechanism. Free-standing films were obtained by growing amorphous Gd-Co alloys on NaCl substrates and dissolving the substrate [16]. The perpendicular anisotropy was virtually unchanged indicating that stress anisotropy was not a major contributor. It was found that both the film composition [17] and the anisotropy [1] are strong functions of the bias voltage applied to the substrate during sputtering. It is known that applying a negative bias to the substrate electrode causes

Figure 2.1 Stripe domains in an amorphous Gd-Co film [15]. Domain contrast obtained with the Magneto-optical Kerr effect. Magnification 200X.

positive argon ions to be extracted from the plasma and causes the ions to bombard the growing film [18]. This ion bombardment can cause some of the arriving atoms to re-sputter so they are not incorporated into the film. It has also been found that in the case of Gd-Co alloys, the Gd atoms re-sputter preferentially. As discussed below, this work provided the first indications that selective resputtering may be involved in the mechanism of growth-induced anisotropy [19].

The magnetization of amorphous Gd-Co alloys was studied as a function of composition and temperature. It was found that compositions with compensation points are found in the vicinity of Gd20–Co80 (compositions are given in atomic percent or atomic fraction in this chapter). The compensation temperature can be varied from 0 K to above room temperature in a fairly narrow range of compositions between Co 84 and Co 78 [20] (see Fig. 2.3). The Kerr and Faraday effects were measured, and it was shown that the sign of these effects changes at the compensation point as it does at a compensation point in a crystalline ferrimagnet [21]. The magnitude of the Kerr effect was shown to have the temperature dependence of the Co subnetwork [21] (the term subnetwork is used in place of sublattice when describing an amorphous ferrimagnet [16]). The coercivity is high in the vicinity of the compensation point but is relatively low, a few oersteds, at other temperatures. The first application proposed for these films was as

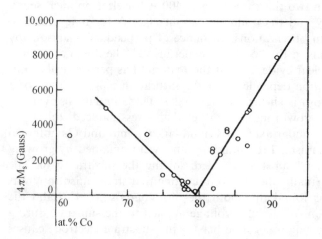

Figure 2.2 Composition dependence of the saturation magnetization at room temperature in a series of Gd-Co amorphous films [15].

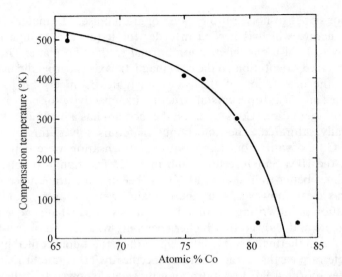

Figure 2.3 Composition dependence of the compensation temperature of a series of amorphous Gd-Co films [1].

magnetic bubble domain materials [12]. The alloy compositions were modified by adding Mo [22] or Au [23] to Gd-Co. The saturation magnetization and exchange stiffness were decreased by these additions so the material could support larger bubble domains in the size range suitable for the lithographic resolution available at that time. These additives also improved the resistance of the amorphous alloy to crystallization and to corrosion. Conventional t-bar patterns of permalloy were deposited on the amorphous film and magnetic bubbles were generated and propagated in a rotating field [24]. The velocity of bubble propagation was measured by Kryder and shown to be very large [24].

Another important study by Cuomo and co-workers was the deposition of the amorphous alloy on polymer substrates [25]. It was shown that the adhesion is good and that anisotropy is still observed. Gambino did the first thermomagnetic writing on amorphous Gd-Co using films close to magnetic compensation [26]. Films on Kapton and glass substrates were used. The laser used was designed for welding so it made spots about 100 μm in diameter. The material in the center of the laser spot was irreversibly damaged, but at the edge of the damage region a reverse domain formed. It was found that the domain formed even in zero applied field. Larger domains could be formed when a perpendicular field of a few hundred oersteds was applied by placing a permanent magnet under the film. Subsequently, controlled writing experiments were made using a focused laser in an apparatus designed for beam writing on amorphous chalcogenide films [27]. It was shown that the threshold for laser beam writing on amorphous Gd-Co is extremely small, about 2 mj/cm^2; this is because compensation point writing was being used. However, the written bits are only stable in a narrow temperature range close to the compensation point.

2.1.2 First Disk Experiments

The IBM group in San Jose was studying MnGaGe polycrystalline films as a magneto-optic medium. This material was the best they had found after a long search, but it had a very poor signal-to-noise ratio because of grain noise. The material has an anisotropic crystal structure which is needed in order for it to have enough magnetocrystalline anisotropy to hold the magnetization normal to the film plane. The films were grown with a preferred orientation so the easy magnetic axis is perpendicular to the film plane. However, the orientation of the c-axis fluctuates from crystal to crystal. Since the material has an anisotropic crystal structure its reflectivity for polarized light is a strong function of orientation. Consequently, the medium has a high noise level even when it is magnetically saturated. The amorphous materials solved this problem immediately. Films of Gd-Co with room temperature compensation were deposited on disks and tested on the IBM San Jose test stand in 1972. The signal-to-noise ratio was greater than 20 times better than that of MnGaGe because the grain noise was negligible [28].

It was clear, however, that the domains were not very stable in Gd-Co using compensation point writing. Huth did an analysis using what is now called the magnetic bubble model and showed that higher coercivity was needed over a larger temperature range to obtain thermally stable bits [29]. In the patent docket filed by IBM the need for non-S-state rare earths in the medium, specifically Tb is taught [30]. Lee and Heiman prepared evaporated RE-Fe amorphous alloys and showed that they have perpendicular anisotropy [31], as do evaporated Gd-Fe films [32].

Sakurai and his coworkers did thermomagnetic writing experiments on amorphous Gd-Co [33] and Ho-Co [34]. In both systems compensation point writing was used. The effect of a magnetic bias field on spot size was investigated. This work was followed by a series of papers by Imamura and coworkers who emphasized RE-Fe amorphous alloys [35], [36] and the advantages of Curie point writing. This work culminated in the 1980 paper by Imamura and Ota, which demonstrated an optical servo system in a magneto-optical disk exerciser [37]. Amorphous TbFe and GdTbFe were used as the recording media. As the decade of the 1980s progressed, improvements in laser power and life made it possible to introduce magneto-optical disk products. Also, the optical servo system perfected for the Audio-CD was carried over into magneto-optical disk technology. Concerns about corrosion of the magneto-optical disk medium were resolved by encapsulation of the medium and methods for injection molding the disks with tracks were perfected. In the injection molding the methods used for Audio-CD were adapted into MO technology with little modification.

Thus it took about 10 years from the discovery of anisotropy in amorphous RE-TM alloys to the development of the first products. Factors in the long lead time were the relatively primitive state of the semiconducting laser in 1972. For example, the initial disk tests on Gd-Co were carried out with a CW laser cooled to liquid nitrogen temperature. Another factor was the need for a servo system including the technology for the injection molding of the servo tracks in the disk. The servo system optics also had to be developed and the cost of the optical head had to be low enough for practical applications.

The amorphous RE-TM alloys are key to the development of this technology. These materials have a combination of properties which make them very well suited for magneto-optic storage media. Some of these properties arise from the fact that they are ferrimagnets. This gives them low saturation magnetization, but at the same time they have a large magneto-optic Kerr rotation. They are amorphous so that they do not produce grain noise, yet, in spite of their amorphous nature, they can be produced with uniaxial anisotropy under certain deposition conditions. Some composition can be produced with very low coercivity but square loop high coercivity materials suitable for storage media can also be obtained. The conditions which produce good media properties are also compatible with deposition on polymer substrates. This feature makes it possible to use low cost injection molded substrates with tracking grooves molded into the surface. Each of these properties will be discussed in greater detail in the following chapters.

2.2 COMPOSITION DEPENDENCE PROPERTIES

The properties of amorphous RE-TM alloys are strongly dependent on composition because they are ferrimagnetic. The amorphous Gd-Co alloys are simple ferrimagnets so it is instructive to consider them first. Most amorphous alloys of iron and all alloys containing non-S-state rare earth elements have more complex spin configurations. The composition dependence in ternary systems must also be considered because most alloys used in magneto-optical recording devices have three or more elements. Finally, a new class of composite materials with ferrimagnetic behavior will be discussed.

2.1.1 Ferrimagnetism

The Néel theory of ferrimagnetism was first used to explain the low saturation magnetization at $T = 0$ K of magnetite and structurally similar iron oxides called ferrites [38]. In magnetite as postulated by Néel and later confirmed by neutron diffraction, the Fe^{3+} on octahedral sites have their magnetic moments antiparallel to the Fe^{3+} on tetrahedral sites. These moments therefore cancel so that the net moment of the system arises from the Fe^{2+} on the octahedral sites. The term ferrimagnetism, derived from ferrite, has been generalized to any system with antiparallel magnetic moments in which there remains a net magnetic moment.

In some of the rare earth-transition metal (RE-TM) intermetallic compounds and amorphous alloys the RE and the TM sublattices (subnetworks) have their magnetic moments antiparallel. The net magnetization thus reflects the difference of the RE and TM magnetic moments rather than the sum. That is,

$$M_{net} = M_{RE} - M_{TM} \qquad (2.1)$$

Where M_{net} is the net magnetic moment per formula unit in Bohr magnetons (μ_B), M_{RE} is the rare earth subnetwork magnetic moment, and M_{TM} is the transition metal subnetwork magnetic moment. This ferrimagnetic behavior is only observed in the compounds and alloys of the heavy rare earths (Gd to Lu).

In the case of similar RE-TM compounds and alloys of the light rare earths (Ce to Eu), ferromagnetic behavior is generally observed. That is for the ferromagnetic, light rare earth systems:

$$M_{net} = M_{RE} + M_{TM} \qquad (2.2)$$

The difference in behavior between the light rare earths and the heavy rare earths is a consequence of the nature of the RE-TM exchange interaction combined with Hund's rule. The light rare earths have a less than half filled $4f$ shell, Gd has seven $4f$ electrons so the heavy rare earths have a more than half filled $4f$ shell. For shells less than half filled, states with lower J values are lower in energy. So for the heavy rare earths

J = L − S. For the light rare earths (less than half filled 4f shell) Hund's rule says states with higher J are lower in energy. It follows that for the heavy rare earths J = L + S. The exchange between the rare earth spin and the transition metal moment is always negative. For the heavy rare earths J and S have the same direction so the net RE moment is antiparallel to the TM moment [see Fig. 2.4(a)]. In the light rare earths L is typically greater than S so J is antiparallel to S but the RE S is antiparallel to the TM moment, which means the net moments of the RE and TM are parallel [see Fig. 2.4(b)]. Thus, the interatomic RE-TM exchange is the same (negative, that is, antiparallel or antiferromagnetic) for all the rare earths but because of Hund's rule the light rare earths couple parallel (or ferromagnetic). As to the reason for the negative exchange between the rare earths and the transition metals, it is likely that the rare earth exchange mainly involves the 6s and 5d electrons which have much greater radial extent than the 4f electrons. The rare earth 5d and the transition metal 3d interatomic exchange is probably positive (ferromagnetic) but the 5d − 4f rare earth intra-atomic exchange is strongly negative. Since most of the rare earth magnetic moment is associated with the 4f electrons the net result is as described above and in Figure 2.4.

In this discussion of the rare earths it is important to consider the case of the half filled 4f shell. For example, the ground state of Gd^0 is $4f^7 5d^1 6s^2$. In forming the trivalent ion, Gd^{3+}, the 5d and 6s electrons are removed leaving the configuration $4f^7$. Hund's first rule is to maximize S so this configuration gives seven unpaired electrons, S = 7/2. The half filled shell is a spherically symmetrical configuration like that of an s electron so it is called an S state. The ground state of Eu^0 is $4f^7 6s^2$ so the divalent ion Eu^{2+} has the $4f^7$ configuration isoelectronic with Gd^{3+} and is also an S-state ion. In the rare earth metals it is usually assumed as a first approximation that the 6s and 5d electrons are delocalized so that the localized magnetic moment arises only from the 4f electrons. However, the Gd magnetic moment in elemental Gd and its alloys is greater than expected from seven spins. This extra moment has been attributed to some spin polarization of the delocalized electrons. Furthermore, metallic Gd has a number of properties associated with spin-orbit interaction; properties which are not

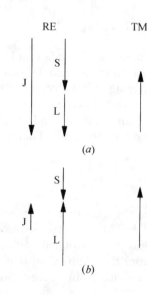

RE   TM

(a)

(b)

Figure 2.4 A simple vector model diagram showing the exchange coupling of the rare earth elements and the magnetic transition metals. With the heavy rare earths (Gd to Lu) the spin (S) is antiparallel to the transition metal TM moment (a). Following Hund's rule J = L + S so J is also antiparallel to the TM magnetization. With the light rare earths (b) S is also antiparallel to the TM moment. However, Hund's rule for the light rare earths is J = L − S and, since L is larger than S, the net rare earth moment J is opposite to S and therefore in the same direction as the TM atomic moment.

expected in an S-state ion. For example, Gd alloys have the largest spontaneous Hall effect of all the rare earths [39], [40]. The situation with respect to Eu alloys is less clear. In some alloys europium acts divalent giving a magnetic moment close to what is expected for seven spins. In other cases the Eu acts more like a trivalent, $4f^6$ configuration.

2.2.2 Gadolinium-Cobalt

One of the most striking features of the amorphous Gd-Co system is the deep minimum in magnetization as a function of composition, as shown in Figure 2.2. This result is a clear indication of ferrimagnetism. The deep minimum can then be explained as a room temperature compensation point. That is, at 79 at.% Co at room temperature the Gd subnetwork moment is just equal and opposite to the Co subnetwork moment. Until the discovery of ferrimagnetism in amorphous RE-TM alloys, compensation had been observed as a function of temperature in a fixed composition. With the amorphous alloys it is possible to vary composition continuously over a wide range and thus to study compensation as a function of composition at a fixed temperature. It is particularly instructive to consider the temperature 0 K. At this temperature it is possible to calculate the compensation composition from atomic magnetic moments. Taking the values 7.10 μ_B for Gd and 1.72 μ_B for Co we can calculate the Co atomic fraction X_{Co} which will be compensated using Equation (2.1). Setting M_{net} equal to zero gives

$$0 = M_{Gd} - M_{Co}$$
$$0 = n_{BGd}(1 - X_{Co}) - n_{BCo}X_{Co} \qquad (2.3)$$
$$0 = 7.10(1 - X_{Co}) - 1.72X_{Co}$$

solving for X_{Co} gives 0.805. The observed $T = 0$ K compensation composition is approximately 0.85 Co atomic fraction, as can be seen in Figures 2.3 and 2.5. While this can be considered reasonable agreement, a simple explanation for the discrepancy is that the Co moment has been decreased by alloying with the trivalent Gd. The transition metals are known to be band magnets and the moment is known to vary systematically with the valence and concentration of the alloying partner. This behavior is the basis of the well-known Slater–Pauling curves [41] and has been extensively

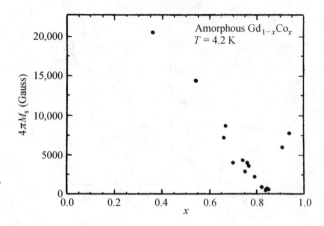

Figure 2.5 Saturation magnetization of amorphous Gd-Co alloys at 4.2 K vs. the atomic fraction of cobalt (X) [20].

reviewed and analyzed recently [42]. We can use the experimentally determined $T = 0\,K$ compensation composition to obtain the Co moment by setting $X_{Co} = 0.85$ and assuming the Gd moment is constant at 7.1. Again using Equation (2.1) we find

$$0 = M_{Gd} - M_{Co}$$
$$0 = n_{BGd}(1 - X_{Co}) - n_{BCo}X_{Co} \tag{2.4}$$
$$0 = 7.10(1 - 0.85) - n_{BCo}(0.85)$$

Solving for n_{BCo} gives 1.25 μ_B. The value obtained is in good agreement with the moment calculated by the model of Williams et al. [42]. It is also interesting to note the composition dependence of the Curie temperature in this system (Fig. 2.6). It appears that the strong Co-Co exchange dominates the behavior of the Co rich compositions. (Note that some of the data points in this figure are for crystalline Gd-Co intermetallic compounds. The amorphous alloys could only be measured up to their crystallization temperature, which is around 700 K.) If we assume that the Curie temperature scales with the Co moment we can estimate the T_C of the composition with compensation at $T = 0\,K$. Taking the ratio of the moment of Co in the alloy to the moment of pure Co, 1.25/1.72, times the Curie point of pure Co, 1400 K gives 1017 K as the estimated Curie point of the alloy with $X_{Co} = 0.85$. The estimated Curie point is very close to that of intermetallic compounds with similar compositions. Another point to be taken from this analysis is that it is not possible to find a Gd-Co composition with compensation near room temperature and a Curie temperature close to room temperature.

Calculating the compensation composition for a finite temperature, say room temperature, requires knowledge of the temperature dependence of the subnetwork magnetizations. A starting point is the mean field analysis which will not be discussed in detail here. Several good references on magnetism address this subject in detail [42]. An example of the temperature dependence of the saturation magnetization of an amorphous GdCoAu alloy is shown in Figure 2.7. To illustrate the mean field method,

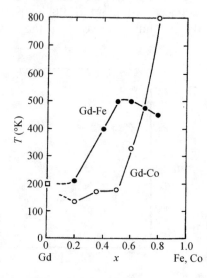

Figure 2.6 Curie temperature (T_c) of amorphous Gd-Co and Gd-Fe alloys vs. atomic fraction of the transition metal (X) [40].

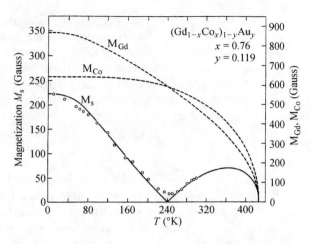

Figure 2.7 Temperature dependence of the saturation magnetization of an amorphous Gd-Co-Au alloy. The data points are experimental, the curves are a molecular field fit to the data as discussed in the text [23].

the calculations used for this M vs. T curve will be illustrated. The amorphous alloys have the general formula $(Gd_{1-x}Co_x)_{1-y}Au_y$. It is assumed that the total magnetization is the sum of the Gd and Co subnetwork magnetizations given by

$$M_s = \mu_B N |(1-y)(1-x)g_1 S_1 + (1-y)x g_2 S_2| \qquad (2.5)$$

where 1 and 2 refer to Gd and Co, respectively, N is 6.3×10^{22} the total number of atoms per unit volume, and g is the g factor. The subnetwork magnetization can be expressed as a function of the effective field H_i and T by the Brillouin function

$$\underline{S}_i = S_i B_{S_i}(g_i \mu_B S_i H_i / k_B T) \qquad (2.6)$$

where S_i is the spin value of atom i and the effective field is expressed by

$$H_1 = 2J_{11}z_{11}\underline{S}_1/g_1\mu_B + 2J_{12}z_{12}\underline{S}_2/g_1\mu_B + H_a \qquad (2.7)$$

$$H_2 = 2J_{21}z_{21}\underline{S}_1/g_2\mu_B + 2J_{22}z_{22}\underline{S}_2/g_2\mu_B + H_a \qquad (2.8)$$

where J_{11}, J_{12} and J_{22} are the exchange constants for Gd-Gd, Gd-Co and Co-Co, respectively and H_a is the applied field. The number of nearest neighbors z_{ij} can be calculated knowing the average coordination number which was taken as 12. Assuming random distribution of atoms, the number of nearest neighbors is given by

$$z_{11} = 12(1-y)(1-x) = z_{21} \qquad (2.9)$$

$$z_{22} = 12(1-y)x = z_{12} \qquad (2.10)$$

The procedure used was to extrapolate the low temperature magnetization data to 0 K. Then assuming $S = 7/2$ for Gd, S_{Co} can be obtained using Equation (2.5). The subnetwork magnetizations are obtained using Equation (2.6) with the exchange constants as adjustable parameters. The best fit to the data is shown in the figure for this composition.

A similar analysis has been used to compare the temperature dependence of the MO Kerr effect with the Co subnetwork magnetization [21]. The fact that the Co spin value is dependent on alloy composition raises some question about the uniqueness of the mean field fit. Nevertheless, the mean field analysis has been helpful in predicting the temperature dependence of magnetization in a limited composition range. It has also been shown that the exchange constants in Gd-Co systems are in the following order:

$$J_{CoCo} > J_{GdCo} > J_{GdGd}$$

The order is quite different in, for example, the Gd-Fe amorphous alloys where the Gd-Fe exchange is comparable in strength to the Fe-Fe exchange.

In the Gd-Co-Au system discussed above, the nonmagnetic alloy addition, Au, has only a slight effect on the Co moment. This behavior is typical of valence one alloy constituents. On the other hand, alloy additions like Mo or Cr have a large effect on the Co moment and tend to decrease the exchange stiffness, the Curie temperature, and the Kerr effect. Polyvalent alloy additions are useful because they impart thermal stability to the alloy. The crystallization temperature increases with Mo addition, for example. Also, Mo additions increase the temperature at which irreversible changes in magnetic properties occur without crystallization.

2.2.3 Gd-Fe and Tb-Fe

When Co is replaced by Fe in the amorphous alloy, greater complexity is introduced. The spins in the Fe subnetwork are not parallel but rather are somewhat fanned out. This type of fanning was postulated to explain the lower than expected magnetization of Tb-Fe alloys. In that system it was suggested that the single ion anisotropy of the Tb causes the fanning. Each Tb site in the amorphous alloy has a crystal field which acts on the Tb atom creating a random local anisotropy field [43]. In the absence of an external field or an exchange field, the Tb spins will be dispersed over all possible directions, a spin structure called spheromagnetic by Coey [44]. In a small applied field, one direction along the local axis will be favored over the other so the spherical distribution will become a hemisphere as shown. As the applied field is increased, the fanning angle decreases. In an alloy with Co or Fe the exchange coupling with the transition metal plays the role of the applied field. The competition between the local random anisotropy and the exchange field determines the fanning angle. In the case of Fe alloys the Fe-Fe exchange is relatively weak so even the Fe subnetwork is somewhat fanned out [Figs. 2.8(b) and 2.8(d)]. With amorphous Dy-Co, the Co subnetwork is collinear but the Dy subnetwork is fanned [Fig. 2.8(c)].

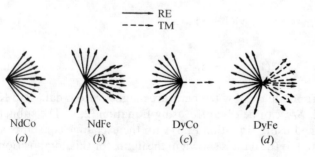

| NdCo | NdFe | DyCo | DyFe |
| (a) | (b) | (c) | (d) |

——— RE
- - - - TM

Figure 2.8 Diagrams showing the effects of competition between the single-ion anisotropy and the exchange in amorphous RE-Co and RE-Fe alloys [44].

Returning to the Gd-Fe system, the local random anisotropy model certainly does not apply and yet there is magnetization evidence that the Fe subnetwork is fanned out somewhat. In amorphous Y-Fe alloys there is neutron diffraction evidence of a spin glass-like state [45]. In some Fe rich compositions in the Zr-Fe system, spin glass behavior has been reported [46]. There is no reason to expect strong local random anisotropy effects in these Fe alloys so another explanation must be sought for the noncollinear subnetwork. In these systems we invoke exchange frustration as the mechanism of the spin glass state.

The TM-TM exchange as a function of interatomic distance is shown schematically in Figure 2.9. Note that Fe is near a zero crossing, at smaller interatom distances the Fe-Fe exchange becomes negative. The combination of positive and negative exchange can give rise to spin glass behavior. This is a different mechanism for spin glass behavior from that of the first concentrated spin glass, amorphous Gd-Al [47]. A comparison of YFe_3 in the amorphous and crystalline states has been discussed in the context of energy-band calculations [48].

In the binary system Fe-Co there is a maximum in transition metal moment [49]. Amorphous ternary systems such as Gd-Fe-Co or Nd-Fe-Co [50], [51] show a maximum in the transition metal moment as well. The TM-TM exchange also appears to be somewhat enhanced in the region of enhanced moment. Because of the stronger exchange, there is also less fanning of the TM subnetwork. All of these factors tend to make for larger magneto-optical Kerr effect but also tend to increase the Curie temperature. Thus, practical compositions tend to be Tb-Fe with some Co addition.

2.2.4 Ternary Systems

A number of ternary amorphous ferrimagnetic systems have been studied. It is useful to plot magnetization at a fixed temperature, usually room temperature, as a function of composition. By connecting compositions of equal saturation magnetization, M_s, a kind of contour plot is obtained. The contours with $M_s = 0$ are of particular significance. One such contour is the Curie line connecting all compositions with the Curie temperature equal to room temperature (the fixed temperature for this diagram). In a ferrimagnetic system there may be another contour with $M_s = 0$, that is, a compensation line, compositions with room temperature compensation. In the vicinity of the

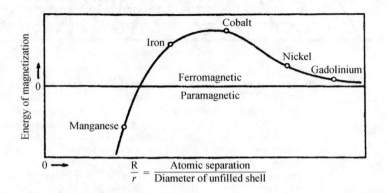

Figure 2.9 The dependence of the exchange energy on interatomic distance for the transition metals (Bethe diagram) [49].

compensation line, the coercivity is high, as shown in Figure 2.10 for the pseudoternary system Gd-Nd-FeCo. Note that the system depicted in Figure 2.10 is actually quarternary, but it can be treated as a ternary if the FeCo ratio is fixed.

The change in sign of the Kerr effect and the Hall effect can also be used to help locate the compensation line. The sign reversal at the compensation point can be understood with reference to Figure 2.11(a), which shows schematically the temperature dependence of the Gd and Co subnetworks in amorphous Gd-Co. At low temperatures, below the compensation point, the Gd subnetwork dominates (broken lines) so the net magnetization at saturation is in the direction of the applied field (up in Fig. 2.11) which is also the direction of the Gd subnetwork magnetization. The spontaneous Hall voltage of ferromagnetic Gd is negative, whereas that of ferromagnetic Co is positive [40]. Since Gd and Co have opposite signs of Hall angle when the subnetwork magnetizations point in opposite directions, the Hall contributions add as shown to give the

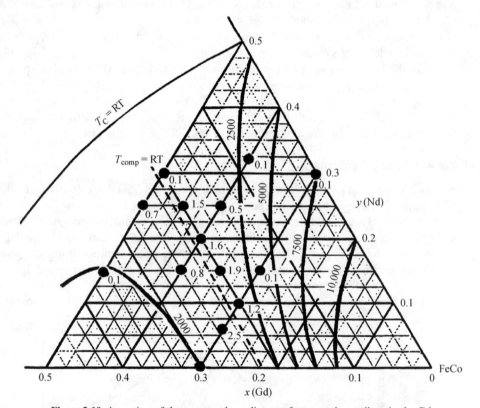

Figure 2.10 A portion of the ternary phase diagram for amorphous alloys in the Gd-Nd-(FeCo) system is shown. The broken line labeled $T_{comp} = $ RT connects compositions with a room temperature compensation temperature, i.e., compositions with 0 saturation magnetization. Compositions which are paramagnetic at room temperature are separated from the ferrimagnetic composition by a solid line (Curie point line), which is approximately perpendicular to the compensation line. The Curie point line represents compositions with a room temperature Curie point ($T_c = $ RT) so it is another line of compositions with saturation magnetization equal to zero at room temperature. Numbers next to the data points are the coercive field in kilo oersteds.

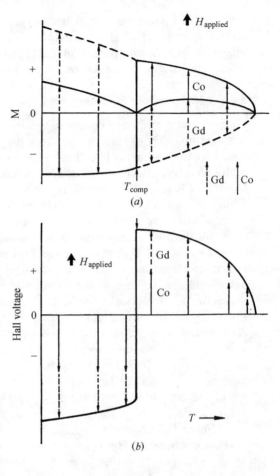

Figure 2.11 Schematic representation of the temperature dependence of the subnetwork magnetizations (*a*) and Hall contributions (*b*) of Gd and Co in an amorphous ferrimagnetic alloy. The magnetization of Gd (broken arrow) and of Co (solid arrow) are in opposition. At low temperature the Gd subnetwork magnetization is larger than the Co so the net magnetization, which always aligns with the applied field, points in the direction of the Gd spins. At the compensation point, the subnetwork magnetizations are equal and opposite so the net magnetization is zero. Above the compensation point, the Co subnetwork dominates so the net magnetization points in the Co direction. The Hall contributions (*b*) of Gd and Co have opposite signs so when the magnetizations oppose the Hall voltages add. The sign of the Hall voltage changes at the compensation temperature when the subnetworks reverse direction with respect to the applied field. The Kerr effect and Faraday effect also change sign at the compensation point.

negative Hall voltage shown in Figure 2.11(*b*). At temperatures above the compensation point the Co subnetwork dominates so the Co magnetization is in the direction of the applied field. The sign of the Hall voltage becomes positive but the magnitude is the same. This is in marked contrast to the saturation magnetization which is always positive but which goes to zero at compensation. In real films there is usually some inhomogeneity which gives regions with opposite signs of Hall voltage and partial cancellation. This effect only occurs in a narrow temperature range within a few degrees of the compensation point as shown, for example, by Shirakawa et al. [52].

The behavior of the Kerr effect and the Faraday effect at compensation is similar to that of the Hall effect. The magneto-optic effects are wavelength dependent so the relative magnitudes and even the signs of the sublattice contributions can change with wavelength. Nevertheless, the compensation point is always associated with a sharp change in the sign of the magneto-optic effect without a large change in the magnitude (neglecting inhomogeneity effects very close to compensation).

These arguments apply equally well to measurements as a function of composition at a fixed temperature. Thus, in Figure 2.10 all of the samples on the FeCo side of the compensation line will have a positive Hall effect and those on the Gd side will have a negative Hall effect. The change in sign is useful for locating the compensation line.

In this system the Tb, a heavy rare earth, couples antiferromagnetically to the transition metal (FeCo) subnetwork whereas the Nd, a light rare earth couples ferromagnetically. The compensation line thus separates Tb dominated regions from regions where the Nd and transition metal combined are dominate.

2.2.5 Macroscopic Ferrimagnets

Ferrimagnetic exchange coupling has been reported in a number of two-phased systems. Multilayers of rare earths alternating with transition metals are known to show compensation behavior [54]. Exchange coupling between Co and EuS was reported in multilayers on the basis of the enhanced T_c of the EuS [55]. However, in 1993, Gambino, Ruf, and Bojarczuk reported compensation temperatures in thin films consisting of an amorphous Co matrix containing 10 nm crystallites of EuS [56]. It was proposed that the negative exchange between Co and EuS at the phase boundary was coupling the EuS magnetization antiparallel to the Co matrix. Subsequent magneto-optical studies have shown that the EuS retains many of the features of its magneto-optical spectrum including the crystal field split main peak [57]. However, in Co dominated samples the sign of the rotation is opposite that of EuS showing that the EuS magnetization is opposite to the Co magnetization. The spectral evidence is shown in Figure 2.12. The change in sign of the Kerr effect at compensation is shown in Figure 2.13. At low temperatures the EuS dominates and the sign of the Kerr loop is negative, as is EuS at this photon energy (2.15 eV). As the temperature is increased the sign of the loop reverses at 20 K. In this system and at this photon energy, the Co and the EuS have opposite signs of Kerr rotation. This can lead to magneto-optical compensation where the two sublattices have equal and opposite Kerr effects so the net Kerr effect gradually decreases, passes through zero, then gradually increases with opposite sign.

Similar evidence of ferrimagnetic behavior has been reported in the system EuO/Tb-Fe-Co where the EuO precipitates out of an amorphous Tb-Fe-Co alloy [57].

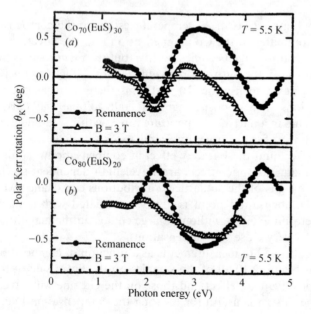

Figure 2.12 Co-EuS spectral dependence of polar Kerr rotation.

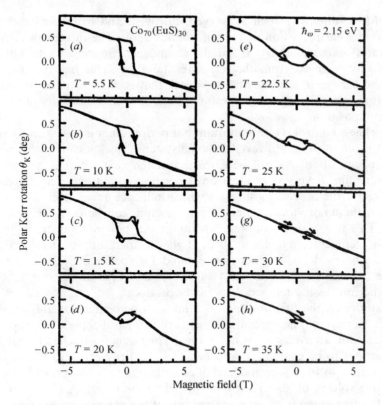

Figure 2.13 $Co_{70}(EuS)_{30}$ Kerr loops vs. temp through compensation.

In this system there are two types of ferrimagnet interactions: macroscopic ferrimagnetism between the FeCo in the amorphous alloy matrix and the EuO particles and microscopic (atomic) ferrimagnetism between the Tb and the FeCo in the amorphous alloy. These more complex systems including Tb-Co-EuS have the advantage from the practical perspective of perpendicular anisotropy at room temperature and even square loops in some cases. The simpler Co-EuS system is better from the perspective of understanding the phenomenon of macroscopic ferrimagnetism. For example, the transition as a function of field to ferromagnetic alignment is actively being studied. The change from antiparallel to parallel Co and EuS magnetizations is accompanied by a large change in electrical resistance [59]. At 5 K the magnetization is not saturated even at 35 kOe. The high field susceptibility observed may be caused by spins which are being rotated into the field direction against the exchange.

2.3 DEPOSITION METHODS

The deposition process for practical MO media must satisfy a number of requirements. Because of the critical dependence of properties on composition as discussed above, control of composition is a major concern. For example, in the Gd-Co system a change in composition of 1 atomic % causes the compensation point to change by more than 50 K. The impurity background in the deposition system is an extremely important factor. Most impurities such as oxygen, nitrogen, and hydrogen react preferentially with the rare earth portion of the amorphous alloy. The rare earth compound which precipitates out (e.g., Gd_2O_3), is usually paramagnetic so some fraction of the rare earth is effectively removed from the ferrimagnetic alloy. This has the same effect as an equivalent change in the alloy composition; that is, approximately 1 atom % oxygen will shift the compensation temperature about 50 K in the vicinity of the 0 K compensation composition.

Thickness control is also important but performance is not as sensitive to thickness as it is to composition. However, in some systems, thickness monitors may be used to control composition. As will be discussed in the next section, the anisotropy of an amorphous film is very dependent on deposition conditions. Therefore, tight control is required of the process parameters which influence anisotropy.

Last, the amorphous magneto-optic medium can be deposited on polymer substrates. This is a major economic advantage but polymer substrates limit the upper processing temperature to about 80°C. Higher temperature substrate materials, such as glass, can be used and in fact are required for such materials as the iron garnets. However, the higher costs of glass substrates outweigh any performance advantages that higher processing temperatures might produce.

Historically, the first amorphous films with perpendicular anisotropy were made by diode sputtering. The apparatus consists of two parallel plate electrodes in a vacuum chamber. Both electrodes are water cooled. The target is attached to one electrode and the substrates to be coated are attached to the other electrode. The chamber is evacuated typically to 10^{-7} Torr and backfilled with argon gas at a pressure of 40–60 mTorr. A negative voltage of about 1 kV is applied to the target. A plasma is excited in the argon. Positive argon ions are extracted out of the plasma and are accelerated toward the target. The bombarding ions impact the target causing a collision cascade in the target. Some of the secondary collisions in the target propagate to the surface causing target atoms to be knocked off the target. The energy of the incident argon ion (of order 1 keV) is distributed over many target atoms in the collision cascade so the sputtered atoms typically have energies of a few electron volts. The target atoms leave the surface with a cosine distribution, and some of them travel across the plasma region to the opposite electrode which supports the substrates. At low argon pressures the target atoms are likely to reach the substrate electrode without collisions (line of sight). As the argon pressure is increased the mean free path decreases so the sputtered atoms undergo numerous collisions as they travel from target to substrate. With each collision the sputtered atom looses energy. In the high pressure limit, the sputtered atom is thermallized, that is, its energy is reduced to the point that it is in equilibrium with the sputter gas (of order 10^{-2} eV). Thus, the energy of the atoms arriving at the substrate can range from several eV to thermal energies depending on pressure. In general, denser films are formed when the atoms forming the film have higher energy.

The plasma used in sputtering is a conductive mixture of ions and electrons which is approximately electrically neutral. Because the electrons have a longer mean free path than the more massive argon ions, electrons tend to be lost from the plasma preferentially causing the plasma to be slightly positive with respect to ground. At low pressures electrons are lost more readily and the plasma potential (V_P) rises rapidly to over 100 eV. The plasma is luminous because of recombination events which form excited atoms that decay with the emission of light. In close proximity to the target electrode, the large negative potential accelerates electrons away from the target and ions toward the target.

As a consequence, there is a dark region between the target and the luminous plasma called the target dark space. Most of the potential drop accelerating the ions is between the target and the plasma across the dark space. Because the plasma is conductive it cannot support large electric fields. Ions drift in the plasma over to the edge of the dark space where they are accelerated into the target. Because of the slightly positive potential of the plasma, all grounded surfaces in contact with the plasma are bombarded with argon ions at the plasma potential. Thus, if the substrates are grounded they experience ion bombardment at an energy that depends on the gas pressure because of the sensitivity of the plasma potential to gas pressure. A negative voltage can be applied to the substrate to increase the energy of the argon ions bombarding the substrates. This applied negative voltage is called the substrate bias (V_A). It should be remembered that the potential accelerating argon ions toward the substrate, the effective bias voltage (V_B), is the sum of the plasma potential and the applied bias [18], [19], as follows:

$$V_B = V_A + V_P \tag{2.11}$$

Thus, decreasing the pressure can cause bombardment effects on the substrate which are similar to the effects caused by applying a bias voltage.

The negative bias voltage at an electrode attracts positive ions. If the electrode is covered with an insulator such as a dielectric substrate the electrons from the electrode may not be able to reach the ions to neutralize the positive charge. A space charge can build up very quickly on the surface of the substrate which opposes the negative bias. By applying an r.f. bias to the electrode, the space charge is neutralized every half (positive potential) cycle by electrons drawn in from the plasma. Because electrons are much more mobile than ions the electrode develops a negative d.c. level which is approximately half the peak-to-peak r.f. voltage. When the target is conductive the voltage can be applied to the target with either a d.c. or r.f. power supply. However, applying a d.c. bias to an insulating or semiconductive substrate is not recommended even when the sputtered film is conductive. The space charge will build up in the initial deposition before the film has become continuous so that the effective bias will vary during the deposition.

Another advantage of r.f. sputtering is that r.f. excitation produces a denser plasma. The plasma is sustained by electron impact ionization of neutral argon. Secondary electrons are produced by argon ion bombardment of the target. These electrons are accelerated across the target dark space where they may collide with a neutral argon causing ionization. If the electron does not collide with a gas atom before it reaches a grounded surface it does not contribute to maintaining the plasma. With r.f. excitation of the plasma the electron travels a zig-zag path under the influence of the r.f. field so that it has a longer path length in the plasma. The longer path length increases the probability of an ionizing collision.

Applying a bias voltage to the substrate can modify the properties of the growing film in a number of ways [60]. The ion bombardment can modify the film composition by preferential resputtering of one component of an alloy [17]. Also, the bombarding ions become incorporated in the film, even the rare gases [61]. Film purity can sometimes be improved by gentle ion bombardment because reactive impurities in the sputter gas are desorbed from the surface before they become incorporated into the film. The ion bombardment can be used to obtain higher density films and to modify the sign and magnitude of the stress in the film.

Many of these effects were discovered using bias sputtering in the diode geometry. Diode sputtering, however, is a complex plasma process which makes it difficult to analyze the deposition conditions. For example, changing the bias on the substrate electrode changes the plasma density which many change the ion current as well as the ion energy. An increased plasma density can also cause an increased flux of sputtered ions from the target. Much of our systematic understanding of the effects of ion bombardment during deposition has been obtained from studies in dual ion beam systems. An ion beam is generated by extracting ions from a dense plasma in a gun and accelerating the ions with grids into the processing chamber. The plasma generation and the deposition process are to a large extent independent of each other. The ion beam bombards the target and sputters atoms which are collected on the substrate. A second ion gun is used to bombard the film during deposition. The ion energy, ion current, even the ion species in the two ion guns can be varied independently. A dual ion beam deposition system is shown schematically in Figure 2.14.

The dependence of alloy composition on fraction re-sputtered in the GdCo system is shown in Figure 2.15. The sputtering yield ratio is found to range from 2.5 to 5 in the alloys studied [62]. The ratio of elemental sputtering yields of Gd to Co is 0.37. Clearly, the sputtering yield ratio of two elements in an alloy is composition dependent and is not simply related to the elemental yield ratio. It has been suggested that surface binding energy differences of Gd and Co can explain the increase in sputtering yield ratio with increasing Co concentration [62].

The deposition method most often used for production is single target magnetron sputtering. In magnetron sputtering a magnetic field is provided in the vicinity of the target. The combined electric and magnetic fields at the target cause the electrons to travel in spiral paths close to the target. The electrons are thus more efficiently utilized in electron impact ionization resulting in a dense plasma close to the target surface. High sputtering rates can be obtained because of this intense ion bombardment. The argon pressure can be low because the secondary electrons are confined by the magnetic field. One disadvantage of magnetron sputtering is that most of the erosion of the target

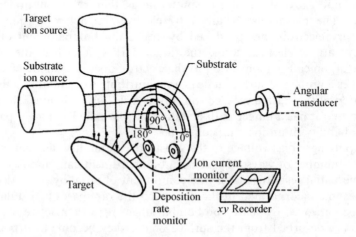

Figure 2.14 Dual-ion beam deposition system (schematic). See Figure 4.3 Harper et al.

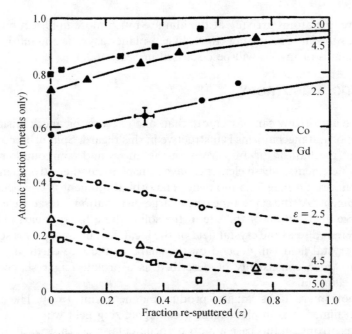

Figure 2.15 Gd-Co alloy composition vs. fraction resputtered. See Figure 4.6 Harper et al.

occurs in a narrow "race track" defined by the location of the strong magnetic field. Target utilization therefore is not very efficient. Since the alloy targets used in single target magnetron are very expensive, target utilization is an important consideration. Because of the low pressure, energetic neutrals from the target have a high probability of reaching the substrate with their full energy. However, the target voltage in magnetron sputtering is usual fairly low, about 500 V. The high rates made possible by magnetron sputtering are an advantage for high manufacturing throughput. In addition, higher purity films can be obtained by high rate deposition when the main source of impurities is the background of the vacuum chamber. High rate deposition, however, may decrease the magnetic anisotropy in the film (anisotropy will be discussed further in the next section of this chapter).

Multitarget magnetron deposition is typically used in a research environment where versatility is more important than throughput. In this method individual sources are provided for each element. The film can be prepared either by codeposition of the elemental constituents or by sequential deposition of very thin (usually submonolayer) films of the alloy constituents. There is evidence of interdiffusion of the rare earth and transition metal components even if the individual layers are thicker than a monolayer [54].

Multisource electron beam evaporation has been used as a research tool for the deposition of amorphous alloys [31], [32]. This method has many of the same advantages as multisource magnetron deposition. Composition control requires rate monitors in a feedback loop to control the electron beam gun power supplies. In vacuum evaporation the source is so far from the substrate it can be approximated as a point source. In all the sputtering methods an area source is the correct approximation.

Therefore, the atoms arriving at the film are much more unidirectional in evaporation. This leads to some interesting effects like in-plane easy axis and hard perpendicular axis magnetic anisotropy, as will be discussed in Section 2.4.

2.4 MAGNETIC ANISOTROPY

Magnetic anisotropy can have more than one microscopic mechanism. A review of the most important mechanisms is instructive in this regard. Spin orbit coupling is often the dominant mechanism of anisotropy in the alloys and compounds of the non-S-state rare earth elements. These elements have nonspherical 4f electron density distributions, that is, an orbital magnetic moment. The orbital moment is coupled to the spin magnetic moment. At the same time, the charge distribution interacts electrostatically with the charge distribution of the site in the solid where the rare earth element is located. This is referred to as the crystal field or the local field in amorphous solids. The effect of a given crystal field will depend on the shape of the rare earth 4f charge density distribution which can usually be described as a prolate (cigar shaped) or oblate (disk shaped) ellipsoid.

Dipole interactions can also produce magnetic anisotropy. The macroscopic shape of a thin film, for example, causes a demagnetizing field which can be described as a shape anisotropy, in this case a hard perpendicular axis. In general, the internal field of a magnetized body, H_{int}, is the sum of the applied field, H_{app}, and the demagnetizing field, H_{demag}, which has the opposite sign. That is,

$$H_{\text{demag}} = -N_{\text{d}}M \qquad (2.12)$$

where N_{d} is the demagnetizing factor which depends on the shape of the sample. In the c.g.s. system of units, the sum of the demagnetizing factors is equal to 4π or in rectilinear coordinates:

$$N_x + N_y + N_z = 4\pi \qquad (2.13)$$

Thus for a sphere, by symmetry, $N_x = N_y = N_z = 4\pi/3$. Another simple case of interest is an infinite sheet with the z-axis perpendicular which has $N_x = N_y = 0$, $N_z = 4\pi$. An infinite cylindrical rod with z along the axis of the rod has $N_z = 0$ so that again, by symmetry, $N_x = N_y = 2\pi$. Real bodies are treated as ellipsoids of revolution and the values of N are tabulated for various ratios of the major axis (a) to minor axis (b) (see, for example, Bozorth [63] or Chikazumi [64]). A prolate ellipsoid with a large a/b approaches the infinite rod case. The shape anisotropy energy is given by

$$K_{\text{s}} = (1/2)(N_x - N_z)M_{\text{s}}^2 \qquad (2.14)$$

which reduces to $K_{\text{s}} = \pi M_{\text{s}}^2$ for a rod with a large a/b ratio.

In discussing dipolar contributions to the anisotropy of amorphous films we are usually concerned with microstructural features. For example, a columnar microstructure can give rise to a perpendicular easy axis anisotropy. In some cases the film can be modeled as an array of prolate ellipsoids arranged with their long axes perpendicular to the film plane. Other microstructural features such as elongated, oriented voids can also cause shape anisotropy.

The rare earth element gadolinium has a spherical 4f electron distribution as expected for the half filled shell, $4f^7$ configuration. Nevertheless, crystalline gadolinium, which is hexagonal, has substantial magnetic anisotropy with the c-axis being the easy axis. The crystal field–spin orbit interaction should not apply to a spherical electron distribution. A possible explanation for the anisotropy of gadolinium is that it retains some 5d character in the metallic state so that its electron density distribution is not really spherical. Another possibility is that the source of the anisotropy is anisotropy of exchange. The Gd-Gd distance is significantly different in the basal plane and along the c-axis in gadolinium. It can be argued that the exchange interactions can be expected to depend on Gd-Gd distance so that different magnetic properties should be expected perpendicular and parallel to the c-axis. It should be noted that the ferromagnetic compounds of divalent europium have very low magnetocrystalline anisotropy. With divalent europium it is clear that the $4f^7$ configuration is present and that the ion is really spherical.

Another treatment of anisotropy considers the individual atomic spins in the crystal structure as dipoles and calculates the energy of the system as a function of the orientation of the atomic dipoles. This treatment generally gives a magnitude of anisotropy much smaller than the observed magnetocrystalline anisotropy. The functional form of a dipole induced anisotropy, however, often fits the observed data relating the anisotropy to the magnetization, however, with much larger coefficients. Systems which show this functional form are said to have a pseudodipolar anisotropy. While this approach is largely phenomenological and does not address directly the microscopic origin of the anisotropy, it does provide a systematic framework for quantifying the sublattice contributions of a ferrimagnetic system.

Last, the magnetic anisotropy can be induced by stress. The mechanism is through the inverse magnetostriction effect [64]. If $\delta l/l$ is the linear magnetostriction and σ is the biaxial (planar) stress, the stress-induced anisotropy is given by [65]

$$K_\sigma = -(3/2)(\delta l/l)\sigma \, (\text{erg/cm}^3) \qquad (2.15)$$

The magnetostriction, like the single ion anisotropy, is a consequence of the spin orbit coupling. Among the rare earths, those elements with the most aspherical 4f charge density distributions have the largest magnetostriction. The S-state rare earths have little or no magnetostriction. The sign of the magnetostriction also depends on the sign of the Stevens factor, that is, whether the 4f charge density distribution is prolate or oblate. The stress-induced anisotropy can be determined by measuring the anisotropy of a film before and after it is removed from the substrate. Since a free-standing film cannot support a macroscopic stress it cannot support a macroscopic stress-induced anisotropy.

Stress in a film on a substrate can come about through differential thermal expansion if the film is grown at a temperature either above or below the temperature at which the film is to be used (e.g., room temperature). Typically the substrate temperature is above room temperature and the thermal expansion of the amorphous metallic film is greater than the thermal expansion of substrates like glass, SiO_2 or Si, so the film is left in tension when cooled to room temperature.

Polymer substrates typically have a larger coefficient of thermal expansion than metallic magnetic films. In crystalline epitaxial films the lattice mismatch between film and substrate can be used to induce anisotropy. In amorphous films, however, the largest contribution to the biaxial stress is the intrinsic growth stress. Most metal films, either amorphous or crystalline, deposited at low substrate temperatures (T_s) tend to grow with intrinsic tensile stress. At temperatures which are low compared with the melting point (T_M) so that surface diffusion of the adatom is inhibited, films tend to grow with some excess free volume. After deposition some annealing occurs even if the substrate temperature is low and the film atoms move closer together, thus taking up some of the free volume and causing an isotropic shrinkage of the film. However, if the film is constrained by a substrate, the decrease in volume will put the film in planar stress. Ion bombardment during growth causes a transition from tensile to compressive stress [60]. Intrinsic stress modification by ion bombardment has been analyzed in terms of a model based on the number of film atoms undergoing rearrangement shortly after deposition as a result of ion impact. In contrast to annealing effects, the volume decrease caused by ion bombardment is not isotropic. Because the ion impact is directional (e.g., normal to the film plane), atomic displacements caused by ion impact compress the film in the direction perpendicular to the film plane and cause the film to expand in the film plane. Since the film is constrained by a substrate, however, the increase in film area is converted to planar compressive stress.

In discussing magnetic anisotropy it is essential to understand the structural origins as well as the microscopic mechanism. In the case of amorphous magnetic materials the anisotropic structural features which produce magnetic anisotropy are formed during preparation of the material. A crystalline material with an anisotropic crystal structure has intrinsic magnetic anisotropy known as magnetocrystalline anisotropy. Cubic materials, such as the rare earth iron garnets, have cubic anisotropy but their crystal structure does not produce a uniaxial anisotropy. However, garnets are known to have growth-induced uniaxial anisotropy, a structural feature produced during growth which produces magnetic anisotropy through one of the microscopic mechanisms outlined above. In the case of amorphous materials the cubic anisotropy is absent but as in the cubic materials, growth-induced uniaxial anisotropy is possible.

We can exclude magnetocrystalline anisotropy in the amorphous case because there is no long-range order. It is possible to prepare amorphous films with columnar microstructure, and if the exchange coupling between the columns is broken and the columns have a high aspect ratio we can expect, as an upper limit, an anisotropy field $H_K = 4\pi M_s$. A columnar microstructure is apparently the main cause of anisotropy in electrodeposited amorphous films of Co-P and NiCo-P [66]. Small angle X-ray diffraction of electrodeposited Co-P revealed the presence of oriented, acicular voids with their long axis oriented perpendicular to the film plane [67]. However, shape anisotropy is not the main cause of anisotropy in amorphous RE-TM films used as magneto-optical media. In the latter case, anisotropy fields many times $4\pi M_s$ have been observed and this is not possible with the simple shape model. Second, Cargill and Mizoguchi showed that in the Gd-Co amorphous alloys, films with the highest density and no evidence of voids had the highest anisotropy [68].

One of the mechanisms of anisotropy in crystalline alloy solid solutions is pair ordering. Néel has shown that when NiFe is annealed in a magnetic field under neutron irradiation it develops a uniaxial anisotropy because of ordering of Fe-Fe pairs [69]. After annealing in a field it is found that more Fe-Fe pairs are oriented with the pair axis perpendicular to the applied field direction. The pair ordering was detected by neutron diffraction. The easy magnetic axis is along the direction that the field was applied during annealing. The theory of pair ordering has been developed by Néel [69] and Taniguchi [70]. Pair ordering is certainly possible in an amorphous alloy because it does not involve long-range ordering. However, more complex forms of short-range ordering are also possible in amorphous materials. In fact, pair ordering can be treated as a limiting case of $\underline{C}$ompositional $\underline{D}$irectional $\underline{S}$hort $\underline{R}$ange $\underline{O}$rdering (CDSRO). Instead of considering the distribution of pairs, in CDSRO we characterize the angular distribution of nearest neighbors of a given element around a central element. For example, in a close-packed f.c.c. alloy like NiFe each Fe has 12 nearest neighbors (nn). In a random solid solution, the average number of Fe having an Fe nearest neighbor, nn_{FeFe}, is the product of the coordination number (CN) and the Fe atomic fraction (X_{Fe}); that is,

$$nn_{FeFe} = CN_{Fe}(X_{Fe}) \tag{2.16}$$

The probability of Fe having an Fe nn is the average over the total number of nn atoms:

$$P_{FeFe} = nn_{FeFe}/CN_{Fe} = CN_{Fe}(X_{Fe})/CN_{Fe} = X_{Fe} \tag{2.17}$$

Chemical short-range ordering is a deviation from this statistical distribution. For example, in amorphous Cu-Zr alloys Mizuguchi has shown that Zr has more Cu nearest neighbors than would be expected on the basis of a random statistical distribution [71].

In directional short-range ordering, CDSRO, the deviation from a random distribution depends on the direction. To visualize CDSRO consider a two-dimensional close packing of circles, as shown in Figure 2.16. In Figure 2.16(a) a random distribution is shown of a close packing consisting of one-third crosshatched circles. Each nearest neighbor has a 0.333 probability of being crosshatched and a 0.666 probability of being an open circle. The probability distribution is shown in the lower part of the

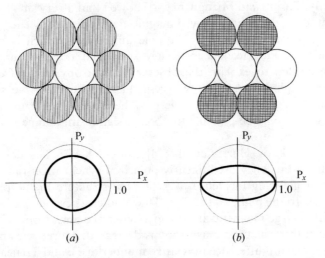

Figure 2.16 Example of chemical directional short-range ordering in two dimensions. An isotropic distribution of 1/3 crosshatched and 2/3 open circles is shown in (a). The lower part of (a) shows the probability of an open circle, $p = 0.666$ in all directions. An anisotropic distribution is shown in (b) with $P_x = 1$ and $P_z = 0.5$.

figure for open circle nearest neighbors. The probability is represented by the distance from the origin and since it is the same in all directions in the xy plane, the probability distribution is a circle. An example of directional ordering is shown in Figure 2.16(b). The center atom only has open circle neighbors in the x direction, and the neighbors in the y direction have an equal probability of being open or crosshatched circles. This distribution can be represented, as shown in Figure 2.16(b) by the distorted ellipse which extends out to the circle representing a probability of one in the x direction and to 0.5 in the y direction. Note that the average number of open circle nearest neighbors has remained the same. The chemical short-range ordering has not changed, so each open circle has on average two crosshatched and four open circle neighbors. What has changed is the probability of finding a given type of neighbor in a particular direction. In crystalline material the distribution of atomic positions in space is dictated by the lattice and the structural parameters. By contrast, in an amorphous two-dimensional packing all directions have an equal probability of being occupied so the geometric Figure in 2.16(b), would be an undistorted ellipse.

Another type of directional ordering called bond-orientational order has been proposed in liquids and glasses [72]. Egami and coworkers have tried to use this type of ordering to explain the anisotropy that develops in amorphous materials after plastic deformation followed by annealing. They propose that the anisotropy comes about because the bond distances are different in different directions in the material. This structural anisotropy has been called Bond Directional Short Range Order (BDSRO). In addition to the deformation/anneal route to this type of anisotropy, Egami et al. have suggested that BDSRO might develop during the deposition of amorphous RE-TM alloys [73]. In contrast to CDSRO which should only be operative in alloys, BDSRO could work in an amorphous element. Of course, it is possible that both CDSRO and BDSRO contribute to the anisotropy in deposited RE-TM films.

All attempts to detect CDSRO by X-ray diffraction have been unsuccessful until very recently. Cargill and Mizoguchi [68] showed that a very small structural anisotropy is sufficient to produce the observed magnitude of anisotropy energy in amorphous Gd-Co. Their estimate was based on dipole anisotropy, which is probably one of the weakest microscopic mechanisms. They state that the structural anisotropy of the magnitude needed to explain the observed anisotropy in Gd-Co is very difficult to detect. In a single-ion anisotropy system like Tb-Fe the same structural anisotropy will produce a higher anisotropy energy. Therefore, in systems involving non-S-state rare earth ions it may be possible to observe significant magnetic anisotropy with even less structural anisotropy.

Recent work by Harris et al. [74] using EXAFS has detected an anisotropic CDSRO in Tb-Fe. They used linearly polarized synchrotron radiation at normal incidence and at glancing incidence to probe the structure in the plane of the film and perpendicular to the plane of the film. They find clear evidence of structural anisotropy in films with a large magnetic anisotropy. When the anisotropy of the film is decreased by annealing, the structural anisotropy is decreased. Moreover, Harris et al. show that there is a significant difference in relative number of Fe and Tb nearest neighbors in the plane vs. out of the plane. This EXAFS method has provided the first clear evidence of structural anisotropy and of CDSRO. It is possible that BDSRO is also present, however, the compositional anisotropy probably makes a very strongly anisotropic crystal field causing a large single-ion anisotropy.

Even more recently, Hufnagel et al. have used X-ray scattering to show that the pair distribution in sputtered amorphous Tb-Fe is anisotropic [75]. They find a larger number of Tb-Fe pairs in the out-of-plane direction than in the plane. The structure anisotropy was detectable in a comparison of the reduced radial distribution functions (RDF) obtained from out-of-plane (reflection) and in-plane (transmission) scattering experiments. The observations were confirmed by the Tb-edge differential distribution function (DDF) from anomalous dispersion data.

The mechanisms which produce an anisotropic structure in an amorphous phase have been discussed in the literature since the discovery of anisotropy in Gd-Co [15]. It is clear that the anisotropy depends on deposition conditions. For example, Tb-Fe produced by high-rate sputtering is not anisotropic [76], whereas amorphous Tb-Fe deposited at more normal rates is anisotropic. In fact, the random anisotropy of amorphous TbFe$_2$ causes the observed decreased Curie point and magnetization according to the theory of Harris, Plischke, and Zuckermann [77]. It is clear, therefore, that the microscopic mechanism of anisotropy which is active is single-ion anisotropy caused by the non-S-state Tb in an anisotropic crystal field. The easy axis of each site is randomly oriented so there is no anisotropy with respect to the film as a whole.

Other experiments have shown that thermal annealing and ion implantation damage both destroy anisotropy [78], [79], [80], [81], [82]. Both of these processes are associated with randomization so these effects are evidence that there is an ordering mechanism during deposition.

One of the first mechanisms proposed to explain the development of anisotropy is the selective re-sputtering model [19]. Re-sputtering can lead to structural anisotropy if the sputter removal of an adatom is dependent on the surface site it occupies. The sputtering threshold depends on the binding energy of the surface atom. In most sputtering models the surface binding energy is estimated from the heat of sublimation. However, in an alloy the surface binding energies of all sites are not equal. This can lead to the selective sputter removal of atoms of one type from particular sites.

REFERENCES

[1] P. Chaudhari, J. J. Cuomo, and R. J. Gambino, "Amorphous Metallic Films for Beam Addressable Applications," *Appl. Phys. Lett.*, vol. 22, p. 337, 1973.

[2] E. A. Nesbitt and J. H. Wernick, *Rare Earth Permanent Magnets*, New York: Academic Press, 1973.

[3] Pol Duwez and R. H. Willens, "Rapid Quenching of Liquid Alloys," *Trans. A.I.M.E.*, vol. 227, p. 362, 1963.

[4] S. Mader and A. S. Nowick, "Metastable Co-Au Alloys; Example of an Amorphous Ferromagnet," vol. 7, p. 57, 1965.

[5] C. C. Tsuei and Pol Duwez, "Metastable Amorphous Ferromagnetic Phases in Palladium-Base Alloys," *J. Appl. Phys.*, vol. 37, p. 435, 1966; Pol Duwez and S. C. H. Lin, "Amorphous Ferromagnetic Phase in Iron-Carbon-Phosphorus Alloys," *J. Appl. Phys.*, vol. 38, p. 4096, 1967.

[6] Pol Duwez, "Structure and Properties of Alloys Rapidly Quenched from the Liquid State," *ASM Trans.*, vol. 60, p. 607, 1967.

[7] J. Orehotsky and K. Schroder, *J. Appl. Phys.*, vol. 43, p. 2413, 1972.

[8] A. H. Bobeck, *Bell Syst. Tech. J.*, vol. 46, p. 1901, 1967.

[9] A. H. Bobeck and H. E. D. Scovil, *Sci. Amer.*, vol. 224, p. 78, 1971.

[10] A. H. Bobeck, E. G. Spencer, L. G. Van Uitert, S. C. Abrahams, R. L. Barns, W. H. Grodkiewicz, R. C. Sherwood, P. H. Schmidt, D. H. Smith, and E. M. Walters, *Appl. Phys. Lett.*, vol. 17, p. 131, 1970.

[11] R. J. Gambino and R. R. Ruf, unpublished.

[12] R. J. Gambino and J. J. Cuomo, unpublished.

[13] E. A. Giess and D. C. Cronemeyer, *Appl. Phys. Lett.*, vol. 22, p. 601, 1973.

[14] E. Klokholm, R. J. Gambino, and J. J. Cuomo, "The Effect of Stress on the Curie Temperature of Gadolinium Films," *A.I.P. Conference Proceedings*, vol. 5, p. 1462, 1972.

[15] P. Chaudhari, J. J. Cuomo, and R. J. Gambino, "Amorphous Metallic Films for Bubble Domain Applications," *IBM J. Res. and Dev.*, vol. 17, p. 66, 1973.

[16] R. J. Gambino, P. Chaudhari and J. J. Cuomo, "Amorphous Magnetic Materials," *A.I.P. Conference Proceedings*, vol. 18, p. 578, 1974.

[17] J. J. Cuomo and R. J. Gambino, "Influence of Sputtering Parameters on the Composition of Multi-Component Films," *J. Vac. Sci. Technol.*, vol. 12, p. 79, 1975.

[18] J. J. Cuomo, R. J. Gambino, and R. Rosenberg, "The Influence of Bias on the Deposition of Metallic Films in R. F. and D. C. Sputtering," *J. Vac. Sci. Technol.*, vol. 11, p. 34, 1974.

[19] R. J. Gambino and J. J. Cuomo, "Selective Resputtering-Induced Anisotropy in Amorphous Films," *J. Vac. Sci. Technol.*, vol. 15, p. 296, 1978.

[20] L-J. Tao, R. J. Gambino, S. Kirkpatrick, J. J. Cuomo, and H. Lilienthal, "Magnetic Properties of Amorphous GdCo Films," *AIP Conference Proceedings*, vol. 18, p. 641, 1974.

[21] B. E. Argyle, R. J. Gambino, and K. Y. Ahn, "Polar Kerr Rotation and Sublattice Magnetization in GdCoMo Bubble Films," *AIP Conference Proceedings*, vol. 24, p. 564, 1975.

[22] P. Chaudhari, J. J. Cuomo, R. J. Gambino, S. Kirkpatrick, and L-J. Tao, "Ternary Amorphous Alloys for Bubble Domain Applications", *AIP Conference Proceedings*, vol. 24, p. 562, 1975.

[23] R. Hasegawa, R. J. Gambino, and R. Ruf, "Magnetic Properties of Amorphous GdCoAu," *Appl. Phys. Lett.*, vol. 7, p. 512, 1975.

[24] M. H. Kryder, K. Y. Ahn, G. S. Almasi, G. E. Keefe, and J. V. Powers, *IEEE Trans. Magn.*, vol. 10, p. 825, 1974.

[25] J. J. Cuomo, P. Chaudhari, and R. J. Gambino, "Amorphous Magnetic Materials for Bubble Domain and Magneto-Optics Applications," *J. Elect. Mat.*, vol. 3, p. 517, 1974.

[26] R. J. Gambino, P. Chaudhari, and J. J. Cuomo, unpublished.

[27] K. Weiser, R. J. Gambino and J. A. Reinhold, "Laser-Beam Writing on Amorphous Chalcogenide Films: Crystallization Kinetics and Analysis of Amorphizing Energy," *Appl. Phys. Lett.*, vol. 22, p. 48, 1973.

[28] C. F. Shelton, "Magneto-Optical Beam Addressable Storage Using MnGaGe and GdCo," *IEEE Trans. Mag.*, vol. 9, p. 398, 1973.

[29] B. G. Huth, "Calculations of Stable Domain Radii Produced by Thermomagnetic Writing," *IBM J. Res. Dev.*, p. 100, March 1974.

[30] P. Chaudhari, J. J. Cuomo, and R. J. Gambino, *U.S. Patent* 3,949,387, "Beam Addressable Film Using Amorphous Magnetic Material," April 6, 1976.

[31] N. Heiman and K. Lee, "Magnetic Properties of Ho-Co and Ho-Fe Amorphous Films," *Phys. Rev. Lett.*, vol. 33, p. 778, 1974.

[32] R. C. Taylor, "Magnetic Properties of Amorphous Gd-Fe Films Prepared by Evaporation," *J. Appl. Phys.*, vol. 47, p.1164, 1976.

[33] S. Matasushita, K. Sunago, and Y. Sakurai, "Thermomagnetic Writing In Gd-Co Sputtered Films," *IEEE Trans. Mag.*, vol. 11, p. 1109, 1975.

[34] S. Matasushita, K. Sunago, and Y. Sakurai, "Thermomagnetic Writing in Ho-Co Films," *Japan J. Appl. Phys.*, vol. 14, p. 1851, 1975.

[35] Y. Mimura, N. Imamura, and T. Kobayashi, "Curie Point Writing in Amorphous Magnetic Films," *Japan J. Appl. Phys.*, vol. 15, p. 933, 1976.

[36] Y. Mimura, N. Imamura, T. Kobayashi, A. Okada, and Y. Kushiro, "Magnetic Properties of Amorphous Alloy Films of Fe with Gd, Tb, Dy, Ho or Er," *J. Appl. Phys.*, vol. 49, p. 1208, 1978.

[37] N. Imamura and C. Ota, "Experimental Study on Magneto-Optical Disk Exerciser with the Laser Diode and Amorphous Magnetic Thin Film," *Japan J. Appl. Phys.*, vol. 19, L731, 1980.

[38] L. Néel, *Ann. Phys.*, vol. 3, p. 137, 1948.

[39] T. R. McGuire and R. J. Gambino, "Magnetic and Transport Properties of Rare-Earth Au and Cu Amorphous Alloys," *J. Appl. Phys.*, vol. 50, no. 11, p. 7653, 1979.

[40] T. R. McGuire, R. J. Gambino, and R. C. O'Handley, "Hall Effect in Amorphous Metals," in *The Hall Effect and its Applications*, C. L. Chien and C. R. Westgate, (eds.), New York: Plenum Press, p. 137, 1980.

[41] Slater-Pauling Curves: *See* R. Bozorth, *Ferromagnetism*, IEEE Press Classic Reissue, 1993.

[42] A. P. Malozemoff, A. R. Williams, K. Terakura, V. L. Moruzzi, and K. Fukamichi, *J. Mag. Magn. Mat.*, vol. 35, p. 192, 1983; *IEEE Trans. Mag.*, vol. 19, p. 1983, 1983.

[43] S. Von Molnar, C. N. Guy, R. J. Gambino, and T. R. McGuire, "Magnetic Phase Diagram of Amorphous Dy-Cu; A Random Anisotropy Axis System," *J. Mag. Magn. Mat.*, vol. 15-18, p. 1391, 1980. S. Von Molnar, T. R. McGuire, and R. J. Gambino, "Random Anisotropy Effects in Amorphous Rare Earth Alloys," *J. Appl. Phys.*, vol. 53, p. 7666, 1982.

[44] J. M. D Coey, and P. W. Readman, *Nature*, vol. 246, p. 476, 1973; *see also* K. Moorjani and J. M. D. Coey, *Magnetic Glasses*, Amsterdam: Elsevier, 1984.

[45] S. J. Pickart, J. J. Rhyne, and H. A. Alperin, *Phys. Rev. Lett.*, vol. 33, p. 424, 1974.

[46] H. Hiroyoshi and K. Fukamichi, *J. Appl. Phys.*, vol. 53, p. 2226, 1982.

[47] T. Mizuguchi, T. R. McGuire, S. Kirkpatrick, and R. J. Gambino, *Phys. Rev. Lett.*, vol. 38, p. 89, 1983.

[48] V. L. Moruzzi, A. R. Williams, A. P. Malozemoff, and R. J. Gambino, "Magnetism in Ordered and Amorphous YCo3 and YFe3," *Phys. Rev.*, vol. B28, p. 5511, 1983.

[49] R. M. Bozorth, *Ferromagnetism*, Piscataway, N.J.: IEEE Press, p. 195, 1993.

[50] R. J. Gambino and T. R. McGuire, "Magneto-Optic Properties of Nd-Fe-Co Amorphous Alloys", *J. Appl. Phys.*, vol. 57, p. 3906, 1985.

[51] R. J. Gambino and T. R. McGuire, "Enhanced Magneto-Optic Properties of Light Rare Earth-Transition Metal Amorphous Alloys," *J. Mag. Magn. Mat.*, vol. 54-57, p. 1365, 1986.

[52] T. Shirakawa, Y. Nakajima, K. Okamoto, S. Matsushita, and Y. Sakurai, *AIP Conference Proceedings*, vol. 34, p. 349, 1976.

[53] W. Reim, R. J. Gambino, R. R. Ruf, and T. S. Plaskett, "TbxNdy(FeCo)$_{1-x-y}$: Promising Materials for Magneto-Optical Storage?," *J. Appl. Phys.*, vol. 61, p. 3349, 1987.

[54] Z. S. Shan, D. J. Sellmyer, S. S. Jaswal, Y. J. Wang, and J. X. Shen, "Magnetism of Rare-Earth-Transition-Metal Nanoscale Multilayers," *Phys. Rev. Lett.*, vol. 63, p. 449, 1989.

[55] R. J. Gambino, "Magneto-Optical Recording Materials – Past, Present and Future," MORIS'91 Proceedings, *J. Magn. Soc. Japan* 15, Supplement S1, 1, 1991.

[56] R. J. Gambino, R. R. Ruf, and N. A. Bojarczuk, "Macroscopic Ferrimagnets as Magneto-Optic Media," *J. Appl. Phys.*, Abstract only, vol. 75, p. 6871, 1994; N. A. Bojarczuk, R. J. Gambino and R. R. Ruf, U.S. Patents 05793711 and 05612131.

[57] R. J. Gambino and P. Fumagalli, "Magneto-Optic Properties of Macroscopic Ferrimagnets," *IEEE Trans. Mag.*, vol. 30, p. 4461, 1994.

[58] R. J. Gambino, "EuO/Tb-Fe-Co Exchange Coupled Films," *J. Magn. Soc. Japan*, vol. 19, Supplement S1, p. 17, 1995.

[59] R. J. Gambino, J. Wang, and T. R. McGuire, "Magnetoresistance of Co-EuS Macroscopic Ferrimagnets," *IEEE Trans. Mag.*, vol. 31, p. 3915, 1995.

[60] J. M. E. Harper, J. J. Cuomo, R. J. Gambino, and H. R. Kaufman, "Modification of Thin Film Properties by Ion Bombardment During Deposition," Chapter 3, *Ion Bombardment Modification of Surfaces*, Vol. I, O. Auciello and R. Kelly (eds.), Amsterdam: Elsevier Science Publishers, 1984.

[61] J. J. Cuomo and R. J. Gambino, "Incorporation of Rare Gases In Sputtered Amorphous Metal Films," *J. Vac. Sci. Technol.*, vol. 143, p. 152, 1977.

[62] J. M. E. Harper and R. J. Gambino, "Combined Ion Beam Deposition and Etching for Thin Film Studies," *J. Vac. Sci. Technol.*, vol. 16, p. 1901, 1979.

[63] R. M. Bozorth, *Ferromagnetism*, IEEE Press, Piscataway, NJ, 1993.

[64] M. Chikazumi, *Physics of Magnetism*, New York: John Wiley, 1964.

[65] P. Chaudhari, J. J. Cuomo, R. J. Gambino, and E. A. Giess, "Magnetic Bubble Films," *Physics of Thin Films*, Vol. 9, George Hass, Maurice H. Francombe, and Richard W. Hoffman (eds.), New York: Academic Press, 1977.

[66] G. S. Cargill, III, R. J. Gambino, and J. J. Cuomo, *IEEE Trans. Mag.*, vol. 10, p. 803 (1974).

[67] G. S. Cargill, III, and R. W. Cochrane, In *Amorphous Magnetism*, H. O. Hooper and A. M. de Graaf (eds.), New York: Plenum, pp. 313–320, 1972.

[68] G. S. Cargill, III and T. Mizoguchi, *J. Appl. Phys.*, vol. 49, p. 1753, 1978, *J. Appl. Phys.*, vol. 50, p. 3570, 1979.

[69] L. Néel, *J. Phys. Radium*, vol. 15, p. 225, 1954.

[70] S. Taniguchi, *Sci. Rep. Res. Inst.*, Tohoku University, A7, p. 269, 1955.

[71] T. Mizoguchi, In *Diffraction Studies on Non-Crystalline Substances*, I. Hargittai and W. J. Orville-Thomas (eds.), Amsterdam: Elsevier, 1981.

[72] P. J. Steinhardt, D. R. Nelson, and M. Ronchetti, *Phys. Rev. B.*, vol. 28, p. 784, 1983.

[73] X. Yan, M. Hirscher, T. Egami, and E. E. Marinero, *Phys. Rev. B.*, vol. 43, p. 9300, 1991.

[74] V. G. Harris, K. D. Aylesworth, B. N. Das, W. T. Elam, and N. C. Koon, *Phys. Rev. Lett.*, vol. 69, p. 1939, 1992; V. G. Harris, K. D. Aylesworth, B. N. Das, W. T. Elam, and N. C. Koon, *IEEE Trans. Mag.*, vol. 28, p. 2958, 1992.

[75] T. C. Hufnagel, S. Brennan, P. Zschack, and B. M. Clemens, Paper AD-02, *Intermag Conference*, Seattle, 1996.

[76] J. J. Rhyne, S. J. Pickart, and H. A. Alperin, *Phys. Rev. Lett.*, vol. 29, p. 1562, 1972.

[77] R. Harris, M. Plischke, and M. J. Zuckermann, "New Model for Amorphous Magnetism," *Phys. Rev. Lett.*, vol. 31, p. 160, 1973.

[78] R. Hasegawa, R. J. Gambino, J. J. Cuomo, and J. F. Ziegler, "Effect of Thermal Annealing and Ion Radiation on the Coercivity of Amorphous GdCo Films," *J. Appl. Phys.*, vol. 45, p. 4036, 1974.

[79] R. J. Gambino, J. Ziegler, and J. J. Cuomo, "Effects of Ion Radiation Damage on the Magnetic Domain Structure of Amorphous Gd-Co Alloys," *Appl. Phys. Lett.*, vol. 24, p. 99, 1974.

[80] T. Mizoguchi, R. J. Gambino, W. N. Hammer, and J. J. Cuomo, "Effects of Ion Implantation Damage on the Magnetic Properties of Amorphous GdCoMo Films," *IEEE Trans. Magn.*, MAG-13, p. 1618, 1977.

[81] T. Katayama, K. Hasegawa, K. Kawanishi, and T. Tsushima, "Annealing Effects on Magnetic Properties of Amorphous GdCo, GdFe and GdCoMo Films," *J. Appl. Phys.*, vol. 49, p. 1759, 1978.

[82] F. E. Luborsky, "Kinetics for Changes in Anisotropy, Coercivity and Argon Content of Transition Metal-Rare Earth Films," *J. Appl. Phys.*, vol. 57, p. 3592, 1985.

NEW MO RECORDING MEDIA BASED ON PT/CO AND PD/CO MULTILAYERS AND PT-CO ALLOYS

Peter F. Carcia, Takao Suzuki

3.1 INTRODUCTION

In magneto-optical (MO) recording [1]–[5], information is stored as perpendicularly magnetized domains in a thin magnetic film. Initially, the disk is magnetized in one direction, and reverse domains are written by locally heating the medium with a laser in a small reversing field (~200 Oe, 15.9 kA/m) from a permanent magnet or an electromagnet. Laser power less than 10 mW, focused to about a micron-size spot, is usually sufficient for writing. The orientation ("up" or "down") of magnetization in a disk is read by detecting the sense, clockwise or counterclockwise, of rotation (Kerr effect) of reflected, linearly polarized light. Only a small laser power, ~1 mW, is used for reading, so as not to change written information. The amplitude of the read signal depends on both the magnitude of the Kerr rotation, which is < 1° for common MO media, and the optical reflectivity.

The minimum bit size that can be read, and thus the ultimate storage density for MO recording, is limited by optical diffraction. A practical limit for minimum domain size detection with standard optics is of the order of the laser wavelength, λ. Currently, the most commonly available compact lasers, used for optical recording, e.g., in an audio CD player and in the current generation of MO disk drives, have a wavelength in the infrared, between 780 and 820 nm. Thus, a 90 mm MO diskette can potentially store as much as ~0.6 Gbyte/side [2], even with current lasers. That is about 500 times more information than magnetic floppy disks and roughly equivalent to that of a CD-ROM. Even with these high storage capacities, it is anticipated that still higher densities will be demanded of optical disks in the future.

A near-term solution to increase the storage density of a MO disk is to use shorter wavelength light. Reducing the wavelength by a factor of two will increase the areal storage density fourfold. To accomplish this, we need to generate blue-green laser light directly [6], [7] or by frequency doubling [8], [9] the light from current, infrared diode lasers in a nonlinear optical device. In fact, practical recording using frequency doubled laser light has already been demonstrated [10].

However, the Kerr signal in the current generation of MO disks, which use a rare-earth transition metal alloy [1], [4], [5], [11] (e.g., TbFeCo), becomes smaller at short optical wavelengths, where higher storage density is possible. The smaller signal and the lower sensitivity of optical detectors at short wavelength make it imperative to find new MO recording media with higher Kerr rotation at blue wavelength.

Of course, a large Kerr rotation is only one of many properties simultaneously required for a new MO recording medium. A new medium also needs perpendicular magnetic anisotropy for storing magnetic bits, a square hysteresis loop for maximum read signal, a large coercivity to preserve written information and allow stable small domains [12] to be written, a modest thermomagnetic switching temperature, and low optical noise. Since the current commercial MO media are susceptible to corrosion, because of easy oxidation of rare-earth elements, improved corrosion resistance in a new medium would also be highly desirable. Finally, a new medium should be a cost-effective manufacturing alternative compared with current media. Although this is a rather formidable list of requirements, metal multilayers of Pt/Co and Pd/Co [11], [13], [14] satisfy most of these criteria. In the following sections, we will describe how to synthesize these multilayers and discuss the relationship of their preparation and micro-structure to magnetic, magneto-optical, and recording properties. There has also been some recent work with alloys [15], [16] of Pt and Co for high-density, MO blue-wavelength recording, and their properties will also be discussed.

3.2 Pt/Co AND Pd/Co MULTILAYERS: GENERAL PROPERTIES

3.2.1 Multilayer Structure

A schematic representation of an ideal multilayer with a periodic structure and chemically sharp interfaces is depicted in Figure 3.1. In contrast to this image, the structure of an actual metal multilayer is often less than ideal and is sensitive to the preparation method and growth conditions. The cross section of vapor-deposited Pt/Co multilayers, viewed by high-resolution, transmission electron microscopy, is shown in Figure 3.2. The wavy light and dark bands in this image correspond to Co-rich and Pt-rich layers, respectively. The rough layers are attributable to the low adatom energy of vapor-deposited Pt and Co, favoring island rather than layer by layer growth.

In general, materials being layered may have different crystal structures and lattice dimensions, which can cause imperfections or incoherence at layer interfaces. For example, there is a relatively large mismatch (10%) in bulk lattice constants [17], $a_o = 3.92$ Å and $a_o = 3.89$ Å for fcc Pt and fcc Pd, respectively, and $a_o = 3.552$ Å for fcc Co. Therefore, formation of chemically sharp, defect-free, coherent (lattice-matched) inter-

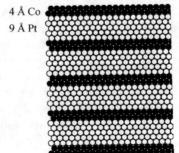

4 Å Co
9 Å Pt

Figure 3.1 Representation of an ideal, periodic, multilayer structure comprised of two atomic layers of Co (filled circles) and five atomic layers of Pt (open circles).

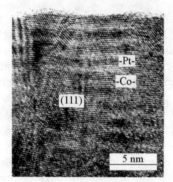

Figure 3.2 High resolution transmission electron micrograph image of the cross section of a vapor-deposited Pt/Co multilayer [93].

faces between Pt or Pd and Co layers is probably not realistic. These structures are thus best visualized as highly chemically modulated with some interfacial accommodation on an atomic scale for the large lattice mismatch. This accommodation may involve chemical (mixing) or physical (e.g., dislocations) defects or both.

The most common tool to characterize the structure of multilayers is X-ray diffraction [18]–[20]. Because of the chemical and lattice modulation of a multilayer, there are additional "superlattice" peaks in the diffraction pattern. The periodicity (D), due to the artificial modulation, can be calculated from the angular positions (φ_i, $\varphi_i + 1$) of consecutive diffracted peaks at an X-ray wavelength λ_x, using Bragg's law of diffraction

$$D = \lambda_x / 2(\sin \varphi_i - \sin \varphi_i + 1) \qquad (3.1)$$

Figure 3.3 illustrates a typical X-ray diffraction pattern, obtained at low angle and high angle from a Pt/Co multilayer film, made by diode sputtering. Because of the longer length scale, the low angle diffraction depends almost exclusively on the chemical modulation of the multilayer. An analysis of the intensities of the low angle peaks can therefore give information about interdiffusion [18]–[20] of the individual layers. We have done this for Pt/Co and Pd/Co multilayers [21], made by rf diode sputtering. Pd/Co multilayers, we concluded, have chemically sharper interfaces than Pt/Co multilayers prepared by this technique. This is consistent with a more favorable heat of alloy formation of Co with Pt than with Pd [22].

More detailed modeling [23]–[25] of X-ray diffraction data from the multilayers can also be used to separate interfacial roughness and chemical interdiffusion between layers. D. C. Johnson and coworkers [25] at the University of Oregon have determined from X-ray analysis the effect of sputter gas mass (Ar, Kr, Xe) on structural properties of Pt/Co multilayers prepared by dc magnetron sputtering. Their analysis indicates that sputtering with a heavier gas (Xe) reduces chemical interdiffusion between Pt and Co but increases the roughness at interfaces, compared with sputtering with a lighter gas (Ar). This is consistent with energetic bombardment of the multilayer by reflected Ar neutrals [26], which apparently enhances interdiffusion and promotes layer by layer growth. Reflected Xe neutrals are much less energetic [26], and Co and Pt layers are consequently rougher and less chemically mixed.

Both Pt/Co and Pd/Co thin film multilayers grow preferentially with (111)-fcc planes normal to the growth direction [21]. The intense X-ray peak at about 40° in Figure 3.3 is the signature of (111)fcc texture in this multilayer. These are the atomic

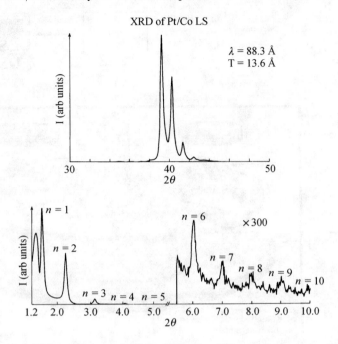

Figure 3.3 High and low angle X-ray diffraction of an rf diode sputtered Pt/Co multilayer, $150\times(13.6\text{Å Co}+74.7\text{Å Pt})$ [21].

planes with the densest packing and lowest surface energy [27] for fcc metals. The degree of texture, as measured by the FWHM from rocking angle X-ray diffraction about the (111) peak, depends on the growth method and conditions during growth. Polycrystalline multilayers, sputtered or e-beam evaporated, commonly have a FWHM $\sim 15°$ [28] and MBE-grown crystalline multilayers $\sim 1°$ [29], [30]. Fortunately, the magnetic properties are also optimum [29], [30] for recording applications, when Pt/Co and Pd/Co multilayers grow along the [111] direction. Although Co can take on either the hcp or fcc structure, Co layers are fcc [21] when they are relatively thin and multilayered with either Pd or Pt, both fcc metals. And multilayers with ultra-thin Co layers have the most attractive properties for MO recording [31]. For about two mono-layers of Co, Li et al. [32] found by high-resolution electron microscopy that Pt/Co multilayer have a fcc structure, characterized by a single lattice constant along the [111] direction, $d(111) = 2.2$ Å. As the Co layer becomes thicker, its structure transforms [32] to mixed fcc and hcp with their characteristic Co-bulk, lattice spacings, and the number of visible defects in the multilayer grows.

In the following sections, we describe the properties of Pt/Co and Pd/Co multi-layers with (111)-fcc texture, unless specific reference is made to another texture.

3.2.2 Deposition Techniques

Sputtering and electron beam evaporation are the two common methods used to synthesize Pd/Co and Pt/Co multilayers. In our sputtering system, schematically illu-strated in Figure 3.4, targets of Co and Pt or Pd are physically separated from one another. Substrates lie on a water-cooled, rotatable table, and an aperture plate

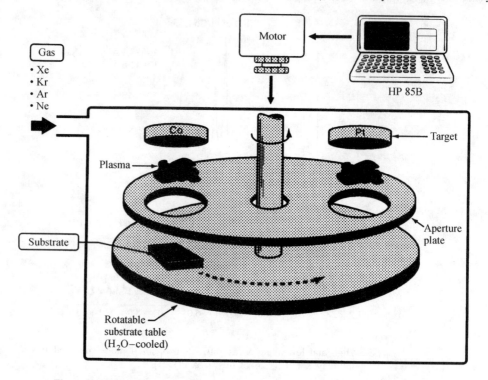

Figure 3.4 Schematic representation of the vacuum sputtering system used to deposit multilayers.

between the targets and table shields substrates from coating, except when they are under a target. The multilayer structure is produced by pausing substrates under each target for a programmed time, independently set to give the desired layer thicknesses. This process can be repeated for a specified number of repetitions. In our particular equipment, the table can also be rf biased, so that substrates can be sputter-etched or cleaned prior to deposition. Multilayers grown on sputter-etched substrates have much better magnetic properties.

In nearly all of our recent experiments, we sputter-deposited multilayers by dc magnetron sputtering. For this method, the Co target must be thin, < 1 mm, to minimize magnetic flux trapping by the ferromagnetic Co target. Some leakage of magnetic flux from the sputtering gun magnet into the vacuum space is necessary to confine the motion of secondary electrons that sustain the plasma by ionizing collisions with gas atoms, near the target. This problem of flux trapping by the target can be circumvented by rf sputtering Co either in a diode or magnetron configuration, since the alternating electric field in the vacuum space accelerates electrons, facilitating ionizing collisions with gas particles, and sustains the plasma.

E-beam evaporated multilayers are made with separate electron guns for each metal. Individual shutters can be used for each gun in order to alternately expose substrates to evaporated metal fluxes. A quartz crystal microbalance controls the metal deposition rates and individual layer thicknesses. Usually, substrate rotation is recommended to ensure uniform deposition, especially when coating larger substrates, such as an optical disk.

For both sputtering and e-beam evaporation, typical deposition rates were between 1 and 5 Å/s. In our experience, background pressures greater than about 5×10^{-7} Torr prior to deposition were generally adequate for making good quality multilayer structures with excellent magnetic properties, whereas poor background pressures, e.g., $> 1 \times 10^{-6}$, compromise the magnetic properties of Pt/Co and Pd/Co multilayers.

3.2.3 Perpendicular Magnetic Anisotropy and Coercivity

A key attribute of Pt/Co and Pd/Co multilayers is a perpendicular easy axis of magnetization [13], [21], [33], [34] that occurs when the Co layer is thin. A large perpendicular anisotropy is necessary in order to store magnetic information with high packing density, to have a large magneto-optic signal via the polar Kerr effect, and for low noise.

Figure 3.5 shows the dependence of magnetic hysteresis loop shape on Co thickness for Pt/Co multilayers. For thin Co, the perpendicular loop is square and the remanent magnetization is equal to its saturation level. As the Co layer thickness increases, the in-plane remanent magnetization becomes larger. Figure 3.6 illustrates how the measured magnetic anisotropy energy (K_{eff}) depends on Co thickness for evaporated Pt/Co multilayers [35] with the Pt thickness fixed at 17 Å. At a Co thickness of about 12 Å, the easy axis of magnetization shifts from in-plane (negative K_{eff}) to perpendicular (positive K_{eff}) as the Co thickness decreases. Pd/Co multilayers exhibit a

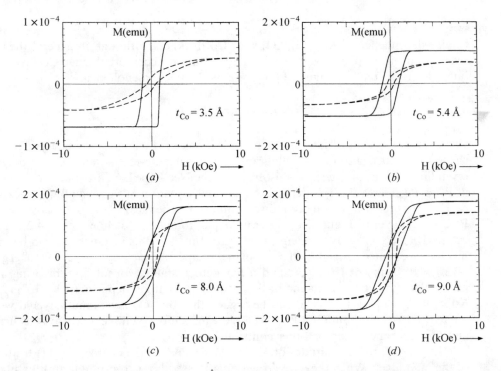

Figure 3.5 Hysteresis loops for $13 \times (t_{\mathrm{Co}} + 17\text{Å Pt})$ multilayers, dc magnetron sputtered in 7 mTorr Kr. Solid curves correspond to loops measured with magnetic field applied perpendicular to film plane and in-plane for dashed curves.

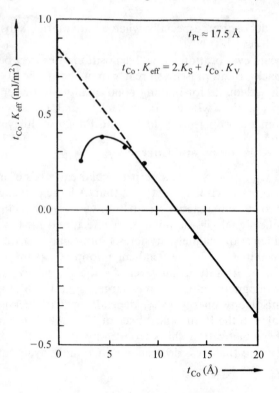

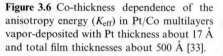

Figure 3.6 Co-thickness dependence of the anisotropy energy (K_{eff}) in Pt/Co multilayers vapor-deposited with Pt thickness about 17 Å and total film thicknesses about 500 Å [33].

similar dependence of K_{eff} [33], [34] with Co thickness, although in general the cross-over to an out-of-plane easy axis of magnetization occurs at thinner Co layers. The linear fit to the data in Figure 3.6 represents the phenomenological equation

$$K_{eff} = K_v + 2\,K_s/t_{Co} \tag{3.2}$$

where K_v is the sum of all volume contributions to the anisotropy energy, including shape (demagnetization), crystallographic, and magneto-elastic, and K_s is a magneto-crystalline surface or interface anisotropy of the Néel-type [36], attributed to Co atoms at Pt or Pd interfaces. The departure from this equation at very small Co thicknesses can be interpreted to be due to a discontinuous or chemically mixed Co layer. For the Pt/Co multilayer of Figure 3.6, Zeper et al. [35] found $K_s = 0.42$ erg/cm^2 (4.2×10^{-4} J/m^2) and $K_v = -6.8 \times 10^6$ erg/cm^3(-6.8×10^5 J/m^3). In this instance, K_v can be conveniently accounted for by the in-plane shape anisotropy (-12.7×10^6 erg/cm^3, -12.7×10^5 J/m^3) of Co layers and a magnetocrystalline anisotropy, favoring a perpendicular easy axis of magnetization, equal to that of hcp Co (6.0×10^6 erg/cm^3, 6.0×10^5 J/m^3) [37]. In fact, it can be argued that thin Co layers multilayered with Pt are fcc [32], which should not have as large a magnetocrystalline anisotropy as hcp Co, and therefore there may be other contributions to K_v.

In general, the magnitudes of K_s and K_v depend on the degree of (111)-fcc texture of the multilayer. When they are grown on a Pt seed layer to promote this texture, Lin et al. [38] find large interface anisotropy energy: $K_s = 0.76$ erg/cm^2 (7.6×10^{-4} J/m^2) for e-beam evaporated Pt/Co multilayers and $K_s = 0.82$ erg/cm^2 (8.2×10^{-4} J/m^2) for MBE growth along the [111] direction. For both films, $K_v \sim -9 \times 10^6\,\text{erg/cm}^3\ (-9 \times 10^5\,\text{J/m}^3)$, smaller than the shape anisotropy of Co layers, which again indicates that there is a volume contribution to a perpendicular easy axis of magnetization. Without a Pt seed layer to promote (111) texture, they find $K_s = 0.31\ \text{erg/cm}^2\ (3.1 \times 10^{-4}\,\text{J/m}^2)$ and $K_v = -10 \times 10^6\,\text{erg/cm}^3\ (-10 \times 10^5\,\text{J/m}^3)$ [38], so that both surface and volume contributions to perpendicular anisotropy are smaller.

The explanation of origin of perpendicular anisotropy in Pt/Co and Pd/Co multilayer is controversial. The various possible contributions to magnetic anisotropy in multilayer structures have been considered in detail by Chappert and Bruno [39], and den Broeder et al. [40]. We originally proposed that the break in chemical symmetry at Pt-Co or Pd-Co interfaces was responsible for perpendicular magnetic anisotropy [33]—i.e., the Néel mechanism [36]. Thus, anisotropy arises from the hybridized character of interfacial Co atoms, and increasing the Co layer diminishes their influence and the magnitude of perpendicular anisotropy. This qualitative explanation is supported by theoretical calculations of Wu, Li, and Freeman [41], who showed that a Co monolayer on Pt(111) has strong perpendicular spin orientation, and by the modified Néel-model calculations of Victora and MacLaren [42] showing strong perpendicular magnetic anisotropy in Pt/Co and Pd/Co multilayer along the [111] direction.

The experimental evidence supporting this Néel-type mechanism is also compelling. Annealing [21], [33], [43–45] these multilayers to deliberately chemically mix the layers, or synthesizing them by more energetic ion-beam sputtering [43], [46], that also causes mixing, reduces K_{eff} and perpendicular hysteresis loop squareness. Further, well-characterized, ultra-thin Co layers, grown in a UHV environment on Pd(111) and Pt(111) single crystal faces [47], [48], exhibit very strong perpendicular magnetic anisotropy that also varies inversely with Co layer thickness. Nonetheless, several groups have argued that an alloyed interface [49]–[52] is the origin of a perpendicular easy axis of magnetization in these multilayers. In this regard, Grütter and Dürig [53], using STM and Auger surface chemical analysis, found no evidence for alloying or interdiffusion of Co two monolayers thick, grown on a Pt(111) surface and then annealed up to 750° K in UHV. They concluded that the interface was sharp, and that Co up to four monolayers thick had perpendicular spin orientation. In spite of this controversy, there is little disagreement among the different groups that compositional modulation is the most direct route to achieve perpendicular magnetic anisotropy in both Pt/Co and Pd/Co systems.

The anisotropy properties of Pd/Co multilayers are very similar to Pt/Co multilayers. For polycrystalline Pd/Co multilayers, the critical Co thickness for perpendicular anisotropy is smaller ($\sim 8\,\text{Å}$) and the magnitude of the surface anisotropy energy [33], [34] also a little smaller than in Pt/Co multilayer. Specific values, however, depend on the details of the synthesis.

The anisotropy energy has been studied as a function of the crystallographic direction [30], [54], [55] for Pt/Co and Pd/Co multilayers. They can be grown along the other two principal cubic crystallographic directions, [001] and [110], by seeding the growth with initiating layers. The perpendicular magnetic hysteresis loops for Pt/Co multilayer with [111], [110], and [001] growth directions synthesized by C. Lee and coworkers [30] by MBE are shown in Figure 3.7. Only the multilayers with [111] growth direction have significant perpendicular magnetic anisotropy. Den Broeder and coworkers [54] reached the same conclusion for MBE grown Pd/Co multilayers, when they compared [001] and [111] growth directions; multilayers with (111) fcc texture had

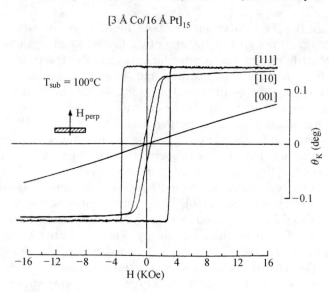

Figure 3.7 Polar Kerr hysteresis loops for Pt/Co multilayers, MBE grown along the [111], [110], and [001] directions [35].

superior magnetic anisotropy. This result for Pd/Co multilayer was confirmed by B. Engel and coworkers [55], although they concluded that, while the perpendicular anisotropy energy was largest for the [111] growth direction, the interfacial anisotropy contribution (K_s) was the same for all growth directions. As previously indicated, without seeding the growth, Pt/Co and Pd/Co multilayers grow preferentially with (111) fcc texture, which fortunately coincides with the direction of maximum perpendicular magnetic anisotropy.

In any magnetic recording medium, a large coercivity is needed to preserve the integrity of written information, and the MO recording medium should have a large enough coercivity compared with typical magnetic writing fields, which are about 200 Oe (15.9 kA/m). A large coercivity is also desirable for stability of small magnetic domains ($d_{min} = \sigma_w/MH_c$, where σ_w is domain wall energy) [12] as is required in a high-density recording medium. Coercivities for RE-TM alloys used in commercial MO media are about 4–7 kOe (318–557 kA/m), whereas multilayers have smaller coercivities: < 1kOe (80 kA/m) for Pt/Co multilayer and < 2 kOe (160 kA/m) for Pd/Co multilayer are typical for both sputtered and evaporated films.

For MO recording, the coercivity (H_c) of Pt/Co multilayer should be at least 2 kOe (160 kA/m). Coercivity and anisotropy energy are connected in that the achievable values of H_c for a magnetic material scale directly with its anisotropy energy [56]. However, H_c can assume large or small values, depending on details of the material's microstructure. These features can be controlled by the multilayer growth process. Thus, the choice of an underlayer, deposition technique (evaporation versus sputtering), and sputtering pressure and gas each separately influence the magnitude of H_c in multilayers. And these influences will be discussed further in the following sections.

Briefly, we observe that large coercivities occur in Pt/Co and Pd/Co multilayer when their microstructure is comprised of discrete columnar boundaries. Growing multilayers on a metal underlayer or sputtering them at high pressure accentuate column boundaries, and the coercivities are then usually larger. We believe that the mechanism for large H_c is hindrance or pinning of magnetic domain wall motion at these boundaries. And this agrees qualitatively with the dynamical domain simulations of Fu et al. [57], which predict an increase in wall motion coercivity as the magnetic exchange interaction between adjacent grains becomes weaker. Clearly, sharp column boundaries that physically separate neighboring column grains in multilayers should weaken the intergranular exchange interaction, which is short range, and increase H_c. Suzuki et al. [58] also concluded that wall pinning was the source of the large coercivities they measure in sputtered Pt/Co multilayer, but attribute pinning instead to small inhomogeneities at Pt-Co interfaces.

3.2.4 Magnetization of Multilayers

Both Pt/Co and Pd/Co multilayers have a magnetization that is enhanced relative to the expected contribution from only Co layers (1422 emu/cm^3, 1422 kA/m). For example, Lin et al. [38] find that at room temperature, the magnetization for e-beam evaporated Co(3Å)/Pt(10Å) multilayer is ~1850 emu/cm^3 (1850 kA/m), a 30% enhancement compared to Co. Spin-dependent X-ray absorption measurements [59], [60] of Pt/Co multilayer indicate that Pt is ferromagnetically polarized with a strength that decreases inversely with distance from the Pt-Co interface. The average magnetic moment of an interfacial Pt atom is estimated to be ~ $0.2 \mu_B$.

There is also evidence that ferromagnetic coupling between Co layers in Pt/Co multilayers is mediated through Pt layers. Zeper et al. [31] found that for a fixed Co thickness, the Curie temperature of Pt/Co multilayers decreased as the Pt layer separating Co increases. From these data, it can be inferred that thin Co (~4Å) layers are magnetically coupled for Pt separation thicknesses up to about 25Å.

Den Broeder et al. [61] and Carcia et al. [62] reported enhanced magnetizations in Pd/Co multilayer. Den Broeder et al. accounted for the enhancement by attributing a $0.6 \mu_B$ induced magnetization to interfacial Pd atomic layers. The enhancement is larger in the Pd/Co multilayer, rf diode sputtered by Carcia, than in the e-beam evaporated multilayers of den Broeder. Carcia and coworkers modeled the magnetization as a constant in the Co layers and an induced Pd magnetization that decays away from the Co-Pd interface. In this model the interfacial Pd's have $-0.9 \mu_B$ induced magnetization.

The ferromagnetic polarization of Pd and Pt layers in multilayers with Co is not surprising, since ferromagnetic polarization of Pd and Pt alloyed with either Co or Fe in dilute concentrations is well known [63]–[65]. The polarization is expected to be weaker in the multilayers than in the alloys because the multilayer architecture is two-dimensional. In fact, there is great variability in the magnitude of enhanced magnetizations measured for Pt/Co and Pd/Co multilayer; this is probably attributable to differences in the extent of interfacial mixing and roughness. A rougher interface, or one that is more chemically mixed, should exhibit a larger magnetization, and thus the details of the multilayer synthesis will play an important role in the magnitude of the induced magnetization in Pd and Pt layers.

3.2.5 Magneto-Optical Properties

When linearly polarized light reflects from the surface of a magnetized material, the polarization rotates and becomes slightly elliptical [66]. For magnetization normal to the reflecting surface and parallel to the propagation direction of the light, this is referred to as the polar Kerr effect. The rotation in most magnetic materials is relatively small, usually much less than 1°. The Kerr rotation is a complex quantity that can be expressed [67] in terms of the dielectric properties of the medium as,

$$\Theta_K = \theta_K - i\eta_K = \varepsilon_{xy}/\sqrt{\varepsilon_{xx}}(1 - \varepsilon_{xx}) \qquad (3.3)$$

where $\varepsilon_{xx} = n^2$ and $n = n + ik$ describe the optical properties in the absence of magnetic effects, θ_K is the Kerr rotation and η_K is the ellipticity, which depend on the off-diagonal elements ε_{xy}, of the medium dielectric tensor. The signal [68] in a magneto-optical recording device is proportional to the magnitude of this complex Kerr rotation, times the optical reflectivity. In the range of MO recording wavelengths, 400–800 nm, the rotation measured for Pt/Co multilayer is usually several times larger [35] than the ellipticity. In Co-base multilayers with fixed Pt (or Pd) thickness, θ_K increases for thicker Co layers (Fig. 3.8) [31]. For thin Co layers, 3–4 Å, using thicker Pt (or Pd) layers reduces θ_K [31]. This reduction is probably associated with a decrease in the Curie temperature (300–400° C) of the multilayers, resulting in a measurably smaller magnetization and θ_K in the vicinity of room temperature.

The spectral [35] dependences of θ_K for Pt/Co multilayer and compositionally equivalent alloys are very similar. Compared to Co, $|\theta_K|$ is larger at short wavelength for alloys and multilayers with Pt and Pd, and the alloy has a larger θ_K than the corresponding multilayer. The difference between the magneto-optical properties of Co and the multilayers or alloys is attributable to a contribution to θ_K from ferromagnetically polarized Pt or Pd atoms. This polarization is stronger for the alloy. From modeling the magneto-optic properties of Pt/Co multilayer, Moog and coworkers [69] concluded that Pt must be magneto-optically active in order to account for the experimental magnitude and wavelength dependence of θ_K in Pt/Co multilayer. This is consistent with an induced magnetization found in Pt and Pd layers, as discussed in the previous section. Alternatively, the inability to account for the MO properties of the multilayers with only a Co contribution and the similarity of spectral properties of the

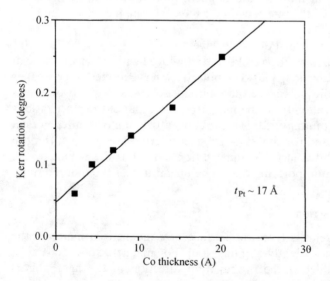

Figure 3.8 Co-thickness dependence to the polar Kerr rotation, θ_K (film/air interface), for vapor-deposited Pt/Co multilayers about 500 Å thick.

alloy and multilayer have led some investigators to conclude that interfacial alloying [49], [70] occurs in these multilayers.

The key advantage of Pt/Co and Pd/Co multilayers compared to RE-TM alloys for MO recording at short wavelength, where higher areal density is possible, is the larger Kerr rotation (θ_K) or MO signal [31], [71]–[73]. Figure 3.9 compares the wavelength dependences of $|\theta_K|$ for thick films of a typical RE-TM alloy, GdTbFe, and Pt/Co and Pd/Co multilayers. Whereas θ_K for the multilayers becomes larger at shorter wavelength, it decreases for GdTbFe. The magnitude of θ_K is larger for Pt/Co Multilayers than for Pd/Co Multilayers, and this accounts for the more extensive investigation of the former for MO recording.

Until recently, very few studies on the Kerr spectroscopic behavior in a wavelength less than 300 nm of any materials have been made because of the experimental difficulties mainly due to the strong absorption of the light by oxygen in air and others related to optical components. Recently, a Kerr spectroscopic apparatus that has overcome this problem was developed by Van Drent and Suzuki who could measure the Kerr spectra of various magneto-optical materials such as fcc cobalt, Co/Pt multilayers, and Co-Pt alloy films in the ultraviolet range [134], [135].

Figure 3.10 shows the photon energy dependence of the Kerr rotation and ellipticity of Co/Pt multilayers, where the thickness of Pt and Co layers are 10 and 3 Å, respectively. The total period of the layers is 20. The Kerr rotation becomes maximum at about 4.2 eV, while the Kerr ellipticity changes its sign from positive to negative with increasing photon energy. This should be compared with the spectra of FCC cobalt (Fig. 3.11(a) and (b)] [135]], where one can find a similarity in Kerr rotation of having the peak at about 4 eV, but not at around 1.5 eV. As to the contribution of Pt to the enhancement of Kerr activity, there seems to be evidence of the enhancement in a wavelength range from 620 to 400 nm, where the Kerr rotation increases with photon energy in Co/Pt multilayers.

A recent work of TbFeCo/Pt multilayers clearly indicates the contribution of Pt on the enhancement of the M-O effect in the ultraviolet region [136]. One of the examples

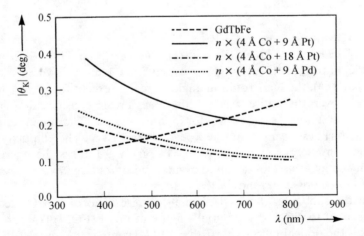

Figure 3.9 Comparison of the wavelength dependence of the magnitude of the polar Kerr rotation in thick films of Pt/Co and Pd/Co multilayers, and GdTbFe [125].

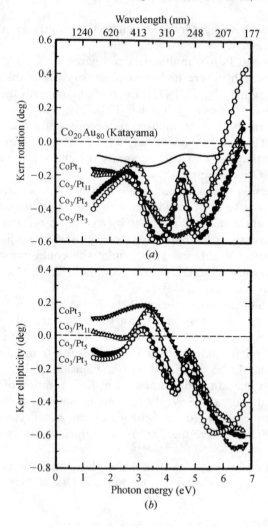

Figure 3.10 The dependences of the Kerr rotation and ellipticity of 20 × {3A Co/10A Pt} multilayer film on photon energy [135].

is shown in Figure 3.12(*a*), (*b*), and (*c*), for the {(5nm Tb$_{23}$ (FeCo)$_{77}$/Y(nm)Pt} × 25. The thickness Y of the platinum is varied from 1 nm to 24 nm. As shown in Figure 3.12(*a*) and (*b*), the Kerr rotation angle increases, except for = 24Å, with increasing Pt thickness over the entire wavelength range under consideration, most significantly enhanced at about 5 eV (240 nm) for all the Y values. The enhancement is pronounced with Pt thickness, being saturated beyond $Y = 12$ Å. The ellipticity is also enhanced with photon energy beyond about 5 eV. Figure 3.12(*c*) is the figure of merit against photon energy. As seen, the figure of merit becomes larger with increasing Pt thickness for photon energies beyond 4 eV.

In the shot noise limit, the signal-to-noise ratio of a MO recording medium is proportional to $R\Theta_K^2$, the material's figure-of-merit (FOM) [74] for optical recording; here R is the optical reflectivity. Table 3.1 [74] compares figures-of-merit for Pt/Co and GdTbFe media for different interference structures, which enhance the overall SNR by increasing θ_K with some overall reduction in disk reflectivity, R. At short wavelength

TABLE 3.1 The Calculated Values (substrate incident) for the Effective Rotation Φ_K, the Reflectivity R, and the Figure-of-Merit $R\Theta_K^2$ at $\lambda = 820$ nm, 633 nm, and 410 nm for Disk Structures With 4 Å CO + 9 Å Pt and GdTbFe of Thickness d

MO layer	disk structure	$\lambda = 820$ nm				$\lambda = 633$ nm				$\lambda = 410$ nm			
		d nm	θ_K °	R %	$R\theta_K^2$ (°)²	d nm	θ_K °	R %	$R\theta_K^2$ (°)²	d nm	θ_K °	R %	$R\theta_K^2$ (°)²
Co/Pt	bare layer	>50	−0.20	70.8	0.028	>50	−0.24	64.8	0.040	>50	−0.36	57.2	0.078
Co/Pt	bilayer	13	−1.39	10.6	0.226	15	−1.41	10.3	0.215	16	−1.53	10.4	0.254
Co/Pt	bilayer	19	−0.94	20.7	0.203	22	−0.95	20.0	0.187	24	−1.05	19.9	0.219
Co/Pt	trilayer	40	−0.51	43.1	0.111	40	−0.63	33.7	0.170	40	−0.88	27.3	0.252
Co/Pt	quadrilayer	15	−1.77	10.4	0.321	15	−1.71	10.5	0.345	15	−1.80	10.7	0.436
GdTbFe	bare layer	>50	−0.25	55.2	0.034	>50	−0.23	52.7	0.034	>50	−0.15	48.5	0.017
GdTbFe	trilayer	40	−0.92	20.4	0.171	40	−0.90	19.0	0.152	30	−0.60	17.9	0.055
GdTbFe	quadrilayer	20	−1.51	10.2	0.230								

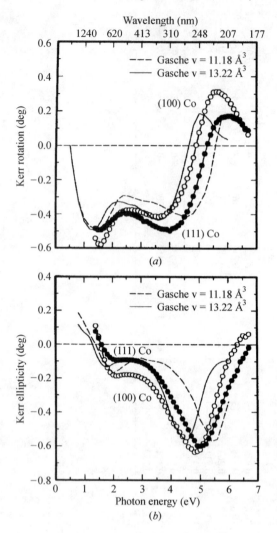

Figure 3.11 The photon energy dependence of the Kerr rotation and ellipticity of fcc cobalt (111) and (100) cobalt (closed and open circle, respectively). The two lines represent calculations by Gasche [143], where the volume of the Co unit cell is varied. The dashed line corresponds to the experimentally determined volume (11.18 Å³).

the FOM for the multilayers is clearly superior. Even at relatively long wavelength, where the Kerr rotation is smaller for Pt/Co multilayers, its FOM is comparable to GdTbFe because of a larger multilayer reflectivity.

When the Kerr rotation of Pt/Co multilayers is measured as a function of the number of bilayer periods of Pt + Co, a maximum [72], [75], [76] in θ_K occurs at a total film thickness of about 100–120Å. This maximum is present over the entire optical recording wavelength range of interest, and is caused by optical interference of reflected waves from the air and substrate interfaces with the partially transparent multilayer. Yusu et al. [77] have exploited this effect, and by judicious choice of Co and Pt layer sequences have achieved Kerr rotations up to 0.8° with good multilayer magnetic properties. This large rotation, without the use of separate, transparent dielectric, optical-interference layers, suggests that a simplified disk construction, comprised of only a substrate and the MO layer, is possible with these multilayers. Although the optical interference effect, itself, is not unique to the multilayers, their superior stability

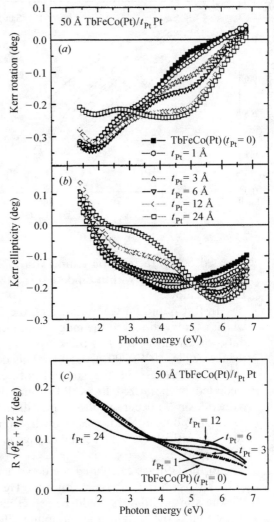

Figure 3.12 The photon energy dependence of (*a*) Kerr rotation, (*b*) ellipticity, and (*c*) Figure of Merit of $5\times\{50$ Å TbFeCo(Pt)/Y Pt$\}$ where Y is varied from 0 to 24Å.

in air enables this effect to be exploited, whereas an equivalently thin layer of an unprotected RE-TM alloy would readily oxidize, becoming nonmagnetic.

3.2.6 Thermomagnetic Properties

To be a candidate for a MO recording medium, reversal or switching of magnetic domains must be possible with modest laser power (<15 mW) and small magnetic field bias (~ 200 Oe, 15.9 kA/m). Since Pt/Co and Pd/Co multilayer are ferromagnetic, they are characterized by a Curie temperature T_c, at which the magnetization becomes vanishingly small. By locally heating the multilayer to near its Curie temperature, the magnetization can be switched by simultaneously applying a small, reversing magnetic field. Figure 3.13 shows the dependence of H_c and θ_K on temperature for Pt/Co multilayers with $t_{Co} = 4$ Å and Pt between 10 Å and 20 Å [31]. Since the temperature dependence of H_c is stronger than for θ_K, the magnetization of these multilayers can be

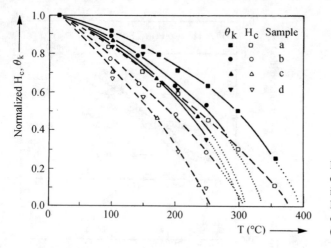

Figure 3.13 Temperature dependence of the coercivity and polar Kerr rotation, normalized to their room temperature values for Pt/Co multilayer with a Co layer thickness of 4 Å and a Pt layer thickness of (a) 10 Å, (b) 13 Å, (c) 16 Å, and (d) 20 Å [80].

reversed below their Curie temperature. These switching temperatures (~250–350°C) are easily achieved with a diode laser, although they are about 100°C above those of RE-TM alloys.

In Pt/Co and Pd/Co multilayers, the Curie temperature and the magnitude of θ_K, which is proportional to the magnetization, depend strongly on Co layer thickness and only weakly on Pt (or Pd) thickness [31]. A 10 Å increase in Pt layer thickness only reduces T_c by 40°C: 390° to 350°C. This dependence of T_c on Pt thickness apparently reflects differences in the strength of ferromagnetic coupling between Co layers, mediated by polarized Pt or Pd atoms. Beyond a Pt thickness of 25 Å, no further reduction in T_c occurs in Pt/Co multilayer with a constant Co thickness. The dependence of T_c on Co thicknesses is much stronger [78]. In a series of Pt/Co multilayer with about 13 Å thick Pt, only a small change in Co thickness (< 2.5 Å) changes T_c by about 200°C [78].

Bruno [79] has calculated the dependence of T_c on Co thickness in ultrathin films of bulk Co and in Co-base multilayers. He concluded that the dependence of T_c on Co thickness in multilayers could be represented by the thickness dependence of T_c in a single bulk Co film, and that coupling effects through Pd and Pt in multilayers were negligible. The calculated T_c decreases from about 725°C for six monolayers of Co to less than 300°C for one monolayer [79]. The experimentally observed reduction in T_c with Pt thickness, Bruno instead attributes to interdiffusion of Pt and Co, since the corresponding alloys have a lower T_c.

In MO recording, if the switching temperature is too high, the disk, which is polycarbonate or glass coated with a polymeric groove structure, can be thermally damaged during the writing process. The damage, which is manifested either as an increase in noise or a reduction in the Kerr signal, limits the number of write/erase cycles before measurable degradation of recording performance (CNR) occurs. Since this occurs in Pt/Co and Pd/Co disks [74], [80], [81], still lower switching or Curie temperatures are desirable. However, changes in Co thickness to reduce T_c are very restrictive, since the magnetic properties are optimum for a very narrow range of Co thicknesses, 3–4 Å. Because multilayers with thicker Pt have smaller Kerr rotations [31] and its effect on lowering T_c is weaker, increasing the Pt thickness to lower T_c is also unattractive.

Alternatively, Hashimoto et al. [81], [82] and van Kesteren and Zeper [78] have chemically doped the Co layer to lower T_c. Van Kesteren and Zeper have tried Os, Re, Rh, Ir, and Ru. The best results are for Os and Re. Fifteen percent Re in a 4Å Co-Re/ 13.5Å Pt multilayer reduces T_c by 250°C without loss of perpendicular magnetic anisotropy. However, the Kerr rotation is reduced by about 25% and there is some loss in Kerr hysteresis loop squareness. Hashimoto et al. [81], [82] find that layering a $Co_{62}Ni_{38}$ alloy with Pt reduces T_c by about 140°C, when compared to equivalent thicknesses of 4Å Co/10Å Pt multilayer ($T_c = 400°C$). Alloying Co with Ni also lowers the threshold laser writing power in a disk, and thereby increases the practical number of write/erase cycles for recording. Although the addition of Ni also reduces the Kerr rotation, disk performance remains satisfactory (CNR > 45 dB) [81].

3.2.7 Thermal Stability and Corrosion Resistance

Another advantage of Pd/Co and Pt/Co multilayers for MO recording is their superior corrosion resistance. Whereas the RE elements (Tb, Gd, or Dy) readily oxidize in air, degrading alloy magnetic properties, the multilayers are far less sensitive to oxidation or corrosion. Storing a very thin, unprotected Pt/Co multilayer in a very aggressive environment (80C/75% RH), which is commonly used to accelerate and estimate the lifetime of a recording medium, causes only a negligibly small change in H_c and θ_K [83], even after more than 200 hours (Fig. 3.14). RE-TM alloys cannot tolerate such an environment without protective layers. With protective layers of a nitride, either SiN_x or AlN, which also function as an optical interference layer to enhance θ_K, RE-TM alloys can satisfactorily tolerate warm, humid environments. Although oxides generally bond better to typical optical disk substrates, nitrides are used because the rare-earth elements in the magneto-optic alloy readily reduce most oxides and degrade the alloy's magnetic properties. But because these nitrides are refractory, when they are deposited at room temperature, they can develop high growth stresses that can drive loss of adhesion to the substrate and other failures of the thin film stack in an optical disk. In contrast, the multilayers are chemically compatible with oxides.

Since the key magnetic properties for recording come from the layered structure, it is important that the structure be thermally stable, since recording involves locally heating it many times. To test only the effects of interdiffusion, several studies [21],

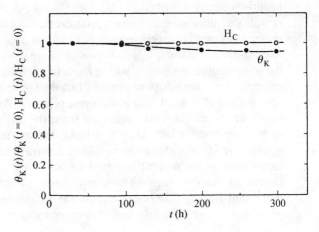

Figure 3.14 Fractional change in the coercivity and Kerr rotation of unprotected 4.8Å Co/10.8Å Pt multilayer, 150Å total thickness, aged at 80°C in 75% relative humidity [83, 103].

[33], [43], [45], [74], [83]–[85] have evaluated the changes in structure and magnetic properties of Pt/Co and Pd/Co multilayer after high temperature annealing. The general results of these experiments are that with annealing below $\sim 300°C$, the multilayer structure and magnetic properties change very little; between $300°C$ and $400°C$ measurable changes occur; above $400°C$, perpendicular magnetic anisotropy is lost and the layers are significantly interdiffused. By comparing the activation energy (1.1 eV) for diffusion in Pd/Co multilayer with Au diffusion in Pd, den Broeder [43] concludes that diffusion in Pd/Co multilayer proceeds primarily along grain boundaries. And this is likely the case for other multilayers. Therefore, to ensure that repeated writing on a multilayer disk will not change magneto-optical properties, it is advisable to choose multilayers with a switching temperature below $300°C$. This demand will involve compromise in the multilayer design, since lower switching temperatures are equivalent to less Co in the multilayer and consequently a smaller θ_K.

As previously discussed, because of superior corrosion resistance, simpler disk structures may be feasible with multilayers. A disk comprised of just a thin (~100 Å) magnetic multilayer on a substrate is possible. Since a thin metal multilayer is semitransparent, it acts as its own optical interference layer. Thus, except for a scratch-resistant overcoat to protect the magnetic multilayer, no other coatings would be necessary.

3.3 INFLUENCE OF PREPARATION METHOD AND GROWTH CONDITIONS ON MAGNETIC AND STRUCTURAL PROPERTIES OF MULTILAYERS

3.3.1 Preparation Method

Since the multilayer architecture is responsible for the attractive magnetic and MO properties of Pt/Co and Pd/Co multilayer, it should not be surprising that the preparation method and growth conditions can affect the structure of the multilayer and significantly influence these properties. Soon after a number of groups began to study these multilayers, it became apparent to us that the magnitude of the perpendicular anisotropy energy of Pt/Co multilayer scales approximately inversely with the energetics of the deposition process. Vapor-deposited films [31], [35] had the largest K_{eff}, followed by magnetron sputtering [86], then diode-sputtering [21], [33], and finally ion-beam sputtered multilayers [43], [46]. In fact den Broeder et al. [43] noted that Pd/Co multilayer, that were ion-beam sputtered, did not exhibit a perpendicular easy-axis of magnetization. The average energy of vapor deposited atoms is ~ 0.1 eV, much smaller than sputtered atoms, which leaves the target with 10–30 eV. However, in sputtering, the most energetic species, which have the greatest potential to influence the multilayer structure, are not sputtered atoms but energetic reflected gas neutrals [87], [88].

Reflected neutrals are gas atoms, typically Ar in most practical sputtering applications, which are elastically reflected from the target and then traverse the vacuum space to the substrate, which they bombard. Depending on the sputtering pressure and the substrate-to-target distance, reflected neutrals can have energies of the order of the target voltage or several hundred eV sufficiently large to exert a strong influence on the multilayer structure. For example, intentionally using only 28 eV Ar-ion bombardment [89] during MBE growth of GaAs on Si suppresses three-dimensional island growth in favor of nearly uniform layer by layer growth.

A reasonable estimate of the mean energy of these back-reflected neutrals can be obtained from the formula for single elastic collision [90]

$$E_r = E_i - (M_g - M_t)^2/(M_g + M_t)^2 \tag{3.4}$$

where E_r and E_i are the reflected and incident gas ion energies, respectively, and M_g and M_t are the corresponding gas ion and target atomic masses. Since E_i, taken equal to the target voltage, is larger for diode and ion beam sputtering than magnetron sputtering, the energy of back reflected gas atoms is less for magnetron sputtering. And since the gas pressure is lower for ion-beam sputtering than diode sputtering, reflected gas neutrals in ion-beam sputtering will arrive at the growing film surface with a greater fraction of their incident energy, since there are fewer energy loss collisions in the more dilute gas environment.

From Equation (3.4), the energy of back scattered gas atoms depends on the difference between their mass and the mass of the target material. When the target is Pt ($M_t = 195$) and the sputtering gas is Ar ($M_g = 40$), reflected Ar ions retain a substantial fraction of their incident energy and therefore can be very influential during the multilayer growth. Since the mass of Co ($M_t = 59$) is relatively close to Ar, ions backscattered from a Co target are far less energetic. Therefore, one strategy to reduce energetic bombardment associated with Pt deposition during multilayer growth and thus increase K_{eff} of sputtered multilayers is to increase the mass [26], [91] of the sputtering gas, e.g., Kr ($M_g = 84$) or Xe ($M_g = 131$). Conversely, sputtering with lighter gas such as Ne ($M_g = 20$) will enhance energetic bombardment and should reduce K_{eff}. Figure 3.15 compares the recoil energy distribution of Ar, Kr, and Xe atoms reflected from a Pt target, as computed by the sputtering simulation code, TRIM [92].

Figure 3.16 compares the dependence of anisotropy energy on Co thickness for Pt/Co multilayers magnetron sputtered in Ar and in Xe to ion-beam sputtered films [46]. From the extrapolation of linear fits to each of these behaviors to obtain K_s, one concludes that it is specifically the magnitude of this interface contribution to K_{eff} that is measurably affected by the sputtering conditions. K_s is largest for Xe-sputtered multilayers.

Sputtering with Xe or Kr not only increases K_{eff} but also H_c [26], [91] of Pt/Co multilayers compared to Ar-sputtering. Similar trends are observed for Pd/Co multilayer, but because of the much smaller mass of Pd ($M_t = 106$) than Pt, degradation of magnetic properties from bombardment by reflected neutrals is less for Ar-sputtered Pd/Co multilayer. Hysteresis loops for nearly identical Pt/Co multilayers sputtered in Ar, Kr, and Xe are shown in Figure 3.17.

Energetic bombardment during the growth of these multilayers has two structural effects: It diminishes the (111)-fcc texture, and it produces flatter layers [93]–[95]. Cross-sectional TEMs of sputtered and vapor-deposited multilayers, shown in Figure 3.18, confirm that, when there is less energetic bombardment, individual Pt (darker bands) and Co (lighter bands) layers become rougher and boundaries between individual columnar grains (~100 Å wide) become more distinct. Corresponding lattice images of these multilayers indicate that the parallelism of (111)-fcc planes with the substrate surface is superior for Xe-sputtered and vapor-deposited films. And whereas a columnar grain in Ar sputtered multilayers is comprised of several crystallites with (111) planes misaligned to the Si substrate surface, Xe-sputtered and vapor-deposited

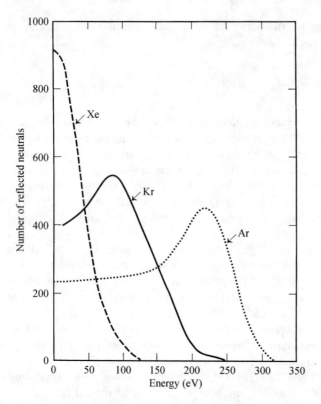

Figure 3.15 Distribution in recoil energy calculated (TRIM) for sputter gas atoms (Ar, Kr, Xe) reflected from a Pt target, when their incident energy is 500 eV [26].

multilayers have superior (111) texture and columnar grains are frequently a single crystal. These observations are corroborated by the corresponding selected area electron diffraction patterns.

One apparent structural effect of the bombardment is to drive the multilayer system toward forming other, less energetically favorable crystallographic orientations. In fact, Dobrev [96] has shown that energetic ion bombardment of fcc metal films converts fiber texture, initially <111>, to <110>, which corresponds to the most

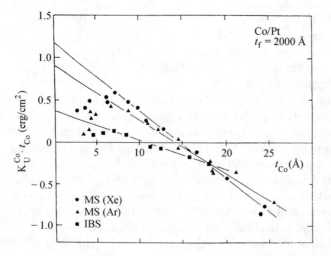

Figure 3.16 Co-thickness dependence of the product of the anisotropy energy and Co thickness for Pt/Co multilayers made by dc magnetron sputtering (MS) in Ar or Xe, and by ion beam sputtering (IBS) in Ar.

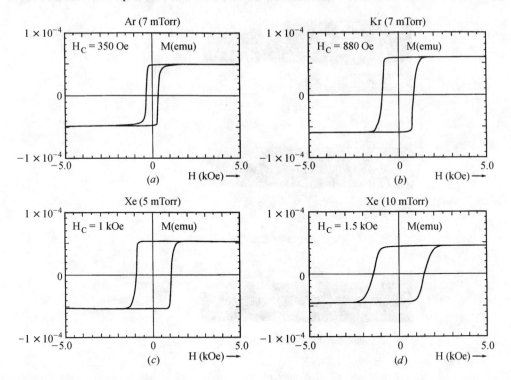

Figure 3.17 Magnetic hysteresis loops of Pt/Co multilayers sputtered in (a) 7 mTorr Ar, (b) 7 mTorr Kr, (c) 5 mTorr Xe, and (d) 10 mTorr Xe. All films have approximate structure: $10\times(4\,\text{Å Co} + 13\,\text{Å Pt})$ [93].

open crystal channeling direction. The densely packed (111) planes do not survive ion bombardment in these experiments.

Flatter layers with less prominent column boundaries for sputtering than for vapor-deposition are consistent with an increase in surface diffusion imparted to sputtered adatoms by energetic, reflected gas neutrals. However, rougher layers do not necessarily imply that Pt-Co interfaces are less sharp chemically, or conversely, that flatter layers are chemically sharper. In fact, D. Johnson and coworkers [25] at the University of Oregon use X-ray diffraction to discriminate layer roughness from chemical interdiffusion by fitting a model to diffraction patterns obtained for equivalent Pt/Co multilayers sputtered in Ar, Kr, and Xe. The results are summarized in Table 3.2. The fits reveal a monotonic increase in layer roughness but a decrease in chemical

TABLE 3.2 Fitting Parameters to X-ray diffracting Patterns for Ar-, Kr-, and Xe-Sputtered Pt/Co MLs. σ_{Co} and σ_{Pt} Are Respective Diffusion Coefficients for Co into the Pt Layer and Pt into the Co Layer. Δ is a Roughness Parameter

Sample $10\times(\sim 4\,\text{Å Co} + 13\,\text{Å Pt})$	Result from fitting X-ray diffraction data
Sputtered with Ar (7 m Torr)	$d_{Pt} = 13\,\text{Å}, d_{Co} = 5\,\text{Å}, \sigma_{Pt} = 2.5\,\text{Å}, \sigma_{Co} = 3.5\,\text{Å}, \Delta = 4\,\text{Å}$
Sputtered with Kr (7 m Torr)	$d_{Pt} = 13\,\text{Å}, d_{Co} = 5\,\text{Å}, \sigma_{Pt} = 3.0\,\text{Å}, \sigma_{Co} = 3.0\,\text{Å}, \Delta = 6\,\text{Å}$
Sputtered with Xe (7 m Torr)	$d_{Pt} = 12.5\,\text{Å}, d_{Co} = 4\,\text{Å}, \sigma_{Pt} = 2.5\,\text{Å}, \sigma_{Co} = 2.5\,\text{Å}, \Delta = 12\,\text{Å}$

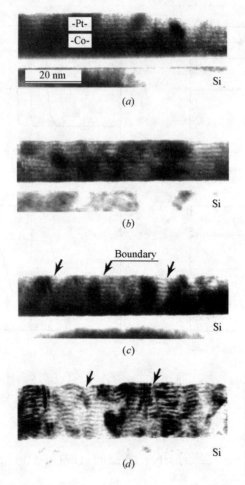

Figure 3.18 TEM cross-sectional micrographs of 10×(4 Å Co + 13 Å Pt) sputtered in (a) 7 mTorr Ar, (b) 7 mTorr Kr, (c) 5 mTorr Xe, and (d) 13×(6 Å Co + 9 Å Pt), vapor-deposited. The light bands correspond to Co-rich and the dark bands Pt-rich layers [93].

interdiffusion for heavier sputter gases. Increased chemical interdiffusion, when growth of the multilayers is accompanied by energetic bombardment, is physically appealing. In contrast, other investigators [50], [97] have also used modeling of X-ray diffraction data to argue for formation of an interfacial alloy of Pt and Co as the origin of perpendicular magnetic anisotropy. However, the smaller anisotropy energy of multilayers grown with energetic bombardment, which should promote interfacial mixing, seems to contradict this interpretation.

Since sputtering with Ar is more economical and more broadly compatible with commercial vacuum pumping equipment, it would seem reasonable to propose sputtering at a high Ar pressure (actually, it is the product of pressure and substrate to target distance that is relevant) to reduce the energy of back reflected neutrals. However, Pt/Co and Pd/Co multilayer, sputtered at high Ar pressure (> 25 mTorr), have less (111)-fcc texture and smaller perpendicular anisotropy energy [93]–[95], [98]. And although coercivities can be as large as several kOe, magnetic hysteresis loops are typically sheared and MO disks we made at high Ar pressure have high disk noise. The origin of the noise may be a variability in structural properties that leads to a variation in optical Kerr effect and reflectivity.

Recently, however, we have made progress in overcoming these deficiencies with Ar sputtering by sputtering multilayers on physically segregated Pt grains, made by controllably etching [99] thin (20–40 Å) Pt underlayers. Pt/Co multilayers grown on these granular Pt underlayers maintain a physically segregated columnar microstructure with excellent (111)-fcc texture, as determined by electron probe microscopies and X-ray diffraction. Multilayers sputtered at 12 mTorr in Ar have a relatively large K_{eff} (1.2×10^7 erg/cm^3-Co, 1.2×10^6 J/m^3-Co) and H_c (3.5 kOe, 2.8×10^2 kA/m). And preliminary MO recording experiments on multilayers grown by this method are encouraging, with CNR > 45 dB at 647 nm.

3.3.2 Underlayers

The magnitude of the perpendicular magnetic anisotropy energy, K_{eff}, of Pt/Co and Pd/Co multilayer depends on (111)-fcc texture [30]. When they are made as thin films, both Pt and Pd grow with strong (111)-fcc texture. On the other hand, the stable phase of Co at room temperature is hcp, and thin films of Co generally grow with mixed hcp and fcc phases; Co films do not have good (111) texture. It is therefore advantageous for good magnetic properties to start the growth of these multilayers with the Pt or Pd layer. In fact, excellent texture and excellent magnetic properties (large K_{eff} and H_c) are assured, when the multilayers are grown on a relatively thick Pt or Pd underlayer [72], [100]–[102]. A prominent microstructural feature of the multilayers grown on Pt is their distinctive granular microstructure [103]. We believe that this granular structure is mainly responsible for the large coercivities [103] that characterize these multilayers, when they are grown on a metal underlayer. Unfortunately, in a practical optical disk structure, laser light is substrate-incident, in order to defocus foreign particles on the disk surface at the MO storage layer. The use of a thick metal underlayer is thus not practical, because it too greatly attenuates the signal.

An alternative to metal underlayers for promoting favorable multilayer texture, and consequently good magnetic properties, is a transparent layer that is lattice matched to (111)-fcc layers of Pt and Co. In fact, the (0001)ZnO surface is an excellent lattice match [104] to (111)Pt, as illustrated by the respective lattice nets shown in Figure 3.19. There is only a 1.6% mismatch in their lattice parameters. Furthermore, because ZnO has a relatively large index of refraction ($n = 2$), it can also act as the optical interference layer in an optical stack design to increase the Kerr effect signal. Figures 3.20 and 3.21 illustrate a typical magnetic hysteresis loop and Kerr effect for Pt/Co multilayers on ZnO films with c-axis texture. When the multilayers are grown on a sputtered ZnO layer [104], [105], the magnetic coercivity is increased by about a factor

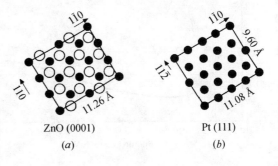

Figure 3.19 Lattice nets of Pt(111) and ZnO(0001) surfaces. For ZnO, solid circles correspond to in-plane Zn atoms and open circles to O atoms at −c/2 [103].

ZnO (0001)
(a)

Pt (111)
(b)

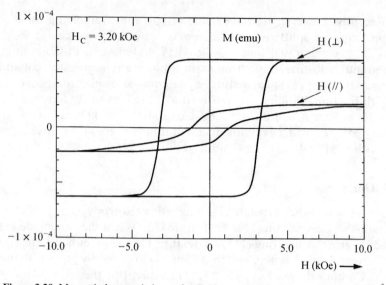

Figure 3.20 Magnetic hysteresis loops for Pt/Co multilayer Kr-sputtered on 1000 Å thick ZnO sputtered on a glass substrate [104].

of four and the anisotropy energy by nearly 50% compared to a glass substrate. From X-ray diffraction, we determined that the growth direction for the sputter-deposited ZnO layer is along the c-axis, which promotes excellent (111)-fcc multilayer growth. Recently, we have grown Pt/Co and Pd/Co multilayers on single crystal ZnO [106] and have corroborated that a large K_{eff} correlates with the structural quality of (111)-fcc growth of multilayers, and large coercivities are due to granular microstructural features. With regard to the practical application of ZnO layers, workers at Sanyo in collaboration with Nagoya University have demonstrated good MO recording proper-

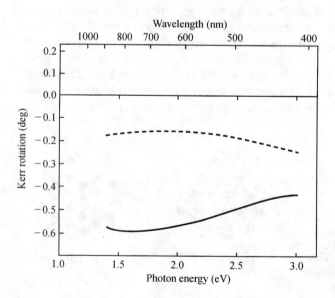

Figure 3.21 Polar Kerr rotation for 10×(4.5 Å Co + 13.3 Å Pt) multilayer deposited on a 1000 Å thick, sputtered ZnO film. Solid curve is for light that is substrate incident; dashed curve is for air-incident light [104].

ties [107] and superior thermal stability [108] for Pt/Co multilayers on a ZnO dielectric layer.

3.3.3 Substrate Etching

Mildly sputter-etching the substrate surface before depositing multilayers has a significant influence on their magnetic properties [91], [104], [109]. For example, Figure 3.22 is a plot that compares perpendicular anisotropy energy of identical Pt/Co multilayers grown on transparent dielectric enhancement layers of AlN, ZnO, and In_2O_3 for different sputter-etch conditions. Generally, as etch conditions become stronger (i.e., larger etch voltage or longer etch time), the anisotropy energy of Pt/Co multilayers increases, magnetic hysteresis loops became more square, and the coercivity decreases. Similar trends are also observed for multilayers directly deposited on glass and Si substrates. We have also found that multilayer disks grown on etched substrates exhibit less disk noise.

We have studied the microstructure of Pt/Co multilayers, sputtered on unetched and etched Si substrates by transmission electron microscopy [91]. We found evidence in multilayers grown on unetched Si for columnar grains comprised of multiple small crystallites, crystallographically misaligned with respect to one another, whereas multilayers grown on etched Si substrates consist of larger, nearly single crystal columns. Thus, sputter-etching the substrate surface apparently increases surface diffusion of subsequently sputtered Pt and Co atoms. Etching may increase adatom mobility by creating a high density of surface defects, and stronger etch conditions may promote a denser multilayer microstructure with fewer boundaries, and consequently a smaller coercivity.

The multilayers grown on etched substrates also have better (111)-fcc texture [91], as determined by selected area electron diffraction, accounting for larger anisotropy energies. From similar structural studies of multilayers grown at high pressure on etched and unetched surfaces [91], we found denser films on etched surfaces, suggesting that etching promotes nucleation.

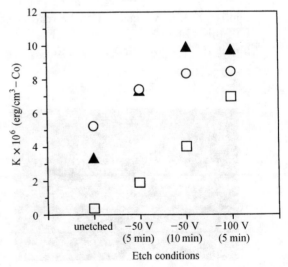

Figure 3.22 Effect of sputter-etching ZnO (O), AlN (▲), In_2O_3 (□) thin film dielectrics on the anisotropy energy of Kr-sputtered (7 mTorr) multilayers, 10×(4 Å Co + 13 Å Pt) [91].

3.4 MO RECORDING PROPERTIES

3.4.1 Recording at 800 nm

The widespread interest in Pt/Co and Pd/Co multilayers is for their potential application as a new high-density, rewritable, optical storage medium. The following sections summarize some recording results on multilayer optical disks.

In the shot noise limit, the signal-to-noise ratio (SNR) for MO recording can be written as [4]

$$SNR = 10 \log[(2\eta P_o R \sin^2 \theta_K)/eB)] \tag{3.5}$$

where η is the sensitivity of the photodiode detector, P_o is the average light intensity, R is the optical reflectivity, θ_K is the Kerr rotation, B is the bandwidth, and e is the electronic charge. For typical recording parameters [4], $\eta = 0.35$ A/W, $P_o = 1$ mW, $R\theta_K = 0.25$, the calculated SNR is 38 dB at $B = 10$ MHz and 66 dB at $B = 30$ kHz. Of course, in an actual disk, noise [110] can arise from electronic as well as media sources, and the SNR will be smaller. Common media sources of noise include fluctuations in optical reflectivity (amplitude noise) and magnetic moment (polarization noise). Film surface roughness can also contribute to polarization noise, because the Kerr rotation is a sensitive function of total film thickness and tilting of the magnetic easy axis.

In MO recording both the magnetic properties of the media and the laser writing parameters determine the written bit size. Figure 3.23 is a Lorentz electron micrograph image [80] of domains written with laser modulation in a Pt/Co multilayer. The domain diameter becomes smaller as the laser writing power is decreased, and the small domains maintain a regular shape. Figure 3.24 is a plot of domain diameter [111], obtained from Lorentz microscopy for vapor-deposited layers, 25×(4.1 Å Co + 19Å Pt), statically written with different laser powers at 514 nm.

Although very small domains can be written in both Pt/Co multilayer and RE-TM alloys, the smallest bit size that can be read is dictated by the optical diffraction limit and is $\sim \lambda$, the wavelength of the read laser. Assuming that the spacing between bits is half this distance and a numerical aperture $N = 0.6$, then densities are $\sim 1/\lambda^2$ [4], or about 10^8 bits/cm^2 for $\lambda = 820$ nm.

P (mW)
- 6.5
- 6
- 5.5
- 5
- 4.5
- 4
- 3.5
- 3
- 2.5
- 2

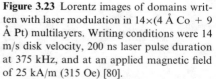

Figure 3.23 Lorentz images of domains written with laser modulation in 14×(4 Å Co + 9 Å Pt) multilayers. Writing conditions were 14 m/s disk velocity, 200 ns laser pulse duration at 375 kHz, and at an applied magnetic field of 25 kA/m (315 Oe) [80].

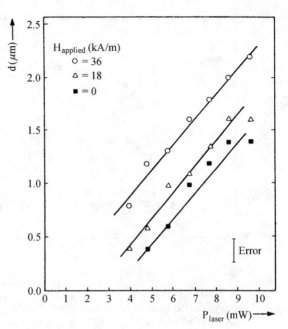

Figure 3.24 Domain size written with laser modulation as a function of laser power and applied magnetic field. The laser pulse duration was 1 μs [81], [111].

Several groups have successfully made Pt/Co multilayer disks and tested their recording properties [72], [74], [80], [112]–[114] in the vicinity of 800 nm. Table 3.3 summarizes some of these recording results. In fact, the best Pt/Co recording results are comparable to the best results reported for RE-TM disks, even at 800 nm.

Typical writing power and bias field dependences [112] of recorded carrier and noise levels for Pt/Co Multilayers, vapor-deposited on 800 Å thick Si_3N_4, are shown in Figures 3.25 and 3.26. In this case, the substrate was a smooth glass disk with very low noise, and tracking and recording of data were achieved with a precision tester. The threshold writing power (~ 7 mW) and the threshold magnetic field bias (~ -200 Oe, 15.9 kA/m) are comparable to those used in commercial MO disk products with a TbFeCo alloy [112] storage layer. Both the carrier and the noise are relatively indepen-

TABLE 3.3 Recording Results (λ − 780–820 nm)

		Recording results (λ − 780–820 nm)			
Group	Prep.*	fc	v	CNR	ML structure
Philips-	e	2 Mhz	10 m/s	57 dB	14×(3ÅCo + 10ÅPt)
Du Pont	s	1 Mhz	5 m/s	54 dB	10×(4ÅCo + 12ÅPt)
IBM [112]	e	2.5 Mhz	20 m/s	64 dB[+]	15×(3.2ÅCo + 11.5ÅPt)
Sony [72]	s	1 Mhz	10 m/s	53 dB	≈8×(4.5ÅCo + 12.5ÅPt)
	s	1 Mhz	10 m/s	46 dB	≈8×(4.5ÅCo + 13ÅPt)
Sanyo-Nagoya U. [114]	s	500 Khz	5 m/s	45 dB[#]	9×(4ÅCo + 16ÅPt)

*e = evaporated
 s = sputtering
[+] glass substrate
[#] PC substrate

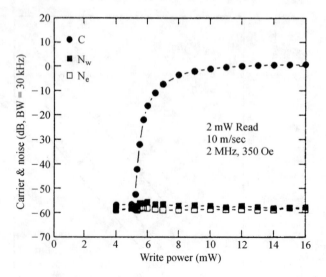

2 mW Read
10 m/sec
2 MHz, 350 Oe

Figure 3.25 Writing power dependence of carrier signal and noise levels before (N_e) and after writing (N_w) on a multilayer disk comprised of 23×(3 Å Co + 10 Å Pt), vapor-deposited on a 80 nm thick Si$_3$N$_4$ layer on a flat glass substrate.

dent of write power beyond about 7 mW, and the small increase in carrier with write power in Figure 3.25 is likely due to an increase in the domain size, which depends on the applied magnetic field and laser writing power. Compared to a TbFeCo disk [112], the noise of this Pt/Co multilayer at small bias fields is quite small.

Recording studies have also been carried out on Pt/Co and Pd/Co multilayers deposited on more practical pregrooved disks [72], [74], [80], [113], [114]. These are typically glass disks coated with a photo-polymerized (2p) lacquer, impressed with 1.6 μm pitch grooves for ease of tracking. Although pregrooved media tend to have higher noise than smooth glass disks without grooves, grooved media simplify the design of a disk drive. In some of these studies recording performance has been carefully correlated with the corresponding microstructural features of written domains, as determined by Lorentz transmission electron microscopy [74] or magnetic force microscopy [116].

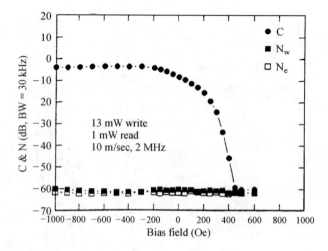

13 mW write
1 mW read
10 m/sec, 2 MHz

Figure 3.26 Bias field dependence of carrier signal and noise levels before (N_e) and after writing (N_w) on a multilayer disk comprised of 23×(3 Å Co + 10 Å Pt), vapor-deposited on an 80 nm thick Si$_3$N$_4$ layer on a flat glass substrate.

Figure 3.27 illustrates magnetic force microscope images of domains written in sputtered Pt/Co disks. The disks were 2 in. diameter glass with a 2p pregrooved structure. For laser modulation, regular domains could be written even without a bias magnetic field, although subdomains are visible within the boundary of written marks, and the CNR and carrier levels are less than with a bias field. Only a small bias (9 kA/m, 113 Oe) is necessary during writing to almost completely eliminate subdomains and increase the CNR by more than 4 dB.

In MO recording with laser modulation, direct overwriting of information is not possible in simple disk structures. Instead, an entire sector or track must be fully erased before writing new information. In this regard, Pt/Co multilayer offer no advantage over other MO media based on RE-TM alloys. Direct overwriting in MO recording can, however, be achieved using magnetic field modulation instead of laser modulation. With magnetic field modulation, information is written by modulating the magnetic field of a small magnetic head close to the disk surface, while the recording medium is heated by the laser, which is usually on continuously. Because of the proximity of the head to disk, some of the inherent advantages of optical recording are obviously compromised.

MO recording on Pt/Co disks has been successfully carried out using magnetic field modulation. Figure 3.28 summarizes typical recording characteristics for magnetic field modulation [80]. When the recording magnetic field strength is 25 kA/m, 315 Oe, the carrier exhibits a maximum at about 4 mW. Below 4 mW the size of written domains and thus also the carrier become smaller, whereas laser power above 4 mW creates subdomains that reduce the modulation depth of the carrier. Increasing the writing

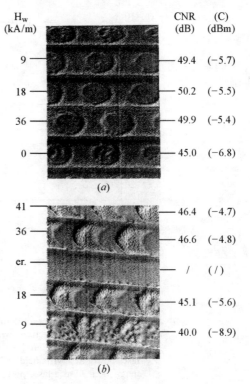

Figure 3.27 Magnetic force microscopy images of domains written in a disk comprised of Kr-sputtered multilayers, $14 \times (4.1$ Å Co + 14.7 Å Pt). Images are for (a) laser modulation with different write-magnetic fields, and (b) magnetic field modulation as a function of field strength with 3.7 mW pulsed laser power. Average domain lengths (L_{eff}) and their average fluctuation or jitter are also shown [31], [112], [116].

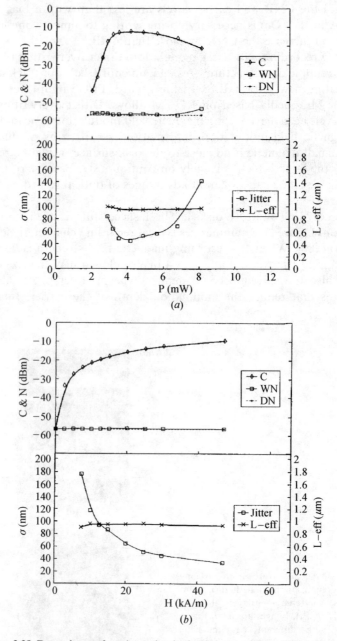

Figure 3.28 Dependence of carrier and noise levels in a multilayer disk with 9× (4 Å Co + 9 Å Pt) structure, written with magnetic field modulation at 1.4 m/s disk velocity and a frequency of 750 kHz (*a*) as a function of laser power at a write field of 25 kA/m (315 Oe), and (*b*) as a function of magnetic field at a laser power of 3.5 mW [31], [80], [112].

magnetic field at an optimum laser power, as illustrated in Figure 3.28(*b*), improves the
carrier modulation depth by eliminating those subdomains. Figure 3.27 includes images
obtained by magnetic force microscopy [116] of magnetic domains written with magnetic field modulation on Pt/Co multilayers. There is a good correlation of the clarity
(absence of subdomains) of written marks and the carrier level.

3.4.2 Blue-Wavelength Recording

Although the figure-of-merit for MO recording at blue wavelength is better for Pt/Co
Multilayers, only recently have actual recording experiments confirmed superior performance. Hurst et al. [117] studied the recording of large marks ($\sim 5\,\mu$m) at 488 nm on
a Pt/Co disk. The substrates were smooth, glass disks without grooves, so that the CNR
of the disk was truly limited by the Pt/Co media noise, which was ascribed to polarization noise, and write noise was minimized by writing in a high magnetic field bias of 800
Oe (63.7 kA/m). Using 3.5 mW of read power in a thermally lossy quadrilayer structure, that needed 22 mW for writing, a CNR of 62 dB was obtained, comparable to the
performance of a RE-TM disk at 780 nm, under similar, idealized conditions. These
experiments prove the efficacy of Pt/Co multilayer as a low noise MO recording medium at blue wavelength.

Several other studies [81], [118]–[120] have compared the recording characteristics
of Pt/Co multilayer and RE-TM alloys at blue wavelength on pregrooved disks, which
give a higher noise contribution. Hashimoto et al. [81] reported that in comparison to
TbFeCo, Pt/Co multilayer disks had a 6–8 dB advantage in carrier level at 488 nm for
0.5 μm written marks; for a 2 μm mark length, the CNR was 42 dB. In these experiments amplifier or electronic noise was cited as the dominant contribution to the total
noise. In similar experiments at 458 nm, Zeper et al. [118] found a CNR of 51.5 dB for
2.5 μm length domains and 40 dB for domains about 0.4 μm in length. These CNRs,
which were disk noise limited, were about 3 dB higher (Fig. 3.29) for Pt/Co disks than
for GdTbFe disks.

3.4.3 Write/Erase Cycling

A practical MO disk product needs to sustain more than 10^6 write/read/erase cycles
without measurable loss of CNR. Under certain conditions, this is achievable, as illustrated in Figure 3.30, in Pt/Co multilayers [81]. In a multilayer medium, degradation in

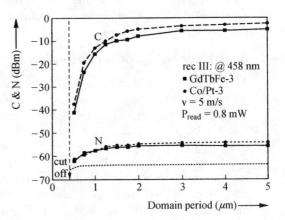

Figure 3.29 A comparison of carrier and
noise levels in Co/Pt and GdTbFe disks vs.
domain size at a recording wavelength of
458 nm [115].

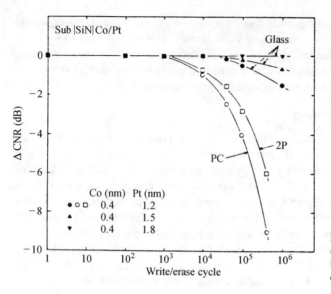

Figure 3.30 Change in CNR vs. the number of write/erase cycles as a function of Co/Pt ratio and disk type: glass, glass-2p, and polycarbonate (PC) [81], [115].

CNR with repeated write/erase cycling [80], [81], [121] occurs primarily due to heating. High local temperatures during writing can interdiffuse the metal layers, changing magnetic and magneto-optical properties, or damage the substrate. Thus, the thermal design of the optical disk stack can mitigate damage. For example, Hashimoto et al. [81], [121] report that a quadrilayer disk structure is more thermally stable with write/ erase cycling than a bilayer structure, and glass disks are more stable than polycarbonate disks. The Al reflective layer, which is one layer in the quadrilayer stack, apparently reduces the temperature experienced by the multilayer, and whereas glass disks are tolerant to heating, PC and disks coated with a polymeric lacquer are more easily damaged during the writing process. This accounts for superior write/erase cycling in glass disks and quadrilayer structures.

Improvements in write/erase lifetime can be achieved by reducing the switching or Curie temperature of the multilayer, so that less laser power and lower peak temperatures are needed to thermomagnetically record on a multilayer medium. Zeper et al. [74] found that Pt/Co multilayers with thicker Pt layers and thus lower T_c could sustain more write/erase cycles, before measurable changes in CNR occur, and Fujimoto and Hashimoto [121] achieve similar improvements when the Co layer is doped with Ni (38%) to reduce T_c.

3.4.4 Near-Field Optical Recording

MO recording at blue wavelengths increases storage densities by pushing the optical diffraction limit to shorter wavelength, which allows smaller recorded features to be read. Near-field optical scanning microscopy [122], [123] circumvents the optical diffraction limit by placing a subwavelength source or detector of visible light in very close proximity ($< 1/50\lambda$) to a sample and raster scanning it to obtain an image. Using near-field optical techniques, Betzig et al. [124] have successfully demonstrated MO recording and imaging of magnetic domains down to ~60 nm in a sputtered Pt/Co multilayer film, $10 \times (4\,\text{ÅCo} + 10\,\text{ÅPt})$. They used a 250 nm Al-coated optical fiber for recording and imaging sub-100 nm domains in the multilayer. Written images were detected by the Faraday effect with the probe positioned to within 10 nm of the Pt/Co surface. Pt/ Co multilayers are unique for this application, since they need no protective layers, which are typically ~ 100 nm thick, and thus permit the necessary close proximity of a near-field probe. The size of domains written by near-field MO recording scales with the writing power, as in conventional MO recording, and the demagnetization field in the multilayers is sufficiently large that domains can be written without an externally applied magnetic field.

With near-field MO recording, storage densities of 45 Gbits/in^2 [124] was previously demonstrated, far surpassing previous records for all forms of magnetic storage. However, the method using fiber optics limits the data rate. Recently, an approach using solid-immersion lens (SIL) indicates a strong feasibility for attaining high rates. Figure 3.31 illustrates how the density can be increased using SIL. The effective numerical aperture increases with using a hemispherical (a) and superspherical lens (b), by a factor of n and n^2, respectively. As compared to a conventional optics, the density can be increased by an order of magnitude with $n = 2$ of the SIL. Figure 3.32 is the schematic diagram using SIL near-field optics [137]. The SIL lens is formed with a hemispherical lens attached to a slider made of the same glass as that of SIL, so that the combined lens system is equivalent to the superspherical lens. Figure 3.33 is the example of written domains in TbFeCo disk using SIL near-field optics, observed by magnetic force microscopy [138]. Written domains as small as 0.2 microns using 780 nm laser were formed.

The approach toward high-density recording using SIL near-field optics is one of the strong candidates. The hard disk technology can be fully applied for this approach. Since the spacing between the SIL and the medium surface must be kept as close as possible so that the evanescent beam can irradiate, the slider technology developed in the hard disk drives will be important for developing the SIL near-field drives.

From another different aspect, this technology is viewed as an alternative approach for high density. As the density in hard disk drives approaches to more than 10 Gigabits/in^2, the thermal density stability of small written domains in the longitudinal recording mode becomes a very serious issue. In this respect, the vertical recording is considered to be the next for beyond 10 Gbits/in^2. Nevertheless, the vertical

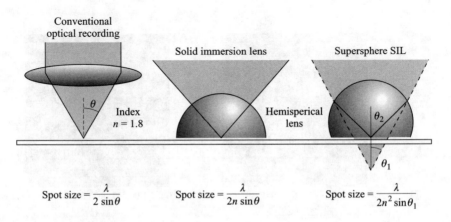

Figure 3.31 Schematic description of the solid immersion lens near-field optics. (a) Conventional, (b) hemispherical lens, and (c) supersphere lens.

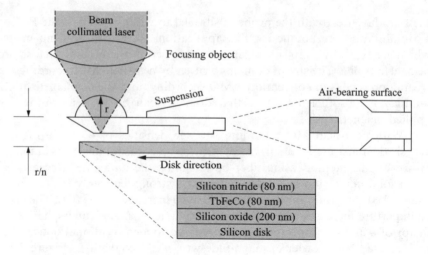

Figure 3.32 Solid immersion lens scheme used in the work [137].

recording mode has also serious issues, such as the relaxation phenomenon of domain magnetizations, and the so-called antenna effects of stray field [139]. Thus, it may take a while before any real drive will be realized in the market. For this reason, the near-field optics using SIL has a potential advantage over the vertical hard disk recording, since it already uses a "vertically magnetized domain state."

3.5 Pt-Co ALLOYS

A deficiency of multilayer MO disks is that they cannot directly be manufactured in most of the currently installed, in-line production equipment for optical disk manufacture [125]. This has been a motivation for renewed investigations of the magnetic and magneto-optical properties of Pt-Co alloys. The same equipment that is currently used to manufacture RE-TM alloy disks could, in principle, be used to make other alloy

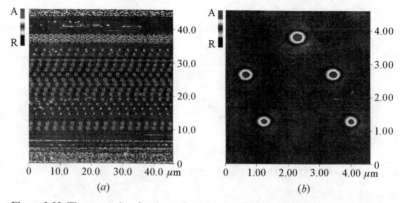

Figure 3.33 The example of written domains in TbFeCo disk using SIL near-field optics, observed by magnetic force microscopy [138].

disks. Further, Pt-Co alloys have a lower Curie temperature and larger Kerr rotation than compositionally equivalent multilayers, advantages for MO recording.

One of the earliest demonstrations of MO recording on a Pt-Co alloy was carried out by Treves et al. [126] in 1975. They synthesized alloy films with perpendicular magnetic anisotropy and large coercivity ($H_c \sim 8$ kOe) by sputter deposition and subsequent annealing of films at 600°C to form the tetragonal phase of $Pt_{50}Co_{50}$. Conversion to the tetragonal phase was critical for perpendicular magnetic anisotropy, which was limited to alloy compositions with 40–50 atomic % Co; more Pt-rich alloys had an in-plane easy axis of magnetization and thus were less attractive for MO recording. Treves et al. were able to dynamically record on a 400 Å thick film, which had a Faraday rotation, $2\theta_F > 0.5°$, even though the film had less than 100% remanence. And more than 10^4 write/erase cycles were achieved without change in the read signal.

More recently, Lin and Gorman [15] and Weller et al. [16] have shown that disordered fcc Pt-Co alloy films, richer in Pt, can be prepared with magnetic properties suitable for MO recording. These films are e-beam evaporated, and perpendicular anisotropy occurs when films have good (111)-fcc texture and an optimum growth temperature between 200 and 300°C. They were prepared either by co-evaporation [15], [16] from Pt and Co sources or by "sub-atomic layering" [16] of Pt and Co, analogous to multilayer synthesis. Lin and Gorman [15] found that between 20 and 360°C, higher growth temperatures increased both the magnetic hysteresis loop squareness and the coercivity of 200 Å thick $Co_{25}Pt_{75}$ alloy films. The coercivity and loop squareness also improved, when alloy films were grown at 200°C on (111)-fcc textured Pt underlayers with increasing thickness; however, films grown *without* substrate heating had only very small perpendicular anisotropy and small coercivity, with or without a Pt underlayer. Etching the substrates before depositing the alloy also promoted better texture. From X-ray diffraction measurements, it was determined that higher anisotropy energies in alloy films correlated with better (111)-fcc texture, analogous to Pt/Co multilayers. A $Co_{25}Pt_{75}$ alloy film grown at 200°C on a 200 Å thick Pt underlayer had an anisotropy energy of 2.5×10^6 erg/cm^3 (2.5×10^5 J/m^3), much smaller ($\sim 4x$) than energies reported for compositionally equivalent Pt/Co multilayers also grown on a Pt underlayer [38]. Identically prepared alloy films with compositions $Co_{57}Pt_{43}$ and $Co_{40}Pt_{60}$ also had net perpendicular anisotropy.

Weller et al. [16], [127]–[130] have characterized the magnetic and magneto-optical properties of polycrystalline Pt-Co alloy films with fcc structure. They found that perpendicular anisotropy occurred in alloy films with Pt concentration greater than 45 atomic % and was maximum near 75% Pt [16]. The magnetization of these thin film alloys is consistent with disordered fcc alloys. At short wavelength, the static MO signal, $R\Theta_K^{1/2}$, is 2.9 dB larger than a compositionally equivalent Pt/Co multilayer and 7.5 dB larger than a TbFeCo film [16]. The spectral dependences for the MO signal and θ_K are shown in Figure 3.34. The larger MO signal of the alloy is attributable to stronger three-dimensional exchange coupling of Pt and Co, compared to two-dimensional coupling in multilayers.

However, the stronger short wavelength MO signal for the alloy has not yet resulted in superior disk performance. A comparison of the dynamic recording performance (2 mW read power, 30 kHz bandwidth, and 10 m/s disk rotation) of multilayer and alloy disks at 488 nm for large written marks (5 μm) shows that Pt/Co multilayer disks have about a 2 dB advantage [127] in CNR (63.5 dB vs. 61.7 dB). The inferior performance of the alloy disk is attributed to higher noise.

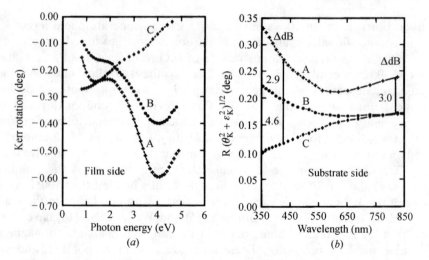

Figure 3.34 (*a*) Kerr rotation spectra of a 100 nm thick $Co_{22}Pt_{78}$ alloy (A), a 77×(3Å Co + 10 Å Pt) multilayer (B), and a 100 nm thick $Tb_{23.5}(Fe_{90}Co_{10})_{76.5}$ film (C) measured at the air/film interface. (*b*) Static MO signal, $R \times (\theta_K^2 + \varepsilon_K^2)^{1/2}$ as a function of wavelength for same films measured at film/substrate interface [16].

In contrast to e-beam evaporated alloys, Farrow et al. [131] found that the anisotropy energy of MBE grown $CoPt_3$ alloy films was independent of growth direction, or texture, and was larger for polycrystalline substrates than for alloy films grown epitaxially on crystalline Al_2O_3 substrates. Specifically, $Ku = 3.8 \times 10^6$ erg/cm^3 (3.8×10^5 J/m^3) for a polycrystalline $CoPt_3$ alloy grown on silica and 1.7×10^6 erg/ cm^3 (3.8×10^5 J/m^3) for epitaxially grown $CoPt_3$, both at 300°C. The coercivity and the anisotropy energy are maximum for MBE growth of the alloy at 300°C. At higher substrate temperatures, Carcia et al. found structural evidence [130] by TEM for ordered $CoPt_3$, and they suggested that this phase might also be present for alloys grown at 300°C and implicated in the mechanism for perpendicular anisotropy. A disk made with this alloy in a quadrilayer structure had a CNR at 488 nm of 57.5 dB, less than the textured alloy disk made by e-beam evaporation.

The mechanism for perpendicular anisotropy in these alloys is as yet undetermined. Whereas evidence for an ordered alloy phase was reported for the MBE grown $CoPt_3$ alloy, no evidence for an ordered alloy was found in the e-beam evaporated films, but (111)-fcc texture [15], [16] was cited as critical for perpendicular anisotropy. One speculation is that local chemical inhomogeneity [129], driven by precipitates of ordered alloy phase in a background of disordered alloy, or by anisotropy in adatom mobility during film growth, is the origin of magnetic anisotropy. This mechanism for magnetic anisotropy is the same one cited in rare-earth transition metal alloys, currently used in commercial MO recording media.

It may be too soon to compare the relative merits of Pt/Co multilayers and Pt-Co alloys for short wavelength MO recording, because, to date, multilayer research and development have been more extensive. The simplicity of using an alloy versus the multilayer architecture in manufacture has already been discussed. However, these alloys require substrate heating that may be incompatible with inexpensive plastic substrates, which will certainly dominate the commercial marketplace. Further, vapor deposition is not likely acceptable for the manufacture of MO disks. And, although there is some earlier work describing perpendicular anisotropy in sputtered Pt-Co alloys [132]–[134], their dynamic recording properties were not tested. With regard to recording properties, the lower CNR for alloy disks than multilayers at 488 nm, in spite of a higher alloy figure-of-merit, suggests that noise may also be a limiting issue for these alloys.

Before closing this chapter, it is worthwhile mentioning a recent work on Co_3Pt ordered phase alloy films. Yamada and Suzuki have recently reported a huge perpendicular magnetic anisotropy of Co_3Pt ordered alloy films [140], [141]. Figure 3.35 (a) and (b) show the concentration and substrate deposition temperature dependence of the

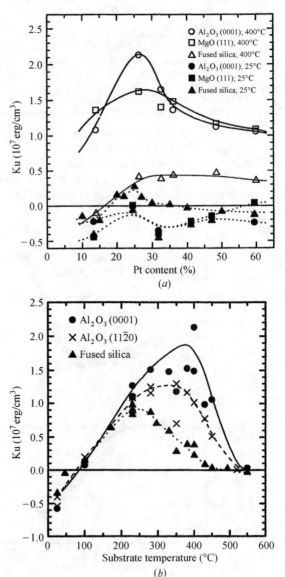

Figure 3.35 (a) The dependence of the perpendicular magnetic anisotropy constant Ku on Pt content of Co-Pt alloy films deposited on various substrates [140].

(b) The dependence of the perpendicular magnetic anisotropy constant Ku on substrate deposition temperature T_s of $Co_{75}Pt_{25}$ films deposited onto various types of substrates [140], [141].

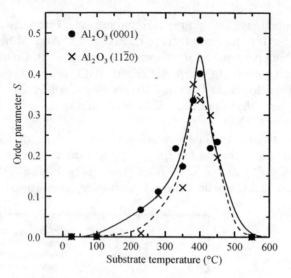

Figure 3.36 Dependence of ther order parameter of Co$_3$Pt on substrate temperature.

perpendicular magnetic anisotropy constant Ku of the Co-Pt alloy films, respectively. As shown in Figure 3.35 (*a*), the perpendicular magnetic anisotropy becomes maximum at about 25%Pt compositions, where the value of Ku reaches about 2×10^7 erg/cm^3 (2×10^6 J/m^3) at room temperature. Figure 3.25 (*b*) shows the dependence of Ku on substrate deposition temperature Ts of 25%Pt in Co-Pt alloys deposited onto various substrates. It is seen that there are the maxima at about 350 to 400C for the various substrates of Al$_2$O$_3$(001), (1120), Si(111). The values of Ku for Al$_2$O$_3$ (0001) reach

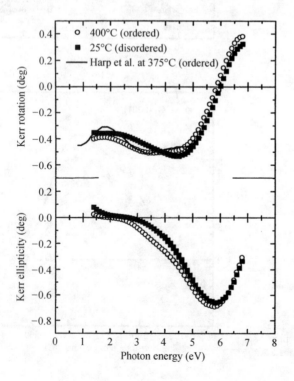

Figure 3.37 The MO spectra of the Co$_3$Pt disordered and ordered phase films [144].

$1 \sim 2 \times 10^7 \, \text{erg/cm}^3$ ($1 \sim 2 \times 10^6 \, \text{J/m}^3$) at room temperature, which is larger by a factor 4 to 5, as compared to that of hcp cobalt. The X-ray diffraction analyses indicate the close correlation between the origin of such a high perpendicular magnetic anisotropy and the ordered Co_3Pt phase, which is shown in Figure 3.36 [142].

The MO spectra of these samples with the order- and disorder phases are shown in Figure 3.37 for a wide photon energy range from 1 to 7 eV. There seems a clear difference between the ordered and disordered samples for photon energy beyond 4 eV, which is previously reported [142].

REFERENCES

[1] M. Hartmann, B. A. J. Jacobs, and J. J. M. Braat, "Erasable Magnetooptical Recording," *Philips Tech. Rev.*, vol. 42, pp. 37–47, 1985.

[2] M. Mansuripur, "Magneto-Optical Disk Data Storage," in *The Electrical Engineering Handbook*, R. C. Dorf (ed.), Boca Raton, FL: CRC Press, 1993, Sec. VIII, pp. 1675–1694.

[3] H. Kryder and A. B. Bortz, "Magnetic Information Technology," *Physics Today*, vol. 37, pp. 20–28, December 1984.

[4] F. E. Luborsky, "Amorphous Transition Metal-Rare Earth Alloy films for Magneto-Optical Recording," *Mater. Res. Soc. Symp. Proc.*, vol. 80, pp. 375–394, 1987.

[5] Ullmann's Encyclopedia of Industrial Chemistry, 5th ed., vol. A14, Weinheim, Germany: Verlag Chemie, "Information Storage Materials," pp. 171–239, 1992.

[6] M. A. Haase, J. Qiu, J. M. DePuydt, and H. Cheng, "Blue-green Laser Diodes," *Appl. Phys. Lett.*, vol. 59, p. 1272, 1991.

[7] J. Qiu, J. M. DePuydt, H. Cheng, and M. A. Haase, "Heavily Doped p-ZnSe:N Grown by Molecular Beam Epitaxy," *Appl. Phys. Lett.*, vol. 59, p. 2992, 1991.

[8] J. D. Bierlein, "Potassium-Titanyl Phosphate (KTP): Properties, Recent Advances and New Applications," *SPIE*, vol. 1104, pp. 2–12, 1989.

[9] C. J. van der Poel, J. D. Bierlein, J. B. Brown, and S. Colak, "Efficient Type I Blue Second-Harmonic Generation in Periodically Segmented $K(TiO)PO_4$ Waveguides," *Appl. Phys. Lett.*, vol. 57, pp. 2074–2076, 1990.

[10] J. E. Hurst and W. J. Kozlovsky, "Optical Recording at 2.4 $Gbit/in^2$ using a Frequency Doubled Diode Laser," *Japan J. Appl. Phys.*, vol. 32, pp. 5301–5306, 1993.

[11] F. J. A. M. Greidanus and W. B. Zeper, "Magneto-Optical Storage Materials," *Materials Res. Soc. Bull.*, vol. XV, p. 31, 1990.

[12] B. G. Huth, "Calculations of Stable Domain Radii Produced by Thermomagnetic Writing," *IBM J. Res. Develop.*, vol. 18, pp. 100–109, March, 1974.

[13] P. F. Carcia, "Layered Coherent Structures for Magnetic Recording," *U.S. Patent* 4 587 176.

[14] W. B. Zeper, H. W. van Kesteren, and P. F. Carcia, "Co/Pt Multilayers for Magneto-Optical Recording," *Adv. Materials*, vol. 3, pp. 397–399, 1991.

[15] C. -J. Lin and G. L. Gorman, "Evaporated CoPt Alloy Films with Strong Perpendicular Magnetic Anisotropy," *Appl. Phys. Lett.*, vol. 61, pp. 1600–1602, 1992.

[16] D. Weller, H. Brandle, G. Gorman, C. -J. Lin, and H. Notarys, "Magnetic and Magneto-Optical Properties of Cobalt-Platinum Alloys with Perpendicular Magnetic Anisotropy," *Appl. Phys. Lett.*, vol. 61, pp. 2726–2728, 1992.

[17] B. D. Cullity, *Elements of X-ray Diffraction*, Reading, MA: Addison-Wesley, pp. 482–483, 1967.

[18] D. B. McWhan, "Structure of Chemically Modulated Films," in *Synthetic Modulated Structures*, L. L. Chang and B. C. Giessen (eds.), Orlando, FL: Academic Press, Chapter 2, pp. 43–74, 1985.

[19] S. A. Barnett, "Deposition and Mechanical Properties of Superlattice Thin Films." In *Physics of Thin Films*, vol. 17, M. H. Francombe and J. L. Vossen (ed.), Boston, MA: Academic Press, Chapter 1, pp. 2–77,1993.

[20] A. Segmuller and A. E. Blakeslee, "X-ray Diffraction from One-Dimensional Superlattices in $GaAs_{1-x}P_x$ Crystals," *J. Appl. Cryst.*, vol. 6, pp. 19–25, 1973.

[21] P. F. Carcia, "Perpendicular Magnetic Anisotropy in Pd/Co and Pt/Co Layered Structures," *J. Appl. Phys.*, vol. 10, pp. 5066–5073, 1988.

[22] A. R. Miedema, "Heat of Formation of Alloys," *Philips Tech. Rev.*, vol. 36, p. 217–231, 1976.

[23] E. E. Fullerton, I. K. Schuller, and Y. Bruynsseraede, "Quantitative X-ray Diffraction from Superlattices," *MRS Bulletin*, vol. XVII, pp. 33–38, 1992.

[24] Z. Xu, Z. Tang, S. D. Kevan, T. Novet, and D. C. Johnson, "Effect of Structural Incoherence on the Low-Angle Diffraction Pattern of Synthetic Multilayer Materials," *J. Appl. Phys.*, vol. 74, pp. 905–912, 1993.

[25] Z. Xu, Z. Tang, S. D. Kevan, T. Novet, and D. C. Johnson, "Distinguishing Between Coherent Interdiffusion and Incoherent Roughness in Synthetic Multilayers Using X-ray Diffraction," *Materials Res. Soc. Symp. Proc.*, vol. 280, pp. 241–244, 1993.

[26] P. F. Carcia, S. I. Shah, and W. B. Zeper, "Effect of Energetic Bombardment on the Magnetic Coercivity of Sputtered Pt/Co Thin-Film Multilayers," *Appl. Phys. Lett.*, vol. 56, pp. 2345–2347, 1990.

[27] H. Wise and J. Oudar, *Material Concepts in Surface Reactivity and Catalysis*, San Diego: Academic Press, p. 33, 1990.

[28] S. Shiomi, T. Nishimura, T. Kobayashi, and M. Masuda, "Dependence of Magnetic Properties of Co/Pt Multilayers on Deposition Temperature of Pt Buffer Layers," *Japan J. Appl. Phys.*, vol. 32, pp. L495–496, 1993.

[29] B. N. Engel, C. D. England, R. A. Van Leeuwen, M. H. Wiedmann, and C. M. Falco, "Interface Magnetic Anisotropy in Epitaxial Superlattices," *Phys. Rev. Lett.*, vol. 67, pp. 1910–1913, 1991.

[30] C. H. Lee, R. F. C. Farrow, C. J. Lin, E. E. Marinero, and C. J. Chien, "Molecular-Beam-Epitaxial Growth and Magnetic Properties of Co-Pt Superlattices Oriented along the [001], [110], and [111] axes of Pt," *Phys. Rev. B*, vol. 42, pp. 11384–11387, 1990.

[31] W. B. Zeper, F. J. A. M. Greidanus, and P. F. Carcia, "Evaporated Co/Pt layered structures for Magneto-Optical Recording," *IEEE Trans. Magn.*, vol. 25, pp. 3764-3766, 1989.

[32] Z. G. Li, P. F. Carcia, and Y. Cheng, "Co Thickness Dependence of the Microstructure of Pt/Co Multilayers," *J. Appl. Phys.*, vol. 73, pp. 2433–2437, 1993.

[33] P. F. Carcia, A. D. Meinhaldt, and A. Suna, "Perpendicular magnetic anisotropy in Pd/Co thin film layered structures," *Appl. Phys. Lett.*, vol. 47, pp. 178–180, 1985.

[34] H. J. G. Draaisma, W. J. M. de Jonge, and F. J. A. den Broeder, "Magnetic Interface Anisotropy in Pd/Co and Pd/Fe Multilayers," *J. Magn. Mat.*, vol. 66, pp. 351–355, 1987.

[35] W. B. Zeper, F. J. A. M. Greidanus, P. F. Carcia, and C. R. Fincher, "Perpendicular Magnetic Anisotropy and Magneto-optical Kerr effect of Vapor-Deposited Co/Pt-layered Structures," *J. Appl. Phys.*, vol. 65, pp. 4971–4975.

[36] L. Néel, *J. Phys. Rad.*, "Anisotropie Magnetique superficielle et surstructures d'orientation," vol. 15, pp. 225–239, 1954.

[37] B. D. Cullity, *Introduction to Magnetic Materials*, Reading, MA: Addison-Wesley, p. 234, 1972.

[38] C.-J. Lin, G. L. Gorman, C. H. Lee, R. F. C. Farrow, E. E. Marinero, H. V. Do, H. Notarys, and C. J. Chien, "Magnetic and Structural Properties of Co/Pt Multilayers," *J. Magn. Magn. Mat.*, vol. 93, pp. 194–206, 1991.

[39] C. Chappert and P. Bruno, "Magnetic Anisotropy in Metallic Ultrathin Films and Related Experiments on Cobalt Films," *J. Appl. Phys.*, vol. 64, pp. 5736–5741, 1988.

[40] F. J. A. den Broeder, W. Hoving, and P. J. H. Bloemen, "Magnetic Anisotropy of Multilayers," *J. Magn. Magn. Mat.*, vol. 93, pp. 562–570, 1991.

[41] R. Wu, C. Li, and A. J. Freeman, "Structural, Electronic and Magnetic Properties of Co/Pd(111) and Co/Pt(111)," *J. Magn. Magn. Mat.*, vol. 99, pp. 71–80, 1991.

[42] R. H. Victora and J. M. MacLaren, "Theory of Anisotropy in Strained Superlattices," *J. Appl. Phys.*, vol. 73, pp. 6415–6417, 1993.

[43] F. J. A. den Broeder, D. Kuiper, and H. J. G. Draaisma, "Effects of Annealing and Ion Implantation on the Magnetic Properties of Pd/Co Multilayers Containing Ultrathin Co," *IEEE Trans. Magn.*, vol. 23, pp. 3696–3698, 1997.

[44] S. Honda, N. Morita, M. Nawate, and T. Kusuda, "Annealing Effects on the Crystallographic and Magnetic Properties of Co/Pt Multilayers," *J. Mag. Soc. Japan*, vol. 15, Supplement S1, pp. 45–48, 1991.

[45] C. D. Wright, W. W. Clegg, A. Boudjemultilayerine, N. A. E. Heyes, P. J. Grundy, R. J. Pollard, S. J. Greaves, A. K. Petford-Long, Y. H. Kim, and J. P. Jakubovics, "Micro-Annealing Studies of Pt/Co Multilayers for Magneto-Optic Recording Applications," *IEEE Trans. Magn.*, vol. 28, pp. 2671–2673, 1992.

[46] S. Hashimoto, A. Maesaka, and Y. Ociai, "Pt/Co Multilayer Magneto-optical Disks," *Proceedings of International Workshop on Magnetic Superstructured Films*, Nagoya, Japan, pp. 10–13, April 24, 1991.

[47] S. T. Purcell, M. T. Johnson, N. W. E. McGee, J. J. de Vries, W. B. Zeper, and W. Hoving, "Spatially Resolved Magneto-optical Investigation of the Perpendicular Anisotropy in a Wedge-Shaped Ultrathin Epitaxial Co Layer on Pd(111)," *J. Magn. Magn. Mat.*, vol. 113, pp. 257–263, 1992.

[48] N. W. E. McGee, M. T. Johnson, J. J. de Vries, and J. van de Stegge, "Localized Kerr Study of the Magnetic Properties of an Ultrathin Epitaxial Co Wedge Grown on Pt(111)," *J. Appl. Phys.*, vol. 73, 3418 , 1993.

[49] K. Sato, H. Hongu, H. Ikekame, J. Watanabe, K. Tsuzukiyama, Y. Togami, M. Fujisawa, and T. Fukazawa, "Magnetooptical Spectra in Pt/Co and Pt/Fe Multilayers," *Japan J. Appl. Phys.*, vol. 31, pp. 3603–3607, 1992.

[50] J. A. Bain, B. M. Clemens, H. Notarys, E. Marinero, and S. Brennan, "X-ray Analysis of Compositional Modulation in Co/Pt Multilayer Films for Magneto-optic Recording," *J. Appl. Phys.*, vol. 74, pp. 996–1000, 1993.

[51] C. J. Chien, R. F. C. Farrow, C. H. Lee, C. J. Lin, and E. E. Marinero, "High-Resolution Transmission Electron Microscopy Studies of Seeded Epitaxial Co/Pt Superlattices," *J. Magn. Magn. Mat.*, vol. 93, pp. 47–52, 1991.

[52] N.-H. Cho, K. M. Krishnan, C. A. Lucas, and R. F. C. Farrow, "Microstructure and Magnetic Anisotropy of Ultrathin Co/Pt Multilayers Grown on GaAs (111) by Molecular-Beam Epitaxy," *J. Appl. Phys.*, vol. 72, pp. 5799–5807, 1992.

[53] P. Grütter and U. T. Dürig, "Growth of Vapor-Deposited Cobalt Films on Pt(111) Studied by Scanning Tunneling Microscopy," *Phys. Rev. B.*, vol. 49, pp. 2021–2029, 1994.

[54] F. J. A. den Broeder, D. Kuiper, H. C. Donkersloot, and W. Hoving, "A Comparison of the Magnetic Anisotropy of (001) and (111) Oriented Co/Pd Multilayers," *Appl. Phys. A*, vol. A49, pp. 507–512, 1989.

[55] B. N. Engel, C. D. England, R. A. Van Leeuwen, M. H. Wiedmann, and C. M. Falco, "Magnetocrystalline and Magnetoelastic Anisotropy in Epitaxial Co/Pd Superlattices," *J. Appl. Phys.*, vol. 70, p. 55873–55875, 1991.

[56] H. Kronmüller, "Coercivity Mechanisms in Modern Magnetic Materials," *J. Magn. Soc. Japan*, vol. 17, Supplement S1, pp. 260–266, 1993.

[57] H. Fu, R. Giles, and M. Mansuripur, "Coercivity Mechanisms in Magneto-Optical Recording Media," *J. Magn. Soc. Japan*, vol. 17, Supplement S1, pp. 2740–2745, 1993.

[58] T. Suzuki, H. Notarys, D. C. Dobbertin, C.-J. Lin, D. Weller, D. C. Miller, and G. Gorman, "Coercivity Mechanisms and Microstructure of Co/Pt Multilayers," *IEEE Trans. Magn.*, vol. 28, pp. 2754–2759, 1992.

[59] G. Schutz, R. Wienke, W. Wilhelm, W. B. Zeper, H. Ebert, and K. Sporl, "Spin-Dependent X-ray Absorption in Co/Pt Multilayers and Co(50)Pt(50) Alloy," *J. Appl. Phys.*, vol. 67, pp. 4456–4462 , 1990.

[60] H. Ebert, S. Ruegg, G. Schutz, R. Wienke, and W. B. Zeper, "Magnetic Properties of Co/Pt Multilayers," *J. Magn. Magn. Mat.*, vol. 93, pp. 601–604, 1991.

[61] F. J. A. den Broeder, H. C. Donkersloot, H. J. G. Draaisma, and W. J. M. de Jonge, "Magnetic Properties and Structure of Pd/Co and Pd/Fe Multilayers," *J. Appl. Phys.*, vol. 61, pp. 4317–4319, 1987.

[62] P. F. Carcia, A. Suna, D. G. Onn, and R. van Antwerp, "Structural, Magnetic, and Electrical Properties of Thin Film Pd/Co Layered Structures," *Superlattices and Microstructures*, vol. 1, pp. 101–109, 1985.

[63] R. M. Bozorth, P. A. Wolff, D. D. Davis, V. B. Compton, and J. H. Wernick, "Ferromagnetism in Dilute Solutions of Cobalt in Palladium," *Phys. Rev.*, vol. 122, pp. 1157–1160, 1961.

[64] J. Crangle and W. R. Scott, "Dilute Ferromagnetic Alloys," *J. Appl. Phys.*, vol. 36, pp. 921–928, 1965.

[65] G. J. Nieuwenhuys, "Magnetic Behavior of Cobalt, Iron, and Manganese Dissolved in Palladium," *Adv. Phys.*, vol. 24, pp. 515–591, 1975.

[66] M. J. Freiser, "A Survey of Magnetooptical Effects," *IEEE Trans. Magn.*, vol. 4, pp. 152–161, 1968.

[67] H. Feil and C. Haas, "Magneto-optical Kerr Effect, Enhanced by the Plasma Resonance of Charge-Carriers," *Phys. Rev. Lett.*, vol. 58, pp. 65–68, 1987.

[68] K. Egashira and T. Yamada, "Kerr-Effect Enhancement and Improvement of Readout in MnBi film Memory," *J. Appl. Phys.*, vol. 45, pp. 3643–3648, 1974.

[69] E. R. Moog, J. Zak, and S. D. Bader, "Kerr Effect from Pt/Co Superlattices and the Role of the Magneto-Optic Activity of Pt," *J. Appl. Phys.*, vol. 69, pp. 880–885, 1991.

[70] K. Sato, "Analysis Of Magneto-Optical Spectra of Pt/Co and Pt/Fe Multilayers Using Optical Constants Determined By Reflectivity Spectra Between 0.5 and 25 eV," *J. Magn. Soc. Japan*, vol. 17, Supplement No. S1, pp. 11–16, 1993.

[71] P. F. Carcia, W. B. Zeper, and F. J. A. M. Greidanus, "Pt/Co Multilayers-a New Magneto-Optical Recording Medium," *Mat. Res. Soc. Symp. Proc.*, vol. 150, pp. 115–120, 1989.

[72] S. Hashimoto and Y. Ochiai, "Co/Pt and Co/Pd Multilayers as Magneto-Optical recording Materials," *J. Magn. Magn. Mat.*, vol. 88, pp. 211–226, 1990.

[73] F. L. Zhou, J. K. Erwin, C. Brucker, and M. Mansuripur, "Wavelength Dependencies of the Kerr Rotation Angle and Ellipticity for the Magneto-optical Recording Media," *J. Appl. Phys.*, vol. 70, pp. 6286–6288, 1991.

[74] W. B. Zeper, F. J. A. M. Greidanus, H. W. van Kestern, B. A. J. Jacobs, J. H. M. Spruit, and P. F. Carcia, "Co/Pt and Co/Pd Multilayers as a New Class of Magneto-Optical Recording Materials," *SPIE*, vol. 1274, pp. 282–292, 1990.

[75] Y. Ochiai, S. Hashimoto, and K. Aso, "Magneto-Optical Properties in Ultrathin Co/Pd and Co/Pt Multilayer Films," *Japan J. Appl. Phys.*, vol. 28, pp. L659–L660, 1989.

[76] S.-C. Shin and A. Palumbo, "Magneto-optical Properties of Co/Pd Superlattice Thin Films," *J. Appl. Phys.*, vol. 67, pp. 317–320, 1990.

[77] K. Yusu, S. Hashimoto, and K. Inomata, "Layer Modulated Co/Pt Multilayers with Enhanced Kerr Rotation Angles," *J. Magn. Soc. Japan*, vol. 17, Supplement No. S1, pp. 56–59, 1993.

[78] H. W. van Kesteren and W. B. Zeper, "Controlling the Curie Temperature of Co/Pt Multilayer Magneto-optical Recording Media," *J. Magn. Magn. Mat.*, vol. 120, pp. 271–273, 1992.

[79] P. Bruno, "Theory of the Curie Temperature of Cobalt-Based Ferromagnetic Ultrathin Films and Multilayers," *J. Magn. Soc. Japan*, vol. 15, Supplement No. S1, pp. 15–20, 1991.

[80] F. J. A. M. Greidanus, W. B. Zeper, B. A. J. Jacobs, J. H. M. Spruit, and P. F. Carcia, "Magneto-Optical Recording in Co/Pt Multilayers," *Japan J. Appl. Phys.*, vol. 28, Supplement 28-3, pp. 37–44, 1989.

[81] S. Hashimoto, A. Maesaka, K. Fujimoto, and K. Bessho, "Magneto-optical Applications of Co/Pt Multilayers," *J. Magn. Magn. Mat.*, vol. 121, pp. 471–478, 1993.

[82] S. Hashimoto, "Adding Elements to the Co Layer in Co/Pt Multilayers," *J. Appl. Phys.*, vol. 75, pp. 438–441, 1994.

[83] S. Hashimoto, Y. Ochiai, and K. Aso, "Ultrathin Co/Pt and Co/Pd Multilayered Films as Magneto-optical Recording Materials," *J. Appl. Phys.*, vol. 67, pp. 2136–2142, 1990.

[84] S. Honda, N. Morita, M. Nawate, and T. Kusuda, "Annealing Effects on the Crystallographic and Magnetic Properties of Co/Pt Multilayers," *J. Magn. Soc. Japan*, vol. 15, Supplement No. S1, pp. 45–48, 1991.

[85] S. Shiomi, T. Nakabayashi, M. Okada, T. Kobayashi, and M. Masuda, "Magnetic Properties and Structure of Co/Pt Multilayered Films Evaporated on Heated Substrates," *Japan J. Appl. Phys.*, vol. 32, pp. 791–795, 1993.

[86] S. Hashimoto, Y. Ochiai, and K. Aso, "Perpendicular Magnetic Anisotropy and Magnetostriction of Sputtered Co/Pd and Co/Pt Multilayered Films," *J. Appl. Phys.*, vol. 66, pp. 4909–4916, 1989.

[87] R. E. Somekh, "The Thermalization of Energetic Atoms During the Sputtering Process," *J. Vac. Sci. Technol.* A, vol. 2, pp. 1285–1291, 1984.

[88] R. E. Somekh, "Calculations of Thermalization During the Sputter Deposition Process," *Vacuum*, vol. 34, pp. 987–990, 1984.

[89] S. T. Picraux, E. Chason, and T. M. Mayer, "Ion-Assisted Surface Processing of Electronic Materials," *MRS Bulletin*, vol. XVII, pp. 52–57, 1992.

[90] R. Resnick and D. Halliday, *Physics for Students of Science and Engineering, Part 1*, New York: John Wiley, p. 182, 1960.

[91] P. F. Carcia, Z. G. Li, and W. B. Zeper, "Effect of Sputter-Deposition Processes on the Microstructure and Magnetic Properties of Pt/Co Multilayers," *J. Magn. Magn. Mat.*, vol. 121, pp. 452–460, 1993.

[92] J. B. Biersack and L. G. Haggmark, "A Monte Carlo Computer Program for the Transport of Energetic Ions in Amorphous Targets," *Nuclear Instr. and Meth.*, vol. 174, pp. 257–269, 1980.

[93] Z. G. Li and P. F. Carcia, "Microstructural Dependence of Magnetic Properties of Pt/Co Multilayer Thin Films," *J. Appl. Phys.*, vol. 71, pp. 842–848, 1992.

[94] Z. G. Li and P. F. Carcia, "HREM Contributions to Microstructural Characterization of Pt/Co Ultra-Thin Magnetic Multilayers," *Ultramicroscopy*, vol. 47, pp. 313–317, 1992.

[95] P. F. Carcia and Z. G. Li, "Growth, Microstructure, and Magnetic Properties of Pt/Co Thin Film Multilayers for Magneto-optical Recording," *Appl. Phys. Comm.*, vol. 11, pp. 531–548, 1992.

[96] D. Dobrev, "Ion-Beam-Induced Texture Formation in Vacuum-Condensed Thin Metal Films," *Thin Solid Films*, vol. 92, pp. 41–53, 1982.

[97] J. F. Ankner, J. A. Borchers, R. F. C. Farrow, and R. F. Marks, "Combined Low- and High-Angle X-ray Structural Refinement of a Co/Pt(111) Multilayer Exhibiting Perpendicular Magnetic Anisotropy," *J. Appl. Phys.*, vol. 73, pp. 6427–6430, 1993.

[98] S-C. Shin, J-H. Kim, and D-H. Ahn, "Effects of Sputtering Pressure on Magnetic and Magneto-optical Properties in Compositionally Modulated Co/Pd Thin Films," *J. Appl. Phys.*, vol. 69, pp. 5664–5666, 1991.

[99] P. F. Carcia, M. Reilly, Z. G. Li, and H. W. van Kesteren, "Ar-Sputtered Pt/Co Multilayers with Large Anisotropy Energy and Coercivity," *6th Joint MMM-Intermag Conference*, Albuquerque, NM, June 20–23, 1994.

[100] C-Y You, J. Hur, and S-C. Shin, "Effects of Pd Predeposition Layer on Magnetic Properties in Compositionally Modulated Co/Pd Multilayers," *J. Appl. Phys.*, vol. 73, pp. 5951–5953, 1993.

[101] P. de Haan, Q. Meng, T. Katayama, and J. C. Lodder, "Magnetic and Magneto-optical Properties of Sputtered Co/Pd Multilayers," *J. Magn. Magn. Mat.*, vol. 113, pp. 29–35, 1992.

[102] S. L. Tang, P. F. Carcia, D. Coulman, and A. J. McGhie, "Scanning Tunneling Microscopy of Pt/Co Multilayers on Pt Buffer Layers," *Appl. Phys. Lett.*, vol. 59, pp. 2898–2900, 1991.

[103] B. Zeper, H. W. van Kesteren, B. A. J. Jacobs, J. H. M. Spruit, and P. F. Carcia, "Hysteresis, Microstructure, and Magneto-optical Recording in Co/Pt and Co/Pd Multilayers," *J. Appl. Phys.*, vol. 70, pp. 2264–2271, 1991.

[104] P. F. Carcia, M. Reilly, W. B. Zeper, and H. W. van Kesteren, "Dielectric Enhancement Layers for a Pt/Co Multilayer Magneto-optical Recording Medium," *Appl. Phys. Lett.*, vol. 58, pp. 191–193, 1991.

[105] P. F. Carcia, Z. G. Li, M. Reilly, and W. B. Zeper, "The Magnetic and Microstructural Properties of Pt/Co Multilayers Grown on ZnO," *J. Appl. Phys.*, vol. 73, pp. 6424–6426, 1993.

[106] P. F. Carcia, Z. G. Li, and H. W. van Kesteren, "Magnetic and Structural Properties of Pt/Co and Pd/Co Multilayers Sputtered on Single-Crystal ZnO," *Thin Solid Films*, vol. 246, pp. 126–130, 1994.

[107] S. Sumi, Y. Kusumoto, Y. Teragaki, K. Torazawa, S. Tsunashima, and S. Uchiyama, "Reliability of Pt/Co Magneto-optical Disk with a Simple Structure," *J. Magn. Soc. Japan*, vol. 17, Supplement No. S1, pp. 151–154, 1993.

[108] S. Sumi, Y. Teragaki, Y. Kusumoto, K. Torazawa, S. Tsunashima, and S. Uchiyama, "Thermal Stability of Pt/Co Multilayered Films," *J. Appl. Phys.*, vol. 73, pp. 6835–6837, 1993.

[109] S. Sumi, K. Tanase, Y. Teragaki, K. Torazawa, S. Tsunashima, and S. Uchiyama, "Microstructures of Pt/Co Films Deposited on Sputter-Etched Underlayers," *Japan J. Appl. Phys.*, vol. 31, pp. 3328–3331, 1992.

[110] A. Maesaka, K. Bessho, and S. Hashimoto, "Sources of Disk Noise on a Co/Pt Disk," *Japan J. Appl. Phys.*, vol. 32, Pt. 1, pp. 3160–3162, 1993.

[111] F. J. A. M. Greidanus, W. B. Zeper, F. J. A. den Broeder, W. F. Godlieb, and P. F. Carcia,"Thermomagnetic Writing in Thin Co/Pt Layered Structures," *Appl. Phys. Lett.*, vol. 54, pp. 2481–2483, 1989.

[112] C. -J. Lin and H. V. Do, "Magneto-Optical Recording on Evaporated Co/Pt Multilayer Films," *IEEE Trans. Magnetics*, vol. 26, pp. 1700–1702, 1990.

[113] S. Hashimoto, H. Matsuda, and Y. Ochiai, "Recording Experiments in Magneto-optical Disks Using Ultrathin Co/Pt and Co/Pd Media," *Appl. Phys. Lett.*, vol. 56, pp. 1069–1071, 1990.

[114] S. Sumi, K. Tanase, K. Torazawa, S. Tsunashima, and S. Uchiyama, "Multilayered Pt/Co Magneto-optical Disk," *IEEE Trans. J. Magn. in Japan*, vol. 6, pp. 141–151, 1991.

[115] H. W. van Kesteren, A. J. den Boef, W. B. Zeper, J. H. M. Spruit, B. A. J. Jacobs, and P. F. Carcia, "Scanning Magnetic Force Microscopy on Co/Pt Magneto-optical Disks," *J. Appl. Phys.*, vol. 70, pp. 2413–2422, 1991.

[116] H. W. van Kesteren, A. J. den Boef, W. B. Zeper, J. H. M. Spruit, B. A. J. Jacobs, and P. F. Carcia, "Scanning Magnetic Force Microscopy on Co/Pt Magneto-optical Disks," *J. Magn. Soc. Japan*, vol. 15, Supplement S1, pp. 247–250, 1991.

[117] J. E. Hurst, D. Weller, and H. A. Notarys, "Short Wavelength MO Recording: System Noise Issues and Performance Optimization," *J. Magn. Soc. Japan*, vol. 17, Supplement S1, pp. 299–302, 1993.

[118] W. B. Zeper, A. P. L. Jongenelis, B. A. J. Jacobs, H. W. van Kesteren, and P. F. Carcia, "Magneto-optical Recording in Co/Pt Multilayer and GdTbFe-Based Disks at 820, 647, and 458-nm Wavelength," *IEEE Trans. Magn.*, vol. 28, pp. 2503–2505, 1992.

[119] S. Hashimoto, A. Maesaka, and Y. Ochiai, " Recording on Co/Pt Magneto-optical Disks Using a 488-nm Wavelength Laser," *J. Appl. Phys.*, vol. 70, pp. 5133–5135, 1991.

[120] S. Sumi, K. Tanase, Y. Fuchigami, K. Torazawa, S. Tsunashima, and S. Uchiyama, "High Density Recording on Pt/Co MO Disk Using Blue Laser," *J. Magn. Soc. Japan*, vol. 15, Supplement S1, pp. 365–368, 1991.

[121] K. Fujimoto and S. Hashimoto, "Write/Erase Cyclability of Co/Pt Disks," *J. Magn. Magn. Mat.*, vol. 126, pp. 587–589, 1993.

[122] E. Betzig, J. K. Trautman, T. D. Harris, J. S. Weiner, and R. L. Kostelak, "Breaking the Diffraction Barrier: Optical Microscopy on a Nanometric Scale," *Science*, vol. 251, pp. 1468–1470, 1991.

[123] J. K. Trautman, E. Betzig, J. S. Weiner, D. J. DiGiovanni, T. D. Harris, F. Hellman, and E. M. Gyorgy, "Image Contrast in Near-Field Optics," *J. Appl. Phys.*, vol. 71, pp. 4659–4663, 1992.

[124] E. Betzig, J. K. Trautman, R. Wolfe, E. M. Gyorgy, P. L. Finn, M. H. Kryder, and C. -H. Chang, "Near-Field Magneto-optics and High Density Data Storage," *Appl. Phys. Lett.*, vol. 61, pp. 142–144, 1992.

[125] P. F. Carcia, W. B. Zeper, H. W. van Kesteren, B. A. J. Jacobs, and J. H. M. Spruit, "Materials' Challenges for Metal Multilayers as a Magneto-optical Recording Medium," *J. Magn. Soc. Japan*, vol. 15, Supplement S1, pp. 151–156, 1991.

[126] D. Treves, J. T. Jacobs, and E. Sawatzky, "Platinum-Cobalt Films for Digital Magneto-optic Recording," *J. Appl. Phys.*, vol. 46, pp. 2760–2765, 1975.

[127] D. Weller, J. Hurst, H. Notarys, H. Brandle, R. F. C. Farrow, R. Marks, and G. Harp, "MO Signal in Co-Pt and Co-Pd Alloy Disks: Comparison to Respective Multilayers and TbFeCo," *J. Magn. Soc. Japan*, vol. 17, Supplement 1, pp. 72–75, 1993.

[128] D. Weller, C. Chappert, H. Brandle, G. Gorman, R. F. C. Farrow, R. Marks, and G. Harp, "Perpendicular Magnetic Anisotropy and Strain in Evaporated Co-Pt and Co-Pd Alloys," *J. Magn. Soc. Japan*, vol. 17, Supplement 1, pp. 76–80, 1993.

[129] D. Weller, H. Brandle, and C. Chappert, "Relationship Between Kerr Effect and Perpendicular Magnetic Anisotropy in $CoPt_x$ and $Co_{1-x}Pd_x$ alloys," *J. Magn. Magn. Mat.*, vol. 121, pp. 461–470, 1993.

[130] H. Brandle, D. Weller, J. C. Scott, S. S. P. Parkin, and C. -J. Lin, "Optical and Magneto-Optical Characterization of Evaporated Co/Pt Alloys and Multilayers," *IEEE Trans. Magn.*, vol. 28, pp. 2967–2969, 1992.

[131] R. F. C. Farrow, R. H. Geiss, G. L. Gorman, G. R. Harp, R. F. Marks, and E. E. Marinero, "Large Perpendicular-Anisotropy, High Coercivity Co-Pt Alloys for Magneto-Optical Recording," *J. Magn. Soc. Japan*, vol. 17, Supplement 1, pp. 140–144, 1993.

[132] P. F. Carcia and W. B. Zeper, "Sputtered Pt/Co Multilayers for Magneto-optical Recording," *IEEE Trans. Magn.*, vol. 26, pp. 1703–1705, 1990.

[133] S. Shiomi, T. Nakakita, T. Kobayashi, and M. Masuda, "Effect of Annealing on Magnetic Properties of Sputtered CoPt Alloy Films," *Japan J. Appl. Phys.*, vol. 32, pp. L1058–L1061, 1993.

[134] S. Shiomi, H. Okazawa, T. Nakakita, T. Kobayashi, and M. Masuda, "Magnetic Properties of CoPt Alloy Films Sputtered on Pt Underlayers," *Japan J. Appl. Phys.*, vol. 32, pp. L315–L317, 1993.

[135] W. Van Drent and T. Suzuki, presented at the Magneto-optical Recording International Symposium (MORIS), The Netherlands, April 1996.

[136] W. Van Drent and T. Suzuki, *J. Magn. Mag. Mat.*, vol. 175, pp. 53–62, 1997.

[137] Y. Ito, W. Van Drent and T. Suzuki, *J. Mag. Soc. Japan*, vol. 22, No. S2, pp. 205–208, 1998.

[138] B. D. Terris, H. J. Maminn, and D. Ruger, *Appl. Phys. Letter*, vol. 68(2), pp. 141–143, 1996.

[139] P. Glijer, T. Suzuki and B. Terris, *J. Magn. Soc. Japan*, vol. 20, no. S1, pp. 297–302, 1996.

[140] W. Cain, A Payne, M. Baldwinson and R. Hemstead, *IEEE Trans. MAG.*, vol. 32, pp. 97–102, 1996.

[141] Y. Yamada, T. Suzuki and E. N. Abarra, *IEEE Trans. MAG*, vol. 33, pp. 3638–3642, 1997.

[142] Y. Yamada, W. P. Van Drent, E. N. Abarra and T. Suzuki, *J. Appl. Phys.*, vol. 83, pp. 6527–6529, 1998.

[143] G. R. Harp, D. Weller, T. A. Rabedeau, R. F. C. Farrow, and M. F. Toney, *Phys. Rev. Lett.*, vol. 71, p. 2493, 1993.

[144] T. Gasche, M. S. S. Brooks, B. Johanson, *J. Magn. Soc. Japan*, vol. 19, No. S1, p. 303, 1995.

[145] Y. Yamada, W. P. Van Drent, T. Suzuki and E. N. Abarra, *J. Magn. Soc. Japan*, vol. 22, No. 2, pp. 81–84, 1998.

Chapter

4

GARNET MEDIA

Takao Suzuki

4.1 GARNET

4.1.1 Introduction

As long as a laser beam is the means to write and read in optical recording, the spot size on a disk is the decisive factor for determining storage capacity. The diffraction limited spot size is given by $0.56\lambda/NA$ (where λ is the wavelength of the laser and NA is the optical aperture of the objective lens). Therefore, a smaller written mark can be obtained by increasing NA and/or using a shorter wavelength. After the visible laser diode (670nm) came to the market in 1988, much progress in laser technology has been made for high power, longer lifetime, better cost performance and toward shorter wavelengths. One of the examples is the work which demonstrated a frequency doubling laser of 40 mW (428 nm) using nonlinear crystal resonator ($KNbO_3$) with high overall conversion efficiency from electrical input to the diode laser to blue output [1].

The magneto-optical (MO) read-out signal is proportional to the effective polar Kerr rotation θ_{eff} which is given by

$$\theta_{\text{eff}} = (\theta_K^2 + \eta_K^2)^{1/2} \qquad (4.1)$$

where θ_K and η_K are the polar Kerr rotation and ellipticity, respectively. Therefore, it is desirable to have a high rotation angle at short wavelengths. Among many candidates that exhibit such characteristics, bismuth-substituted garnet is the material of which much effort has been made to apply for magneto-optical recording [2]–[8]. The main reason for this choice is the strong Kerr activity at a wavelength of about 500 nm which future magneto-optical recording drives are expected to use for high-density storage. The magneto-optical effect in rare earth-transition metal films, by comparison, becomes worse at shorter wavelengths. Figure 4.1 shows the read signal of garnet films, together with the case of typical TbFeCo film and Co/Pt multilayers, which are discussed in Chapters 2 and 3, respectively. Here, the signal is proportional to $2d\theta_{\text{eff}} \exp(-2\alpha d)$ for garnet, and $R\theta_{\text{eff}}$ for TbFeCo and Co/Pt, respectively [9], where α is the absorption coefficient, d the thickness of a garnet film, R reflectivity and θ_{eff} is defined by Equation (4.1). It is clear that the signal is far larger for garnet film than those of TbFeCo and Co/Pt at wavelengths around 500 nm.

The main drawback of garnets is the fact that they, like all magnetic oxides, are crystalline. When fabricated onto amorphous substrates such as glass or even single crystals like GGG (gadolinium gallium garnet), they are amorphous, and need to be crystallized at high temperatures ($\approx 650°C$). The grain boundaries and/or impurities present in such crystalline films are believed to be the cause of the noise in the readout

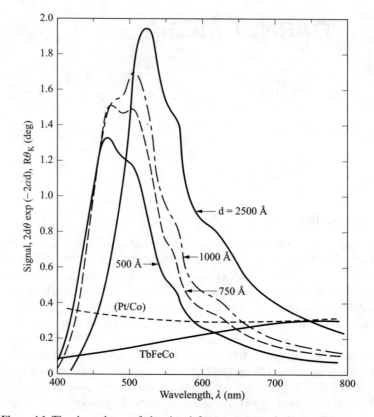

Figure 4.1 The dependence of the signal for magneto-optical recording on wavelength in Bi-substituted garnet films, together with the data for TbFeCo
amorphous films and Co/Pt multilayer films. Here, the angle θ is defined
by the combination of the Faraday rotation angle θ_F and the ellipticity η_F.
(d is the film thickness, α: absorption coefficient, R: reflectivity, and T_K:
Kerr rotation angle) [9].

signal, because the domain walls tend to follow the grain boundaries and/or impurities
and because scattering of light caused by the randomly oriented crystallites and the
grain boundaries changes the polarization of the light. Another drawback is the high
temperature processing for crystallization. A typical crystallization temperature of Bi-
substituted garnet is about 650°C, and thus conventional glass is unsuitable for garnet
films. This limitation may be crucial for cost performance of media.

In this chapter, the crystallographical aspect of garnets is first given. Then, the
magnetic and magneto-optical properties are discussed. Finally, the recording performance of garnet films is presented.

4.1.2 Crystal Structure

The name garnet was originally applied to certain silicates which occur naturally having a formula $\{A_3^{2+}\}[B_2^{3+}](Si_3)O_{12}$. A garnet belongs to space group la3d(O_h^{10}) and
contains eight formula units in the unit cell. The arrangement of cations in the garnet
structure is shown in Figure 4.2. Here, c, a and d denote the dodecahedral, octahedral
and tetrahedral site, respectively. The arrangement about an oxygen ion is shown in

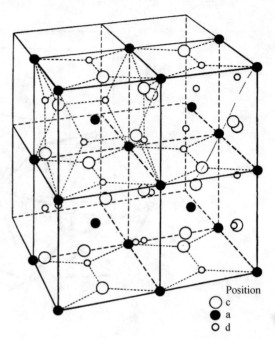

Figure 4.2 Arrangement of cations in the
garnet structure [10].

Position
◯ c
● a
○ d

Figure 4.3 [10], [11], [12]. There are 24 A-ions, 40 B-ions and 96 oxygen atoms in the cell
described in Figure 4.2, where { } is called the dodecahedral site or 24c, [ ] the octahedral site or 16a and ( ) is called the tetrahedral site or 24d, respectively. At the { }
positions, Y^{3+}, 4f rare earths, Bi^{3+}, Pb^{2+}, Ca^{2+}, Sr^{3+}, Ba^{2+}, Cd^{2+} and Na^{2+} are the
possible elements to locate. For [ ] sites, Fe^{3+}, Ti^{4+}, Zr^{4+}, Al^{3+}, Ga^{3+} and Ge^{4+} are
possible. For ( ), V^{5+}, Si^{4+}, Ge^{4+}, Fe^{3+}, Al^{3+}, and Ga^{3+} are located. Each oxygen ion
is at the corner of four polyhedra, one tetrahedron, one octahedron and two dodeca-
hedra only one of which is shown in Figure 4.3. The important magnetic interactions
are the a–d or [Fe]-O-(Fe) interactions in YIG and the c–d or {R}-O-(Fe) as well as the
a–d interactions in the magnetic rare earth iron garnets.

Among many garnets, rare earth iron garnets are well known for magnetic bubble
memory applications. The formula is $\{R_3{}^{3+}\}[Fe_{2-x}{}^{3+}M_x{}^{3+}](Fe_3)O_{12}$. For R^{3+}, Y,
La, Sm, Eu, Gd, Er, Tm, Yb, Lu and Bi are common, and for M^{3+}, Ga and Al are
used. Figure 4.4 shows the lattice constant vs. atomic number for various rare earth
elements [13]. The figure shows the small crystal field effects at room temperature on the
rare earth ions not having spherical electronic configuration and the expected cusp at
the Gd^{3+} ion. The maximum lattice constant attainable in the equilibrium phase diagram by any iron garnet is 12.540 Å [13]. The closest value to this is that of
$\{Y_{1.12}Bi_{1.89}\}[Fe_2](Fe_3)O_{12}$ which has a lattice constant of 12.531 Å; SmIG has a lattice
constant of 12.529 Å. However, recent work using the alternating ion-beam sputtering
method showed that a thin film of $Bi_3Fe_5O_{12}$ was successfully fabricated [14], whose
lattice constant is 12.62 Å, much larger than that possible in bulk form. Furthermore,
using this technique, Al- and Ga-substituted $Bi_3Fe_5O_{12}$ films were also successfully
made [15]. The lattice constant of those garnets is given in Figure 4.5. A detailed
description of this study is given in Section 4.1.4.

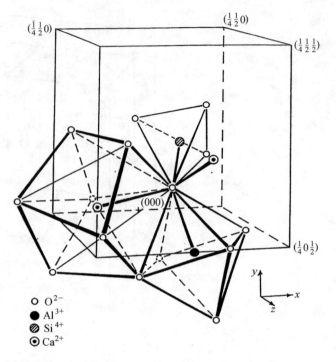

Figure 4.3 Coordination about an oxygen ion in a garnet [10].

For magneto-optical recording, $(BiDy)_3(FeGa)_5$ thin films were most widely studied [16]–[20]. Most of the work utilized the sputtering technique and pyrolysis method, and were concerned with morphology, especially grain size in conjunction with recording performance.

Another interesting system, which is important in the magneto-optical effect, is Ce-substituted iron garnet [50]. Gomi et al. have successfully fabricated epitaxially grown single crystals of $Y_{3-x}Ce_xFe_5O_{12}$ onto GGG (for $x \leq 1.0$) and NGG (for $x \geq 1.0$) [50]. They reported that the Faraday rotation in a range from 1.5 to about 3 eV increases with increasing x. The lattice constant of this system is given in Figure 4.6 [50]. The lattice constant is found to increase at a rate of 0.1 Å/Ce, which is due to a large ionic radius of Ce^{3+}. The maximum content of Ce to be substituted is about $x = 2.0$. The magneto-optical effect of this system is discussed in Section 4.1.3.2.

4.1.3 Magnetic and Magneto-Optical Properties

4.1.3.1 Magnetic Property

Yttrium iron garnet (YIG) is an ideal Néel ferrimagnet. Through the super-exchange interaction, the moments of the Fe^{3+} ions in the octahedral (a) and tetrahedral (d) sites interact antiferromagnetically. At 0 K, each Fe^{3+} ion contributes $5\mu_B$. Because there are three Fe^{3+} ions in tetrahedral (d) sites and two in octahedral (a) sites, the resultant must be $5.0\mu_B$ per formula unit from the Fe^{3+} ion sublattices. The value first reported were $4.72\mu_B$ [21] and $4.69\ \mu_B$ [22] and later on 4.96 and $5.01\mu_B$ [23], [24].

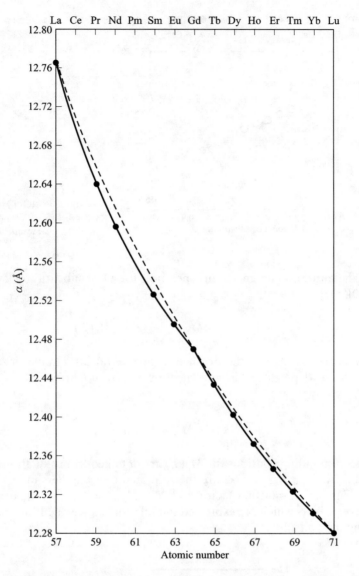

Figure 4.4 Lattice constant vs. atomic number for rare-earth iron garnets. The dashed curve passes through values for the trivalent rare earths with special electronic configuration [10].

The slight discrepancy is believed to be due to purity of single crystals used. The substitution of Fe^{3+} ions by nonmagnetic ions has been greatly studied by many workers [24~29] for the magnetic and magneto-optical properties. For a low substitution level of nonmagnetic ions in garnets $Y_3\{Fe_{2-x}A_x\}(Fe_{3-y}D_y)O_{12}$, the temperature dependence of the saturation magnetization can be expressed by the Néel model, where D and A denote nonmagnetic ions on tetrahedral and octahedral sites, respectively. For high concentrations ($y > 2$ and $x > 0.7$), the canting of the sublattice magnetization is significant, and strong deviations from the simple Néel model occur [25], [31].

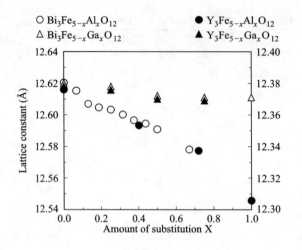

Figure 4.5 Lattice constants of Al- or Ga substituted BIG films ($\bigcirc$, $\triangle$) and Al- or Ga-substituted YIG films ($\bullet$, $\blacktriangle$) as a function of the amount of substitution X [15].

The saturation magnetization per mole for a low substitution level can be described by [30], [32], [33] as

$$M_S = M_d(T) - M_a(T) \tag{4.2}$$

where a and d refer to the octahedral and tetrahedral sublattices, respectively. The temperature dependence is governed by the Brillouin functions B_S^d (z_{ad}) and B_S^d (z_{da}) given by

$$M_a = M_a(0)B_S^d(z_{ad}) \tag{4.3}$$

The corresponding relations for $M_d(T)$ are obtained from Equation (4.3) replacing a by d and d by a. $S_a = S_d = 5/2$ are the spin quantum numbers of the Fe^{3+} ions, $g = 2$ is the spectroscopic-splitting factor and N_{aa}, N_{dd}, and $N_{ad} = N_{da}$ denote the molecular-field coefficients which are expressed in mole cm^{-3}. μ_B is the Bohr magnetron, and k the Boltzmann constant.

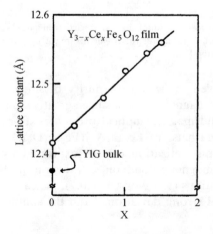

Figure 4.6 Lattice constant of $Y_{3-x}Ce_x$ Fe_5O_{12} epitaxial films [49].

At $T = 0\,\mathrm{K}$, the sublattice magnetization can be expressed by

$$M_a(0) = g\mu_B S_a N(2-x)\{1 - (y/3)^{5.4}\},$$
$$M_d(0) = g\mu_B S_d N(3-y)\{1 - 0.05x\}, \tag{4.4}$$

where N is Avogadro's number. The expression in the second bracket of each equation represents a correction to the pure Néel model obtained from a fitting procedure to the experimental data [33] and may originate from canting of the sublattice magnetizations. The molecular-field coefficients vary as [30]

$$N_{aa} = -65.0(1 - 0.42y),$$
$$N_{dd} = -30.4(1 - 0.43x), \tag{4.5}$$
$$N_{ad} = N_{dd} = 97.0(1 - 0.125x - 0.126y)$$

From Equations 4.2 through 4.5, one can calculate the temperature dependence of the saturation magnetization for a given distribution of the nonmagnetic ions, which fits to the experimental data [26], [33].

Figure 4.7 shows the temperature dependence of the saturation magnetization of gallium-substituted yttrium iron garnet. The solid lines represent the molecular field theory using Equations (4.2) through (4.5). Figure 4.8(a) and (b) show the concentration dependence of the saturation magnetization of gallium-substituted yttrium iron garnet at (a) $T = 4.2\,\mathrm{K}$ and (b) $T = 295\,\mathrm{K}$. The dashed line (pure tetrahedral occupation) and the solid line (distribution on tetrahedral and octahedral sites) represent the molecular field theory. $\bigcirc$, $\triangle$ from work [30]: $\bullet$, $\blacktriangle$ from the data given in [25], [32]–[40]. The saturation magnetization of pure YIG at $T = 295\,\mathrm{K}$ is $4\pi M_S = 1794 \pm 15\,\mathrm{G}$. This value is in agreement with the experimental value [30]. Figure 4.9(a) illustrates the temperature dependence of the saturation magnetization of gallium-substituted yttrium iron garnet calculated from Equations (4.2) through (4.5) for different gallium distributions for $x + y = 1.3$. The compensation temperature calculated from Equations (4.2) through (4.5) for different gallium concentrations and different gallium distributions is shown in Figure 4.9(b). The dotted line represents the distribution deduced from the saturation magnetization at $4.2\,\mathrm{K}$ [30]. With decreasing octahedral occupation, T_{comp} increases up to the Curie temperature and with increasing values of x, T_{comp} decreases to zero.

A recent work by Okuda et al. [14] showed that the saturation magnetization $4\pi M_S$ of $Bi_3Fe_5O_{12}$ films which were fabricated onto $Nd_3Ga_5O_{12}$ substrates by ion-beam sputtering method is about $1500\,\mathrm{kG}$, much smaller than that of YIG ($+ 1740\,\mathrm{G}$). A representative magnetization curve of the film at room temperature is given in Figure 4.10. It is also reported that the internal field $H_{in}(d)$ for 24a estimated by conversion electron Mossbauer spectroscopy is about 421 kOe, which is larger by 30 kOe for $Y_3Fe_5O_{12}$, while the internal field for 16a sites is 491 kOe, nearly the same as that (486 kOe) for $Y_3Fe_5O_{12}$ [14]. The smaller magnetization value in $Bi_3Fe_5O_{12}$ is believed to be due to the antiferromagnetic coupling of the magnetic moment at the Bi sites with the net moment of Fe^{3+} ions at 24d and 16a sites.

It is also of interest to note that a perpendicular magnetic anisotropy was observed in a $Bi_3Fe_5O_{12}$ film, which is about $7.3 \times 10^4\,\mathrm{erg/cc}$. The origin of the perpendicular

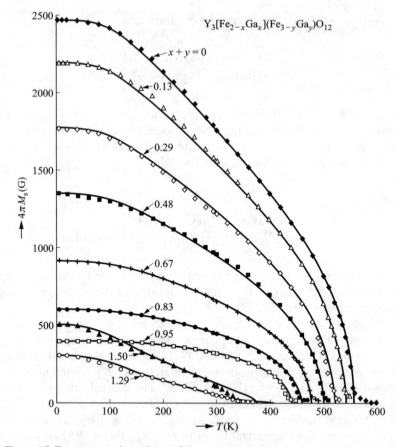

Figure 4.7 Temperature dependence of the saturation magnetization of gallium-substituted yttrium iron garnet. The solid curves represent the molecular field
theory (Equations 4.2–4.5).

anisotropy may result from the stress caused by the thermal expansion between the film
and the substrate [14].

The Ce-substituted films made by sputtering were reported to exhibit perpendicular magnetic anisotropy. Figure 4.11 shows the domain pattern and the Faraday
hysteresis loop of a $Y_{2.3}Ce_{0.7}Fe_{4.2}Al_{0.8}O_{12}$ film fabricated on GGG substrate. The
mazed domain pattern clearly indicates the presence of perpendicular magnetic anisotropy. The Curie point of the film is about 180°C, and the coercivity is about 35 Oe
[49].

The summary of the magnetization behavior with temperature for various
$R_3^{3+}Fe_5^{3+}O_{12}$ is given in Figure 4.12, and the magnetic properties are shown in
Table 4.1. In Figure 4.12, R stands for Gd, Tb, Dy, Ho, Er, Tm, Yb, Lu, and Y. All
the garnets show nearly the same Néel point ($\approx$ 540–570 K), but the compensation
point varies strongly, depending on R.

It is worth describing the origin of the stress-induced magnetic anisotropy in garnet
thin films. Garnet films are grown by LPE, sputtering, or pyrolysis methods onto
various kinds of substrates. Because of the difference in lattice constant between sub-

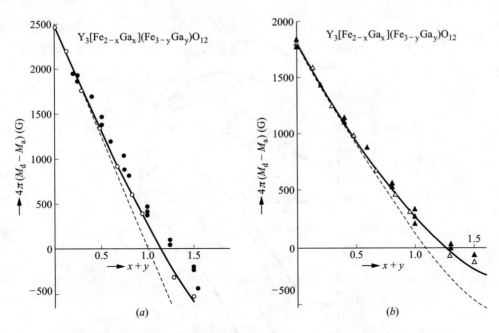

Figure 4.8 Concentration dependence of the saturation magnetization of gallium-substituted yttrium iron garnet at (*a*) $T = 4.2$K and (*b*) $T = 295$K. The dashed line (pure tetrahedral occupation) and the solid line (distribution on tetrahedral and octahedral sites) represent the molecular field theory ($\bigcirc$, $\triangle$, from [30], $\bullet$, $\blacktriangle$, from [25], [32], [33], [34]).

strate and film, stress is induced. The stress due to the mismatch may be expressed by $\sigma = \{Y/(1 - \mu)\}\{(a_s - a_f)/a_f\}$, where a_s and a_f are the lattice constants of the substrate and film, respectively, Y is the Young's modulus, and μ the Poisson ratio. If $a_f < a_s$, the stress is a tension, and if $a_f > a_s$, then it is a compression. Through the magneto-elastic coupling, this stress will induce a magnetic anisotropy. The magnitude and the sign of the magnetic anisotropy are dependent on the magnetostriction constants λ_{100} and λ_{111}, which are listed in Table 4.1. In Table 4.2, the stress-induced magnetic anisotropy field H_K for the different film planes is summarized [50].

4.1.3.2 Magneto-Optical Effects

(*a*) **Y₃Fe₅O₁₂** For technical applications the magneto-optical effect/absorption ratio for YIG is low at most wavelengths of interest. Therefore, the effect of many substitution elements on the properties has been studied. We will not discuss all of this work, but only those results related to magneto-optical recording.

First, it is important to briefly discuss the magneto-optical effect of $Y_3Fe_5O_{12}$ since substitutions of bismuth, rare earth, or other ions are regarded as perturbations of YIG, though ultimate interest in their properties may far exceed that in YIG. We will start summarizing some important aspects of the energy levels of YIG [10].

(*i*) **Energy Levels** Figure 4.13 shows the energy levels important in optical properties of ferrimagnetic YIG. The feature of the energy levels may be summarized as follows:

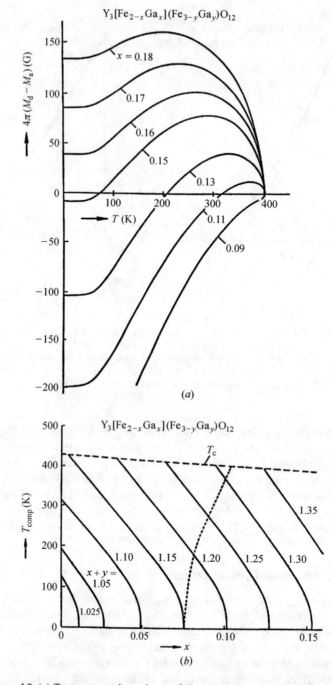

Figure 4.9 (*a*) Temperature dependence of the saturation magnetization of gallium-substituted yttrium iron garnet calculated from Equation 2 through 5 for different gallium distributions for $x + y = 1.3$. (*b*) The compensation temperature calculated from Equations (4.2) through (4.5) for different gallium concentrations and different gallium distributions. The dotted line represents the distribution deduced from the saturation magnetization at 4.2K [30].

TABLE 4.1 Magnetic Properties of Garnets [61]

R	Y	Sm	Eu	Gd	Tb	Dy	Ho	Er	Tm	Yb	Lu
Compensation point T_c (°K)	–	–	–	290	246	220	136	84	$4 < T_c < 20$	–	–
Néel temperature T_N (°K)	560	560	570	564	568	563	567	556	549	548	539
Saturation moment (μ_B)	9.44	9.3	5.0	30.3	31.4	32.5	27.5	23.1	2.0	0	8.30
Saturation magnetization (G)	1767	1675	1172	56	198	376	882	1241	1397	1555	1815
Density (g/cm³)	5.169	6.235	6.276	6.436	6.533	6.653	6.760	6.859	6.946	7.082	7.128
Magnetostriction constant $\lambda_{111} \times 10^{-6}$	−2.4	−8.5	1.8	−3.1	12.0	−5.9	−4.0	−4.9	−5.2	−4.5	−2.4
Magnetostriction constant $\lambda_{100} \times 10^{-6}$	−1.4	21	21	0	−3.3	−12.5	−3.4	2.0	1.4	1.4	−1.4
Lattice constant (Å)	12.376	12.530	12.498	12.479	12.477	12.408	12.380	12.349	12.325	12.291	12.277

TABLE 4.2 Stress-induced Magnetic Anisotropy of Garnet Films [50]

Film Plane	H_K	
{100}	$\dfrac{2K_1 - 3\sigma\lambda_{100}}{M_s}$	
{110}	$\dfrac{2K_1 - 3\sigma(\lambda_{100} + \lambda_{111})}{2M_s}$	$(M_s\ (100))$
	$\dfrac{-2K_1 - 3\sigma\lambda_{111}}{M_s}$	$(M_s\ (100))$
{111}	$\dfrac{-4K_1 - 9\sigma\lambda_{111}}{3M_s}$	

1. A filled valence band of oxygen 2p states.
2. Localized 3d states of Fe^{3+}. These are associated with octahedral and tetra-hedral sites.
3. 3d bands. These have density of state peaks corresponding to the molecular orbitals, which are important components of the band states. These peaks are identified as e and t_2 states of tetrahedral and e_g and t_{2g} of octahedral Fe^{3+}.
4. 4s bands. These are thought to begin well above the lower edge of the 3d bands.

The valence band is completely filled, and the crystal field levels are partly filled. Therefore, the lowest-energy electronic transitions to be encountered are within the crystal field states. If only the single ion is considered, these are spin forbidden since they involve reversing a spin. For octahedral sites, they are in addition parity forbidden. Therefore, these lines are intrinsically very weak. At higher energies, we expect very

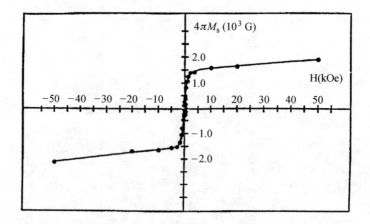

Figure 4.10 Hysteresis loop of $Bi_3Fe_5O_{12}$ film at room temperature [14].

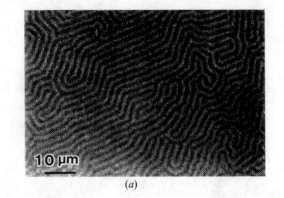

(a)

$Y_{2.3}Ce_{0.7}Fe_{4.2}Al_{0.8}O_{12}$ film

Thickness: 0.85 μm

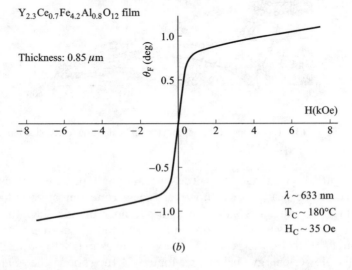

$\lambda \sim 633$ nm
$T_C \sim 180°C$
$H_C \sim 35$ Oe

(b)

Figure 4.11 (a) Magnetic domain and (b) Faraday hysteresis loop of $Y_{2.3}Ce_{0.7}Fe_{4.2}Al_{0.8}O_{12}$ film on SiO_2 coated GGG [49].

strong electric dipole allowed interband transitions in which an electron would go from a state with 2p character to a 3d state.

(ii) Absorption Spectrum of YIG Figure 4.14 shows the optical absorption spectrum of YIG [52]. The absorption increases with increasing photon energy. The two prominent peaks at 1.37 and 2.0 eV are due to crystal field transitions of Fe^{3+} in octahedral and tetrahedral sites.

(b) (YBi)$_3$Fe$_5$O$_{12}$ The attractive feature for Bi-garnet films for magneto-optical recording is the enhancement in the magneto-optical effect. Figure 4.15(a) and (b) show the Kerr rotation spectra and real and imaginary parts of ε_{12} of $Y_3Fe_5O_{12}$ and $Y_2BiFe_5O_{12}$ [53]. The Kerr rotation at around 2.7 eV is very much enhanced in BiYIG, by almost a factor of 40, as compared to YIG.

Figure 4.15(b) indicates the Bi substitution in the dodecahedral site. The dominant feature in the ε'_{12} curve of YIG is the negative peak at about 4.1 eV. The substitution of a modest amount of Bi, $x = 0.25$ increases this peak as well, but the most remarkable effect is in the appearance of peaks at about 2.8 and 3.3 eV. As x goes from 0 to 1.0, the

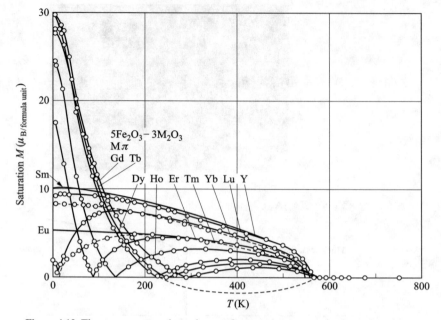

Figure 4.12 The temperature dependence of saturation magnetization of various garnets.

peak in ε'_{12} at 4.9 eV changes very little, but that at about 4.1 eV increases from -0.04 to -0.05. The peak near 3.3 eV, however, goes from almost zero to about 0.05. The maximum in ε'_{12} at 2.8 is still seen as a shoulder on the side. In YIG the negative peak in ε'_{12} at 4.1 eV was the dominant factor, and ε'_{12} has been determined down to the infrared. With Bi, the peak a ~ 3.3eV becomes magneto-optically active. It determines the lower-energy behavior. Figure 4.16 shows the Faraday spectra of $Y_{3-x}Bi_xFe_5O_{12}$ for the various Bi contents [48]. The Faraday rotation θ_F increases drastically at wavelengths less than 600 nm with increasing Bi content x. Recent work by Okuda et al. [47] indicates the value θ_F to be about $4 \sim 5 \times 10^{4\circ}$/cm at $x = 2.0$, which is far larger than those given in Figure 4.16.

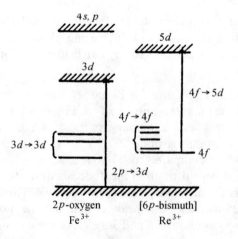

Figure 4.13 Schematic of energy levels important in optical properties of ferrimagnetic garnets [10].

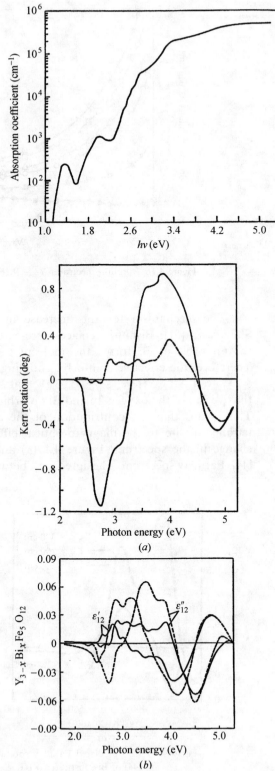

Figure 4.14 Optical absorption of YIG at 300K [52].

Figure 4.15 (*a*) Kerr rotation Φ_K vs. photon energy for $Y_3Fe_5O_{12}$ (dashed line) and for $Y_2BiFe_5O_{12}$ (solid line) [10]. (*b*) Real and imaginary parts of ε_{12} for $Y_{3-x}Bi_xFe_5O_{12}$ with $x = 0$ (solid line), 0.25 (dashed line) [53].

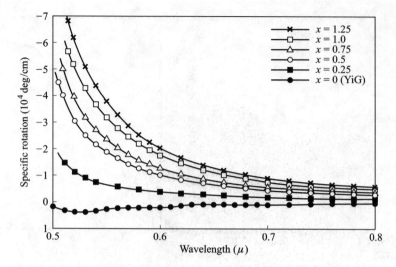

Figure 4.16 Rotation spectra of $Y_{3-x}Bi_xFe_5O_{12}$ [48].

The mechanism for this increase in θ_F with Bi has been accounted for by Shinagawa [51]. Bismuth replaces rare-earth elements at the dodecahedral site, and the 6p orbit of Bi forms the molecular orbit with the 2p orbit of oxygen ions. Therefore, the effective spin-orbit coupling ξ_{2p} of the oxygen 2p orbit is changed as $\xi_{2p}^* = \xi_{2p} + S^2\xi_{2p}$. Here, $\xi_{2p} \sim 0.03\,\text{eV}$ and $\xi_{6p} \sim 2.1\,\text{eV}$. S is the quantity representing the overlap of the oxygen 2p and Bi 6p orbits. For $S = 0.1$, ξ_{2p} becomes about 0.05 eV. This means that the contribution of the charge transfer transition of Fe^{3+} at the tetrahedral site to the magneto-optical effect becomes more significant, causing the change in the spectrum. Figure 4.17(a) and (b) shows the calculated and measured [44] Faraday spectrum. The agreement between measurement and theory is reasonable,

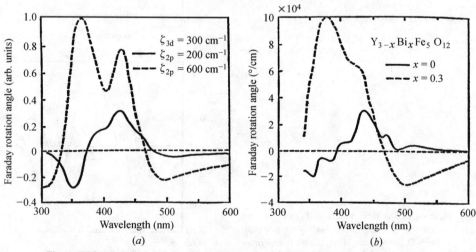

Figure 4.17 (a) Calculated Faraday rotation spectra [51] and (b) measured spectra [44] of Bi-substituted YIG.

and thus the enhancement is accounted for based on the increase of the effective spin-orbit coupling of the 2p orbit in Bi garnet.

(c) $Y_3(FeGa)_5O_{12}$

(i) Faraday Rotation θ_F The magneto-optical effects originate from the magnetic and electric dipole transitions. Both can be expressed in terms of the sublattice magnetizations [29], and especially the tetrahedral and octahedral contributions are significant for $Y_3Fe_5O_{12}$ at $\lambda = 633$ nm. Therefore, a gallium substitution leads to an increase of Faraday rotation θ_F at $\lambda = 633$ nm at 295K for up to $x + y \approx 0.6$, as shown in Figure 4.18 [29]. This increase is believed to be due to the reduction of the tetrahedral contribution via that of M_d. For higher substitutional levels the reduction of the exchange interaction causes a decrease of θ_F approaching zero if the Fe^{3+} ions of the tetrahedral sublattice have been completely replaced by Ga^{3+}.

The temperature dependence of θ_F calculated [29] with temperature-independent magneto-optical coefficients is shown in Figures 4.19(*a*) and (*b*) [29]. The sublattice magnetization was inferred from [43]. There is a reasonable agreement between experiment and theory. If the temperature dependence of the magneto-optical coefficients was taken into account, better agreement would be obtained.

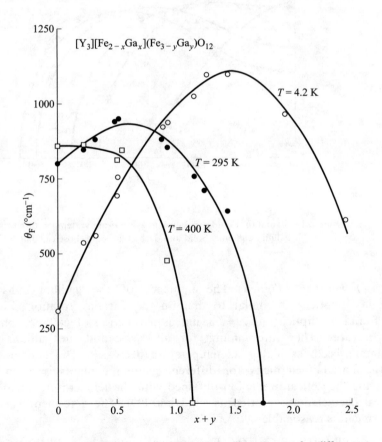

Figure 4.18 Faraday rotation at $\lambda = 633$ nm vs. gallium content for different temperatures [29].

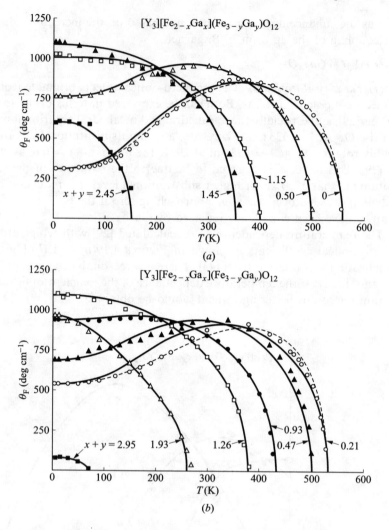

Figure 4.19 (*a*) and (*b*) Faraday rotation at $\lambda = 633$ nm vs. temperature for different gallium contents. Solid and dashed lines are those calculated [29].

(ii) Faraday Ellipticity The influence of the gallium substitution on the Faraday ellipticity is similar to that on the Faraday rotation. Figure 4.20 shows the Faraday ellipticity at $\lambda = 633$ nm as a function of gallium content at different temperatures. There are minima for all cases, and the gallium content for the minimum becomes higher as temperature decreases. The temperature dependence of the Faraday ellipticity for different gallium contents is given in Figure 4.21. Here the theoretical prediction obtained with the temperature-independent magneto-optical coefficients is plotted as solid line [29]. The agreement between theory and experiment is reasonable.

(d) (BiDy)₃ (FeGa)₅O₁₂ For magneto-optical recording purposes, it is important to have a strong perpendicular magnetic anisotropy and high coercivity and

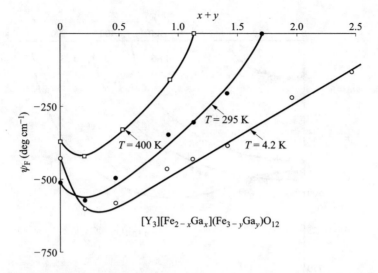

Figure 4.20 Faraday ellipticity at $\lambda = 633\,\mathrm{nm}$ vs. gallium content for different temperatures [29].

also the hysteresis must exhibit high squareness. For this reason, the substitution of Y by Dy has been studied. A typical spectrum of $Dy_1Bi_2Fe_{3.6}Ga_{1.4}O_{12}$ thin films is shown in Figure 4.22 [54]. The Faraday rotation θ_F has two peaks, both $1 \times 10^{5\circ}/cm$ at 430 and 520 nm. The ellipticity η_F obtains a maximum value of about $2 \times 10^{5\circ}/cm$ at 460 nm.

4.1.4 Film Fabrication

4.1.4.1 Sputter Deposition

Much work has been performed using sputtering technique so as to incorporate a large amount of Bi substituted in garnet films. Since a film in the as-deposited condition is amorphous unless the substrate is heated to about 600°C or higher, an annealing must be made to crystallize it. Suzuki et al. [9], [54] have found that rapid thermal annealing (RTA) is very effective for the crystallization of garnet with small grains less than 300 Å in size. In RTA, the ramp-up rate to a temperature around 650°C is 100°C/s or even higher so that grain growth is suppressed, leaving only small crystalline nuclei. Figure 4.23 shows the scanning electron microscope images of the samples annealed at 1°C/s and 50°C/s. The surface smoothness is much improved for the samples for 50°C/s, compared with 1°C/s. The photographs demonstrate the difference in grain size between 1 and 50°C/s. The summary of grain size as a function of ramp-up rate in $(Bi_2Dy_1)(Fe_{3.6}.Ga_{1.4})O_{12}$ is given in Figure 4.24 [54]. The result was obtained from X-ray diffraction line width measurements. In this case, the effect of the stress on the line broadening was neglected, since its contribution is estimated to be negligible. The grain size decreases with heating ramp rate Γ. This result is also confirmed by electron microscopy.

For further reduction in grain size, a multilayer of garnet with Cr, Co, or SiO as separator has been studied [9]. A typical structure is {70Å garnet/5 ÅM} × N where M is Co, Cr and SiO, and N is the number of layer pairs, typically 30–35. The idea of

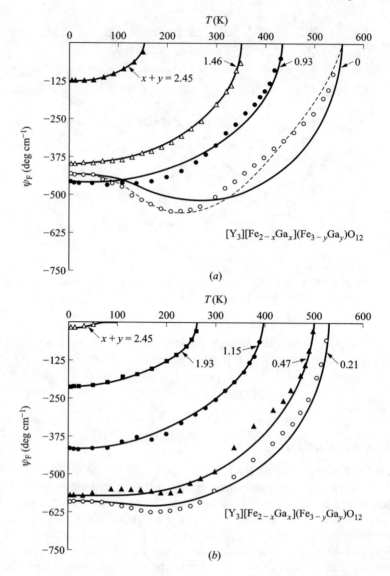

Figure 4.21 (a) and (b) Faraday ellipticity at $\lambda = 633\,\text{nm}$ vs. temperature for different gallium contents. Solid and dashed lines are those calculated [29].

having the separator in between garnet layers is to prevent grain growth from taking place once the crystallization has started. This has been confirmed by electron microscopy.

Another approach to obtain a crystalline film is an in-situ crystallization. Shono, Kano, et al. [6], [8], [55], [56] fabricated garnet disks crystallized during deposition at about 650°C. The grain size is a few hundred Å. The disks thus obtained performed well at blue wavelengths, the CNR of which was reported to be 60 dB at 514 nm with 30 kHz bandwidth [56].

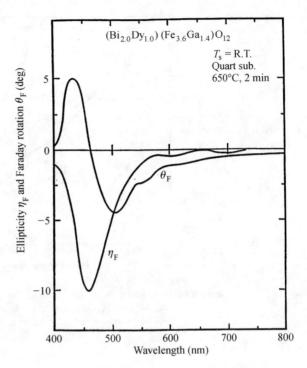

Figure 4.22 Faraday rotation and ellipticity as a function of wavelength for $(Bi_{2.0}Dy_{1.0})(Fe_{3.6}Ga_{1.4})O_{12}$ films annealed at 650°C for 2 min. by rapid thermal processing [54].

4.1.4.2 Pyrolysis Method [7], [57], [58]

A pyrolysis method has several advantages. It can control a film composition almost continuously, compared with sputtering where the film composition is not easy to control. It does not require any vacuum system and it is easy to fabricate samples in volume.

The film-fabrication process consists of several steps: First, an acetylacetone solution is spin-coated onto substrates. The solution contains about a few moles of $(BiDy)_3(FeGa)_5O_{12}$ per liter. Then the spin-coated film is to be preheated at a

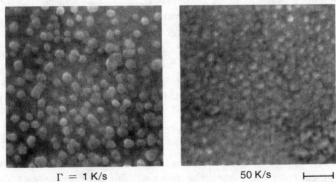

Figure 4.23 The SEM micrographs of the film surface in $(Bi_{2.0}Dy_{1.0})(Fe_{3.6}Ga_{1.4})O_{12}$ films made onto fused quartz at 60°C during deposition [54].

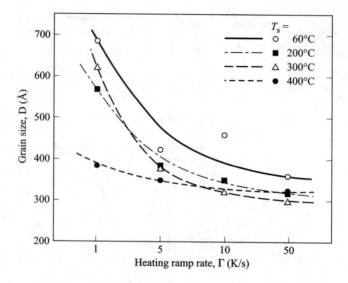

Figure 4.24 The grain size as a function of heating ramp-up rate in $(Bi_{2.0}Dy_{1.0})(Fe_{3.6}Ga_{1.4})O_{12}$ films deposited onto fused quartz substrate held at various temperatures during deposition [54].

temperature T in a range from 80 to 300°C for drying, followed by the heating at about 350°C for a few hours. Then, the film is annealed at about 650°C for a few hours. The films thus fabricated exhibit high squareness and high coercivity of around 1 kOe [7]. A recent study of a double-layer garnet disk in which an underlayer was made using a pyrolysis method and an upper layer was fabricated by sputtering reported a CNR of 52 dB at 514 nm [58].

4.1.5 Recording Performance

As shown in Figure 4.1, the readout signal in the magneto-optical recording in garnet films is expected to be much higher than those of rare earth-transition metal films and Co/Pt multilayers. However, if the detector noise results from a shot noise only, then the media noise is the governing factor for the recording performance. The media noise is proportional to the effective rotation defined by Equation (4.1), and thus it is important to minimize the media noise.

The origin of the media noise has been the subject of study by many workers. Phenomenologically speaking, any depolarization effect is the source for the media noise. The depolarization effect results from nonuniformity of both magnetic and optical properties, which are closely related to microcrystalline structure of the film under consideration. Since the high temperature crystallization process is mandatory for garnet, the key issue is how one can form the garnet crystalline phase from the as-deposited amorphous phase. An in-situ crystallization during deposition and a rapid thermal annealing process are the methods by which one can successfully fabricate small-grain crystalline garnet films [8], [9]. The grain size thus obtained is of the order of 100 Å, and can be made even smaller for a multilayer structure, as proposed [9].

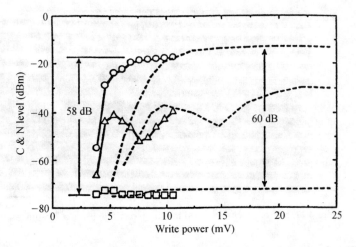

Figure 4.25 Write power dependence of carrier and noise level measured at 488 nm
[8]. (The levels observed for 514 nm are shown as dashed lines.)

Figure 4.25 shows the write power dependence of carrier-and-noise level measured at 488 nm (solid line) and at 514 nm (dashed line) [8]. The testing condition for 488 nm was the linear velocity 10 m/s, the read power 2.5 mW, the bandwidth 30 kHz, and the recording frequency of 600 kHz. The very high CNR values of 60 and 58 dB were reported [8]. Those numbers are very comparable to those reported in Co/Pt multilayers (64 dB at 488 nm) [59] and TbFeCo films [60]. There is a little difference in media noise between 488 and 514 nm. Figure 4.26 shows the readout signal voltage as a function of wavelength for the garnet disk using Ar laser [8]. The experiment was performed using sideband wavelengths of an Ar laser, by tuning the resonator mirror. The numbers in parentheses indicate the CNR values. The signal output increases with wavelength, as expected from the increase in the effective Faraday rotation as shown in Figure 4.1. Figure 4.27 shows the written marks at 785 nm, 3.1 m/s and read power of 1 mW [8].

The overwrite performance was also demonstrated by Shono et al. [8]. Figure 4.28 are the photographs of the spectrum analyzer, showing an initial signal (0.5 MHz signal) which was overwritten by a 0.7 MHz signal in a garnet disk.

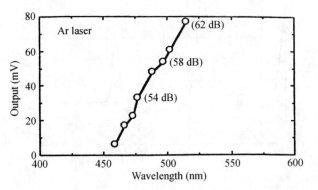

Figure 4.26 Reproduced output voltage vs. wavelength [8].

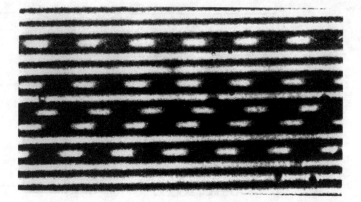

Figure 4.27 Bits on tracks recorded in a Bi-garnet film using a 785-nm laser diode [8].

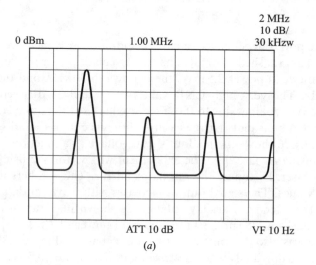

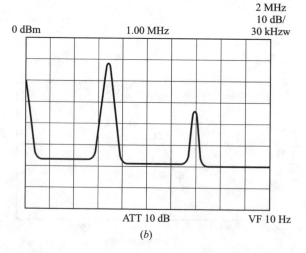

Figure 4.28 The spectrum analyzer display of the signal of a Bi-substituted film. Recording frequencies after (*a*) a 0.5 Mhz signal was overwritten by (*b*) a 0.7 MHz signal [8].

REFERENCES

[1] W. Kozlovsky, W. Lenth, E. E. Latta, A. Moser, and G. L. Bona, *Appl. Phys. Lett.*, vol. 56, p. 2291, 1990.

[2] W. D. Doyle, G. K. Goldberg, and W. E. Flannery, *IEEE MAG*-6, p. 548, 1970.

[3] B. Petek, E. A. Giess and R. T. Hodgson, *J. Appl. Phys.*, vol. 52 (6), p. 4170, 1981.

[4] T. Mizuno and M. Gomi, *IEEE MAG*-22, p. 1236, 1986.

[5] A. Itoh, Y. Toriumi, T. Ishii, M. Nakada, F. Inoue, and K. Kawanishi, *IEEE MAG*-23, p. 2964, 1987.

[6] K. Shono, H. Kano, N. Koshino, and S. Ogawa, *IEEE MAG*-23, p. 2970, 1987.

[7] J. Cho, M. Gomi, and M. Abe, *Japan J. Appl. Phys.*, vol. 28, p. 1593, 1989.

[8] K. Shono, S. Kuroda, and S. Ogawa, *IEEE MAG*-27, p. 5130, 1991.

[9] T. Suzuki, *J. Appl. Phys.*, vol. 69, p. 4756, 1991.

[10] *Physics of Magnetic Garnets*, A. Paoletti (ed.), New York: North-Holland, 1978.

[11] S. Geller and M. A. Gilleo, *Acta Cryst.*, vol. 10, p. 239, 1957.

[12] S. Geller, *Zeits. Kristall.*, vol. 125, p. 1, 1967.

[13] G. P. Espinosa, and J. Chen, *Phys.*, vol. 37, p. 2344, 1966.

[14] T. Okuda, T. Katayama, H. Kobayashi, N. Kobayashi, K. Satoh, and H. Yamamoto, *J. Appl. Phys.*, vol. 67, p. 4944, 1990.

[15] S. Nishida, T. Okuda, H. Ohsato, Y. Kato, and T. Suzuki, *J. Mag. Soc. Japan*, vol. 18, p. 157, 1994 (Japanese).

[16] J.-P. Krumme, V. Doorman, and P. Willich, *J. Appl. Phys.*, vol. 57, p. 3885, 1985.

[17] M. Gomi, T. Tanida, and M. Abe, *J. Appl. Phys.*, vol. 57, p. 3888, 1985.

[18] M. Gomi, K. Utsugi, and M. Abe, *IEEE MAG*-22, p. 1233, 1986.

[19] M. Gomi, H. Furuyama, and M. Abe, *J. Mag. Soc. Japan*, vol. 13, p. 163, 1989 (in Japanese).

[20] T. Suzuki, F. Sequeda, H. Do, T. C. Huang, and G. Gorman, *J. Appl. Phys.*, vol. 67, p. 4435, 1990.

[21] R. Aleonard, J. C. Barbier, and R. Pauthenet, Compt. Rend., vol. 242, p. 2531, 1956.

[22] S. Geller and M. A. Gilleo, *Acta Crystall.*, vol. 10, p. 239, 1957.

[23] M. A. Gilleo and S. Geller, *J. Appl. Phys.*, vol. 29, p. 380, 1958.

[24] S. Geller, H. J. Williams, R. C. Sherwood, and G. P. Espinosa, *J. Appl. Phys.*, vol. 33, p. 1195, 1962.

[25] S. Geller, J. A. Cape, G. P. Espinosa, and D. J. Leslie, *Phys. Rev.*, vol. 148, p. 522, 1966.

[26] G. Winkler, P. Hansen, and P. Holst, *Philips Res. Rept.*, vol. 27, p. 151, 1972.

[27] H. J. VanHook and F. Euler, *J. Appl. Phys.*, vol. 40, p. 4001, 1969.

[28] P. Hansen, *J. Appl. Phys.*, vol. 45, p. 3638, 1974.

[29] P. Hansen and K. Witter, *Phys. Rev. B*, vol. 27, p. 1498, 1983.

[30] P. Hansen, P. Roshmann, and W. Tolksdorf, *J. Appl. Phys.*, vol. 45, p. 2728, 1974.

[31] A. M. Gilleo, *J. Phys. Chem. Solids*, vol. 13, p. 33, 1960.

[32] E. E. Anderson, *Phys. Rev.*, A134, p. 1581, 1964.

[33] G. F. Dionne, *J. Appl. Phys.*, vol. 40, p. 1839, 1969.

[34] M. A. Gilleo and S. Geller, *Phys. Rev.*, vol. 110, p. 73, 1958.

[35] G. R. Harrison and L. R. Hodges, Jr., *J. Am. Ceram. Soc.*, vol. 44, p. 214, 1961.

[36] E. E. Anderson, J. R. Cunningham, Jr, G. E. McDuffie, Jr., and R. F. Stander, *J. Phys. Soc. Japan*, Suppl. 17, p. 365, 1962.

[37] E. A. Giess, B. A. Calhoun, E. Klokholm, T. R. McGuire, and L. L. Rosier, *Appl. Phys. Lett.*, vol. 18, p. 287, 1971.

[38] B. A. Calhoun, E. A. Giess, and L. L. Rosier, *Appl. Phys. Lett.*, vol. 18, p. 287, 1971.

[39] S. Visnovsky and V. Prosser, *Phys. Status Solidi*, A10, K97, 1972.

[40] H. Matthews, S. Singh, and R. C. LeCraw, *Appl. Phys. Lett.*, vol. 7, p. 165, 1965.

[41] P. Hansen, H. Heitman, and K. Witter, *Phys. Rev. B*, vol. 23, p. 6085, 1981.

[42] P. Roschmann, *J. Phys. Chem. Solids*, vol. 41, p. 569, 1980.

[43] P. Roschmann and P. Hansen, *J. Appl. Phys.*, vol. 52, p. 6257, 1981.

[44] S. Wittekoek, T. J. A. Popma, and J. M. Robertson, *AIP Conference Proceedings*, No. 18 (2), 944, 1973.

[45] S. Wittekoek, J. M. Robertson, T. J. A. Popma, and P. F. Bongers, *AIP Conference Proceedings*, No. 10, 1418, 1973.

[46] S. Wittekoek, T. J. A. Popma, J. M. Robertson, and P. F. Bongers, *Phys. Rev. B.*, vol. 12, p. 2777, 1975.

[47] T. Okuda, N. Koshizuka, K. Hayashi, T. Takahashi, H. Kotani, and H. Yamamot, *IEEE MAG*-23, p. 3491, 1987.

[48] H. Takeuchi, K. Shinagawa, and S. Taniguchi, *Japan J. Appl. Phys.*, vol. 12, p. 465, 1973.

[49] M. Gomi, K. Satoh, and M. Abe, *Japan J. Appl. Phys.*, L1536, 1988, M. Gomi, K. Sato, H. Furuyama, and M. Abe, J. Mag. Soc. Japan, vol. 13, p. 163, 1989, M. Gomi, H. Furuyama, and M. Abe, *Japan J. Appl. Phys.*, vol. 29, p. 351, 1990.

[50] J. E. Mee, G. R. Pulliam, J. L. Archer, and P. J. Besser, *IEEE MAG*-5, p. 717, 1969.

[51] K. Shinagawa; The 38th *Topical Meeting of Mag. Soc. Japan*, 7, 1985.

[52] S. H. Wemple, S. L. Bank, J. A. Seman, and W. A. Biolsi, *Phys. Rev. B*, vol. 9, p. 2134, 1974.

[53] S. Wittekoek, T. J. A. Popma, J. M. Robertson, and P. F. Bongers, *Phys. Rev. B*, vol. 12, p. 2777, 1975.

[54] T. Suzuki, F. Sequeda, H. Do, T. C. Huang, and G. Gorman, *J. Appl. Phys.*, vol. 67(9), p. 4435, 1990.

[55] K. Shono, H. Kano, S. Kuroda, N. Koshino, and S. Ogawa, *IEEE MAG*-25, p. 3737, 1989.

[56] H. Kano, K. Shono, S. Kuroda, N. Koshino, and S. Ogawa, *IEEE MAG*-25, p. 3737, 1989.

[57] K. Nakagawa, K. Odagawa, and A. Itoh, *J. Magn. Soc. Japan*, vol. 15, S1, p. 231, 1991.

[58] K. Nakagawa and A. Itoh, *J. Magn. Soc. Japan*, vol. 17, S1, p. 278, 1993.

[59] D. Weller, J. Hurst, H. Notarys, H. Brandle, R. F. C. Farrow, R. Marks, and G. Harp, *J. Mag. Soc. Japan*, vol. 17, S1, p. 72, 1993.

[60] J. Hurst, D. Weller, and H. Notarys, *J. Mag. Soc. Japan*, 299, 1993.

[61] *Magnetic Bubble*, S. Iida, S. Iwasaki, Y. Iwama, H. Kobayashi, Y. Sakurai, T. Nagashima, and S. Watanabe (eds.), Maruzen Pub. Co., 1976, p. 82. (In Japanese.)

Chapter

5

INTERMETALLIC COMPOUNDS AND FERRITES

Takao Suzuki (5.1, 5.2), Masanori Abe (5.3), James C. Suits (5.4)

5.1 MnBi

MnBi is the first material that was used to demonstrate thermo-magnetic writing [1] and since then, this material has been considered to be a very promising candidate for applications because of the high perpendicular magnetic anisotropy along the c-axis [3] and a high Kerr rotation angle [4]. However, because of the structural instability of the phase transformation between a low temperature phase (LTP) and a quenched high temperature phase (QHTP) [5], very little real application for magneto-optical recording media has ever been achieved. Nevertheless, continuous effort has been made to stabilize the LTP MnBi phase since it has a higher Kerr rotation angle [6]–[13]. Work is still in progress to stabilize the structure for better performance in magneto-optical applications [14]. This section will summarize the studies of MnBi in conjunction with magneto-optical recording applications.

5.1.1 Structure

MnBi has the NiAs structure with a = 4.26 Å and c = 6.08 Å, c/a = 1.42 [2]. The space group is $P_{6_3}/mmc-D_{6h}^4$. Figure 5.1 shows the NiAs hexagonal structure of MnBi [5]. It consists of two equivalent Mn atoms at the sites (0, 0, 0) and (0, 0, ½ c) and two equivalent Bi atoms at the sites ($\frac{1}{3}a\sqrt{3}$, 0, (1/4)c) and ($\frac{1}{6}a/2\sqrt{3}$, (−1/2)a, (3/4c)) in a Cartesian frame.

Guillaud [3] showed the X-ray evidence indicating a drastic change in the lattice constants a and c of MnBi quenched from above and below the transformation temperature of about 360°C to room temperature. Roberts [5] also obtained results consistent with the observation by Guillaud [3], which is shown in Figure 5.2 [5].

5.1.2 Magnetic Properties

Guillaud [3] was the first to perform a careful study of the magnetic properties of MnBi and reported that MnBi is ferromagnetic from very low temperatures to 360°C. Also, he showed that there was a hysteresis in the magnetization variation with temperature between heating and cooling. It is the fact that this hysteresis behavior in magnetization has been and is still an active subject of research because for practical applications the thermal hysteresis must be overcome.

The temperature dependence of the saturation magnetization of the quenched bulk MnBi was also studied by Heikes [6]. He has found MnBi quenched from above the transformation temperature (which corresponds to QHTP) to be ferromagnetic at room temperature with approximate saturation moment of $1.7\mu_B$ per Mn atom and a Curie

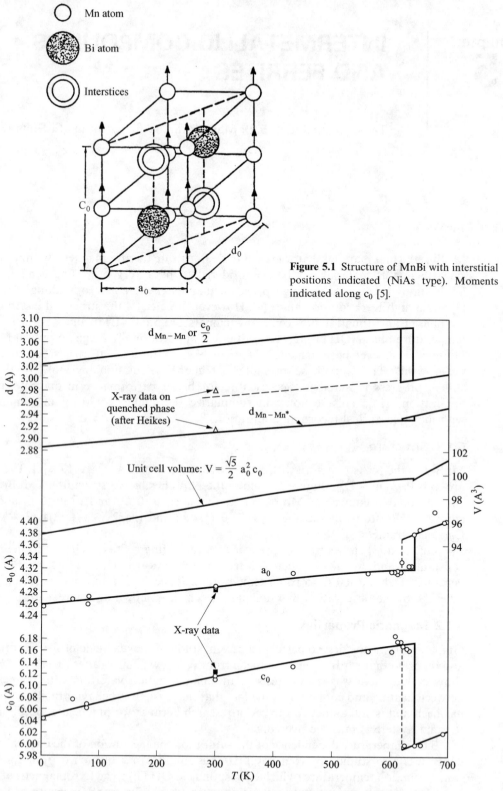

Figure 5.1 Structure of MnBi with interstitial positions indicated (NiAs type). Moments indicated along c_0 [5].

Figure 5.2 MnBi lattice constants, volume and Mn-Mn distance with temperature [5].

temperature near 200°C. Upon heating above 200°C, the saturation moment recovered to the equilibrium state value (which corresponds to LTP). The results by Guillaud [3] and by others [21] were at variance with this observation (3.95 μ_B). Adam and Standley [22] have estimated a g value at −180°C to be 2.4 for MnBi.

A careful analysis of the magnetization with temperature by Roberts [5] using neutron diffraction suggested a disordered arrangement of Mn atoms on regular and interstitial lattice sites, which explained reasonably well the temperature dependence of the magnetization. Figure 5.3 shows the model proposed by Roberts to explain the quenched high temperature phase (QHTP), which has a contraction in lattice constant c. Consider those atoms on (110) planes in the NiAs-type structure in Figure 5.3. Columns of Mn atoms alternate with staggered arrangements of Bi atoms and interstitial sites. In the disordered (NiIn$_2$) structure, the same arrangements of the Bi atoms persist but Mn atoms jump at random into the interstitial sites (Mn*). Each column of Mn atoms over very long distances would be expected on the average to contract. In Figure 5.2, about 3% contraction with increasing temperature and an equal expansion upon cooling of c is observed, which qualitatively coincides with the magnetization hysteresis [5]. The magneto-crystalline anisotropy constant K measured by Guillaud [3] is shown in Figure 5.4 The magnetic anisotropy constant decreases with increasing temperature, and is about 1.1×10^7 erg/cc at room temperature. The observed change in sign of K in Fig.5.4 is likely due to the error in measurements, and the dotted line below 84K suggested by Roberts is more accurate [5]. The saturation magnetostriction constant was reported [23] to be about 8×10^4.

The first self-consistent spin-polarized band-structure calculation of LTP MnBi using the augmented spherical (ASW) method was made by Coehoorn and de Groot [20]. The density of states obtained is shown in Figure 5.5. Also, shown is the band structure at Γ as a function of spin-orbit parameter λ for (a) spin along the c-axis, and (b) along the a-axis in Figure 5.6. The electronic structure of MnBi in the LTP is very similar to that of MnSb. The calculated spin contribution to the total magnetic moment

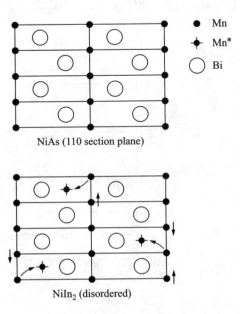

NiAs (110 section plane)

NiIn$_2$ (disordered)

Figure 5.3 Atomic arrangement on (110) planes of NiAs and disordered NiIn$_2$ models [5].

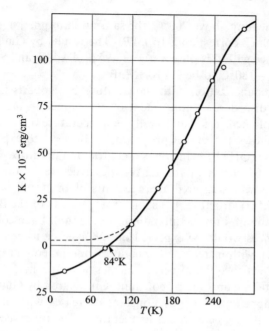

Figure 5.4 Magneto-crystalline anisotropy energy constant, K, as a function of temperature. Possible nature of K from neutron diffraction observations made in zero magnetic field [5].

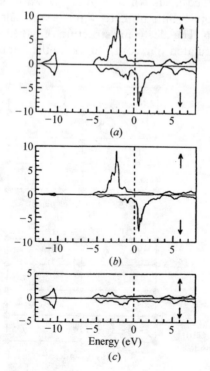

Figure 5.5 (a) Total density of states of ferromagnetic MnBi; scalar-relativistic calculation, (b) partial Mn density of states, (c) partial Bi density of states in states/(eV unit cell) [20].

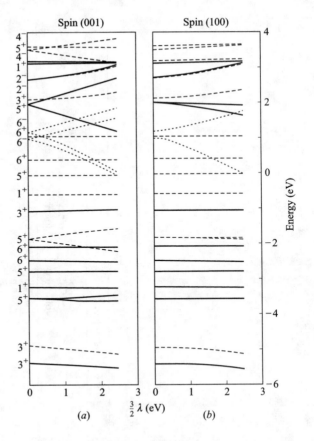

Figure 5.6 Band structure at Γ as a function of the spin-orbit parameter λ. (*a*) Spins along the *c*-axis, (*b*) spins along the *a*-axis. Solid lines correspond to majority-spin character; dashed lines are for minority spin character and dotted lines are for a strongly mixed majority-minority spin character [20].

is $3.53\,\mu_B$/Mn, and if one takes g to be 2.1, then the orbital contribution to the magnetic moment is about $0.17\,\mu_B$. The total moment of $3.7\,\mu_B$ is in reasonable agreement with that at 4.2K [19]. Also, it should be mentioned that due to the larger Mn-Mn distance the d bands are somewhat narrower than in MnSb. This leads to larger spin contributions to the local magnetic moments on the Mn atoms $3.61\,\mu_B$ and $3.30\,\mu_B$ for MnBi and MnSb, respectively. The intra-atomic contribution to the exchange splitting of the d band is also larger than in MnSb: 2.9eV as opposed to 2.7eV.

The magnetic properties and structure, can be summarized as follows: Upon heating the LTP MnBi to 628K, a first-order ferromagnetic-to-paramagnetic transition takes place, which corresponds to the phase decomposition of MnBi into $Mn_{1.08}$ Bi and free Bi. In the high temperature phase (HTP) of $Mn_{1.08}$Bi, 10~15% of the Mn atoms occupy the bipyramidal interstitial positions of the NiAs structure, as described above. Upon cooling, the phase transition $Mn_{1.08}$Bi$\rightarrow$MnBi + Mn was observed at 613K, but if single crystals of the HTP are quenched, this decomposition does not occur. Crystals in this metastable quenched high temperature phase (QHTP) show a Curie point at about 440K [19]. The summary of the physical properties of the two phases is given in Table 5.1 [10].

5.1.3 Magneto-Optical Effects

The magneto-optical effect of MnBi films was first measured by Chen and Gondo [4]. A very strong dependence of polar Kerr rotation on temperature was reported [4] (Fig. 5.7).

TABLE 5.1 Summary of LTP and HTP MnBi [8], [10]

Sample	Tc	$4\pi Ms(G)$	Unit Cell Parameter				Density calc (g/cm^3)	Density measured (g/cm^3)	2 F/α (°)
			a(Å)	b(Å)	c(Å)	Cell volume (Å^3)			
LTP	360°C	7500	4.285 (±0.002)		6.113 (±0.002)	97.23 (±0.08)	9.013^a		3.05~2.45
QHTP	180°	580	11.941	8.861	7.520	779.51	8.994^b	9.145	1.4 ~ 1.03

^{a} Based on 2 MnBi molecules per unit-cell volume of 97.31 Å^3.
^{b} Based on 16 MnBi molecules per unit-cell volume of 779.51 Å^3.

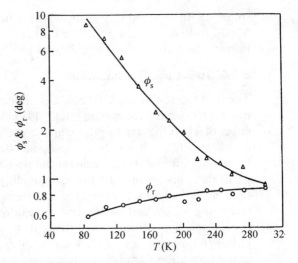

Figure 5.7 Magneto-optic Kerr rotation of MnBi film as function of temperature. ϕ_s—film in saturation, ϕ_r—film in remanent state [4].

The angles at 633 nm are $-0.7°$ and $-4.5°$ at 300 and 90K, respectively. This behavior has not been well understood until now. The wavelength dependence of the specific Faraday rotation angle F for both LTP (MnBi) and QHTP (MnTiBi) is shown in Figure 5.8. The Faraday rotation angle is about $5.6 \times 10^{5}°/cm$ at 700 nm, which is almost equivalent to that at 500 nm of $(BiDy)_3(FeGa)_5O_{12}$, as shown in Figure 4.22. This large magneto-optical effect is believed to result from a large spin-orbit coupling ~ 2.5 eV) of the 6p orbit of Bi.

Figure 5.6, which is the band structure at Γ as a function of λ, calculated by Coehoorn and de Groot [20], indicates that all initial states for interband transitions at Γ have positive parity. The only final states that are magnetically active are 6^- and 4^- states. These states are exchange-split, show a large spin-orbit interaction, and have

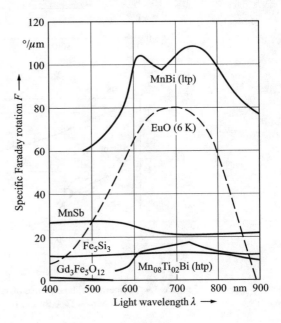

Figure 5.8 Specific Faraday rotation angle for LTP MnBi and HTP $Mn_{0.8}Ti_{0.2}Bi$, together with EuO, MnSb, Fe_5O_{12} [16].

some Mn 4p or Bi 6d character, which is needed for large transition probabilities from Mn 3d or Bi 6p initial states. The former and latter correspond to 1 and 3 eV, which are believed to be those (600 and 750 nm) in Figure 5.8 [16].

5.1.4 Structural Stabilization

The stabilization of the LTP phase is important for applications. For this reason, voluminous work has been carried out [7], [9]–[13]. Unger et al. [7] made a careful study of the effect of Ti on the structural, magnetic and magneto-optical properties of $Mn_{1-x}Ti_xBi$ evaporated films. It was found that the effect of Ti was significant in the phase transformation kinetics. It slows down the transformation of the HT-phase to LT-phase by up to three orders of magnitude, depending on the Ti concentration and the temperature. Both the Curie temperature and the specific Faraday rotation are decreased with increasing Ti content, however. For example, the Faraday rotation for LT (HT) at 633 nm changes from $9.8 \times 10^{5\circ}/cm$ ($4.3 \times 10^{5\circ}/cm$) for $x = 0$ to $3.8 \times 10^{5\circ}/cm$ ($1.6 \times 10^{5\circ}/cm$) for $x = 0.18$. Figure 5.9(a) and (b) shows the temperature dependence of the saturation Faraday rotation angle φ for (a) a 60 nm thick $Mn_{0.96}Ti_{0.04}Bi$ film and (b) a 60 mm thick $Mn_{0.82}Ti_{0.18}Bi$ film, where "m" denotes the metastable phase. The effect of Ti on the Faraday rotation is clearly demonstrated in these figures. The Curie temperature for $x = 0.18$ is lower by about 25°C as compared to that of $x = 0.04$.

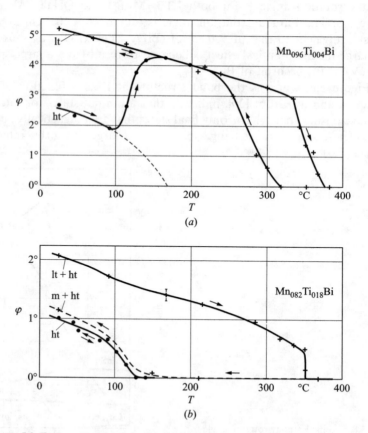

Figure 5.9 Temperature dependence of saturation Faraday rotation angle at 633 nm for (a) $Mn_{0.96}Ti_{0.04}Bi$ and (b) for $Mn_{0.82}Ti_{0.18}Bi$ [7].

Because of the mixed phase of LTP and HTP for $x = 0.18$, the Faraday rotation measured immediately after preparation is smaller than that for $x = 0.04$.

Wang et al. [11], [13] reported the effect of various elements on the magnetic and magneto-optical properties of MnBi. By adding an appropriate amount of Al, structural stability was claimed to be obtained. Also, enhancement of the Kerr rotation was obtained, and read/write cycling was found to improve the magneto-optical recording performance. However, Shen et al. reported no effect of Al on the magnetic and magneto-optical properties [12]. The discrepancy has not been resolved as yet.

5.1.5 Magneto-Optical Recording Performance

Despite the fact that MnBi was the material with which the first thermomagnetic writing demonstration was made in 1957, and in spite of voluminous work performed to stabilize the LTP MnBi structure, there has been little progress made in magneto-optical recording performance. The best CNR ever reported in the literature is CNR 35 dB for 30 kHz bandwidth $\lambda = 830$ nm [14]. The main cause for the low performance is a large media noise, which results from large grains and the presence of the multiphase structure. Nevertheless, a continuous effort is still being made for better performance.

REFERENCES

[1] H. J. Williams, R. C. Sherwood, F. G. Foster and E. M. Kelley, *J. Appl. Phys.*, vol. 28, p. 1181, 1957.

[2] M. Hansen, *Constitution of Binary Alloys*, New York: McGraw Hill, 1958, p. 318; R. Hocart and C. Guillaud, *Compt. Rend.*, 209, 443, 1939.

[3] C. Guillaud, Thesis, University of Strassbourg, 1943 (unpublished).

[4] D. Chen and Y. Gondo, *J. Appl. Phys.*, vol. 35, 1024, 1964.

[5] B. W. Roberts, *Phys. Rev.*, vol. 104, p. 607, 1956.

[6] R. R. Heikes, *Phys. Rev.*, vol. 104, p. 607, 1956.

[7] W. K. Unger, E. Wolfgang, H. Harms and H. Handek, *J. Appl. Phys.*, vol. 43, p. 2875, 1972.

[8] D. Chen, R. L. Aagard and T. S. Liu, *J. Appl. Phys.*, vol. 41, p. 1395, 1970.

[9] D. Chen, *J. Appl. Phys.*, vol. 45, p. 2358, 1974.

[10] Y. J. Wang, C. P. Luo, L. C. Kong, X. S. Qi, D. Huang and Y. Chen, *J. Mag. Soc. Japan*, vol. 17, S1, p. 294, 1993.

[11] J. X. Shen, R. Kirby and D. Sellmyer, *J. Magn. Magn. Mat.*, vol. 81, p. 107, 1989; *J. Appl. Phys.*, vol. 69, p. 5984, 1991.

[12] Y. Chen, C. P. Luo, Z. T. Guan, Q. Y. Lu and Y. J. Wang, *J. Magn. Magn. Mat.*, vol. 115, p. 55, 1992.

[13] M. Nakada and M. Okada, presented at *Magneto-optical Recording International Symposium*, 1994, Tokyo, 27B-03.

[14] H. Haudek and W. K. Unger, *Physica Status Solidi (a)*, vol. 7, p. 393.

[15] E. Feldtkeller, *IEEE MAG*-8, p. 481, 1972.

[16] M. Masuda, I. Izawa, S. Yoshino, S. Shiomi, and S. Uchiyama, *Japan J. Appl. Phys.*, vol. 26, p. 707, 1987.

[17] R. Kanglet, *IEEE MAG*-8, p. 489, 1972.

[18] T. Chen and W. E. Stutius, *IEEE MAG*-10, p. 581, 1974.

[19] R. Coehorn and R. A. de Groot, *J. Phys. F: Met. Phys.*, vol. 15, p. 2135, 1985.

[20] T. McGuire and J. O. Varela, Naval Research Laboratory, Silver Spring, Maryland, unpublished data. Also, see A. J. P. Meyer and P. Taglang, *J. Phys. Radium*, vol. 12, p. 63S, 1951.

[21] G. D. Adam and K. J. Standley, *Proc. Phys. Soc.* (London) A66, p. 823, 1953.

[22] H. J. Williams, R. C. Sherwood, and Boothby, *Bull. Am. Phys. Soc. Ser. II*, vol. 1, p. 132, 1956.

5.2 PtMnSb HEUSLER ALLOY

PtMnSb is one of the Heusler alloys [1], which exhibits a strong magneto-optical effect at wavelengths for applications [2]. This section discusses the structure and magnetic- and magneto-optic properties of PtMnSb.

5.2.1 Structure and Magnetic Properties

Heusler is a general name for the ordered body-centered cubic structure whose composition is A_2MnX, which was first found by Heusler in 1903 [1]. Cu_2MnAl is one of the representative compositions. There are two different crystallographical structures for Heusler; namely, ferromagnetic type and antiferromagnetic type, which are shown in Figure 5.10. Here, on the A site Au, Pd, Ni, and Co are possible, and X is Al, In, Sn, Ga, Ge, Sn, Sb, and Si. In this structure, Mn forms a face-centered cubic cell, and the distance between Mn and Mn is $a\sqrt{2} \approx 4$ Å. For many cases, the spins of the Mn atoms are parallel to each other; they have a magnitude of about $4\,\mu_B$. The electronic structure of Mn atoms is $(3d)^5(4s)^2$, but that in alloys is believed to be $(3d)^6(4s)^1$.

The crystal structure of PtMnSb was studied by a number of workers, and one representative result is given in Table 5.2 [3], together with the data for PtMnSn. The following may be summarized for PtMnSb [3]:

1. The CaF_2 structure PtMnSb was obtained when quenched from above 1300°C. The lattice constant is 6.263 Å.

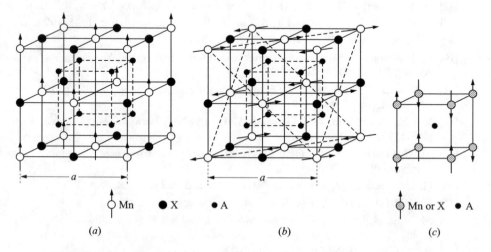

        Mn   X   A   Mn or X   A

         (a)   (b)   (c)

Figure 5.10 Structure of A_2MnX. (*a*) Heusler type ferromagnetic structure ($K_1 > 0$);
(*b*) Heusler type antiferromagnetic structure; and (*c*) CsCl-type antiferromagnetic structure.

TABLE 5.2 Lattice Parameters and Densities of PtMnSn and PtMnSb [3]

Alloy	Heat Treatment	Lattice Parameter (Å)	Density (g/cc)	
			Measured	Calculated
$Pt_{1.01}Mn_{0.99}Sn_{1.00}$	Water-quenched after heating at 1325°C for 1 h	6.263	10.00	10.06
$Pt_{1.01}Mn_{0.99}Sb_{1.00}$	Cooled at rate of 50°C/h after heating at 850°C for 50 h	6.201	10.38	10.40

2. The ordered PtMnSb was obtained when slowly cooled from 850°C, the structure of which is Cl_b . The lattice constant is 6.201 Å.

3. The water-quenched PtMnSb alloy has a Curie point of 360K and a saturation moment of 55.1 emu/g with 3.65 μ_B/mole. The Mn-Mn distances are 4.43 and 3.13 Å.

4. The slowly cooled PtMnSb alloy has a Curie point of 582K, and a saturation moment of 62.0 emu/g with 4.14 μ_B.

Since the magnetic moment in Heusler alloys is largely localized at Mn atoms [4], the magnetic properties are strongly dependent on the Mn-Mn distance, which is summarized in Table 5.3 [3].

5.2.2 Magneto-Optical Properties

The magneto-optical Kerr effect was first studied by van Engen et al. [2]. Figure 5.11 shows the wavelength dependence of both Kerr rotation angle and ellipticity of PtMnSb bulk, which compound was prepared by means of arc melting in an atmosphere of purified argon gas. The Kerr rotation ϕ_K is very high (about 1.3°) at about 1.7eV. The ellipticity ε_K is also very high (0.7° at 1.5 eV). Table 5.4 summarizes the data at 633 nm, together with those of MnBi reported [5], [6]. Here, θ_{eff} is defined by Equation (4.1). The effective Kerr rotation θ_K is about 1.1°, whereas it is about 0.72° for MnBi. Figure 5.12

FIGURE 5.3 The Mn-Mn Inter-Atomic Distance, Number of Bohr Magneton, and Curie Temperature [3]

	Alloy	Mn-Mn Inter-Atomic Distance (Å)	Number of Bohr Magneton (μ_B/mol) at 0°K	Curie Temperature (°K)
	PtMnSb	4.43 (3.13)	3.65	360
	PtMnSb	4.38	4.14	582
(a)	NiMnSb	4.18	3.65	750
	PdMnSb	4.43	3.0	535
	CuMnSb	4.30	3.9	55 (Néel temp.)
	Cu_2MnAl	4.21	4.12	603
(b)	Cu_2MnIn	4.39	3.95	506
	Cu_2MnSn	4.37	4.11	–

TABLE 5.4   Kerr Rotation θ_K, ε_K, Effective Rotation Θ_{eff} and Reflectivity R for PtMnSb and MnBi [2]

Compound	φ_K (°)	ε_K (°)	θ_{eff} (°)	R
MnBi[a]	−0.56	−0.48	0.73	0.39
MnBi[b]	−0.70	−0.16	0.72	0.57
PtMnSb	−0.93	−0.61	1.11	0.42

shows the Kerr rotation and ellipticity of other types of Heusler alloys, replacing Pt or Sb by Pd or Sn. All the alloys of PdMnSb, PtMnSn, and NiMnSb exhibit Kerr rotation and ellipticity much smaller than those of PtMnSb [2].

De Groot and Mueller [7] calculated the electronic structure of PtMnSb in order to explain this very high magneto-optical Kerr effect. The band structure calculation was made using the self-consistent augmented spherical wave (ASW) method [8]. Figure 5.13 shows the calculated band structure, and Figure 5.14 is the total density of states for the majority and minority spin directions [8]. The unique feature from this result is that it is a metal for the majority spin electrons, while at the same time it is a semiconductor for the minority spin electrons, called "half-metallic ferromagnetism." This feature is similar to that of NiMnSb [9]. One important difference for PtMnSb from NiMnSb is that the position of the Fermi level with respect to the top of the valence band of the minority spin direction, and that the top of the spin-orbit-split valence band for the minority spin direction is just above the Fermi level. As shown in Figure 5.15, the Fermi level is between those for $m = 0$ and $+1$ of Γ_4 which are split into four levels, leading to the absence of one type of excitation. This leads to the large Kerr effect

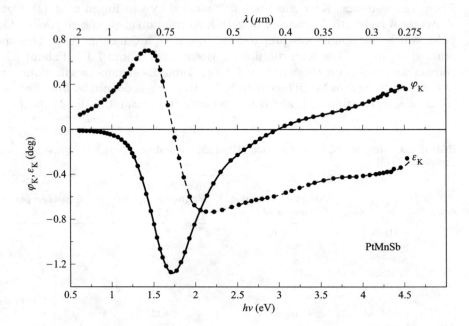

Figure 5.11 Kerr rotation (full line) and Kerr ellipticity (broken line) of PtMnSb vs. photon energy [2].

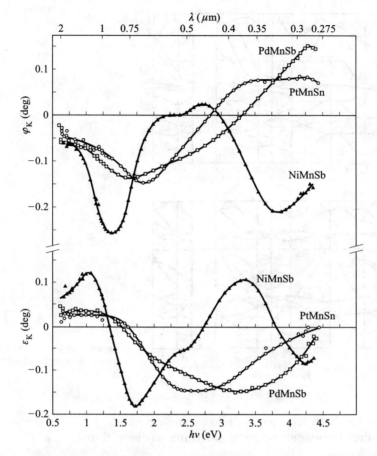

Figure 5.12 Kerr rotation (upper part) and Kerr ellipticity (lower part) of PdMnSb, NiMnSb, and PtMnSn vs. photon energy [2].

experimentally observed. On the other hand, the Fermi level of NiMnSb is on the top of the $m = +1$ level, leading to a weak magneto-optical effect.

A recent work [10] reported that $Mn_{0.5}Pt_{0.06}Sb_{0.44}$ films of Cl_b structure exhibited a high Kerr rotation of $1°$ at about 500 nm. This finding is important in understanding the magneto-optical mechanism in conjunction with the role of the Pt element in Cl_b structure.

5.2.3 Media Fabrication

Efforts have been made to use PtMnSb thin films for magneto-optical recording purposes. Since the magneto-crystalline anisotropy of PtMnSb is weak (1×10^4 erg/cc at room temperature), how one might induce perpendicular magnetic anisotropy along the film normal in PtMnSb films is a major issue. Koyama et al. [11] fabricated a double layer of PtMnSb/TbFe so as to take advantage of the magneto-static and exchange coupling effects to induce perpendicular magnetic anisotropy. In an attempt to induce magnetic anisotropy and make the grain-size small, Carey et al. [14] used a rapid thermal annealing technique to crystallize PtMnSb films. So far only very limited

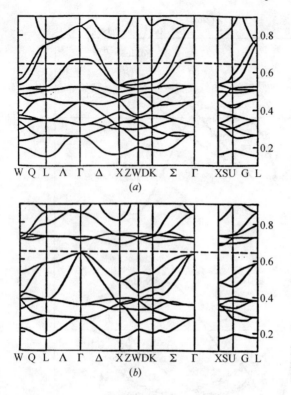

WQL Λ Γ Δ XZWDK Σ Γ XSU G L
(a)

WQL Λ Γ Δ XZWDK Σ Γ XSU G L
(b)

Figure 5.13 Calculated band structure [7] (a) majority spin band and (b) minority spin band.

success has been reported, and no promising way to fabricate perpendicularly magnetized films for magneto-optical recording has been found.

REFERENCES

[1] F. Heusler, *Verh. Deutsch Phys. Ges.*, vol. 5, p. 219, 1903.

[2] P. G. van Engen, K. H. J. Buschow, R. Jonngebreur, and M. Evan, *Appl. Phys. Lett.*, vol. 42, p. 202, 1983.

[3] K. Watanabe, *J. Phys. Soc. Japan*, vol. 28, p. 302, 1970.

[4] G. P. Felcher, J. W. Cable, and M. K. Wilkinson, *J. Phys. Chem. Solids*, vol. 24, p. 1663, 1963.

[5] S. Edokoro and M. Nagao, *Oyo Butsuri*, vol. 39, p. 1172, 1970 (in Japanese).

[6] K. Egashira and T. Yamada, *J. Appl. Phys.*, vol. 45, p. 3643, 1974.

[7] R. A. de Groot, F. M. Mueller, P. G. van Engen, and K. H. J. Buschow, *J. Appl. Phys.*, vol. 55, p. 2151, 1984.

[8] A. R. Williams, J. Kuebler, and C. D. Gelatt, Jr., *Phys. Rev. B*, vol. 19, p. 6094, 1970.

[9] R. A. de Groot, F. M. Mueller, P. G. van Engen, and K. H. J. Buschow, *Phys. Rev. Lett.*, vol. 50, p. 2024, 1983.

[10] M. Takahashi, H. Shoji, Y. Hozumi, and T. Wakiyama, *J. Magn. Magn. Mat.*, vol.130, p. 67, 1994.

[11] M. Koyama, R. Ohyama, T. Koyanagi, Y. Watanabe and K. Matsubara, *J. Magn. Soc. Japan*, vol. 11, p. 173, 1987.

[12] T. Inukai, M. Matsuoka and K. Ono, *Appl. Phys. Lett.*, vol. 49, p. 52, 1986.

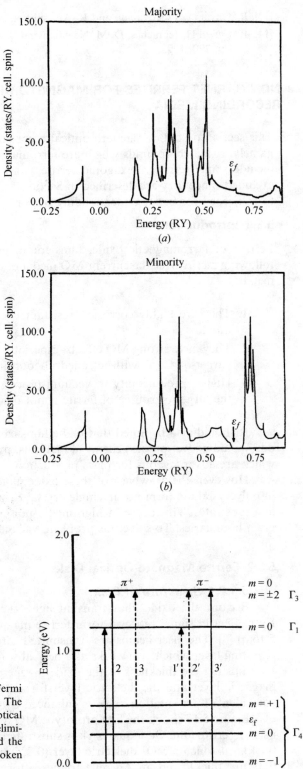

Figure 5.14 Total density of states of PtMnSb for the majority and minority spin directions [7].

Figure 5.15 Energy levels around the Fermi energy for the minority spin direction. The arrows indicate the various allowed optical transitions. The excitations which are eliminated by crossing the $m = +1$ level and the Fermi level have been drawn with broken lines [7].

[13] R. Ohyama, T. Koyanagi and K. Matsubara, *J. Appl. Phys.*, vol. 61, p. 2347, 1987.

[14] R. Carey, H. Jenniches, D. M. Newman and B. W. J. Thomas, *J. Magn. Soc. Japan*, vol. 17, S-1, p. 290, 1993.

5.3 NON-GARNET FERRITES FOR MAGNETO-OPTICAL RECORDING MEDIA

This section describes magneto-optical recording materials of ferrites in a wide sense, namely, oxide compounds which are ferromagnetic at room temperature [1]–[6]. They include spinel ferrites, hexagonal ferrites, and perovskite ferrites. Garnet ferrites are excluded, since they are described in Section 5.1, and are only supplementarily referred to as needed for better understanding of non-garnet-ferrites.

5.3.1 Introduction

Ferrite, or ferromagnetic oxide, films for magneto-optical recording media have the following merits over the current MO media of amorphous rare earth transition (a-RT) metals:

1. They are highly corrosion resistant because an oxide cannot be oxidized any more.
2. They have strong MO effects, especially when enhanced by such ions as Bi^{3+} in garnet or Co^{2+} with tetrahedral coordination.
3. High reproducibility in vacuum-process film preparation is expected, because the target or source of ferrite is not oxidized even when exposed to air.

It should also be noted that oxide films can be prepared by "non-vacuum" methods, including wet-process chemical methods, pyrolysis methods, and aerosol methods, which are advantageous for mass production.

However, the drawback of these oxide materials is that they can only be obtained in polycrystalline form not in single crystal form, on glass or other non-single-crystalline substrates. This causes a high media noise in MO readout due to light scatter at grain boundaries. To solve this problem, various measures have been proposed [1], [3], [6].

5.3.2 Ferrite Magneto-Optical Disk

5.3.2.1 Structure of Disk

Because the oxide films transmit light, the Faraday effect is used instead of the Kerr effect in signal retrieval form ferrite magneto-optical media, as shown in Figure 5.16(*a*) [3]. The laser beams are transmitted through the oxide film and reflected by a reflecting layer which also works as a heat-absorbing layer for thermomagnetic writing. By adjusting the thickness of the oxide magnetic layer, or the thicknesses of both the magnetic layer and the dielectric layer formed on it [Figure 5.16(*b*)], the virtual (i.e., equivalent) Kerr rotation angle is enhanced by multireflection of light.

Figure 5.17 shows the first prototype MO recording disk made by Martens et al. [7] using a ferrite film. On a quartz glass substrate they deposited a $CoFe_2O_4$ film (0.21 μm thick), on which a SiO_2 dielectric layer (0.22 μm thick), a lacquer "after-groove" layer (0.08 μm thick), and an Ag reflector were formed successively. The thickness of the

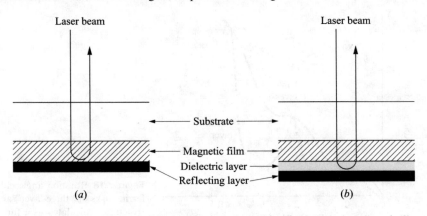

Figure 5.16 Structure of oxide magneto-optical disk of (*a*) "two-layer" and (*b*) "three-layer" structures [3].

ferrite layer was optimized to enhance the Faraday rotation by multireflection of light. The SiO_2 dielectric layer moderates the thickness dependence of the Faraday rotation, as Figure 5.18 shows. Due to the enhancement, the Co-ferrite medium exhibits a MO rotation angle as large as $\pm 8°$ at $\lambda = 780$ nm.

Since the optical absorption in the oxide films is much weaker than in the a-RT films, the MO enhancement by the multireflection of light obtained in the former is much stronger than in the latter. This is another merit of oxide MO films over the a-RT films. The MO enhancement by multireflection is not adopted in most of the current MO recording disks in practice, partly because the enhancement is realized only if the a-RT films are very thin ($< \sim 0.03$ μm), which reduces the corrosion resistance of the films greatly.

5.3.2.2 Perpendicular Magnetic Anisotropy

In MO recording media the easy axis of magnetization must be directed perpendicular to the plane of the film. In the polycrystalline ferrite films deposited on non-single-crystalline substrate, the perpendicular anisotropy may be established by crystal magnetic anisotropy and/or inverse magnetostriction effect by thermally induced stress.

The uniaxial anisotropy constant K_u pertaining to the thermal stress is proportional to the magnetostriction coefficient λ of the film and the thermal stress σ in the film, expressed as

$$K_u = 3\lambda\sigma/2 = -3\lambda(\alpha_f - \alpha_s)E\Delta T/[2(1-\nu)] \qquad (5.1)$$

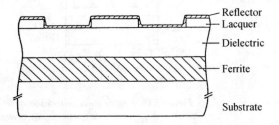

Figure 5.17 Cross section of "after-groove" disk using $CoFe_2O_4$ ferrite film [7].

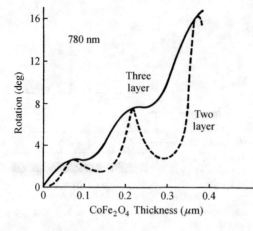

Figure 5.18 Rotation angle enhanced in Co-ferrite disks of "three-layer" and "two-layer" structures, calculated as a function of ferrite film thickness [7].

Here, ΔT is difference between substrate temperature (at which film is crystallized) and room temperature, α_f and α_s: thermal expansion coefficients of film and substrate, respectively, and E and ν are Young's modulus and Poisson's ratio, respectively, of the film [1], [36].

As shown in Figure 5.19, we can obtain perpendicularly magnetized films for ferrites with $\lambda < 0$ (e.g., $CoFe_2O_4$ and $Dy_3Fe_5O_{12}$) on glass substrates ($\alpha_f < \alpha_s$), while for ferrite with $\lambda > 0$ (e.g., $CoCrFeO_4$ and $Tb_3Fe_5O_{12}$) on metal substrates ($\alpha_f < \alpha_s$), provided

$$K = K_u - 2\pi M_s^2 > 0 \qquad (5.2)$$

Here K_u is the effective perpendicular magnetic anisotropy constant and M_s the saturation magnetization. Reducing M_s increases the perpendicular magnetic anisotropy.

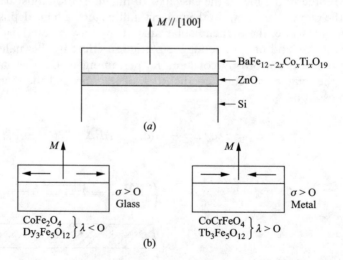

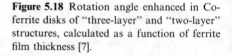

Figure 5.19 Aligning magnetization of ferrite film perpendicular to film plane by (a) crystal magnetic anisotropy and (b) inverse magnetostriction [6].

Glass substrate is preferred to metal substrate, because the former has a higher heat resistance than the latter.

The crystal magnetic anisotropy contributes to the perpendicular magnetic anisotropy when a magnetic easy axis such as $\langle 100 \rangle$ axis in $CoFe_2O_4$ or c-axis in $BaFe_{12-2x}Co_xTi_xO_{19}$ is preferentially oriented perpendicular to the film plane in textured films.

5.3.3 Magneto-Optical Effect in Ferrite

5.3.3.1 Light Absorption in Ferrite

As shown in Figure 5.20, the absorption coefficient for various ferrites is small in a spectral interval $\hbar\omega$ (photon energy) = 0.1~2 eV, or λ(wavelength) = 0.6~15 μm, which is often referred to as a "window." Thus, ferrites transmit light in visible and near infrared regions, which enables ferrites to be applied to optical devices including MO memory. The lower energy edge of the window is ascribed to absorptions by lattice vibrations, while the higher energy edge to those by electronic transitions of $Fe^{2+,3+}$ and other metal ions, which we describe as M^{n+}.

There are three principal electronic transitions in ferrites, (I) charge transfer transitions, (II) internal transitions, and (III) crystal field transitions [5], [6]. The transitions are closely related to the fact that the $Fe^{2+,3+}$ and M^{n+} ions are coordinated with the O^{2-} ions, as follows.

(I) *Charge transfer transitions* — Electrons hop from O^{2-} to M^{n+} [Fig. 5.21(a), Fig. 5.22(a)]. In case $M^{n+} = Fe^{3+}$, 2p valence electrons of O^{2-} transfer to 3d orbitals of Fe^{3+}. The transitions are electric-dipole-allowed, which cause

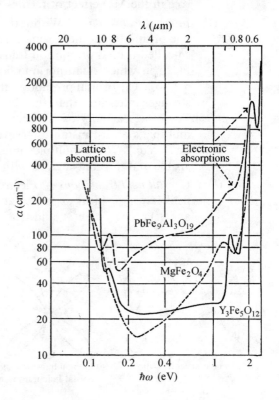

Figure 5.20 Spectra of light absorption coefficient for various ferrites [5].

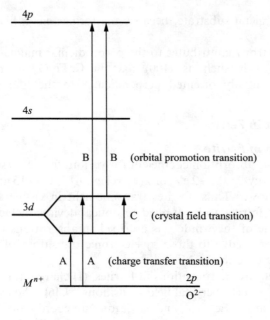

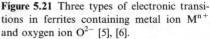

Figure 5.21 Three types of electronic transitions in ferrites containing metal ion M^{n+} and oxygen ion O^{2-} [5], [6].

strong light absorptions in the ultraviolet region of $\hbar\omega > \sim 2.5\,\mathrm{eV}$, with accompanying strong MO effects. The enhanced MO effect has a tail extending down to the visible and infrared regions, which plays the most important role in the MO effect of ferrites from the stand point of application.

(II) *Internal transitions* — Within the metal ion M^{n+}, electrons are excited from one orbital to another orbital, which are divided into two categories. One is so-called orbital promotion transitions, e.g., 3d→4p in Fe^{3+} and 4f→5d in Pr^{3+}, in which quantum number is promoted during the transitions [Fig. 5.22(b)]. The orbital promotion transitions occur in higher energy range with stronger intensities than the charge transfer transitions do.

The other category of the internal transitions is those occurring between J-multiplets of, for instance, 4f levels of rare earth ions ($R^{3+} = Eu^{3+}$, Dy^{3+}, Pr^{3+}, etc.). The J-multiplet internal transitions cause light absorptions in visible and infrared regions with very sharp spectral shapes.

(III) *Crystal field transitions* — Electrons are excited from lower to higher crystal field levels. Typical examples are transitions between crystal field levels (e and t^2) of Fe^{2+}, Fe^{3+}, and Co^{2+} ions. The crystal field transitions of Fe^{3+}

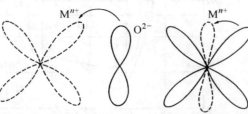

(a) Charge transfer transition   (b) Internal transition and crystal field transition

Figure 5.22 Transfer of electron in three types of electronic transitions in ferrites [5], [6].

determine the structure of the higher energy edge of the window in ferrites (Figure 5.19). The crystal fields transitions of Co^{2+} are partially allowed, which, however, give strong MO effects, as described in the next section.

In ferrites, major MO effects are mostly classified as the "double transition type," which is also called "diamagnetic type." Double transition type MO effect arises because, as shown in Figure 5.23, the excited state of an allowed transition is split into "double levels" by LS coupling. This polarizes the electric dipole transition, and higher and lower energy transitions are allowed for left and right circularly polarized transitions, respectively, or vice versa. Superimposing the contributions form the two transitions with small energy difference due to the LS coupling, off-diagonal dielectric permeability tensor element ε_{xy} (which is proportional to the MO effect) has the spectral shape, as shown in Figure 5.24.

5.3.3.2 Magneto-Optical Enhancement in Ferrites

Prominent magneto-optical enhancement has been observed for the following ferrites, associated with the electric transitions written in the parentheses [5].

1. Bi-substituted garnets (charge transfer transitions)
2. Pr-substituted garnets (orbital promotion transitions)
3. Various ferrites containing tetrahedrally-coordinated Co^{2+} (crystal field transitions).

Since non-garnet ferrites are our major concern, only item 3 is discussed here. As shown in Figure 5.25, the MO enhancement by tetrahedrally coordinated Co^{2+} [denoted $Co^{2+}(Td)$] is observed for various kinds of ferrites: spinels $Co^{2+}M_x^{3+}Fe_{2-x}^{3+}O_4$ (M = Cr, Mn, Al, Rh, etc.) [8], hexagonal ferrites $Ba^{2+}Fe_{12-2x}^{3+}Co_x^{2+}Ti_x^{4+}O_{19}$ [9], and garnets [10]. The enhancement occurs in two spectral regions where light is strongly absorbed, one in the visible range centered at $\lambda \approx 0.6\,\mu m$ ($\hbar\omega \approx 1.8\,eV$), called the P band, and the other in near infrared range centered at $\lambda \approx 1.5\,\mu m$ ($\hbar\omega \approx 1.2\,eV$), called the F band [11]. The light absorptions in the P and F bands arise from electric dipole transitions between the crystal field 3d levels. As Figures 5.26 and 5.27 show, in F (or P)

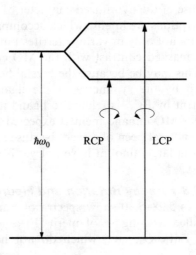

$\hbar\omega_0$ RCP   LCP

Figure 5.23 Allowed electric dipole transitions giving magneto-optical effect of double-transition type.

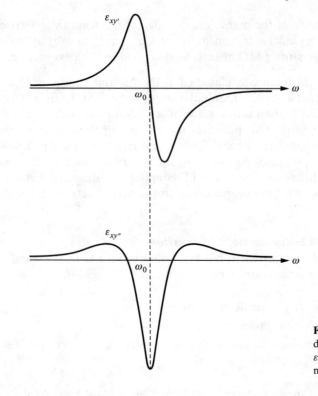

Figure 5.24 Spectrum shape for non-diagonal dielectric permeability tensor element $\varepsilon_{xy} = \varepsilon'_{xy} + i\varepsilon''_{xy}$ in double transition (or diamagnetic) type magneto-optical effect [4]–[6].

band transition electronic state changes from the ground $^4A_2(F)$ state with $e^4t_2^3$ configuration to the excited $^4T_1(F)$ (or $^4T_1(P)$ state with hybridized configuration $e^3t_2^4$ and $e^2t_2^5$.

Both F and P band absorptions are highly polarized; in either F or P band absorptions, $\Delta J = -1$ transition is allowed for left circular polarization (LCP), while $\Delta J = +1$ transition is allowed for right circular polarization (RCP). Because the $\Delta J = +1$ transition for RCP is further split into three transitions, while the $\Delta J = -1$ transition for LCP remains unsplit, MO effect associated with either F or P band absorption has spectral shape in which three "double transition type" spectra are superimposed [12].

Because of the hybridized character of the $^4T_1(F)$ and $^4T_1(P)$ orbitals, the F and P band absorptions are intense which accompany strong MO enhancement. The enhancement occurs not only in various ferrites but also in chalcogenides, (e.g., $CoCr_2S_4$) [11], making a marked contrast with the MO enhancement by Bi^{3+} which occurs only in garnets. This may be because the crystal field transitions of the $Co^{2+}(Td)$ is primarily determined by the symmetry of the ligand field at the tetrahedral site, while the enhancement by Bi^{3+} is related to ligand fields not only of Bi^{3+} but also of Fe^{3+}.

Similar MO enhancement is expected for Ni^{2+} on tetrahedral sites, which, however, have not yet been observed, because ferrites containing tetrahedrally coordinated Ni^{2+} ions in large amount have not yet been synthesized.

5.3.3.3 Faraday Rotation and Figure of Merit

Figures 5.28–5.30 show spectra of Faraday rotation F, absorption coefficient α, and so-called MO figure of merit $|F|/\alpha$ for various ferrites. Such spinel ferrites as $NiFe_2O_4$, $ZnFe_2O_4$, etc., which do not have $Co^{2+}(Td)$, show very small Faraday

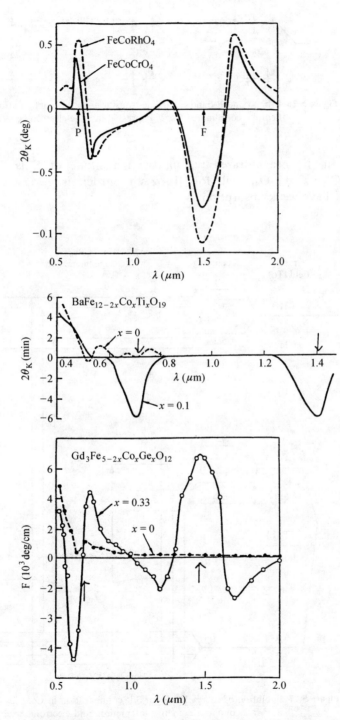

Figure 5.25 Enhancement of magneto-optical effect associated with P and F band absorptions (shown by arrows) of Co^{2+} (Td) for various ferrites [8]–[10].

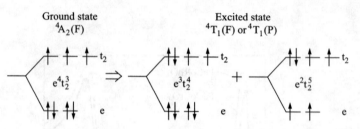

Figure 5.26 F-band and P-band electronic transitions of $3d^7$ configuration in tetrahedrally coordinated Co^{2+}, expressed in "one-electron" energy scheme.

rotation. In the near-infrared region, the magnitude of F is in the order YIG
$<BaFe_{12}O_{19}<CoFe_2O_4$, but for $|F|/\alpha$ the order is reversed since YIG and
$BaFe_{12}O_{19}$ have weak absorption.

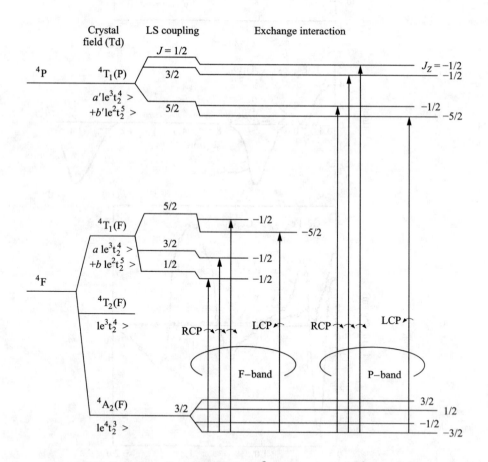

Figure 5.27 Evolution of energy levels for $3d^7$ configuration in Co^{2+} by Td crystal
field, LS coupling, exchange interaction, and electronic transition of F
and P bands. For $^4T_1(F)$ and $^4T_1(P)$ states exchange interaction is shown
only for the excited states of the transitions.

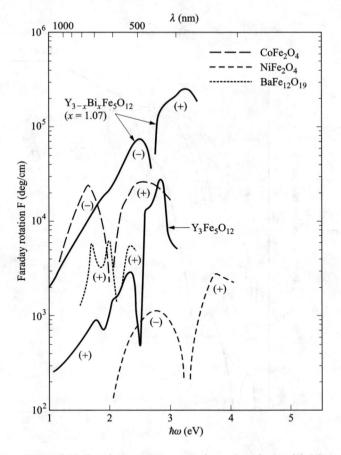

Figure 5.28 Faraday rotation spectra for various ferrites [3], [4].

Partial substitution of Fe with Rh in $CoFe_2O_4$ [which increases the amount of Co^{2+} (Td), as described in Section 5.3.4.1, and decreases light absorption] increases the figure of merit in the infrared region. However, Bi-substituted YIG is about two orders of magnitude higher in figure of merit than $CoRhFeO_4$. Ce-substituted YIG exceeds Bi-substituted YIG in figure of merit in the range $\hbar\omega >\sim 2.3\,eV$.

Here it should be noted that $|F|/\alpha$ is not a satisfactory figure of merit for oxide MO recording media [6]. Taking only shot noise generated in the photodetector into account, the signal-to-noise ratio in MO readout from a magnetic layer (in which the laser beams go and return, as shown in Figure 5.16(a)) satisfies the relation

$$S/N \propto |F| \cdot 2l \exp(-\alpha \cdot 2l) \leq F/\alpha \qquad (5.3)$$

Here l is the thickness of the film, and $|F| \cdot 2l$ and $\exp(-\alpha \cdot 2l)$ express Faraday rotation angle and rate of light intensity loss, respectively, which occur in the film. In Equation (3), $|F| \cdot 2l \exp(-\alpha \cdot 2l)$ takes the maximum value $|F|/\alpha$ when $l = 1/2\alpha$, as shown in Figure 5.31. This thickness is too large or too small to be realized for oxide media; e.g. for YIG and $CoFe_2O_4$ with $\alpha = 10^2 cm^{-1}$ and $10^5 cm^{-1}$, respectively (Fig.

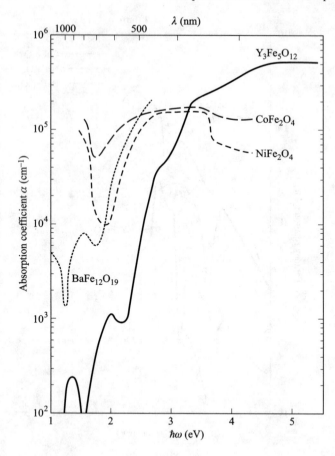

Figure 5.29 Absorption coefficient spectra for various ferrites.

5.29), we obtain $1/2\alpha = 50\mu m$ and $0.05\mu m$, which are larger and smaller than the desirable thickness $(-1\mu m)$ of the oxide MO recording media. Therefore the figure of merit for oxide MO recording media should be figured by $2|F|l\exp(-2\alpha l)$ instead of $|F|/\alpha$.

Figure 5.32 shows spectra of $2|F|l\exp(-2\alpha l)$ for Bi-substituted YIG, Co-ferrite, and Co-substituted barium ferrite. For $Y_{3-x}Bi_xFe_5O_{12}(x = 1.07)$, $2|F|l\exp(-2\alpha l)$ increases with $\hbar\omega$, reaching a maximum of $-2°$ around $\hbar\omega = 2.3\,eV(\lambda = 540\,nm)$, while $|F|/\alpha$ decreases with increasing $\hbar\omega$ (Fig. 5.30). Therefore, Bi-substituted iron garnet becomes more advantageous as shortening of laser diode wavelength proceeds. Furthermore, $2|F|l\exp(-2\alpha l)$ for the Bi-substituted iron garnet is much larger than for $BaFe_{12-2x}Co_xTi_xO_{19}$ and $CoFe_2O_4$.

5.3.4 Ferrite Magneto-Optical Recording Media

This section describes typical non-garnet ferrites which can be potentially applied to MO recording media. They are spinel ferrites, hexagonal ferrites, perovskite ferrites, and amorphous ferrites. As novel MO recording media, particulate films with ferrite particles dispersed in non-magnetic matrices are also described.

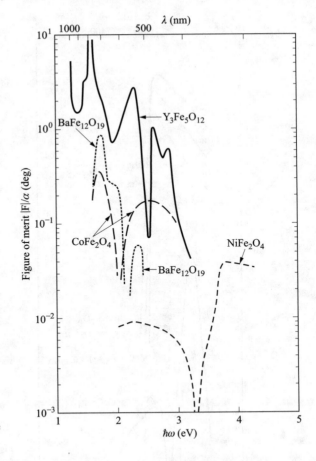

Figure 5.30 Spectra of magneto-optical figure of merit for various ferrites [3], [4].

5.3.4.1 Spinel Ferrites

Among a number of ferrites with spinel structure, Co-ferrite ($CoFe_2O_4$) has attracted much attention as MO recording media. This is because (1) it has a strong MO effect in the visible range due to Co^{2+} (Td), and (2) perpendicularly magnetized films are obtained by virtue of its strong crystal magnetic anisotropy and magnetostriction.

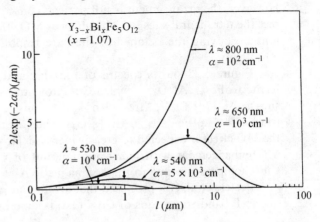

Figure 5.31 Dependence of $2l\exp(-2\alpha l)$, a factor appearing in Equation (5.3), on film thickness l for Bi-substituted YIG [6].

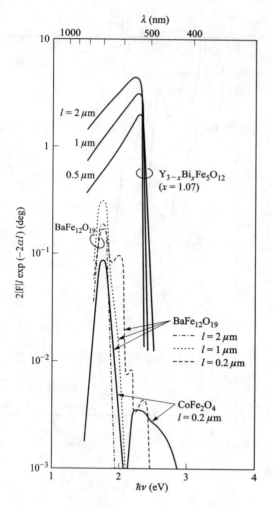

Figure 5.32 True figure of merit $2|F|l\exp(-2\alpha l)$ for MO recording on $Y_{3-x}Bi_xFe_5O_{12}$, $CoFe_2O_4$, and $BaFe_{12-2x}Co_xTi_xO_{19}$ films with various thickness l.

Co-ferrite is an inverse spinel with an ionic arrangement $[Fe^{3+}]_{tet}[Fe^{3+}Co^{2+}]_{oct}$. However, the arrangement is not perfect; consequently, a small amount of Co^{2+} occupies the tetrahedral sites, which enhances MO effect in F and P bands. The major Co^{2+} ions occupying the octahedral sites are responsible for the strong crystal magnetic anisotropy.

Figure 5.33 shows spectra of Faraday and Kerr rotations for Al-substituted Co ferrite $CoFe_{2-x}Al_xO_4$, in which Co^{2+} ions transfer from the octahedral to tetrahedral sites as Al^{3+} (or Cr^{3+}, Mn^{3+}, Rh^{3+}, etc.) ions occupy the octahedral sites preferentially ($[Fe_{1-x}^{3+}Co_x^{2+}]_{tet}[Fe^{3+}Co_{1-x}^{2+}Al_x^{3+}]_{oct}O_4$). Thus, as the amount, x, of Co^{2+}(Td) increases, the MO effect is expected to greatly increase. However, this does not occur, because the MO enhancement with increasing amount of Co^{2+}(Td) is offset by the decrease in Curie temperature due to the nonmagnetic Al^{3+} ions occupying the octahedral sites.

Peeters et al. [13] proposed that around $\hbar\omega = 2\,eV$ the diamagnetic type MO effect due to P band transitions of Co^{2+}(Td) is superimposed by a broad paramagnetic type

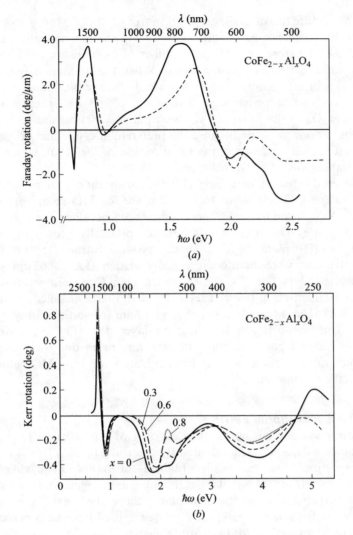

Figure 5.33 Spectra of (*a*) Faraday rotation and (*b*) Kerr rotation at room temperature for polycrystalline $CoFe_{2-x}Al_xO_4$ films [13].

MO effect, which is probably ascribed to a $Co^{2+} \rightarrow Fe^{3+}$ charge transfer transition on the octahedral sites.

Having degenerate energy levels of $3d^7$ configurations, the Co^{2+} ions on the octahedral sites give very strong crystal magnetic anisotropy and magnetostriction. The easy axis of the magnetization is parallel to the $\langle 100 \rangle$ axis, and the magnetostriction coefficient along the $\langle 100 \rangle$ axis is as large as $\lambda_{100} = -250 \times 10^{-6}$, negative in sign [14]. Therefore, in (100) textured $CoFe_2O_4$ films deposited on glass substrates, both the crystal magnetic anisotropy and inverse magnetostriction contribute to the perpendicular magnetic anisotropy.

The $CoFe_2O_4$ films of the prototype MO disks shown in Figure 5.17 were deposited by the spray pyrolysis method on quartz glass substrates in polycrystalline form with (100) texture (private communication from J. W. D. Martens, one of the authors of [7]). The films did not give high squareness in the magnetization curve, as shown in Figure 5.34. Therefore, the MO disks utilizing Co-ferrite films did not give high carrier-to-noise ratio (CNR) in signal retrieval. When the squareness is poor, a recorded bit domain is split into a multidomain state and also the bit domain becomes irregular in shape, which causes media noise. This is one of the main reasons why the MO disks using $CoFe_2O_4$ media have not yet been put to practical use. It is supposed that the hysteresis is poor in shape because the preferential crystalline orientation of the ⟨100⟩ axis is not perfect, and, therefore, the direction of the ⟨100⟩, which is the easy axis of magnetization in $CoFe_2O_4$, is dispersed.

The establishment of a perfect ⟨100⟩ orientation is a requisite for putting the polycrystalline $CoFe_2O_4$ films to practical use for MO recording, which is yet to be attained. A high squareness hysteresis has been obtained for a single crystalline Co-ferrite ($Co_{0.7}Fe_{2.3}O_4$) film of (100) plane epitaxially grown by chemical transport method on (100) plane of MgO single crystal substrate [15]. On these films bits 1–2 μm in diameter were thermomagnetically written at $\lambda = 0.63$ μm.

Despite the fact that $CoFe_2O_4$ has a high Curie temperature (520° C) and no magnetic compensation point, a relatively high thermomagnetic writing threshold sensitivity (0.45 nJ/m²) was obtained at $\lambda = 752$ nm for static writing of bits 1×3 μm² in size [7]. This was attained for the three-layer disk (Fig. 5.17) with optimized film thickness where a rotation angle takes a maximum due to multireflection of light. Thus, the multireflection in oxide films enhances not only MO rotation but also thermomagnetic writing sensitivity.

5.3.4.2 Hexagonal Ferrites

Among various hexagonal ferrites, only M-type barium ferrite ($BaFe_{12}O_{19}$) has been studied extensively as an oxide MO recording media. This is because perpendicularly magnetized films are easily obtained for $BaFe_{12}O_{19}$ having a strong uniaxial magnetic anisotropy along its hexagonal c-axis, which tends to be preferentially oriented perpendicular to the film plane. Since the c-axis is an optical axis along which no birefringence occurs, the c-plane textured films with perpendicular magnetization can be applied to MO recording media.

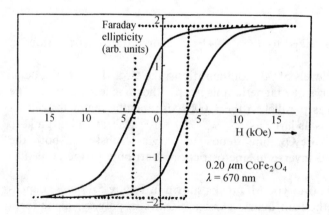

Figure 5.34 Magnetic hysteresis loop of $CoFe_2O_4$ film measured from Faraday ellipticity perpendicular to film plane [7]. Dotted line indicates an ideal loop perfectly square in shape, which is required in MO recording.

A film of $BaFe_{12}O_{19}$ with a good *c*-plane texture has been prepared by sputtering on an oxidized Si wafer intermediated by an Au reflector and a dielectric layer of ZnO (which enhances the *c*-plane orientation), as shown in Figure 5.35 [16]. The easy axis of magnetization was directed normal to the film plane by the uniaxial magnetic anisotropy. For a fixed thickness (i.e., 0.25 μm) of the film, the Faraday rotation was enhanced by the multi-reflection effect, reaching maximum values of 0.55° and 0.30° at $\lambda = 0.63$ μm and 0.75 μm, respectively. Since even these values were not enough to get a high readout CNR, the intrinsic Faraday rotation was enhanced by substituting Fe^{3+} by $Co^{2+} + Ti^{4+}$ [16], [17]. As shown in Figures 5.36 and 5.37, the Faraday rotation increased linearly with *x* in $BaFe_{12-2x}Co_xTi_xO_{19}$, but at the same time coercive force and anisotropy field decreased, while the saturation magnetization did not decrease much. This deteriorated square shape in magnetic hysteresis offset the effect due to the Faraday rotation enhancement.

Bits of 2.0 μm diameter were thermomagnetically written at $\lambda = 780$ nm on a *c*-plane textured $BaFe_{10.42}Co_{0.8}O_{19}$ ($x = 0.8$) film with an Nd reflector on it [17]. This film was deposited by sputtering, 1 μm in thickness, on a ⟨111⟩ oriented GGG substrate, which exhibited relatively large Faraday rotation of 0.75°, though magnetic hysteresis loop was poor in squareness.

5.3.4.3 Other Non-Garnet Ferrites

This section describes novel ferrite materials which are of interest because they have features advantageous for application to MO recording media, though yet to be realized. They are perovskites $(La, Sr)MnO_3$, amorphous ferrites, and particulate films with ferrite fine particles dispersed in nonmagnetic transparent matrices.

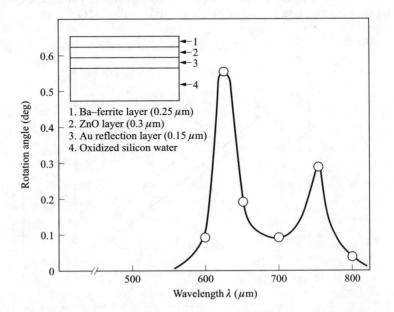

Figure 5.35 Wavelength dependence of enhanced rotation angle in $BaFe_{12}O_{19}$ media [16].

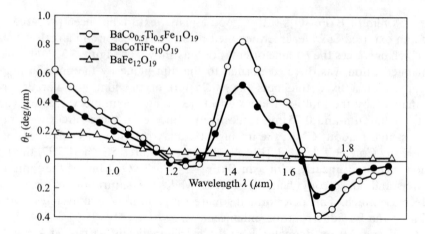

Figure 5.36 Spectra of Faraday rotation for single crystalline films of $BaFe_{12-2x}Co_xTi_xO_{19}$ [16].

(a) Perovskites Sr-substituted lanthanide manganese perovskite $La_{1-x}Sr_xMnO_3$ ($La_{1-x}^{3+}Sr_x^{2+}Mn_{1-x}^{3+}Mn_x^{4+}O_3$) with $x = 0.2 \sim 0.4$ exhibits metallic conductivity and ferromagnetism due to double exchange interaction between Mn^{3+} and Mn^{4+}. Partial substitution of La with Bi ($Bi_yLa_{1-x-y}Sr_xMnO_3$) in this compound enhances MO Kerr rotation in a ultraviolet range around $\lambda = 0.27\,\mu m$ ($\hbar\omega = 4.6\,eV$), as shown in Figure 5.38 [18]. The enhancement is prominent only at low temperature, because the Bi-substitution reduces the Curie temperature, which offsets the MO enhancement at room temperature.

As in Bi-substituted garnets, the MO enhancement in (Bi,La, Sr)MnO_3 is ascribed to strong LS coupling in 6p orbitals of Bi^{3+}. The MO offset in the perovskite is

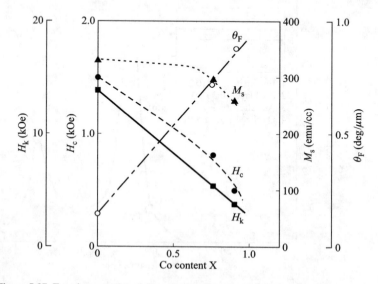

Figure 5.37 Faraday rotation $\theta_F(\lambda = 0.63\,\mu m)$, saturation magnetization M_s, coercive force H_c, and anisotropy field H_k in $BaFe_{12-2x}Co_xTi_xO_{19}$ [17].

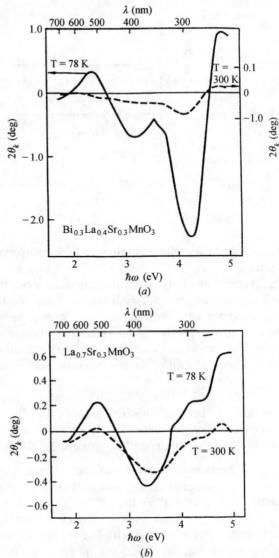

Figure 5.38 Kerr rotation spectra for (a) $Bi_{0.3}La_{0.4}Sr_{0.3}MnO_3$ and (b) $La_{0.7}Sr_{0.3}MnO_3$, at 300K and 78K [18].

enhanced either by (1) internal orbital promotion of Bi^{3+}, from ground state $^1S_0(6S^2)$ to excited state $^3P_1(6s6p)$ having a large splitting due to the strong LS coupling, or by (2) charge transfer transition from O^{2-} to M^{3+} or Mn^{4+} in which oxygen 2p orbitals are admixed with bismuth 6p orbitals with the strong LS coupling [18].

A (100) textured polycrystalline film of $La_{0.79}Sr_{0.21}MnO_3$ deposited by sputtering on a (111) oriented GGG substrate had its magnetization aligned perpendicular to the film plane, and exhibited hysteresis loops with good squareness, as shown in Figure 5.39 [19].

(b) Amorphous Ferrites If amorphous oxide films having a ferromagnetic moment aligned perpendicular to the film plane at room temperature are fabricated, they will be the most advantageous media for MO recording. With a strong corrosion resistance and having no grains, they are free from the problem of media noise due to light scatter at

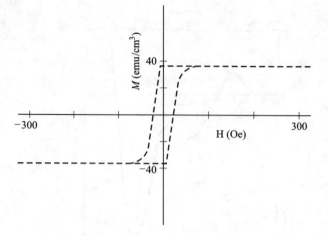

Figure 5.39 The magnetization curve for (La, Sr)MnO$_3$ film measured perpendicular to film plane [19].

grain boundaries which is inherent in all polycrystalline oxide recording media so far reported.

Amorphous ferrites, ferromagnetic at room temperature, have been synthesized by adding glass forming materials such as P$_2$O$_5$, V$_2$O$_5$, and SiO$_2$ to spinel ferrites [20], [21]. The ferromagnetic moment is not ascribed to genuine amorphous structure, but is ascribed to very fine ferromagnetic crystalline particles embedded in nonmagnetic amorphous matrices. Therefore, the magnetization in the amorphous ferrites is small in magnitude and different in temperature dependence as compared to magnetization in bulk samples.

Amorphous ferrite films with magnetization aligned perpendicular to film plane have not yet been synthesized successfully, though CoFe$_2$-P$_2$O$_5$ films show uniaxial anisotropy of $K_u = 1.8 \times 10^5$ erg/cm^3, which is, however, one order of magnitude smaller than that of crystalline CoFe$_2$O$_4$ [21].

(c) Particulate Films From the practical view point, oxide MO recording media have an additional disadvantage that they require high temperature (> several hundred°C) to crystallize the ferrite. This makes it hard to use plastics as substrates. To solve this problem as well as the problem of light scatter at grain boundaries, particulate films with magnetic fine particles, either of ferrites or metals, dispersed in nonmagnetic matrices (Fig. 5.40) are proposed to be used for MO recording media [22], [23]. When the size of the inhomogeneity of the particulate films, as well as the size of the particles, is much smaller than the wavelength, light is not scattered by the particles; the particulate film behaves for light waves as if it were a continuous medium with an

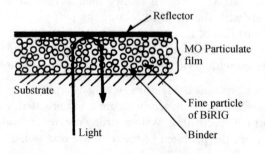

Figure 5.40 Magneto-optical recording medium of particulate film with magnetic fine particles [22].

effective dielectric permeability tensor [24]. The effective permeability tensor has been derived by extending the Maxwell-Garnett effective permeability to non-diagonal tensorial form [25], [26]. However, the Maxwell-Garnett permeability is applicable only when the particles are dispersed sparsely, or the volume fraction occupied by the particles is small. For large volume fraction a better description of the effective tensor for magnetized composite has been achieved based on the symmetrized effective medium theory [27].

Particulate films with fine particles of Bi-substituted DyAl iron garnet dispersed in a matrix, or binder, having a large stiffness constant exhibited magnetic hysteresis with good squareness, when measured perpendicular to the film plane. The binder induces strong stress on the particles during curing (at 100°C) the binder, which causes the perpendicular magnetic anisotropy through inverse magnetostriction effect in the garnet. On these films static and dynamic (84 kHz) thermomagnetic recordings were performed at $\lambda = 633$nm, obtaining a CNR of 25.5 dB [23].

REFERENCES

[1] M. Abe and M. Gomi, "Oxide Films for Magneto-Optical Applications," Proceedings of International Symposium Magneto-optics, *J. Magn. Soc. Japan*, vol. 11, Supplement, pp. 299–304, 1987.

[2] M. Abe and M. Gomi, "Advanced Materials for Magneto-Optical Disk," *Proceedings SPIE*, vol. 1316, Optical Data Storage, pp. 216-220, 1991.

[3] M. Abe and M. Gomi, "Magneto-Optical Recording on Garnet Films," *J. Magn. Magn. Mat.*, vol. 84, pp. 222–228, 1990.

[4] M. Gomi, "Thin Films for Magneto-Optical Applications," *J. Ceramic Soc. Japan*, vol. 99, pp. 852–861, 1991.

[5] M. Abe and M. Gomi, "Oxide Magneto-Optical Materials: Theory and Applications," *Oyobuturi (Applied Physics)*, vol. 57, pp. 723–737, 1988 (in Japanese).

[6] M. Abe and M. Gomi, *Magneto-optical Disk Materials*, Kogyo Chosakai Publishing, 1993, Chapter 5, pp. 137–191 (in Japanese).

[7] J. W. D. Martens and A. B. Voermans, "Cobalt Ferrite Thin Film for Magneto-Optical Recording," *IEEE Trans. Magn.*, vol. MAG-20, pp. 1007–1012, September 1984.

[8] R. Ahrenkiel and T. Coburn, "Magneto-Optic Insulators Utilizing the Optical Activity of Co^{++}(Td)," *IEEE Trans. Magn.*, vol. MAG-11, pp. 1103–1108, September 1975.

[9] M. Abe and M. Gomi, "Magneto-Optical Kerr Effect in $CoFe_{2-x}M_xO_4$(M = Mn, Cr, Al) and $BaFe_{12-2x}Co_xTi_xO_{19}$ with terahedrally coordinated Co^{2+}," *J. Appl. Phys.*, vol. 53, pp. 8172–8174, November 1982.

[10] K. Egashira and T. Manabe, "Effects of Some Transition Metal Ions on the Visible and Infrared Faraday Rotation of Gadolinium Iron Garnet," *IEEE Trans. Magn.*, vol. MAG-8, pp. 646–648, September 1972.

[11] R. K. Ahrentiel, S. Lyu, and T. J. Coburn, "Reflectance-Circular Dichroism of the Magnetic Insulator $Co_xCd_{1-x}Cr_2S_4$," *J. Appl. Phys.*, vol. 46, pp. 894–899, February 1975.

[12] T. Saito, K. Shinagawa, and T. Tsushima, "Magneto-Optical Effects of Tetrahedrally Coordinated Co^{2+} in Ferrites," *IEEE Trans. J. Magn. Japan*, vol. TJMJ-2, pp. 687–692, 1987.

[13] W. L. Peeters and J. W. D. Maetens, "Magneto-Optical Effects of Aluminum and Ferrous Substituted Cobalt Ferrite," *J. Appl. Phys.*, vol. 53, pp. 8178–8180, 1982.

[14] R. M. Bozoroth, E. F. Tilden, and A. J. Williams, "Anisotropy and Magnetostriction of some Ferrites," *Phys. Rev.*, vol. 99, pp. 1788–1798, 1955.

[15] N. N. Evtihiev, N. A. Economov, et al., "Co-Ferrite New Magnetooptic Recording Materials," *IEEE Trans Magn.*, vol. MAG-12, pp. 773–775, November 1976.

[16] H. Machida, F. Ohmi, et al., "Magneto-Optical Properties and Thermomagnetic Recording of M-type Ba-ferrite," *J. Magn. Magn. Mat.*, vols. 54–57, pp. 1399–1400, 1986.

[17] H. Nakamura, F. Ohmi, et al., "Cobalt-Titanium Substituted Barium Ferrite Films for Magneto-Optical Memory," *J. Appl. Phys.*, vol. 61, pp. 3346–3348, April 1987.

[18] T. J. A. Popma and M. G. J. Kamminga, "The Polar Magneto-Optic Kerr Rotation of Ferromagnetic Perovskites (La, Bi, Sr)MnO$_3$," *Solid State Commun.*, vol. 17, pp. 1073–1075, 1975.

[19] J. Cho, M. Gomi, and M. Abe, "Ferromagnetic (LaSr)MnO$_3$ Films Deposited by rf Sputtering," *Japan J. Appl. Phys.*, vol. 29, pp. 1686–1689, September 1990.

[20] M. Sugimoto, T. Takahashi, et al., "Preparation of Ferrimagnetic Amorphous Oxides and Their Properties," *Advances in Ceramics*, vol. 16, Proceedings of the 4th International Conference on Ferrites, Part II, pp. 609–615, 1986.

[21] N. Hiratsuka and M. Sugimoto, "Preparation of Amorphous Cobalt Ferrite Films with Perpendicular Anisotropy and their Magneto-Optical Properties," *IEEE Trans. Magn.*, vol. MAG-23, pp. 3326–3328, September 1987.

[22] M. Gomi and M. Abe, "Particulate Films for Magneto-Optical Recording II. Design and Characteristics of the Film," Proceedings of the International Symposium on Magneto-optics, *J. Magn. Soc. Japan*, vol. 15, Supplement S1, pp. 227–230, 1991.

[23] Y. Kumura, T. Kawano, T. Fujimoto, M. Gomi, and M. Abe, "Oxide Particulate Media for Magneto-Optical Recording," Proceedings IUMRS-ICAM'93 Symposium V, "Materials for Information Storage Media," Tokyo, *Trans. Mater. Res. Soc. Japan Ad. Mat.* '93 II B, Elsevier: North-Holland, pp. 1129–1134.

[24] M. Abe and M. Gomi, "Particulate Films for Magneto-Optical Recording I. Theory of the Magneto-Optical Effect," Proceedings of the International Symposium on Magneto-optics, *J. Magn. Soc. Japan*, vol. 15, Supplement S1, pp. 259–262, 1991.

[25] P. H. Lissberger and Saunders, "Optical and Magneto-Optical Properties of Thin Film Cermets," *Thin Solid Films*, vol. 34, pp. 323–333.

[26] M. Abe, "Effective dielectric tensor for composites with magnetic fine particles dispersed," Proceedings of the Magneto-optical Recording Symposium '94, Tokyo, *J. Magn. Soc. Japan*, vol. 19, Supplement S1, pp. 433–434, 1995.

[27] M. Abe, "Derivation of Non-Diagonal Effective Dielectric Permeability Tensors for Magnetized Granular Composites," 1998 to be submitted.

5.4 THE EUROPIUM CHALCOGENIDES

5.4.1 Introduction

The europium chalcogenides consist of the four europium compounds EuO, EuS, EuSe, and EuTe. These materials exhibit fundamentally interesting and unique properties. Some fundamental interest relates to the fact that this group contains several of the first ferromagnetic semiconductors ever discovered. Some practical interest relates to the fact that these compounds exhibit some of the largest magneto-optical effects ever observed. This interest relates back to earlier days when the prospect of creating a magneto-optical disk storage device using these materials was first envisioned and actively pursued.

A great deal of research and development has been done on the Eu chalcogenides. This review is not meant to be all-inclusive — in this short section we will review only a few of the highlights and we will focus our discussion mainly on the pure undoped chalcogenides. There are earlier reviews of these materials [1], [2], [3], [4], [5], [6] which emphasize the basic magnetic, electrical, and optical properties. These reviews usually do not extensively discuss thin films nor do they discuss device efforts using these films. In this section we will start with a description of some of the early work. Then we briefly review some bulk properties, including structural, magnetic, and optical. We give a basic description in terms of eigenmodes of magneto-optical effects including Faraday, Cotton–Mouton, and Kerr effects. We give examples of some of these effects measured in EuSe and EuS. We discuss work done on thin films of EuO and doped EuO. Finally, we describe some device work in which the first magneto-optical rotating disk device was made and tested.

5.4.2 Early Work

Interest in the Eu chalcogenides began when Matthias et al. [7] in 1961 found that EuO is ferromagnetic. Some of the magnetic and electrical properties were measured. It was found that EuO is a *ferromagnetic semiconductor* with a large magnetization (larger than that of iron or cobalt metal) with a Curie temperature of about 69 degrees Kelvin (K). Prior to the discovery of $CrBr_3$ in 1960, it was believed that all semiconductors and insulators with magnetic constituents were antiferromagnetic. EuO was the second ferromagnetic semiconductor to be discovered.

Not long after the discovery of the ferromagnetism of EuO, some magneto-optical measurements were made on a europium compound which is not a chalcogenide but which nevertheless contains divalent europium like the chalcogenides. This transparent ferromagnet, europium orthosilicate, Eu_2SiO_3, was found to exhibit large magneto-optical activity [8].

Soon after this, single crystals of EuSe became available and measurements were made of the Faraday rotation of these crystals [9]. The Faraday rotation is the rotation of the plane of polarization of plane polarized light after it has traversed through the crystal during application of a magnetic field. On one early crystal of EuSe it was found that the magnitude of this rotation was about 1500 degrees. In other words, by applying a large magnetic field to this crystal, the plane of polarization of the incident light was rotated 1500 degrees, or approximately four complete revolutions by the time the light exited the crystal. This may be compared with the Faraday rotation of less than 1° of today's most popular magneto-optical material, TbFe. Of course, we must hasten to note that the rotation of EuSe was measured at 4.2 K, whereas the Faraday rotation of TbFe is generally measured at room temperature.

EuO has a much higher Curie temperature than EuSe. As will be described later, by doping EuO one can achieve still higher Curie temperatures. However, the fact that, at least to this date, no one has succeeded in bringing the Curie temperature of these compounds above room temperature has been the single greatest obstacle to the use of these compounds in practical disk drive storage devices.

5.4.3 Structural and Magnetic Properties

In general, the europium ion exists in two different valence states: Eu^{2+}, and Eu^{3+}. It turns out that the trivalent form is non-magnetic, i.e., has no net magnetic moment. However, the divalent form, Eu^{2+}, has an $^8S_{7/2}$ ground state which exhibits a large

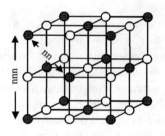

Figure 5.41 Sodium chloride crystal structure. Dark atoms are Eu, and light atoms are O, S, Se or Te.

magnetic moment. Europium oxide, EuO, has the simple ionic form $Eu^{2+}O^{2-}$. In other words, the two valence electrons of the europium atom transfer to the oxygen atom forming an ionic compound.

The crystal structure is the cubic NaCl rock salt structure shown in Figure 5.41. We note for future reference that the nearest neighbor Eu ions are on a $\langle 110 \rangle$ diagonal (nn in Fig. 5.41), and the next nearest neighbor Eu ions lie along a $\langle 100 \rangle$ direction (nnn direction in Fig. 5.41).

All the europium chalcogenides, EuO, EuS, EuSe, and EuTe, have the same crystal structure. Since the ionic size increases going from O to S to Se to Te, the lattice constant also increases as shown in Table 5.5 [1], [2]. These compounds are so ionic in nature, that the lattice constants of the compounds may be calculated quite readily from the ionic radii of the constituent ions. Table 5.5 also gives the density which decreases as the ions become more widely separated.

The Eu chalcogenides exhibit a variety of magnetic properties. EuO and EuS are ferromagnetic, EuSe is metamagnetic (shows several magnetic states), and EuTe is antiferromagnetic. The compound with the highest Curie temperature, or spontaneous magnetic ordering temperature, is EuO with a T_c of 69 K. This is just below the liquid nitrogen boiling temperature of 77 K. EuS has a ferromagnetic Curie temperature of 16 K. EuTe is antiferromagnetic with a Néel temperature, or antiferromagnetic ordering temperature, of 9.6 K. EuSe is something of a hybrid exhibiting ferromagnetism in high magnetic fields and ferrimagnetism and antiferromagnetism in low fields. Some of the magnetic properties are collected in Table 5.6. These compounds are strongly magnetic. For comparison, the saturation magnetizations $4\pi M$ of some common ferromagnetic metals like iron, cobalt, and nickel are 21,450 Gauss, 17,590 Gauss, and 6,080 Gauss, respectively.

The magnetic structure of EuTe was found from neutron diffraction experiments to be of the MnO kind with ferromagnetic (111) planes aligned in a NSNS spin structure [10]. This is a common form of antiferromagnetic spin orientation.

The spin structure of EuSe is more complicated. Figure 5.42 shows a spin structure phase diagram [11]. Temperature is given along the horizontal axis and applied mag-

TABLE 5.5 Crystallographic Properties [2]

Compound	Lattice Constant (A)	Density (g/cm³)
EuO	5.141	8.20
EuS	5.968	5.75
EuSe	6.195	6.44
EuTe	6.598	6.45

TABLE 5.6 Magnetic Properties [2]

	$4\pi M$ (Gauss)	T_c, T_N (K)	Magnetic Order	J_1 (K)	J_2 (K)
EuO	24,007	69	Ferro	$+0.6$	$+0.1$
EuS	15,346	16	Ferro	$+0.2$	-0.1
EuSe	13,720	4.6	Ferri, Anti	$+0.07$	-0.01
EuTe	11,356	9.6	Antiferro	$+0.04$	-0.15

netic field along the vertical axis. Above the magnetic ordering temperature of 4.6 K, the material does not show spontaneous magnetization, i.e., it is paramagnetic. Just below 4.6 K the material is antiferromagnetic below a field H_1. This critical field H_1 varies between 0 and several hundred oersteds depending on the temperature. At higher fields but below field H_2 EuSe is ferrimagnetic where spins are aligned antiparallel, but there is still a net spin or moment in the direction of the applied field. For fields higher than H_2, EuSe exhibits a ferromagnetic moment where all the spins are aligned in the direction of the applied field.

At temperatures below 1.8 K and below a critical field labeled H_3, the material is antiferromagnetic. The two areas where antiferromagnetism exists show different kinds of antiferromagnetism. The spin arrangement, although still antiferromagnetic, is different in the two cases.

This complex magnetic behavior of the europium chalcogenides may be conveniently thought of in terms of magnetic exchange coupling between neighboring Eu spins. J_1 is a measure of the exchange energy between nearest neighbor spins (nn in Figure 5.41), and J_2 is a measure of the exchange energy between next nearest neighbor spins (nnn in Fig. 5.41). A positive value of J_1 or J_2 means that the two spins in question tend

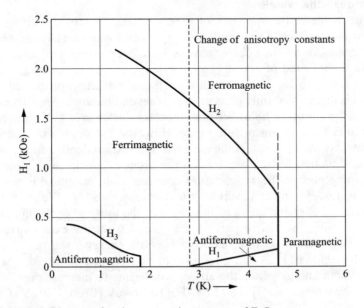

Figure 5.42 Diagram of various magnetic structures of EuSe.

to align parallel to each other and therefore the exchange is ferromagnetic. A negative value of J_1 or J_2 means that the spins tend to align antiparallel and the exchange is antiferromagnetic.

J_1 and J_2 values for the chalcogenides as determined from various experiments [12] are listed in Table 5.6. One sees that for EuO, both J_1 and J_2 are positive—all spins are expected to be aligned parallel with each other, and therefore EuO is expected to be ferromagnetic. With EuS the next nearest exchange, J_2, is negative; however, J_1 is larger and positive and dominates causing EuS to be also ferromagnetic.

For EuTe, negative exchange dominates and the material is antiferromagnetic. For EuSe, metamagnetic behavior is consistent with the observed exchange values.

5.4.4 Optical Properties

5.4.4.1 Optical Absorption

One of the striking optical properties of the Eu chalcogenides is the high transparency of these materials for certain optical wavelengths. We can measure optical absorption in terms of the absorption coefficient α, which is defined in terms of the light intensity I_0 incident upon a material of thickness t and the light intensity I exiting the material (neglecting reflections)

$$I = I_0 e^{-\alpha t} \tag{5.1}$$

From Equation (5.1), one sees that if the thickness is equal to the reciprocal of I, i.e., $It = 1$, then about one-third of the incident light is transmitted ($e^{-1} = 0.3678$).

For a sample of EuSe to be discussed later the absorption coefficient I was equal to $89 \, \text{cm}^{-1}$ in the deep red part of the visible spectrum (at 700 nm). This means that the thickness of material which would transmit about one-third of the incident light would equal 1/89 or about 0.01 cm. The actual sample thickness was 0.0157 cm so the magneto-optical effects illustrated were accompanied by substantial transmission of light through the sample.

The degree of transparency of these materials is strongly related to the stoichiometry of the samples. The sample just mentioned was an early sample. More recently, single crystals of all four chalcogenides have been grown [13] with absorption coefficients in the infrared of about $1 \, \text{cm}^{-1}$ or less.

For comparison, TbFe has an absorption coefficient in the red of about 700,000 cm^{-1}. This means that only films as thin as several hundred Angstroms will transmit an appreciable amount of light. We note that, for device use, TbFe is used in a reflectance mode rather than a transmission mode. However, the same general arguments apply—in reflectivity, the light enters the material to a certain depth and is reflected within this distance. This penetration depth is on the order of $1/\alpha$ in magnitude.

Turning now to the wavelength dependence of the optical properties, Figure 5.43 shows the absorption coefficient for the four materials [14]. We see that all four materials show an absorption going to near zero at the low end of the light energy spectrum. For orientation, the visible part of the optical spectrum extends from 2 eV to 3 eV, where 2 eV is visible red and 3 eV is visible blue; energy lower than 2 eV is the infrared. This is the region of high transparency that we have just discussed. The absorption edge is the incident energy where the absorption begins to increase rapidly. The absorption edge for these materials [1] is 1.12 eV (EuO), 1.64 eV (EuS), 1.80 eV (EuSe), and 2.00 eV (EuTe).

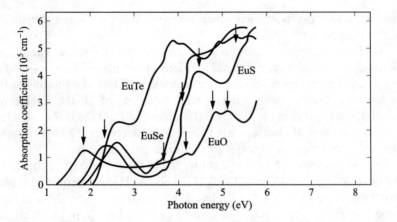

Figure 5.43 Absorption coefficient of europium chalcogenides at room temperature.

These measurements of optical absorption coefficient in undoped EuX show that the lowest energy peak corresponds to a high value of absorption coefficient—on the order of $100,000$ cm^{-1}. Therefore, these materials not only have regions where the optical absorption is very low and characteristic of insulators or semiconductors in the band gap, but also other regions where the absorption is more comparable to that of metals.

5.4.4.2 Band Structure

Identification of the optical transitions shown in Figure 5.43 by the development of a consistent band structure has been the subject of a great deal of effort by many people. One of these band structures for the four chalcogenides [2] is illustrated in Figure 5.44.

To explain this band structure, let us begin with the free atoms of oxygen and europium. The electronic structure of a free oxygen atom may be represented by

$$[He]2p^4 \tag{5.2}$$

where [He] represents the closed electron shells of the helium atom (2 1s electrons) and the outer shell is a partially filled 2p shell which contains four out of a maximum of six electrons.

The electronic structure of a free europium atom may be represented by

$$[Xe]4f^7 6s^2 5d^0 \tag{5.3}$$

where [Xe] represents the closed shells of the xenon atom. The 4f shell is half full containing seven out of a maximum of 14 electrons, and the 6s shell is full with two electrons. For future reference we have also shown an empty 5d shell.

When free Eu and O atoms are combined together to form EuO, an ionic compound is formed. The two outer 6s electrons of Eu transfer to the 2p shell of oxygen filling the 2p shell. Thus all shells are full (or empty), except for the half-full 4f shell of europium, and it is this 4f shell which is responsible for the magnetism of EuO and the other chalcogenides.

All the 4f electrons within each Eu ion have parallel spins. Therefore, in ferromagnetic EuO, the saturation magnetic moment of the material corresponds to the sum of these seven 4f electrons on each Eu ion summed over all the Eu ions of the material. At very low temperature, where the 4f spin moments of all the Eu atoms are lined up parallel, these spins sum up to the total moment of EuO (24,007 G, Table 5.6). It should be noted that these 4f electrons are buried quite deeply in the europium ion and are not perturbed very much by changes in the outer electron shells.

Looking at Figure 5.44, for EuO we see in the lower part of the picture the full $2p^6$ band of the oxygen and the half-full $4f^7$ levels. At higher energy are some empty bands. When light is incident on the material, electrons from the 2p and the 4f bands are excited to these empty bands. The optical energy of the light at which these transitions are excited corresponds to the peaks in absorption shown in Figure 5.43.

We have already noted that europium in EuO has an empty 6s shell, and also an empty 5d shell. These two shells are quite similar in energy. These outer 5d and 6s shells make up the unoccupied upper energy states shown in Figure 5.44. In contrast to the 4f shell which remains unperturbed and atomic in nature, the 5d and 6s shells are modified during compound formation. The 5d shell is split into two bands, a t_{2g} and an e_g band, as shown in the figure. This is caused by crystal field splitting which is due to interaction of the outer 5d electrons with the electric field of the oxygen ions. The 6s shell is perturbed even more by compound formation and it spreads out into a wide band as shown.

A number of experiments have gone into the determination of this structure, and the reader is referred to earlier review articles for the details [15]. In essence, the two major transitions at lower energy in Figure 5.43 may be identified as $4f^7$ to 5d transi-

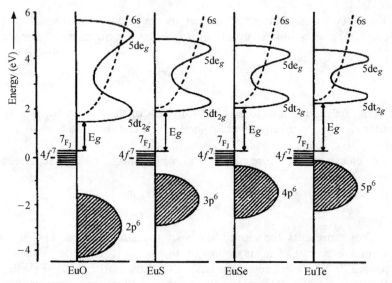

Figure 5.44 Electronic structure of the europium chalcogenides mapped as energy E
on the vertical axis vs. density of electronic states $\Psi(E)$ on the horizontal
axis.

tions. The lowest optical transition is a transition from the $4f^7$ band to the lowest of the crystal field split 5d level, the $5dt_{2g}$ band. The second lowest large absorption peak in Figure 5.43 corresponds to transitions from the $4f^7$ band to the upper 5d band, the $5de_g$ band.

As will be discussed in the section on magneto-optical properties, Faraday rotation measurements on single crystals over a wide wavelength range have suggested that two additional major transitions in this spectrum may be identified as being transitions between 2p and 5d bands ($2p^6$ to $5dt_{2g}$, and $2p^6$ to $5de_g$) [16].

5.4.4.3 Red Shift

We have already noted that EuO has an absorption edge in the near infrared, and for shorter wavelengths the material becomes highly transparent. It was discovered by Busch and co-workers [17] that the location in optical energy of this absorption edge was a strong function of temperature. Most insulators *on cooling* show a small shift of the band edge toward higher optical energy (a blue shift). The europium chalcogenides do show a blue shift above the ordering temperature. Below the ordering temperature the ferromagnetic or ferrimagnetic chalcogenides show a shift of the absorption edge toward the red. Thus, the name "magnetic red shift."

An example of measurements of this red shift is shown in 5.45 [18]. In the case of EuO, just above the Curie temperature, the band gap is about 1.17 eV. At temperatures much lower than this the band gap has decreased by approximately 0.24 eV. Therefore, the band gap has decreased by over 20%. The reason why the band gap behaves this way has been a subject of considerable discussion. It is rather generally agreed that as

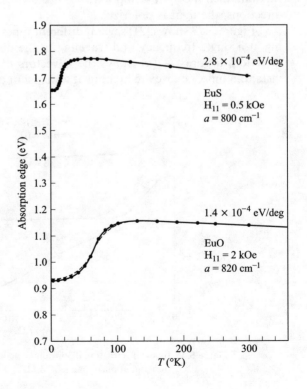

Figure 5.45 Magnetic red shift in single crystals of EuO and EuS.

discussed above, the optical transition involved is a 4f to $5dt_{2g}$ transition. The red shift appears to be caused by splitting of the $5dt_{2g}$ band by exchange into two bands (not shown in Figure 5.44) which move apart as the temperature cools [19]. The lowering of the lower t_{2g} sub-band thus reduces the energy gap, $4f^7$ to $5dt_{2g}$, in Figure 5.44.

Accompanying this red shift in absorption, is also a red shift in index of refraction [20], Figure 5.46. For EuO, the change in index of refraction upon application of a field is seen from the figure to be about 0.05. This has implied practical applications in the areas of optical beam deflection and modulation.

5.4.5 Magneto-Optical Properties

In preparation for a later discussion of various magneto-optical effects observed in the Eu chalcogenides, this section will present a description of the Faraday, Kerr, and Cotton-Mouton effects in terms of eigenmodes. This will allow one to understand the conditions under which these effects are observed and the relations between them.

5.4.5.1 Basic Description

Polarization. Let's begin by discussing some properties of polarized light. Light may be described in terms of electromagnetic waves whose vibration directions are perpendicular to the direction of propagation of the waves. Although each wave consists of an electric field vector **E** and a magnetic field vector **H**, we will refer only to the vibration direction of the electric field; this is in agreement with convention as well as being reasonable since the **E** field plays the dominant role in magneto-optical effects. If the vibration directions in the plane perpendicular to the direction of propagation are random, then the light is unpolarized. If the vibrations are limited to specific transverse directions, the light is polarized.

Figure 5.47 shows [21] several different types of polarization of a light wave vibrating at a single frequency and traveling in the direction of the z-axis, the propagation direction. Figure 5.47(*a*) shows the **E** vectors of a *linearly* polarized wave at a single instant in time, i.e., we are looking at a snapshot of the wave. Each vector represents the

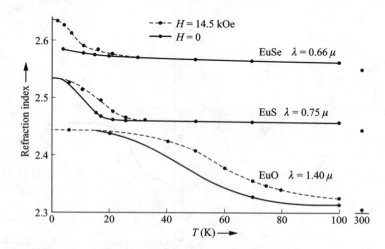

Figure 5.46 Index of refraction of europium chalcogenides as a function of temperature and applied magnetic field.

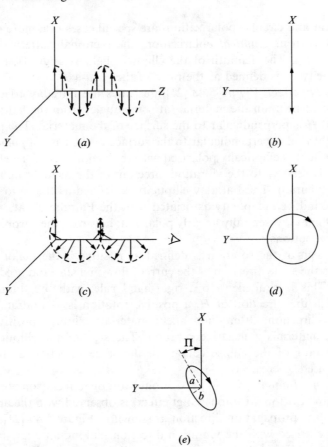

Figure 5.47 A linearly polarized wave as it appears (*a*) at a particular instant in time, and (*b*) as it appears at a particular position on the *z*-axis looking back toward the wave. Similarly, a right circularly polarized wave is depicted in (*c*) and (*d*), and an elliptically polarized wave is shown in (*e*).

magnitude and direction of the electric field **E** at various points along the *z*-axis. As time goes on, this entire wave pattern moves as a whole to the right. This wave vibrates in the *xz*-plane and is said to be linearly polarized in the *x* direction. We may have a wave linearly polarized in any other direction normal to the *z*-axis.

Figure 5.47(*b*) is a sectional pattern of the wave shown in Figure 5.47(*a*). This pattern is observed by an observer sitting a long way out on the *z*-axis and looking back toward the light source.

Figure 5.47(*c*) and (*d*) depicts *circularly* polarized light. Here, the arrowheads of the *E* vectors form a right-handed helix similar to the thread on a typical machine screw. We define this as right-handed circularly polarized light. The sectional pattern of circularly polarized light [Fig. 5.47(*d*)] consists of a circle whose sense of rotation is determined by imagining the helix to be translated (without rotation) toward our observer and noting the rotation of the point of intersection of the helix with a fixed plane perpendicular to the *z*-axis.

Linear and circular polarizations are special cases of a more general type of polarization known as *elliptical* polarization, the sectional pattern of which is shown in Figure 5.47(*e*). The azimuth of the elliptical light is angle Π, and the magnitude of the ellipticity *M* is defined as the ratio of the semi-axes *b/a*.

Faraday effect. Figure 5.48 [21] illustrates the Faraday effect. Linearly polarized light is incident upon the material (at some angle) from the left and the applied magnetic field *H* is perpendicular to the surface of the material. The propagation direction of the light is also perpendicular to the surface in the case of *polar* Faraday effect. The emergent light is elliptically polarized with the major axis of the ellipse rotated through an angle Π relative to the vibration direction of the incident light. The angle Π is the Faraday rotation. The Faraday ellipticity is defined as the ratio of the semi-axes *b/a*. Often the induced ellipticity associated with the Faraday rotation is so small that the emergent light is essentially linearly polarized; however, the europium chalcogenides are notable exceptions.

The sign of the rotation is defined as positive if the major axis of the ellipse is rotated in the same direction as the current flow in a solenoid used to create the applied field *H*. This is equivalent to a right-hand rule: with the thumb of the right hand pointing in the direction of *H*, a positive rotation is a rotation of the major axis in the finger direction. Often diamagnetic materials exhibit a positive rotation and paramagnetic materials a negative rotation. The sign of the ellipticity is positive if the electric vector of the ellipse rotates in the same direction as the current flow in a solenoid used to create *H*.

Cotton–Mouton effect. The Cotton–Mouton effect (sometimes called the Voigt effect or the Cotton–Mouton–Voigt effect) is observed with the applied field *H perpendicular* to the propagation direction as shown in Figure 5.49 [21]. The incident light is linearly polarized with the vibration direction making an angle of 45 degrees with *H*. Similar to the Faraday effect, the emergent light is elliptically polarized with the major axis of the ellipse rotated through an angle Π. In this case, however, the dominant effect is the ellipticity rather than the rotation of the major axis of the ellipse. The Cotton–Mouton effect in solid materials is generally much smaller than the Faraday effect and, therefore, only a few measurements exist of this effect in magnetic materials.

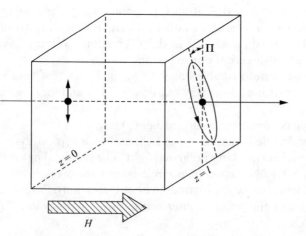

Figure 5.48 Polar Faraday rotation and ellipticity (the signs are both positive as shown).

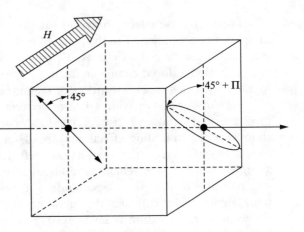

Figure 5.49 Cotton–Mouton ellipticity and rotation.

Kerr effect. When linearly polarized light is incident upon the surface of a magnetic material, the reflected light in most cases is elliptically polarized with the major axis of the ellipse rotated through some angle Π from the vibration direction of the incident beam. The portion of this ellipticity and rotation which is induced by the magnetization of the material is known as the Kerr magneto-optical effect. The Kerr effect is classified as polar, longitudinal, or transverse depending on the direction of the magnetization relative to the surface and the plane of incidence.

The polar Kerr effect is illustrated in Figure 5.50(a) [21]—the magnetization is perpendicular to the surface. The plane of incidence is defined as the plane containing the incident and reflected light paths. E_s and E_p are the vibration directions of the components of the incident light beam which are perpendicular and parallel to the plane of incidence. Usually, the incident light is linearly polarized of either E_p or E_s type. The polar Kerr effect is measured with the angle of incidence ϕ equal to zero. The polar Kerr effect usually gives the largest rotation of the three types.

The longitudinal Kerr effect has the magnetization in both the plane of the surface and the plane of incidence, Figure 5.50(b). Maximum Kerr rotation is observed for intermediate values of ϕ (about 60 degrees), and the observed rotations here are typically three to five times smaller than those observed for the polar effect. However, because of the large demagnetizing factor inherent to the thin films usually required for practical devices, a large external field must be applied for saturation in the polar effect (e.g., about 10 kOe for Permalloy) but not in the longitudinal effect (about 2 Oe for Permalloy).

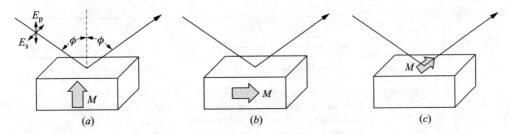

Figure 5.50 Kerr effect—(a) polar, (b) longitudinal, and (c) transverse.

The transverse effect, shown in Figure 5.50(c), is where M is in the plane of the sample and perpendicular to the plane of incidence. This effect behaves quite differently from all of the preceding effects. E_p light is not rotated but only undergoes a small magnetization induced change in intensity upon reflection. E_s light undergoes a change in intensity which is several orders of magnitude smaller than the change for E_p light.

Eigenmodes. To provide a bridge between the experimental observations and the preceding description, we discuss eigenmodes or normal modes of vibration. We wish to show that the preceding effects may be described in terms of the velocity (index of refraction) and attenuation (extinction coefficient) of eigenmodes and that these effects are interrelated by the velocity and attenuation parameters.

In magneto-optics, an eigenmode is a mode of polarization (e.g., vertical linear, right circular, elliptical) such that upon passage of the light beam through the material the *mode* of polarization is unchanged. For example, Figure 5.48 shows that for the Faraday effect, linearly polarized light incident upon the crystal emerges as elliptically polarized light, and therefore linearly polarized light is not an eigenmode. It turns out that right circularly polarized light (**R**) and left circularly polarized light (**L**) are the two eigenmodes for the Faraday effect.

One may represent linearly polarized light as the superposition of two circularly polarized beams of light, one right-hand polarized (**R**) and one left-hand polarized (**L**). The dotted vectors of Figure 5.51 [21] represent the amplitude of **R** and **L** electric

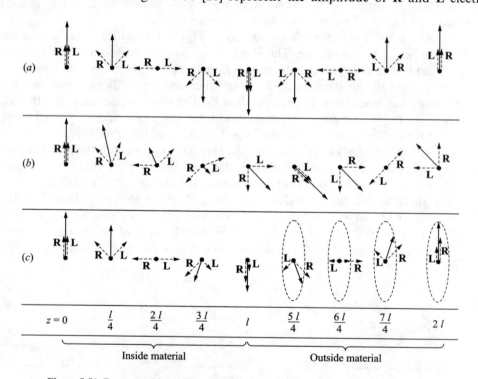

Figure 5.51 Decomposition of linearly polarized light into right circularly polarized light (**R**) and left circularly polarized light (**L**). **R** and **L** travel through the material (*a*) with equal velocities and no attenuation, (*b*) with unequal velocities and no attenuation, and (*c*) with equal velocities and unequal attenuation.

vectors for the Faraday effect [see also Fig. 5.47(c) and 5.47(d)]. The solid vector is the resultant or sum of the **R** and **L** vectors. All the vectors in Figure 5.51 represent vibration amplitude at the same instant in time. Each vector diagram corresponds to a particular position along the z-axis; $z = 0$ and $z = 1$ are the faces of the material as in Figure 5.48.

The simplest case is illustrated in Figure 5.51(a) in which it is postulated that **R** and **L** both travel through the material at the velocity of light in free space and suffer no attenuation. Arbitrarily, at $z = 0$, **R** and **L** are vertical and the wavelength of the light has been chosen as $2l$. At $z = 1/4$, **R** and **L** are rotated in opposite directions through the same angle and unattenuated, and the resultant is shortened but not rotated. Following the diagrams through successive values of z one sees that the emergent light is still linearly polarized and is not rotated; i.e., as expected, the incident light is unaffected by the material.

Now suppose that the velocity of **R** and **L** are not equal in the material. This is the case sketched in Figure 5.51(b). In this case the resultant electric vector is rotated by the material away from its $z = 0$ position; and at $z = 1$ this rotation, the Faraday rotation, is 45 degrees. The ellipticity is zero.

We may make this quantitative by letting the velocity of the **R** and **L** waves be v_r and v_l, respectively. Then, since the index of refraction of the material is the velocity of light in free space c divided by the wave velocity, we may write the indices of refraction of left- and right-hand circular light as

$$n_r = \frac{c}{v_r} \qquad n_l = \frac{c}{v_l} \tag{5.4}$$

It may be shown that the magnitude of the Faraday rotation angle (in radians) is just proportional to the *difference in indices of refraction* of **R** and **L** [22]

$$\theta = \pi \frac{l}{\lambda_0} \Delta n_F \tag{5.5}$$

where $\Delta n_F = n_r - n_l$, λ_0 is the wavelength in vacuum and l is the sample thickness.

Now let us suppose that the velocity of **R** and **L** are equal in the material, e.g., $\Delta n_F = 0$. However, suppose that **L** is attenuated or absorbed compared to **R**. This case is shown in Figure 5.51(c) where **R** rotates without attenuation but **L** is gradually absorbed by the material. We note that at $z = 1$ the resultant in Figure 5.51(c) is very similar to the resultant in Figure 5.51(a) but the unequal length of **R** and **L** causes the resultant emerging light to be elliptically polarized. The major axis of the emerging elliptical light, however, is not rotated. Therefore, we may describe the ellipticity inherent in the Faraday effect in terms of a difference in absorption between **R** and **L**.

The extinction coefficient k is related to the absorption coefficient α defined earlier by

$$k = \left(\frac{\lambda_0}{4\pi}\right)\alpha \tag{5.6}$$

If we represent the extinction coefficients of **R** and **L** by k_r and k_l, it may be shown that the Faraday ellipticity is given by

$$\varepsilon_F = \tanh\left(\pi\frac{l}{\lambda_0}\Delta k_F\right) \tag{5.7}$$

where $\Delta k_F = k_r - k_l$ and l is the sample thickness. Instead of measuring M_F directly, one may measure the absorption coefficients I_r and I_l, and obtain M_F from the preceding two equations. Materials for which I_r is not equal to I_l are said to exhibit circular dichroism.

The Cotton–Mouton effect may be described in a similar manner. The principal difference is that the two eigenmodes are linearly polarized light polarized parallel and perpendicular to the applied external field. With the incident light polarized at 45° to H, as shown in Figure 5.49, the incident light may be decomposed into the two linear eigenmodes—one parallel and one perpendicular to the field. We may define an index of refraction for the perpendicular eigenmode, $n_\perp$, and for the parallel eigenmode $n_\parallel$. The applied field induces a difference in indices, $\Delta_{CM} = n_\perp - n_\parallel$ which causes an ellipticity in the emergent beam. Rather than the ellipticity, the Cotton–Mouton effect is often specified in terms of the field-induced phase difference δ between the two eigenmodes. This phase difference is related to the difference in indices of refraction by

$$\delta_{CM} = 2\pi\frac{l}{\lambda_0}\Delta n_{CM} \tag{5.8}$$

The ellipticity is given by

$$\varepsilon_{CM} = \tan\left(\frac{\delta_{CM}}{2}\right) \tag{5.9}$$

A rotation of the major axis of the ellipse of the emergent light is caused by the differential absorption of the two eigenmodes, and is given by

$$\theta_{CM} = \frac{\pi}{4} - \tan^{-1}\exp\left(-2\pi\frac{l}{\lambda_0}\Delta k_{cm}\right) \tag{5.10}$$

where $\Delta k_{CM} = k_\perp - k_\parallel$. Materials for which Δk_{CM} is not equal to zero may be said to exhibit linear dichroism.

Kerr Effect. The polar Kerr rotation may be expressed in terms of these same quantities by

$$\theta_K = \frac{A(\Delta k_F) - B(\Delta n_F)}{A^2 + B^2} \tag{5.11}$$

and the associated ellipticity by

$$\varepsilon_K = \frac{-A(n_F) - B(\Delta k_F)}{A^2 + B^2} \tag{5.12}$$

where A and B are given by

$$A = n_r n_l - k_r k_l - 1 \tag{5.13}$$

$$B = n_1 k_r + n_r k_1 \tag{5.14}$$

Thus, the Faraday, Cotton–Mouton, and polar Kerr effects may all be described in terms of four quantities: the field-induced birefringence, Δn_F and Δn_{CM}, and the field induced dichroism, Δk_F and Δk_{CM}. These quantities are not all unrelated. For example, if one knows the wavelength dependence of Faraday rotation over a very wide region, one can use a Kramers–Kramer type relation to calculate the Faraday ellipticity from the rotation data [22]. A calculation and comparison with experiment of the longitudinal Kerr effect determined from data of Faraday rotation and ellipticity data has also been made [30].

For a theoretical treatment of Δn_F and Δk_F in terms of the atomic properties of a ferromagnetic material, see Freiser [23].

5.4.5.2 EuSe

Soon after single crystals of EuSe became available, measurements were made of their Faraday rotation [24]. An example of this data is shown in Figure 5.52. This figure shows the rotation of the plane of polarization on exiting the sample as a function of applied magnetic field. For this sample the rotation of the incident light was 1500 degrees, approximately four complete revolutions. Thus, for example, one had to increase the field carefully during the measurement in order to be sure one or more complete 360 degree revolutions was not missed.

The field dependence shows a kink in the curve at low fields which corresponds to the change in magnetic phase of EuSe at the field labeled H_1 in Figure 5.52. The magnitude of this critical field in Figure 5.52 is much larger than what is shown in Figure 5.52 because of the large demagnetizing field which must be overcome to magnetize a sample with this geometry. When the rotation data are plotted against magnetization instead of applied field, the rotation is found to be linearly dependent on magnetization.

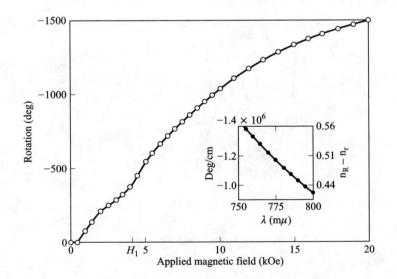

Figure 5.52 Faraday rotation of EuSe single crystal (thickness 157 microns) at 4.2 K.

Magneto-optical measurements are extremely sensitive to the optical wavelength chosen for the measurements. Figure 5.53 shows some absorption measurements made on chalcogenide films spanning a wavelength range of interest for device applications [25]. By comparing Figure 5.53 with Figure 5.43, one can see an example of how film data compares with bulk data. The peak illustrated here is the $4f5dt_{2g}$ transition discussed earlier with regard to the band structure diagram of Figure 5.44. Since these curves are not corrected for reflection losses, values of absorption coefficient lower than about $3 \times 10^4 \, cm^{-1}$ are unreliable, e.g., the low-lying peak in absorption at 800 nm for the EuSe film is not observed in the bulk crystalline data of Figure 5.43.

The measurements of Faraday rotation shown in Figure 5.52 were made at a wavelength of 800 nm. As seen in Figure 5.53, this wavelength is far removed from the absorption peak for EuSe. The wavelength dependence over a short wavelength range is shown in the insert of Figure 5.52, showing a rapid increase as one approaches the absorption peak. Due to this strong absorption, even very thin crystals could not be measured at wavelengths shorter than about 600 mμ. Also shown in Figure 5.52 is the circular birefringence Δn_F calculated from Equation (5.5).

One method of comparing materials is in terms of saturation rotation per decibel (db) of optical absorption. At 755 nm, the absorption coefficient for this sample of EuSe is 45 cm^{-1} after correction for reflection losses. (At 20 kOe for this sample the magnetization is approximately 83% of saturation.) The saturation rotation of EuSe is then 850 deg/db. This may be compared with 800 deg/db for YIG ($\lambda = 1.2 \, \mu$) [26], 30 deg/db for CrBr$_3$ ($\lambda = 493$ nm) [27], and 0.7 deg/db ($\lambda = 1 \, \mu$) for iron.

We may note that attempting to measure Faraday rotation at shorter wavelengths in single crystals is difficult not only because of increased absorption but also because of variations in sample thickness. For example, a 5% variation in sample thickness will cause a variation in rotation of 75 degrees across the sample (at 20 kOe and 800 nm) which will almost completely depolarize the light.

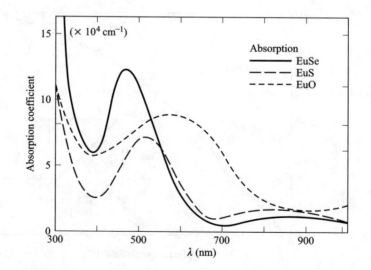

Figure 5.53 Absorption of Eu chalcogenide evaporated films.

The experimental dependence of the Cotton–Mouton phase difference upon H is plotted in Figure 5.54 along with corresponding values of $\Delta n_{CM} = n_{\perp} - n_{\parallel}$, calculated from Equation (5.8) [28]. For H approximately equal to 2 kOe, the phase difference is hard to measure because the light is largely depolarized. The bump in the curve due to the magnetic phase change occurs at a much smaller field here than for the Faraday effect because the demagnetizing field is much smaller for this geometry. It may be seen that at these wavelengths the linear birefringence Δn_{CM} is much smaller than the circular birefringence for the case of Faraday rotation.

Figure 5.55 shows the absorption coefficients (α_r and α_l) for right and left circularly polarized light at wavelengths 680, 700, and 800 nm vs. the magnetic field H for EuSe [29]. The field H is applied parallel to the direction of light propagation and normal to the crystal plate. These absorption data are not corrected for reflection losses. We note that EuSe exhibits three distinct regions of optical behavior which seem to correlate with the three types of spin configuration illustrated in Figure 5.42.

The magnetic linear dichroism of EuSe is shown in Figure 5.56 which gives the absorption coefficients for light of wavelengths 680, 700, and 800 nm propagating normal to the plane of the specimen while the applied field lies in the plane of the specimen. The curves labeled $\alpha_{\parallel}$ and $\alpha_{\perp}$ refer to the plane of polarization of the incident light being parallel and perpendicular, respectively, to the field. The structure at low fields again appears to reflect the transitions between magnetic phases, but the critical applied fields are again much smaller than in the Faraday geometry case because of smaller demagnetization. The regions of characteristic behavior appear at about the same internal fields as may be noted from the top scale in the two figures.

With increasing wavelength of the incident light the dichroism diminishes rapidly. Figure 5.57 gives the variation with wavelength of the absorption coefficients α_r, α_l, $\alpha_{\parallel}$, and $\alpha_{\perp}$ measured in an applied field of 15 kOe [29]. The absorption coefficient in zero field for unpolarized light $\alpha(0)$ is also given for 292 K (room temperature), 77 K, and 4.2 K. All curves are normalized to the room temperature absorption at 800 nm.

In the paramagnetic temperature region the absorption curve shifts toward shorter wavelengths with decreasing temperature as observed for other (nonmagnetic)

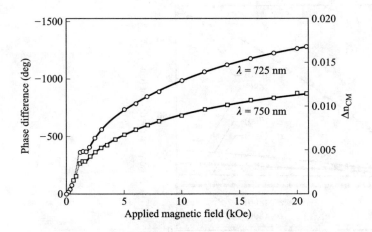

Figure 5.54 Cotton–Mouton phase difference and birefringence of EuSe single crystal (157 microns thick) at 4.2 K.

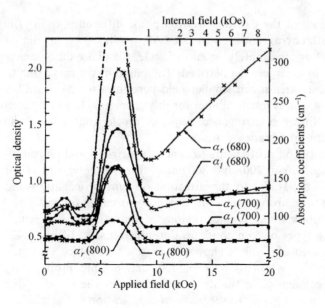

Figure 5.55 Magnetic circular dichroism of EuSe single crystal (157 microns) at 4.2 K.

materials. (Compare $\alpha(0)$ at 292 K with $\alpha(0)$ at 77 K.) However, the curve of $\alpha(0)$ at 4.2 K shows that in the temperature region of spin ordering a reverse shift (to longer wavelengths with decreasing temperature) occurs in agreement with observations of red shift described earlier.

It is noteworthy that Figure 5.57 [28] shows a large red shift of all 4.2 K absorption curves toward longer wavelengths when the field becomes large enough to produce the ferromagnetic phase. For right circularly polarized light the shift in the absorption curve at 4.2 K produced by an applied field of 15 kOe (an internal field of about 5

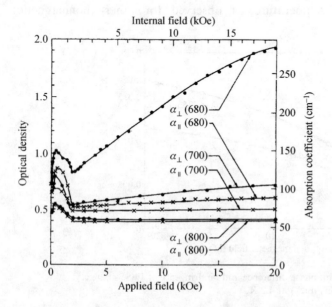

Figure 5.56 Magnetic linear dichroism of EuSe single crystal (157 microns) at 4.2 K.

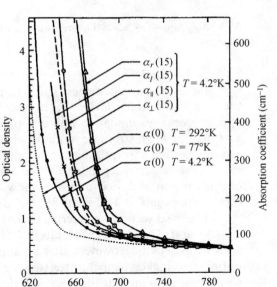

Figure 5.57 Absorption edge of EuSe single crystal (157 microns thick). $\alpha(15)$ is data taken at 15 kOe field, and $\alpha(0)$ is data taken at zero field.

kOe) is close to 1000 cm^{-1}. The exchange splitting inferred from T_c of the $(4f^7)^8S$ *ground* state of Eu^{++} is for EuSe only of the order of 10 cm^{-1} and for EuO, of the order of 100 cm$^{-1.}$ Therefore, the splitting of the *excited* states rather than the ground states must be responsible for the absorption shift in agreement with an exchange splitting of the $5dt_{2g}$ band postulated to explain the observed magnetic red shift.

5.4.5.3 EuS

An example of magneto-optical effects in EuS is shown in Figure 5.58 [30]. The Faraday rotation and dichroism is illustrated over a wide wavelength range. The circular dichroism was calculated from the rotation data. The maximum Faraday rotation in the visible red at 2.1 eV is 2×10^6 deg/cm, and the maximum rotation in the ultraviolet at 4.3 eV is 2.7×10^6 deg/cm. An analysis of this data was done by the authors in terms of line shapes which tends to confirm the assignment of the optical transitions in terms of the band structure of Figure 5.44. The two highest peaks in rotation are due to

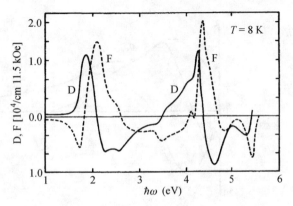

Figure 5.58 Spectral dependence of the circular dichroism (D) and the Faraday rotation (F) of EuS at 8 K.

$4f \rightarrow 5dt_{2g}$ and $4f \rightarrow 5de_g$. The remaining major transitions are from the 3p band to the 5d band.

5.4.5.4 EuO

Since EuO has the highest Curie temperature of all the chalcogenides, it claimed the most attention for device related research. In broad outline, EuO exhibits magneto-optical properties similar to EuS and (ferromagnetic) EuSe. One can see from Figure 5.44 that the band structure of all the chalcogenides are similar. From Figure 5.43 one can see that the absorption curves of all the chalcogenides are broadly similar.

The wavelength dependence of the Faraday rotation and ellipticity of an EuO film over the region of device interest is shown in Figure 5.59 [30]. The maximum Faraday rotation/thickness at 1.55 eV is 850,000 deg/cm for this film.

In the next section we describe some device work in which the light source used was a GaAs laser. The GaAs laser emits at 1.46 eV. Figure 5.59 shows that θ_F is near a peak at this wavelength. However, after an approximately 0.2 eV red shift of this curve on warming to higher temperatures (toward the blue on warming) the zero crossing of rotation will end up near the GaAs wavelength. It may be shown that one may use both the rotation and ellipticity for signal output [31]. In this case the total signal is shown in Figure 5.59 as θ_{total}. In this case one sees that ample signal is available over a wide range of wavelengths even under the conditions of shifting curves due to temperature. The method of using both rotation and ellipticity is applicable to today's storage devices which operate at room temperature.

While there is more than adequate magneto-optical activity in EuO at a few degrees Kelvin, for device application a practical device must operate at much higher temperatures. Therefore, for device work a major shortfall of EuO was the fact that its Curie temperature (69 K) was below the boiling point of liquid nitrogen (77 K). Additional concerns about EuO as a device material related to coercivity and remanence.

One clue to raising the Curie temperature was an early discovery which showed that the Curie temperature of EuSe could be raised by a factor of three by doping with gadolinium [32]. Doping EuSe with a trivalent rare earth such as Gd^{+++} essentially adds a d electron to the previously empty d band so that exchange between the f electrons of the Eu^{++} is enhanced by an additional f to d exchange. Attempts to raise the Curie temperature of EuO were made first with bulk samples by reacting EuO with excess Eu and trivalent rare earth oxides [33]. By doing this the Curie

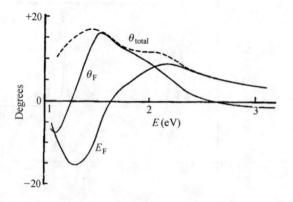

Figure 5.59 Faraday rotation θ_F, Faraday ellipticity E_F, and total rotation θ_{total} for an EuO film. Temperature = 5 K and film thickness = 1890 Å.

temperature was raised to about 135 K. However, in these cases the remanent rotation at 77 K was not as large as desired. Shortly afterward, similar results were reported for films [34].

Then, it was discovered by K. Ahn that doping EuO films with iron not only raised the Curie temperature, but also maintained square loops desired for device application at 77 K [35], [36]. An example of the temperature dependence of the rotation is shown in Figure 5.60 [37]. One sees that very substantial remanent rotation ($2\phi_R$) exists well above liquid nitrogen temperature. These films had somewhat modest coercive force (about 17 Oe). It was shown later that by doping EuO with both iron and gadolinium [38] one could increase the coercivity without degrading other properties.

As a final example using EuO, we wish to show the effect of combining the polar Kerr effect of EuO with an optical interference surface to enhance the Kerr rotation and ellipticity [39]. The process was to deposit a silver film on a glass substrate followed by an EuO film. The composition of the EuO film was adjusted to give the Curie temperature of bulk EuO. Polar Kerr measurements made on single crystals of EuO gave a maximum Kerr rotation of 6 degrees (at a wavelength of 600 microns). Figure 5.61 shows that a Kerr rotation as high as 70 degrees may be obtained with this film composition and geometry. The Kerr ellipticity and the reflectivity of the combination film are also shown. By combining reflections from multiple surfaces in a Kerr effect geometry one may substantially enhance the Kerr rotation of EuO.

There are number of other interesting applications of magneto-optical effects in EuO which will not be described in this work. Several that have been reported include fabrication of magnetic holograms in EuO [40] and the diffraction of light by magnetic domains in EuO and EuS [41].

5.4.6 Magneto-Optical Storage Device

In discussions of today's inductive and magneto-resistive disk drives one often sees a reference to the first disk drive ever built, the **IBM RAMAC** (Random Access Method of Accounting and Control). This drive was built in 1957. The motivation for such reference is to give some perspective on the remarkable progress made in disk drives over the past relatively few years. In this same spirit, I conclude this chapter with a brief description of the first magneto-optical drive, built in 1973.

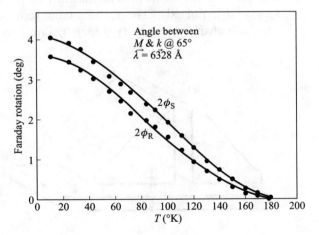

Figure 5.60 Faraday rotation of a 170-nm thick film of iron doped EuO. The ϕ_s is the saturation Faraday rotation for $H = 400$ Oe, and ϕ_r is the remanent rotation. The angle of incidence of the light is 65°.

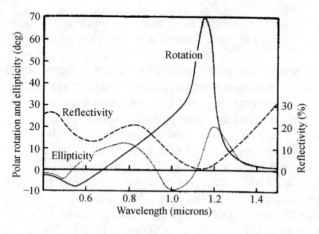

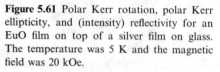

Figure 5.61 Polar Kerr rotation, polar Kerr ellipticity, and (intensity) reflectivity for an EuO film on top of a silver film on glass. The temperature was 5 K and the magnetic field was 20 kOe.

Magneto-optical recording offers some distinct advantages over conventional magnetic recording. These advantages are largely in the reduction or elimination of problems in the head-film region.

Figure 5.62 gives a head-film schematic showing some of the important parameters in magnetic recording. The head gap is given as g, the film thickness by D, and the flying height by d. It may be shown for conventional inductive recording that the smallest recorded bit length (L) is given by [42]

$$L = 2\sqrt{g^2 + (d + a)(d + a + D)} \qquad (5.15)$$

where a is the transition parameter given by the film characteristics $a = 2MD/H_c$, M being the film magnetization, and H_c is the coercive force.

It turns out that all of the parameters in Equation (5.15) are similar in magnitude. One must reduce all the parameters to reduce L significantly. In 1973, typical gap size g was about 2 microns. (Today the gap on thin film heads is typically 0.4–0.6 microns.)

One important justification for an optical memory is that many of these mechanical tolerance problems are eliminated. For example, the head gap g and head to film spacing d do not exist. The attendant and serious problems of head wear and film wear are eliminated and reliability is thereby improved. The film corrosion problem and the

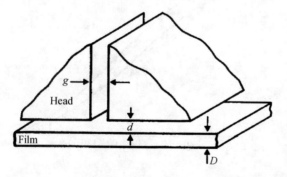

Figure 5.62 Schematic of a magnetic recording film-head geometry.

surface smoothness problem are reduced. Of course, in place of these problems, other problems may appear such as depth of focus.

To determine what some of these new problems might be, a magneto-optical disk file was proposed [43] and constructed [44]. This file used the Faraday effect with iron doped EuO as the magneto-optical material. The spinning disk with film was cooled to liquid nitrogen temperature. The light source was the GaAs laser (Fig. 5.63). With regard to the laser, in those days cooling of the disk was an advantage since the GaAs laser did not operate at room temperature! The laser and the disk were both cooled to liquid nitrogen temperature.

The GaAs laser supplies optical energy for both writing and reading. The laser output is quite divergent so that lenses are required to focus the laser junction onto the film surface. Writing information on the film is accomplished by pulsing the laser at the same time a magnetic bias field is applied to the film. The laser intensity must be sufficient to locally heat the film to a temperature such that the coercive force of the film is reduced below the level of bias field. This allows the magnetization of a localized region to line up parallel to the bias field during heating, and remain in this state after cooling. Light transmitted by the film is collected by a lens and focused on a differential detection system.

A design for the physical system including refrigeration is shown in Figure 5.64. The 3 in. diameter disk rotates in an atmosphere of helium gas used for heat transfer. The disk drive consists of a motor with the rotor at 77 K in the exchange gas, while the stator is outside at room temperature. The refrigerator is an electrically driven mechanical device available commercially. Its only mechanical connection with the system is to provide a cold surface to condense gaseous nitrogen from boil-off back to liquid

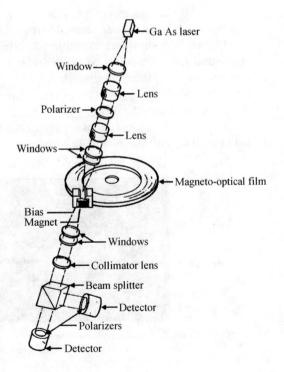

Figure 5.63 The optics of a magneto-optical disk file device.

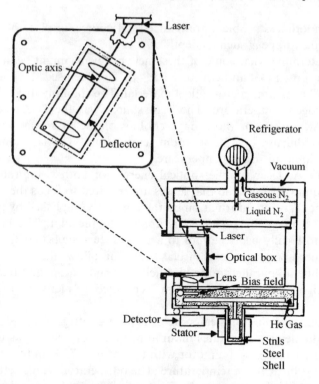

Figure 5.64 The mechanical arrangement of the cryogenic disk system [43].

nitrogen. This arrangement provides a liquid nitrogen bath which will keep the disk cool for some time in the event of refrigerator or power failure.

Figure 5.65 shows an example of system readout signal measured by Brown [45]. The signal (peak-to-peak) to noise (rms) is about 25 to 1. The bit size is 200 square microns. The amplifier bandwidth is 5 Mhz, and the data rate is about 2 Mb/s. The bits are approximately 10 microns apart. Also shown in Figure 5.65 is the output signal after threshold detection.

Figure 5.66 presents some results of a noise analysis by Brown for the cryogenic disk file. The circles show measured values of noise which are seen to be in good

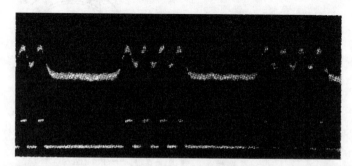

Figure 5.65 Output signal from cryogenic model. Upper trace—output signal from differential detector. Lower trace—output of threshold detector.

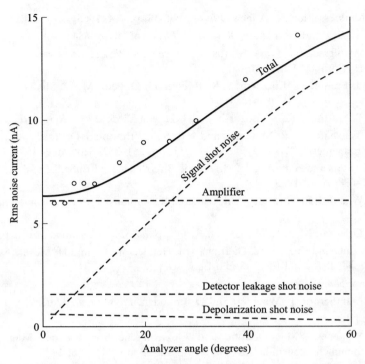

Figure 5.66 System noise current. Circles—measured values; dotted lines—calculated contributions to noise; solid line—total of calculated contributions.

agreement with the total calculated noise (solid line). Various calculated contributions to the noise are also shown. At an analyzer angle of 30° (which happens to give the best signal-to-noise ratio with this system), the amplifier noise and the photocurrent shot noise are similar in magnitude, and they dominate over other noise sources.

5.4.7 Summary

In this section we have given a brief description of some of the research and development carried out on the class of materials known as the europium chalcogenides. These materials are truly remarkable. Their study has increased our knowledge of basic magnetic, electrical, optical, and magneto-optical properties of materials. In this chapter we have described only a relatively small part of the research into the fundamental properties of these materials. In addition to basic properties, and devices related properties, we have reviewed the development of the first magneto-optical disk drive to have been fabricated.

REFERENCES

[1] A. Mauger and C. Godart, "The Magnetic, Optical, and Transport Properties of Representatives of a Class of Magnetic Semiconductors: The Europium Chalcogenides," *Physics Reports*, vol. 141, pp. 51–176, 1986.

[2] P. Wachter, *Handbook of Physics and Chemistry of Rare Earths*, A. Gschneidner, Jr. and L. Eyring (eds.), chapter 19, Amsterdam: North Holland, 1978.

[3] S. Methfessel and Z. Angew. *Physik*, vol. 18, p. 414, 1965.

[4] T. Kasuya and A. Yanase, *Rev. Mod. Phys.*, vol. 40, p. 684, 1968.

[5] S. Methfessel and D. C. Mattis, *Handbuch der Physic*, vol. 18, p 1, S. Flugge (ed.), New York: Springer Verlag, 1968.

[6] M. J. Freiser, F. Holtzberg, S. Methfessel, G. D. Petit, M. W. Shafer, and J. C. Suits, *Helv. Phys. Acta*, vol. 41, p. 832, 1968.

[7] B. T. Matthias, R. M. Bozorth, and J. H. van Vleck, *Phys. Rev. Lett.*, vol. 7, p. 160, 1961.

[8] M. W. Shafer, T. R. McGuire, and J. C. Suits, "Europium Orthosilicate, a New Transparent Ferromagnet," *Phys. Rev. Lett.*, vol. 11, pp. 251–252, September 1973.

[9] J. C. Suits and B. E. Argyle, "Magnetic Birefringence of EuSe," *Phys. Rev. Lett.*, vol. 14, pp. 687–688, April 1965.

[10] G. Will, S. J. Pickart, H. A. Alperin, and R. Nathans, *J. Phys. Chem. Solids*, vol. 24, p. 1679, 1963.

[11] R. Griessen, M. Landolt, and H. R. Ott, *Solid State Commun.*, vol. 9, p. 2219, 1971.

[12] For EuO and EuS: O. W. Dietrich, A. J. Henderson, Jr., and H. Meyer, *Phys. Rev.*, vol. B12, p. 2844, 1975, and for EuS and EuSe see [2].

[13] See p. 538 of [2].

[14] G. Guntherodt, P. Wachter, and D. Imboden, *Phys. Kond. Materie*, vol. 12, p. 292, 1971.

[15] See [1] and [2].

[16] J. Schoenes, "Magnetooptic und Elektronische Struktur der Magnetisch Ordnenden Europiumchalkogenide," *Z. Physik B*, vol. 20, pp. 345–368, 1975.

[17] G. Busch, P. Junod, and P. Wachter, *Phys. Lett.*, vol. 12, p. 11, 1964.

[18] M. J. Freiser, F. Holtzberg, S. Methfessel, G. D. Pettit, M. W. Shafer, and J. C. Suits, "The Magnetic Red Shift in Europium Chalcogenides," *Helvetica Phys. Acta.*, vol. 41, pp. 832–838, 1968.

[19] See [2].

[20] P. Wachter, *Phys. Kondens. Mat.*, vol. 8, p. 80, 1968.

[21] J. C. Suits, "Magneto-Optical Properties," RC 1520, *IBM Research Internal Publication*, pp. 35–38, 1965.

[22] J. Schoenes, *Z. Physik*, vol. B20, p. 345, 1975.

[23] M. J. Freiser, "A survey of Magneto-optic Effects," *IEEE Trans. Magn.*, vol. MAG-5, pp. 152–161, June 1968.

[24] J. C. Suits and B. E. Argyle, "Magnetic Birefringence of EuSe," *Phys. Rev. Lett.*, vol. 14, pp. 687–688, April 1965.

[25] J. C. Suits, B. E. Argyle, and M. J. Freiser, "Magneto-optical Properties of Materials Containing Divalent Europium," *J. Appl. Phys.*, vol. 37, p. 1391, 1966.

[26] R. C. LeCraw, D. L. Wood, J. F. Dillon, Jr., and J. P. Remeika, *Appl. Phys. Lett.*, vol. 7, p. 27, 1965.

[27] J. F. Dillon, Jr., H. Kamimura, and J. P. Remeika, "Magneto-optical Properties of Ferromagnetic Chromium Trihalides," *J. Phys. Chem. Sol.*, vol. 27, pp. 1531–1549, 1966.

[28] D. O. Smith, *Optical Information Processing* Chapter 28, Cambridge, MA: Technology Press, 1965.

[29] B. E. Argyle, J. C. Suits, and M. J. Freiser, "Magnetic Dichroism in EuSe," *Phys. Rev. Lett.*, vol. 15, p. 822, 1965.

[30] J. Schoenes and P. Wachter, *Phys. Lett.*, vol. 61A, p. 68, 1977.

[31] J. C. Suits, "Magneto-Optics of EuO," *FERRITES Proceedings of the International Conference*, Y. Hoshino, S. Iida, and M. Sugimoto (eds.), University of Tokyo Press, 1971, pp. 396–399.

[32] F. Holtzberg, T. R. McGuire, S. Methfessel, and J. C. Suits, "Effect of Electron Concentration on Magnetic Exchange Interaction in Rare Earth Chalcogenides," *Phys. Rev. Letters*, vol. 13, pp. 18–21, July 1964.

[33] M. W. Shafer and T. R. McGuire, "Studies of Curie-Point Increases in EuO," *J. Appl. Phys.*, vol. 39, pp. 588–590, February 1968.

[34] K. Y. Ahn and T. R. McGuire, "Magnetic and Magneto-optic Properties of EuO Films Doped with Trivalent Rare-Earth Oxide," *J. Appl. Phys.*, vol. 39, pp. 5061–5065, October 1968.

[35] K. Y. Ahn, "Increase of Curie Temperature in EuO Films by Fe Doping," *Appl. Phys. Lett.*, vol. 17, p. 347–349, October 1970.

[36] K. Y. Ahn, K. N. Tu, and W. Reuter, "Preparation and Structure of Eu-Doped EuO Films," *J. Appl. Phys.*, vol. 42, pp. 1769–1770, March 1971.

[37] K. Y. Ahn, Kn. N. Tu, and W. Reuter, "Preparation and Structure of Fe-Doped EuO Films," *J. Appl. Phys.*, vol. 42, pp. 1769–1770, March 1971.

[38] K. Y. Ahn, "EuO Films Doped with Fe and Gd," *J. Appl. Phys.*, vol. 43, pp. 231–232, January 1972.

[39] J. C. Suits and K. Lee, *Giant Magneto-Optical Kerr Effect in EuO*, vol. 42, pp. 3258–3250, July 1971.

[40] G. Fan, K. Pennington, and J. H. Greiner, "Magneto-Optic Hologram," *J. Appl. Phys.*, vol. 40, pp. 974–975, March 1969.

[41] J. C. Suits, "Optical Diffraction by Magnetic Domains in Europium Chalcogenides," *J. Appl. Phys.*, vol. 38, pp. 1498–1489, March 1967.

[42] B. K. Middleton, "The Dependence of Recording Characteristics of Thin Metal Tapes on their Magnetic Properties and on the Replay Head," *IEEE Trans. Magn.*, vol. MAG-2, pp. 225–229, September 1966.

[43] G. Fan and J. H. Greiner, *J. Appl. Phys.*, vol. 41, p. 1401, 1970. A. H. Eschenfelder, *J. Appl. Phys.*, vol. 41, p. 1372, 1970.

[44] A. M. Patlach, "Design Consideration for a Magneto-Optic Cryogenic Film Memory," *IBM J. Res. & Dev.*, vol. 16, pp. 16–18, 1972.

[45] B. R. Brown, "Readout Performance Analysis of a Cryogenic Magneto-Optical Data Storage System," *IBM J. Res. & Dev.*, vol. 16, pp. 19–26, 1972.

Chapter 6

DOMAIN DYNAMICS
AND RECORDING PHYSICS
IN MAGNETO-OPTICAL
RECORDING MEDIA

Dieter Mergel*

In this chapter, the creation and erasure of magnetic domains in MO storage layers is discussed. Our aim is to present a variety of experimental results, computer simulations, and theoretical models in order to discuss them on a common ground. The emphasis is put on rare-earth transition-metal (RE-TM) alloys that allow a tuning of their magnetic properties toward the requirements of MO-recording, but sometimes we compare with Pt/Co multilayers.

The historical background is sketched by comparing MO recording with bubble-domain memories that were intensively investigated in the 1970s. The magnetodynamic theory (Landaus–Lifschitz–Gilbert formalism) is illustrated by computer simulations of the thermomagnetic write process.

A micromagnetic bubble-like model of the forces on an existing domain wall is described and serves as a theoretical reference for the discussion of various recording experiments. In addition to the forces on a classical bubble domain, there is an essential coercive force and a force due to the wall energy gradient in the temperature profile induced by the laser spot.

Experiments on the magnetic reversal in single and exchange-coupled layers at a given temperature as well as computer simulations are discussed with respect to micromagnetic concepts of coercivity like domain nucleation, domain wall motion, and thermal activation of these processes.

Two types of recording experiments are treated in detail. (1) Domain formation in the thermomagnetic write process, illustrated by four phenomenological models, and (2) destabilization and erasure of domains with emphasis on the stroboscopic observation of domain expansion and contraction in a polarizing microscope and on the wall mobility.

The noise in MO media is also discussed. Domain irregularities are related to the parameters of the write process and to the material properties and deposition parameters of thin MO films.

*The author would like to thank the following persons for having helped him in the preparation of this contribution. A. Hubert constructively criticized the initial concept. J. P. C. Bernards, R. Carey, K. Immink, M. H. Kryder, M. Mansuripur, D. Raasch, and A. M. J. Spruijt discussed and commented on different sections of the text. R. Labusch made fruitful suggestions for the final version. T. Koller carefully prepared most of the figures. H. Pärschke typed part of the script.

In the Appendix (Section 6.8) we calculate the demagnetizing field of a cylindrical domain because the formulae reported in the literature are not consistent. Furthermore, the achievable linear bit density depending on optical resolution and signal-to-noise ratio is presented in a tutorial way. This is important to estimate the performance of recording systems but often ignored in the materials science community.

The simultaneous use of two magnetic unit systems is common practice in the literature and is sometimes also applied here. As this can easily confuse the inexperienced reader, the main conversion formulae for magnetostatic quantities in the SI and cgs (Gauss) systems are listed in Table 6.1.

6.1 INTRODUCTION: THE SCOPE OF RECORDING PHYSICS

6.1.1 Principle of MO Recording

In a simplified way, a magneto-optical (MO) recording system can be regarded as a CD player with a laser beam focused onto a disk but with the two main distinctions that *polarized laser light* of tunable intensity together with polarizing components in the light path are used and that the disk comprises a *hard magnetic layer* with perpendicular magnetization. The information is stored as a domain pattern in the magnetic film.

Marks are written in the thermomagnetic write process illustrated in Fig. 6.1. A focused laser beam heats the magnetic layer to its Curie temperature such that within the laser spot a paramagnetic region ("Curie cylinder," "Curie disk") is built within the laser spot. During cooling down, a magnetic mark is created, normally under the influence of an applied magnetic field, and frozen in. Typically, laser powers of about 8 mW and magnetic fields of about 16 kA/m (200 Oe) are used.

Two write modes are in use: laser power modulation at a constant magnetic field (LM) and magnetic field modulation at a constant laser power (*MFM*). LM produces

TABLE 6.1 Correspondence Between Magnetic Units in the SI and cgs Systems

	SI	cgs
field strength H	A/m	$4\pi 10^{-3}$ Oe
	80 kA/m	≈ 1 kOe
	10 kA/m	≈ 125 Oe
dipole moment, Bohr magneton μ_B	$0.927 * 10^{-23}$ Am^2	$0.927 * 10^{-20}$ emu
magnetization M_s (dipole moment per volume)	1 A/m	10^{-3} emu/cm$^3 = 10^{-3}$ G
flux density B	$B = \mu_0 H + \mu_0 M$	$B = H + 4\pi M_s$
	T = Vs/m^2	10 kG
	$\mu_0 = 4\pi 10^{-7}$ Vs/Am	
polarization	$\mu_0 M_s$	$4\pi M_s$
susceptibility χ	$M = \chi H$	$M = \chi H$
	e.g. $\chi = 4\pi$	e.g. $\chi = 1$
energy density of magnetic field	$BH/2$	$BH/8\pi$
	J/m^3	10 erg/cm^3
energy of magnetic matter in an external field	$\mu_0 H dM = \mu_0 H M_s dV$	$H dM = H M_s dV$
Coulomb-law for a magnetic charge at		
$r = 0$, $\qquad H(r) =$	$-\mathrm{div} M_s/(4\pi r^2)$	$-\mathrm{div} M_s/r^2$
demagnetizing field in a thin film and its energy	$-M_s$	$-4\pi M_s$
density	$\mu_0 M_s^2/2$	$2\pi M_s^2$

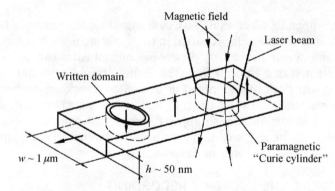

Figure 6.1 Creation of magnetic domains in the thermomagnetic write process. A paramagnetic region (*Curie cylinder* or *Curie disk* or *Curie hole*) builds within the laser spot where $T > T_{Curie}$. A reverse domain is formed and frozen in during cooling. The disk moves to the left.

domains in the form of a (distorted) disk whereas MFM yields crescent-shaped domains, see Figure 6.2. In MFM, the old domains are erased and new domains are written in the same run. Standard LM, on the other hand, does not allow such a direct overwrite; only new marks are written; the old domains have to be erased before, in a separate pass with constant laser power under a reversed magnetic field. The advantage of LM over MFM is its higher data rate, for laser power switching is much faster than field modulation which is limited by the heat production in the coil. MFM, on the other hand, allows higher linear domain densities than LM.

Direct overwrite can also be achieved for two modes of modified LM ("LIMDOW" = light intensity modulation, direct overwrite). In one method, a MO-medium consisting of two or more exchange-coupled magnetic layers is used. One of the layers is for storage and contains thermomagnetically written domains. A second one is homogeneously magnetized in its initial state such that an interface wall to the domains in the storage layer exists. The wall is an energy source that drives the erasure of the domains in the storage layer in a certain temperature range. The LIMDOW process on exchange-coupled layers is described in Chapter 9 of this book in detail. The other LM-

MFM

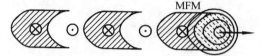

LM

Temperature distribution

Figure 6.2 Shape of marks, thermomagnetically written with laser modulation (LM) and magnetic field modulation (MFM). Gray area within the laser spot is paramagnetic.

method uses single layers that become magnetically soft enough well below the Curie temperature so that the old domains collapse like a bubble (see Section 6.5.3).

The read process utilizes the same laser beam as the write process but with reduced intensity. It makes use of the magneto-optical polar Kerr effect: The polarization plane of the laser beam is rotated on reflection at the perpendicularly magnetized layer, clock- or counterclockwise according to the orientation of the magnetic moments in the domain pattern. Therefore, the setup in the optical head contains polarizing components.

For test purposes, the signal is written in the form of a *carrier*, i.e., periodic repetitions of 1 and 0. The readout signal is decomposed into its Fourier components by a spectrum analyzer and a *carrier-to-noise ratio (CNR)* is determined as the ratio of the signal at the write frequency and the intensity of the background. The CNR is higher than the signal-to-noise ratio (SNR) by the ratio of the signal bandwidth to the resolution bandwidth of the spectrum analyzer, typically $10*\log(10\,\mathrm{MHz}/30\,\mathrm{kHz}) = 25\mathrm{dB}$.

A cross section of a typical disk in quadrilayer configuration is shown in Figure 6.3. The MO layer is embedded in dielectric layers (Si_3N_4 commonly known as SiN in this case) to enhance the magneto-optical figure-of-merit. The laser beam is incident from the polycarbonate (PC) substrate. The light is partly reflected at every interface and finally at the Al layer. The first dielectric layer may be regarded as an antireflection layer and the Al layer as a mirror. Light reflected at the Al layer passes the MO layer twice. Historically, only the MO effect upon reflection is called the Kerr effect, whereas the MO effect in transmission is called the Faraday effect. The design of the layer stack determines also the thermal properties of the disk.

Marks (magnetic domains) are usually written in the "land" between the grooves that guide the laser beam. There is currently a trend to make land and groove equally wide to use both for ("land/groove") recording.

From the principles of thermomagnetic writing and magneto-optic readout exposed so far, some requirements of magnetic materials are appropriate for MO media. We need:

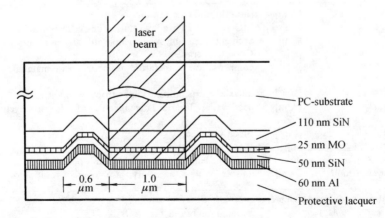

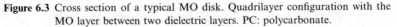

Figure 6.3 Cross section of a typical MO disk. Quadrilayer configuration with the MO layer between two dielectric layers. PC: polycarbonate.

1. a perpendicular (uniaxial) magnetic anisotropy, described by an anisotropy constant K_u and

2. a sufficiently high signal, determined by the polar Kerr effect and the layer stack and characterized by the MO figure-of-merit $\sqrt{R} \bullet \theta_K$ (R = reflectivity, θ_K = Kerr rotation angle)

3. a Curie temperature T_C ranging between 400 K and 600 K, because of the limited write laser power, and

4. a high coercive field H_c at room temperature and at readout temperature to ensure stable domains.

The parameters used to describe magnetic materials for MO recording are listed in Table 6.2, grouped according to whether they are phenomenological or derived from a theoretical model.

In the remainder of this introduction, we compare MO recording with the earlier bubble memory, present a magnetostatic model of the force equilibrium at a cylindrical domain boundary, and illustrate magnetodynamic theory by a computer simulation of domain formation during the thermomagnetic write process.

6.1.2 Comparison with Bubble Domain Memories

Magnetic bubble domain memories were intensively studied in the 1970s. The state of knowledge is well described in textbooks [1]–[5]. In such memories, the information is stored as *bubbles*, i.e., cylindrical magnetic domains, in a thin magnetic film with perpendicular magnetization. Contrary to MO-recording, however, the medium is held fixed and the bubbles are moved in the magnetic layer along tracks defined by an overlay drive circuit of permalloy.

The bubbles have to be stabilized against collapse by a bias field, usually provided by a permanent magnet. The driving force for their propagation arises from a rotating in-plane field produced by coils. They are detected electronically when they pass a

TABLE 6.2   Magnetic Parameters Describing Materials for MO and Bubble-domain Storage. SI-units Are Used

M_s	[A/m]	saturation magnetization
θ_K and θ_F	[degree]	MO Kerr and Faraday rotation angle, respectively
A_x	[J/m]	exchange constant, macroscopic stiffness constant
T_C	[K]	Curie temperature
T_{comp}	[K]	compensation temperature of ferrimagnetic materials
K_u	[J/m^3]	uniaxial (perpendicular) anisotropy constant
H_c, H_a, H_d	[A/m]	coercive, applied, and demagnetizing field, respectively
$\sigma_w = 4\sqrt{(AK_u)}$	[J/m^2]	Bloch wall energy
$\delta_w = \pi\sqrt{(A/K_u)}$	[m]	Bloch wall width
$\Delta_w = \sqrt{(A/K_u)}$	[m]	exchange length, domain-wall width parameter
$H_{anis} = 2K_u/(\mu_0 M_s)$	[A/m]	anisotropy field, necessary for a coherent rotation of the magnetization

Normalized to demagnetizing energy:
$Q = 2K_u/(\mu_0 M_s^2)$		material quality factor, $= H_{anis}/M_s$
$l = \sigma_w/(\mu_o M_s^2)$		material length parameter

magnetoresistive strip. New bubbles are created by dividing a seed bubble with local magnetic fields produced by electrical currents in the overlay structure.

A bubble storage unit is a chip comprising a bubble layer covered with a laterally structured permalloy overlayer. A typical bubble storage device consists of several storage chips wrapped in magnetic coils and sandwiched between permanent magnets. Bubble memories are currently used in space craft because they are radiation insensitive.

6.1.2.1 Bubble Materials

A material suited for a bubble memory has to fulfill the following three requirements, formulated in terms of the micromagnetic parameters of Table 6.2 (from [3], but here in SI-units):

1. The quality factor $Q = 2K_u/\mu_0 M_s^2$ must be larger than 1,

$$1 < Q < 10,$$

   i.e., the demagnetizing energy $\mu_0 M_s^2/2$ has to be smaller than the anisotropy energy, so that the magnetization generally points perpendicular to the film plane. The upper limit arises from the fact that the wall mobility is inversely proportional to Q.

2. The thickness of the film, h, should be about four times the material length parameter, $l = \sigma_0/\mu_0 M_s^2$, with σ_0 being the magnetic wall energy:

$$h \approx 4l$$

   The minimum domain size is then about $2h$. For $h < l$, bubbles collapse because, for decreasing radius, the decrease in wall energy is larger than the increase in demagnetizing energy. Typical values for h are about 0.5 μm. Bubble films are thus typically one order of magnitude thicker than MO layers. A magnetic bubble is typically 1–4 μm in diameter.

3. The coercive field, H_c, is only 5% of the demagnetizing field H_d of the thin film ($H_d = M_s$ in SI-units):

$$H_c/M_s < 0.05,$$

   so that a bubble can easily be moved around in the film by a magnetic field gradient. Point (3) constitutes the main difference to MO media for which a large coercive field at room temperature is required to fix the domain structure at its site on the disk.

Epitaxial garnet films with uniaxial anisotropy were studied most as potential bubble media [6]; but also amorphous metallic RE-TM films such as Gd-Co were considered (see Chapter 2).

6.1.2.2 Magnetostatic Equilibrium of a Normal Magnetic Bubble

In the cgs system, the net effective magnetic field H_w on the wall of an isolated bubble with radius r in a uniform applied field H_a is given by [7]:

$$H_w = H_a + 4\pi M_s \left(\frac{l}{2r} - \frac{1}{1 + 3r/2h} \right) \quad \text{(cgs)} \tag{6.1}$$

provided $1 < r/h < 10$ with h being the thickness of the magnetic layer and l the material length parameter, see Table 6.2. This can be rewritten in the SI-system as

$$H_w = H_a + \frac{\sigma_w}{2\mu_0 M_s r} - \frac{M_s}{1 + 3r/2h} \quad \text{(SI)} \tag{6.2}$$

The second term on the right-hand side represents a (contracting) field arising from the wall curvature. It is derived from a surface energy tending to minimize the surface area just like in the case of a soap bubble. The third term is the approximate demagnetizing field $H_d(r)$ at the domain boundary [8] and always tends to expand the bubble domain (for details see Appendix 6.8.1).

The external field H_a has an expansive effect for an orientation parallel to the magnetization inside the bubble and a contractive effect for an antiparallel orientation. In bubble materials normally a contractive bias field has to be applied, compensating the demagnetizing field, to hold the bubble at a stable radius.

For contracting fields below a critical value, there exists a stable solution of Equation (6.2) with a well-defined bubble diameter. Above the critical value the bubble collapses. There is also a lower critical value, below which the bubble runs out into a stripe domain. Under typical conditions, the midrange bias field H_B is about a quarter of the value of the demagnetizing field of the (homogeneously magnetized) thin film, $H_B/M_s \approx 0.25$.

In the above formulae, the following phenomena are not taken into account.

1. Any variation of the wall energy density, σ_w, with the radius of the domain, which is important for "hard" magnetic walls.
2. Local variations of the magnetic parameters such as those induced by a temperature distribution during the thermomagnetic write process.
3. Any pinning of the wall (coercive effects).
4. Any nucleation of reverse domains. The existence of a domain surrounded by a well-defined wall is preassumed. This is trivial, but one must be aware of it when applying the bubble model to thermomagnetic writing.

The effects (2) to (4) have to be avoided in bubble domain memories but play an important role in MO recording, so that the equations for the driving force must be modified before they can be applied to MO materials.

6.1.2.3 Wall Structure and Wall Motion

Experimentally, stable domains were found with radii up to a factor of 5 smaller than the critical collapse radius and at fields higher than the collapse field, both calculated from the equilibrium conditions discussed in connection with Equation (6.3). This discrepancy between theory and experiment was attributed to a special structure of the domain wall, a *hard* wall with *vertical Bloch lines*, not considered by the theory. Bloch lines are 1-dimensional boundaries between parts of the wall with different screw sense (chirality).

For the equilibrium equations it is implicitly assumed that the wall energy is given by the product of an energy per unit length, σ_w, and the circumference of the domain. However, when a hard domain shrinks, the wall magnetization along the wall becomes more tightly wound and the wall energy per unit length increases. Before the domain collapses, the wall structure has to change, which requires a higher field than calculated for a normal bubble.

Under a field gradient a bubble moves, generally not in the direction of the gradient, but at an oblique angle to it the size of which depends on the fine structure of the wall. Hard bubbles move almost at right angles to the field gradient.

6.1.3 Forces on a Domain Wall Subjected to a Temperature Gradient

In this subsection, the radial forces on a cylindrical domain in a thin MO film under recording conditions are derived for a quasistatic process [7]. The most important difference to a domain in a bubble material is that temperature profiles and corresponding local variations of the magnetic parameters must be taken into account. The domain nucleation process is not considered here.

The total energy of a cylindrical domain is given by the sum of three energies: the wall energy E_w, Zeeman energy E_H, and demagnetizing energy E_d. They are listed below for a cylindrical domain subjected to a temperature profile, together with the related radial forces F on the domain wall obtained by differentiation with respect to the radial coordinate. The parameters r and h specify the radius of the domain and the thickness of the film, respectively. Differing from the formulae for the classical bubble, the magnetization and the Bloch wall energy now depend indirectly on the radial coordinate, because a central, radial symmetric temperature profile (independent of the z-coordinate) has been assumed.

1. wall energy (contracting): $E_w = 2\pi r h \sigma_w$ (6.3)

$$F_w = 2\pi h \sigma_w + 2\pi h r \frac{\partial \sigma_w}{\partial r} \tag{6.4}$$

2. Zeeman energy: $E_H = 2h\mu_0 H_a \int_0^r M(\rho) 2\pi \rho d\rho$ (6.5)

$$F_H = 4\pi h r \mu_0 M_s(r) H_a \tag{6.6}$$

3. demagnetizing energy (expanding):

$$E_d = \frac{1}{2}\mu_0 \int_0^\infty \int_0^{2\pi} \int_0^h M(r, \Theta, z) H_\perp(r, \Theta, z) r\, dr\, d\Theta\, dz \tag{6.7}$$

$$F_d = 4\pi h r \mu_0 |M_s(r)| \overline{H_d(r)} \qquad (6.8)$$

$M_s(r)$ denotes the magnetization at the domain boundary. $H_d(r)$ denotes the average over z of the demagnetizing field of a cylindrical domain with radius r and with $M(\rho) = M_s(\rho)$ for $\rho < r$ and $M(\rho) = -M_s(\rho)$ for $\rho > r$. The factor 2 in Equation (6.5) arises because switching a dipole moment m from antiparallel to parallel orientation with respect H_a yields an energy gain of $2\mu_0 m H_a$.

To obtain the force f_t per unit area of domain wall, i.e., the pressure on the wall, the above equations are divided by $2\pi r h$. The resulting expressions have the dimension of energy density.

$$f_t = 2\mu_0 M_s(r)H_a + 2\mu_0 M_s(r)H_d(r) - \frac{\sigma_w(r)}{r} - \frac{d\sigma_w(r)}{dr} \quad \text{(SI)} \qquad (6.9)$$

The equivalent of Equation (6.9) in the (cgs) system is

$$f_t = 2M_s(r)H_a + 2M_s(r)H_d(r) - \frac{\sigma_w(r)}{r} - \frac{d\sigma_w}{dr} \quad \text{(cgs)} \qquad (6.10)$$

The wall energy gives rise to two types of force: the *wall tension* tending to reduce the wall length and the *wall gradient force* tending to shift the wall to regions with lower σ_w, i.e., along the temperature gradient into warmer regions.

H_d represents the vertical component of the demagnetizing field at the domain boundary generated by all the dipoles in the film. It depends on the geometry of the domain structure. For a cylindrical bubble in a homogeneously magnetized film we get

$$H_d(r) + M_s\left(\frac{1}{1 + 3r/2h}\right) \quad \text{(SI)} \qquad (6.11)$$

The wall moves if the total force overcomes a coercive force given by

$$f_c(r) = 2\mu_0 M_s(r)H_c(r) \qquad (6.12)$$

At T_{comp}, M_s and consequently the terms f_H and f_d become zero, so that the balance is determined by the wall forces and the coercive force alone. We shall discuss f_c in the next section in more detail but emphasize here that, with its dimension being an energy density, it exhibits no singularity, not even at the compensation temperature T_{comp} of ferrimagnetic materials where the coercive *field* H_c becomes infinite because M_s becomes zero.

The quantities M_s, σ_w, and H_c are material parameters depending, in addition to the temperature, on the composition and the microstructure. They will be discussed in Section 6.2. The demagnetizing field of a radially varying distribution of the magnetization is calculated in Appendix 6.8.1.

6.1.4 Magnetodynamic Model of Thermomagnetic Domain Formation

6.1.4.1 LLG Formalism

The bubble-like model presupposes a specific, highly symmetric domain structure and is derived from a quasistatic process. More general micromagnetic calculations are often performed for an ensemble of magnetic dipoles whose dynamic behavior is described by the Landau–Lifshitz Gilbert (LLG) equation [3], [5]. A magnetic body is modeled as a net of interacting magnetic moments m_i, each representing a cell of that body. The dimensions of the cell have to be small compared to atomic distances such that the cell can be regarded as a magnetic continuum described by the macroscopic parameters M_s, K_u and A.

The magnetic moments possess an angular momentum m/γ with γ being the gyromagnetic ratio (γ is negative). A torque is exerted by the vector product of m and a magnetic field H. The dynamics of a magnetic moment m is described by the torque (LLG) equation:

$$\frac{dm/dt}{\gamma} = -\frac{1}{|\gamma|}\frac{dm}{dt} = m \times H_{\text{eff}} + \alpha \frac{m}{|m|} \times \frac{dm/dt}{\gamma} \tag{6.13}$$

The different terms can be illustrated by means of Figure 6.4. The first term on the right-hand side represents the applied torque due to the component of an effective magnetic field normal to the moment direction. It causes the dipole to precess around the direction of H_{eff} with a constant angular velocity. In the micromagnetic model of a thin film, H_{eff} comprises several contributions:

$$H_{\text{eff}} = H_a + H_{Ku} + \sum_{\text{n.n}} H_{x\,\text{chg}} + \sum_{\text{all}} H_d \tag{6.14}$$

H_a is the externally applied field, assumed to be uniform over the thin film. H_{Ku} is the anisotropy field that is assumed to be exerted individually upon each dipole and, in thin films of interest for our application, described by a uniaxial anisotropy constant K_u. $H_{x\,\text{chg}}$ is the exchange field, which is of short range, so that only the nearest neighbors (n.n.) are relevant. It is described by a macroscopic stiffness constant A_x.

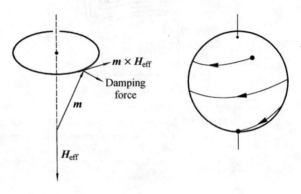

Figure 6.4 Torque and damping force on a magnetic moment m in a magnetic field (left). Rotation of the magnetic moment into the direction of the applied field (right). The origin of m is in the center of the sphere.

H_d is the magnetostatic demagnetizing field whose source is the negative divergence of M. Contributions from all other dipoles in the film must be considered and this makes H_d the most difficult term to handle.

The second term in Equation (6.13) represents a torque proportional to the time rate of change of the angular momentum. It characterizes a viscous damping that changes the polar angle θ continuously until m is aligned with H_{eff}, see Figure 6.4, right. The dimensionless constant α describes the damping and is named after Gilbert (Gilbert damping factor).

From the LLG equation important dynamic parameters such as mobility and mass of a wall may be derived. The formulae are valid, however, only if coercive effects can be neglected. This is justified for bubble materials but generally not for MO materials.

After sufficient time, the magnetic moments align with the effective magnetic field and the torque becomes zero everywhere, i.e., a magnetostatic equilibrium configuration is reached. With respect to this configuration, the LLG simulation can be compared with an iterative numerical procedure with nonrestrictive boundary conditions and slow convergence.

6.1.4.2 Computer Simulation

The thermomagnetic write process has been simulated, based on the LLG equation, within a cylindrical calculation region of 800 nm radius and a central laser spot [9]. Temperature dependences of $M(T)$, $A(T)$ and $K_u(T)$ typical for Tb-FeCo with $T_C = 200°C$ and $T_{comp} = 0°C$ were imposed. The film thickness was 80 nm. The simulation is done in two dimensions, r and z. A cell had the size $\Delta z = 2$–$5\,nm$ and $\Delta r = 2\,nm$, the time increment was 1 ps. The temperature distribution after 60 ns laser irradiation was calculated by assuming appropriate values for the thermal conductivity and the specific heat of the disk. At the boundary of the calculation region the magnetization is fixed upwards as a boundary condition.

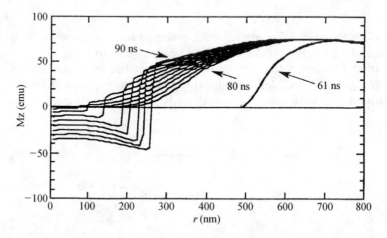

Figure 6.5 [8] Computer simulation (LLG) of the thermomagnetic write process. Temporal development of the perpendicular component of magnetization, M_z, in the middle plane of the recording layer. Cooling process after laser switch-off at 60 ns. Beam radius 750 nm, magnetic field -500 Oe.

Figure 6.5 shows the results for a laser beam of radius 0.75 μm and an applied write field of 500 Oe (40 kA/m). The laser has been switched off at 60 ns. The Curie radius r_C, belonging to the isothermal circle $T = T_C$, shrinks during cooling down. A permanent magnetization reappears at r_C. In the computer simulation, its magnitude was given $M(T)$ and its initial direction was chosen parallel to the direction of $H_a + H_d$ (external plus demagnetizing field). This corresponds to a virtual nucleation of a reverse ring domain at r_C. The domain wall is of Néel type due to the chosen radial symmetry.

In the first phase of the cooling process, the magnetization is reestablishing in the original direction, against the external field, i.e., the virtual nucleus was not stable; but at 83 ns, when the temperature at the center is close to T_C, a domain wall is permanently created at the temporal Curie radius and moves outward until it reaches the boundary of the calculation region, beyond which the magnetization is kept in the initial state (upward) as boundary condition. In other words, a domain forms in the central part of the temperature profile, very close to the Curie radius, and grows by wall motion. The domain wall velocity at $t = 90$ ns is about 20 m/s, bigger than the velocity of the Curie radius. Coercive effects due to inhomogeneous magnetic parameters were not taken into account.

The described domain formation with wall motion is schematically depicted in Figure 6.6. During heating, a maximum Curie radius is reached (a) but no domain is nucleated. In the cooling phase, the Curie radius shrinks, a ring-shaped nucleus forms (b). In phase (c) the magnetization inside the domain increases and the domain expands by wall motion. This is not the general model of the thermomagnetic write process but just one out of four presented here.

We can interpret these results in terms of the magnetostatic bubble-like model. The virtual nucleation at r_C considers the external and the demagnetizing fields. If it is not successful, this is due to the wall forces, especially the wall gradient force, that becomes weaker when the temperature profile smoothes during cooling.

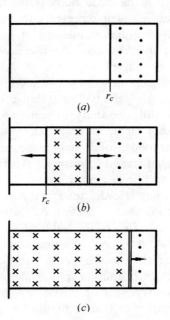

Figure 6.6 Nucleation and expansion of a domain in the cooling phase according to Figure 6.5. (a) Maximum Curie radius, (b) nucleation, (c) expansion. Top view. Wall curvature not drawn for simplicity.

In an equivalent simulation for a beam radius of only 0.1 μm, no domain is nucleated for applied fields below 5 kOe. This is due to the steep T-gradient inducing a strong collapsing wall gradient force. Above 5.5 kOe, two ring-shaped nuclei much larger than the Curie radius are generated at the surfaces of the layer immediately after laser switch-off. This surface nucleation process is a rotation of the magnetization creating Néel walls parallel to the film plane, that move toward the central plane.

The T-dependence of the magnetic parameters of the storage medium, especially the exact behavior near T_C, severely influences the mark formation process. The simulations described above do not take into account coercive effects and must thus be considered as strongly idealized. Coercive effects due to inhomogeneous magnetic parameters facilitate domain nucleation and hamper wall motion.

6.1.5 Outline of this Chapter

We have compared MO recording with the older bubble storage technology. In bubble storage, cylindrical domains are created by dividing existing domains and are moved in "soft" magnetic layers by means of rotating external magnetic fields. The forces on a bubble domain wall arise from the demagnetizing energy (expanding effect), the tension of the curved wall (contracting effect), and the external field.

In MO recording, domains are created in regions of "hard" magnetic layers that are locally heated above the Curie temperature by a laser beam (thermomagnetic write process). A temperature profile is induced giving rise to a wall energy gradient and a corresponding contracting force, in addition to the forces on a bubble. At storage temperatures the domains are immobile.

The Landau–Lifshitz–Gilbert (LLG) equation describes the dynamics of magnetic moments in an applied field. It considers the torque exerted by an effective magnetic field and a viscous damping of the resulting precession of the magnetic moment (*magnetohydrodynamic* theory). In computer simulations of magnetic reversal based on the LLG equation, a magnetic body is modeled as a network of interacting magnetic moments. Each moment represents the magnetic properties of small volume of the body. Such a computer simulation of the domain nucleation and the domain wall motion in the thermomagnetic write process reveals that domains are created and expand in the cooling phase.

Coercive effects have not yet been considered, in detail. In MO recording, however, coercive forces are essential to stabilize the domains. In order to support physical models of recording, we study, in Section 6.3, magnetic reversal processes in MO layers at homogeneous temperature, i.e., not in the thermomagnetic write process. Micromagnetic models of domain nucleation and domain wall motion, computer simulations (LLG), and results of reversal experiments in single layers and exchange-coupled double layers will be discussed.

The recording relevant magnetic parameters of MO materials, especially RE-TM alloys are summarized in Section 6.2, with the aim being to estimate the forces on a domain wall according to the bubble-like model.

Section 6.4 deals with the thermomagnetic write process. We set up prototype curves for the signal and the noise levels of a set of written domains as a function of the write laser power and the applied magnetic field and discuss the minimum field that is necessary to suppress or create reverse domains. Three more domain formation models, in addition to that of Figure 6.6, are presented.

Section 6.5 is devoted to domain instability and erasure. We discuss in detail a direct overwrite process in single layers (single-layer direct overwrite) based on the erasure of domains, against an expansive magnetic field, by a laser-induced temperature gradient. The direct observation of the expansion and contraction of domains in this process allows a comparison with the wall dynamics in bubble domain materials.

In Section 6.6, we relate the noise of the readout signal to the domain formation in the thermomagnetic write process and the magnetic parameters and the microstructure of the MO layer. In an "if–then" analysis, we try to extrapolate the current performance of the media to future recording with blue laser light.

In MO recording, coercive forces are essential to stabilize the domains, just as in magnetic recording but contrary to bubble storage. In order to support the physical models of the write process, we study in Section 6.5 magnetic reversal processes in MO layers at constant temperature, i.e., not in the thermomagnetic write process. First, we concentrate on coercive effects in single layers and discuss the results of computer simulations of magnetic reversal based on the Landau–Lifshitz equation and the experimentally observed magnetic aftereffect. Second, we review the phenomenology of the magnetic reversal in exchange-coupled double layers with emphasis on the role of the interface magnetic wall.

6.2 RECORDING-RELEVANT PARAMETERS OF MO MEDIA

In this section we discuss the recording-relevant properties of rare-earth transition-metal (RE-TM) thin films that have emerged during the last 20 years of research and development as the materials of choice for magneto-optical recording. This preeminence results from a fundamental understanding of their basic magnetic material properties that are exposed in Chapter 2. Here we briefly sketch those magnetic properties that are directly relevant for MO recording, describe the microstructure of thin films and discuss in more detail the parameters that are directly related to magnetic domains and the forces on their boundary.

6.2.1 Magnetic Properties of Amorphous RE-TM Thin Films

We will first discuss some magnetic properties of binary RE-TM alloys that are well described in the literature [11]–[20] (see also Chapter 2 of this book) and then see why specific ternary compositions are used for practical disks.

In Table 6.3 [20] some recording-relevant magnetic parameters of the three binary systems Gd-Fe, Tb-Fe, and Dy-Fe are listed, together with the values desired for recording. These alloys are ferri*magnetic* with the TM magnetization antiparallel to the (heavy) RE magnetization and exhibit, in a certain compositional range, a compensation temperature T_{comp}, at which the net magnetization is zero. At this temperature the coercive field H_c becomes infinite. In comparison, the magneto-optic effects (Kerr and Faraday rotation angles θ_K and θ_F, respectively), which are mainly due to the TM sublattice, are a continuous function of temperature. In order to get low magnetization above room temperature, necessary to suppress demagnetizing effects like subdomain formation, a compensation temperature around room temperature is favorable. This is obtained for about 75–82 at% Fe.

TABLE 6.3 [20] Magnetic Parameters of Amorphous RE-TM Thin Films. The Term dT_{Curie}/dy Specifies the Rise in Curie Temperature upon Adding Co to the RE-Fe Alloy

	$Gd_{1-x}Fe_x$	$Tb_{1-x}Fe_x$	$Dy_{1-x}Fe_x$	Desired
Compensation point at 295 K for:	$x = 0.77$	$x = 0.75$	$x = 0.82$	
$dT_{comp}/dx[K/at.\%]$	114	30	23	Medium
K_u [$10^5 J/m^3$]	−0.2(in-pl.)	6	1	> 0.3
T_{Curie}	500 K	405 K	340 K	≈ 450 K
dT_{Curie}/dy, [K/at.%]	7	7	10	
y = Co-addition				

None of the binary compounds with this composition is well matched to the needs of MO recording. Gd-Fe has a too high Curie temperature T_c and an in-plane anisotropy. The Curie temperature T_c is too low for Tb-Fe and Dy-Fe. Co-based alloys which exhibit a T_{comp} have a too high Curie temperature. Practical MO RE-TM alloys are therefore ternary: GdTb-Fe, where the Tb introduces perpendicular anisotropy, increases the coercive energy, and decreases T_c; Tb-FeCo and Dy-FeCo, where the Co increases T_c and the Kerr rotation angle θ_K at room temperature. The Co-Fe exchange is stronger than the Fe-Fe exchange [12]. This effect allows fine-tuning of the Curie temperature in the composition range relevant for MO recording.

These ternary alloys differ in the dependence of the uniaxial anisotropy constant K_u on temperature, see Figure 6.7 [20], which in turn determines the recording relevant dependence of H_c on T. For Tb-FeCo, the curve is steep close to T_c, so that thermomagnetic writing of domains can only be achieved close to the Curie temperature. This is in contrast to Dy-FeCo and GdTb-Fe where H_c approaches zero at T_c much less steeply such that domain writing is possible well below T_c. For Dy-FeCo new choices of T_{comp} (greater than room temperature) and T_c exploit this effect and lead to good recording performance.

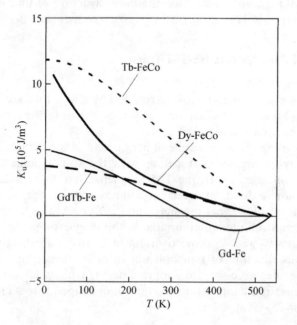

Figure 6.7 [21] Temperature dependence of the uniaxial (perpendicular) anisotropy constant K_u for several RE-Fe alloys. Negative values indicate in-plane anisotropy.

6.2.2 Influence of the Deposition Process on the Microstructure of the Deposited Films

The density of sputtered RE-TM films depends on the sputter pressure p_{Ar}, see Figure 6.8, top curve, due to the different energy of the species arriving at the growing film [21]. At 1 Pa, the mean free path is about 0.6 cm, an order of magnitude less than the target-substrate distance. The energy of the sputtered target atoms, originally about 10 eV, is thermalized to 0.025 eV. Under these conditions the films become porous and exhibit a pronounced columnar structure. Upon decreasing the pressure, the mean free path increases and the target atoms arrive at the substrate with higher energy favoring surface diffusion and densification of the film.

The anisotropy constant K_u increases together with the density. This is explained by improved layer-by-layer growth leading to an increased formation of Tb-Fe pairs perpendicular to the film plane [22]. $Ec = 2\mu_0 M_s H_c$ is maximum at $p_{Ar} = 1.2$ Pa. E_c has the dimension of an energy and is sometimes called coercive energy. It represents the energy to create a reverse magnetic nucleus or a coercive force per domain wall area. At higher pressure, the curve $E_c(p_{Ar})$ follows $K_u(p_{Ar})$. The decrease of E_c with decreasing pressure is explained by the gradual disappearance of the columnar structure due to improved growth, as discussed above, and related magnetic inhomogeneities. These results show that E_c is determined by both, the value of K_u and the microstructure.

The intercolumnar boundaries are not only less dense than the interior of the columns but may also be different chemically. This has been shown for thin Tb-Fe films, d.c. magnetron sputtered at different pressures (0.13–0.93 Pa), by chemical imaging using electron energy loss spectroscopy (EELS) with high spatial resolution (about 2 nm) [23]. The distributions of both Fe and Tb are not homogeneous. There are chemical fluctuations at a scale of about 10–20 nm with Tb-rich intercolumnar

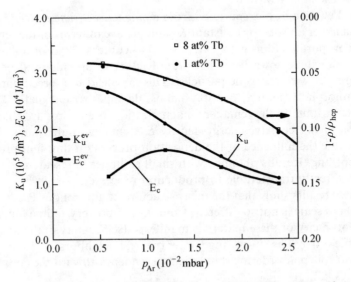

Figure 6.8 [22] Deviation of the density ρ from the crystalline value, anisotropy constant K_u and coercive force E_c (proportional to $M_s H_c$) of GdTb-Fe as a function of the Ar pressure during sputtering. $T = 300$ K. 10^{-2} mbar $= 1$ Pa.

boundaries of a thickness of about 2–4 nm. They are stronger in the films sputtered at higher pressure. K_u is maximum for 0.4 Pa. The coercive field increases when the segregation is more pronounced, e.g., when the sputter pressure is increased. The driving force for the chemical segregation can be: (1) oxidation of Tb at the intercolumnar boundaries. This is ruled out because no evidence for any oxygen enriched locations has been found. (2) A deviation of the film composition from those of intermetallic RE-TM phases.

Using spin-polarized photoemission, in-plane magnetic layers were observed at the surface of TbFeCo films. The films were prepared by evaporation in high vacuum and covered with protection layers [Al (10 nm)/SiO$_2$ (25 nm)] that were removed by Ar-sputtering in the UHV apparatus [24]. The results are explained with a three-layer structure generated by surface oxidation and segregation of Tb. It consists of: (1) an oxidized, RE-rich surface layer with in-plane anisotropy, (2) a TM-rich subsurface layer with reduced K_u, and (3) the bulk with perpendicular anisotropy.

There are also compositional fluctuations Δx in RE$_x$TM$_{1-x}$ layers on a larger geometrical scale inducing a variation in the compensation temperature of about 20 K, corresponding to $\Delta x < 0.5$ at%. This has been shown by reversal experiments on exchange-coupled double layers at measuring temperatures scanning the range of T_{comp} [25].

It is interesting to compare with the microstructure of thin film media for low-noise longitudinal magnetic recording on hard disks, e.g., polycrystalline Co-Pt-Cr layers [26]. Computer simulations reveal that the crystalline grains must be exchange-decoupled to yield a low write noise because they can then individually be reversed and form sharp domain boundaries. This is experimentally achieved either by a *geometric separation* of the grains in porous films obtained when evaporated or sputtered at high pressure and at low enough temperature or by a *chemical separation* when the films segregate (at high enough deposition temperatures) forming a grain boundary phase with low exchange-constant.

Dy-FeCo films, d.c. sputtered from a *magnetically unbalanced* magnetron cathode, exhibit a lower anisotropy constant K_u and behave in terms of the ferrimagnetic properties like evaporated films with 5 at.% less TM content [27]. For unbalanced magnetrons the plasma extend toward the substrate leading to an enhanced bombardment of the growing layer with energetic particles. This may lead to a precipitation of TM clusters in the amorphous matrix, possibly nanoscale superparamagnetic TM crystallites that do not contribute to the remanent magnetization. Such films are characterized by a low K_u and a higher coercive energy density E_c than evaporated films. These effects again demonstrate the influence of the deposition process on thin film properties relevant to MO recording. Results obtained with small cathodes in research laboratories are therefore not directly transferable to production processes.

These results show that the microstructure of amorphous RE-TM thin films on the 10 to 20 nm scale is not so different from that of polycrystalline films as often assumed. The amorphicity of these materials manifests itself mainly in the absence of long-range crystalline order. The short-range order (nearest neighbors, < 1 nm) is characterized by an anisotropic pair ordering that reflects a tendency toward the coordination of crystalline alloys [22].

The microstructure, the magnetic and recording properties of Pt/Co multilayers are also strongly affected by the parameters of film deposition. See Chapter 3 of this book.

6.2.3 Domain Wall Energy and Structure

The domain wall energy σ_w can be obtained from minor hysteresis loops of exchange-coupled double layers, see Section 6.3.5. Another method uses films with thermomagnetically written domains [28]–[30]. The principle is illustrated in Figure 6.9 [30] where hysteresis loops on MO disks are displayed. The exterior loop corresponds to reversals between saturated magnetic states; the coercive field, H_C, is determined by domain nucleation. The interior curve results from two experiments on the same disk with thermomagnetically written domains. The Faraday rotation angle θ_F is reduced in magnitude as compared to the exterior loop, because now 22% of the MO layer consists of thermomagnetically written domains with opposite magnetization. Both curves start at $H = 0$. The right part ($H > 0$) corresponds to an expansion, the left part ($H < 0$) to a collapse of domains. Both parts together do not belong to a reversal *loop* because the domains disappear at saturation.

The switching fields, H_1 and H_2, for respectively expanding and contracting the domains differ in magnitude. The conditions for reversal are formulated in the absolute values of magnetic fields,

$$\text{expansion:} \qquad H_1 = H_c^w - H_d + H_w \qquad\qquad (6.15a)$$

$$\text{contraction:} \qquad H_2 = H_c^w + H_d + H_w \qquad\qquad (6.15b)$$

$$\text{difference:} \qquad H_1 - H_2 = 2(H_w - H_d) \qquad\qquad (6.16)$$

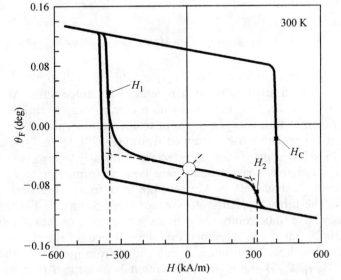

Figure 6.9 [30] Magnetic reversal curves of MO disks (GdTb-Fe) as monitored by the Faraday effect. The interior curve is observed on disks with cylindrical domains and consists of two parts, $H > 0$: domain expansion and $H < 0$: domain contraction.

where H_c^w is the coercive field for wall motion, H_d the demagnetizing field, and $H_w = \sigma_w/(2\mu_0 M_s r)$.

The wall gradient force need not be considered because the temperature is constant throughout the film. The coercive field for wall motion, H_c^w, given by

$$H_c^w = \frac{(H_1 + H_2)}{2} \tag{6.17}$$

is smaller than the static coercive field measured in complete loops where the reverse domains still have to be nucleated.

The difference between the switching fields for expanding (H_1) and collapsing (H_2) the cylindrical domains is evaluated according to

$$\sigma_w = 2\mu_0 M_s r \left(\frac{|H_1| - |H_2|}{2} + \frac{M_s}{1 + 3r/2h} \right) \quad \text{(SI)} \tag{6.18}$$

where r is the domain radius and h the film thickness.

This expression is derived from Equation (6.16) and Equation (6.2) by considering three points:

1. The sign of H_1 (expansion) is positive (as that of H_d), and that of H_2 (collapse) negative (as that of the wall force).
2. The demagnetizing field can be expressed by Equation (6.11) because no temperature gradient is involved and the domains are assumed to be perfectly cylindrical.
3. The wall moves when the driving force is larger than a coercive force:

$$2\mu_0 M_s H_c^w > |f_c|.$$

If the domain edge is or becomes jagged during motion, the domain wall length is greater than $2\pi r$ this method no longer yields reasonable results. As will be seen later in Section 6.6, this is the case for disks with a carrier-to-noise ratio CNR $<$ 50 dB.

Experimental wall energies at room temperature, reported for different compositions, are listed in Table 6.4 (compiled from [31]–[33], [29]). Typical values are about $3\,\text{erg/cm}^2$ ($3 \times 10^{-3}\,\text{J/m}^2$). They decrease about linearly to zero between room temperature and T_C. Reliable measurements have been performed up to $T_C - 40\,\text{K}$. The Bloch wall thickness, calculated as $\delta_w = (\pi/4)(\sigma/K_u)$ from measured quantities, is also reported in the table. Typical values range from 5 nm (Tb-FeCo to 18 nm (GdDy-FeCo). They have to be compared with the lateral scale of the columnar microstructure of about 10–20 nm. Typical temperature dependences of the characteristic parameters, entering the Bloch wall formulae, as calculated from mean-field theory, are shown in Figure 6.10 [34]. K_u, A and σ_w are approximately linear in T from room temperature to T_c where they all vanish, whereas the domain wall thickness $\delta_w = \pi\sqrt{(A/K_u)}$ is relatively independent of temperature.

The classical equation for the energy of a Bloch wall is $\sigma_w = B\sqrt{(AK_u)}$ with $B = 4$. The domain wall energy increases under an applied magnetic field [35]–[37]. For the

TABLE 6.4 Domain Wall Energy Density σ_w and Thickness δ_w in Amorphous RE-TM Alloys at Room Temperature. Units: 10^{-3} J/m^2 (SI) or erg/cm^2 (cgs)

	σ_w [erg/cm^2 or 10^{-3} J/m^2]	K_u [10^5 J/m^3]	δ_w [nm]
TbFeCo ([a,b])	3.1–4.4, average 3.8	6	5
Tb$_{28}$Fe$_{63}$Co$_9$ ([b])	2.7		
Gd$_{20.6}$Tb$_{4.5}$Fe$_{75.9}$ ([a])	1.9	2.5	6
Gd$_{13}$Tb$_{16}$Fe$_{49}$Co$_{18}$Ar$_4$ ([b])	1.4		
DyFeCo ([a,c])	2.7–3.8, average 3.5	2.5	10
Gd$_{19.5}$Dy$_{5.5}$Fe$_{75}$ ([a])	1.8	0.8	18
Tb-Nd$_x$-FeCo ([c])	0.6–4	0.9–5.6	(3–7)

Sources: References: [a][31], [33], [b][29], [c][38], [d][33], [e][32]. The Bloch Wall Width Was Calculated as $\delta_w = (\pi/4)(\sigma_w/K_u)$. The values for K_u were taken from [31].

systems (Gd,Tb)-(Fe,Co) and (Gd,Dy)-(Fe,Co), the variation of σ_w with the Tb and Dy content can be explained by the measured variation of K_u [31]–[33].

The experimentally determined parameters K_u and A_x are values averaged over the whole specimen. A domain wall is, however, expected to be located in regions with low energy, i.e., with low K_u or low A_x. Possible candidates are boundaries between columns, characteristic for thin films, where a reduced exchange may be expected. The measured value of σ_w should therefore be lower than the one calculated from K_u and A_x. The difference could tell about the pinning power of the defects. The measurements are, however, not precise enough to allow quantitative conclusions.

In the case of the system Tb-Nd$_x$-(Fe,Co), the factor B decreases continuously from 4 for Tb-FeCo to 1.5 for a Nd content $\geq$ 10 at.% [38]. This is not yet satisfactorily understood but is thought to arise from a big noncolinearity of the magnetic moments introduced by the strong spin-orbit coupling of Nd.

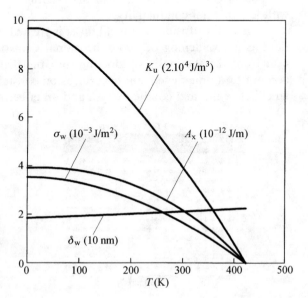

Figure 6.10 [34] Exchange stiffness constant A_x, uniaxial anisotropy constant K_u, wall energy density $\sigma_w = 4\sqrt{(AK_u)}$ and wall thickness $\delta_w = \pi\sqrt{(A/K_u)}$ for Tb$_{21}$Fe$_{79}$ as a function of temperature. Theoretical estimate, by mean-field theory.

The structure of a domain wall in polycrystalline Pt/Co multilayers (average grain size = 30 nm) has been calculated by means of a two-dimensional LLG simulation. The results for a saturation polarization $J = J_{Co} + J_{Pt} = (1.76 + 0.16)\,\text{T}$ are shown in Figure 6.11 [39]. The wall structure is of Bloch type in a grain with $K_u = 1.9\,\text{MJ/m}^3$ (right) but of Néel type for $K_u = 1.7\,\text{MJ/m}^3$ (left).

The resolution in a recently developed differential phase contrast imaging mode of Lorentz microscopy is so high (10 nm in favorable cases, for high M_s) that magnetic domain walls can be detected [40]. In the case of Pt/Co multilayer films, the simulated *Bloch* wall contrast was much stronger than the experimentally observed one. A computer simulation based upon the LLG equation in two dimensions (representing the cross section of an infinitely long film stripe) has been used to obtain more information about the micromagnetic wall structure [40]. The results are similar to the left part (Néel type) of Figure 6.11.

In Néel walls there is no in-plane magnetization parallel to the wall and the in-plane components perpendicular to the wall cancel out in a vertical sum-up. The Lorentz contrast, which is determined by the in-plane components, is therefore very weak. The magnetic moments are aligned in a curl-like structure minimizing the divergence of M and therefore the demagnetizing energy. This wall structure is representative of films with high magnetization and low anisotropy. As there is no exchange-coupling between the layers (especially of alternating magnetic and nonmagnetic layers), an antiparallel alignment in the curl-center is possible without a singularity in the energy density. In a homogeneous film the minimum configuration is an asymetric Bloch wall [1].

6.2.4 Laser-Induced Temperature Profiles on the Disk

In the layer stack of a MO disk, heat conducting metallic layers, such as the MO layer and the reflection layer (Al or Ti) are, generally, embedded in poor heat conductors (dielectric layers, substrate, lacquer). Laterally, the heat spreads mainly within the metallic layers, but there is also an essential vertical heat flow through the layers with less thermal conductivity.

The heat diffusion in optical disks is treated, within an effective-layer approximation, as a broadening of two-dimensional Gaussian profiles [41]. The penetration of heat from the thermally conducting into the thermally isolating layers is taken into account by a time-dependent heat diffusion constant $D(t)$ calculated as the quotient of an effective thermal conductivity λ and an effective thermal capacity c:

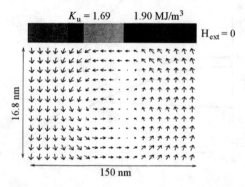

Figure 6.11 [39] Wall structure in a polycrystalline Pt/Co multilayer with perpendicular anisotropy (12 bilayers, $d_{Co} = 0.35$ nm, $d_{Pt} = 1.05$ nm). K_u changes from grain to grain. Its value is indicated on the gray scale map. The maximum deviation angle is $5°$.

$$D(t) = \frac{\sum_i \lambda_i \delta_i + \sum_c \lambda_c h_c}{\sum_i \rho_i c_i \delta_i + \sum_c \rho_c c_c h_c} \qquad (6.19)$$

The summation over i and c concern the thermally isolating and conducting layers, respectively. The h_c denote the physical thickness of the conducting layers and the δ_i the time-dependent penetration depth into the isolating layers:

$$\delta_i(t) = \sqrt{\pi D_i t} \qquad (6.20)$$

with $D_i = \gamma_i/(\rho_i c_i)$ being the heat diffusion coefficient of the respective layers. The specific thermal capacity c in the thin layers is expected to be the same as in the bulk material and a good estimate of ρc can be obtained by taking the densities ρ of the films as 95% of their bulk crystalline values. The thermal conductivity λ, however, depends strongly on the microstructure of the medium and must be determined experimentally.

Two experimental methods to determine the thermal conductivity of the layers of a MO disk have been reported: (1) fitting recording results to theoretical models and (2) evaluating Kerr images of the hot laser spot.

(a) The domain instability can be determined in a test recorder in dependence on laser power and magnetic field, as will be discussed later in Section 6.5. When comparing the experimental results with the predictions of the bubble-like model, the temperature profile is calculated with the thermal conductivity of the disks as a fitting parameter. In order to determine the thermal conductivity of one of the layers in a stack, series of disks are prepared with the thickness of the respective layer varied while the thickness of the other layers is kept constant [30]. Results thus obtained and others are summarized in Table 6.5.

(b) A spinning disk, heated by a laser beam and subjected to a magnetic bias field to prevent thermomagnetic writing, is monitored in a polarizing microscope [42]. The spatial resolution is better than 0.4 μm. The Kerr image is transformed into a temperature distribution via the measured temperature dependence of the Kerr rotation angle, $\theta_K = \theta_K(T)$. The result for a 145 nm thick GdTb-Fe based disk moving with a velocity of 6 m/s and a 2 μs, 5.5 mW laser pulse is shown in Figure 6.12, together with theoretical calculations based upon a thermal conductivity $\lambda = 7\,W/(mK)$ for the GdTb-Fe layer.

At the leading edge of the laser spot, the temperature gradient is about 170 K/μm and at the trailing edge 45 K/μm. Values in the order of 100 K/μm have been reported also for several theoretical calculations [43], [31], [41]. For thinner layers (12 nm MO)

TABLE 6.5 Measured Thermal Conductivity λ of Thin Films and Theoretical Thermal Capacities per Volume, ρc, Calculated from Literature Values of the Specific Heat c of Crystals and Assuming 95% Dense Films. (am) Means That the AlN Layer is Amorphous

λ[W/(K m)]	RE-TM	Al	Ti	AlN
Sputtered film[a]	17	190	8	23 (am)
Sputtered film[b]	whole stack: 7			
Evaporated film[c]	15.4			
Bulk crystal	54	240	22	300
ρc [10^6 J/(K m^3)]	2.6	2.1	2.1	2.1

Sources: References: [a][31], [30], [b][42], [c][30].

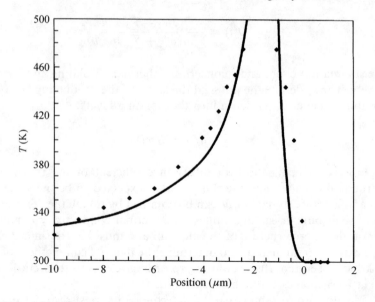

Figure 6.12 [42] Temperature profile of a rotating MO layer induced by a laser pulse (2 µs, 5.5 mW). Model results for $\lambda = 7$ W/(mK) (curve) and experimental data (points). Linear disk velocity 6 m/s.

and shorter pulses (50 ns), about a factor of 3 higher values can be obtained (see, e.g., [10], Section 11.3).

6.2.5 Representative Values of the Bubble Parameters

In the following, we consider in detail a set of four Tb-FeCo compositions comprising 21 to 30 at.% Tb that differ magnetically in their compensation temperature. The composition, Curie, and compensation temperatures are given in Table 6.6 [44] together with the demagnetizing temperature defined as the temperature where the magnetic layer looses its 100% remanence. The decrease of the remanence in the vicinity of T_c is a demagnetizing effect and not due to an in-plane magnetization.

The magnetization and the coercive field of these samples is shown in Figure 6.13 [44]. The uniaxial anisotropy constant K_u is about 4×10^5 J/m^3 at room temperature for all samples and decreases linearly to zero at T_c.

We can transform values from these curves into forces per area representing the pressure on a bubble domain wall. The results for a bubble with a radius of 0.5 µm in a film of thickness 50 nm at $T = 400$ K are in Table 6.7. A wall energy density $\sigma_w = 2.5 * 10^{-3}$ J/m^2 has been assumed which represents less than 20% error for the

TABLE 6.6 [44] Composition and Magnetic Data of Four Typical Tb-FeCo Samples

Sample	Composition	T_C	T_{comp}	T_{demag}
1	$Tb_{29.9}Fe_{62.6}Co_{7.5}$	450	$> T_C$	$> T_C$
2	$Tb_{27.2}Fe_{65.5}Co_{7.3}$	461	310	455
3	$Tb_{23.6}Fe_{67.6}Co_{8.8}$	473	214	465
4	$Tb_{21.2}Fe_{71.9}Co_{6.9}$	473	0	440

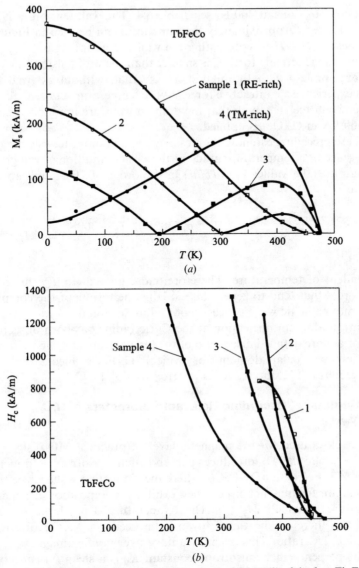

Figure 6.13 [44] Magnetization M_s (a) and coercive field H_c (b) of the four Tb-FeCo
samples of Table 6.6 with different compensation temperature T_{comp} and
about the same Curie temperature T_C. $M_s(T_{comp}) = 0$, $H_c(T_{comp}) = \infty$.

TABLE 6.7 Pressure (forces per unit area) on a Domain Wall. Tb-FeCo Films of 50 mm Thickness,
Samples of Table 6.6, $T = 400$ K, Diameter 1 μm. Formulae: $f_c = (2\mu_0 M_s)H_c$, $f_d = (2\mu_0 M_s)(M_s/16)$, $f_w = \sigma_w/r$. The Wall Gradient Force f_{wg} is About 2 kJ/m³ for a Temperature Gradient Outside the Curie Radius
of 100 K/μm, Independent of the Temperature (see text)

#	M_s [kA/m]	H_c [kA/m]	f_c [kJ/m³]	f_d [kJ/m³]	f_w [kJ/m³]
1	160	100	40	4.0	5
2	90	350	80	1.3	5
3	35	450	40	0.2	5
4	25	700	42	0.1	5

chosen compositions at 400 K, see Table 6.4. The wall tension f_w is about 10% of the coercive force f_c. Approximately the same ratio can be seen in Figure 6.9 [30] between the values of $|H_1-H_2|$, representing the wall energy force, and H_c.

The demagnetizing force f_d is smaller than the wall tension f_w and comparable to it only for sample 4 with the highest M_s, so that, without external field, the domains always experience a contractive force. At the temperature chosen, about 70 K below T_C, the coercive force is so high that the domain walls are immobile unless a field of more than 100 kA/m (1kOe) is applied.

These preceding estimated forces concern a homogeneously magnetized sample. In the presence of a temperature gradient there is an additional wall gradient force f_{wg}. In the literature, the values for (dT/dr) in the order of 100 K/µm are reported. We can estimate

$$f_{wg} = \frac{d\sigma_w/dT}{dT/dr} = \frac{\sigma_w(300\text{K})/(T_c - 300\text{K})}{100\text{K/µm}} = 2\text{kJ/m}^3 \tag{6.21}$$

independent of temperature. Therefore, close enough to T_c, this force dominates all other forces that tend to zero. This explains the results of the computer simulation of the thermomagnetic write process reported in Section 6.1.4 where for a thin laser beam (0.1 µm) no domain nucleation at the Curie radius has been observed.

For a more detailed discussion of the temperature and the radial dependence of the forces on a circular domain for typical Tb-FeCo media with $T_c = 500$ K and $T_{comp} = 360$–420 K, the reader is referred to [45], [46].

6.2.6 Summary "Recording-Relevant Parameters of MO Media"

RE-TM alloys used for the magnetic layer of practical MO disks are ternary such as GdTb-Fe where the Tb introduces perpendicular anisotropy and increases the coercive field and Tb-FeCo and Dy-FeCo, where the Co increases the Curie temperature. These materials are ferrimagnetic; i.e., they exhibit a composition dependent compensation temperature at which $M_s = 0$. The temperature dependence of the magnetization, $M_s(T)$, can therefore be tuned toward the needs of MO-recording by choosing the proper RE/TM ratio. This is an advantage over nonferrimagnetic materials.

The perpendicular anisotropy constant K_u is a steep function of the temperature when Tb is the dominant RE element, but a flat one when Dy or Gd dominates. When Gd is the only RE element, K_u even becomes in-plane above room temperature. This difference in behavior defines roughly two classes of MO media: magnetically hard ones (with enough Tb) and magnetically "less hard" ones.

The coercive force E_c is determined by the value of K_u and by magnetic inhomogeneities of the film. The microstructure of amorphous RE-TM thin films on the 10–20 nm scale is often characterized by columns, sometimes with RE-rich segregates in the intercolumnar regions, depending on the preparation conditions. When the density of the films increases and the intercolumnar boundaries become less pronounced, E_c decreases although K_u still increases.

The domain wall energy σ_w can be obtained from hysteresis loops of films with thermomagnetically written domains. Its value at room temperature ranges from 2 to $4 \cdot 10^{-3}$ J/m^2 (SI), (= 2–4 erg/cm^2) for all RE-TM MO-media. It is well described by the

Bloch wall formula $\sigma_w = 4\sqrt{(AK_u)}$, except for Nd-containing materials where it is found to be lower.

The wall gradient force outside the Curie radius, induced by the T-gradient, is approximately independent of the temperature and should dominate, close enough to the Curie temperature, over the M_s-related forces arising from the external and the demagnetizing fields. This overweight may even prevent the domain formation in the first stage of the cooling phase.

6.3 MAGNETIC REVERSAL PROCESSES AND COERCIVE EFFECTS IN SINGLE AND EXCHANGE COUPLED LAYERS

In this section we discuss several concepts of coercivity. First, micromagnetic models of the domain nucleation and the domain wall pinning in materials with structural defects are reviewed. Scaling laws of the coercive force with K_u of the type $\mu_0 M_s H_c = C_n K_u^n$ with characteristic coefficients n are derived and compared with experimental results. Experiments on the magnetic after-effect are presented and evaluated according to theoretical models of thermally activated wall motion.

Then the results of computer simulations based on the LLG equation are reported and compared with the predictions of the micromagnetic models presented before. Finally, the domain formation in exchange-coupled layers is discussed with emphasis on the role of the interface wall in the various reversal processes.

6.3.1 Domain Nucleation and Domain Wall Pinning as a Function of K_u

Table 6.8 summarizes the scaling powers n in the law $\mu_0 M_s H_c = C_n K_u^n$ for various models of coercivity to be discussed and compared with experiments in this subsection.

6.3.1.1 Micromagnetic Models Founded Scaling Laws

Nucleation by Coherent Rotation We consider a body, homogeneously magnetized in an easy direction described by a uniaxial anisotropy constant K_u, embedded in a magnetic material. A magnetic field is applied opposite to the magnetization. The critical value, H_n, necessary to rotate the magnetization coherently into the direction of the applied field is given by [47]:

$$H_n = H_{anis} - H_d = \frac{2K_u}{\mu_0 M_s} - N_{eff} M_s \quad \text{(SI)} \tag{6.22}$$

TABLE 6.8 Theoretical Scaling Powers of the Coercive Force with the Anisotropy constant K_u According to: $\mu_0 M_s H_c = C_n K_u^n$

$n = 4$	Eq. (6.26), nanocrystalline materials
$n = 1$	Eq. (6.25), domain nucleation controlled
$n = 3/2$	Eq. (6.28), wall pinning at small defects
$n = 1/2$	Eq. (6.31), wall pinning at large defects
	Eq. (6.32), expansion of residual domain

$$H_{\text{anis}} = \frac{2K_u}{\mu_0 M_s} \tag{6.23}$$

The first term on the right-hand side, reproduced in Equation (6.23), is called the *anisotropy field*, H_{anis}. The second term is the component of the demagnetizing field parallel to H_{anis} and arises from magnetic charges (defined as $- \, div \, M$). In the case of an ellipsoidal body in a homogeneously magnetized matrix, the demagnetizing field is uniform over the body and is described by a demagnetizing tensor N. N_{eff} is its value in the direction of the applied field. Effects due to domain walls are neglected in Equation (6.22) that is, therefore, strictly valid only for single domain particles that are exchange-decoupled from the surrounding material.

Other types of magnetic reversal with a non-uniform rotation of the magnetization like curling or buckling occur only in low-K_u materials and are, therefore, not of interest here.

Experimentally observed values of H_n are generally one or even two orders of magnitude smaller than expected from Equation (6.22). In the case of amorphous RE-TM alloys the factor is about 10 [31]. This discrepancy is known as Brown's paradox [48]. It is attributed to magnetic inhomogeneities leading to locally low anisotropy constants and high demagnetizing fields. These effects may be taken account of by a microstructural parameter α:

$$H_n = \alpha \frac{2K_u}{\mu_0 M_s} - N_{\text{eff}} M_s \quad \text{(SI)} \tag{6.24}$$

The parameter α has been calculated analytically in a one-dimensional model, assuming quasi-harmonic spatial variations in $K_u(z)$ [51], [52]. Its value depends on the amplitude and the wavelength $2r_0$ of the K_u-variations, $\alpha = 1$ is found if the "defect width" $2r_0$ is much smaller than the wall width parameter $\Delta_w = \sqrt{(A/K_u)}$. This means that, in the presence of small defects, the anisotropy field is determined by the *average* K_u. In the inverse situation, $2r_0 \gg \delta_w$, *large defects*, the anisotropy field is determined by the *minimum* value of K_u. For intermediate values of $2r_0$, the value of α depends on the assumed model of the inhomogeneities. This one-dimensional model should be adequate for the nucleation at planar defects like grain boundaries or inter-columnar boundaries.

The demagnetizing field becomes strong in the vicinity of nonmagnetic regions (big div **M**). Small nucleation fields can therefore be expected in regions of low K_u, that are larger than the wall width, adjacent to nonmagnetic regions.

Equation (6.24) can be reformulated to provide a scaling law of the coercive force with K_u:

$$\mu_0 M_s H_c + \mu_0 N_{\text{eff}} M_s^2 = (2\alpha) K_u^1 \tag{6.25}$$

For compositions of amorphous RE-TM alloys typically used for MO recording the demagnetizing term can be neglected so that the scaling power is 1.

Nanocrystalline Materials The coercivity of bulk nanocrystalline materials with randomly oriented easy magnetic axes of the grains is explained by a statistical variant of Equation (6.22) in which K_u is replaced by an effective anisotropy $\langle K \rangle$ [49]. $\langle K \rangle$ is obtained as the average over the number N of grains (of diameter D) within a volume whose diameter is the wall width parameter Δ_w. $\langle K \rangle$ is not zero only if the nanocrystals are not uniformly oriented in all directions. The deviation from equidistribution can be estimated as $\frac{\sqrt{N}}{N}$. The magnetocrystalline anisotropy of the material is assumed to be cubic and given by a parameter K_1. We get the three interdependent equations $N = D^3/\Delta_{ex}^3$, $\langle K \rangle = K_1 \sqrt{N}/N = K_1/\sqrt{N}$, and $\Delta_{ex} = \sqrt{(A/\langle K \rangle)}$, yielding

$$\langle K \rangle = \left(\frac{D^6}{A^3} \right) K_1^4 \tag{6.26}$$

This expression is valid when D, the average grain diameter, is small against Δ_w. The scaling power n is 4. When D exceeds Δ_w, $\langle K \rangle = K_1$ and $n = 1$.

Wall pinning. Due to magnetic and structural inhomogeneities, the domain wall energy depends on position and the walls tend to be fixed in locations with minimum energy. Therefore, even if a sample already contains reverse domains, the further reversal is still hampered by *wall pinning*. Two cases are distinguished: the wall width is small against the defect width and vice versa.

A large variation in the wall energy, $\sigma_w = 4\sqrt{(AK)}$, requires large variations in A and/or in K. For a planar barrier of width Δ_b and values A_b and K_b of the exchange and anisotropy constant in the barrier, respectively, the following equation has been derived within a one-dimensional variational calculation of Bloch wall structure and energy [50]:

$$H_w = 0.6 H_{anis} \frac{\Delta_b}{\Delta_w} \left(\frac{A}{A_b} - \frac{K_b}{K} \right) \tag{6.27}$$

which is valid when the defect width Δ_b is small compared to the wall width parameter: $\Delta_b \ll \Delta_w = \sqrt{(A/K)}$. In this case the pinning becomes stronger with increasing defect thickness. Applying this equation to films with perpendicular anisotropy and substituting for H_{anis} and Δ_b (Table 6.2), we see that the coercive force $\mu_0 M_s H_w$ scales with K_u like:

$$\mu_0 M_s H_w = C * K_u \sqrt{K_u} = C * K_u^{3/2} \tag{6.28}$$

valid for a comparison of films with the same A, i.e., with the same T_c, and measured at the same temperature. A similar formula has been derived for the quasi-harmonic spatial variations of $K_u(z)$ referred to above [51] (δ_w = wall width = $\pi \Delta_w$, r_0 = defect width):

$$H_w = H_{anis} \pi \left(\frac{r_0}{\delta_w} \right) \qquad \text{for } 2\pi r_0 \ll \delta_w \tag{6.29}$$

yielding the same scaling law [Equation (6.28)] with $n = 3/2$. On the other hand, a formula for large barriers was derived in the same formalism:

$$H_w = H_{anis}\frac{2}{3}\left(\frac{\delta_w}{r_0}\right) \qquad \text{for } \delta_w < 2\pi r_0 \qquad (6.30)$$

The pinning becomes stronger when the wall thickness approaches the defect thickness. Equation (6.30) yields a scaling law:

$$\mu_0 M_s H_w = \frac{\pi}{r_0}\sigma_w = C * \frac{K_u}{\sqrt{K_u}} = C * K_u^{1/2} \qquad (6.31)$$

valid under the same assumptions as above: same T_c, same measuring temperature.

Expansion of Residual Domains The expansion of an existing small domain nucleus (1) requires wall energy according to the increase of surface area and (2) yields Zeeman energy according to the increase in volume. These opposite effects define an energy barrier that has to be overcome by a critical field H_{ex}. For a conical nucleus of radius r_0 this is [53]:

$$H_{ex} = \sqrt{\frac{3}{2}}\frac{\sigma_w}{\mu_0 M_s r_0} = 0.4 H_{anis}\left(\frac{\sigma_w}{r_0}\right) \qquad (6.32)$$

For the second equation the formulae for energy and width of a Bloch wall (see Table 6.2) have been used. The field for expansion is proportional to δ_w and consequently to $\sqrt{K_u}$. For $r_0 \approx \delta_w$ this model yields a coercive field, $H_{ex} \approx 0.4 H_a$, in the order of magnitude of the anisotropy field. Equation (6.32) is essentially the same as Equation (6.30) so that the scaling law is given by Equation (6.31), $n = 1/2$.

For the perpendicular magnetic recording media, $Co_{80}Ni_{20}$ and $Co_{73}Pt_{27}$, the experimental values of the coercive field can be reproduced by computer simulations of residual domain expansion based on the LLG equation [54]. The magnetic films are modeled as bundles of long columnar grains separated by substantial grain boundaries that interrupt the exchange interaction. Each grain contains a small cubic nucleus whose magnetization is flipped, at the start of the calculation, along the direction of the applied field. The coercive field is then obtained as the minimum field under which the nucleus expands. An alternative model for the coercivity in CoPt alloy films is given below in Section 6.3.3.3.

6.3.1.2 Experimental Values of the Scaling Power

The experimental values of n for different amorphous RE-TM alloy systems are listed in Table 6.9 (data from [31]–[33]). At higher temperatures, values $n \approx 1.3$–1.7 are found indicating that wall pinning at small defects dominates the coercivity in all recording-relevant RE-TM systems. The situation at lower temperatures is not so uniform. For Tb-FeCo, the reversal is nucleation controlled, which fits well to the square hysteresis loops generally observed in these materials.

The coercivity in Nd-containing materials is determined for all temperatures by wall motion. This indicates easy nucleation that may be explained by a strong non-colinearity of the magnetic moments introduced by the Nd so that each Nd ion may be regarded as a nucleation center. The reason for the noncolinearity is the sensitivity of the Nd moments to local anisotropies, due to a strong spin-orbit coupling. Compare

TABLE 6.9 Experimental Scaling Powers n in the Relation $\mu_0 M_s H_c = C_n K_u^n$ for Amorphous RE-TM Alloys

Tb-FeCo	$T > 200$ K	$n = 1.3$
	$T - > 0$ K	$n = 1$
Dy-FeCo, GdDy-Fe, GdDy-FeCo	$T > 140$ K	$n = 1.4$
	$T < 140$ K	$n = 0.7$
TbNd-FeCo	all T	$n = 1.7$

Sources: Data assembled from [31], D. Raasch, dissertation Aachen, 1995.

also the deviation of the experimental domain wall energies from values predicted by the classical Bloch wall formula (Section 6.2.3).

For the magnetically "less hard" Dy-containing materials the behavior is different below 140 K. A scaling power $n = 0.7$ is observed, and it is not clear whether this is due to a control by nucleation ($n = 1$) or by wall pinning at large defects or expansion of residual domains ($n = 0.5$). The wall width for such composition 10–18 nm (Table 6.14), is of the same order as the lateral dimensions of the columnar microstructure and considerably larger than that of the other compositions. This may explain the different behavior.

6.3.2 Models of Thermally Activated and Time-Dependent Magnetic Reversal

6.3.2.1 Phenomenological Introduction

Figure 6.14 shows the domain wall velocity v in a 20 nm thick GdTb-Fe film as a function of the applied field [55]. Above a critical field, H_p, $v(H)$ approaches a straight line and can be described by

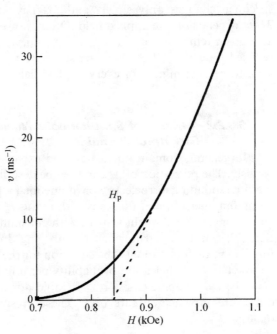

Figure 6.14 [55] Domain wall velocity v as a function of the applied field H. GdTb-Fe film with $H_c = 700$ Oe (= 56 kA/m).

$$v = \mu_w(H - H_p) \tag{6.33}$$

where μ_w and H_p are called the domain wall mobility and the propagation field, respectively. The mobility is related to a viscous damping of the spin precession described in the LLG formalism. The corresponding formula will be discussed later in Section 6.5 together with experiments.

Below H_p, the velocity varies exponentially with the field and is thermally activated:

$$v = v_0 \exp\left(-\frac{W_p - 2\mu_0 H M_s V_p}{kT}\right) \tag{6.34}$$

This behavior described by Equation (6.34) arises from a statistical, jumplike wall motion. A jump is characterized by an activation volume V_p and an activation energy W_p. The activation volume measures the region that the Bloch wall scans on its way from the minimum to the maximum of the potential energy under an applied field. It is generally not identical to the elementary jump volume that can be larger.

A thermally activated nucleation-rate N follows the same type of law

$$N = N_0 \exp\left(-\frac{W_N - 2\mu_0 H M_s V_N}{kT}\right) \tag{6.35}$$

with V_N and W_N being, respectively, the activation volume and the energy for nucleation.

Under an applied field less than the coercive field, the magnetization M of a specimen changes only slowly and $M(t)$ is called a relaxation curve. The form of $M(t)$ depends on the applied field. Often, however, all relaxation curves of a specimen at a given temperature fall in a unique curve, irrespective of H, when plotted versus reduced time $t/t_{0.5}$. The characteristic time $t_{0.5}$ is the time to reach the demagnetized state to be determined for every applied field separately [56].

6.3.2.2 A Model of Simultaneous Nucleation and Growth of Domains

In general, domain nucleation and expansion of existing domains occur simultaneously. The relaxation of M can then be described by a model originally developed for the corresponding ferroelectric phenomenon [57]. It is based upon two assumptions: (1), a random nucleation of domains with radius r_c, described by $N(t) = N_0[1 - \exp(-Rt)]$, and (2) a circular domain growth with constant radial velocity v. The second assumption is certainly not true when neighboring domains exert a repulsive demagnetizing force upon each other [58]. The equation for the relaxation curve is governed by the two parameters R, a nucleation probability per unit time, and $k = v/(Rr_c)$ (dimension-less).

The two extreme cases, $k \gg 1$ (rapid domain wall motion) and $k = 0$ (nucleation only), are shown in Figure 6.15. The corresponding formulae is given in Equation (6.36):

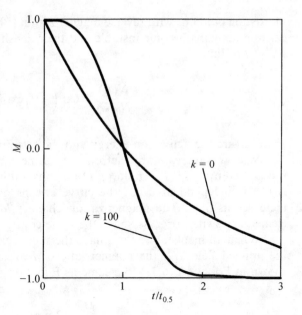

Figure 6.15 [56] Theoretical curves of the magnetic relaxation, $M(t/t_{0.5})$, for $k = 0$ (nucleation only, constant probability) and $k = 100$ (slow nucleation followed by rapid domain growth). The time axis is normalized with $t_{0.5}$, the time necessary to reach the demagnetized state, $M = 0$.

$$k \gg 1 : M(t) = 2\exp\left[-\left(\frac{k^2}{3}\right)R^3 t^3\right] - 1$$

$$k = 0 : M(t) = 2\exp[-Rt] - 1 \tag{6.36}$$

We have modified the equations in [56] such that $M = 1$ in the initial state, $M = 0$ in the demagnetized state, and $M = -1$ when the magnetization is completely aligned parallel to the external field.

The corresponding hysteresis loops are shown in Figure 6.16. Slow domain nucleation followed by rapid domain wall motion leads to a square hysteresis loop whereas continuous nucleation leads to a sheared hysteresis loops.

6.3.2.3 *Models of Thermally Activated Magnetic Reversal*

When the magnetic field applied to a partly reversed specimen is suddenly incremented, the magnetization follows in many cases a logarithmic time law: $M(t) = S^* \ln(t) + \text{const}$. This can be explained by a thermally activated reversal rate

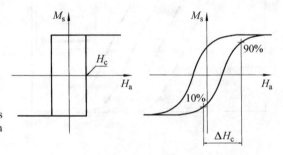

Figure 6.16 Square and sheared hysteresis loop. ΔH_c characterizes the deviation from squareness.

of existing domains with reverse magnetization [59], [60]. No new nuclei are created but existing domains become instable and their density of states, $N(E)$ decreases exponentially with time:

$$\frac{N(E)}{N_0(E)} = \exp\left(-tf_0 \exp\left(-\frac{E}{kT}\right)\right) \tag{6.37}$$

E and f_0 are the activation energy and the attempt frequency, respectively.

When t is increased by factor ε^n, the same curve $N(E)/N_0(E)$ is observed, however it is shifted by $\Delta E/kT = n^* \ln(\varepsilon)$. For a constant initial distribution of states, i.e., when $N_0(E)$ is independent of E, the curve sweeps out equal areas in equal logarithmic increases in time. The magnetization changes *logarithmically* with time when every elementary switch process yields the same contribution.

When all metastable states have the same activation energy E (depending only on the applied field H_a) the magnetization M/M_s reverses exponentially with time, as shown in Equation (6.38) [the same as Equation (6.37)].

$$\frac{M}{M_s} = 2\exp\left(-\frac{t}{\tau}\right) - 1$$
$$\tau = \frac{1}{f_0}\exp\left(\frac{E(H)}{kT}\right) \tag{6.38}$$

The variation of M/M_s as a function of $\ln(t)$ with $E(H_a/kT)$ as parameter are shown in Figure 6.17. The times t' obtained from different curves for the same M/M_s (e.g., $= -0.6$ in Fig. 6.17) are related to one another by $\ln(t') - E(H_a/kT) =$ const. For Stoner–Wohlfart domains (reversal by homogeneous rotation of M_s) we get $\partial E/\partial H = \mu_0 V M_s$ (SI), where V is the volume of the domains. For a plot H_a vs. $\ln(t')$ straight lines with a negative slope $H_f = kT/(\partial E/\partial H)$, the "fluctuation field," are expected.

Experimental results for $Tb_{22}Fe_{70}Co_8$ under fields $H_a = 8545$ to 8721 Oe look very similar to the curves in Figure 6.17. Their evaluation yields a fluctuation field of about 87 Oe and an activation volume of $5.5 \times 10^{-18} cm^3$ [60].

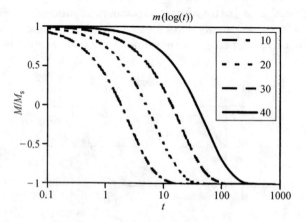

Figure 6.17 Magnetic reversal vs. $\ln(t)$ at various fixed values of applied field. Equation (6.38), τ is given in the inset.

6.3.2.4 Monte Carlo Simulations of Dendritic Domain Growth

Relaxation curves of thin films with perpendicular magnetic anisotropy have been calculated by Monte Carlo simulations and compared to experimental results for Dy/Fe compositionally modulated multilayers [61]. The magnetic medium has been modeled as an array of cells in the shape of hexagonal prisms extending through the thickness of the film. The magnetic relaxation is affected by a series of coherent rotations of individual cells so that no regular wall motion is involved. This type of reversal can be characterized as *dendritic domain growth*. The main parameters of this model are the cell volume and the domain wall energy. The probability that cell j reverses its magnetization in time Δt is thermally activated:

$$P_j = R \exp\left[-\frac{E_j^B}{kT}\right]\Delta t \qquad (6.39)$$

where R is an attempt frequency chosen to be $2 \times 10^9 \, s^{-1}$ (2 GHz). During the simulation, cells are chosen at random and their magnetization is reversed if their P_j exceeds a random number.

The energy barrier E_j^B of each cell is calculated during the simulation from the following micromagnetic model. The energy of cell j during the reversal process is taken to be

$$E_j = K_u V_c \sin^2\Theta_j - \mu_0 M_s V_c (H_z + \langle H_{dj}\rangle)\cos\Theta_j + \frac{1}{3}\left(3 - \frac{1}{2}S_j\cos\Theta_j\right)E_w \text{ (SI)} \qquad (6.40)$$

where Θ_j is the angle of the magnetization of cell j measured from the $+z$-axis, the film normal. The first term represents the anisotropy energy. The second term represents the Zeeman energy due to the external field H_z and the average demagnetizing field $\langle H_{dj}\rangle$ defined by the magnetic state of all other cells. The anisotropy and the Zeeman terms define an energy barrier that vanishes if the total magnetic field is larger than the anisotropy field $H_{anis} = 2K_u/(\mu_0 M_s)$.

The third term considers the creation and annihilation of domain walls. E_w is the energy to form walls on all six edges of the cell. S_j is a sum over the six nearest neighbors of cell j and ranges in value from -6 (walls created at all six interfaces) to $+6$ (walls annihilated at all six interfaces). Below a critical value of the magnetic field, Equation (6.40) has minima at $\Theta_j = 0$ and π with a maximum in between defining the energy barrier to reversal, E_j^B, for cell j.

Under the assumption of a coherent rotation, it is justified to take the average demagnetizing field of the cell configuration when considering effects due to the magnetostatic energy. However, H_d is only strong within a distance to a domain boundary comparable with the film thickness. If H_d is important relative to the external field, the assumption of a coherent rotation is perhaps no longer justified. The Dy/Fe multilayers are, however, ferrimagnetic and exhibit a low M_s so that this neglect may not be important.

The cell volume V_c and the wall energy E_w are varied. V_c is adjusted to give a realistic coercive field (about 7 kOe in the case of the Dy/Fe multilayers). Optimal values of V_c are in the order of magnitude of $(12.5 \text{ nm})^3$. The wall energy E_w is chosen to reproduce the experimental relaxation curves. Nucleation is accompanied by the creation of magnetic walls at all interfaces, whereas during domain growth existing walls are annihilated and new ones created. This explains why, for a relatively low E_w, the relaxation curves are similar to that for $k = 0$ (continuous nucleation) in Figure 6.15, whereas for a relatively high E_w they look like the curve for $k = 100$ (slow nucleation followed by rapid growth).

6.3.3 Experimental Results on Coercivity and their Correlation with the Microstructure of Thin Films

6.3.3.1 The Magnetic Aftereffect in RE-TM Films

In typical experiments on the magnetic aftereffect, nucleation and growth of domains are separated. First, reverse nuclei are created and "frozen-in," e.g., by interrupting the magnetic reversal process in an early stage, and second, various fields are applied. In MO films, thermomagnetically written domains can also act as nuclei.

For a study on the regularity of the domain growth, Tb-FeCo films have been prepared by d.c. magnetron, r.f. magnetron, and r.f. diode sputtering. Their composition has been varied such that M_s values ranging from 50 to 300 emu/cc (4 kA/m–24 kA/m) are obtained [53]. Domains have been written thermomagnetically and the reversal curves, observed in a Kerr microscope, have been evaluated in terms of the deviation from the coercive squareness defined by ΔH_c, the range of the magnetic field over which 80% of the reversal occurs see (Fig. 6.16).

Magnetization and uniaxial anisotropy are the most significant parameters to affect the coercive squareness. The deposition process has only a slight influence. Three types of magnetic reversal are distinguished. They are phenomenologically correlated to ΔH_c and to the anisotropy field $H_{anis} = 2K_u/M_s$ (cgs) in the following way.

1. Spontaneous nucleation all over the film when $H_c > H_{anis}/5$, i.e., when the observed H_c approaches the field for coherent rotation. This occurs for low values of H_{anis} and even when the samples are presaturated by 50 kOe (5 T).
2. Dendritic growth for $H_c < H_{anis}/10$.
3. Regular domain wall motion, characteristic for high squareness ($\Delta H_c < 0.15$ kOe) and observed for small M_s (< 100 emu/cm^3 = 8 kA/m).

The regular domain wall motion is attributed to the low demagnetizing field. Nuclei need a higher applied field to be built but expand easily by wall motion. Under a high demagnetizing field, on the contrary, regions of opposite magnetization are easily built and the domain boundaries become jagged during motion.

The expansion and contraction of thermomagnetically written domains at room temperature have been observed in situ using Lorentz microscopy. The results are schematically represented in Figure 6.18 [63]. For $Tb_{19}Fe_{81}$ a wall motion creep is observed. The domains expand or contract more or less radially with the domain walls becoming increasingly jagged. This corresponds best to case (2), dendritic growth, of the preceding paragraph. The demagnetizing field ($H_{demag} = 4\pi M_s \approx 1.3$ kOe as compared to $H_a = 4.2$ kOe) is not so important, in contrast to $Tb_{32}Fe_{68}$ with $H_{demag} \approx 3.14$ kOe. In this second specimen, the initial domains do not change when an external field is applied. Instead, new nuclei are created between the marks (for

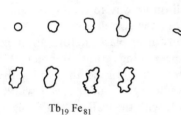

Tb$_{19}$Fe$_{81}$ Tb$_{32}$Fe$_{68}$

Figure 6.18 Shapes of originally circular domains after applying an expansive magnetic field at room temperature. Schematically after in-situ Lorentz micrographs [63]. The eight different shapes in the Tb$_{19}$Fe$_{81}$ film characterize the temporal development.

expansive fields) or within the marks (for erasive fields), run out into jagged stripe domains and expand under increasing field. This is similar to case (1) of the preceding paragraph. The easy nucleation may be attributed to the high M_s that decreases the anisotropy field.

The behavior illustrated in Figure 6.18 is typical for the respective compositions. The following macroscopic experiments confirm this behavior and, furthermore, yield more quantitative information on the activation process.

A square hysteresis loop is found for an r.f.-sputtered film with a Tb content of 20.7 at.% [64], [65]. In the initial stage of the aftereffect, multi-edged (cornered) domain nuclei are created. They grow irregularly under an applied field, and at the same time new nuclei are formed. This process of dendrite-like growth looks, at this scale, more like the creation of new nuclei at the edges of existing domains than like a wall motion. This behavior seems well modeled by the Monte-Carlo simulations on single-domain cells described in Section 6.3.2.4. The evaluation of the magnetic aftereffect as a thermally activated process yields an activation volume $V_a = 1.4*10^{-4}$ (μm)^3 corresponding to a cube of 52 nm side length or to a column in the 100 nm thick film with a cross section of 35 nm × 35 nm.

A sheared hysteresis loop is found for samples with 32.8 at.% Tb. Round nuclei are initially formed and run out into stripe domains to form a maze-like structure. No new nuclei are created; the whole magnetization reversal occurs by wall motion only [65]. The same behavior was observed on a 1000 nm thick Tb$_{37}$Fe$_{63}$ film [66] in which the mean wall velocity v has been determined as a function of the applied field and the temperature. It varies from 0.32 to 6.24 mm/s in the temperature range 298 K to 370 K. Also in this case, the magnetic aftereffect is interpreted as thermally activated wall motion. The activation volumes V_a are 4.2 to 21.4*10^{-18} cm^3, an order of magnitude less than the value presented above.

6.3.3.2 Interpretation of Activation Volumes in Amorphous RE-TM Thin Films

The models of thermally activated wall motion assume that the domain wall moves piecewise through the medium. The activation volume is introduced to consider the magnetic reversal energy that reduces the energy barrier for wall motion [see Equation (34)]. Its correlation with the microstructure of the material is not unique in the literature. Sometimes it is identified with "Barkhausen entities" implying that the activation volume corresponds to the volume of an elementary jump. This is, however, not generally true because the wall might move a considerable distance toward the next potential minimum after having overcome the pinning center. Sometimes, the lateral extension of the activation volume is identified with the defect width. Most precise is an identification with the volume swept by the wall on its way to the maximum of the potential. For a discussion on the related problem of the correlation of the activation entities to defect or jump widths of dislocation motion during plastic deformation see [70].

In Section 6.3.1.2, we conclude that the probable pinning centers are intercolumnar boundaries. Their width is small compared to the wall width so that the activation width for overcoming a straight intercolumnar boundary is half the wall width. The lateral scale of the columns, 10–20 nm, is comparable with the wall width (Table 6.4) so that we qualitatively get the situation sketched in Figure 6.19 where the wall is following the course of the intercolumnar boundaries. These boundaries are regions of low K_u and consequently low wall energy so that the wall center tends to be positioned there.

The supposed elementary wall motion step between intercolumnar boundaries covers one column. The energy maximum is expected to occur when the wall has left the lower intercolumnar boundary. Consequently, the activation width is the column diameter D and the activation step length is half the Bloch wall width, $\delta_w/2$. In this case, the activation volume is given by $\delta_w Dh/2$ with h being the thickness of the film.

The activation volumes obtained in the experiments presented above are gathered in Table 6.10. From them the lateral extension of the activation volumes, assumed to be quadratic slabs extending through the thickness of the films, has been calculated. It is in the range 10–20 nm which is the same order of magnitude as both the wall width and the lateral extension of the columns that are characteristic of the microstructure of amorphous RE-TM films. Conclusions on the details of the activation step are, therefore, not possible. However, these results, together with the experimental scaling powers of Table 6.9, suggest that the elementary Barkhausen jump is over a column and that the domain walls are pinned at the intercolumnar boundaries.

There are two exceptions: (1) the small estimated width of the slab in the 1000 nm thick film, and, (2) its high value in Gd-Fe. (1): Assuming that the minimum wall motion step is of the order of the wall width (about 10 nm), we suppose that in the thin (< 100 nm) films the wall moves in planar steps whereas in the thicker (1000 nm) film, the wall motion is inhomogeneous in the vertical direction. The stiffness of the wall is generally higher in the magnetization direction than perpendicular to it, so that horizontal steps with magnetic charges are avoided. In ferrimagnetic materials vertical steps may nevertheless occur due to the low value of M_s. Compare the nucleation at the surface observed in the computer simulations of the thermomagnetic write process discussed in connection with Figure 6.5.

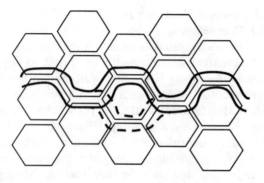

Figure 6.19 Movement of a domain wall in the columnar structure of thin films with intercolumnar boundaries as pinning defects.

TABLE 6.10 Activation Volumes V_a of Domain Wall Motion. Equivalent Lateral Extension b of Corresponding Slabs Extending Through the Thickness d of the films

Material	d/nm	V_n/(10 nm)^3	b/nm	Reference
Tb$_{20.7}$FeCo, rf sputtered	115	1400	35	a
Tb$_{37}$Fe$_{63}$, dc sputtered	1000	4.2 (298 K)	2	b
		21.4 (370 K)	4.6	
Tb$_{22}$Fe$_{70}$Co$_8$, sputtered	16	8	22	c
	66	8	11	
Tb$_{22}$Fe$_{70}$Co$_8$	48.5	5.5	11	i
Tb$_{20}$Fe$_{72}$Co$_8$ (commercial)	49	1	4.5	d
Tb$_{26}$Fe$_{66}$Co$_8$	250	5 (290 K)	4.5	e
		25 (460 K)	10	
GdTb-Co (nucleation)	26	11.5	21	f
Gd-Fe, co-evaporated (wall motion)	20	150	87	
Dy/Fe multilayers, dc sputtered	≈ 20	2	10	g
Co, UHV-evap.	0.6		10	h
	1		15	

Sources: References [a][64], [65], [b][66], [c][67], [d][68], [e][69], [f][56], [g][61], [h][71], [i][60]

(2): In Gd-Fe, a relatively soft magnetic material, a *large* step width is observed. This can be compared to the situation in Dy-containing materials that are also less hard. There, the low value of the scaling power of the coercive force with K_u may be explained by pinning at *large* defects. According to Table 6.4 the wall in these materials is thicker than 10 nm so that it covers more than one intercolumnar boundary. In this case the pinning effect is not due to single boundaries but due to fluctuations of their density.

6.3.3.3 Ultra-Thin Co Layers

Domain nucleation and wall propagation in ultra-thin Co layers (2–9 atomic layers, embedded in Au) have been found to be thermally activated, according to the model described above, Equation (6.34) or (6.35) [71]. Structurally, these layer stacks are better characterized than the amorphous RE-TM films and there is a good chance to relate the activation volumes to defects.

For a Co thickness $d_{Co} = 0.6$ nm (1 nm), the lateral size of the activation volume is 10 nm (15 nm). This has to be compared to a domain wall thickness of 6 nm (10 nm), a distance between steps in atomically flat terraces of 8 nm and a grain size of 20 nm. A conclusion from the activation volume on the dominant pinning defect is not possible.

The experimentally observed variation of H_c with d_{Co} at T = 2 K has then been compared with the predictions of two different models.

In the first model, the pinning centers are grain boundaries. Equation (6.28) or (6.31) is applicable. The coercive field is proportional to $K_u^{3/2}$ [Equation (6.28)] if the grain boundary is smaller than the wall width or to $K_u^{1/2}$ [Equation 6.31)] in the inverse situation. K_u varies in such layer systems like K_s/d_{Co}. H_c is then predicted to vary like $d_{Co}^{-3/2}$ or $d_{Co}^{-1/2}$, respectively, which cannot be fitted to the experimental data.

In the second model, the pinning arises from the abrupt variation of K_u at the terrace steps. For small layer thicknesses, H_c is proportional to $t_{Co}^{-5/2}$. This relationship fits the experimental data best for an assumed roughness of 3 Å (about 1.5 atomic layers) and an extension of the terraces of 10 nm, which is consistent with the experimental data.

6.3.3.4 Magnetic Reversal in CoPt Alloy Films

CoPt alloy films (typically $Co_{28}Pt_{72}$) with perpendicular magnetic anisotropy, have also been proposed as MO medium [72]. They are polycrystalline with an average grain size of about 10 to 20 nm. The magnetic reversal in such films has been investigated experimentally and simulated numerically [73].

The films have been deposited by evaporation onto Si/SiN_x substrates at 230°C and observed in a polarizing microscope. For $d = 10$ nm thick films, the hysteresis loops are square. During reversal large domains with jagged boundaries are produced. For $d = 30$ nm thick films, the reversal loops are non-square with an initial step in M_s at H_c followed by a gradual change upon increasing external field. The optical micrographs show many small domains with partial common boundaries.

This behavior could be reproduced in micromagnetic computer simulations where the films were modeled by a two-dimensional quadric grid, each cell representing one grain supposed to behave as a single domain. The micromagnetic assumptions are similar to those for the Monte-Carlo simulation of the relaxation curves discussed at the end of Section 6.3.2.1. The size of the anisotropy field has been calculated from the experimental values of K_u and M_s. A random fluctuation of about 3% is introduced to account for the experimentally found distribution of the crystalline orientation of the grains around the plane normal. The demagnetizing field is calculated in an approximate way from all cells. The demagnetizing factor of a cell is approximated by that of an ellipsoid with half axes corresponding to the cell diameter and film thickness.

The exchange coupling between the cells is taken into account by a magnetic wall energy. The wall energy density, derived from the experimental values of K_u and A, amounts to $\sigma_w = 4(AK_u)^{0.5} = 3.7^*10^{-3}$ J/m^2. The best fit of the simulated hysteresis curves to the experimental ones is obtained by taking 30% of the experimental value of σ_w. This discrepancy is attributed to a reduced exchange-coupling across the grain boundaries and a reduced wall width. Remember that such conclusions are not possible for RE-TM layers due to lack of measuring precision (Section 6.2.3). In the thicker film the wall energy is larger due to a larger intergranular interface area and the demagnetizing factor of a cell is smaller because the ellipsoid is more stretched.

The activation volume of the magnetic after effect corresponds to one grain. This is consistent with the fact that the elementary process is not a wall motion step but a reversal of a grain.

6.3.4 Computer Simulations of Magnetic Reversal Based on the Landau–Lifshitz Equation

In order to understand the mechanism of magnetic reversal in RE-TM films, computer simulations on the basis of the phenomenological Landau, Lifshitz, and Gilbert (LLG) equation (see Section 6.1.4) have been performed [74], [10, chapters 15 and 16].

6.3.4.1 Lattice Geometry and Material Parameters

The MO films are modeled by a two-dimensional hexagonal lattice with 256×256 dipoles. Each dipole represents a hexagonal based prism of the thin film with side distance 10 Å and a length of 500 Å corresponding to the film thickness, so that the whole lattice covers an area of 256 nm × 222 nm of a 50 nm thick film. The calculations are performed on a connection machine with 65,536 (64K) processors where each processor handles one dipole. Periodic boundary conditions are imposed avoiding finite size demagnetizing effects and enabling the use of fast Fourier transformation in calculating the demagnetizing field.

Upon changing the applied magnetic field H_a, each dipole first precesses around a local effective field H_{eff} determined by H_a, and the instantaneous status of the other dipoles. This precession is damped by the Gilbert term and in the steady state all dipoles align with their local effective field.

The parameters chosen to represent typical RE-TM films are in cgs units (SI units in parentheses):

$$M_s = 100 \text{ emu/cm}^3 \ (= 8 \text{ kA/m})$$

$$K_u = 10^6 \text{ erg/cm}^3 \ (= 10^2 \text{ kJ/m}^3)$$

$$A_x = 10^{-7} \text{ erg/cm} \ (= 10^{-12} \text{ J/m})$$

$$\alpha = 0.5$$

They result in a wall energy, σ_w, and a wall thickness parameter Δ_w:

$$\sigma_w = 4(A_x K_u)^{1/2} = 1.25 \text{ erg/cm}^2 \ (= 1.25 \times 10^{-3} \text{ J/m}^2)$$

$$\Delta_w = (A_x/K_u)^{1/2} = 31.6 \text{ Å},$$

and in a Walker breakdown field H_w and an anisotropy field H_{anis}:

$$H_w = 2\pi\alpha M_s = 314 \text{ Oe} \ (= 25 \text{ kA/m})$$

$$H_{anis} = 2K_u/M_s = 20 \text{ kOe} \ (= 1600 \text{ kA/m}).$$

The wall velocity is proportional to the applied field below H_w and reduces abruptly above H_w.

6.3.4.2 Relative Energy During Reversal

In a series of simulations, the coercivity in the basic lattice has been modeled by a random distribution of the easy axis from site to site within a cone of half-angle θ. For $\theta = 20°$, $30°$, $40°$, coercive nucleation fields of, respectively, 17, 15.6, and 14 kOe are obtained, which must be compared to the 20 kOe predicted by the coherent rotation theory for $\theta = 0°$.

Figure 6.20 [74] shows the temporal development of the magnetization together with different energy terms when an external field equivalent to the coercive field ($H_c = 15.6$ kOe for $\theta = 30°$) is applied. After a nucleation time of about 0.15 ns, a nucleus is formed and grows, decreasing the demagnetizing energy, and creating wall area with a constant rate until the domains touch each other. This is consistent with the assumption of a constant velocity v_w for radial domain growth assumed in the model for the $M(t)$ relaxation curve (Section 6.3.2.2). The domain wall velocity can be estimated from the figures given in [74] to be $v_w = 160$ m/s. A similar value is obtained from Figure 6.20 assuming that the domain occupies half of the computational area at minimum demagnetizing energy ($\pi r^2 = 0.5(256 \times 222) \text{ nm}^2$, $v_w \approx r/\Delta t = 95 \text{ nm}/0.65 \text{ ns}$).

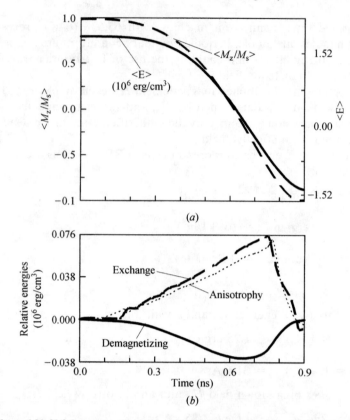

Figure 6.20 [74] Computer simulation (LLG) of the magnetic reversal in Tb-FeCo at the coercive field, $H_c = 15.6$ kOe. (a) average magnetization $\langle M_z/M_s \rangle$ and average energy $\langle E \rangle$ vs. time. (b) individual contributions to $\langle E \rangle$.

The total energy change during reversal is 3×10^6 erg/cm^3. The sum of exchange and anisotropy energy, representing the wall energy after nucleation (maximally 0.15×10^6 erg/cm^3), amounts to only 5% of the total energy. The demagnetizing energy is always less than 25% of the wall energy or only about 1% of the total energy change.

6.3.4.3 Structure of Domains and Walls

The structures of a circular and a stripe domain in the patchy lattice are shown in Figure 6.21 (schematically after [75]). The wall exhibits sometimes a Bloch character (in-plane moments are parallel to the wall) and sometimes a Néel character (in-plane moments are perpendicular to the wall). Also vertical Bloch lines between Bloch walls of different chirality are found so that the wall structure corresponds to a hard bubble in bubble materials.

6.3.4.4 Nucleation in the Patchy Lattice

The site-to-site random deviation of the easy axis from the film normal cannot account for the experimentally observed order of magnitude reduction of the coercive field (Brown's paradox). More realistic coercivity models must take the microstructure of

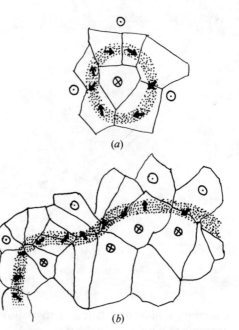

Figure 6.21 Wall contours in a planar net of magnetic moments representative of Tb-FeCo. Schematically after computer simulations based on the LLG equation [75]. "Patchy" lattice, boundaries with reduced exchange. (*a*) Circular domain during expansion (magnetization "down" inside). (*b*) Static configuration (magnetization "down" in lower half).

the film into account. In [75] the microstructure has been modeled by dividing the basic lattice into patches with typical diameters 60 Å (2,073 patches) to 200 Å (195 patches). The anisotropy field is allowed to fluctuate randomly from patch to patch between 1 and 40 kOe with the maximum of the distribution at 20 kOe. The easy axis fluctuates from site to site with a maximum angle of 45° to the plane normal. The exchange constant at the patch boarders has also been varied, from 0 to 100% of the inside value $A_x = 10^{-7}$ erg/cm $(= 10^{-12}$ J/m).

Under zero applied field, all dipoles in the lattice are aligned nearly parallel to one another and the magnetization corresponds to more than 90% of the maximum theoretical value. Due to the strong exchange coupling, there is nearly no magnetic dispersion, contrary to experimental results where the M_s in amorphous RE-TM is sometimes only 50% of the crystalline value [76].

Nucleation occurs in two steps:

1. An *in-plane domain* is formed covering about four adjacent patches (of 10 nm diameter each).
2. The domain enlarges, and its magnetization aligns to the external field.

Compare with the computer simulation of the thermomagnetic write process reported in Section 6.1.4. A surface nucleus is formed at fields above 5.5 kOe. Such surface effects are a priori excluded in the two-dimensional planar lattice.

Figure 6.22 [75] shows the dependence of the coercive field for nucleation, H_n, i.e., the external field necessary to reverse the magnetization in a small volume, on the average patch size. If the patches become smaller than the domain wall width (10 nm), H_n will approach the *average* anisotropy field. For increasing patch size, a nucleus can eventually be formed in the "easiest" patch alone and H_n approaches the

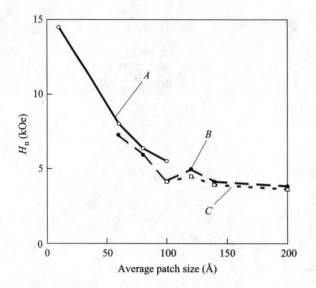

Figure 6.22 [75] Coercive field H_n for domain nucleation as a function of the average patch size of the patchy lattice. The exchange constant A_{xb} at the patch boundaries is randomly varied. The minimum and maximum values of this variation are different for the three types of lattices, type A: A_{xb} = value inside patch, type B: A_{xb} = 0 to 0.5 of patch value, type C: A_{xb} = 0 to 0.2 of patch value.

minimum anisotropy field, in this simulation equal to 3.6 kOe. These results are in agreement with the nucleation models presented in Section 6.3.1, although the case of an in-plane domain nucleus has not been considered there.

6.3.4.5 Wall Motion in a Patchy Lattice

The wall motion coercive field H_w is defined as the external magnetic field necessary to move an existing domain wall. In the *basic* lattice, with site-to-site variations in the easy axis with a maximum angle of 45° to the film normal, H_w is found to be 0.65 kOe, about a factor of 20 smaller than the nucleation field. Experimentally, the factor is only 1.25 (see Fig. 6.9). In the *patchy* lattice, H_w is mostly caused by fluctuations in the exchange constant at the patch borders (see Fig. 6.23 [75]) and is nearly independent of the patch size.

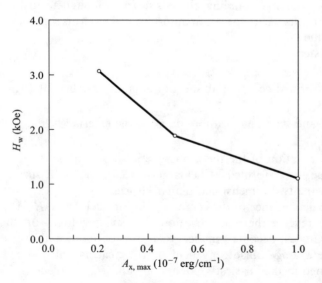

Figure 6.23 [75] Coercive field H_w for wall motion in the patchy lattice as a function of the exchange strength at the patch borders relative to the value $A_x = 10^{-7}$ erg/cm $= 10^{-12}$ J/m within the patches.

The curve shows that H_w decreases when the boundary exchange strength approaches the value inside the patches, just opposite to the trend for H_n. H_w does not go to zero because of the patch-to-patch variations of the easy axis. For the extreme values of the parameters, a maximum patch-to-patch dispersion of the easy axis of $45°$ (half angle of a cone) and zero exchange at the boundaries, $H_w = 4.4$ kOe is found. For such a disturbance of the dipole lattice and a patch size larger than 10 nm, the ratio H_w/H_n approaches the experimental value of about 0.8.

In the wall configuration of Figure 6.21(a). The domain wall is trapped at low-exchange regions and encircles regions of high K_u. We expect that, when the wall has swept over that region, a circular domain remains around the high K_u obstacle, being a nucleus for a new reversal into the opposite direction. This resembles the Cottrell mechanism in the plastic deformation of materials [77]. These effects cannot be produced in one-dimensional models of wall pinning. Scaling laws of the coercive force with the defect width and the anisotropy constant for this type of domain wall pinning at large defects have not yet been derived from computer simulations. This seems to be worthy of further study.

6.3.5 Domain Formation in Exchange-Coupled Layers

It is very difficult to obtain rare-earth transition-metal thin films that exhibit all the desired magneto-optic and micromagnetic properties necessary for high-performance MO recording media. In most cases, the optimization of one property affects another property adversely. New and interesting possibilities in this regard are offered by layer structures with two or more RE-TM films (ECLs, exchange-coupled layers) (see Chapters 7 to 9 of this book).

Exchange-coupled double layers (ECDLs) consist of two layers with different magnetic properties, e.g., different coercive fields so that the magnetic moments can be directed oppositely in the two layers. When the exchange coupling is maintained across the interface, magnetic walls of macroscopic area can exist at the interface. For ferrimagnetic RE-TM alloys there are two types of ECDLs, A and P (see Fig. 6.24). Type A occurs when the ambient temperature is between the compensation temperatures of the two layers, such that in one layer the TM sublattice magnetization M_{TM} is parallel to the net magnetization M and in the other layer, it is antiparallel. At high enough applied magnetic fields the magnetizations align parallel to the external field such that the TM sublattice magnetizations are antiparallel to one another and a magnetic wall is formed. Type P occurs in all other cases.

ECDLs and also sandwich structures with more than two magnetic layers are important media for MO recording, exhibiting features that cannot be obtained with single-layer media, e.g., direct overwrite with laser modulation (see Chapter 8) or magnetically induced superresolution (see Chapter 9). In these applications, the energy

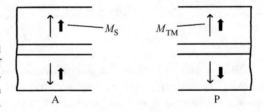

Figure 6.24 Two types of exchange-coupled double layers. M_{TM}: magnetic moment of the TM sublattice (thin arrows), M: net magnetic moment (bold arrows). In type A an interface wall exists at infinite magnetic fields.

stored in the interface wall is used to reverse one of the magnetic layers when it is heated by the laser beam of the MO recorder. ECDLs with strong exchange coupling may also be used to optimize the storage and readout functions in two layers separately.

Due to the different growth conditions, the coercive fields in a double layer may not be the same as in the layers deposited separately even if the preparation conditions are the same [78]. The main difference comes, however, from the interface wall. In the following section we show how the existence of an interface wall and its energy influences the reversal behavior of ECLs.

6.3.5.1 Experimental Method and Theoretical Analysis

Magnetic reversal curves on ECDLs reported in the literature are usually obtained by a full cycle of the magnetic field between its extremal values. A theoretical analysis of the resulting hysteresis curves is given in Chapter 7.

The curves presented below have been obtained by systematically including two experimental variations in addition to the full cycle [25], [36], [79]. In one of these the magnetic field is reversed between two processes (after the complete reversal of one layer and before the beginning of the reversal of the other layer) to obtain a minor loop, which corresponds to switching the same layer to and fro with subsequent creation and annihilation of an interface wall. The dashed parts of the following experimental hysteresis curves represent these minor loops. A second variant of the reversal experiments is obtained when the external field is reversed in the middle of a reversal process, i.e., when one layer is in a partly demagnetized state. From these experiments models for domain formation are deduced.

The interpretation of the hysteresis curves is based upon three basic reversal processes that are allowed by the energy balance [79]. Three terms are involved in this balance: the Zeeman energy density E_Z, the coercive force E_c, and the interface wall energy σ_w. With reference to unit area of the interface wall, we obtain for the Zeeman energy E_z of layer z, i.e., the energy in the external field H_{ext}:

$$E_{Zz} = 2\mu_0 M_{sz} d_z H_{ext}, \tag{6.41}$$

where M_z denotes the magnetization of layer z and d_z its thickness, and for the coercive force E_c, representing the dissipation of energy during reverse domain nucleation or wall motion

$$E_{cz} = 2\mu_0 M_{sz} d_z H_{cz}, \tag{6.42}$$

where H_{cz} is the coercive field of layer z. E_c is always positive. E_Z and E_c have the dimension of energy density.

A reversal of the magnetization of one layer with the magnetization of the other layer remaining unchanged is possible if energy is gained:

$$0 > 2\mu_0 M_{sz} d_z H_{cz} + v\, 2\mu_0 |M_{sz} d_z H_{ext}| + w\sigma_w, (v, w = \pm 1) \quad (SI) \tag{6.43}$$

with $v = +1/-1$ when the magnetization is rotated, against/[ag] into [in] the external field (M_z and H_{ext} are antiparallel/parallel after the process) and with $w = +1/-1$ when an interface wall is created [c]/annihilated [a] by the process. In the following we will use the abbreviations in the square brackets to designate magnetic reversal processes.

Equation (6.43) can only be fulfilled when v or w or both are negative. Three processes are therefore allowed:

- $[a, in, z]$: annihilation of the interface wall with rotation of M_s of layer z into the external field,
- $[a, ag, z]$: annihilation of the interface wall by rotation of M_{sz} against the external field,
- $[c, in, z]$: creation of the interface wall by rotation of M_{sz} into the external field.

In the first process σ_w and E_Z compensate E_c. This should be observed for high coercive forces. In the second process, σ_w alone compensates both E_Z and E_c. In the third process, E_Z is used to overcome E_c and to create a wall. A process $[c, ag, z]$ does not exist because the energy change would always be positive.

6.3.5.2 Domain Formation Models

The reversal behavior of a (GdTb-Fe) double layer (with layer numbers 1 and 2) at 20 K is shown in Figure 6.25 [79]. The interpretation of these curves is performed with the help of Figure 6.26.

In the horizontal parts of the hysteresis curve, the domain structure is in a (meta)-stable state. The magnetic configurations for high positive fields and intermediate fields are sketched in Figure 6.25 and labeled $+$II and $-$I, respectively. Vertical parts of the curves correspond to state transitions and are labeled with the notations in brackets explained above.

A creep-like process, $[a, in, 2]$, is observed at high magnetic fields. We interpret this as a vertical motion of the interface wall through layer 2 (Fig. 6.26, left). GdTb-Fe is magnetically rather soft, compared with Tb-FeCo, or "less hard" in our terminology. The reversal behavior in single layers containing Dy and Gd may also be interpreted by a motion of domain walls pinned at large defects (see Table 6.9).

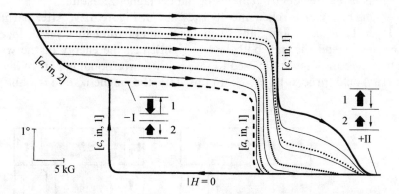

Figure 6.25 [79] Reversal behavior of a double layer at 20 K as observed by the Faraday effect. (Both layers GdTb$_{12}$-FeCo with different T_{comp}, $M_{s1} = 155$ G, $M_{s2} = 38$ G). The measuring temperature is below the compensation temperatures of both layers so that an inverted Faraday curve results.

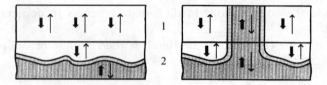

Figure 6.26 Interpretation of Figure 6.25. Left: vertical motion of the interface wall through layer 2 ([*a*, in, 2], initial stage); right: common reversal of both layers, [*a*, in, 1].

The process [*a*, *in*, 1] may be understood as common reversal of both layers, as sketched in Figure 6.26 (right).

Another frequently observed reversal behavior is shown in Figure 6.27 [79]. In the absence of an external field, common domains extend through both layers. When applying a field, only the domains in the relatively "soft" upper layer expand or contract according to the direction of the applied field, while the part of the domains in the "hard" lower layer remains unchanged [78], [79].

If all walls in a double layer are immobile, the domain formation, in both layers, is by nucleation only. This is the case for the double layer represented in Figure 6.28 [79] and interpreted in Figure 6.29. The measuring temperature is between the compensation temperatures of the two layers so that an interface wall is stable under high magnetic fields (state + II). The energy of the interface wall drives the process [*a*, *ag*, 2], a rotation of the magnetization of layer 2 against the external field, observed when the magnetic field is reduced.

If the magnetic field is reversed between the two processes, the wall is again created by a reversal of layer 2, [*c*, *in*, 2] (dashed line in Fig. 6.28). The steepness of the curves indicates that both the creation and the annihilation of the interface wall are nucleation controlled.

When the magnetic field is reversed within [*c*, *in*, 1] [to the left in Fig. 6.28(*a*)] so that the creation of the wall is not completed, layer 1 remains in a partly demagnetized state (Fig. 6.29, left). Subsequently only reversals of layer 2, the processes [*a*, *ag*, 2] and [*c*, *in*, 2] are observed (two steps in the dotted lines), completely reversing layer 2, whereas layer 1 evidently remains in the demagnetized state.

This behavior is schematically sketched in Figure 6.29. After partial wall creation in layer 1, [*c*, *in*, 1], and subsequent wall annihilation in layer 2, [*a*, *ag*, 2], common domains extend through both layers (right), i.e., the energy of the wall area created in the reversal of layer 1 is used to reverse the corresponding part of layer 2 against the external field (process [*a*, *ag*, 2]). In this state, the magnetization is stable with respect to

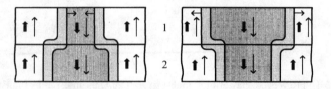

Figure 6.27 Bloch-wall motion in one layer, while the domain in the other layer remains unchanged.

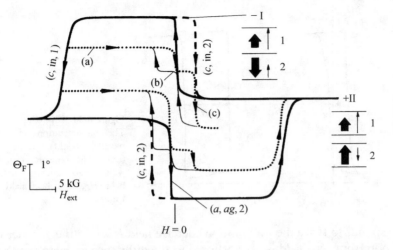

Figure 6.28 [79] Reversal behavior of a double layer at 230 K as observed by the
Faraday effect. Layer 1: GdTb$_4$-FeCo; layer 2: GdTb$_8$-FeCo. The measuring temperature is between the compensation temperatures of the two
layers so that an interface wall exists at infinite magnetic fields (e.g., in
state $+$II).

small changes of the magnetic field corresponding to the plateau of the thin and dotted
curves in Figure 6.28.

6.3.5.3 Coercivity Model for a Trilayer System

The reversal mechanisms in the two branches of a minor loop are different: In one
branch, an interface wall is nucleated whereas in the other branch such a wall already
exists and the reversal may take place by a motion of the interface wall through a layer.

This difference in the reversal mechanisms becomes evident in experiments with
trilayers. The coercivity of the intermediate layer, as observed in minor loops, depends
on the relative direction of the (transition metal subsystem) magnetization of the adjacent layers (see Fig. 6.30, [80]). This can be explained by the coercivity model for the
intermediate layer sketched in Figure 6.31 [20], [21], [79].

For antiparallel orientation of the magnetic moments of the outer layers (Fig. 6.31,
left), an interface wall is always present and is probably shifted across the intermediate
layer for both branches of the minor reversal loop. The width of the hysteresis loop

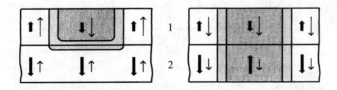

Figure 6.29: Interpretation of Figure 6.28. Left: domains in layer 1 after partial
reversal [c, in, 1], (a) in Figure 6.28. Right: common domains with
immobile Bloch walls after subsequent reversal of layer 2 by [a, ag, 2],
(c) in Figure 6.28.

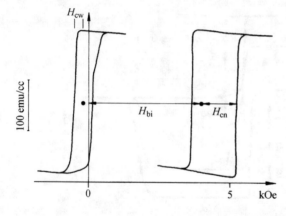

Figure 6.30 [80] Minor loops in a trilayer. The magnetizations in the outer layers are parallel (right), respectively, antiparallel (left). The interpretation of the curves by wall motion coercive field H_{cw}, nucleation field H_{cn} and bias field H_{bi} is based on Figure 6.31.

corresponds to twice the wall motion coercive field H_{cw} and the distance of the center of the loop from zero field is proportional to the difference in energy of the interface wall at the two positions. For comparison, we mention here, that the energy of interface walls in exchange-coupled double layers also depends on their position relative to the interface [36], [81].

For parallel orientation of the outer magnetizations (Fig. 6.31, right) the reversal mechanisms for the two branches of the hysteresis loop are different. For the high-field branch it is necessary for the domains to be nucleated and for the interface walls to be created at both interfaces. This results in a higher coercivity (nucleation field H_{cn}). For the low-field branch, the magnetic reversal occurs again via interface wall motion, and the coercive field is expected to be, to a first approximation, the same as that for the left loop in Figure 6.30. The width of the hysteresis loop corresponds to the sum of nucleation field and wall motion coercive field. The bias field H_{bi} is proportional to the sum of the wall energies at the two interfaces.

6.3.6 Summary "Reversal Processes"

During the magnetic reversal of thin films, domain nucleation and expansion of already existing domains generally occur simultaneously. For amorphous RE-TM thin films the observed relaxation curves $M(t)$ practically fall into three categories.

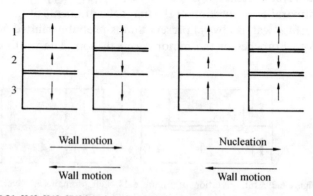

Figure 6.31 [20], [21], [79] Model of magnetic reversal for the intermediate layer in a trilayer. Left = antiparallel, right = parallel orientation of the (TM) magnetic moments in the outer layers.

1. Slow domain nucleation followed by rapid domain wall motion, leading to a square hysteresis loop and observed for low M_s.
2. Continuous nucleation of domains that do not grow further, leading to a sheared hysteresis loop and observed for high M_s.
3. Dendritic domain growth that resembles the nucleation at already existing domains, leading to hysteresis loops that are steep in the initial part and sheared in the final part.

Scaling laws of the coercive force with K_u, $\mu_0 M_s H_c = C K_u^n$, have been derived from some micromagnetic models of nucleation and wall pinning. Experimentally, the magnetic reversal at high T is, for all RE-TM media, controlled by wall pinning at small (relative to the wall thickness) defects ($n \approx 1.5$). Candidates for such pinning defects are primarily intercolumnar boundaries.

At low T, the reversal in Tb-FeCo is nucleation controlled ($n = 1$), whereas in the Nd-containing media it is wall motion controlled. The easy nucleation, necessary in the second case, is explained by the noncolinear arrangement of the magnetic moments due to the strong spin-orbit coupling of Nd. When the wall thickness is larger than the lateral dimensions of the columnar microstructure the reversal behavior is different.

Wall motion in RE-TM media is thermally activated. In most cases the lateral size of the activation volumes is found to be 5–20 nm when it is assumed that the activation entities are slabs extending through the thickness of the film. This is the typical size of the diameter of the columns characteristic of the thin film microstructure and of the domain wall width. These results suggest that, at temperatures above room temperature, the elementary jump is between intercolumnar boundaries and covers one column. If the walls are pinned by intercolumnar boundaries, whose thickness is small against the domain wall width, the activation step length is half the Bloch wall width. The experimental values are, however, not precise enough, to decide on details of the model.

The results of computer simulations are consistent with the assumptions and predictions of the presented micromagnetic models. The domains expand with a constant radial velocity. The nucleation is determined by the *average* anisotropy field for defects that are smaller than the domain wall width and by the *minimum* anisotropy field for large defects. The following effects are observed in the simulations but not considered in the theoretical models presented above. (1) An *in-plane* domain is formed in the initial stage of nucleation. (2) The domain wall encircles regions of high K_u before it breaks away from them leaving a residual domain behind.

In hysteresis experiments with exchange coupled double layers, minor loops around a bias field can be obtained, corresponding to reversing the same layer to and fro with creation and annihilation of an interface magnetic wall, respectively. The wall energy can be derived from such a bias field. The reversal mechanisms in the two branches of a minor loop are different: in one branch, an interface wall is nucleated, whereas in the other branch such a wall already exists and the reversal can be affected by a motion of the interface wall through a layer. The energy of the interface wall results in a driving force for the magnetic reversal of one layer, sometimes against the external field. This is important for direct overwrite mechanisms on disks with exchange-coupled layers.

The models presented in this section should not be applied, without further examination, to the thermomagnetic write process, because there the time-varying temperature profile may introduce additional effects.

6.4 THERMOMAGNETIC WRITE PROCESS

We specify the below parameters for write, read, and erase processes in a MO recorder and set up prototype curves for the signal and the noise levels as a function of the write laser power and the magnetic write field. The characteristics of these prototype curves are related to physical models of domain formation and to material parameters of the MO layer. Of special interest is whether the domain walls move during the write process as predicted by the bubble-like model.

In this section, we concentrate on the write process and especially on the critical external field for the initiation/suppression of the magnetic reversal in the thermomagnetic write process. Domain erasure and the noise of MO media will be treated in Sections 6.5 and 6.6, respectively.

6.4.1 MO Test Recorder, Write Control, and Readout Measurements

In a test recorder, marks are written under well-controlled conditions characterized by the parameters laser power P_{wr}, magnetic field H_{wr}, and linear velocity of the disk, v_{wr} at the site of the laser spot.

The parameters of the read process are the laser read power and the magnetic field. The magnetic field is not necessary for the read operation but is sometimes accidentally or, for testing, purposely applied and may influence the domain stability. The relationship between the spatial extent of the magnetic domains and the readout signal is sketched in Figure 6.32. The signal is maximum when the domain is completely within the laser spot. The domain width is determined as the half width of the readout signal multiplied by the linear velocity of the disk. The spatial fluctuations on the disk are transformed into temporal noise during readout.

The signal and the noise of the optical pickup channel can be obtained by spectrally analyzing the readout signal. In order to compare results obtained on different systems, the linear disk velocity and the resolution bandwidth of the spectrum analyzer have to be set accordingly. When the marks are written periodically, the readout signal occurs at a single frequency and is called a *carrier C*. Then, the ratio of the signal peak to the noise level at its base is called *carrier-to-noise ratio CNR*. The relation of the CNR to the signal-to-noise ratio SNR will be discussed below in Section 6.6.

In a time-length analyzer, the distribution of domain lengths can be measured. For optimum resolution, marks must be separated by at least the optical diffraction limit. The relative position of the marks, defined by the leading and trailing edges of the signal, can then be determined with an accuracy of better than 10 nm, much less than the optical diffraction limit. The accuracy of the mean deviation of the domain length ("the jitter") depends on the number of marks. For a typical assembly of 10^4 marks, it is ± 1 nm. Therefore, the characterization of disk homogeneity by jitter is much more precise than any other method.

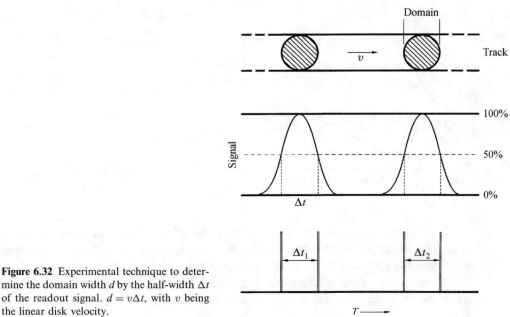

Figure 6.32 Experimental technique to determine the domain width d by the half-width Δt of the readout signal. $d = v\Delta t$, with v being the linear disk velocity.

6.4.2 Characteristic Recording Parameters

The write process in a MO medium is controlled by the write power P_{wr} and the write field H_{wr}. Prototype curves for the dependence of the carrier and the noise on these parameters are shown in Figures 6.33 and 6.34, respectively.

The following characteristic power levels for laser modulation are obtained (see Fig. 6.33):

P_{min}, the minimum power to write detectable domains, also called the "onset power,"

P_{sat}, the power needed to obtain a saturated (maximum) signal, e.g., when the effective mark length is as large as the laser spot diameter,

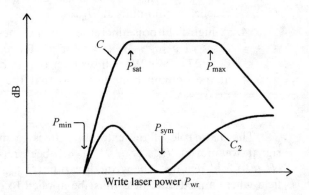

Figure 6.33 Characteristic laser powers for the carrier C and its second harmonic C_2 of thermomagnetically written periodic domain pattern. Laser modulation.

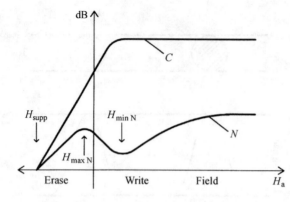

Figure 6.34 Characteristic magnetic fields for the carrier C and the noise N of thermomagnetically written domains. Laser modulation.

P_{sym}, the power for symmetric writing, when the effective distance between marks is as large as the effective mark length ($=$ half the carrier period) and the second harmonic becomes minimum, and

P_{max}, this power defines when the signal level begins to decrease, which occurs when the distance between the marks becomes smaller than the size of the laser spot.

In order to obtain a well-defined mark length, laser power modulation with P_{sym} may be used. For magnetic field modulation, the domain length is determined by the switching period of the field. It is the same for all recording powers. However, the domains become wider with increasing power (see Chapter 10).

The magnetic field dependence of the carrier and write noise levels (Fig. 6.34) for laser modulation is characterized by the following features.

1. For the great majority of disks investigated, a domain formation even under erase fields ($H < 0$) is reported. The driving force is the demagnetizing field. The thermomagnetic mark formation can be suppressed by a critical field H_{supp}, which is usually in the erase direction.

2. For $H_{ext} < H_{max\,N}$, the noise increases with the signal. Irregular domain shapes are often observed.

3. For $H_{ext} > H_{max\,N}$, the noise decreases with increasing write field until it reaches a minimum at $H_{min\,N}$.

4. A high-field noise increase is sometimes observed, especially for the extreme cases of a high M_s (e.g., for an RE content $x < 20$ at.%) and of $M_s = 0$ ($x = 27$ at.%). We will see later that in both cases there is no force equilibrium at the domain boundaries so that the domain walls move during the write process.

The main role of the external field is to make the domains more regular (high signal, low noise). $H_{max\,N}$ or H_{supp} has been reported to be at write ($H > 0$) or erase ($H < 0$) field regions. The write direction ($H_{supp} > 0$) is found for small demagnetizing field where an external field must be applied to create domains.

We have chosen the term "suppression field" for the critical field H_{supp} of Figure 6.34, but in the literature the terms "erase field" and "onset field" are often used. When applying these terms it is necessary to be conscious of the different implicit concepts. The name "onset field" does not express the fact that it has in most cases to be applied in the erase direction. "Erase field," on the other hand, suggests that a domain is first written and subsequently erased. The only observable effect is, however, that no mark remains after the write attempt when applying this bias field. We therefore prefer the expression "suppression field" H_{supp}.

6.4.3 Domain Nucleation and/or Wall Motion

As shown in Figure 6.34, the carrier level C usually increases with increasing write field before it saturates. This behavior can be explained by two models of thermomagnetic mark formation:

1. Perfect marks are written for every field but their size increases with H_{wr} (bubble model),
2. Mark size is independent of H_{a} but the mark area is only completely reversed for large enough write fields (model of rigid nuclei).

Much information concerning this question has been obtained by investigations of thermomagnetically written marks with Lorentz microscopy. In this mode of electron microscopy, an image is observed following the Lorentz force deflection of electrons by the components of the magnetic induction in the specimen perpendicular to the beam. In principle it is possible to image those moments inside a domain wall that has a component perpendicular to the electron beam. However, in the classical method, the wall thickness is too small to be resolved (compare, however, Section 6.2.3 and Figure 6.11, the observation of domain walls in Pt/Co multilayers). Therefore, samples with perpendicular magnetization have to be tilted, and the image is obtained by the interference between electrons scattered from the two different sides of the domain boundary.

6.4.3.1 Shapes of Thermomagnetically Written Domains

In the following, we discuss a systematic investigation of thermomagnetically written domains in specimens of four different compositions [44]. We have selected this reference as an instructive example because the TEM samples have been prepared by a technique that does not require a removal of the MO layer from the substrate. In addition, the samples have been completely characterized magnetically (see Section 6.2, Figure 6.13, and Table 6.6).

The domains were written in a test recorder on a silicon wafer disk covered with a SiN layer (10 nm) and provided with four sectors of Tb-FeCo layers with different compositions. In the silicon a matrix of 2 mm × 2 mm blocks with pyramidal holes was etched resulting in SiN windows with a surface area varying between 25×25 μm^2 and 100×100 μm^2 to be used later, without further processing, as TEM windows. On top of the (unetched) SiN protection layer the MO layers (about 45 nm) and an additional Al protection layer (10 nm) were deposited by evaporation. After recording, the disks were cut into small (2 mm × 2 mm) TEM samples.

Figure 6.35 [44] shows domains written by laser modulation at a write power of 9.6 mW and at different magnetic field strengths. In the Tb-rich film (Nr. 1) with the very steep $H_c(T)$ but flat $M_s(T)$ curve, the written marks consist of a number of small domains ("multidomain mark"). Their size is independent of H_a. A similar behavior was observed in sputtered $Tb_{32}Fe_{68}$ films [82]. The domain walls seem to be immobile in these films, and the mark formation seems to be controlled by nucleation. A possible domain formation model is shown in Figure 6.36.

For the Fe-rich sample [Nr.4, high M_s, flat $H_c(T)$], the written marks mostly contain subdomains that are suppressed only by strong fields (32 kA/m = 400 Oe) in the write direction. This can be explained by the high M_s in this film and a correspondingly high demagnetizing field which also shows up in the large difference between T_c and the demagnetizing temperature T_{demag} ($T_c - T_{demag} = 33$ K, Table 6.6). A possible domain formation model is shown in Figure 6.37.

In films 2 and 3, with compositions between these extremes, single domains are observed when write fields are applied. An erase field does not decrease the mark size but rather splits the single domain into a multidomain pattern and finally, for $H_a > 24$ kA/m, completely suppresses domain formation.

In dc-magnetron sputtered $Tb_{23}Fe_{77}$, contrary to the above (evaporated) sample 3 with a similar composition, a strong dependence of the resulting domain size on H_a was observed. For $H_a = 0$ Oe the radius was only 70 nm as theoretically expected from the bubble model [83]. The magnetization of this sample, close to T_c, is small due to a small $\Delta T = T_c - T_{comp} = 60$ K. Consequently, the magnetostatic driving force is small and the (contracting) wall forces are relatively more important. Sputtered samples are generally less porous than evaporated ones so that a lower wall coercive force may be expected. For the other compositions studied ($Tb_{19}Fe_{81}$, $Tb_{28}Fe_{72}$, and $Tb_{32}Fe_{68}$), the

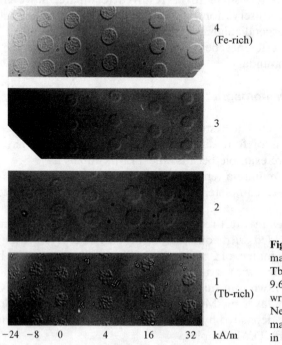

4
(Fe-rich)

3

2

1
(Tb-rich)

−24 −8   0   4   16   32   kA/m

Figure 6.35 Lorentz micrographs of thermomagnetically written marks in (evaporated) Tb-FeCo samples. Laser power modulation, 9.6 mW, write period 2.8 μm. The magnetic write field increases from left to right. Negative values indicate erase direction. The magnetic parameters of the samples are given in Table 6.6, section 6.2.

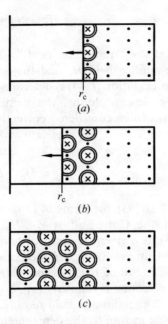

Figure 6.36 Nucleation of small *rigid* domains at the Curie radius r_C, observed for steep $H_c(T)$. The material is paramagnetic inside r_C. Top view.

mark forms were similar to those on the evaporated samples (films 4, 2, 1) described above and shown in Figure 6.35.

6.4.3.2 Domain Nucleation at the Curie Radius

In order to account for the often observed independence of the domain size on the external field, a nucleation field model, as opposed to the bubble-like model, has been proposed [83]. The following criterion for nucleation is chosen:

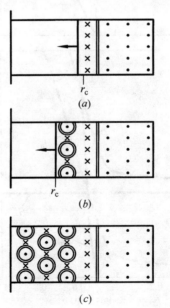

Figure 6.37 Creation of *subdomains* within the written mark, observed for high M_s. Top view.

$$H_t = H_d + H_a > H_n \tag{6.44}$$

H_n is called the "nucleation field." The total field H_t at the site of the nucleus consists of the applied field H_a and the demagnetizing field H_d of the Curie "hole." When the H_n of Equation (6.44) is determined experimentally from the coercive field H_c of macroscopic reversal loops, the demagnetizing field of the homogeneous film ($4\pi M_s$ in cgs) has to be considered correctly:

$$H_n = H_c + 4\pi M_s \quad \text{(cgs)}$$
$$H_n = H_c + M_s \quad \text{(SI)} \tag{6.45}$$

In Figure 6.38 [83], the terms of Equation (6.44) are shown for a $Tb_{32}Fe_{68}$ layer in the vicinity of the Curie radius r_C. H_n, determined experimentally according to Equation (6.45), is a steep function of temperature (due to the high Tb-content) and vanishes at the Curie radius r_C. H_d decreases at r_C but does not vanish because of the (relatively) long range of the magnetostatic field, see Appendix 6.8.1. Therefore, the condition for nucleation is fulfilled at r_C, even for small external fields H_a applied in the erase direction. The minimum field required to suppress nucleation is equal in magnitude but opposite in sign to the demagnetizing field at r_C.

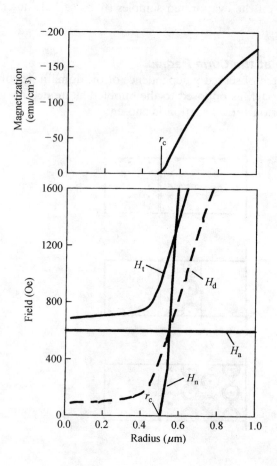

Figure 6.38 [83] Upper: radial dependence of magnetization in a $Tb_{32}Fe_{68}$ layer at the end of a 50-ns, 8.7-mW laser pulse. Lower: corresponding radial dependence of the demagnetizing field H_d, the applied field H_a (600 Oe), the total field H_t, and the nucleation field H_n.

In this nucleation model it is implicitly assumed that the domain walls cannot move. As a consequence, wall forces are not effective and the nuclei remain stable during cool down ("rigid nuclei," Fig. 6.36). If this is not the case, the wall gradient force, which is expected to be stronger than the demagnetizing force, collapses the nuclei.

Once a nucleus is formed, its demagnetizing field inhibits the creation of other nuclei in its vicinity. This resembles the behavior of free bubbles in magnetically soft materials that repel each other. Such inhibition explains the regular arrangement of small domains in the written mark, sometimes in a hexagonal array, sometimes in concentric rings.

6.4.4 Influence of Material Properties and Process Conditions

6.4.4.1 Dependence of H_{supp} ("Suppression Field," "Erase Field," "Onset Field") on RE-TM Composition

Domains recorded on two Tb-FeCo disks, one with a Fe-rich layer ($Tb_{22}Fe_{68}Co_{10}$) and the other one with a Tb-rich layer ($Tb_{28}Fe_{60}Co_{12}$), were observed in a high-resolution polarized microscope [84]. The layers were rf-magnetron sputtered and were 100 nm thick. Magnetization and coercivity are comparable to samples 4 (Fe rich) and 1 (Tb rich) of Figure 6.13. The resulting domain sizes are displayed in Figure 6.39 [84] vs. the applied field together with theoretical results of the bubble-like model. $T_c - T_{comp}$ of these specimens is listed in the figure caption. The authors obtain agreement between the theoretical curves and the experimental data by setting the demagnetizing field $H_d = 700$ Oe in the Fe-rich sample and $H_d = 0$ Oe in the

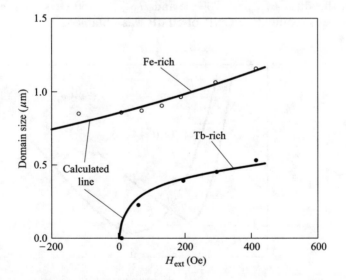

Figure 6.39 [84] Diameter of thermomagnetically written domains in Tb-FeCo storage layers as a function of the applied field. Fe-rich: $T_C - T_{comp} > 250$ K, Tb-rich: $T_C - T_{comp} = 60$ K.

Tb-rich layer. The size of the domains in the Tb-rich film is thought to be smaller due to a stronger coercivity. This argument implies a domain expansion during the write process.

From the discussion in Section 6.4.3, we know that H_d should be the demagnetizing field at the Curie radius. For comparison: in the homogeneously magnetized sample, $H_d = 4\pi M_s = 2\,\text{kOe}$ for the Fe-rich film 60 K below T_c and $H_d = 250$ Oe for the Tb-rich sample 30 K below T_c as can be estimated from the data given in [84]. The demagnetizing field at the edge of a paramagnetic disk of diameter D in a thin film of thickness h and saturation magnetization M_s is given by (see Appendix 6.8.1):

$$\frac{H_d^{\text{edge}}}{-4\pi M_s}(\text{cgs}) = \frac{1}{2} * \frac{0.75(D/h)}{1 + 0.75(D/h)} \tag{6.46}$$

With the above given data we obtain $H_d^{\text{edge}} \approx 860$ Oe for a 0.8 μm domain in the Fe-rich film and $H_d^{\text{edge}} \approx 80$ Oe in the Tb-rich film consistent with the fit parameters of Figure 6.39.

Figure 6.40 [85] shows the dependence of the write suppression field H_{supp} on the RE-content x in disks with $\text{Tb}_x(\text{FeCo})_{1-x}$ layers. The minimum of the curves is found for $\text{Tb}_{21}(\text{Fe}_{78}\text{Co}_{22})_{79}$ and $\text{Tb}_{26}(\text{Fe}_{55}\text{Co}_{45})_{74}$. T_c and T_{comp} of the samples are not reported, but it is stated that the curves in Figure 6.40 are analogous to $M_s(x)$ attaining their minimum when the composition leads to a compensation temperature at room temperature. This demonstrates that the increase of $H_{\text{supp}}(x)$ on both sides of the minimum is mainly due to the increasing demagnetizing field. The magnetic field H_{sat} necessary to saturate the CNR is found to be proportional to H_{supp} and is attributed to the suppression of demagnetizing effects within the written mark.

A disk comprising an MO layer requiring the minimum H_{supp} (stack: ZnS/$\text{Tb}_{21}(\text{Fe}_{78}\text{Co}_{22})_{79}$/ZnS) was then prepared for recording by magnetic field modulation [85]. For this disk, $H_{\text{supp}} = -200$ Oe and $H_{\text{min}\,N} = 150$ Oe so that a modulation width of ±200 Oe is required. A CNR of 50 dB was obtained.

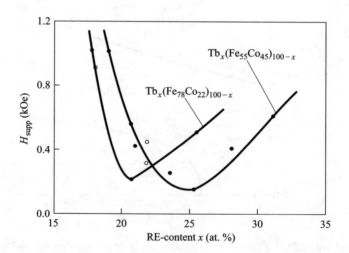

Figure 6.40 [85] Domain suppression field H_{supp} vs. the Tb-content x of Tb-FeCo storage layers.

In another study [86] on a series of disks with $Tb_x(Fe_{82}Co_{18})_{100-x}$ layers, the minimum in H_{supp} (< 50 Oe(4 kA/m) was found for $x = 27$. In this case, $H_{min N}$ (the field for minimum noise) was found to be larger than 1000 Oe which is attributed to the small M_s ($T_c - T_{comp} = 27$ K, $\mu_0 M_s H_c =$ const.) (see Section 6.4.4.2).

6.4.4.2 Compositional Dependence of the Field for Minimum Write Noise, H$_{min N}$

Fig. 6.41 [46] shows the external magnetic write field necessary to obtain minimum write noise, $H_{min N}$ in our terminology, as a function of $T_c - T_{comp}$, for GdTb-Fe compositions with 5 to 26 at.% Tb. Interpreting the result in the bubble model, the hyperbolic curve in Figure 6.41 indicates that the pressure onto the domain wall due to the external field is about the same in all samples: $2\mu_0 M_s H_a =$ const. $= 2.5$ kJ/m^3. This is estimated from the values for $\Delta T = 150$ K: $M_s = 35$ kA/m at a temperature of 50 K below the Curie temperature (Fig. 6.13, sample 2) and $H_{min N} = 30$ kA/m (Fig. 6.40). Note that the maximum magnetization of the samples is roughly proportional to $\Delta T = T_c - T_{comp}$.

The value of 2.5 kJ/m^2 corresponds roughly to the typical wall gradient force outside the Curie radius (see Table 6.7 and the corresponding explanation in Section 6.2.5). We therefore conclude that the domain formation takes place close to the Curie temperature where mainly the forces due to the external field and the wall gradient force are important. The condition for minimum noise is then mainly determined by the balance between the external write field and the wall gradient force.

6.4.4.3 Roughness of the Dielectric Underlayer

From the model of rigid nuclei we have concluded that suppression of domain formation during a write attempt is related to the neutralization of the demagnetizing effect of the "Curie disk" (also called "Curie cylinder" or "Curie hole"). The Curie disk is the paramagnetic region in the center of the laser spot where $T > T_c$. In Section 6.4.4.2 we saw that the minimum write noise is obtained when the external field balances the wall forces such that the domain wall does not move during the write process. We shall now discuss the role of wall motion coercivity in the write process.

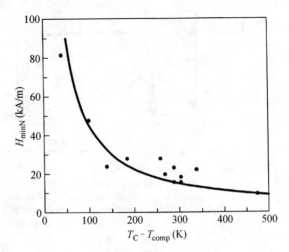

Figure 6.41 [46] Field to obtain minimum write noise, $H_{min N}$, as a function of $T_C - T_{comp}$ for GdTb-Fe storage layers. The curve represents a hyperbolic relationship $\mu_0 H_{min N} M_s =$ const.

In Figures 6.42 and 6.43 [87], recording results are shown for disks with a magnetically less hard (relative for MO recording) Tb-FeCo-Cr MO layer, deposited on SiN underlayers that are polished by sputter etching or not, respectively. On the same materials, the wall motion coercivity and the wall energy have been determined by the method of bubble expansion (see Section 6.2.3) so that a rather complete set of parameters necessary for an interpretation of recording results is available. The salient experimental results are summarized in Table 6.11.

Sputter etching reduces the surface roughness of the films. This reduces the wall motion coercivity, but leaves the nucleation field constant (2 kOe). We will see below that the experimental recording results shown in Figures 6.42 and 6.43 can be explained by domain wall motion during the creation and suppression of domains in the thermomagnetic write process.

Figure 6.42 [87] shows carrier and second harmonic levels as a function of the write power P_{wr} for the two parameters SiN etched (e)/not etched (ne) and $H_{wr} = 200$ Oe/500 Oe (16 kA/m per 40 kA/m). Increasing the write field leads to a more rapid rise of C at the onset power 5.5 mW and to a reduction of the power for symmetric writing, P_{sym}. At 200 Oe no difference in recording characteristics for etched and unetched underlayers is observed. At 500 Oe, however, the etched sample exhibits a more rapid rise in C at the onset power 5.5 mW. The minimum in the second harmonics at P_{sym} (corresponding to a domain length of 0.94 μm) is reached at a lower laser power, $P_{opt} = 6.5$ mW, as compared to 7.5 mW for the unetched sample.

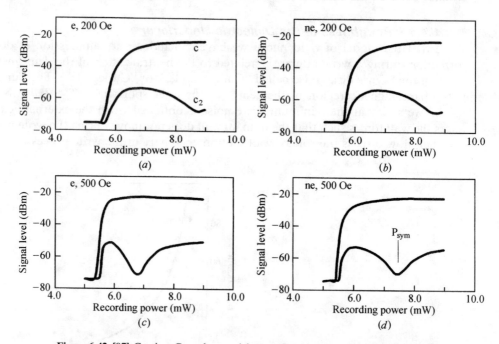

Figure 6.42 [87] Carrier, C, and second harmonic, C2, levels as a function of the recording power. Tb-FeCo-Cr recording layer deposited on a SiN underlayer that was sputter-etched (e) or not (ne). Laser modulation, pulse width 110 ns, recording frequency 3 MHz. Write fields 200 Oe and 500 Oe.

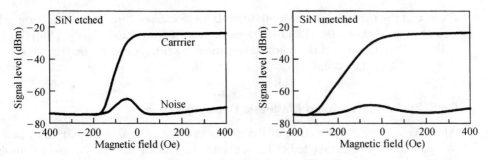

Figure 6.43 [87] Carrier C and noise N as a function of the external field for Tb-FeCo-Cr recording layers on etched and unetched SiN underlayers, respectively. Recording power 7.7 mW, pulse width 110 ns.

Increasing the write field to 500 Oe and etching the SiN underlayer both decrease P_{sym}, the power necessary to write domains of optimum length. Both measures increase the probability of wall motion. We therefore suppose that, in these samples, there is a *bubble expansion* during writing, driven by the external field, which is less hampered in the film on the etched underlayer.

The magnetic field dependence of the carrier and write noise levels are displayed in Figure 6.43 [87], [88] for the two cases "SiN (underlayer) etched" and "SiN unetched." For the etched sample, H_{supp} becomes smaller in magnitude. This can only be explained if wall motion coercive effects, expected to be reduced upon polishing of the underlayer, also play a role in the write suppression. Therefore, we conclude that, in the MO layers on etched SiN, domains are first formed in the write process but then collapse during cooling down under the external erase field. Such effects are indeed directly observed for "soft" single-layer direct-overwrite media, as will be discussed later in Section 6.5.4 (domain formation model of Figure 6.52).

The field for minimum write noise, $H_{min\,N}$, is also reduced in magnitude in samples on etched underlayers. This may also be due to a reduced coercive field for wall motion. In conclusion, the domain walls in samples on polished underlayers begin to move at lower drive fields.

Curves for the carrier $C = C(H)$ similar to those in Fig. 6.43 are reported by a second group [89]. Recorded marks in Tb-FeCo films deposited onto smooth and rough SiN underlayers [stack: SinN (85 nm)/Tb-FeCo (25 nm)/Al (10 nm)] were imaged by spin-polarized scanning electron microscopy. The marks on the rough underlayer are all multidomain but of the same total size, independent of the (erase) field. Contrary,

TABLE 6.11 Influence of Polishing the SiN Underlayer in a Stack SiN (120 nm)/Tb$_{18}$Fe$_{71}$Co$_8$Cr$_3$ (20 nm)/SiN (30 nm) by Sputter Etching

	(b) Unetched	(a) Etched
Surface roughness	2 nm	1 nm
Wall motion coercivity at R.T.	1.3 kOe	0.8 kOe
Erase field H_{supp}	300 Oe	180 Oe
Wall energy	5.1 erg/cm^2	4.3 erg/cm^2

Source: Data from [87].

the size of the marks on the smooth underlayer decreases with increasing erase field and is, also at $H = 0$, smaller than for the marks on the rough underlayer. This is consistent with our hypothesis that the thermomagnetically written domains on the smooth underlayer shrink in the cooling process.

6.4.5 Exchange-Coupled Magnetic Capping Layers

An LLG computer simulation of the thermomagnetic domain formation in two layers was performed in an extended cell model [90]. Technically it is similar to the simulations discussed in Section 6.3.4. One of the layers (C2) had a compensation temperature of about 220 K, whereas the other one (N) had a compensation temperature below 0 K such that its $M_s(T)$ was essentially ferromagnetic. When the two layers were exchange-decoupled, the domain size was much larger in N than in C2. Introducing an exchange coupling between the layers results in a nearly equal domain size, less jagged domain in N (due to less wall motion) but more irregular domains in C2 (due to more wall motion).

A thin film with in-plane magnetic anisotropy deposited onto the MO layer is called a *magnetic capping layer*. Such a layer is found to increase the field sensitivity of the stack. For example, a 2 nm PtCo alloy film reduces the noise and the size of the suppression field (H_{supp} in Fig. 6.34) from 600 Oe to 200 Oe for a Tb-FeCo film (20 nm thick, $T_c = 190°C$, $T_{comp} = 130°C$) [91]. A purely magnetostatic origin of this effect was ruled out because it does not occur when a very thin nonmagnetic layer is deposited between the capping and the MO layer. A possible schematical model of the magnetic moments in an exchange-coupled capping layer is shown in Figure 6.44. A detailed analytical micromagnetic model is developed in [92].

Also a 5 nm thick $Gd_{21}Fe_{74}Co_5$ ($H_c = 0.2$ kOe, in-plane anisotropy) capping layer could reduce the size of H_{supp} of a $Tb_{21}Fe_{70}Co_9$ film from 300 Oe to 100 Oe without any degradation in CNR. With increasing Gd-FeCo thickness, H_{supp} is even shifted to positive (write) values [93].

The reduction of H_{supp} due to a capping layer is attributed to an increased effective wall energy due to the interface magnetic wall [91]. From the discussion in Section 6.2,

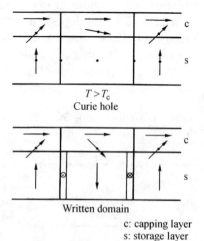

$T > T_c$
Curie hole

Written domain

c: capping layer
s: storage layer

Figure 6.44 Magnetic moments in an exchange-coupled double layer consisting of a storage layer s and a capping layer c (with in-plane magnetization). Heated in a laser spot (top) and at storage temperature (bottom).

we can expect in this case a higher wall tension and therefore a higher driving force for domain collapse, leading to a lower erase field (as found) but also to lower readout stability (not yet investigated). The interface wall may also move vertically through the storage layer (see Section 6.3.5).

A very thin Co layer can also help to suppress domain formation [94]. A thickness of 0.3 to 0.5 nm corresponding to one or two atomic layers is most effective. It changes H_{supp} of a RE-rich ("hard") Tb-FeCo layer (25 nm) from -800 Oe to -200 Oe. On the other hand, Fe layers with a thickness ranging from 0.1 to 3 nm do not change the magnetic field sensitivity at all.

The different behavior of Fe and Co layers is not yet well understood. From the work on RE/TM multilayers it is known that TM layers up to a thickness of 11 atomic monolayers can be amorphous, depending on the deposition process parameters. On the other hand, it is known that amorphous Fe has a Curie temperature below room temperature and is therefore paramagnetic during the thermomagnetic write process, contrary to amorphous Co [12]. This could possibly explain the difference between very thin Fe and Co layers.

A capping layer may also be realized in a Pt/Co multilayer by just increasing the thickness of the top Co layer to 0.7 nm as compared to 0.3 nm in the interior of the stack [80]. In this way, H_{supp} is reduced from -400 Oe to -150 Oe.

Often the capping layer decreases $|H_{supp}|$ and $|H_{\min N}|$ the same way. It offers then an important possibility to increase the field sensitivity in magnetic field modulation through the design of the layer stack.

6.4.6 Summary "Thermomagnetic Write Process"

Three types of reversal behavior are observed in the thermomagnetic write process.

1. Perfectly cylindrical domains are written, the size of which increases with the magnitude of the write field. Only in this case is the domain formation described by the bubble-like model. Occurs in "less hard" MO media such as GdTb-Fe or Tb-FeCo-Cr on ion-polished SiN underlayers. Domain wall motion during the write process is possible.

2. Small domains are, repetitively formed, outside-in, within the shrinking Curie radius during cooling. Observed for hard media under low write fields, e.g., in evaporated Tb-FeCo on rough surfaces.

3. Cylindrical domains with small reverse subdomains are formed. Observed in media with high magnetization.

The effect of a write field on (2) and (3) is to make the written mark a single domain. In MO storage technology the MO medium must be designed, by choosing the proper composition, to assure writing of single domain marks under the specified write field of recorders.

The mark formation can be suppressed by an external field H_{supp}. For most media the suppression field must be applied in erase direction. In this case, the primary driving force for mark formation is the demagnetizing field H_d within the paramagnetic "Curie disk," close to its edge. There is an optimum field $H_{\min N}$ for which the noise becomes minimum. A second role of the write field is, therefore, to make the domain shape regular.

Magnetic field modulation requires low values of H_{supp} and $H_{min\,N}$. They are achieved by making the medium magnetically softer ("less hard"), for example, by adding Cr to Tb-FeCo or by smoothing the dielectric underlayer (by ion etching or "soft" preparation with optimized sputter cathodes). An additional thin magnetic film with in-plane anisotropy on top of the storage layer (*a capping layer*) has the same effect because of the interface magnetic wall that increases the wall force.

6.5 DOMAIN INSTABILITY AND SINGLE-LAYER DIRECT OVERWRITE

6.5.1 Readout Stability

When domains are subjected to a laser spot and/or a magnetic field, they tend to be destabilized and are eventually erased.

Figure 6.45 [96] shows the carrier C and the noise N for a Dy-FeCo disk as a function of the cw read laser power. For a linear disk velocity of 10 m/s, the carrier C begins to decrease and N peaks at about 4 mW. At 6 mW the domains are completely erased. When exposed to repeated irradiation by the laser beam above a stability power limit (under defined applied field and operating temperature, e.g., 400 Oe and 55°C), the CNR deteriorates in proportion to the logarithm of the readout time [96]:

$$CNR(t) = CNR_0 - \alpha \log(t) \tag{6.47}$$

$$N = N_0 + \beta \log(t) \tag{6.48}$$

where β is called the *noise deterioration factor*. The logarithmic time dependence indicates a creep-like domain wall motion with a broad ("white") spectrum of activation energies as described in Section 6.3.2.3.

Figure 6.46 [96] shows the noise increase, as characterized by β, vs. the read laser power P_r for different external fields H_a. The stability of the domains is maximum for

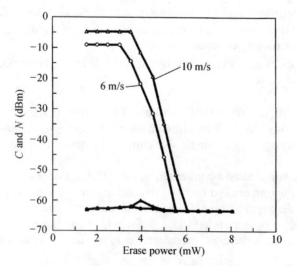

Figure 6.45 [96] Carrier C and noise level N vs. (read/erase) laser power (at H_a = 300 Oe). Written with 8 mW and at 200 Oe. Layer stack: Ce-SiO$_2$ (85 nm)/Dy$_{26}$Fe$_{55.5}$Co$_{18.5}$ (25 nm)/Ce-SiO$_2$ (25 nm)/Al (40 nm).

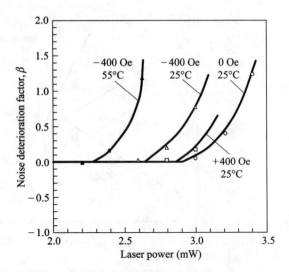

Figure 6.46 [96] Noise increase of recorded marks, characterized by a deterioration factor β, due to repeated read at a disk velocity of 6 m/s. Experimental parameters are the laser read power P_r, the operating temperature of the disk and the applied field H_a.

$H_a = 0$ and minimum when an erase field (-400 Oe) is applied. For $P_r = 3.0$ mW, at 6 m/s, only N increases, whereas C remains constant indicating that the domain boundaries become jagged but the average domain size remains constant.

During readout, a temperature distribution passes over the domains and the domain wall experiences forces different from the stable situation at ambient temperature. In order to compare with the bubble-like model, the domain stability under repeated read was determined as a function of laser power and magnetic field [30]. Figure 6.47 [30] shows the stability limits for four GdTb-Fe specimens with different Tb content and different compensation temperatures. The specimens are magnetically "less hard" due to the low Tb content, and the domains may be expected to erase by wall motion. 100,000 domains with a diameter of 1.2 μm were measured, and every domain was sampled 1000 times. As a criterion for destabilization a loss in CNR by 1 dB for 100 read cycles was chosen corresponding to an average motion of the domain walls by about 20 nm.

The curves in Figure 6.47 were calculated from the bubble-like model using the calculated temperature profiles of Figure 6.48 [30] and the measured values of $M_s(T)$, $H_c(T)$, and $\sigma_w(T)$. For a general discussion and details of this method see [45], [46]. The wall energy $\sigma_w(T)$ was obtained by the bubble expansion method (see Section 6.2.3). The theoretical curve conforms best to the experimental data when assuming a thermal conductivity of the RE-TM films of $\lambda = 17$ W/mK (for the sputtered films as compared to the bulk value of 54 W/mK, compare Section 6.2.4) and a wall motion coercivity H_c^w of 70% of the static coercive field as measured in complete hysteresis loops.

To a first approximation we identify the laser read power with a local temperature increase above room temperature and assume that the temperature is constant throughout the domain area. The instability values H_{in} are mainly determined by the coercive field at the corresponding temperature, $H_c[T(P_r)]$. The main error in this constant temperature consideration is the neglect of the contracting wall gradient force. For contracting (erase) field direction, the forces add and the size of H_{in} is lower than for expanding (write) field direction. This is most pronounced in the curve for 395 K in Figure 6.47.

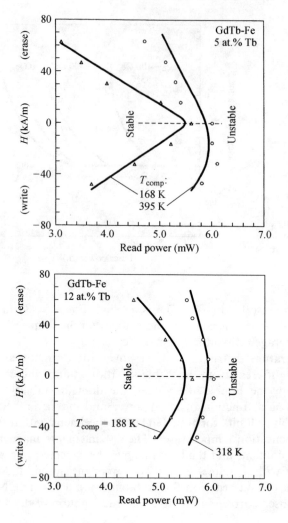

Figure 6.47 [30] Stability limit of recorded marks in a read power (P_r) applied field (H) diagram. The curves have been obtained from the bubble-like model, experimental values of the magnetic parameters and fitted temperature profiles. Layer stack: AlN (80 nm)/ GdTb-Fe (50 nm)/Al (40 nm); disk velocity $v = 5$ m/s. Four samples were studied with 5 at.% Tb ($T_{comp} = 168$ K and 395 K) and 12 at.% Tb ($T_{comp} = 188$ K and 318 K).

The readout stability becomes less field-dependent with increasing Tb content (increasing the coercivity), and with increasing T_{comp} (lowering the magnetization and therefore f_d and f_a, due to the demagnetizing and external fields, respectively). The stability at zero applied field increases with increasing T_{comp} due to a decrease of the demagnetizing force. The maximum stability is theoretically and experimentally obtained for the low-M_s disk ($T_{comp} = 395$ K) at a field of 20 kA/m in write direction compensating the contracting wall forces.

The temperature profiles in Figure 6.48 [30] are drawn in a position relative to the domain center at the moment when the wall displacement theoretically starts under an erase field, a write field, and zero field. The position of the wall is indicated by the vertical dotted line. The wall displacement does not start at the passage of the temperature peak when H_c becomes minimum but before or after when the wall experiences a temperature gradient. Under write or zero field, the domains expand at the leading edge of the T profile. Under an erase field, the domains shrink at the trailing edge. In

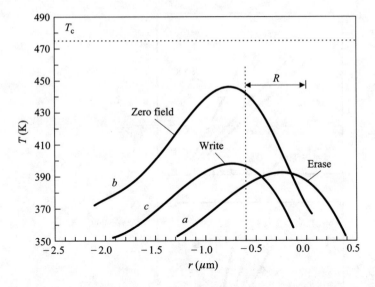

Figure 6.48 [30] Calculated temperature profiles at which domain wall displacement starts. Domain center at $r = 0$, domain radius R. "Erase": $H_a = 46$ kA/ m, $P_r = 3.7$ mW. "Zero field": $H_a = 0$, $P_r = 5.6$ mW. "Write": $H_a = -46$ kA/m, $P_r = 3.9$ mW. GdTb-Fe disk with 4.5 at.% Tb and $T_{comp} = 168$ K.

both cases the wall gradient force, tending to shift the wall to regions with higher temperature, points into the same direction as the force due to the external field or, for $H_a = 0$, the demagnetizing field.

6.5.2 Domain Erasure

When increasing the laser power to a critical value P_{er} depending on the applied magnetic field (erase field H_{er}), the domains are completely erased. The basic process can be an outside-in wall motion or a creation of subdomains within the written mark.

Figure 6.49 [46] shows the correlation of P_{er} and H_{er} for GdTb-Fe disks with 5 and 12 at.% Tb and various values of the compensation temperature. Without applied field, the erase-power level is nearly the same for all specimens corresponding to heating the domains to T_c. The highest erase-field sensitivity is observed for the lower Tb-content and the lowest T_{comp}. This is caused by a lower coercivity (due to the lower Tb-content) and a higher field pressure, $2\mu_0 M_s H_a$ due to a higher M_s (due to the lower T_{comp}).

It is, a priori, not clear whether the erasure of domains occurs uniquely via an outside-in collapse with wall motion or a generation of subdomains within the written mark. During the write process in Tb-FeCo films, a field applied in the erase direction does not generally lead to circular domains with smaller radius but in many cases to domains of the size of the laser spot with subdomains (high-M_s samples) or to a multi-domain mark (steep H_c), see Section 6.4.3. In some erase experiments the domain length jitter was found to increase from initially 14 nm to 110 nm (domain period about 2 μm) whereas the signal decreased by a factor of 10 [97]. This indicates that the mark size does not shrink to zero and subdomains are formed. The best method to establish the mechanism of erasure would be to observe the shapes of half-erased domains, e.g., by

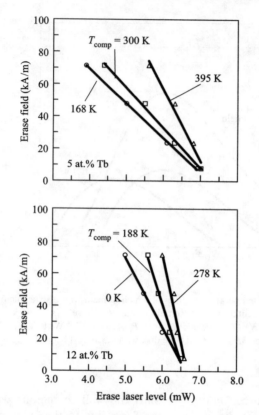

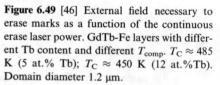

Figure 6.49 [46] External field necessary to erase marks as a function of the continuous erase laser power. GdTb-Fe layers with different Tb content and different T_{comp}. $T_C \approx 485$ K (5 at.% Tb); $T_C \approx 450$ K (12 at.%Tb). Domain diameter 1.2 μm.

Lorentz microscopy, spin-polarized scanning electron microscopy, or magnetic force microscopy, which has not yet been attempted.

6.5.3 Principle of Stroboscopic Polarized Light Microscopy and Single-Layer Direct Overwrite

The classical thermomagnetic write process needs two passes of the laser beam to overwrite old information, a first one to erase old domains and a second one to write new domains with the bias field being reversed in-between. In stroboscopic experiments, it was discovered by accident that written domains could vanish when pulsed by a laser beam in the absence of a magnetic field [98], [43]. As domains can also be created in zero applied magnetic field due to the effect of the demagnetizing field, this offers the possibility of a one-pass direct overwrite in single layers (SL-DOW) without magnetic field modulation, even without a bias field. Suitable materials are $(Gd_{0.5}Tb_{0.5})_x(FeCo)_{1-x}$ with x about 0.25. They are "less hard" or "MO-soft" in our terminology.

Two main variants of SL-DOW have been developed:

1. erasure with laser *pulses*, where the position of the old domains have to be localized either in a *read-before-write* step or by predefining possible locations on the disk ("*cell-bit-method*"),

2. "true" direct overwrite by *power modulation* of only one laser such that old domains are erased by a low continuous power level and new domains are created by high power pulses.

As shown in Figure 6.50 [99], the setup for stroboscopic polarized light microscopy consists of

1. a polarized light microscope suitable for observing the domains by the polar magneto-optic Kerr effect,
2. a high-speed sampling camera system;
3. a viewing laser, typically a Q-switched (Nd:YAG pumped) dye laser (pulse duration 5–10 ns, command rates 60 Hz–1030 Hz); and
4. a heat laser to induce a temperature profile in the layer (e.g., a 30 mW diode laser [100]).

A heat laser pulse pattern (e.g., a write pulse or a write/erase sequence) is periodically repeated. It has to be assured that the induced changes in the domain pattern of the samples are reproducible. Typically, the positional jitter is about 0.1 μm at a linear disk velocity of 20 m/s [42]. The viewing laser pulse is synchronized to the heat laser to the order of ±1 ns. A temporal image averaging is applied to remove camera and electronic noise. Background subtraction is used to reduce optical errors and spatial variation in the illumination.

The setup allows time-resolved observation of laser-induced temperature profiles and of the formation and erasure of domains. The spatial resolution of magnetic information is typically better than 0.4 μm [42]; domains of 0.3 μm diameter were

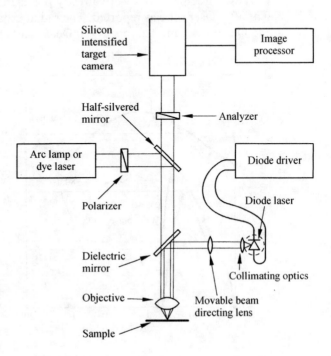

Figure 6.50 [99] Experimental setup for the stroboscopic observation of domain dynamics in a Kerr microscope. The diode laser induces a temperature profile in the sample. The arc lamp or the dye laser is used for (time-delayed) viewing. Rotating disks can also be observed.

also observed [100]. An image of temperature distribution can be obtained by applying a bias magnetic field high enough to prevent magnetic reversal. The transient Kerr contrast in the laser spot can then be transformed into a temperature contrast using the known $\theta_K(T)$ relationship [42].

6.5.4 Observation of Domain Formation and Erasure

In a typical experiment on SL-DOW media, a domain area is perodically heated by laser pulses and the domains are observed by stroboscopy. Domain diameters thus obtained on a sputtered GdTb-FeCo film under static conditions are displayed in Figure 6.51 as a function of the time after switching the laser on [100].

Pulse durations up to 60 ns create temporary domains of about 1 µm diameter that disappear again upon cooling, whereas pulse durations longer than 80 ns create residual domains of more than 1 µm diameter that are frozen in during shrinking. For short pulses, the peak temperature is lower and during cooling, the high coercivity region is reached earlier. This favors domain stability contrary to the observation. For short pulses, however, the temperature gradient is steeper and the wall gradient force stronger. We therefore suppose that domain collapse is mainly due to the wall gradient force.

The salient features of the curves in Figure 6.51 and also of those obtained in similar experiments are

1. visible nucleation (0.3 µm) starts within 15 ns,
2. the domains expand during heating and reach maximum size within 5 ns after the laser has been switched off, they then contract upon further cooling,
3. stable domains (diameter 0.7–1.3 µm) are only obtained for long enough pulses (> 80 ns) as already discussed above.

These three processes were already postulated in [43] where domain growth up to 100 ns after laser off was reported. The radial expansion rate reported in [100] is 2.2 m/s at (45 Oe, 7 mW) and 6.3 m/s at (90 Oe, 9.5 mW). The radial contraction rate is 3 to 8

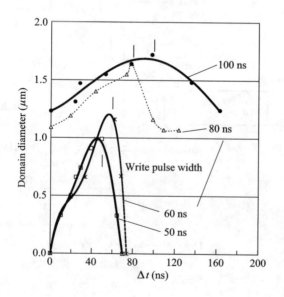

Figure 6.51 [100] Domain diameters as a function of time after starting a laser (write) pulse. Sputtered GdTb-FeCo, laser power 9.5 mW, H_a = 90 Oe (write direction). The vertical bars at the curves indicate the pulse duration.

times larger. The external field influences the domain size but not the growth rates. A model of this type of domain formation is shown in Figure 6.52. It is typically observed in magnetically "less hard" MO materials.

Two models have been proposed to explain the erasure of a magnetic domain when heated by a laser beam.

1. A new domain is created in the old domain and "consumes" it. This process would be driven by demagnetization during cooling. It was postulated in the first papers on SL-DOW and theoretically predicted to occur for specific values of the compensation temperature [101].
2. The old domain collapses outside-in by wall motion.

Only outside-in collapses have been observed in all experiments so far, e.g., domains that were created by 900 ns pulses (in a 104 nm $Gd_{12}Tb_{12}Fe_{62}Co_{14}$ film) were, in the course of erasing, still complete after 105 ns, half collapsed after 130 ns and completely gone after 155 ns, before the pulse ends [102]. The erasure, therefore, occurs in the heating period and not during cooling.

A similar sort of SL-DOW in $Tb_{32}Fe_{68}$ was discovered in Lorentz micrographs [103]. By applying long (L) and short (S) laser pulses under the same write field (250 Oe = 20 kA/m), a cycling between two domain sizes was achieved.

(L): a domain of diameter 1.1 μm was created during cool down from the maximum (calculated) Curie diameter $d_C = 1.9$ μm.

(S): the domain shrinks to 0.4 μm from a Curie diameter of 1.1 μm (size of the larger domain).

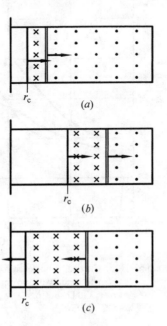

Figure 6.52 Domain formation model to illustrate the processes of Figure 6.51. (a) Nucleation outside the Curie radius. (b) Domain expansion during heating. (c) Domain contraction during cooling. Top view. Wall curvature not shown.

In both cases, the resulting domain radius is smaller than the maximum Curie radius reached at the end of the laser pulse. Due to the high T_{comp}, demagnetizing effects play only a minor role. The drive for the domain collapse is the thermally induced wall energy gradient, which should be stronger for shorter pulses (S).

6.5.5 Operating Margins and Recording Performance

In the first recording experiments with SL-DOW using constant frequency pulses, only a moderate CNR of 29 dB at a write field of 50 Oe was obtained [104]. In power-controlled ("true") direct overwrite on a series of disks with GdTb-FeCo and GdTb-Fe layers, maximum CNR was observed for 24–25 at.% rare-earth content (see Fig. 6.53). The best performance (32 dB at 1800 rpm = 30 Hz) was obtained for MO films thicker than 150 nm and a (relatively low) $T_c = 240°C$ due to a high carrier level.

Quadrilayer disks of the structure substrate/AlSiN (110 nm)/ $Gd_{6.5}Tb_{19.5}Fe_{66.6}Co_{7.4}$/AlSiN (135nm)/Al-alloy (60nm) were then prepared and further optimized. A higher thermal conductivity is expected for this layer stack leading to a more symmetric T-profile and consequently more regular domains. Sputter etching of the underlayer resulted in 8 dB improvement in CNR (40 dB at 1.2 µm domain length), but only at higher write field and higher laser power. Sputter etching polishes the underlayer and reduces the wall pinning force, and domain shrinkage has to be prevented by a higher magnetic field.

Although this represents a considerable improvement of more than 10 dB over the first results, SL-DOW media have not yet met the 45 dB CNR requirement for today's commercial disks. A CNR > 46 dB is obtained but only for H_a > 500 Oe (40 kA/m). This improvement arises probably from less domain shrinkage during the write process

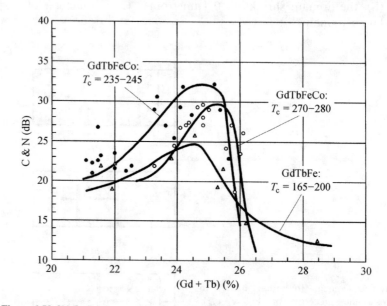

Figure 6.53 [105] Carrier-to-noise ratio CNR obtained in the single-layer direct-overwrite mode with power modulation. Disks with different composition: ○, GdTb-FeCo, $T_C = 270 - 280°C$; •, GdTb-FeCo, $T_C = 235 - 245°C$; △, GdTb-Fe, $T_C = 165 - 200°C$. Domain diameter 1.5 µm.

because the external field compensates the contracting wall forces. Under such high fields, however, the margin of the laser pulse width for domain erasure becomes impracticably small.

A critical assessment of this type of direct overwrite in single layers compared to direct overwrite with exchange-coupled layers is given in [106].

6.5.6 Domain Collapse Rate and Wall Mobility

Domain wall motion plays an important role in the erasure of domains. Results for a $Gd_{11.5}Tb_{11.5}Fe_{77}$ film are shown in Figure 6.54 [107]. In these erase experiments, a thermomagnetically written domain is subjected to a bias erase field just below the coercive value such that an additional erase field pulse starts the collapse. The process is stroboscopically observed with a fast laser (0.5 ns, 1080 Hz repetition rate).

The radial shrinkage velocity increases during the collapse due to the increase of the wall tension (σ_w/r) with decreasing domain radius. When the wall is moving, its driving force is reduced by a coercive force and its velocity is proportional to an effective field $H_{er} = H_a - H_c$:

$$v_w = \mu_w(H_a - H_c). \tag{6.33}$$

The proportionality factor μ_w is the domain wall mobility. It is clear from the discussion of Figure 6.54 that Equation (6.33) applies only to the beginning of the collapse of large domains. The reason is that only then is H_a the dominant driving force much larger than the wall tension and the demagnetizing field.

Plots of the initial velocity vs. the total collapse field yield a domain wall mobility $\mu = 0.3$ cm/sOe (sample of Fig. 6.54, domain diameter $> 5\,\mu m$). When the mobility is deduced from measurements of the total time necessary to shrink the domain to the critical radius (about $1\,\mu m$), an order of magnitude larger (incorrect) values are obtained. The observed wall mobility is much smaller than the 1–30 cm/sOe typical for bubble domain materials. The velocity is one to two orders of magnitude smaller

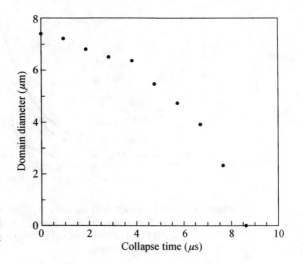

Figure 6.54 [107] Collapse of a cylindrical domain under an erase field $H_a = 240$ Oe at $T = 160°C$. $Gd_{11.5}Tb_{11.5}Fe_{77}$ layer.

than those deduced from the computer simulations represented in Figure 6.5 (20 m/s at 500 Oe) and in Figure 6.20 (160 m/s at 15.6 kOe, the coercive field).

Figure 6.55 [108] shows the wall mobility in several GdTb-Fe samples as a function of the temperature distance to T_c. In samples with high $M_s (T_c - T_{comp} > 170$ K), μ_w increases toward infinity when T_c is approached, whereas in the samples with 18 at.% Tb and $T_c - T_{comp} < 85$ K, the mobility remains low.

The mobility is discussed on the basis of a formula calculated from the LLG equation:

$$\mu_w = \frac{|\gamma|}{\alpha} \sqrt{\frac{A}{K_u}} = \frac{|\gamma|}{\alpha} \Delta_w \qquad (6.49)$$

with γ being the gyromagnetic ratio and α the Gilbert damping constant. It could successfully explain some experimental results for bubble domain materials. The lower mobility in RE-TM films can be attributed, within the LLG model, to the smaller wall width parameter Δ_w and an increased damping parameter α, both due to the presence of Tb.

The increase in μ_w for the magnetically "less hard" materials, represented in Figure 6.55, is discussed by examining the factors in Equation (6.49). The damping factor α is expected to increase with temperature because more damping mechanisms become effective. The exchange stiffness A decreases with increasing temperature. Both trends lead to a decrease of μ_w. Other possible explanations for the order of magnitude increase in wall mobility are either more than an order of magnitude increase in the gyromagnetic factor γ or in the wall width (equivalent to more than two orders of magnitude decrease in K_u). This does not fit, however, to the experimental trends presented in Section 6.2. The wall width, e.g., is expected from the formula for Bloch

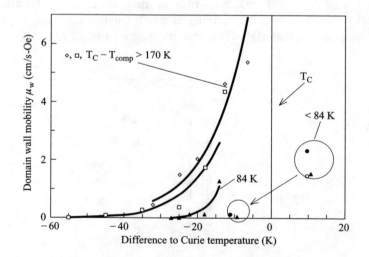

Figure 6.55 [108] Domain wall mobility μ_w, [Eq. (33)], close to the Curie temperature. Samples with approximate composition $Gd_{11}Tb_{11}Fe_{78}$ (only ◊) and
$Gd_6Tb_{18}Fe_{73}Co_3$ (all others); their temperature difference $T_C - T_{comp}$ is
given in the figure.

walls to be nearly independent of the temperature. The validity of the formula for the Bloch wall energy up to $T_C - 40$ K seems plausible from the experimental results presented in Section 6.2.3. It is, however, not certain that this formula and Equation (6.49) remain valid closer to T_c where fluctuations of the magnetic moments play an important role.

MO recording materials are characterized by strong coercive effects that are not taken into account by the LLG equation. They exhibit a thermally activated magnetic aftereffect (see Section 6.3.2) that could also be the origin of an exponential increase of the domain wall mobility for T approaching T_c. Such effects should, however, only be important for fields below H_c. A very fast thermally induced switching was observed on GdTbFe layers when they are rapidly heated through the compensation temperature. The observation method was spin-polarized photoemission [109, 110]. When the magnetization is small, as is the case close to T_{comp}, reversal involves only a small transfer of angular momentum to the lattice and may be fast but under static conditions the high coercive field prevents reversal. When samples are heated rapidly through the compensation temperature, however, the spin temperature lags behind the lattice temperature because heat transfer to the lattice is much faster than to the spin system. At a certain time, therefore, both the magnetization is low and the coercive field (related to the lattice) is low enough for switching. A similar situation may occur under static conditions when the sample temperature approaches the Curie temperature.

6.5.7 Summary "Domain Instability"

The instability of cylindrical domains in "less hard" MO media under the combined action of an applied field and a moving temperature profile is well described by the bubble-like model of the forces on a domain boundary. The effect of the wall gradient force becomes evident. The maximum stability is theoretically and experimentally obtained for MO layers with small M_s under a field in the write direction that compensates the contracting wall forces.

In stroboscopic experiments in a Kerr microscope, it has been observed that the domains in magnetically "less hard" MO layers expand when heated by a laser beam and contract after the laser has been switched off. Laser-induced outside-in collapse of domains can be used to obtain direct overwrite in single layers. This method yields a maximum CNR of 35 dB under practical conditions.

The domain wall mobility can be determined from the collapse of domains under an erase field. It increases in some cases toward infinity when the measuring temperature approaches T_c. The domain wall velocity is generally lower than the values observed in bubble materials or those obtained from computer simulations based on the LLG. This indicates that in MO layers coercive effects are stronger than in the two cases compared.

6.6 SIGNAL AND NOISE, DOMAIN IRREGULARITIES

In this section, we analyze the relationship of the shape of the domains, especially the regularity of their boundary, with the signal-to-noise ratio in MO readout and try to connect the findings with the magnetic properties and the microstructure of the films.

The most important task of digital recording is to avoid bit errors. A bit error occurs when, within the detection window, the noise becomes larger than the distance of the signal to the decision threshold. The bit-error rate (BER) is a function of the signal-to-noise ratio (SNR). The SNR is, however, difficult to determine. Instead, the recording performance of a disk is estimated by analyzing the signal of a periodic mark pattern (a carrier) in a spectrum analyzer. The carrier-to-noise ratio (CNR) is determined as the ratio of the signal peak and the base intensity near the signal frequency. The CNR is higher than the SNR by the ratio of the signal bandwidth to the resolution bandwidth of the spectrum analyzer, typically $10*\log(10\,MHz/30\,MHz) = 25$ dB.

In order to illustrate the mutual implications of system requirements, materials research, and recording physics for the development of an optimum medium, we review the discussion "Pt/Co multilayers vs. RE-TM amorphous films" for blue recording on the basis of a "what if" analysis. We will see (Section 6.6.1) that it is important to distinguish between various noise sources when extrapolating from current to future performance. In Section 6.6.2, the main emphasis is on disk noise that arises from an initialized disk without written domains and in Section 6.6.3 it is on write noise mainly arising from irregularities of the domain boundary. In Section 6.6.4, we discuss the recording performance of RE-TM media.

6.6.1 Distinction between Different Noise Sources

In a MO test recorder, the signal and the noise can be measured under various experimental conditions [111]. First, (1), the noise can be determined with the light switched off and the disk at rest. Then, successively, (2) the light is switched on, (3) the (magnetically initialized) disk is rotated, and (4) marks are written and reread.

From an evaluation of the respective noise spectra, the following noise sources can be distinguished.

1. Electronic noise, measured without light, including amplifier noise and thermal noise.

2a. Laser noise.

2b. Detector shot noise associated with the photocurrent in the detector.

3. Disk noise measured on a rotating disk in a magnetically initialized state (without marks).

4. Write noise arising mainly from irregularities of written marks.

Items (2a) and (2b) add to the electronic noise when the disk is irradiated but at rest. The sum of (1), (2a), and (2b) is often called **system noise**. Its origin is *temporal* fluctuations. For blue recording, the detector noise constitutes a serious problem.

The sum of disk (3) and write (4) noise is often called **medium noise**. Its origins are *spatial* fluctuations of disk properties that are optically transferred to the detection system, so that the frequency spectrum contains the optical transfer function, as a factor.

The total noise is the sum of all noise contributions. Often, one noise source N_d dominates the other ones. Then the signal-to-noise ratio CNR is determined by the ratio C/N_d.

The performance of a drive-medium system depends on the relative size of the different noise contributions. As an illustration consider a fictitious competition for the highest CNR between two disk families with different carrier and noise levels that are schematically shown in Figure 6.56. If the sum of laser and detector noise is dominant

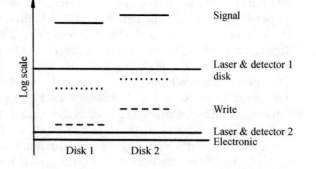

Figure 6.56 Comparison of signal and noise levels for two "competing" MO media. Disk 1 ("F", finer microstructure) and disk 2 ("S", higher signal level). The relatively better performance with respect to CNR depends on the position of the sum of laser and detector noise.

(indicated by "laser & detector 1"), disk 2 (S) with the higher signal level performs better. If this noise can be sufficiently reduced ("laser & detector 2"), e.g., by increasing the laser power and improving the detector sensitivity, the disk becomes the dominant noise source and both disk families yield the same CNR for the values chosen in the figure. Upon reducing the disk noise, e.g., by making more perfect grooves and more homogeneous layers, disk 1 (F) with the lower write noise performs better. If the write noise is reduced on both disk families below the level *laser & detector 2*, e.g., by improving the microstructure of the layers, disk 2 (S) prevails again as in the beginning of our Gedanken experiment.

6.6.2 Disk Noise, Illustration: Pt/Co Multilayers and RE-TM Films for Blue Recording

Disk noise generally consists of an amplitude and a polarization noise due to local changes in reflectivity and the polarization state, respectively. The amplitude noise is normally canceled by differential detection (*common mode rejection*) so that the disk noise is mainly polarization induced. Polarization noise can be due to inhomogeneities in the MO layer, but also due to the roughness of the dielectric underlayer because it changes the optical enhancement locally and therefore generates local variations of the Kerr rotation. The latter effect becomes relatively more important when very thin MO storage layers are used (e.g., 25 nm Tb-FeCo or 18 nm Pt/Co ML on an underlayer with a roughness of 2–7 nm).

Disk noise spectra have been measured at 488 nm for Co/Pt samples prepared by different sputtering techniques together with a Tb-FeCo disk and an exchange-coupled double layer [Co/Pt]/Tb-FeCo disk [112]. The laser power was adjusted, so that the reflected light intensity was the same for every disk. The amorphous Tb-FeCo layer exhibits the lowest noise level. The higher disk noise of Pt/Co is attributed to its crystallinity because it is clearly related to the degree of dispersion of the crystallographic (111) axis, the magnetically easy axis. This noise can be reduced by sputtering the SiN with Xe instead of Ar or by sputter etching of the SiN underlayer which both make the surface smoother. The [Co/Pt]-Tb-FeCo exchange coupled double layer has as low a disk noise as the Tb-FeCo disk, probably because the dispersion of magnetic moments of Co/Pt is reduced by the exchange interaction with the more perfectly aligned TM moments in Tb-FeCo.

In the recording experiments with low read laser power, the amplifier noise was 8 dB higher than the disk noise due to the low sensitivity of the photodiode detector at

488 nm [112]. This corresponds to the situation sketched in Fig. 6.56 with the noise level "laser & detector 1." The maximum CNR is therefore obtained at maximum carrier C. As C is proportional to the figure-of-merit $\theta_K \sqrt{R}$, the Co/Pt disks possess a 6–8 dB higher carrier level at 488 nm than the Tb-FeCo disk.

In a feasibility study of high-density MO recording, high-sensitivity detectors and a high-power (60 mW), low-noise, green (532 nm) laser were used so that the system noise no longer dominates [113]. A standard Tb-FeCo layer, a double layer Gd-FeCo (higher MO signal)/Tb-FeCo (higher coercivity), and a Pt/Co multilayer were compared as media. Figure 6.57 [113] displays the CNR of the three disks as a function of the recording frequency or the corresponding mark length.

For marks longer than 0.7 μm, the GdTb-Fe/Tb-FeCo disk performs better than Pt/Co, but below 0.7 μm it is vice versa. The reason for this crossover is the reduction of the medium noise in the frequency analyzer, by the optical transfer function, below the detector noise level at 0.7 μm. The CNR is, therefore medium-noise limited for mark lengths above 0.7 μm and system-noise limited for mark lengths below that value.

The implications of this crossover shall now be discussed in more detail by means of Figure 6.58 [113] where the noise spectra of the disks are shown together with the shot noise of the detector (for 2 mW readout laser power) and the electronic noise.

The carrier appears at 12.5 MHz corresponding to a mark length of 0.4 μm. At this frequency the medium noise of the Co/Pt storage layer and the detector shot noise are about equal. Consequently, the CNR does not increase when the detector noise is further reduced by increasing the readout laser power. For the (Gd-FeCo/TbFeCo)-based disk, however, increasing the readout power to 3 mW improves the CNR by 1 dB because here the medium noise is well below the detector noise.

In order to obtain a CNR > 48 dB at a mark length of 0.4 μm, an estimated readout power of 5 mW is needed. To keep sufficient domain stability, the layer stack would have to be redesigned with the consequence that the write power would have to be more than 20 mW. The same relative decrease of the shot noise can be obtained by a higher detector sensitivity.

The influence of the optical transfer function on both the carrier and the noise is clearly demonstrated in Figure 6.59 [115]. It concerns a comparison between an evaporated Pt/Co and a GdTb-Fe disk, where the carrier and noise levels were measured as

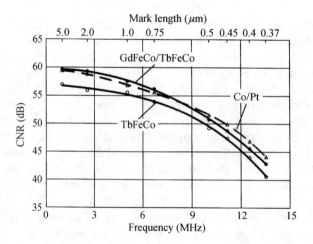

Figure 6.57 [113] Carrier-to-noise ratio CNR of three MO media as a function of the mark length. Laser wavelength 532 nm.

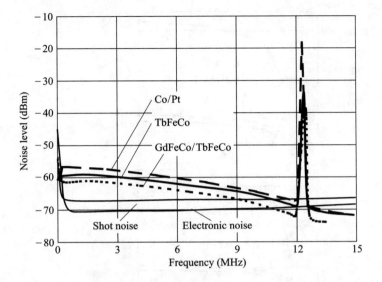

Figure 6.58 [113] Noise spectra for the media of Fig. 6.57. Mark length 0.4 μm. Shot noise measured with the Gd-FeCo/Tb-FeCo based disk.

a function of the domain period for the three wavelengths 820 nm, 647 nm, and 458 nm. When the optical frequency is approached, both the carrier and the noise go to zero. At cutoff, the domain period becomes equal to the laser spot diameter. The cutoff period is, therefore, given as $\lambda/(2\times$ numerical aperture) with λ being the readout wavelength.

For both disk families the disk noise dominates with the write noise adding always less than 2 dB. The disk noise of Pt/Co is always higher in this comparison (e.g., 3 dB at 820 nm read laser wavelength) but the difference becomes smaller at shorter wavelengths similar to the situation in Figure 6.57 [113, 114].

At $\lambda = 820$ nm and 647 nm, GdTb-Fe performs better, but at 458 nm, the higher magneto-optical figure-of-merit of Co/Pt causes a higher carrier level (+ 3 dB) and results in a correspondingly higher CNR (40 dB for 0.38 μm domain length). For both disks the CNR at 458 nm is not as high as at the other wavelengths, presumably due to an increased disk noise at the shorter wavelength arising mainly from the tracking grooves.

If the disk noise is suppressed by improved manufacturing procedures, the predominant noise is expected to arise from irregularities of the domain boundaries (domain jitter). In this situation, signal and noise are equally enhanced by a higher figure-of-merit and the CNR is independent of the figure-of-merit if it is only above a critical value to overcome the system noise. In this range ("write-noise" limited region) RE-TM based disks should have an advantage because of their finer microstructure.

6.6.3. Write Noise Due to Domain Irregularities

6.6.3.1 Shapes of Thermomagnetically Written Domains

In Section 6.4, we have discussed domain shapes observed by Lorentz microscopy to illustrate the write process. Already in the early stage of research on MO recording, however, thermomagnetically written domains were observed by the Bitter method in

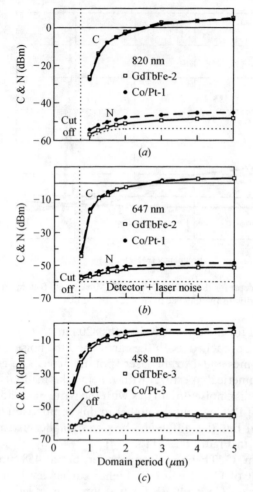

Figure 6.59 [115] Carrier C and noise N for Co/Pt and GdTb-Fe memory layers as a function of the written domain period for different laser wavelengths, (a): 820 nm, read power P_r = 0.9 mW, (b): 647 nm, P_r = 1.0 mW, (c) 458 nm, P_r = 0.8 mW. Disk velocity v = 5 m/s. Magnetic write fields have been optimized to yield maximum CNR.

an optical microscope [116]. As the magnetic characteristics of the specimens were also reported, we can use these early experiments to illustrate the development of domain wall irregularities during the write process.

A Tb-rich and a Fe-rich film (200 nm thick) were prepared by r.f.-sputtering. The exact compositions were not given, but the magnetic characteristics look like those of specimen 1 (30 at.% Tb) and specimen 4 (21 at.% Tb) of Figure 6.13. The domain structures of large marks (12 μm diameter) written under zero bias magnetic field are shown in Figure 6.60 [116].

In the Tb-rich film characterized by a steep $H_c(T)$ curve, a multidomain structure similar to Figure 6.36 is observed. The small domains are arranged in a coaxial multiring structure that reflects the symmetry of the temperature profile during cooling and a successive nucleation and inhibition of the magnetic reversal around the nuclei both induced by the respective demagnetizing field. In the Fe-rich film, characterized by a flat $H_c(T)$ curve and a high M_s, a maze-like demagnetizing structure is found within the mark. In addition, radially outward extending stripe domains are observed indicating wall motion during cooling.

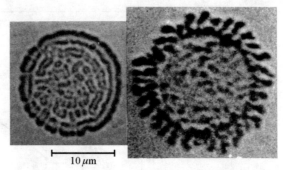

Figure 6.60 [116] Domain structure of marks
in a Tb-Fe film written under zero bias field.
Observation in a Kerr microscope.

$\overline{\qquad 10\,\mu m \qquad}$

(*a*) Tb-rich   (*b*) Fe-rich

6.6.3.2 Irregularity of the Domain Boundary

From the discussion of the domain destabilization during repeated read in Section 6.5, we know that domain wall irregularities of the order of 20 nm are detectable as an increase in the noise. Such ranges could only recently be resolved magnetically by scanning Lorentz microscopy [40]. However, macroscopic methods of domain expansion were developed some time ago and yielded valuable quantitative information about the jaggedness of the domain boundaries.

In one type of such experiments, domains of about 1 µm diameter are thermomagnetically written in a polarization microscope modified to perform static recording and domain observation (a "static tester"). They are then expanded at constant temperature under an applied field H_a to a size of typically 100 µm such that the boundaries can easily be measured by optical means.

The fractal dimension D of the domain boundary is then computed by the ruler method [117]. D is defined via $L(\theta) = L_0\theta^{(1-D)}$, where L is the measured domain boundary length and θ the measuring scale. It is representative for the as-written mark provided the domains grow according to a fractal law. Figure 6.61 [118] shows the temperature dependence of the fractal dimension D for two Tb-FeCo samples, B1 and B2. B1 (20.3 at.% Tb) is TM-dominated and B2 (26.4 at.% Tb) RE-dominated. The respective dependence $M_s(T)$ is similar to that of $D(T)$ in Figure 6.61 which confirms a fractal model [119] that shows that $D \sim M_s^2/T$.

A quantitative characterization of the domain boundary on a smaller scale can be obtained from the wall energy determined by the bubble growth method described in Section 6.2.3. The evaluation of the experimental data assumes a perfectly cylindrical domain shape that is, however, only guaranteed for domains that yield a CNR in recording of more than 50 dB. This can be deduced from Figure 6.62 [33] where the wall energy σ_w, determined on five different disks is displayed vs. the carrier-to-noise ratio. The variation in CNR is obtained by writing the marks under different recording conditions.

For CNR > 50 dB, identical values of σ_w are observed, whereas for CNR < 50 dB, the apparent value of σ_w increases with decreasing CNR. This is due to an increasing irregularity of the domain boundary and to subdomains leading to a corresponding increase in wall length (up to 5 times at 40 dB) so that the bubble model is no longer

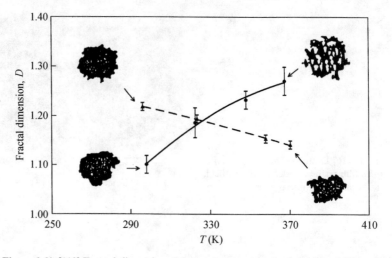

Figure 6.61 [118] Fractal dimension D versus temperature for boundary of domains in two Tb-FeCo films, expanded to about 100 μm diameter. (•) sample B1, 20.3 at.% Tb, $T_C = 230°C$; (▲) sample B3, 26.4 at.% Tb, $T_C = 195°C$.

valid. For a reliable determination of σ_w , high-performance disks with a CNR > 50 dB have, therefore, to be prepared.

6.6.3.3 Domain Length Jitter and Write Noise

In recording experiments, an effective domain length l_{eff} can be determined by measuring the time interval between two pulses (see Fig. 6.32) [120]. This is called the FWHM method (full width at half maximum). The half widths normally form a Gaussian distribution with a standard deviation σ that is generally called (temporal) jitter. The spatial jitter is obtained by multiplying with the linear disk velocity.

Figure 6.63 [120] shows the average domain length l_{eff} and its scatter σ as a function of the applied field H_a as determined on 10,000 domains (for every point) on a $Gd_{21}Tb_4Fe_{75}$ storage layer. The error in each point is estimated to be 20 μm. Between

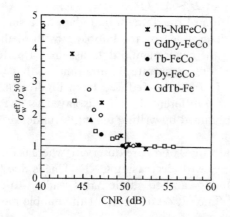

Figure 6.62 [33] Apparent domain wall energy σ_w^{eff}, determined on thermomagnetically written domains as a function of the signal-to-noise ratio CNR obtained with these domains, normalized to the value σ_w^{50dB} for a CNR = 50 dB in the same medium.

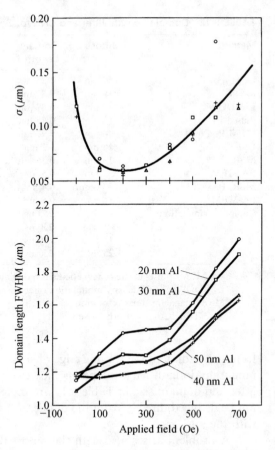

Figure 6.63 [120] Average domain length (bottom) and domain length scattering σ (top) vs. the applied field. GdTb-Fe recording layers. Write energy 0.6 nJ. Al-layer thicknesses are indicated in the figure.

about 200 and 300 Oe, l_{eff} is nearly independent of H_a. A similar dependence of the domain length on the write field was observed by Lorentz microscopy [44].

This behavior can be interpreted as follows. In the plateau, the driving force for wall motion is lower than the coercive force and the domain walls do not move. The domain length is the maximum Curie diameter reached during the write process. The Curie diameter is reduced when a thicker Al layer is used due to a higher thermal conductivity of the layer stack. Below $H_a = 200$ Oe, the domains shrink in the cooling phase due to the dominance of the wall forces. The domain dynamics are described by the model Figure 6.52. Above $H_a = 400$ Oe, the domains grow larger than the Curie radius, driven by $H_a + H_d$, where H_a is the applied write field and H_d the demagnetizing field.

In the plateau, the domain jitter σ reaches its minimum of about 50 nm and recording experiments yield the lowest noise. The increase in the write noise at both sides of the plateau is evidently due to the fact that moved domain walls have become jagged.

We now try to compare recording results reported by different authors. Table 6.12 summarizes experiments for which the domain length jitter was reported together with CNR values. In the original references the definition of jitter is not unique. Often $\Delta T/T$ is reported where T is the detection window and ΔT the standard deviation of the time

TABLE 6.12 Domain Length Jitter and CNR for Several Recording Experiments

Method, Disk	Jitter j	Domain Length l	$20 \log(l/j)$	CNR	Year of Publication	Reference
GdTb-Fe	50 nm	1.3 μm	28.3 dB	47 dB	1988	[120]
MFM	18 nm	0.5 μm	28.9 dB	49 dB	1990	[121]
LIMDOW	30 nm	0.67 μm	26.9 dB	46 dB	1993	[127]
Pulsed LIM	110 nm	0.75 μm	16.7 dB	51 dB	1993	[126]
MFM Pt/Co-ML	40 nm	0.97 μm	27.7 dB	50 dB	1993	[125]
DyFeCo	15 nm	1.2 μm	38 dB	55 dB	1993	[124]
MSR	15 nm	0.36 μm	27.6 dB	45 dB	1996	[123]
PA-MFM	23 nm	0.5 μm	26.7 dB	45 dB	1996	[122]
MSR, PA-MFM	33.6 nm	0.4 μm	21.5 dB	40.2 dB	1996	[128]
PA-MFM	16 nm	0.5 μm	29.9 dB	46 dB	1996	[135]
Computer simulation	3 ns	250 ns	38.4 dB	53 dB	1995	[10]
	5 ns	250 ns	34 dB	48 dB		
	15 ns	250 ns	24.4 dB	38 dB		
	25 ns	250 ns	20 dB	34 dB		

Note: PA-MFM: pulse-assisted magnetic-field modulation
LIMDOW: light-intensity modulation direct-overwrite
MSR: magnetic super resolution
disk: Tb-FeCo, if not otherwise stated

from the leading to the trailing edge of signals from domains with minimum length. The minimum domain length depends, however, on the modulation scheme. The values of jitter and domain size in Table 6.12 are therefore reported as lengths. When they could not be deduced directly from the publications, they were obtained from correspondence with the authors.

A problem arises also with the reported CNR values because they depend on the measurement conditions. The medium and write noise measured in a spectrum analyzer is proportional to RBS/v (RBS = residual band width, v = linear disk velocity). Values of v = 5 m/s and RBS = 30 kHz are often used. If the reported conditions differ from this standard we modify the CNR by adding a ΔCNR given by Equation (6.50).

$$\Delta\text{CNR} = 20 * \log\left(\frac{\text{RBS} * 5\,\text{m/s}}{v * 30\,\text{kHz}}\right) \tag{6.50}$$

The CNR values generally increase with domain length. To estimate this dependence quantitatively, the CNR values corrected to Equation (6.50) are plotted in Figure 6.64 versus 20*log(domain length/jitter). The two entities are roughly proportional to one another indicating that C/N is proportional to d/l. The domain length jitter j is, therefore, a good entity to predict the CNR that can be obtained for different domain length.

In recording experiments with MFM, the amplitude and the rise time of the magnetic field modulation as well as the linear disk velocity have been varied [121]. The spatial jitter is governed over a wide range of experimental conditions by a quadrature relation comprising the inverse field gradient $(dH_b/dx)^{-1}$ and a term that is independent of the external field:

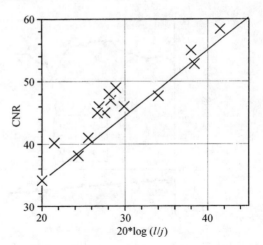

Figure 6.64 Carrier-to-noise ratio CNR vs. [(domain length l) / (jitter j)] for the specimens of Table 6.11. Data points below the line result from computer simulations.

$$\sigma = \sqrt{\sigma_0^2 + \frac{k}{dH_b/dx}} \qquad (6.51)$$

For a disk with a CNR of about 55 dB, σ_0 is found to be 18 nm, similar to the minimum jitter of 15 nm found in Table 6.12. This is about the lateral scale of the columnar microstructure. The jitter values characteristic of high performance MO disks confirm, therefore, the model that the domain walls are pinned at the boundaries in the columnar microstructures.

6.6.4 Recording Performance of RE-TM Media

6.6.4.1 Compositional Dependence of the Recording Noise

The compositional dependence of the recording noise was systematically studied for Tb-FeCo and TbDy-FeCo media. The results are shown in Figure 6.65 [129]. The noise increases drastically for about 27.5 at.% Tb in Tb-FeCo and about 30 at.% TbDy in TbDy-FeCo. For these compositions, $T_c - T_{comp}$ becomes smaller than 70 K.

In another study [86], the recording behavior of $Tb_x(Fe_{82}Co_{18})_{100-x}$ layers has been investigated. The suppression field for writing, H_{supp} in our terminology, is found to have a minimum for $x = 27$. The maximum of N together with a minimum of C is found for 28 at.% Tb ($T_c - T_{comp} = 30$ K), similar to the value reported above.

The minima in C can be explained as follows. For decreasing magnetization, the (M_s-related) expanding forces due to H_a and H_d become weaker, whereas the contracting (domain wall) forces remain constant. This situation results in smaller domains or incomplete domains because the applied field is not increased. The noise increase for T_{comp} approaching T_c is explained by stronger fluctuations in the coercivity radius due to a steeper $H_C(T)$ curve and caused by compositional fluctuations. The coercivity radius is defined by the circle in the temperature profile where the total force is equal to the coercive force.

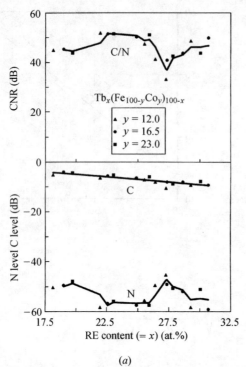

(a)

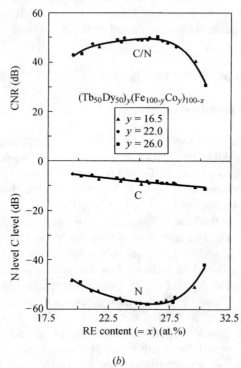

(b)

Figure 6.65 [129] Compositional dependence of C, N, and CNR (= C/N) for films of Tb-FeCo (a) and TbDy-FeCo (b) films. The curves are drawn for visual convenience.

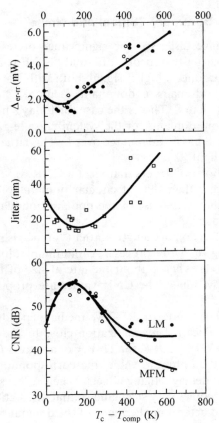

Figure 6.66 [130], [124] Recording performance of Dy-FeCo layers vs. $T_c - T_{comp}$. Domain length 1.2 μm. Top: Difference in laser power between stable readout and complete erasure for an external field $H_a = 32$ kA/m (400 Oe) in erase direction. Middle: Domain length jitter, LM, write field $H_{wr} = 16$ kA/m, $v_{disk} = 15$ m/s. Bottom: CNR, $H_{wr} = 16$ kA/m, $v_{disk} = 15$ m/s. ○ MFM (magnetic field modulation), ● LM (laser modulation).

6.6.4.2 *Dependence of CNR on* $T_c - T_{comp}$

Figure 6.66 [130], [124] shows the maximum CNR values for a series of Dy-FeCo disks of different compositions [$Dy_{17}(FeCo)_{83}$ to $Dy_{33}(FeCo)_{67}$] together with the domain length jitter and the difference between the minimum laser power for complete erasure and the maximum power under which the domains remain stable. As characteristic material parameter, the difference between the Curie and the compensation temperatures, $\Delta T = T_c - T_{comp}$, has been chosen. It determines the steepness of the magnetization $M_s(T)$ in the high temperature range. Write power and write frequency were adjusted to obtain domain lengths of approximately 1.2 μm.

The curves CNR vs. (ΔT) for Tb-FeCo and GdTb-Fe are qualitatively similar to those in Figure 6.66. The best performance (defined by the maximum in CNR and the minimum in the jitter) is obtained for Dy-FeCo at $\Delta T \approx 120$ K [124], for Tb-FeCo at $\Delta T \approx 220$ K [86], and for GdTb-Fe at $\Delta T \approx 280$ K [31].

The decrease of the CNR at higher ΔT is attributed to demagnetizing subdomains in the written marks that are favored by a higher M_s. The decrease in CNR at lower ΔT is attributed to fluctuations in ΔT due to compositional inhomogeneities which become more important when $H_c(T)$ becomes very steep. In that case the fluctuations in the coercive radius and consequently the irregularity of the domain boundaries increase.

6.6.5 Summary "Signal and Noise"

We have discussed the significance of results on the carrier-to-noise ratio CNR by comparing two media, "F" and "S." F is assumed to have a finer microstructure and S to produce a higher signal, both with respect to the other medium. When the noise of written domains is dominant, medium F, causing less domain length jitter, performs better than S. This is the case for today's high performance disks. When the disk noise (without domains) or the system noise (e.g., the detector noise) is larger than the write noise, S has an advantage over F. This situation is currently found for reading with blue laser light.

For MO layers that yield a CNR < 50 dB, the wall energy of the written domains is bigger than that of circular domains of the same size. This is due to subdomains and the jaggedness of the domain boundaries that lead to a longer effective domain boundary.

The domain length scatter ("jitter") is minimum when *the domain walls do not move* during the write process. A minimum value of 15 nm is found for different recording methods. This is about the lateral size of the columnar microstructure of amorphous RE-TM films. The CNR values are proportional to the ratio of domain length and jitter.

The CNR of RE-TM media depends on the difference $\Delta T = T_c - T_{comp}$ that determines the magnetization close to T_c. It is maximum at $\Delta T = 280$ K for GdTb-Fe, at $\Delta T = 220$ K for Tb-FeCo, and at $\Delta T = 120$ K for Dy-FeCo. When ΔT is bigger than the optimum value, the correspondingly higher M_s causes domain irregularities due to demagnetizing effects. When ΔT is smaller than the optimal value, the curve H_c (T) becomes very steep and spatial fluctuations of T_{comp} become relatively more important to determine the shape of the domain boundary. Both types of irregularity increase noise.

6.7 SUMMARY AND CONCLUSIONS

The magnetic reversal of RE-TM media at a given temperature above room temperature is characterized by a pinning of domain walls at defects that are small compared with the wall width (about 5 nm in Tb-FeCo films), probably boundaries in the columnar microstructure of the thin films. An elementary jump of a wall covers probably one column. When the films are prepared to become dense with no columnar structure, the coercive force decreases although the anisotropy constant increases. A similar effect is observed when the underlayer in a layer stack is smoothened. Therefore, a minimum microstructural inhomogeneity is necessary to stabilize the written domains.

The scatter of the length of thermomagnetically written domains (the jitter) also reflects the columnar microstructure of the medium. A minimum of about 15 nm has been observed so far. In order to improve the signal-to-noise ratio, the future development of MO media should aim at a pronounced microstructure on a smaller scale. However, if the lateral scaling length of the microstructure becomes smaller than the domain wall width the pinning becomes weaker because of statistical averaging over many obstacles. Consequently, the minimum jitter for a medium class is defined by the domain wall width.

The forces on a domain wall are described by a bubble-like model that considers, in addition to the forces on a classical bubble, a wall gradient force due to the temperature profile induced by the laser spot. Close to the Curie radius a linear temperature profile is expected during the thermomagnetic write process. There the wall gradient force is constant and contractive and prevails over the other forces that tend to zero when the Curie temperature is approached. This can even prevent the domain formation in the first stage of the cooling phase.

Four models of thermomagnetic domain formation have been presented to describe the variety of results of experiments and computer simulations. In two of these the domain walls move. In *model 1* the domain is nucleated in the cooling phase and expands when the external field together with the demagnetizing field overcome the wall forces. This is predicted by a magnetohydrodynamic simulation of the thermomagnetic write process, based upon the LLG equation, without considering coercive effects.

In "less hard" MO media, moving domain walls are indeed observed. The mechanism of domain formation (*model 2*) differs, however, from the simulation. The domain nucleates and expands in the heating phase but contracts in the cooling phase until it is frozen in by coercive effects. The domain diameter depends on the external field. The wall mobility in such media tends toward infinity when the Curie temperature is approached.

Theoretically, the minimum write field depends on the temperature gradient. In the above-mentioned computer simulation, the temperature gradient was bigger than induced in the experiment. This may be the reason for the different domain formation. Systematic recording experiments on the influence of the temperature gradient, determined by the diameter, the pulse length, and the intensity of the laser beam together with the thermal properties of the layer stack, are valuable to clarify this question but have not yet been reported.

In *hard* MO media (high Tb content, rough interfaces) the domain walls are immobile during the write process. The size of written marks is only determined by the Curie radius, and the bubble-like model does not apply. The driving force for reverse domain formation is the demagnetizing field of the paramagnetic Curie cylinder. Domains written under suboptimal external fields consist of many small domains (*model 3*). The multidomain pattern arises because the demagnetizing field is reduced in the neighborhood of already existing reverse domains so that the nuclei repel each other. In media with high M_s, subdomains are formed for suboptimal write fields due to demagnetizing effects (*model 4*). The main role of the magnetic write field in these media (models 3 and 4) is, therefore, to ensure single-domain marks by overcoming demagnetizing effects.

Moving domain walls become jagged, perhaps according to a fractal law. This increases the write noise and has to be avoided, either by choosing hard media or by properly balancing the contracting wall forces by the expanding demagnetizing and external fields. The latter possibility is most conveniently realized by tuning the magnetization of the MO layer because the write field of the recording drives is prespecified in industrial standards. Therefore, ferri*magnetic materials have an advantage over ferro*magnetic materials.

Reading with blue instead of IR light yields a higher linear bit density along the track only if the SNR remains high. In current read experiments with blue laser light, the noise induced by spatial inhomogeneities of the disk or the detector noise is often stronger than the write noise that is due to irregularities of the domain boundaries. Consequently, media that produce a higher signal, yield a better signal-to-noise ratio. If these noise sources are suppressed by improved disk manufacturing and more sensitive detectors (or higher laser power), media that produce less domain length jitter are expected to perform better even if their signal is lower than that of competing media.

6.8 APPENDIX

6.8.1 Demagnetizing Field of a Cylindrical Domain

In this subsection the demagnetizing field of a cylindrical domain in a film with perpendicular anisotropy is calculated (in the SI system). In order to represent the situation during the thermomagnetic write process, a radially varying magnetization is eventually considered.

The source of the magnetostatic field due to a dipole density M is the negative divergence of M, called "magnetic charge" ρ_m analog to the electrostatic case: $\rho_m = -\text{div } M$. The global magnetic charge of a dipole distribution is, of course, zero. The field of a magnetic charge is Coulomb-like:

$$H(w) = \frac{\rho_m w}{4\pi |w|^3} \tag{6.52}$$

with w being the vector originating at the charge position.

The magnetic charges of a thin film with perpendicular magnetization M_s are localized at the surfaces if the magnetization inside the film is the same through the thickness of the film. If the magnetization points "up," the magnetic charge density is $+M_s$ and $-M_s$ at the top and bottom surface, respectively.

6.8.1.1 Homogeneous Magnetization

For a homogeneously magnetized and infinitely extended film the magnetostatic field is zero outside and $-M_s$ (SI system) everywhere inside the film.

We now calculate the Coulomb-like field arising from a strip charged with M_s. Let the strip be located in the plane $z = z_0$ and extend parallel to the y-axis from $-y_0$ to $+y_0$, and let its infinitesimal width be Δx. Equation (6.53) represents the field of such a strip along the x-axis.

$$H_z(x) = -\int_{-y_0}^{y_0} \frac{(M_s \Delta x) z_0}{4\pi |r|^3} dy$$

$$= -C \int_{-y_0}^{y_0} (a^2 + y^2)^{-\frac{3}{2}} dy = -C \frac{y_0}{a^2 \sqrt{a^2 + y_0^2}} \quad \text{(charged strip)} \tag{6.53}$$

with $a^2 = (x - x')^2 + z_0^2$ and $C = \frac{(M_s \Delta z) z_0}{4\pi}$

The field of a circular area charged with M_s and located in the $z = z_0$ plane (center on the z-axis) with radius r, obtained by integration over Equation (6.53), is given by Equation (6.54).

$$\frac{H_z(x)}{M_s} = -\frac{z_0}{4\pi} \int_{-r}^{+r} \frac{\sqrt{r^2 - x'^2}}{a^2\sqrt{a^2 + r^2 - x'^2}} \, dx' \quad \text{(charged circular area)} \qquad (6.54)$$

The perpendicular component of the demagnetizing field of a homogeneously magnetized cylinder (magnetization M_s up inside, zero outside) is given by linear superposition of the Coulomb-like fields of the (positive) charges at its top surface and the (negative) charges at the bottom surface. In the medial plane we get twice the value of Equation (6.54). This expression has been integrated numerically for $h/D = 0.2$ where h and D are the height and the diameter of the cylinder, respectively. The resulting function $H_z(x)/M_s$ is shown in Figure 6.67 together with the demagnetizing field H_z^{plate}/M_s of a semiinfinite plate of the same thickness d ending at $x = r$. This field is analytically derived from Equation (6.53) as

$$\frac{H_d^{\text{plate}}(x)}{M_s} = -\arctan\left(\frac{2(x - x_0)}{h}\right) \qquad (6.55)$$

Its slope at the edge defines an approximate width, $x = h\pi/2$, of the "response" of the magnetic field to an abrupt change in the magnetization. If the local variation of M_s is smoother than that, the demagnetizing field will approximately follow the magnetization, $H_d \approx -M_s$ (SI).

The demagnetizing field of a cylindrical domain is qualitatively similar to that of a semiinfinite plate at its edge but exhibits two quantitative differences. At $x = 0$ (center of the cylinder) its slope is zero due to symmetry and at the edge its value is bigger than $-0.5\,M_s$.

The demagnetizing field of a cylindrical domain or a semi-infinite stripe domain of magnetization M_s in a laterally infinite film of magnetization $-M_s$ is obtained by linear superposition of the fields of an isolated cylinder in vacuum with magnetization $2\,M_s$

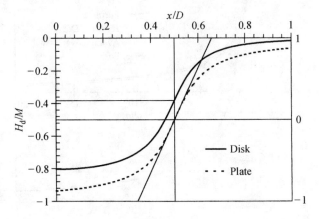

Figure 6.67 Demagnetizing field H_d of a disk (diameter D) with homogeneous magnetization M and height $h = 0.2D$, compared to that of a semiinfinite plate.

and an infinite film of the same thickness with magnetization $-M_s$. This amounts to a simple rescaling of the H-axis as done at the right abscissa of Figure 6.67.

The field at the center of such a domain can be evaluated analytically to:

$$\frac{H_d}{M_s}(r = 0) = \frac{2}{\sqrt{1 + (D/h)^2}} - 1 \qquad (6.56)$$

if $D \gg h$. The driving force on a domain wall is derived from the demagnetizing field at the domain boundary averaged over the thickness of the film. An analytical expression for the field at the edge of the domain is more difficult to obtain and comprises the complete elliptical integral of the second kind [130]. It can be approximated by [8]:

$$\frac{H}{M_s}(r = D/2) = \frac{1}{1 + 0.75(D/h)} \qquad (6.57)$$

Both fields are given in Figure 6.68 as a function of D/h. For D/h approaching 0, the domain vanishes and both fields become equal to M_s, antiparallel to the magnetization of the film. For increasing diameter D the field approaches the demagnetizing field of the semi-infinite stripe domain with $H_d(0) = -M_s$ and H_d (edge) $= 0$.

6.8.1.2 Radially Varying Magnetization

During the thermomagnetic write process the magnetization is not uniform but changes according to the temperature distribution. This situation is modeled in the simplest way by a cylindrical distribution of the magnetization, $M(r, \theta, z) = M(r)$, inside the film. The Coulomb-like potential of a charged circular area is now calculated using cylindrical coordinates r, Θ, z as

$$H(w) = \int_0^\infty \int_0^{2\pi} \frac{M(r')(w - w')}{4\pi |r - r'|^3} r' d\Theta' dr' \qquad (6.58)$$

The perpendicular field H_z is now:

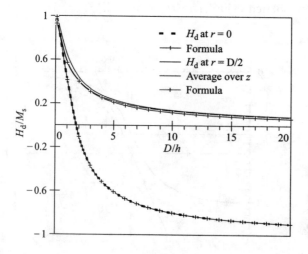

Figure 6.68 Demagnetizing field H_d in the center and at the edge of cylindrical domain (magnetization M_s, diameter D) in an infinite film (thickness h). Results of numerical integration for $z = h/2$ are compared to analytical formulae.

$$H_z(r, z) = \frac{z}{4\pi} \int\limits_{0}^{\infty} \int\limits_{0}^{2\pi} \frac{M(r')r'}{(r^2 + r'^2 - 2rr'\cos(\gamma) + z^2)^{3/2}} d'\Theta'dr' \qquad (6.59)$$

where $\gamma = \theta - \theta'$ is the angle between r and r'. The length z in the second equation specifies the horizontal distance between the charged surface and the test point. The integration over θ' leads to the complete elliptical integral of the second kind, $E(\xi)$ [Eq. (6.60)]:

$$H_z(r, z) = \frac{z}{\pi} \int\limits_{0}^{\infty} \frac{M(r')E(\xi)r'd'r}{[(r - r')^2 + z^2][(r + r')^2 + z^2]^{1/2}}$$

$$\text{where } \xi = \frac{4r'r}{[(r + r')^2 + z^2]} \qquad (6.60)$$

The demagnetizing field of a cylindrical domain of height h is obtained as the superposition of the fields arising from magnetic charges on the top and on the bottom surface [Eq. (6.61)]:

$$H_z^{\text{cyl}}(r, z) = H_z(r, z - h) - H_z(r, z) \qquad (6.61)$$

The sign in Equation (6.61) is valid when a magnetization $M(r')$ pointing from the bottom to the top surface is counted positive. Formulae similar to Equation (6.60) have been reported in the literature several times {[132] Eq. 13), [7] Equation (A6)}, yet not with consistent results. The equation given above yields the correct dimension, $[H_d] = [M]$, and, for a cylindrical domain with homogeneous perpendicular magnetization, a field identical to that in Figure 6.67.

6.8.2 SNR and Linear Data Bit Density

In this section, the linear data bit density δ[bit/μm] along the track is related to medium noise and domain length jitter. First, efficiencies of some modulation codes are reported and then SNR requirements for the application of these codes are discussed.

In nearly all recording systems, the "data" bit stream is modulated such that a "channel" bit stream is obtained that best fits the peculiarities of the write/read channel. In general, a block of m consecutive data bits is mapped onto n ($> m$) consecutive channel bits. This modulation is called block-based channel coding.

In optical recording, run-length limited codes, designated by $(m/n)(d,k)$ – RLL, are often applied, allowing only bit sequences with a minimum of d and a maximum of k 0s

TABLE 6.13 Comparison of Some (d, k)-RLL Codes

d	k	bits/$L_{\min}$ (max)	$w/L_{\min}$
0	∞	1	1
1	7	1.358	0.5
3	9	1.750	0.25

Note: w = length on the disk corresponding to the time window.

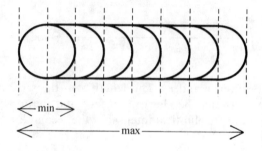

Figure 6.69 Possible shapes of recorded marks for (1.7)-RLL modulation. The minimum (maximum) length corresponds to a 101 (100000001) channel bit sequence.

between consecutive 1s. With such codes the data density on the disk can be maximized and the low frequency component of the readout signal can be minimized. Figure 6.69 shows the domain lengths that occur for a (1, 7) RLL code when the write mode is laser intensity modulation. At every 1 in the channel bit stream a transition in the magnetization is generated in the write process. The minimum distance between transitions corresponds to the channel bit distance on the disk or the channel clock period T during readout. The minimum domain length for (1, 7) RLL is $L_{min} = 2Tv$, where v is the linear disk velocity.

A (1, 7) RLL code allows for seven different mark lengths corresponding to $ld(7) = 2.81$ channel bits. If, for a specific coding scheme, all lengths are equally probable, an average message length of $5T$ or $2.5L_{min}$ is obtained yielding a code efficiency $\rho = 2.81 \text{ bit}/(2.5\, L_{min}) = 1.12 \text{ bit}/L_{min}$. The maximal efficiency, obtained for an optimal distribution of length probabilities, is $\rho_{max} = 1.358 \text{ bit}/L_{min}$. Actual codes achieve currently $1.33 \text{ bit}/L_{min}$. These data are summarized in Table 6.13 together with corresponding values for $(0, \infty)$ and $(3, 9)$ RLL codes (all from [134]). The $(0, \infty)$ RLL reproduces the original data bit sequence.

When the readout signal of a statistical bit sequence is displayed on an oscilloscope that is triggered with the channel clock frequency, "eye patterns" are observed. The eye pattern for a (1, 7) code is shown in Figure 6.70. The dashed curve with minimal amplitude is obtained for the channel bit sequence 10101.

Eye width ($= T$ corresponding to $L_{min}/(d + 1)$) and eye height depend on the modulation code chosen. Fig. 6.71 [135] shows the eye height for modulation codes with different d as a function of the normalized linear information density δ (data bits/ μm) along the track. δ is inversely proportional to the geometrical length of L_{min}. The

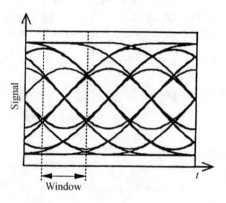

Figure 6.70 Possible signal contours of (1,7)-RLL mark patterns.

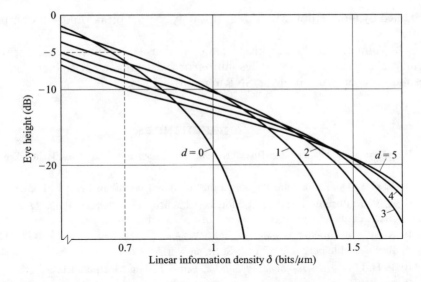

Figure 6.71 [135] Eye height of the signal contours of some (d, k)-RLL modulation codes vs. the normalized linear information density along the track (data bits/mm).

curves are calculated for values typical of the audio CD, namely a wavelength of $\lambda = 790$ nm and a numerical aperture NA $= 0.45$ giving a laser focus size of $0.5\lambda/$NA $= 0.88\,\mu$m and consequently an optical cutoff frequency $f_c = 1/0.88\,\mu$m $= 1.14/$ μm. The curve for $d = 0$ is equivalent to the optical transfer function that approaches zero at f_c. Modulation with $d > 0$ allows higher densities, proportional to the higher code efficiencies, but yields lower eye heights at low δ.

For ideal noise-free signals the eye pattern is always open, a decision on 1 (zero-level crossing) or 0 can always be taken, so that δ can be made arbitrarily big by choosing a sufficiently big d. In reality, noise and domain length jitter blur the eye opening and limit the information density. The signal-to-noise ratio and the jitter determine, therefore, the minimal eye width and eye height.

Suppose that for some channel an eye height of -20 dB is sufficient to remain below the acceptable bit error rate BER. According to Figure 6.71, a $d = 3$ modulation code is well suited in this situation and yields a maximum linear information density of 1.5 bit/μm. An increased optical resolution can be considered a rescaling of the horizontal axis such that a corresponding increase in density is obtained, yet only if the SNR remains high. Consider, as an illustration of this restriction, a resolution increase by a factor of 2 (e.g., due to the use of a blue laser or to magnetically induced super-resolution), at the cost of a decrease in SNR by 15 dB. In this situation, an eye height of -5 dB is required to yield the same BER as before. The maximum linear density is

TABLE 6.14 Statistics of the Publication Years of the References

Before 85	86/87	88/89	90/91	92/93	94/95	96/97
19	12	17	33	28	19	9

obtained by modulation with $d = 1$. It is only $\delta = 0.7$ bit/0.5 μm = 1.4 bit/μm, less than before.

In summary, a higher linear data bit density (or linear data capacity) can be achieved by a higher optical resolution or by a higher SNR. Increasing the optical resolution is only useful if the SNR remains high.

REFERENCES

[1] A. Hubert, *Theorie der Domänenwände in geordneten Medien*, Berlin: Springer Verlag, 1974.

[2] T. H. O'Dell, *Magnetic Bubbles*, London: The Macmillan Press Ltd., 1975.

[3] A. P. Malozemoff and J. C. Slonczewski, *Magnetic Domain Walls in Bubble, Materials Applied Solid State Science*, New York: Academic Press, 1979.

[4] A. H. Eschenfelder, *Magnetic Bubble Technology, Springer Series in Solid-State Sciences*, Berlin, Heidelberg, New York: Springer Verlag, 1980.

[5] T. H. O'Dell, *Ferromagnetodynamics*, London: The Macmillan Press Ltd., 1981.

[6] G. Winkler, *Magnetic Garnets*, Viewing Tracts in Pure and Applied Physics, Braunschweig, 1981.

[7] B. G. Huth, "Calculations of Stable Domain Radii Produced by Thermomagnetic Writing," *IBM J. Res. Dev.*, vol. 18, p. 100, 1974.

[8] H. Callen and R. M. Josephs, "Dynamics of Magnetic Bubble Domains with an Application to Wall Mobilities," *J. Appl. Phys.*, vol. 42, p. 1977, 1971.

[9] Motoko Hasegawa and Katsumi Moroga, Mitsuya Okada and Osamu Okada, Yasuharu Hidaka, "Computer Simulation of the Dynamic Process of Mark Formation for Magneto-optical Memory," *J. Appl. Phys.*, vol. 75, p. 2149, 1994.

[10] M. Mansuripur, *The Physical Principles of Magneto-optical Recording*, Cambridge: Cambridge University Press, 1995.

[11] P. Hansen and H. Heitmann, "Media for Erasable Magnetooptic Recording," *IEEE Trans. Magn.*, vol. 25, p. 4390, 1989.

[12] P. Hansen, "Magnetic Amorphous Alloys," *Handbook of Magnetic Materials*, vol. 6, Chapter 4, K. H. J.Buschow (ed.), Elsevier Science Publishers B.V., 1991.

[13] P. Hansen, C. Clausen, G. Much, M. Rosenkranz, and K. Witter, "Magnetic and Magneto-optic Properties of Amorphous Rare-earth Transition-metal Alloys Containing Gd, Tb, Fe, Co," *J. Appl. Phys.*, vol. 66, p. 756, 1989.

[14] P. Hansen, S. Klahn, C. Clausen, G. Much, and K. Witter, "Magnetic and Magneto-optic Properties of Amorphous Rare-earth Transition-metal Alloys Containing Dy, Ho, Fe, Co," *J. Appl. Phys.*, vol. 69, p. 3194, 1991.

[15] P. Hansen, D. Raasch, and D. Mergel, "Magnetic and Magneto-optic Properties of Amorphous Rare-earth Transition-metal Alloys Containing Pr, Nd, Fe, Co," *J. Appl. Phys.*, vol. 75, p. 5267, 1994.

[16] D. Mergel, P. Hansen, and S. Klahn, "Magnetic Materials and Exchange-Coupled Layer Structures For Magneto-Optic Information Storage," International Symposium MASHTEC '90, Materials Science for High Technologies, Dresden, G.D.R., April 23–27, 1990, *Materials Science Forum*, Vols. 62–64, p. II, p. 547, 1990.

[17] D. Mergel, P. Hansen, S. Klahn, and W. B. Zeper, "The Switching Process for Thermo-magneto-optical Recording and its Relation to Material Properties and Preparation Conditions of Thin Films," *Electro-Optic and Magneto-Optic Materials II*, SPIE 1274, p. 270, 1990.

[18] D. Mergel, P. Hansen, S. Klahn, and D. Raasch, "MO-recording: The Switching Process and its Relation to the Magnetic Properties of Thin Films," *Science and Technology of Nanostructured Magnetic Materials*, G. C. Hadjipanayis and G. A. Prinz (eds.), New York: Plenum Press, NATO ASI *B259*, p. 249, 1991.

[19] M. Hartmann, A. Spruijt, J. Disbergen, G. H. Johnson (PDO), D. Mergel (Philips Research Hamburg), "Rare-Earth Transition-Metal alloys: the road of industrialisation," *J. Mag. Soc. Japan*, vol. 15, Supplement S1, p. 165, 1991.

[20] D. Mergel, P. Hansen, and D. Raasch, "The Physical Basis of Magneto-optic Recording," Topical meeting on Optical Data Storage, San José, February 10–13, 1992, Donald B. Carlin, David B. Kay, (ed.), *Proc. SPIE* 1663, p. 240, 1992; G. Kaempf, D. Mergel, "Optical information storage materials," *Kirk-Othmer Encyclopedia of Chemical Technology*, 4th ed., New York: John Wiley & Sons, vol. 14, p. 277, 1995.

[21] S. Klahn, *Langzeitstabilität Amorpher Magnetooptischer Seltenerd-Übergangsmetall-Dünnfilmschichten*, Dissertation, Hamburg, 1990.

[22] D. Mergel, H. Heitmann, and P. Hansen, "A Pseudo-crystalline Model of the Magnetic Anisotropy in Amorphous Rare-earth Transition-metal Thin Films," *Phys. Rev.*, vol. B47, p. 882, 1993.

[23] M. J. Kim, J. S. Bow, R. W. Carpenter, and J. Liu, Soon Gwang Kim, Seh Kwang Lee, Won Mok Kim and Jong Shik Yoon, "Nanostructure and Chemical Inhomogeneity in TbFe Magneto-Optical Films," *IEEE Trans. Magn.*, vol. 30, p. 4398. 1994.

[24] M. Aeschlimann, M. Scheinfein, J. Unguris, F. J. A. M. Greidanus, and S. Klahn, "Magnetic-field-modulated Written Bits in TbFeCo Thin Films: Transmission Electron Lorentz Microscopy and Scanning Electron Microscopy with Polarization Analysis Studies," *J. Appl. Phys.*, vol. 68, p. 4710, 1990. M. R. Scheinfein, J. L. Blue, and M. Aeschlimann, "Micromagnetics of Surface Segregation Regions in Domain Written in TbFeCo Alloys," *IEEE Trans. Magn.*, vol. 27, p. 5124, 1991.

[25] D. Mergel, "Domain Formation in Exchange-coupled Double Layers," *J. Appl. Phys.*, vol. 69, p. 4520, 1991.

[26] K. E. Johnson, "Fabrication of Low Noise Thin-film Media," Chapter 2 in Arnoldussen, Nunnely (eds.), *Noise in Digital Magnetic Recording*, 1992, World Scientific Publishing Co.

[27] D. Mergel, H. Bentin, and D. Raasch, "Sputtering of RE-TM Layers with an Unbalanced Magnetron," *Thin Solid Films*, vol. 259, p. 72, 1995.

[28] M. Mansuripur, "Domain wall energy in the media of MO-recording," *J. Appl. Phys.*, vol. 66, p. 6175, 1989.

[29] R. A. Hajjar and H.-P. D. Shieh, "Measurement of Domain-wall Energy for Amorphous Rare Earth – Transition Metal Thin Films," *J. Appl. Phys.*, vol. 68, p. 4199, 1990.

[30] S. Klahn and D. Raasch, "The Role of Wall Coercivity and Energy on the Read-out Stability of GdTb-Fe Based MO Disks," *IEEE Trans. Magn.*, MAG-26, p. 1918, 1990.

[31] D. Raasch, *Magnetische Wandenergien und Austauschkonstanten in amorphen Seltenerd-Übergangsmetall-Dünnfilmschichten*, Aachener Beiträge zur Physik der kondensierten Materie, Band 14, "D82 (Dissertation RWTH Aachen)," 1995.

[32] D. Raasch and J. Reck, "Anisotropy, Wall Energy Density, and Exchange Stiffness of Amorphous (Gd,Dy)-(Fe,Co) Films," *Appl. Phys.*, vol. 74, p. 1229, 1993.

[33] D. Raasch, J. Reck, C. Mathieu, and B. Hillebrands, "Exchange Stiffness Constant and Wall Energy Density of Amorphous GdTb-FeCo Thin Films," *J. Appl. Phys.*, vol. 76, p. 1145, 1994.

[34] M. Mansuripur, "Magnetization Reversal, Coercivity, and the Process of Thermomagnetic Recording in Thin Films of Amorphous Rare Earth Transition Metal Alloys," *J. Appl.*

Phys., vol. 61, p. 1580, 1987. M. Mansuripur and M. Ruane, "Mean-field Analysis of Amorphous Rare Earth-transition Metal Alloys for Thermomagnetic Recording," *IEEE Trans. Magn.*, MAG-22, p. 33, 1986.

[35] P. Hansen, "New Type of Compensation Wall in Ferrimagnetic Double Layers," *Appl. Phys. Lett.*, vol. 55, p. 200, 1989.

[36] D. Mergel, "Magnetic Interface Walls Under Applied Fields," *J. Appl. Phys.*, vol. 70, p. 6433, 1991.

[37] R. Labusch, "Trapping of Bloch Walls at the Interface of Ferrimagnetic Double Layers," *Phys. Stat. Sol. (a)*, vol. 137, p. 525, 1993.

[38] D. Raasch, D. Mergel, and P. Hansen, "Bloch Wall Energy in Nd-TbFeCo Thin Films," *J. Appl. Phys.*, vol. 76, p. 8022, 1994.

[39] T. Schrefl and J. Fidler, "Micromagnetic Simulation of Multilayers," *J. Magn. Soc. Japan*, vol. 20, Supplement S1, p. 223, 1996

[40] R. Ploessl, J. N. Chapman, M. R. Scheinfein, J. L. Blue, M. Mansuripur, and H. Hoffmann, "Micromagnetic Structure of Domains in Co/Pt Multilayers. I. Investigations of Wall Structure," *J. Appl. Phys.*, vol. 74, p. 7431, 1993.

[41] A. H. M. Holtslag, "Calculations on Temperature Profiles in Optical Recording," *J. Appl. Phys.*, vol. 66, p.1530, 1989.

[42] M. D. Schultz, Tsing Xue, and M. H. Kryder, "Direct Observation of Magnetization Dynamics in Spinning Magneto-optic Discs," *J. Appl. Phys.*, vol. 73, p. 5776, 1993.

[43] Han-Ping D. Shieh and M. H. Kryder, "Dynamics and Factors Controlling Regularity of Thermomagnetically Written Domains," *J. Appl. Phys.*, vol. 61, p. 1108, 1987.

[44] F. J. A. M. Greidanus, B. A. J. Jacobs, J. H. M. Spruit, and S. Klahn, "Recording Experiments on Rare-earth Transition-metal Thin Films Studied with Lorentz Microscopy," *IEEE Trans. Magn.*, MAG-25, p. 3524, 1989.

[45] P. Hansen, "Thermomagnetic Switching in Amorphous RE-TM Alloys with High Compensation Temperature," *J. Appl. Phys.*, vol. 63, p. 2364, 1988.

[46] J. H. Crasemann, P. Hansen, M. Rosenkranz, and K. Witter, "Thermomagnetic Switching on RE-TM alloy MO disks," *J. Appl. Phys.*, vol. 66, p. 1273, 1989.

[47] A. Aharoni, "Theoretical Search for Domain Nucleation," *Rev. Mod. Phys.*, vol. 34, p. 227, 1962.

[48] W. F. Brown, Jr., "Micromagnetics," *Interscience Tracts on Physics and Astronomy*, New York, London, 1963.

[49] G. Herzer, "Grain Size Dependence of Coercivity and Permeability in Nanocrystalline Ferromagnets," *IEEE Trans. Magn.*, vol. 26, p. 1297, 1990.

[50] R. Friedberg and D. I. Paul, "New Theory of Coercive Force of Ferromagnetic Materials," *Phys. Rev. Lett.*, vol. 34, p. 1234, 1975.

[51] H. Kronmüller, "Coercivity Mechanisms in Modern Magnetic Materials," *J. Magn. Soc. Japan*, vol. 17, Supplement S1, p. 260, 1993.

[52] H. Kronmüller, "Theory of Nucleation Fields in Inhomogeneous Ferromagnets," *Phys. Stat. Sol. (b)*, vol. 144, p. 385, 1987.

[53] D. Givord, Q. Lu, and M. F. Rossignol, "Coercivity in Hard Magnetic Materials," *Science and Technology of Nanostructured Magnetic Materials* (eds.), G. C. Hadjipanayis and G. A. Prinz, New York: Plenum Press, NATO ASI, B259, 1991, p. 635.

[54] R. H. Victora, "Micromagnetic Approach to Magnetic Hysteresis," *Science and Technology of Nanostructured Magnetic Materials* (eds.), G. C. Hadjipanayis and G. A. Prinz, New York: Plenum Press, NATO ASI, B259, 1991.

[55] F. Rio, P. Bernstein, M. Labrune, "Magnetization Process in RE-TM Alloys: Wall Mobility and Nucleation," *IEEE Trans. Magn.*, vol. 23, p. 2266, 1987.

[56] M. Labrune, S. Andrieu, F. Rio, and P. Bernstein, "Time Dependence of the Magnetization Process of RE-TM Alloys," *J. Magn. Magn. Mat.*, vol. 80, p. 211, 1989.

[57] E. Fatuzzo, "Theoretical Considerations on the Switching Transient in Ferroelectric," *Phys. Rev.*, vol. 127, 1962, p. 1995.

[58] A. Lyberatos, J. Earl, and R. W. Chantrell, "Model of Thermally Activated Magnetization Reversal in Thin Films of Amorphous Rare-earth-transition-metal Alloys," *Phys. Rev.*, B53, p. 5493, 1949.

[59] R. Street and S. D. Brown, "A Study of Magnetic Viscosity," *Proc. Phys. Soc.*, A62, p. 562, London, 1949.

[60] R. Street and S. D. Brown, "Magnetic Viscosity, Fluctuation Fields, and Activation Energies," *J. Appl. Phys.*, vol. 76, 1949, p. 562.

[61] R. D. Kirby, J. X. Shen, R. J. Hardy, and D. J. Sellmyer, "Magnetic Reversal in Nanoscale Films with Perpendicular Anisotropy," *Phys. Rev.*, B49, p. 10810, 1994.

[62] A. A. Merchant and M. H. Kryder, "Investigation of Coercive Squareness in TbFeCo Films," *IEEE Trans. Magn.*, vol. 27, p. 3690, 1991.

[63] C.-J. Lin and D. Rugar, "Observation of Domain Expansion and Contraction in TbFe Films by Lorentz Microscopy," *IEEE Trans. Magn.*, vol. 24, p. 2311, 1988.

[64] S. Winkler, W. Reim, and K. Schuster, "Domain Nucleation and Wall Movement in TbFeCo," *Thin Solid Films*, vol. 175, p. 265, 1988.

[65] S. Winkler, "Charakterisierung des Temperaturabhängigen Verhaltens Magnetischer Domänen in Amorphen TbFeCo-Schichten," Dissertation, Erlangen, 1992.

[66] A. Forkl, M. Hirscher, T. Mizoguchi, and H. Kronmüller (MPI Metall), "Magnetic properties of FeTb Amorphous Thin Films," *J. Mag. Magn. Mat.*, vol. 93, p. 261, 1991.

[67] T. Thomson and K. O'Grady, "Activation Volumes of Reversal in Tb-Fe-Co Thin Films," *IEEE Trans. Magn.*, vol. 28, p. 2518, 1992.

[68] T. Thomson and K. O'Grady, "Optical and Magnetic Measurements of Time Dependence Effects in Magneto-optic Thin Films," *IEEE Trans. Magn.*, vol. 28, p. 2515, 1992

[69] T. Thomson and K. O'Grady, "Temperature Dependence of Activation Volumes in Tb-Fe-Co Magneto-optic Thin Films," *IEEE Trans. Magn.*, vol. 32, p. 286, 1996.

[70] R. Labusch, "Quantum Effects in Low Temperature Plastic Deformation," *Crystal Res. & Technol.*, vol. 19, p. 315, 1984.

[71] J. Ferré, V. Grolier, A. Kirilyuk, J. P. Jamet, and D. Renard, "Magnetization Reversal in Ultra-thin Films with Perpendicular Anisotropy," *J. Magn. Soc. Japan*, vol. 19, Supplement S1, p. 79, 1995.

[72] D. Weller, H. Brändle, G. Gorman, C. J. Lin, and H. Notarys, "Magnetic and Magneto-optical Properties of Cobalt-Platinum Alloys with Perpendicular Magnetic Anisotropy," *Appl. Phys. Lett.*, vol. 61, p. 2726, 1992.

[73] J. Valentin, Th. Kleinefeld, and D. Weller, "Micromagnetic Analysis of Magnetization Reversal in CoPt Alloy Films," *J. Phys.*, D 29, p. 1111, 1996.

[74] M. Mansuripur and R. Giles, "Simulation of the Magnetization-reversal Dynamics on the Connection Machine," *Comput. Phys.*, p. 291, May/June 1990.

[75] Hong Fu, R. Giles, and M. Mansuripur, "Coercivity Mechanisms in Magneto-optical Recording Media," *Comput. Phys.*, vol. 8, p. 80, 1994.

[76] J. M. D. Coey, J. Chappert, J. P. Rebouillat, and T. S. Wang, "Magnetic Structure of an Amorphous Rare-Earth Transition-Metal Alloy," *Phys. Rev. Lett.*, vol. 36, p. 1061, 1976.

[77] A. H. Cottrell, *Dislocations and Plastic Flow in Crystals*, Oxford, 1953.

[78] F. Stobiecki, T. M. Atmono, S. Becker, H. Rohrmann, and K. Röll, "Investigation of Interface Wall Energy σ_w and Coercivity H_c in Exchange-coupled Double Layers (ECDLs)," *J. Magn. Magn. Mat.*, vol. 148, p. 497, 1995.

[79] D. Mergel, "Magnetic Reversal Processes in Exchange-coupled Double Layers," *J. Appl. Phys.*, vol. 74, p. 4072, 1993. The energy considerations in this paper are an extension of: T. Kobayashi, H. Tsuji, S. Tsunashima, and S. Uchiyama, *Japan J. Appl. Phys.*, vol. 20, p. 2089, 1981.

[80] T. Fukami, Y. Kawano, T. Tokunaga, Y. Nagaki, and K. Tsutsumi, "Direct Overwrite Technology Using Exchange-coupled Multilayers," J. Magn. Soc. Japan, vol. 15, Supplement S1, p. 293, 1991.

[81] D. Raasch, "Wall Energies of Amorphous GdTb-FeCo Single and Exchange Coupled Double-layer Films," *J. Magn. Magn. Mat.*, vol. 101, p. 202, 1991.

[82] J. C. Suits, "Lorentz Microscopy of Micron-sized Laser-written Magnetic Domains in TbFe," *Appl. Phys. Lett.*, vol. 49, p. 419, 1986.

[83] J. C. Suits, "Thermomagnetic Writing in TbFe: Modeling and Comparison with Experiment," *J. Appl. Phys.*, vol. 64, p. 252, 1988.

[84] M. Takahashi, N. Ohta, S. Takayama, Y. Sugita, M. Yoshihiro, and K. Shigematsu, "Submicron Domain Observation and Write-read Characteristics of Magneto-optical TbFeCo Discs," *IEEE Trans. Magn.*, MAG-22, p. 931, 1986.

[85] F. Tanaka, S. Tanaka, and N. Imamura, "Magneto-optical Recording Characteristics of TbFeCo Media by Magnetic Field Modulation Method," *Japan J. Appl. Phys.*, vol. 26, pp. 231–235, 1987.

[86] C.-J. Lin and A. E. Bell, "Domain Formation Model for Thermomagnetic Recording," Oral presentation at MMM/Intermag Vancouver, AE-02, 1988.

[87] T. Yorozu, T. Satoh, K. Nagato, Y. Yoneyama, and Y. Takatsuka, "Characterization of Thin Film Media for Magneto-Optical Recording," *Appl. Phys. Comm.*, vol. 11, p. 513, 1992.

[88] T. Satoh, Y. Takatsuka, H. Yokoyama, S. Tatsukawa, T. Mori, and T. Yorozu, "Control of Wall Coercivity and its Effect on Dynamic Characteristics in Magneto-Optic Materials," *IEEE Trans. Magn.*, vol. 27, p. 5115, 1991.

[89] T. Kohashi, H. Matsuyama, Ch. Haginoya, K. Koike, H. Miyamoto, J. Ushiyama, and H. Awano, "Recorded Mark Observation by Spin-polarized Scanning Electron Microscopy," *J. Magn. Soc. Japan*, vol. 20, Supplement S1, p. 303, 1996.

[90] C. Peng, S. K. Lee, and S. G. Kim, "Computer Simulation of Thermomagnetic Recording Process in Exchange-coupled Magneto-optical Bilayer Films," *IEEE Trans. Magn.*, vol. 31, p. 3268, 1995.

[91] Y. Yamada, S. Ohnuki, N. Ohta, K. Shimazaki, M. Yoshihiro, and H. Fujiwara, "Thermal and Magnetic Design of 8 MB/s MO Disk," *IEEE Trans. Magn.*, vol. 6, p. 5121, 1991.

[92] X. Hu, T. Yorozu, S. Honma, Y. Kawazoe, S. Ohnuki, and N. Ohta, "An Analytical Study of the Capping Effect in Magnetic Super Resolution Magneto-optic Recording," *IEEE Trans. Magn.*, vol. 29, p. 3790, 1993.

[93] K. Ichitani, S. Tsunashima, and S. Uchiyama, "Recording Field Sensitivity of Magneto-optical Disks Using Very Thin Exchange-coupled Films," *J. Magn. Soc. Japan*, vol. 17, MORIS 92, p. 196, 1993.

[94] S. Ohnuki and N. Ohta, "Magnetic Capping Layer Effect of Very Thin Cobalt Film on TbFeCo," *J. Magn. Soc. Japan*, vol. 19, Supplement S1, p. 149, 1995.

[95] J. Ushiyama, H. Awano, and M. Takahashi, "Improved Magnetic Sensitivity of Pt/Co Multilayer Magneto-optical Disks," *J. Magn. Soc. Japan*, vol. 19, p. 149, 1995.

[96] Kazunori Naito, Takehiko Numata, Kazuo Nakashima, Miyozo Maeda, and Nagaaki Koshino, "DyFeCo Magneto-Optical Disks with a Ce-SiO$_2$ Protective Film," *SPIE* Vol. 1499, Optical Data Storage '91, p. 386, 1991.

[97] R. Yardy, B. I. Finkelstein, and T. W. McDaniel, "Read Stability in Magneto-optical Storage," *SPIE* Vol. 1316, Optical Data Storage, p. 106, 1990.

[98] Han-Ping D. Shieh and Mark H. Kryder, "Magneto-optic Recording Materials with Direct Overwrite Capability," *Appl. Phys. Lett.*, vol. 49, p. 473, 1986.

[99] M. D. Schultz and M. H. Kryder, "The Erase Process in Direct Overwrite Magneto-optic Recording," *IEEE Trans. Magn.*, vol. 25, p. 3530, 1989.

[100] H.-P. D. Shieh, "Time Resolved Thermomagnetic Recording Process in GdTbFeCo Films," *J. Appl. Phys.*, vol. 69, p. 4951, 1991.

[101] P. Hansen, "Thermomagnetic Switching in Amorphous Rare-earth Transition-metal Alloys," *J. Appl. Phys.*, vol. 62, p. 216, 1987.

[102] M. D. Schultz and M. H. Kryder, "Domain Erasure and Formation in Direct Overwrite Magneto-optic Recording," *J. Appl. Phys.*, vol. 68, p. 5293, 1990.

[103] D. Rugar, J. C. Suits, and C.-J. Lin, "Thermomagnetic Direct Overwrite in TbFe Using Thermally Induced Domain Wall Energy Gradient," *Appl. Phys. Lett.*, vol. 52, p. 1537, 1988.

[104] Y. Hashimoto, K. Nakashima, M. Maeda, H. Inoue, and S. Ogawa, "Direct Overwriting Capability of Magneto-optical Disks," *J. Appl. Phys.*, vol. 67, p. 4420, 1990.

[105] M. D. Schultz, M. H. Kryder, M. Sekiya, and K. Chiba, "True Direct Overwrite in Single Layer Magneto-Optic Recording," *IEEE Trans. Magn.*, vol. 29, p. 3772, 1993.

[106] C. J. Lin., "Critical Assessment of the Physics Underlying Direct Overwrite in Magneto-optic Recording," *J. Appl. Phys.*, vol. 67, p. 4409, 1990.

[107] Mann Du, M. D. Schultz, and M. H. Kryder, "Measurement of Domain Wall Mobility in Magneto-Optic Media," *Japan J. Appl. Phys.*, vol. 32, p. 5202, 1993.

[108] Mann Du and M. H. Kryder, "Domain Wall Mobility Measurements in Magneto-Optic Media," *IEEE Trans. Magn.*, vol. 30, p. 4401, 1994.

[109] M. Aeschlimann, A. Vaterlaus, M. Lutz, M. Stampanoni, and F. Meier, "Ultrafast Thermomagnetic Writing Process in Rare-earth Transition-metal Thin Films," *J. Appl. Phys.*, vol. 67, p. 4438, 1990.

[110] M. Aeschlimann, A. Vaterlaus, M. Lutz, M. Stampanoni, F. Meier, and H. C. Siegmann, "High-speed Magnetization Reversal Near the Compensation Temperature of Amorphous GdTbFe," *Appl. Phys. Lett.*, vol. 59, p. 2189, 1991.

[111] A. G. Dewey, "Measurement and Modelling of Optical Disk Noise," *SPIE* Vol. 695, Optical Mass Data Storage II, p. 72, 1986.

[112] S. Hashimoto, A. Maesaka, K. Fujimoto, and K. Bessho, "Magneto-optical Applications of Co/Pt Multilayers," *Japan J. Appl. Phys.*, vol. 121, p. 471, 1993.

[113] Y. Sabi, M. Kaneko, K. Fujimoto, and S. Hashimoto, "Characteristics of Co/Pt and GdFeCo/TbFeCo for Short Wavelength MO Disks," *3rd IUMS Symposium V*, Tokyo, 1993, Vaa.4.4.

[114] M. Kaneko, "Magnetic Multilayer Films for High Density MO Recording," *J. Mag. Magn. Mat.*, vol. 148, p. 351, 1995.

[115] W. B. Zeper, A. P. J. Jongenelis, B. A. J. Jacobs, H. W. van Kesteren, and P. F. Carcia, "MO Recording in Co/Pt Multilayer and GdTbFe-based Disks at 820, 647 and 458-nm Wavelength," *IEEE Trans. Magn.*, vol. 28, p.2503, 1992.

[116] S. Honda, J. Hirokane, M. Ohkoshi, and T. Kusuda (Hiroshima U), "Static and Dynamic Properties of Thermomagnetic Writing in Amorphous TbFe Films," *J. Mag. Magn. Mat.*, vol. 35, p. 208, 1983.

[117] B. B. Bernacki and M. Mansuripur, "Characterization of MO-recording Media in Terms of Domain Boundary Jaggedness," *J. Appl. Phys.*, vol. 69, p. 4960, 1991.

[118] Wu Te-ho and M. Mansuripur, "Observations of Domain Nucleation and Growth in Magneto-optical Recording Media," *J. Magn. Soc. Japan*, vol. 17, Supplement S1, p. 131, 1993.

[119] G. V. Sayko, "Fractal Domain Structures in Thin Amorphous Films," *IEEE Trans. Magn.*, vol. 28, p. 2931, 1992.

[120] W. B. Zeper and A. M. J. Spruijt, "Domain Size Measurements on GdTbFe-based Thin-Film Structures for Magneto-optical Recording," *J. Appl. Phys.*, vol. 63, p. 2141, 1988.

[121] D. C. Cheng, T. W. McDaniel, and C. R. Davis, "Domain Edge Formation and Jitter Characteristics in Thermomagnetic Recording with Magnetic Field Modulation," *IEEE Trans. Magn.*, vol. 26, p. 1903, 1990.

[122] N. Aoyama, Y. Morimoto, and T. Miyahara, "High Density Land & Groove Recording with Modified Optics and PA-MFM Recording," *J. Magn. Soc. Japan*, vol. 20, Supplement S1, p. 233, 1996.

[123] A. Nakaoki, M. Kanno, I. Naka, T. Sakamoto, M. Shinoda, and M. Kaneko, "Recording on Land and Groove with Magnetically Induced Super Resolution," *J. Magn. Soc. Japan*, vol. 20, Supplement S1, p. 243, 1996.

[124] D. Raasch, "Recording Characteristics of Dy-FeCo-based Magneto-optical Disks in Comparison to Other MO Materials," *IEEE Trans. Magn.*, vol. 29, p. 34, 1993.

[125] Y. Teragaki, Y. Kusumoto, S. Sumi, K. Torazawa, S. Tsunashima, and S. Uchiyama, "Magnetic Field Modulation Recording on Pt/Co Magneto-optical Disks," *IEEE Trans. Magn.*, vol. 29, p. 3796, 1993.

[126] M. Yoshihiro, K. Shimazaki, N. Ohta, T. Toda, H. Awano, and M. Ojima, "Write/erase cyclability of TbFeCo for mark-edge recording," *Japan J. Appl. Phys.*, vol. 32, p. 5441, 1993.

[127] K. Tsutsumi, Y. Nakaki, T. Tokunaga, T. Fukami, and Y. Fujii, "High Density Recording with a Visible Laser Diode in Direct Overwrite MO Disk," *IEEE Trans. Magn.*, vol. 29, p. 3760, 1993.

[128] Y. Suzuki, K. Tanase, A. Yamaguchi, S. Murata, S. Sumi, and K. Torazawa, "High Density Recording on Magnetically Induced Superresolution Disk with Magnetic Field Modulation and Pulsed Laser Irradiation," *IEEE Trans. Magn.*, vol. 32, p. 4067, 1996.

[129] K. Nagato, A. Kawamoto, T. Sato, and T. Yorozu, "Compositional Dependence of Recording Noise in Amorphous RE-TM MO Disks," *J. Appl. Phys.*, vol. 63, p. 3856, 1988.

[130] D. Raasch, "Recording Characteristics of Dy-FeCo-based MO Disks," *J. Magn. Soc. Japan*, vol. 17, Supplement S1, p. 192, 1993.

[131] A. A. Thiele, "Theory of the Static Stability of Cylindrical Domains in Uniaxial Platelets," *J. Appl. Phys.*, vol. 41, p. 1139, 1970.

[132] Enrique Bernal G., "Mechanism of Curie-point Writing in Thin Films of Manganese Bismuth," *J. Appl. Phys.*, vol. 42, p. 3877, 1971.

[133] A. B. Marchant, *Optical Recording: A Technical Overview*, Reading, MA: Addison-Wesley, 1990.

[134] K. Shouhamer Immink, "Channel Coding for Optical Disc Systems," G. Bouwhuis et al. (eds.), *Principles of Optical Disc Systems*, Chapter 7, Bristol and Boston: Adam Hilger Ltd., 1986.

[135] K. Aratani, T. Narahara, A. Fukumoto, and S. Masuhara, "High Density Recording Using an Ordinary Structured MO Disk with Field Modulation," *J. Magn. Soc. Japan*, vol. 20, Supplement S1, p. 83, 1986.

Chapter 7

EXCHANGE-COUPLED FILMS

Shigeru Tsunashima

7.1 INTRODUCTION

An exchange interaction between electron spins is essential for the appearance of ferromagnetism. Attempts to control material properties through an exchange coupling probably began in the late 1960s, when work on magnetic thin film memories was gaining momentum. Then, multilayer films were studied with the aim of improving the properties of magnetic thin films for developing new functional devices [1]. The films studied had the magnetization in the film plane. The objective of controlling the coercivity and critical switching magnetic field through the exchange force between magnetic layers was the same as that for today's exchange-coupled multilayer films for magneto-optical recording applications. Since 1969, there have been a number of other exchange-coupled multilayer films. Some of them have involved the coupling of a low T_c and high H_c magnetic layer with a high T_c and low H_c layer, to obtain a temperature characteristic of coercivity suitable for thermomagnetic recording [1]; others have involved the combination of a material with a low Curie temperature and large magneto-optic effect such as EuO with a magnetic film which stores the recorded data at room temperature [2], [3]. In addition, the laminations of magnetic garnet or other oxide films and metal magnetic films, which are probably not exchange coupled, but instead magnetostatically coupled, have been studied [4]. However, the technology utilizing such multilayer magnetic thin films has not been realized for optical storage.

As discussed in detail in Chapter 2, rare earth-transition metal (RE-TM) amorphous alloy films were discovered in 1973. Their coercivity and Curie temperatures can be in principle controlled through controlling compositions, making such films suitable for magneto-optical recording applications [5]–[10].

Because of the uniqueness in controlling magnetic properties, exchange-coupled multilayer films are so important for both light modulation direct overwrite [11] and for magnetic super-resolution [12] purposes, that a detailed discussion is presented in this chapter.

7.2 PROPERTIES OF EXCHANGE-COUPLED FILMS

7.2.1 Exchange Coupling and Interface Domain Walls

When two magnetic layers (I and II) are in contact on an atomic scale, the electron spins of magnetic atoms A and B in the layers I and II, respectively, are coupled through an exchange interaction. This exchange interaction is extremely strong: Between atoms in proximity its magnetic field equivalent reaches 10^4 kOe, which is

298

several orders of magnitude higher than magnetostatic coupling forces. While a magnetostatic force is a long-range type, a direct exchange force is short range and only for nearest-neighbor atoms. In what follows only exchange interactions between nearest-neighbor atoms are considered, as shown schematically in Figure 7.1.

As discussed in Chapter 2, if the RE element is a heavy rare earth in an RE-TM amorphous film, the magnetic state is ferrimagnetic, in which case, the RE and TM magnetic moments are antiparallel. The net magnetization of the film is given by the difference of the magnetizations between the RE and TM sublattices. If the rare earth magnetization is dominant in one layer and the transition metal magnetization dominates in the other layer, and if a sufficiently strong magnetic field is applied, then the net magnetization of both layers will align themselves parallel to the magnetic field. Here the atomic magnetic moments (spins) of the first and second layer are oppositely directed, so that a region will appear between the layers in which the spin gradually changes in its direction. As shown in Figure 7.2 , a domain wall similar to a Bloch wall (in the case of perpendicular magnetization, the wall differs from the usual Bloch wall type in the sense that the magnetization on both sides of the wall is perpendicular to the wall) will appear at the interface between the two layers. This is called an interface wall. Similar to Bloch walls, exchange and anisotropy energies are stored in this region. In perpendicularly magnetized films, as shown in Figure 7.2, the demagnetization energy is also stored in the interface wall.

If the magnetic film is regarded as a continuous medium, the static spin structure can be determined from the condition under which the sum of exchange energy E_{ex}, the anisotropy energy E_a, the demagnetizing field energy E_d, and the Zeeman energy E_z is minimized. If the direction of magnetization within the film plane is uniform in a uniaxially anisotropic material with the easy axis in the direction normal to the film plane, the total energy E_t takes the same form as that of a Bloch wall:

$$E_t = E_a + E_d + E_{\text{ex}} + E_z$$

$$= \int \left[(K_u - 2\pi M_s^2) \cos^2 \theta + A \left(\frac{\partial \theta}{\partial z} \right)^2 + M_s H \cos \theta \right] dz \tag{7.1}$$

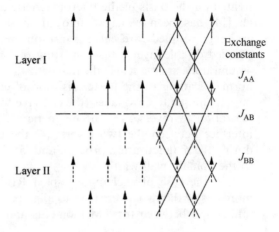

Layer I

Layer II

Exchange constants

J_{AA}

J_{AB}

J_{BB}

Figure 7.1 Schematic illustration of the interface of exchange-coupled films.

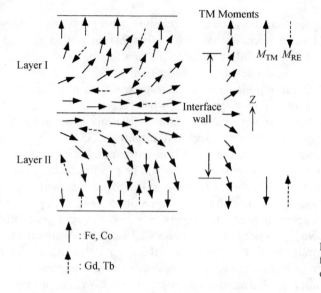

Figure 7.2 Schematic illustration of the interface wall in a rare earth-transition metal exchange coupled film.

Here, K_u is the perpendicular magnetic anisotropy constant, M_s is the saturation magnetization, A is the exchange stiffness, H is the external magnetic field, and θ is the direction of the magnetic moment of the transition metal with respect to the film normal. An interface wall differs from a simple domain wall in a number of respects: the above physical parameters change in the thickness direction and the boundary conditions are imposed at the layer interfaces and at the film surfaces.

A micromagnetic analysis of interface walls has been performed by Kaneko et al. [13]. Their results indicate that the interface wall energy depends on the wall position, and the lowest energy is obtained where the wall position is shifted from the center of the interface toward the layer side with the lower anisotropy energy.

7.2.2 Magnetization Process

Even when each layer of the film is in a single-domain state, exchange-coupled films exhibit complicated magnetization processes because of the appearance of the interface wall. In principle, the magnetization process of the exchange coupled films should be treated on the basis of the micromagnetic theory. A model proposed by Kobayashi et al. [14] has been widely employed in the analysis of magnetization processes of exchange-coupled rare earth-transition metal films. The model deals with exchange-coupled double-layer films consisting of ferrimagnetic materials, where the following assumptions are made: (1) the magnetization within each layer is directed along the film normal, leading to the hysteresis loop of each layer completely square; (2) an energy barrier unique to each layer (the coercive force energy) exists, which opposes the magnetization to reverse; (3) the magnetic walls are created and annihilated only at the interface between the two layers; (4) the interface wall energy σ_w remains constant during the magnetization process; and (5) the thickness of each layer is large compared to the domain wall width.

In the case of exchange-coupled RE-TM double-layer films, the TM magnetic moments of the two layers tend to align parallel because of the ferromagnetic exchange interaction between the TM moments and because of the antiferromagnetic coupling between the TM and heavy RE moments. As a result, the magnetization states (a) or (c) on the left-hand side in Figure 7.3 are stable under zero magnetic field. Here, the double-layer film (a) is called the A(antiparallel) type where each layer has the composition opposite to that of the other layer relative to the compensation composition; that is, if the TM magnetization is dominant in one layer, the RE is dominant in the other. The double-layer film (c) is called the P (parallel) type; both the layers have their compositions on the same side with respect to the compensation composition. In A type films, the magnetizations of the two layers tend to be antiparallel, while in P type films they tend to be parallel.

When a strong magnetic field is applied in the upward direction to the A type film, as shown in Figure 7.3(b), the magnetization of the first layer is also directed upward, and the magnetizations of the two layers become parallel. Since the magnetic moments in the first and second layers are oppositely directed, an interface wall should form between the two layers. Even in a P-type film, an interface wall will be formed, as shown in Figure 7.3(d).

Under the assumptions described before, the magnetization process can easily be obtained for exchange-coupled ferrimagnetic double-layer (ECDL) films. In a magnetic field, the double-layer film can be in one of four magnetization states (Fig. 7.4). Here, an interface wall exists in states 1 and 4 for an A type film, and in states 2 and 3 for a P type film. In an infinitely large field $H = +\infty$, the magnetization of both the layers is directed upward as in the state 1. As the field is reduced from this state to $H = -\infty$, the magnetization state changes through various paths toward the state 4. The actual magnetization process is determined by comparing the magnitude of the switching field H_{ij} at which the change of magnetization state from i to j will take place.

In order to obtain the switching field H_{ij} from the state i to j, we consider the free energy of the film. The total free energy per unit area E_i for the state i is given as

$$E_i = \pm M_{s1} h_1 H \pm M_{s2} h_2 H + \sigma_w \tag{7.2}$$

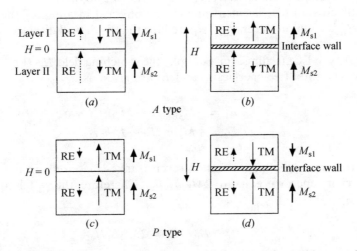

Figure 7.3 Magnetization states of exchange-coupled rare earth-transition metal double layer films.

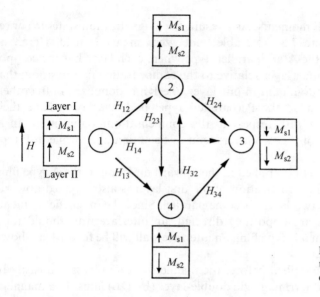

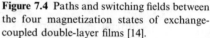

Figure 7.4 Paths and switching fields between the four magnetization states of exchange-coupled double-layer films [14].

where h_1 and h_2 are the thicknesses of the first and the second layers, H is the applied field, and σ_w is the interface wall energy density. If the interface wall does not exist, then σ_w is equal to zero. Then, the switching field H_{ij} is given by the field at which the free energy difference $E_i - E_j$ exceeds the coercivity energy designated in the following. In single-layer films, the magnetization reversal takes place at coercive field H_c, where the difference of the free energy between the two states is equal to $2M_s h H_c$. This is the energy that is required for the irreversible magnetization reversal, designated as the coercivity energy. Then, the coercivity energy of the ith layer of ECDL film is assumed to be equal to that of the corresponding single-layer film. Namely, when only the ith layer magnetization reverses, the coercivity energy is equal to $2M_{si}h_i H_{ci}$, where H_{ci} is the coercive force of the isolated ith layer. When the magnetizations reverse in both the layers, the coercivity energy is equal to $2M_{s1}h_1 H_{c1} + 2M_{s2}h_2 H_{c2}$. According to the Bloch wall displacement model, the physical meaning of the coercivity energy $2M_{si}h_i H_{ci}$ is equal to the energy required for the Bloch wall displacement of the isolated ith layer.

In A type ECDL films, for example, the switching field H_{12} (Fig. 7.4) is obtained as follows. The total free energies E_1 and E_2 are given as

$$E_1 = -M_{s1}h_1 H - M_{s2}h_2 H + \sigma_w \qquad (7.3)$$
$$E_2 = +M_{s1}h_1 H - M_{s2}h_2 H \qquad (7.4)$$

In this transition, the magnetization reversal takes place only in the first layer, so that the coercivity energy is equal to $2M_{s1}h_{c1}H_{c1}$. Therefore, the switching field H_{12} is given from

$$E_1 - E_2 = 2M_{s1}h_1 H_{c1} \qquad (7.5)$$

as

$$H_{12} = \frac{\sigma_w}{2M_{s1}h_1} - H_{c1} \tag{7.6}$$

In the same manner, the switching fields H_{ij} are given for A TYPE as well as for P TYPE films. The results are given in the following.

$$H_{12} = \pm\frac{\sigma_w}{2M_{s1}h_1} - H_{c1} \tag{7.7}$$

$$H_{13} = \pm\frac{\sigma_w}{2M_{s2}h_2} - H_{c2} \tag{7.8}$$

$$H_{14} = -\frac{M_{s2}h_2H_{c2} + M_{s1}h_1H_{c1}}{M_{s2}h_2 + M_{s1}h_1} \tag{7.9}$$

$$H_{23} = -\frac{M_{s2}h_2H_{c2} + M_{s1}h_1H_{c1}}{M_{s2}h_2 - M_{s1}h_1} = -H_{32} \tag{7.10}$$

$$H_{24} = \pm\frac{\sigma_w}{2M_{s2}h_2} - H_{c2} \tag{7.11}$$

$$H_{34} = \pm\frac{\sigma_w}{2M_{s1}h_1} - H_{c1} \tag{7.12}$$

where the upper and the lower signs correspond to A type and P type films, respectively.

Finally, the paths along which the actual magnetization reversal takes place is discussed. The conditions to realize a certain specified process are determined by comparing the magnitudes of the switching fields given by Equations (7.6)–(7.11). Hereafter, the magnetic moment of the second layer is assumed larger than that of the first layer; that is,

$$M_{s2}h_2 > M_{s1}h_1 \tag{7.13}$$

For the A-type films under an applied field decreasing from $+\infty$ to $-\infty$, the first transition starting from state 1 is either $1 \to 2$, $1 \to 3$, or $1 \to 4$. The condition for the transition $1 \to 2$ is that $H_{12} > H_{13}$ and $H_{12} > H_{14}$, rewritten as

$$\frac{\sigma_w}{2M_{s1}h_1} - \frac{\sigma_w}{2M_{s2}h_2} > H_{c1} - H_{c2} \tag{7.14}$$

The next transition starting from state 2 is either $2 \to 3$ or $2 \to 4$, which can be realized since both H_{23} and H_{24} are smaller than H_{12}. The condition for the transition $2 \to 3$ is $H_{23} > H_{24}$, that is,

$$\frac{\sigma_w}{2M_{s1}h_1} - \frac{\sigma_w}{2M_{s2}h_2} > H_{c1} - H_{c2} \tag{7.15}$$

In this case, the final transition is $3 \to 4$. Thus, the condition for the process $1 \to 2 \to 3 \to 4$ is given by Equation (7.15). If $H_{24} > H_{23}$, then the transition $2 \to 4$ is realized. Thus, the condition for the process $1 \to 2 \to 4$ is given as

$$H_{c1} + H_{c2} > \frac{\sigma_w}{2M_{s1}h_1} - \frac{\sigma_w}{2M_{s2}h_2} > H_{c1} - H_{c2} \tag{7.16}$$

The condition for the transition $1 \to 3$ is that $H_{13} > H_{12}$ and $H_{13} > H_{14}$, that is,

$$H_{c1} - H_{c2} > \frac{\sigma_w}{2M_{s1}h_1} - \frac{\sigma_w}{2M_{s2}h_2} \tag{7.17}$$

In this case, since $H_{32} > H_{13}$ according to Equation (7.17), the transition $3 \to 2$ does not occur. Therefore, the process $1 \to 3 \to 4$ is realized under the condition of Equation (7.17). The process $1 \to 4$ is not realized since it requires σ_w to be negative. In the films of A type, the processes $1 \to 2 \to 3 \to 4$ [Fig. 7.5(a)], $1 \to 2 \to 4$ [Fig 7.5(b)], and $1 \to 3 \to 4$ [Fig. 7.5(c)] are realized under the conditions of Equations (7.15), (7.16), and (7.17), respectively.

The conditions for the possible processes in the films of P type are summarized as follows. The process $1 \to 4$ [Fig. 7.5(d)] is realized for

$$\frac{\sigma_w}{2M_{s1}h_1} + \frac{\sigma_w}{2M_{s2}h_2} > |H_{c1} - H_{c2}|$$

the process $1 \to 2 \to 4$ [Fig. 5(e)] for

$$H_{c2} - H_{c1} > \frac{\sigma_w}{2M_{s1}h_1} + \frac{\sigma_w}{2M_{s2}h_2} \tag{7.19}$$

and the process $1 \to 3 \to 4$ [Fig. 5(f)] for

$$H_{c1} - H_{c2} > \frac{\sigma_w}{2M_{s1}h_1} + \frac{\sigma_w}{2M_{s2}h_2} \tag{7.20}$$

It should be noted here that the theory for P type films is applicable to "ferromagnetic" double-layered films.

The magnetization curves (M-H loop) and the switching fields of both A- and P type films are summarized in Figure 7.5, together with the Kerr hysteresis loops observed from the surfaces of the first and the second layers. The ordinate in the M-H loops gives the total magnetization $M_1h_1 + M_2h_2$ in arbitrary units while that in the Kerr loops gives either M_1 or M_2 in arbitrary units as well. The polarity of the Kerr loops is determined so that the Kerr signal becomes positive for TM dominant layers. It is noted in Figure 7.5(a) that the Kerr loop from the first layer has the same form as that often observed for Gd-Co or Gd-Fe films close to the compensation temperature [15]–[17]. In Figure 7.5(b) and (c), the Kerr hysteresis of one layer exhibits an inverted loop which has also actually been reported [15]–[17].

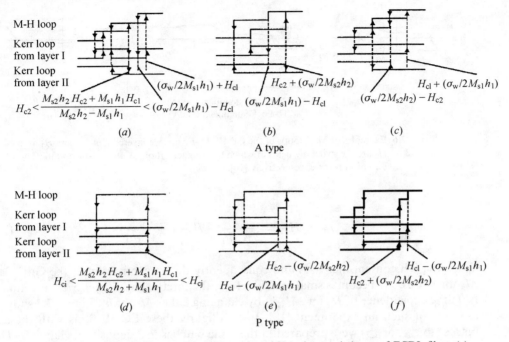

Figure 7.5 Calculated magnetization curves and Kerr hysteresis loops of ECDL films: (*a*) process $1 \rightarrow 2 \rightarrow 3 \rightarrow 4$, (*b*) $1 \rightarrow 2 \rightarrow 4$, (*c*) $1 \rightarrow 3 \rightarrow 4$; (*d*) $1 \rightarrow 4$, (*e*) $1 \rightarrow 2 \rightarrow 4$, and (*f*) $1 \rightarrow 3 \rightarrow 4$ [14].

The saturation magnetization of ferrimagnetic materials exhibits four distinct types of temperature dependences as described in Néel's theory. Therefore, exchange-coupled films consisting of ferrimagnetic layers show a very peculiar temperature dependence of the switching (coercive) fields and sometimes exhibit even a change of the type of magnetization process with temperature. This may easily be understood since the magnetization process is determined not only by the coercivity of constituent layers but also by their magnetizations. Near the Curie point, the coercivity changes with the saturation magnetization while it changes inversely with the saturation magnetization near the compensation point of ferrimagnetic materials. Thus, the temperature dependence of the magnetization process can be controlled more easily using ferrimagnetic multilayers rather than ferromagnetic ones.

7.2.3 Exchange Bias and Interface Wall Energy

Figure 7.6 is an example of measured magnetization curves for GdFe/TbFe doubled-layer films of type (b) in Figure 7.3; the curves indicate the changes resulting from the difference of compositions. Here, H_1 and H_2 are the magnetic fields at which the magnetization is reversed in the GdFe and TbFe layers, respectively. The value of H_1 observed is of the order of several KOe and the coercive force of Gd-Fe film is of the order of 100 Oe or less except for temperatures very close to the compensation point, where the apparent coercivity is greatly increased.

Since the coercivity of the GdFe layer itself is small, H_1 given by Equation (7.7) may be approximated as

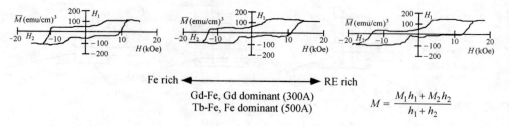

Fe rich ◄——————————————————► RE rich

Gd-Fe, Gd dominant (300A)
Tb-Fe, Fe dominant (500A)

$$M = \frac{M_1 h_1 + M_2 h_2}{h_1 + h_2}$$

Figure 7.6 Examples of M-H loops of the Gd-Fe/Tb-Fe double-layered films, where H_1 and H_2 are the switching fields at which the magnetizations of the Gd-Fe and the Tb-Fe layers reverse, respectively [14].

$$H_1 = H_{12} = \frac{\sigma_w}{2M_{s1}h_1} - H_{c1} \approx \frac{\sigma_w}{2M_{s1}h_1} \qquad (7.21)$$

When the RE content increases and consequently the magnetization of the GdFe layer M_{s1} increases, H_1 becomes smaller. Therefore, the interface wall energy σ_w is estimated from the dependence of H_1 on $2M_{s1}h_1$ by changing either M_{s1} or h_1. Figure 7.7 shows an example of such an experiment [13]. In this figure, these ECDL films with the same marks (●, ▲, or ○) were prepared in the same batches in a deposition chamber. Thus, as far as the same marks are concerned, the switching field H_1 is proportional to $1/(2M_{s1}h_1)$. From the slope of the line of H_1 vs. $1/(2M_{s1}h_1)$, the interface wall energy density is estimated to be 1–2 erg/cm². The value of σ_w thus obtained may be compared with that of the Bloch wall in Gd-Co, which is estimated to be 1–3 erg/cm² from the stripe domain width [18]. The difference between the wall energies may be attributed to the property of the interface. For example, if the interface between the layers is partially oxidized, the interface wall structure is greatly influenced.

Here, the quantity given by $\sigma_w/2M_{s1}h_1$ can be estimated from the shift of the center of the minor loop corresponding to magnetization reversal in the GdFe layer alone. This loop shift called the exchange bias effect occurs depending on whether or not there is an interface wall.

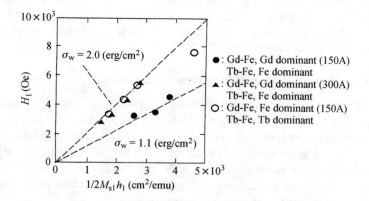

Figure 7.7 Relation between the magnetizations M_{s1} of the Gd-Fe layer in the Gd-Fe/Tb-Fe double-layered films and the switching fields H_1 of the Gd-Fe layer, where h_1 is the thickness of the Gd-Fe layer [14].

Exchange coupling can be used to control the apparent coercivity, but this method is only effective over a certain layer thickness range. When the layer to be controlled becomes thicker, the coercivity (magnetization reversal field) will decrease in inverse proportion to the product of the layer magnetization and thickness, as seen from Equation (7.21). On the other hand, when both layers are thin compared to the wall width, the above model cannot be applied, and the magnetization reversal should simultaneously occur in both layers. And, when either one of the two layers is thinner than the wall width, the center of the wall is displaced to the opposite layer, and this is expected to have an effect on the magnetization process. A rigorous treatment of such phenomena requires a micromagnetic analysis.

The exchange coupling strength, namely the exchange bias or the interface wall energy, can be reduced adequately by inserting a very thin ferromagnetic or paramagnetic layer between two magnetic layers to be coupled with each other. In some applications of magneto-optical recording media, the coupling strength between two magnetic layers is required to disappear at a temperature below the Curie temperature of the magnetic layers. For this purpose, a triple-layer structure is used [19], where an intermediate ferromagnetic layer with a lower Curie temperature is inserted between the two layers. Figure 7.8 shows the temperature dependence of the interface wall energy in triple-layer films, where a DyFe layer with $T_C = 350\,K$ is inserted between GdFe and TbFe($T_C = 400\,K$) layers. As seen from the figure, if the thickness of DyFe layer is around 50 Å, the wall energy at room temperature is roughly the same as that of direct coupling without the intermediate layer, while the wall energy becomes very small at the Curie temperature of DyFe layer compared with direct coupling. However, the wall energy is not zero at T_c, which is probably due to the spin polarization of DyFe layer induced by adjacent GdFe and TbFe layers, as described later in Section 7.2.5.

When a paramagnetic layer is used for the intermediate layer, the interface wall energy changes in a way a little different from the case of a ferromagnetic intermediate layers. Figure 7.9 shows the temperature dependence of the interface wall energy of GdFe/Pt/TbFe triple-layer films [19]. As seen from the figure, the wall energy rapidly decreases with increasing thickness of the Pt layer, but its temperature profile changes very little. Therefore, this structure can be used only to reduce the coupling force but not to control the thermomagnetic properties.

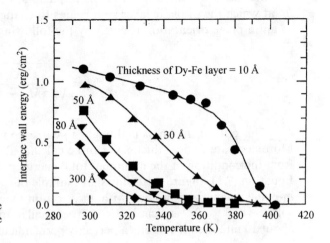

Figure 7.8 Temperature dependence of the interface wall energy in Gd-Fe/Dy-Fe/Tb-Fe triple-layer films [19].

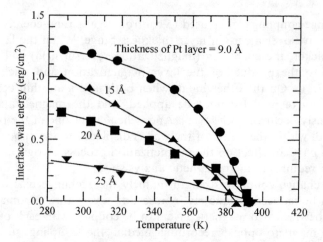

Figure 7.9 Temperature dependence of the interface wall energy in Gd-Fe/Pt/Tb-Fe triple-layer films [19].

7.2.4 Control of the Spin Orientation (Magnetic Anisotropy)

High-density magneto-optic recording requires a material with perpendicular magnetization and a squareness of magnetization loops close to unity. On the other hand, materials with high magneto-optic performance, namely large Kerr or Faraday rotation, do not always exhibit large perpendicular magnetic anisotropy. For this reason, attempts have been made to combine the film of such materials with other materials exhibiting a large perpendicular anisotropy [20]–[23]. In order to make the magnetization perpendicular to the film plane in the entire film, it is necessary not only that the perpendicular magnetic anisotropy averaged over the entire film and including the demagnetizing field energy be positive (easy axis in the perpendicular direction), but also that the in-plane magnetization layer be fairly thin.

If the spins at the interface are all aligned along the perpendicular direction to the film normal and the spin direction changes linearly as a function of the distance from the interface from the normal to the in-plane direction, then the critical film thickness h_{cr} at which the in-plane layer spin begins to change its direction from a perpendicular to an in-plane orientation is given by the following relation [20]:

$$h_{cr} = \sqrt{\frac{3A}{2\pi M_s^2 - K_u}} \tag{7.22}$$

This critical thickness is thought to correspond to the width of 90° interface wall. More accurate critical thickness can be calculated numerically [24] or analytically [25] from the condition of the minimum total energy, based on the micromagnetic model of Equation (7.1). Figure 7.10 shows an example of the spin orientation calculated for the in-plane magnetization layer with a saturation magnetization of 200 emu/cc, exchange stiffness of 3×10^{-7} erg/cm and no perpendicular anisotropy. If the layer is thinner than about 10 nm, then it exhibits a perfectly perpendicular magnetization. This thickness of

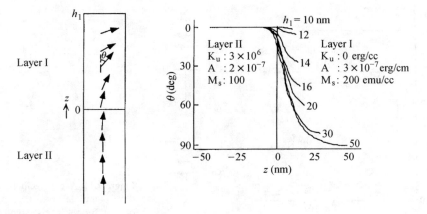

Figure 7.10 Spin orientation of the exchange-coupled double-layer film consisting of in-plane and perpendicular magnetization layers, where the thickness of the in-plane layer is varied as a parameter [21].

about 10 nm is considerably smaller than the critical thickness of 19 nm given by Equation (7.22). This difference is probably attributed to a tendency for the magnetization within the perpendicular magnetization layer to be inclined toward in-plane directions under the influence of the in-plane magnetization layer. The critical layer thickness for materials without perpendicular magnetic anisotropy is roughly 10 nm or less for the higher saturation magnetization case. Since light penetrates through 10 nm or more even when the material is a metal, the use of such a structure in magneto-optical recording media is a critical issue.

7.2.5 Control of Spin Polarization (Curie Temperature)

Many materials which exhibit a large magneto-optic effect are 4f and 5f transition metal compounds like EuO and USb whose Curie temperatures are below room temperature [26]. The idea of using such materials in magneto-optical recording has long been considered; a structure of magneto-optical memory using EuO, operating normally at low temperatures was proposed at the beginning of the 1970s, where EuO is exchange-coupled with iron or permalloy, of higher Curie temperatures to protect recorded information at elevated temperatures [27]. Further efforts were made to find compounds of Eu and U with higher Curie temperatures, and the addition of iron and cobalt was tried [26], [28].

Recently, attempt has been made to raise the Curie temperature of EuS through an exchange-coupling with cobalt, and the T_c of EuS was reported to increase from 16K to 100K [29]. However, this effect may be attributed to a change in the electronic state of EuS due to proximity with Co, rather than due to an exchange interaction.

No experimental result which directly demonstrates a rise in the Curie temperature T_c due solely to the effect of exchange coupling has been found in the literature. However, a theoretical prediction was made by applying the molecular field model to the multilayer structure [30], [31].

A stack of N monoatomic layers of Gd with low Curie temperature ($T_c = 293$ K) sandwiched between high-T_c cobalt layers is considered, as in Figure 7.11. At a finite

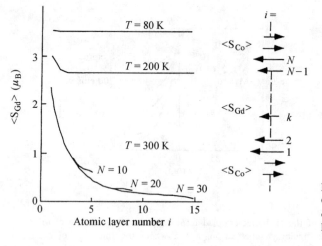

Figure 7.11 Average Gd spin calculated for Gd/Co multilayers, where N is the number of Gd mono layers involved in each Gd layer [30].

temperature, the Gd spin expectation value $\langle S_i \rangle$ in an atomic plane i is given in terms of the Brillouin function B_s by

$$\langle S_i \rangle = S_{Gd} B_s(g_{Gd} \mu_B S_{Gd} H_i / RT) \tag{7.23}$$

The molecular field H_i is given in terms of the exchange interaction of the atomic planes i, $i+1$ and $i-1$ as follows.

$$H_i = \bar{z}_j \frac{z_{ij} J_{ij}}{g_{Gd} \mu_B} \langle S_i \rangle \tag{7.24}$$

Here z_{ij} is the number of nearest-neighbor atoms in the jth atomic plane as seen by a Gd atom in the ith atomic plane. Figure 7.11 shows the expectation values of Gd moment, as a function of the distance from the interface. Even at 300 K, nearly equal to the Curie temperature of Gd, the magnetic moments virtually vanishes on Gd sites a few atomic planes distant from the interface. This demonstrates the difficulty in raising the Curie temperature of thick magnetic layers only through the exchange coupling. However, it does show the possibility of a very thin exchange switching layer which thermally controls the coupling force between adjacent magnetic layers on the both sides. The application of such a switching or exchange-control layer has been suggested both for light-modulation overwriting [32] and for magnetic superresolution [12]. For the control of the Curie temperature, It is more realistic to utilize proximity effects together with the exchange coupling.

7.3 APPLICATION TO MAGNETO-OPTIC RECORDING MEDIA

7.3.1 Separation of Recording and Readout Functions for High-Performance Media

Magneto-optic recording media must provide two separate functions: (1) thermo-magnetic data storage, and (2) readout. The recording layer which provides the thermomagnetic recording function must have a Curie temperature appropriate for recording and a high coercivity, and the readout layer should have a large magneto-optic effect and a high Curie temperature. In addition, the two magnetic layers must be coupled so that there is a one-to-one correspondence between data-stored and data-readout. Possible couplings between the two layers include the exchange force and the magnetostatic force; when using a metal film for magneto-optic recording, however, a stronger coupling can be obtained through the exchange force, owing to the extreme thinness of the film.

The GdFe/TbFe (readout/recording layers) exchange-coupled double-layer film is one of these examples [8]. TbFe has a high coercivity as well as an appropriate Curie temperature, but its Kerr rotation angle is relatively small at room temperature. On the other hand, GdFe has a relatively high Curie temperature and a large Kerr rotation angle, but has a low coercivity. The exchange-coupled double-layer film combines the merits of these two materials. The advantage of such a double-layer film lies in the use of a material with a high Curie temperature as the readout layer to improve readout performance. Here we use a simple model to compare such two-layer films with single-layer films [33].

When the noise source is limited to shot noise only, then the signal-to-noise ratio (S/N) is given as

$$\frac{S}{N} = (\eta/2Bh\nu)^{1/2}(RI_0)^{1/2} \sin 2\langle\theta_k\rangle \tag{7.25}$$

Here, η is the photodetector quantum efficiency, B is the frequency bandwidth of the amplifier, h is the Planck's constant, ν is the frequency of the light, R is the film reflectivity, I_0 is the optical intensity of incident light on the film, and $\langle\Theta_k\rangle$ is the effective Kerr rotation angle, which is defined by $(\theta_K^2 + \eta_K^2)^{1/2}$. Thus, the S/N rises as $I_0^{1/2}$; but increasing I_0 brings about a rise in the film temperature, so that $\langle\Theta_k\rangle$ becomes smaller. Because the rise in film temperature is proportional to I_0, S/N varies with the film temperature T during readout as

$$S/N \propto \langle\theta_k\rangle(T)(T - T_{amb})^{1/2} \tag{7.26}$$

Here T_{amb} is the ambient temperature and $T - T_{amb}$ is the rise in temperature due to the laser irradiation during readout.

In the films, RE and TM elements have atomic magnetic moments antiparallel to each other both contributing to the Kerr rotation, but it is thought that most of the magneto-optic effect at wavelengths near 800 nm for present application is due to the TM magnetization [34]. The Kerr rotation Θ_K is, therefore, proportional to the magnetization of TM sublattice. Then, the temperature dependence of Θ_K from the TM magnetization determined using a molecular field approximation can be calculated. Figure 7.12 shows the resulting relative S/N obtained for various RE-TM films using Equation (7.26). At an ambient temperature near 300 K, the horizontal axis with the origin at 300 K indicates the readout optical power. If the double-layer films with TbFe as the recording layer and GdFeCo as the readout layer are used, approximately 6 dB higher S/N than TbFe single-layer films can be obtained at the optimum readout power for TbFe. The TbFe/GdFeCo double-layer film was actually examined showing a higher S/N than that of TbFe single-layer film by about 7 dB [35].

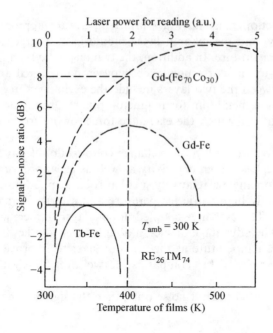

Figure 7.12 Signal-to-noise ratio of various RE-TM films as a function of the film temperature during readout [33].

Exchange-coupled films of the separate function type have been used for high-speed (high bit rate) magneto-optic recording media [36] since they can achieve higher recording sensitivities without sacrificing readout performance. As described in Chapter 9, exchange-coupled films, with GdFeCo as the readout layer, have also been used in magnetically induced super high-resolution [12].

7.3.2 Thermomagnetic Domain Replication and Bias Effect

Ordinarily, the magnetization is reversed through the external magnetic field and/or the demagnetizing field. In exchange-coupled films, the thermomagnetic recording process is different from that in single-layer films. It is conceivable that a variety of thermomagnetic recording processes appear, depending on the combination of the thermomagnetic properties of each layer. The most important process is a thermomagnetic domain replication, which occurs in the separate function type double layers mentioned above as well as other exchange-coupled films.

As shown in Figure 7.13, an external field H_b is applied to write data to a TbFe/GdFe double-layer film and the laser irradiation causes the spot region of radius R to be heated above the Curie temperature of the TbFe layer [37]. Then, the GdFe layer becomes free from the exchange force from the TbFe layer and the magnetization of GdFe layer can be reversed. Here, a domain nucleus of radius r ($< R$) appears in the GdFe layer. This nucleus expands to a domain of radius R when the following condition is satisfied.

$$\frac{\sigma_{w1}}{2R_o M'_{s1}} + \frac{1}{2M'_{s1}}\frac{\delta\sigma_w}{\delta r} + H_{s1} + H_{s2} + H_b > H'_{c1} \qquad (7.27)$$

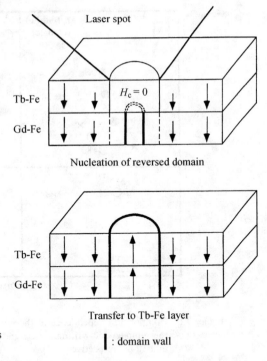

Figure 7.13 Thermomagnetic writing process in exchange-coupled double-layer films [37].

$\blacksquare$: domain wall

where σ_w is the domain wall energy density for the GdFe layer, M'_{s1} and H'_{c1} are the saturation magnetization and coercivity of the GdFe layer during heating, H_{s1} and H_{s2} are the stray fields from TbFe and GdFe layers, respectively, and H_b is the applied field. The bit appearing in the GdFe layer will then be duplicated in the TbFe layer through the exchange interaction when the magnetization appears in the TbFe layer during cooling, and will be retained owing to the high coercivity.

The validity of the above consideration based on Equation (7.27) might be tested by measuring the field dependence of the thermomagnetic recording characteristics. In Figure 7.14, the minimum bias field strengths are written in Oersted which are necessary for recording on the GdFe/TbFe exchange-coupled films of respective composition. For the points shown by $\bigcirc$ and $\square$, the direction of the fields is parallel to that for writing on the TbFe layers, while for the points $\bullet$ and $\blacksquare$ which are for A type films, it is not for writing on TbFe, but for GdFe layers. This supports the above consideration.

Figure 7.15 is the result of numerical calculation of Equation (7.27), which should be compared with the experimental results of Figure 7.14. Here, y_0 is assumed equal to $R(= 1.3 \ \mu m)$, $\sigma_{w1} = 1 \ erg/cm^3$, $M'_{s1}H_{c1} = 1.3 \times 10^4 \ erg/cm^3$, $\delta\sigma_w/\sigma r = 0$ and the thickness of GdFe and TbFe layers 30 nm and 50 nm, respectively. It is noted from the figures that the calculated values agree well with the experiment. However, this simple consideration failed to explain the process of thermomagnetic erase [37]. This may be due to the lack of the consideration of phenomena occurring below the Curie temperature of the TbFe layer.

In the case of double-layer films for overwriting or magnetic super resolution (actually such films consist of three or more layers), the temperature characteristics of coercivity of the two layers must be adjusted such that data transfer occurs under a weak magnetic field on heating to a certain temperature [11], [12], [32].

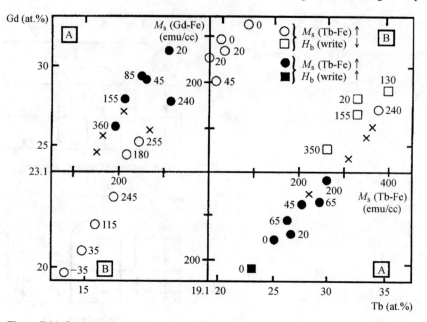

Figure 7.14 Composition dependence of the minimum bias field (in Oersted) necessary for thermomagnetic writing, where the laser power and pulse duration are 3 mW and 10 μs, respectively [37].

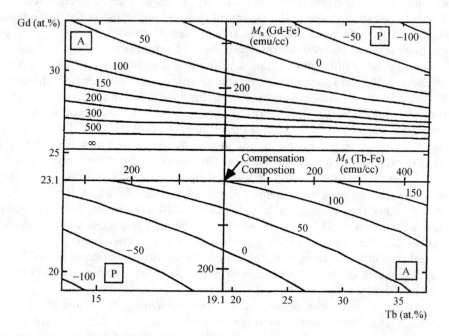

Figure 7.15 Calculated bias field (in Oersted) necessary for thermomagnetic writing on Gd-Fe/Tb-Fe double-layer films as a function of the composition of the layers [37].

The thermomagnetic transfer effect in exchange-coupled films makes possible a variety of new functions for magneto-optic recording media; but there have been very few micromagnetic analyses of the transfer process itself [38]. This is probably because of the difficulty involved in micromagnetic description of the coercivity and its temperature dependence, which remains a theme for future work.

7.3.3 Short-Wavelength Recording Media

The alloys of iron with Gd, Tb, Dy, and other heavy rare earth currently used in magneto-optic recording media have magneto-optic effect maxima in the infrared range, and the Kerr rotation angle tends to diminish with decreasing wavelength. This tendency is more pronounced in alloys of Tb and Dy than for Gd. In the future, if blue-light lasers or SHG devices are used for optical writing and reading at wavelengths near 400 nm in order to achieve further high recording densities, a considerable drop in S/N is inevitable. Hence, the development of PtCo superlattice films, oxide films, and other new materials with a large magneto-optic effect is underway; but the excellent thermomagnetic recording characteristics and low noise property of TbFe and other amorphous alloys still remain very attractive.

Amorphous alloys of iron with Nd, Pr, and other light rare earth metals have a larger magneto-optic effect at short wavelengths than do amorphous alloys of heavy rare earth elements, owing to the contribution of 4f electron transitions to the magneto-optic effect [41], [42]. However, since the magnetic moment of light rare earth is parallel to the iron moment, the saturation magnetization is large and the perpendicular magnetization state is not readily obtained. Hence, the exchange coupling with TbFe and other materials has been tried as a means of controlling the spin orientation and obtaining the perpendicular magnetization. Initially a two-layer film with an Nd alloy on the substrate (readout) side was tried, as in Figure 7.16(*a*), but it was not possible to simultaneously attain both a completely square hysteresis characteristic and good magneto-optic properties at short wavelengths [20]. Afterward three-layer films supplemented with an extremely thin TbFeCo layer on the substrate side have been examined [Fig. 7.16(*b*)]. In this structure, complete perpendicular magnetization is achieved by using the highly anisotropic TbFeCo layer at the film surface (substrate side) where the spin orientation is the most unstable [23].

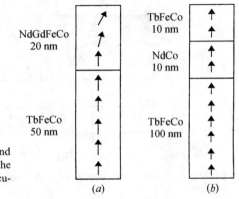

Figure 7.16 Exchange-coupled (*a*) double-and (*b*) triple-layer films designed to control the spin orientation of Nd alloy layer perpendicular to the film plane.

7.3.4 Magnetic Superresolution

The bit density of optical recording is generally determined by the spot size of the readout light beam since signals from adjacent marks which exist in the same beam spot interfere with each other and become difficult to read out. Magnetic superresolution can reduce the interference of the readout signal and enables the magneto-optical readout of recorded bits much smaller than the diffraction limited spot size. As a result, magneto-optical memory is expected to achieve much higher bit density than conventional optical memories.

Various types of magnetic superresolution (MSR) techniques have been developed since the first one was reported by Aratani et al. [12] . As will be described in Chapter 9, MSR was attained using exchange-coupled films consisting of readout and recording layers. During the readout, the readout layer forms mask and aperture areas in the beam spot according to the temperature profile and applied field, where the exchange coupling is utilized for controlling the temperature dependence of the switching fields of the readout layer.

In the original MSR technique, the mask consists of an area uniformly magnetized in a direction that was determined by an external field applied during and before the readout, respectively, for front aperture detection (FAD) and rear aperture detection (RAD). In both cases, the magnetization of the readout layer is always perpendicular to the film plane and the exchange coupling with the recording layer determines only the spin direction either up or down.

Recently another type of magnetic superresolution has been developed by Murakami et al. [39], where exchange-coupled films similar to the separate function type is utilized. As shown in Figure 7.17, the GdFeCo readout layer has in-plane magnetization except for the center of the readout beam spot where the temperature of the film is higher than the surrounding and exceeds a certain value. As a result, the readout layer of the center area becomes magnetized perpendicular to the film plane, being parallel to that of the recording layer. Then, the polar Kerr signal comes only from the high temperature region, achieving superresolution. This method does not need any magnetic fields for forming the mask area and thus can achieve recording

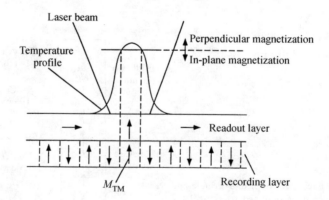

Figure 7.17 Schematic illustration of readout mechanism using in-plane magnetization layer [39].

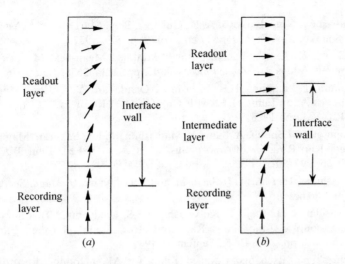

Figure 7.18 Schematic illustration of the spin orientation in MSR films using in-plane magnetization layers; (*a*) double-layer structure, (*b*) triple-layer structure [40].

density much higher than conventional MO disks without changing principal parts of conventional disk drive systems.

The difficulty of this technique is that the transition from in-plane to perpendicular magnetization is not so sharp to obtain sufficiently high CN ratio. This is partly due to the strong exchange coupling between the readout and recording layers existing in the mask area. As shown in Figure 7.18(*a*) [40], the interface 90 deg wall will penetrate significantly to the readout layer which has smaller wall energy. If the read beam is reflected by the readout layer with magnetization component perpendicular to the film plane, the masking effect will not be sufficient. The masking effect is thought to be improved by reducing the width of the transition area keeping it large at the readout temperature. As described in Section 7.2.4, the width of the transition area, namely the wall width, is inversely proportional to the square root of the effective anisotropy. Thus, the wall structure with a width which is small in the mask area while large in the aperture area can be realized by introducing an intermediate layer. For this purpose, a GdFe layer with lower T_C and larger M_S than those of the readout layer was examined as the intermediate layer [40]. On readout of the data, the spin orientation of the mask area is controlled, as shown in Figure 7.18(*b*), which reduces the Kerr signal of the mask area. By using this triple layer structure, high performance has been achieved.

There are several other schemes proposed for high-density recording. They are "Magnetic Domain Expansion" [43] and "Magnetic Multi-valued Recording" [44]. They utilize exchange-coupled layers and promise likely paths for extending density beyond 10 Gbit/in^2.

REFERENCES

[1] J. C. Bruyere and O. Massenet, *IEEE Trans. Magn.*, 5, 292, 1969, and references therein.

[2] K.Y. Ahn and G. S. Almasi, *IEEE Trans. Magn.*, vol. 5, p. 944, 1969.

[3] Knerr and W. Zinn, *Z. Angrew. Phy.*, vol. 26, p. 152, 1969.

[4] M. Balbashov, N. D. Baikova, A. P., Gubarev, S. N. Marchenko, A. Ya. Chervonenkis, and A. A. Shimko, *Sov. Tech. Phys. Lett.*, vol. 3, p. 529, 1977.

[5] N. Heiman, K. Lee, and R. I. Potter, "Modified Mean-field Model for Rare-earth-Iron Amorphous Alloys," *J. Appl. Phys.*, vol. 47, pp. 2634–2638, June 1976.

[6] Y. Mimura, T. Imamura, T. Kobayashi, A. Okada, and Y. Kusiro, "Magnetic Properties of Amorphous Alloy Films of Fe with Gd, Tb, Dy, Ho, or Er," *J. Appl. Phys.*, vol. 49, pp. 1208–1214, March 1978.

[7] H. Tsujimoto, M.Shouji, A. Saito, S. Matsushita, and Y. Sakurai,"Magnetic Properties and Magnetic Kerr Rotation of Amorphous TbFeCo and TbFeCr Films," *J. Mag. Magn. Mat.*, vol. 35, pp. 199–201, 1983.

[8] S. Tsunashima, H. Tsuji, T. Kobayashi, and S. Uchiyama, *J. Magn. Soc. Japan*, vol. 5, p. 73, 1981 (in Japanese).

[9] S. Tsunashiama, H. Tsuji, T. Kobayashi, and S. Uchiyama, "Thermomagnetic Writing on Exchange-coupled Amorphous Rare-earth Iron Double Layered Films," *IEEE Trans. Magn.*, vol.17, pp. 2840–2842, September 1981.

[10] S. Tsunashima,"Exchange Coupled Films for Magnetooptic Recording Applications," *J. Mag. Soc. Japan*, vol. 15, pp. 822–830, 1991.

[11] J. Saito, M. Sato, H. Matsumoto, and H. Akasaka, *Japan J. Appl. Phys.*, 26, Supplement 26-4, p. 155, 1987.

[12] K. Aratani, A. Fukumoto, Ohta, M. Kaneko, and K. Watanabe, *Proceedings of SPIE*, 499, 209, 1991.

[13] K. Kaneko, K. Aratani, Y. Mutoh, A. Nakaoki, K. Watanabe, and H. Makino, *Japan J. Appl. Phys.*, 28, Supplement 28-3, p. 27, 1989.

[14] T. Kobayashi, H. Tsuji, S. Tsunashima, and S. Uchiyama, *Japan J. Appl. Phys.*, vol. 20, p. 2089, 1981.

[15] S. Esho, Proceedings of the 7th Conference on Solid State Devices, Tokyo, 1975, *J. Appl. Phys.*, vol. 15, Supplement 15-1, p. 93, 1975.

[16] M. Amatsu, S. Honda, and T. Kusuda, *IEEE Trans. Magn.*, vol. 13, p. 1612, 1977.

[17] O. S. Lutes, J.O. Holmen, R. L. Kooyer, and O. S. Aadland, *IEEE Trans. Magn.*, vol. 13, p. 1615, 1977.

[18] R. Hasegawa, *J. Appl. Phys.*, vol. 45, p. 3109, 1974.

[19] T. Kobayashi, A. Okayama, H. Morioka, S. Shiomi, and M. Masuda, "Exchange-coupling in Triple-layered Films," *J. Mag. Soc. Japan*, vol. 19, Supplement S1, pp. 53–56, 1995.

[20] S. Tsunashima, Y. J. Choe, K. Ito, and S. Uchiyama, *MRS Int'l. Mtg. on Adv. Mats.*, 10, 355, 1989, Materials Research Society.

[21] K. Ichitani, K. Ito, S. Tsunashima, and S. Uchiyama, IEICE Tech. Rep., *MR89-47*, 1990.

[22] H. Wakabayashi, H. Notarys, J. C. Suits, and T. Suzuki, *Materials for Magneto-Optic Data Storage*. Materials Research Society, Symposium Proceedings, vol. 150, C. J. Robinson, T. Suzuki, and C. M. Falco (eds.), p. 95.

[23] H. Iiyori and S. Takayama, *J. Appl. Phys.*, vol. 69, p. 4761, 1991.

[24] H. Wakabayashi, H. Notarys, and T. Suzuki, "Distribution of Magnetization in Exchange-coupled Co/TbFeCo Double-layered Films," *J. Mag. Soc. Japan*, vol. 15, Supplement S1, pp. 87–90, 1991.

[25] X. Hu and Y. Kawazoe, "Theory of Capping Effect in Magnetic Double-layer Film Systems," *Phys. Rev. B*, vol. 49, pp. 3294–3302, 1994.

[26] W. Reim and J. Schoenes, Chapter 2 in *Ferromagnetic Materials*, vol. 5, K. H. J. Buschow and E. P. Wohlfarth (eds.), Elsevier Science Publishers B. V., 1990, and references therein.

[27] G. S. Almasi and E. R. Genovese, *IBM Technical Disclosure Bulletin*, vol. 14, p. 342, 1971.

[28] H. Brandle, J. Schoenes, F. Hulliger and W. Reim, *J. Magn. Magn. Mat.*, vol. 83, p. 29, 1990.

[29] R. J. Gambino, *J. Magn. Soc. Japan*, vol. 15, Sl, p. 1, 1991.

[30] S. Tsunashima, T. Ichikawa, M. Nawate, and S. Uchiyama, *J. de Phys.*, C8, p. 1803, 1988.

[31] R. E. Camley and D. R. Tilley, *Phys. Rev.*, vol. 37, p. 3413, 1988.

[32] Y. Nakaki, T. Fukami, T. Tokunaga, M. Taguchi, and K. Tsutsumi, *J. Magn. Soc. Japan*, vol. 14, p. 165, 1990.

[33] S. Tsunashima, *Res. Rep. Mag. Soc. Japan*, vol. 27, p. 33, 1982.

[34] Y. J. Choe, S. Tsunashima, T. Katayama, and S. Uchiyama, *J. Magn. Soc. Japan*, 11, Supplement Sl, p. 273, 1987.

[35] H. Akasaka, *Function and Materials*, p. 24, October 1984 (in Japanese).

[36] T. Nomura, 1986 *Optical Memory Symposium papers*, p. 1. 1986.

[37] A. Nodo, T. Kobayashi, S. Tsunasima, and S. Uchiyama, *J. Magn. Soc. Japan*, vol. 6, p. 131, 1982.

[38] M. Hasegawa, K. Moroga, M. Okada, and Y. Hidaka, "Computer Simulation for Reverse Domain Formation Process in Magneto-optical Memory," *J. Mag. Soc. Japan*, vol. 17, Supplement S1, pp. 249–254, 1993.

[39] Y. Murakami, N. Iketani, J. Nakajima, A. Takahashi, K. Ohta, and T. Ishikawa, "Super Resolution Readout of a Magneto-optical Disk with an In-plane Magnetization Layer," *J. Mag. Soc. Japan*, vol. 17, Supplement S1, pp. 201–204, 1993.

[40] N. Nishimura, T. Hiroki, and T. Okada, "MSR Disks with Three Magnetic Layers Using In-plane Magnetization Films," *J. Mag. Soc. Japan*, vol. 19, Supplement S1, pp. 417–420, 1995.

[41] R. J. Gambino and T. R. McGuire, *J. Appl. Phys.*, vol. 57, pp. 3906–3908, 1985.

[42] T. Suzuki and T. Katayama, *IEEE Trans. MAG-22*, pp. 1230–1232, 1986.

[43] H. Awano, S. Ohnuki, H. Shirai, N. Ohta, A. Yamaguchi, S. Sumi, and K. Torazawa, *Appl. Phys. Lett.*, vol. 69, no. 27, pp. 4257–4259, 1996.

[44] K. Shimazaki, N. Ohta, M. Yoshihiro, N. Nagai, S. Imai, and H. Takao, *J. Magn. Soc. Japan*, vol. 20, Supplement S1, pp. 67–72, 1996.

Chapter 8

LIGHT INTENSITY MODULATION DIRECT OVERWRITE

Jun Saito

8.1 GENERAL INTRODUCTION

8.1.1 Direct Overwrite Function

In the twenty-first century, an information apparatus is expected to be a personal belonging, it is not professional gear anymore. In the daily life of the twenty-first century, many kinds of electrical information apparatus will be used by ordinary people. Personal computers will be able to handle and process large amounts of stored data at high speed. Optical fibers and digital communication will enable telecommunication of large and high-speed data streams. Magneto-optical disk memory will achieve high capacity, high transfer rate, and interchangeable data storage.

Such progress in the technologies of information data processing, telecommunication, and storage will lead us to a so-called multimedia era. In the multimedia era, anyone will be able to process, telecommunicate, and store any kind of data anytime, anywhere. Just as electric power is easily available from electric outlets and batteries today, so document data, coded data, graphic data, vocal data, video data, animation data, image data, and all such kinds of data will be available at will in the multimedia era.

A potential candidate for future multimedia storage is the magneto-optical disk memory judging from its data capacity, recording density, data transfer rate, data accessibility, interchangeability, mass producability, data reliability, durability, and read/write cyclability. Phase-change disk memories and flash memories like EEPROM are also other attractive candidates. However, they have disadvantages with respect to recording density and read/write cyclability, and are not superior to magneto-optical disk memories. At present, CD-ROM memories are taken as the multimedia storage, though read-only memories. When multimedia technologies become more sophisticated in the coming century, rewritable type magneto-optical disk memories will take the main role of multimedia storage, it is believed.

In 1988, the first products of magneto-optical disk memory (ISO-standardized) appeared in the market. The information bit size can be as small as the laser wavelength; approximately $0.7\,\mu m$, so that even the first products have a large capacity; —650 megabyte/130 mm double side. Magneto-optical disks are interchangeable— that means, magneto-optical disks are so standardized that every disk is compatible with every other. While hard disk memories are called "on-line memories," and magnetic tape memories "off-line memories," magneto-optical disk memories are now called "near-line memories"(see Table 8.1).

TABLE 8.1 Two Main Features of Multimedia Storage

Storage	Expandability	Accessibility
Hard disk memory	N.G	O.K
MO disk memory	O.K	O.K
Magnetic tape memory	O.K	N.G

Magneto-optical disk memories have been demonstrated to be ideal for multimedia storage, except that the direct overwrite function has not been achieved. Direct overwrite is indispensable for high-speed data transfer, especially for real-time recording of large, high-speed sequential data, such as, video data. Two methods for direct overwrite have been proposed. One is magnetic field modulation direct overwrite (MFM-DOW). This method may not be suitable for high-speed data transfer (several megabytes per second), because the magnetic field cannot be switched at a high frequency. The flying magnetic head is located close to the recording surface of magneto-optical disk. (The gap between the head and the disk surface is typically several μm.) In this case, the disk rotates at a relative low speed, to prevent head crashes. In a hard disk drive, both the disk and the head are packed in a sealed space in order to avoid such a crash. The other method for the direct overwrite is light intensity modulation direct overwrite (LIM-DOW), which is described in this chapter.

So far, only the LIM-DOW method has achieved high-speed data direct overwriting in magneto-optical disk memories for computers. The MO disk which is used for the LIM-DOW method is called a direct overwrite magneto-optical disk (DOW-MO disk).

8.1.2 Outline of Light Intensity Modulation Direct Overwrite

A DOW-MO disk uses the same readout mechanism as that of an ordinary MO disk. Figure 8.1 shows the readout mechanism. As discussed in Chapter 2, it utilizes the polar Kerr effect, the strength of which depends on the wavelength to be used. A plane polarized, focused beam of typically 1 mW DC laser light irradiates magnetic domains which are written marks of a micron size in an amorphous magneto-optical thin film, for example, a Terbium Iron Cobalt (TbFeCo) rare-earth transition metal alloy. After reflecting from the written marks, the plane of polarization of the light rotates by a Kerr rotation angle (θk), for example, $+\theta k$ from the written marks, regions of upward magnetization and $-\theta k$ from the downward written marks. An optical analyzer (polarizer) can convert the difference in the plane of polarization into the modulation of light intensity. A photo diode can convert the modulation of light intensity into an electrical signal, so that the written marks; written data can be read out.

DOW-MO disks use a different erase/write mechanism from that of an ordinary MO disk. Figure 8.2 shows the erase/write mechanism for ordinary MO disks. In the erase mechanism of ordinary MO disks, a magneto-optical thin film (typically TbFeCo) is irradiated and scanned by a focused beam of laser DC light (approximately 10 mW DC) and a magnetic field is applied for erasure (upward directed field in the figure). The temperature of the irradiated spot is elevated by the laser above the Curie point where the coercivity is zero. The direction of the magnetization of the

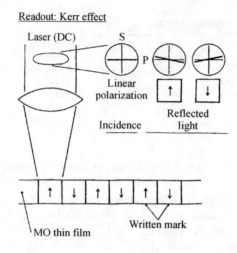

Figure 8.1 Readout mechanism of Magneto-Optical disks.

irradiated and scanned track is uniformly directed along that of the magnetic field for erase. In the write mechanism of ordinary MO disks, a laser beam whose intensity is modulated according to data is directed to the MO thin film. The spot irradiated by the modulated high intensity beam is heated above the Curie point. The magnetization is directed by the magnetic field for writing whose direction is opposite to that for erasure. In the figure, the erasure produces upward magnetic domains and the write process makes downward magnetic domains. Since ordinary MO disks have one value for the Curie point, the operation of light intensity modulation direct overwrite is impossible. However, LIM-DOW can be achieved using a medium having two operation temperatures. As shown in Figure 8.3, rare earth transition metal alloy thin films used for ordinary MO disks exhibit a hysteresis loop with 100% squareness space. By changing

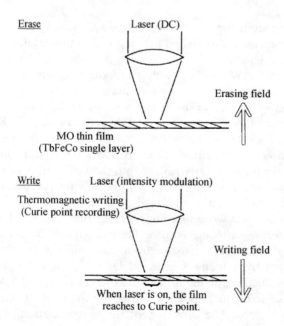

Figure 8.2 Erase/write mechanism of ordinary MO disks.

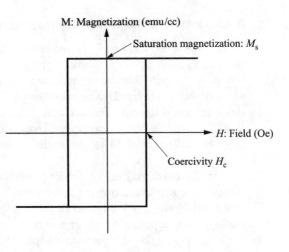

Figure 8.3 Schematic hysteresis loop of rare earth transition metal alloy thin film.

its elemental content and the composition, a rare earth transition metal alloy thin film can have various values of coercivity (Hc), saturation magnetization (Ms), coercivity energy (2MsHc [erg/cc]), Curie point (Tc), and Kerr rotation angle (θ_K). A typical coercivity energy is several to several tens of erg/cm^2 at room temperature. The controllability of the magnetic properties is important for materials for data storage media, since one can control and generate a submicron-size cylindrical domain. If very thin films of various rare earth transition metal alloys are laminated, they can be coupled through a magnetic exchange interaction.

It is possible for an exchange-coupled multilayered thin film to have an erase operation temperature (T_L) and a write operation temperature (T_H). As shown in Figure 8.4, if such an exchange-coupled multilayered MO thin film is irradiated and scanned by a laser beam whose intensity is modulated between P_H and P_L, corresponding to the temperatures of T_H and T_L, then temperature modulation occurs in the scanned track of the thin film. The sequential processes write and erase occur, and thus, LIM-DOW can be complete. It should be noted that the applied magnetic field has one direction throughout the LIM-DOW process.

The details of LIM-DOW outlined above is given in Section 8.2.

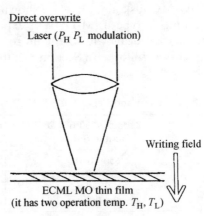

Figure 8.4 Outline of LIM-DOW operation.

8.1.3 Outline of High-Density Recording Technique

Since 1988 when the first generation ISO standardized MO disk became available in the market (Table 8.2), the wavelength of the laser diode has been decreased and the recording density has been increased. So-called 4X and 5X MO disk memories have already been achieved. The wavelengths of 2X and 3X are the same, though, the densities are different. The 1X and 2X use a mark position recording method (PPM). The 3X and the higher capacity drives use a mark edge recording method. The mark edge recording method is also called the pulse width modulation (PWM) recording method.

In the mark position recording method, digital information of "1" and "0" corresponds to a mark and a gap between marks, respectively, so that the length of a mark is constant. In the mark edge recording method, as shown in Figure 8.5, digital information "1" corresponds to either a trailing or leading edge of the written marks, so that the length of mark and gap varies with the run length of "0." Though 1X and 3X use the same mark length, the bit length of 3X is a half of that of 1X. One can see that the mark edge recording method can achieve about twice the recording density as the mark position recording method. It should be noted that the bit length in 3X and 4X examples in Table 8.2 does not correspond directly to the length of a "1" or a "0" in Figure 8.5, because a coding scheme called run length limited (R.L.L.) coding is executed between them. In an R.L.L. coding scheme, the information digital data are converted so that the run length of "0" is limited; for example, one to seven in 1–7 R.L.L. and two to seven in 2–7 R.L.L.

To practice the mark edge recording scheme, it is necessary to solve the thermal interference problem. As shown in Figure 8.6, thermomagnetic writing with heating by a simple waveform of laser intensity makes a tear drop shaped mark. In this case, mark edge loci are shifted and it is difficult to reproduce the data. This is also the case with the LIM-DOW operation. The improved waveform of a laser intensity shown in Figure 8.6 has solved this problem, which is discussed in detail in Section 8.3.

8.1.4 Objective and Structure of this Chapter

Since 1984 when the idea of LIM-DOW was developed, major improvements have been made. The current LIM-DOW MO disk memories perform the function specified for the next generation ISO MO disk memories. For the ISO 3X MO disk memories shown in Table 8.2, LIM-DOW products are available in the market. The first products of 3X LIM-DOW MO disk and drive are shown in Figure 8.7. For the ISO 4X and the later product, a media type, LIM-DOW is expected to be officially supplied.

This chapter deals with the main research issues of LIM-DOW. The structure of this chapter is as follows. In Section 8.2, the principles of LIM-DOW are discussed and

TABLE 8.2 Densities and Capacities of MO Disk Memories

Density	Capacity/130mm Ø Double-Sided	Track Pitch	Bit Length	Laser Wavelength
1X	650 Mbyte	1.60µ	1.00µ	0.83µ
2X	1.3 GByte	1.39µ	0.83µ	0.78µ
3X	2.0 GByte	1.34µ	0.56µ	0.78µ
4X	2.5 GByte	1.15µ	0.50µ	0.68µ

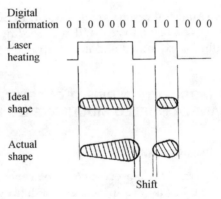

Digital
information 0 1 0 0 0 0 1 0 1 0 1 0 0 0

Laser
heating

Ideal
shape

Actual
shape

Shift

Figure 8.5 Thermal interference problem in high-density mark edge recording.

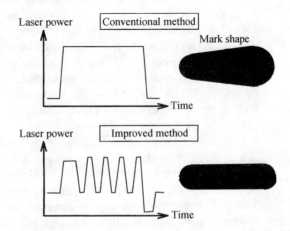

Laser power   Conventional method

Mark shape

Time

Laser power   Improved method

Time

Figure 8.6 Improved waveform of laser light modulation to solve thermal interference problem.

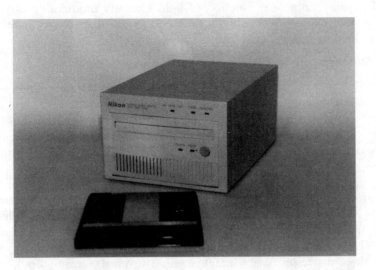

Figure 8.7 3X LIM-DOW MO disk and drive.

the experimental results are described. In Section 8.3, the thermal properties of a LIM-DOW disk are analyzed and a recording compensation technique for high-density recording is explained and demonstrated.

8.2 LIGHT MODULATION DIRECT OVERWRITE ON EXCHANGE-COUPLED MULTILAYERED MO DISK

8.2.1 Introduction

An MO erase/write process could be generally explained as a kind of cyclic process. It could be taken as a reciprocal-engine-like cyclic process; between the maximum and the minimum energy levels which correspond to the upward and downward moment magnetic domains, respectively, the magnetic moment is going back and forth by the action force of both the magnetic field applied for erase/write and the heat supplied by the modulated light intensity.

If one would try to make a direct overwrite mechanism by using the action force of modulated magnetic field, which is called a vector quantity having both direction and magnitude, it would be easy. This is the so called, Magnetic Field Modulation Direct Overwrite (MFM-DOW) [1]–[8]. This could be taken as a hybrid technology between hard disk and MO disk. As mentioned previously, this is not suitable for high speed data transfer. On the other hand, if one would try to make a direct overwrite mechanism on an ordinary single layered rare earth transition metal MO disk by using the action force of modulated temperature or heat, which is a scalar quantity, it would not be easy. It was recently reported that it is feasible to achieve a light intensity modulation direct overwrite function on a single layered rare earth transition metal MO material. The disk structure is especially designed for this method: The erase/write condition is determined by both the duration and the power value of the laser pulse for recording [9], [10]. To make this method practical, it is essential to have the degree of freedom to set the erase/write condition over a wide margin.

To make a practical function of light intensity modulation direct overwrite, the erase/write cyclic processes should be modified. In other words, a new partial process having three or more energy levels is necessary.

8.2.2 Process of LIM-DOW

LIM-DOW process described here is a cyclic process iterating among the three energy levels of four energy levels corresponding to the magnetization state of the exchange-coupled double-layered thin film of rare earth transition metal. This LIM-DOW process has a new partial process; an initialization process besides the erase/write process. The maximum energy level among the three levels is realized when the initialization process pumps up the magnetization energy state.

The write process included in LIM-DOW is substantially the same as the existing write process; a magnetization reversal process caused by the applied magnetic field and heating by laser irradiation. On the other hand, the erase process included in the LIM-DOW process utilizes a copy process observed in exchange-coupled double-layered thin films. This erase process is caused by the coupling force and heating by laser irradiation. These three processes, write (magnetization reversal), erase (copy), and initialization processes are the essential LIM-DOW functions.

Figure 8.8 shows the process of LIM-DOW, going from the left side (initializing) to the right side. The following list explains how the exchange-coupled double-layered thin film works in the LIM-DOW process.

(a) As the disk rotates, one layer, the writing layer (abbreviated as W layer) of the two layers is initialized by the initialization field (H_{ini}), so that the magnetization of the W layer is directed in one direction.

(b) The high/low power laser beam makes a reversed/not reversed magnetic domain on the W layer.

(c) As the disk rotates and thus the heated local area moves outside the laser spot, its temperature decreases. Another layer (the memory layer or M layer) copies the magnetic domain written in (B). The information is transferred from the W layer to the M layer. The temperature where this copy process is carried out is the erase operation temperature (T_L) mentioned in Section 8.1.

8.2.3 Three Elemental Techniques

Figure 8.9 shows three elemental techniques in LIM-DOW technology. They are (1) the exchange-coupled double-layered media designed for LIM-DOW, (2) the intensity modulated laser pulse, and (3) the initialization field (H_{ini}). The LIM-DOW media could be made of at least the M layer and W layer. However, for higher performance and improved function, the present LIM-DOW media have more layers. The laser power for LIM-DOW is modulated between two levels: higher level (P_H) and lower level power (P_L). These two levels correspond to the LIM-DOW operation temperatures: T_H (write temperature) and T_L (erase temperature). The P_H irradiation heats the point over T_H, and P_L irradiation heats the point over T_L. Any other modulation in

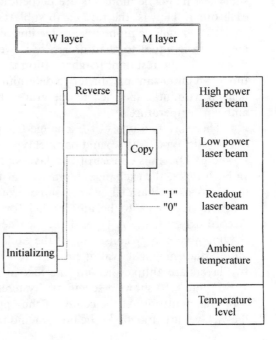

Figure 8.8 Process structure of LIM-DOW.

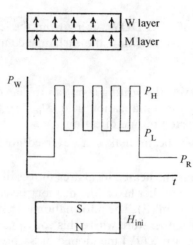

Figure 8.9 Three elemental techniques in LIM-DOW.

intensity, if it works in the same function, would be acceptable. P_R stands for the readout power level. An external field is needed for the initialization. There are other methods of initialization, such as using an initializing layer [11]–[14] included in the constitution of the exchange coupled multi-layered thin film.

8.2.3.1 LIM-DOW Exchange-Coupled Multilayered MO Material

LIM-DOW exchange-coupled multilayered thin films are all rare earth transition metal alloys. The thickness of each layer is in the range of several hundred to a thousand angstroms. As discussed in Chapters 2 and 7, both the rare earth atoms and the transition metal atoms have their own sublattice magnetic moments in the alloy. Both sublattice magnetic moments are perpendicular to the film surface, but antiparallel to each other. That is, the rare earth sublattice magnetic moments and transition metal sublattice magnetic moments are ferrimagnetically coupled. Accordingly, the net magnetization is equal to the difference between the two sublattice magnetizations. The direction of the resultant magnetization is the sense of a written domain. The temperature is an important parameter to determine the magnetization direction. If the sense is defined without a specified temperature, the temperature is room temperature or the ambient temperature.

There are two types of Exchange-Coupled Double-Layer (ECDL) films [15], [16]; antiparallel type (A type) and parallel type (P type) (refer to Chapter 7). The A type and P type ECDL films consist of two layers of different and the same senses, respectively. In both types, the exchange interaction at the interface works so as to make magnetic moments to be parallel for the same group (TM or RE) atoms (ferrocoupling) and magnetic moments to be antiparallel for the different group atoms (ferricoupling). Accordingly, for the A type, if the two net magnetizations of two layers are parallel, the potential energy consisting of the exchange interaction at the interface is high and an interface magnetic wall is present. For the P type, if the two net magnetizations of two layers are antiparallel, an interface magnetic wall is present at the interface.

Figure 8.10 shows a schematic hysteresis loop of an A type LIM-DOW ECDL at room temperature. At the center of the figure, the loops of ECDL of the M layer and the W layer are drawn. At the bottom and top, the loops of the W layer and M layer are

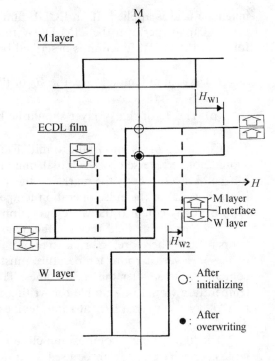

Figure 8.10 Schematic M-H hysteresis loop of LIM-DOW ECDL film.

given. The magnetization states are drawn beside the center loop. The blank arrow shows the net magnetization. The top column in the subfigure is for the M layer. The bottom is the loop for the W layer. In this figure, the "down/down" (downward directed moment in M layer/downward directed moment in W layer) and "up/up" are realized when the large positive and negative magnetic fields are applied, respectively. It should be noted that the down/down and up/up state are stable at zero field. In the down/down and up/up state, there is an interface magnetic wall. The double line between the top and bottom columns represents the interface magnetic wall.

The hysteresis loops of an ECDL film exhibit both major and minor loops, as shown in Figure 8.10, except for a highly coupled ECDL P type film. The magnetic field where the net magnetization reversal of a layer of ECDL film occurs is called a reversal field or a switching field: H_{sw}. The H_{sw} is different from the intrinsic H_c where the layer is not coupled within an ECDL film. The difference ($H_w = |H_{sw} - H_c|$) is proportional to the coupling energy, which is identical to the interface wall energy (σ_w [erg/cm^2]).

The H_{sw} and H_w are then given as

$$H_{sw} = H_c \pm H_w \tag{8.1}$$

$$H_w = \sigma_w/(2M_s t) \tag{8.2}$$

where σ_w is the interface magnetic wall energy, t is the thickness of the layer, and M_s is the magnetization of the layer. In Figure 8.10, the H_w of the M layer is H_{w1}, and the H_w of the W layer is H_{w2} [16].

Similar to the tightly coupled P type ECDL film explained above, both the layers of an ECDL film could have the reversal at the same time when a certain magnitude of magnetic field is applied. If an ECDL film exhibits such a coupling at room temperature, it cannot perform the LIM-DOW function at all. The main condition necessary for the LIM-DOW function is described below, with the help of Figure 8.11.

(a) At room temperature, the H_c of the M layer should be larger than that of the W layer.

(b) The T_c of the W layer should be higher than that of the M layer.

Condition (a) is important to initialize the W layer, not the M layer. The M layer should not be reversed by the initializing magnetic field. The condition (b) is necessary for the M layer to copy the marks on the W layer. The Curie point of the M layer (T_{c1}) is nearly equal to the erase operation temperature (T_L). The Curie point of the W layer (T_{c2}) is nearly equal to the write operation temperature (T_H).

The initializing field reverses the magnetization direction of the W layer at room temperature. Therefore, in order to reduce the magnitude of the initializing field, the H_c of the W layer at room temperature must be made small. The higher the dominant content is, the smaller the H_c becomes. The TM-rich W layer with small H_c at room temperature would be suitable for writing microdomains. On the other hand, the RE-rich W layer with small H_c at room temperature is suitable for uniform circular shape domains.

The film having a composition close to the compensation composition and with a large coercivity energy can be used as an M layer. The reason is as follows. The large coercivity energy makes written marks stable. In the case of the film with a composition close to the compensation composition, the coercivity at room temperature is large and thus the switching field, H_{sw}, could also be large.

An example which satisfies the conditions (a) and (b) is an A-type ECDL film of TM-rich M layer and RE-rich W layer. Such an ECDL film could be useful for direct overwrite under the condition given below.

1. The H_{sw} of the W layer should be larger than the H_{sw} of M layer at room temperature.

$$H_{c1} - \sigma_w/(2M_{s1}t_1) > H_{c2} - \sigma_w(2M_{s2}t_2) \qquad (8.3)$$

2. The H_{ini} should initialize W layer without any effect on M layer.

$$H_{c1} + \sigma_w/(2M_{s1}t_1) > H_{c2} + \sigma_w/(2M_{s2}t_2) \qquad (8.4)$$

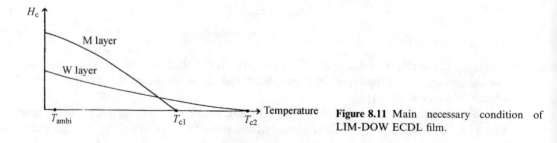

Figure 8.11 Main necessary condition of LIM-DOW ECDL film.

3. The W layer should keep the initialized direction of magnetization under zero field at room temperature.

$$H_{c2} > -\sigma_w/(2M_{s2}t_2) \tag{8.5}$$

where σ_w is the interface magnetic wall energy, H_{c1} is the H_c of the M layer, H_{c2} is the H_c of the W layer, t_1 is the thickness of the M layer, t_2 is the thickness of the W layer, M_{s1} is the magnetization of the M layer, and M_{s2} is the magnetization of the W layer.

8.2.3.2 Light Intensity Modulation (LIM)

The laser power for the LIM-DOW operation is modulated between the two levels P_H and P_L, when the target temperatures of P_H and P_L irradiation are near T_{c2} (the Curie point of the W layer) and T_{c1} (the Curie point of the M layer), respectively. The readout laser power, P_R should be lower than P_H and P_L, but large enough that the shot noise in the photo diode is small compared to P_R.

The laser power controller (LPC) in an MO disk drive should have enough tolerance to set the laser power levels. The laser power margins of levels P_H, P_L, and P_R of the LIM-DOW disk drive, should have enough tolerance for reliable operation. An ordinary MO disk drive without LIM-DOW function has only two power setting margins for the write power, P_W and read power, P_R. The absolute value of P_H, is usually 40 to 50% larger than P_W for an ordinary MO disk drive. However, the erase power P_E for an ordinary MO disk drive, which is DC power, is nearly equal to the write pulse power, P_W. There is no need for such a large DC erase power in the LIM-DOW operation. Ultimately, the load given to the laser diode by the LIM-DOW operation is not so different from that of the ordinary erase/write operation. Therefore, the laser diodes used for an ordinary erase/write operation is still usable for the LIM-DOW operation.

8.2.3.3 Initialization

Figure 8.12 shows the schematic hysteresis loop, where the vertical axis is the free energy level of each state of magnetization in the LIM-DOW process. The left-hand side of the horizontal axis is the temperature, and the right-hand side represents the field strength of the initialization. The solid and dotted lines are for the P_H- and P_L processes, respectively. The temperatures T_H and T_L correspond to those for P_H and P_L, respectively. (In the case of the LIM-DOW MO disk with the additional initializing and switching layers [11]–[14], the heating and cooling processes could increase the free energy.) If the state is "up/down" (upward and downward directions of the moment in the M- and W layers, respectively), the initialization gives the interface magnetic wall energy after initializing the W layer direction. One of the four states of magnetization of ECDL film, which is "down/down" in Figure 8.12, is not used in the LIM-DOW process.

8.2.4 Mechanism of LIM-DOW

The three essential processes mentioned in the previous Section 8.2.3 are presented in Figure 8.13. While a disk rotates as indicated by an arrow, every point of the disk undergoes the initializing field (H_{ini}), and the magnetization direction of the W layer is oriented along the initializing field. During the initialization, the magnetization direction of the M layer is unchanged, because of its high H_c. After that, the laser light from

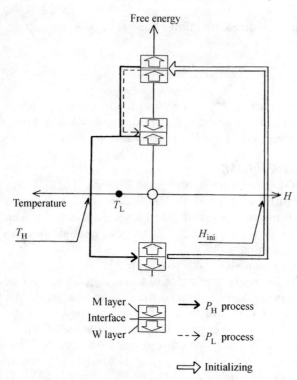

Figure 8.12 LIM-DOW cyclic process loop.

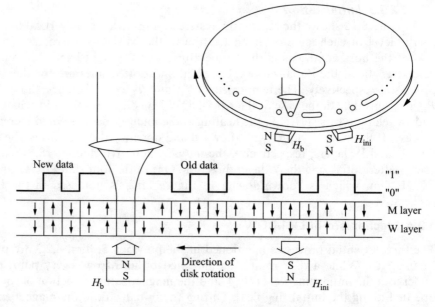

Figure 8.13 Layout of LIM-DOW components.

the optical head objective lens irradiates the disk. The laser power is modulated between the two levels (P_H and P_L) according to the data to be stored.

In the case of Figure 8.13, the writing bias field is upward and the disk has a P-type ECDL film, and thus, P_H and P_L pulse irradiation produces the upward state and the downward state, respectively, of directed microdomains on the M layer.

The P_H process is explained as follows. Each point where the P_H laser power is focused is heated over T_H. The direction of magnetization of the W layer over T_H is reversed by the H_b field, so that a written mark is made on the W layer. This process is the same as that of an ordinary MO disk. During the cooling after heating, the M-layer copies these written marks.

The P_L process is explained as follows. Each point where the P_L laser power is focused is heated over T_L but under T_H, so that W-layer magnetization is unchanged and keeps the initialized direction. The M layer coupled to this area of the W layer, during cooling after this process, copies the unchanged magnetization state determined by the initialization.

Figure 8.14 shows the states of magnetization during the LIM-DOW process. The film is A-type ECDL. The important results given in Figure 8.14 may be summarized as follows. Immediately after the initialization, the first state is either up/up or down/up. The magnetization direction of the W layer is up, but that of the M layer is either up or down. For both cases, the direction of magnetization of the W layer for the copy operation depends on whether the laser power level is either P_H or P_L. P_H process makes it downward, and P_L process makes it upward. After that, M layer copies the W layer, so that the states of magnetization immediately before initializing are either up/down or down/up. The initializing process keeps the values of the M layer unchanged,

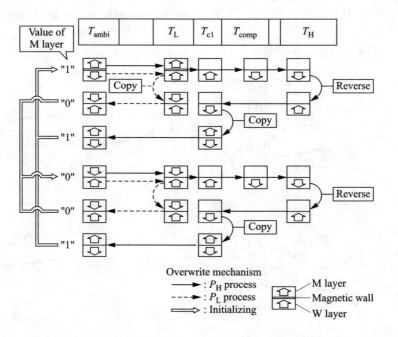

Figure 8.14 State transition of magnetization during LIM-DOW process.

but orients the magnetization of the W layer upward. At anytime after the P_H process, the magnetization direction of the M layer is upward and at anytime after P_L process, it is downward.

In Figure 8.15, the M-H hysteresis loops of a LIM-DOW ECDL film observed with a TM-rich TbFeCo M layer and a RE-rich GdFeCo W layer at the four characteristic operational temperature levels T_{ambi}, T_L, T_{c1} and T_H are shown. It should be noted that, the minor loop at T_{ambi} is from the W layer. However, the minor loop at T_L is from the M layer.

Since the coercivity and the magnetization of the M layer vanish at T_{c1}, only the W layer loop can be observed at T_{c1} and high temperatures. At T_H, H_b overcomes the H_c of the W layer and thus marks can be written. It should be noted that the initialized states; up/up and down/up made by the upward initializing field at T_{ambi} would be automatically up/down and down/down, respectively, at T_H due to the T_{comp} of the W layer. So, the magnetization of the W layer is reversed by upward H_b.

The minor loop of the M layer at T_L observed shifted away from the vertical axis in Figure 8.15 suggests that the exchange coupling energy overcomes the coercivity energy of the M layer. On the other hand, the coercivity energy at T_{ambi} overcomes the exchange coupling energy so that the state having the interface magnetic wall; up/up is energetically stable at zero field. Accordingly, as shown in Fig. 8.16, the coercivity energy of the M layer at T_L becomes smaller than the exchange coupling energy.

8.2.5 Experiment and Result

Figure 8.17 shows the frequency dependence of readout carrier-to-noise ratio (C/N) of a LIM-DOW MO disk with TbFe M layer and TbFeCo W layer. The linear velocity of the laser spot is 13.4 m/s, the wavelength of the laser diode 830 nm, the

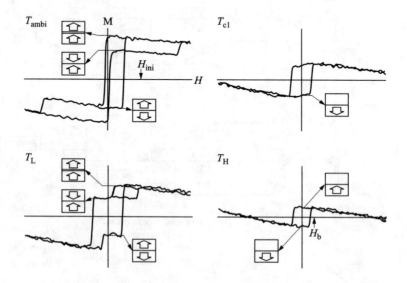

Figure 8.15 Observed hysteresis loops at characteristic temperature levels.

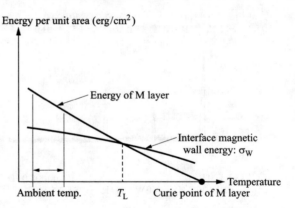

Figure 8.16 Inversion between exchange coupling energy and coercivity energy of M layer.

numerical aperture (NA) of the objective lens 0.55, and the laser power levels of P_L and P_H are 4.6 and 8.6 mW, respectively. The written signal is a repetitive one of rectangular shape with duty cycle of 50%. The rise time and fall time of the laser power are both about 10 ns, and the reading power P_R is 1.5 mW. H_b and H_{init} are 200 and 7000 Oe, respectively. The readout C/N with a mark size about 0.8 mm is about 45 dB.

Figure 8.18 shows the LIM-DOW recorded signal. The top spectrum (a) shows that the 1 MHz signal direct overwritten on certain data can have 53.8 dB readout C/N. The bottom spectrum (b) shows that the 2 MHz signal direct overwritten on the 1 MHz signal can have a C/N of 52.3 dB. Though the 2 MHz written mark is smaller than the 1 MHz written mark, the 1 MHz signal is not observed in the bottom spectrum. The crosstalk of the residual signal, overwrite crosstalk, is not observed. In other words, prerecorded marks are completely erased by this LIM-DOW operation. It is an important feature that the erasability of pre-recorded marks is 100%.

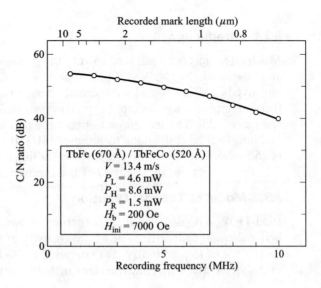

Figure 8.17 An example of frequency dependence of readout C/N.

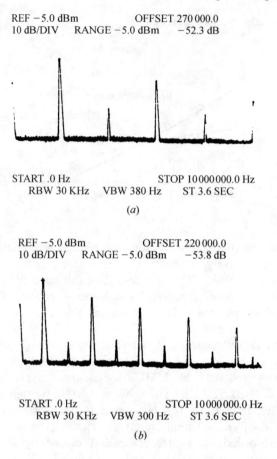

REF −5.0 dBm   OFFSET 270 000.0
10 dB/DIV   RANGE −5.0 dBm   −52.3 dB

START .0 Hz   STOP 10 000 000.0 Hz
    RBW 30 KHz   VBW 380 Hz   ST 3.6 SEC
                    (a)

REF −5.0 dBm   OFFSET 220 000.0
10 dB/DIV   RANGE −5.0 dBm   −53.8 dB

START .0 Hz   STOP 10 000 000.0 Hz
    RBW 30 KHz   VBW 300 Hz   ST 3.6 SEC
                    (b)

Figure 8.18 An example of the readout spectrum of a LIM-DOW recorded signal.

8.3 HIGH-DENSITY RECORDING ON A LIM-DOW DISK

8.3.1 Introduction

Much effort has been put into solving the problems for high density, high performance and low cost LIM-DOW [17]–[22]. One of several issues impacting practical use of such improved LIM-DOW disks, a thermal interference is the one which must be solved. The thermal interference should be precompensated for [23], or made uniform [24], or eliminated [25]. The technique to make the thermal interference uniform is called thermal interference uniforming technique (TIU). It eliminates the data pattern dependence of the locus shift of leading edges and trailing edges of written marks.

In this section, the analysis of the thermal interference, is first discussed [26].

8.3.2 Model of Thermal Diffusion

LIM-DOW MO disks with the structure, shown in Figure 8.19, could be modified for better thermal properties. The heat diffusivity of thin film MO material was reported to be 1/3–1/4 of that of bulk MO material [27]. Both the specific heat C_ρ and the thermal diffusivity κ are nearly independent of temperature, slightly increasing over the Curie

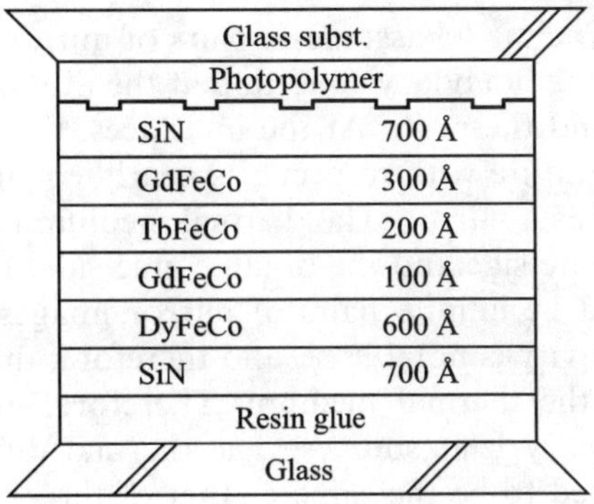

Glass subst.	
Photopolymer	
SiN	700 Å
GdFeCo	300 Å
TbFeCo	200 Å
GdFeCo	100 Å
DyFeCo	600 Å
SiN	700 Å
Resin glue	
Glass	

Figure 8.19 An example of the thin-film structure of a LIM-DOW MO disk.

temperature, since the Curie temperature is a second-order phase transition temperature. In this chapter, they are assumed to be unchanged. As shown in Figure 8.19, the thin films are sandwiched by two organic resin layers. In this chapter, a stack of the RE-TM amorphous films, and the dielectric films are considered as a thermal medium which has uniform thermal properties. The two organic resin layers insulate the heat flow from the thermal medium.

Figure 8.20 shows a SEM photograph of MO cross section perpendicular to the direction of the grooves.

We assume that the laser spot scanning axis in the thermal medium is the x-axis, and the y-axis is the axis orthogonal to the x-axis. The z-axis is the thermal medium depth axis. At the center of the thermal medium, z equals zero. The laser spot scanning velocity along the groove direction (x) is v [m/s]. The center of the laser spot is located at $(x\ y\ z) = (v \cdot s\ 0\ 0)$ when time $=$ s [s]. The heat input at time $=$ s [s] is given by $Q(s)$ [W/m^3] which is the product of the one- and two-dimensional Gaussian function:

$$Q(s) = W(s) \cdot \frac{1}{D_{\mathrm{M}} \cdot \sqrt{2\pi}} \cdot \exp\left(\frac{-z^2}{2 \cdot D_{\mathrm{M}}^2}\right) \cdot \frac{2}{\pi \cdot w_0^2} \cdot \exp\left(\frac{-2[(x - v \cdot s)^2 + y^2]}{w_0^2}\right) \quad (8.6)$$

where $W(s)$ is a laser power absorbed at time $=$ s, w_0 is a radius of laser spot, and D_{M} is the skin depth of the laser.

Figure 8.20 SEM cross section of a MO film on the grooves of a disk substrate.

The model assumes n pairs of mirror images of the heat source of $Q(s)$ in order to meet the boundary condition at the discontinuous interfaces between the thermal medium and the resin. At the interfaces, the boundary condition is that the derivative of temperature with respect z is nearly equal to zero. The discontinuous interface can be taken as a mirror. The thermal medium has two interfaces, i.e., at the organic material substrate side and the organic glue side. If the reflectance of the mirror is 100%, there should be infinite pairs of mirror images of the heat source $Q(s)$. However, the real reflectivity is not 100%, and therefore, the resin could not perfectly shut the heat flow from the thermal medium. Therefore, the model has a finite number of n pairs of imaginary heat sources. The thermal diffusivity of the organic material substrate is assumed to be the same as that of the organic glue. The larger the number of pairs n is, the more adiabatic the resin becomes. d [m] is the total thickness of thin films; MO and dielectric films. The temperature increment $\theta(t\,x\,y\,z)$ is the output given at t for a point (x, y, z), which is given as described.

$$\theta(t\,x\,y\,z) = \int_{\arctan\sqrt{t_M/t_{00}}}^{\arctan\sqrt{(t+t_M)/t_{00}}} \Theta_{00} \cdot \theta_z \cdot \theta_H\, d\varphi \tag{8.7}$$

$$t_M = \theta_M^2/2\kappa \tag{8.8}$$

$$t_{00} = t_0 - t_M \tag{8.9}$$

$$t_0 = W_0^2/8\kappa \tag{8.10}$$

$$\varphi = \varphi(s) = \arctan\sqrt{(t-s+t_M)t_{00}} \tag{8.11}$$

$$\Theta_{00} = \frac{W(s)}{C_\rho} \cdot \frac{1}{2\sqrt{2}} \cdot \left(\frac{1}{\pi}\right)^{1.5} \cdot \frac{1}{\kappa} \cdot \sqrt{\frac{1}{(W_0^2/4) - D_M^2}} \tag{8.12}$$

$$\theta_z = \sum_{i=-n}^{i=n} \exp[-(z-iD)^2/4\kappa t_{00}\tan^2\varphi] \tag{8.13}$$

$$\theta_H = \exp[-C_2 \cdot (F \cdot \cos^2\varphi + G_{00} + H_{00}/\cos^2\varphi)] \tag{8.14}$$

$$C_2 = 2/(1 - t_M/t_0) = 2(t_{00} + t_M)/t_{00} = 2(1 + t_M/t_{00}) \tag{8.15}$$

$$F = (X1 - V)^2 + Y^2 \tag{8.16}$$

$$X1 = x/W_0 - v \cdot t/W_0 \tag{8.17}$$

$$V = v \cdot t_0/W_0 \tag{8.18}$$

$$Y = y/W_0 \tag{8.19}$$

$$G_{00} = 2 \cdot V_{00} \cdot (X1 - V) \tag{8.20}$$

$$V_{00} = v \cdot t_{00}/W_0 \tag{8.21}$$

$$H_{00} = V_{00}^2 \tag{8.22}$$

Here, $W(s)$ is the product of the absorption coefficient of the disk and the laser power at $t = s$. When the laser power is a constant DC power, $W(s)$ is constant. Thus, when the laser power is constant, the saturated temperature increment is proportional to the laser power. In addition, a two-dimensional scalar field (temperature profile $\theta(x, y)$) is introduced which is derived from the $\theta(t, x, y, z)$ at t and $z = 0$. As the time of heating and cooling goes on, the heating and cooling temperature profiles can be defined. For heating with laser irradiation of long duration, the saturated temperature profile can be calculated. The steep and sharp ridgelines of the profiles are needed for high-density recording. The controllability of the mask shape is important to minimize edge jitter and also the laser power dependence of mark shape.

8.3.3 Parameter Fitting

8.3.3.1 Fitting Specific Heat; Measuring Thermal Efficiency

For fitting parameter C_ρ, the thermal efficiency E_T [°C/W] of the peak temperature on the saturated temperature profile raised by long duration laser heating was measured. Here, E_T is the slope of the measured lines, given in Figure 8.21. The threshold powers of P_H and P_L by long duration laser irradiation are subject to the disk ambient temperature, which is the base temperature. The higher the disk ambient temperature is, the lower the necessary write power becomes. In the figure, the minimum write power for each process is plotted.

The interception of the two lines of P_L and P_H with the x-axis corresponds to T_H (W-layer reversal temperature) and T_L (M-layer copy temperature), respectively, as mentioned in Section 8.2. When a disk is irradiated by a long duration P_L (threshold) power, a saturated temperature profile is formed whose peak is T_L at the laser spot. In the same manner, when a disk is irradiated by the long duration P_H (threshold) power, a saturated temperature profile is formed whose peak is T_H at the laser spot. It could be assumed that those two critical processes shown in the figure are both carried out at the peak temperature points on the saturated temperature profiles.

As mentioned previously, the temperature increment of each location on a saturated temperature profile is in proportion to the irradiated laser power. Therefore, P_H and P_L line have the same slope: [°C/W] and are parallel to each other. For Figure 8.21, $E_T = 43$ [°C/mW], and the specific heat C_ρ is fitted to be 6×10^6 [J/°C m³].

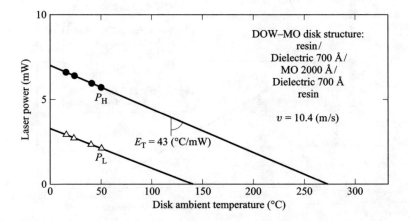

Figure 8.21 Disk ambient temperature dependence of the thresholds P_H and P_L.

8.3.3.2 Fitting Heat Diffusivity; Measuring Thermal Time Constants

For fitting κ, the thermal response function [27] of a disk must be measured. Figure 8.22 shows an example of the thermal response function of LIM-DOW MO disk. A thermal response function is obtained as follows. Periodically repetitive and plural laser pulses with duration D_p are irradiated onto a disk at a linear velocity v. The periodic cycle time is long enough so that the diffused heat from one pulse to the adjacent irradiation point can be negligible. For each D_p, the corresponding writing threshold power, P_{th} is measured. In Figure 8.22, the horizontal axis is D_p. In the top figure, the vertical axis is $1/P_{th}$ normalized by the saturated $1/P_{th}$ for sufficiently long D_p.

The top figure tells us how the peak temperature at each moment changes during heating with laser power irradiation which rises or steps up at time = zero and keeps a constant power for time > zero. It is a kind of a step response function called a thermal response function. In other words, it is the heating curve of a spot exposed to a step in laser power irradiation while the spot is scanning at velocity, v. On the vertical axis of the bottom figure, $(1 - 1/P_{th})$ is plotted in a logarithm scale showing a linear dependence. Therefore, LIM-DOW MO disks have an exponential thermal response function; $[1 - \exp(-t/\tau)]$. τ is a thermal time constant [26] of the response function. For the case of Figure 8.22, τ is 46 ns.

Based on various simulations with this model, one can say that κ is a function of τ. In this case, it is found by fitting that $\kappa = 7 \times 10^{-7}$ [m^2/s].

As mentioned in [26] and [28], τ dominates also the cooling process after the heating process by a laser pulse irradiation. It could be said that the bottom figure of Figure 8.22 shows such a cooling process.

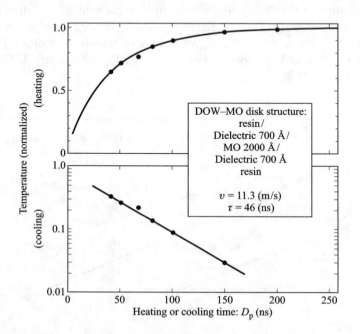

Figure 8.22 An example of the thermal response function of a LIM-DOW MO disk.

When κ is fitted according to τ, it is important that the velocity v decides whether the correlation between κ and τ is plus type or minus type. When v is relatively small, the smaller κ is, the larger τ is. On the other hand, when v is relatively large, the smaller κ is, the smaller τ is. In addition, $1/\tau$ is a linear function of v, which is mentioned in [28] and later in Section 8.3.4.

8.3.3.3 Fitting Adiabatic Index; Measuring Velocity Dependence of Writing Threshold Laser Power

For fitting n, we measure the velocity dependence of writing threshold of long duration laser power. In this measurement, the long pulse duration was used to saturate the thermal response at each v. In Figure 8.23, the pulse duration was 500 ns, and the period was 1000 ns, respectively. The threshold writing power for the P_L process as a function of velocity v is measured with a 1 MHz laser pulses. The vertical axis is the threshold laser power in a logarithm scale. The horizontal axis is the velocity v. An example of the fitting procedure is shown in Figure 8.24.

The threshold laser power is found to be in proportion to v^{α}. Judging from simulations with this model, one could say that n is a function of α, and that α becomes larger within the range of $0 < \alpha < 1$, when n becomes larger. The number of pairs of mirror images of the heat source, n, mentioned at Section 8.3.2 and Equation (8.13), and κ mentioned previously are both related to the heat diffusion. κ represents the averaged heat diffusivity in the thermal medium, and implies the relative difficulty of heat diffusion in the resin which is sandwiching the thermal medium. If n is zero, the heat diffusivity of the resin is equal to that of the thermal medium. The larger n is, the more the resin insulates the heat flow from the thermal medium. When n is large, the resin is taken as heat insulator and the heat supplied by laser power is confined in the thermal medium. α is found to be 0.75 for the measured values given in Figure 8.23. The parameter fitting the observed data yields the value of n to be 1, which is consistent with the value $\alpha = 1$. It is noted that this model could well simulate the actual diffusion of heat supplied by laser power focused and scanned onto LIM-DOW MO disks.

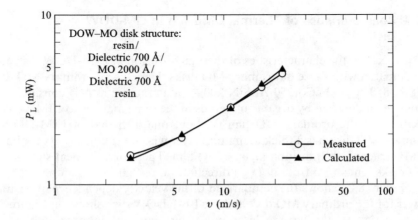

Figure 8.23 The velocity v dependence of writing threshold P_L of long duration laser power.

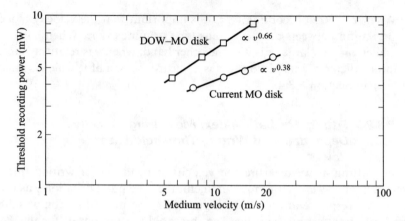

Figure 8.24 Comparison of the velocity dependence of writing threshold power.

It should be noted that the LIM-DOW MO disk used in these three parameter fitting experiments is a primitive type, two-layered one. The total thickness of MO films is 2000 Å, as shown in Figures 8.21, 8.22, and 8.23, while the disk shown in Figure 8.19 has a 1200 Å thick MO layer. The parameter fitting to the 1200 Å thick disk gives results as follows:

$$C_\rho = 3.9 \times 10^6 [\text{J/}^\circ\text{C m}^3] \tag{8.23}$$

$$\kappa = 4.0 \times 10^{-6} [\text{m}^2/\text{s}] \tag{8.24}$$

$$n = 11 \tag{8.25}$$

In addition, as mentioned previously, a heat sink or a heat radiator layer like an aluminum layer has recently been added to improve the thermal property of LIM-DOW MO disk. In such cases, the fitted parameters are different from these mentioned above.

8.3.4 Characteristics of Thermal Diffusion in LIM-DOW Disk

In this section, the characteristics of thermal diffusion in LIM-DOW disk are discussed, as compared with those of ordinary MO disks. Here, as an ordinary MO disk structure of SiN 850 Å, TbFeCo 250 Å, SiN 200 Å, aluminum 500 Å is considered. These thin films are sandwiched by organic materials in the same manner to LIM-DOW disks. The thickness of the ordinary MO film is about one fifth that of LIM-DOW disks. The ordinary MO disk has a thick aluminum layer whose heat diffusivity is about twice that of MO (rare earth transition metal alloy) film. Therefore, the heat supplied to ordinary MO disks tends to diffuse in (x-y) direction more than z direction.

Figure 8.24 shows the comparison of the velocity dependence of writing threshold power for the ordinary MO disk and the LIM-DOW disk shown in Figure 8.19. Also in this experiment, the writing laser pulse duration was long enough to saturate the thermal response. The vertical axis and horizontal axis are both scaled in logarithm.

The LIM-DOW disk has the $v^{0.66}$ dependence, whereas the ordinary MO disk has dependence of $v^{0.38}$.

When the velocity v is relatively slow, the transport of heat takes place mainly through heat diffusion. Then, the temperature increment due to the laser irradiation becomes almost independent of velocity, v, and thus the writing threshold power is in proportion to v^0. On the other hand, when the velocity is relatively large, the heat transport occurs mainly by the laser spot scanning on the disk, not by heat diffusion. Then, the temperature increment by laser irradiation depends on the scanning velocity, and thus the writing threshold power is proportional to v^α. If the scanning velocity is fast enough to neglect the diffusion of heat in materials, the temperature increment by laser irradiation is in inverse proportion to the velocity. When the velocity becomes larger, α converges to unity, where the slope is unity. $\alpha\,(0 \leq \alpha \leq 1)$ is related to the total diffusivity of heat in the disk. As mentioned, α is corresponding to n. When α is close to zero, the resin allows the heat flow to some extent. When α is close to unity, the resin almost insulates the heat flow from the thermal medium.

Figure 8.25 shows the comparison of the velocity dependence of the thermal time constant for DOW and ordinary MO media. The horizontal axis is the scanning velocity, v in linear scale. The vertical axis is the inverse of the thermal time constant, $1/\tau$. It is found that $1/\tau$ is a linear function of v for both the media, indicating that the thermal response becomes faster, when the velocity becomes faster. Figure 8.25 indicates that τ of LIM-DOW disk is larger than that of an ordinary MO disk for small velocity, and that it becomes smaller than that of an ordinary MO disk for larger velocity. Judging from this fact, one may say that the LIM-DOW disk is more heat-accumulative than an ordinary MO disk.

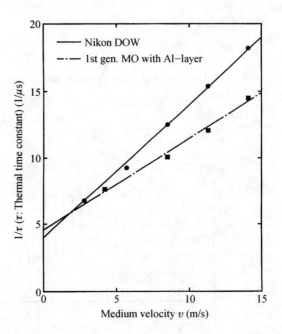

Figure 8.25 Comparison of the velocity dependence of thermal time constant.

8.3.5 High-Density Recording Experiment and Result

The TIU (thermal interference uniforming) technique on ordinary MO disks was first developed by Maeda et al. [29]. In this section, another explanation of the TIU mechanism is presented using the time constant of the thermal response function. As shown in Figure 8.26, the TIU consists of pulse train writing followed by a combination of heat shutoff and bias power heating. The TIU eliminates the variation in thermal interference in forming marks coded as various lengths of the mark and gap. Pulse train writing can make the thermal interference uniform when forming trailing edges. The combination of heat shutoff and bias power heating can make uniform the thermal interference when forming leading edges. In the figure, the pulse whose power is P_{w1} is the first pulse, and the pulses whose power are P_{w2} are the pulse-train pulse. A combination of the first pulse followed by a pulse-train pulse makes a mark. The dormant power P_{LB} is for the heat shutoff, and the bias power P_L is for the bias power heating. In this section, the TIU is discussed in detail and, it is demonstrated that the TIU works for the LIM-DOW disks as well as ordinary MO disks.

Since the LIM-DOW disk has a simple thermal response function which can be represented by a time constant τ, the conditions to produce such a uniform thermal interference are given as follows.

The conditions to produce uniform thermal interference in forming leading edges is first examined. The laser power changes as shown in Figure 8.27. The initial temperature of the disk is assumed to be zero. After forming a mark using a long DC P_W irradiation which gives the temperature increment, $E \cdot P_w$ at the center of laser spot (E corresponds to the thermal efficiency referred to in Section 8.3.3.1).

The following decay in temperature (T) takes place:
When $0 < t < t_{LB}$,

$$T = E \cdot [P_{LB} + (P_W - P_{LB}) \cdot \exp(-t/\tau)] \tag{8.26}$$

When $t_{LB} < 1$,

$$T =$$
$$E \cdot [P_{LB} + (P_W - P_{LB}) \cdot \exp(-t/\tau) + (P_L - P_{LB}) \cdot \{1 - \exp(-(t - t_{LB})/\tau)\} \tag{8.27}$$

Thus, if

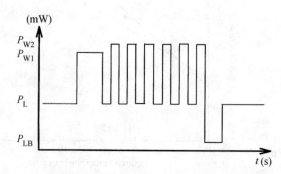

Figure 8.26 Waveform of laser power for TIU.

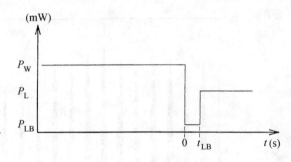

Figure 8.27 Waveform of laser power for heat shutoff and bias power heating.

$$(P_W - P_{LB}) \cdot \exp(-t_{LB}/\tau) = P_L - P_{LB} \tag{8.28}$$

then one has

$$T(t > t_{LB}) = E \cdot P_L \tag{8.29}$$

When Equation (28) is satisfied, the temperature is constant after $t = t_{LB}$. In other words, Equation (28) ensures the uniform thermal interference when forming the leading edge of the next mark at $t_{W1} + N \cdot t_0$. Thus, the condition is that t_{LB} in Equation (28) should be set smaller than the minimum gap length used in coding. In practical cases, a relaxation must be allowed, because a slight fluctuation of temperature in forming the leading edge of the next mark could be allowed. In addition, when the LIM-DOW disk is used, the temperature during the heat shutoff and bias power heating should be high enough to erase prerecorded marks.

The condition to produce a uniform thermal interference in forming trailing edges is given as follows. Suppose that the laser power changes as shown in Figure 8.28, and that, the disk initial temperature is zero. The bias power heating gives at the saturated temperature $E \cdot P_L$ at the center of the laser spot on the disk.

When $0 < t < t_0 - t_{w2}$,

$$T = E \cdot \lfloor P_L + (P_{w1} - P_L) \cdot \{1 - \exp(-t_{w1}/\tau)\} \cdot \exp(-t/\tau) \rfloor \tag{8.30}$$

When $t_0 - t_{w2} < t < t_0$,

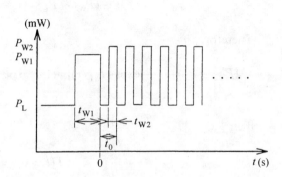

Figure 8.28 Waveform of laser power for pulse train recording.

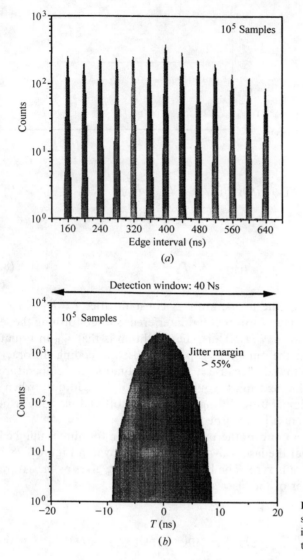

Figure 8.29 Practical usage of TIU. In (*a*) the signal for various edge intervals is shown and in (*b*) the distribution of edge locations, in the time domain, is shown for 10^5 samples.

$$T = E \cdot [P_L + (P_{w1} - P_L) \cdot \{1 - \exp(-t_{w1}/\tau)\} \cdot \exp(-t/\tau)$$
$$+ (P_{w2} - P_L) \cdot \{1 - \exp\{-(t - (t_0 - t_{w2}))/\tau\}\}] \tag{8.31}$$

Therefore, if

$$(P_{w1} - P_L) \cdot \{1 - \exp(-t_{w1}/\tau)\} \cdot \{1 - \exp(-t_0/\tau)\} = (P_{w2} - P_L) \cdot \{1 - \exp(-t_{w2}/\tau), \tag{8.32}$$

then

$$T(t = 0) = T(t = t_0) \tag{8.33}$$

Thus, when Equation (8.32) is satisfied,

$$T(t = Nt_0) = \text{a constant} \tag{8.34}$$

where N is zero or a positive integer and t_0 the clock period used in coding. In other words, when the pulse train shown in Figure 8.28 forms marks, Equation (32) ensures uniform thermal interference in forming trailing edges at $t = t_{w1} + N \cdot t_0$.

Miyamoto et al. [30] discussed the first experimental result of TIU for high-density recording using the LIM-DOW disk. Figure 8.29 shows the result for so called 3X high density. The LIM-DOW disk exhibits the detection window margin of 55% of the clock period of 40 ns for its recorded random data coded with 0.56 μm/bit (1–7) R.L.L. PWM recording.

Figure 8.29(*a*) shows the appearance frequency of each data pattern in the random data at 40 ns interval. The time interval from mark edge to mark edge is plotted on the horizontal axis. The minimum of pattern length is four times the clock period; 160 ns. Figure 8.29(*b*) shows the distribution for all the overlapped fragments given in the top figure.

It is found that the total distribution of edge locus occupies 45% of the clock period of 40 ns, and the readout window margin of 55% of the clock period.

The ordinary MO disk has also been examined in the same manner. It is found that the readout window margin is 50% of the clock period, 40 ns. Therefore, it is confirmed that the TIU works on LIM-DOW MO disks as well as on ordinary MO disks.

REFERENCES

[1] F. Tanaka, S. Tanaka, and S. Suzuki, "The Overwriting Characteristics of Magneto-Optical Disk by Magnetic Field Modulation Method," Invited Presentation, *IEEE Trans. Magn.*, MAG-23, no. 5, p. 2695, 1987.

[2] T. Nakao, M. Ojima, Y. Miyata, S. Okamine, H. Sukeda, N. Ohta, and Y. Takeuchi, "High Speed Overwritable Magneto-Optic Recording," Proceedings of ISOM'87, *Japan J. Appl. Phys.*, 26, Supplement 26-4, p. 149, 1987.

[3] F. Tanaka, S. Tanaka, and N. Imamura, "Magneto-Optical Recording Characteristics of TbFeCo Media by Magnetic Field Modulation Method," *Japan J. Appl. Phys.*, vol. 26, no. 2, p. 231, 1987.

[4] D. Rugar, "Magnetooptic Direct Overwrite Using a Resonant Bias Coil," *IEEE Trans. Magn.*, vol. 24, no. 1, p. 666, 1988.

[5] H. Miyamoto, T. Niihara, H. Sukeda, M. Takahashi, T. Nakao, M. Ojima, and N. Ohta, "Domain and Write-Read Characteristics for Magnetic Field Modulated Magneto-Optical Disk with High Data Transfer Rate," *J. Appl. Phys.*, vol. 66, no. 12, p. 6138, 1989.

[6] D. C. Cheng, T. W. McDaniel, and C. R. Davis, "Domain Edge Formation and Jitter Characteristics in Thermomagnetic Recording with Magnetic Field Modulation," *IEEE Trans. Magn.*, vol. 26, no. 5, p. 1903, 1990.

[7] M. Aeschlimann, M. Scheinfein, J. Unguris, F. J. A. M. Gredanus, and S. Klahn, "Magnetic-Field-Modulated Written Bits in TbFeCo Thin Films: Transmission Electron Microscopy Lorentz and Scanning Electron Microscopy with Polarization Analysis Studies," *J. Appl. Phys.*, vol. 68, no. 9, p. 4710, 1990.

[8] S. Kawasaki, K. Ishizuka, S. Katsuda, and M. Soumuta, "Magneto-Optical Disk for Magnetic Field Modulation Recording Method with Multi-Pulsed Laser Irradiation," *Japan J. Appl. Phys.*, vol. 32, p. 3163, 1993.

[9] M. D. Schultz and M. H. Kryder, "Domain Erasure and Formation in Direct Overwrite Magneto-Optic Recording," *J. Appl. Phys.*, vol. 68, no. 10, p. 5293, 1990.

[10] M. D. Schultz, Tsing Xue, and M. H. Kryder, "Direct Observation of Magnetization Dynamics in Spinning Magneto-optic Disks," Invited Presentation, *J. Appl. Phys.*, vol. 73, no. 10, p. 5776, 1993.

[11] T. Fukami, Y. Nakaki, T. Tokunaga, M. Toguchi, and K. Tsutsumi, "Novel Direct Overwriting Technology for Magneto-Optical Disks by Exchange-Coupled RE-TM Quadrilayered Films," *J. Appl. Phys.*, vol. 67, no. 9, p. 4415, 1990.

[12] T. Tokunaga, Y. Nakaki, T. Fukami, and K. Tsutsumi, "Overwrite Characterisitics of Magneto-Optical Disks by Exchange-Coupled RE-TM Quadrilayered Films," *IEEE Trans. Magn.*, vol. 27, no. 6, p. 5112, 1991.

[13] Y. Nakaki, T. Fukami, T. Tokunaga, Y. Kawano, and T. Tsutsumi, "High Density Overwriting in Exchange-Coupled Magneto-Optical Multilayer Films," *IEEE Trans. Magn.*, vol. 28, no. 5, p. 2509, 1992.

[14] T. Tokunaga, Y. Nakaki, T. Fukami, and K. Tsutsumi, "Exchange-Coupled Quadrilayer Films for Overwrite MO Disks," Invited Presentation, Proceedings of MORIS'92, *J. Magn. Soc. Japan*, vol. 17, Supplement S1, p. 357, 1993.

[15] S. Tsunashima, T. Kobayashi, H. Tsuji, and S. Uchiyama, "Thermomagnetic Writing on Exchange-Coupled Amorphous Rare-Earth Iron Double-Layer Films," *IEEE Trans. Magn.*, MAG-17, p. 2840, 1981.

[16] T. Kobayashi, H. Tsuji, S. Tsunashima, and S. Uchiyama, "Magnetization Process of Exchange-Coupled Ferrimagnetic Double-Layered Film," *Japan J. Appl. Phys.*, vol. 20, p. 2089, 1981.

[17] T. Hosokawa, J. Saito, H. Matsumoto, H. Iida, A. Okamuro, S. Kokai, and H. Akasaka, "C/N Improvement of Direct Overwrite Magneto-Optical Disk by Adding a GdFeCo Readout Layer," *Japan J. Appl. Phys. Series 6*, Proceedings of ISOM'91, p. 55, 1991.

[18] K. Aratani, Y. Muto, M. Kaneko, K. Watanabe, and H. Makino, "Overwriting on a Magneto-Optical Disk with Magnetic Triple Layers by Means of the Light Intensity Modulation Method," *Proceedings of SPIE*, ODS'89, p. 258, 1989.

[19] M. Kaneko, K. Aratani, Y. Mutoh, A. Nakaoki, K. Watanabe, and H. Makino, "The Interface Wall Structure of Magnetic Triple-Layer Film for Overwriting by Light Intensity Modulation," Proc. ISOM'89, *Japan J. Appl. Phys.*, vol. 28, Supplement 28-3, p. 27, 1989.

[20] K. Hayashi and O. Okada, "Improvement in Recording Power Sensitivity for Overwritable MO media by RE-rich GdNdFeCo Control Layer," *IEEE Trans. Magn.*, vol. 27, no. 6, p. 5100, 1991.

[21] Y. Muto, T. Shimouma, A. Nakaoki, K. Suzuki, and M. Kaneko, "Design of the Intermediate Layer in the Overwritable Magnetic Triple-Layer Disk," *Proceedings of MORIS'91*, p. 311, 1992.

[22] A. Nakaoki, M. Arai, H. Owa, and M. Kaneko, "Double-Capacity Overwritable Magneto-Optical Disk Using Magnetic Triple-Layer Film," Invited Presentation, Proceedings of MORIS'92, *J. Magn. Soc. Japan*, vol. 17, Supplement S1, p. 363, 1993.

[23] J. Saito, H. Akasaka, H. Birecki, and C. Perlov, "Demonstration of High Data Density Recording on Direct Overwrite Magneto-Optical Disk," *IEEE Trans. Magn.*, vol. 28, p. 2512, 1992.

[24] J. Saito, K. Morita, S. Kurita, M. Doi, Y. Aoki, and H. Akasaka, "Modeling Thermal Diffusion of Scanned and Focused Laser Power on Direct Overwrite Magneto-Optical Disk," *Japan J. Appl. Phys.*, vol. 32, no. 11B, Proceedings of ISOM/ODS'93, p. 5197, 1993.

[25] H. Wakabayashi and F. Yamada, "Short-Pulsed Laser Writing in Magneto-Optical Recording," Proceedings of MORIS'92, *J. Magn. Soc. Japan*, vol. 17, Supplement S1, p. 218, 1993.

[26] J. Saito, H. Matsumoto, T. Hosokawa, A. Okamuro, K. Miyata, and H. Akasaka, "Direct Overwrite Magneto-Optical Disk and High Data Density Recording," Proceedings of MORIS'92, *J. Magn. Soc. Japan*, vol. 17, Supplement S1 p. 353, 1993.

[27] H. Nakagawa, S. Nakamura, M. Takahashi, and A. Arimoto, "Estimating The Conductivity of Magneto-Optical Recording Media," *Applied Optics*, vol. 31, no. 22, p. 4559, 1992.

[28] K. Miyamoto, J. Saito, and H. Akasaka, "High-speed Response to Laser Heating and Cooling in Thermo-magnetic Writing on Magneto-Optical Disk Memory," *Proceedings of SPIE ODS'94*, vol. 2338, p. 333, 1994.

[29] T. Maeda, F. Kirino, T. Toda, and H. Ide, "Write Control Method for High Density Magneto-Optical Disk System," *IEEE Trans. Mag.*, vol. 29, pp. 3787–3789, 1993.

[30] H. Miyamoto, M. Ojima, T. Toda, T. Nishihara, T. Maeda, J. Saito, H. Matsumoto, T. Hosokawa, and H. Akasaka, "2GB/130mm Capacity Direct Overwrite Magneto-Optical Disk," *Japan J. Appl. Phys.*, vol. 32 no. 11B, p. 5457 1993.

MAGNETICALLY INDUCED SUPERRESOLUTION

Masahiko Kaneko

9.1 INTRODUCTION

Magneto-optical (MO) disks with a capacity of 650 MB per double-sided 130 mm disk appeared in the market in 1988, with a capacity of 128 MB per single-sided 90 mm disk in 1991, and 1.0 GB per 130 mm single-sided disk in 1994, which is so called 3X disk (3 times that of the first generation capacity). The capacity of the first two disks is based on the areal density which is given by a bit length of 0.8–0.9 μm and a track pitch of 1.6 μm. The evolution of the density and capacity is discussed in Chapter 1. Higher capacity is required for applications such as digital moving pictures and multimedia. Various techniques to increase capacity have been investigated including mark length recording, zoning, short wavelength recording. In addition to these techniques, magnetically induced superresolution (MSR) technique [1], [2] was first demonstrated in 1991. MSR is the technique by which the resolving power can be much increased with little change in the current optical system. Three detection methods were invented for MSR. They were the front aperture detection (FAD) method, the rear aperture detection (RAD) method, and the center aperture detection method (CAD). These methods are made possible by using exchange-coupled magnetic multilayer films described in Chapter 8.

After the introduction of the conventional detection in Section 9.2, the principles and characteristics of MSR disks will be discussed in detail.

9.2 LIMIT OF CONVENTIONAL DETECTION

9.2.1 Limit of Density Caused by the Recording Process

The magneto-optical recording is thermomagnetic recording which is caused by light pulses irradiated on the media under an external magnetic field H_{rec}. A recorded mark is determined as an area where the temperature is raised so high that the coercivity H_c of the magnetic layer becomes equal to the external magnetic field. Since the coercivity is a function of the temperature as shown in Figure 9.1, the contour of the recorded mark is an isotherm at T_w where $H_c(T_w) = H_{rec}$. A mark can be recorded on an MO disk as shown in Figure 9.2, if the amplitude and width of the light pulse is carefully controlled for the writing precompensation technique. Another technique using magnetic field modulation is also available for recording a mark which is not determined by the irradiated dc light but can be controlled by the modulated magnetic field [3]. A theore-

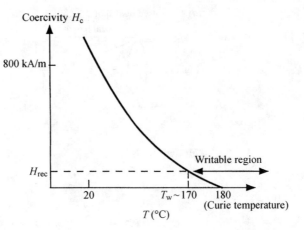

Figure 9.1 Typical temperature dependence of coercivity for a TbFeCo film. Data are written in the region where the coercivity has been reduced to below the external magnetic field H_{rec}.

tical minimum mark size diameter D which can be recorded is given by the magnetic bubble theory [4] as

$$D = \frac{\sigma_B}{M_s H_c} \tag{9.1}$$

where σ_B is the Bloch wall energy, M_s is the saturation magnetization.

9.2.2 Limit of Density Caused by the Readout Process

The diameter d of the first Airy disk for the light spot focused on the media through an objective lens is given by $2.44\ \lambda/(2NA)$ as shown in Figure 9.3(a), where λ is the light

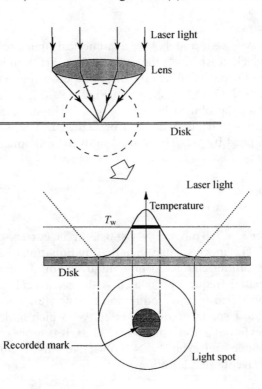

Figure 9.2. Method for recording a minute mark less than a light spot based on the principles of thermomagnetic recording.

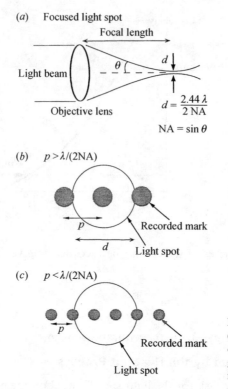

(a)   Focused light spot

(b) $p > \lambda/(2NA)$

(c) $p < \lambda/(2NA)$

Figure 9.3 Limit of conventional detection: (a) focused light spot on the disk through an objective lens; (b) recording wavelength p is greater than the optical limit $\lambda/(2NA)$; (c) p is less than the optical limit.

wavelength and NA is a numerical aperture of the objective lens. Recorded marks which move along the rotating disk direction are detected out by the light spot focused on the media. When the distance between two recorded marks is larger than the optical limit $\lambda/(2NA)$ as shown in Figure 9.3(b), a signal can be detected. When p is smaller than the optical limit as shown in Figure 9.3(c), however, optical diffraction theory states that no signal can be detected. The minimum mark length is the domain size defined by $p/2$. The mark length for the optical limit is given by

$$\frac{\lambda}{4(NA)} = 0.37 \ \mu m \tag{9.2}$$

for $\lambda = 780$ nm and NA = 0.53 in the current optics. Since the value given by Equation (9.1) is much smaller than that by Equation (9.2), the linear density is not determined by recording characteristics but by readout characteristics. From the viewpoint of the spatial frequency n which is the reciprocal of p, the amplitude of the signal can be evaluated by the modulation transfer function as will be described in Section 9.6. The cutoff spatial frequency is $2NA/\lambda$ which limits the absolute linear density for a conventional detection scheme. Thus, it is more effective to use a shorter wavelength light source and a higher NA objective lens to obtain higher areal recording densities in conventional detection.

9.3 OUTLINE OF MAGNETICALLY INDUCED SUPERRESOLUTION

9.3.1 Superresolution in Optical System Using a Pinhole

The resolving power of a microscope can be increased by placing an optical stop with a tiny pinhole at a position sufficiently close to the object [5]. This means that even a minute structure of an object smaller than the diffraction limited size could be observed, as shown in Figure 9.4. This system with a pinhole for superresolution would be applicable to an optical disk if a sufficiently small pinhole could be located close to the object and within the focused light spot [1], [2].

9.3.2 Two Methods for Superresolution in Magneto-Optical Disks

The interaction between heat and light enables effective pinholes to be formed in magnetic layers. As a whole, two types of effective pinholes were first invented, as shown in Figure 9.5. Examining Figure 9.5(b) first, the effective pinhole which is shaped like an ellipse is formed at the right side or rear part of the light spot for the disk moving to the right. The area outside the pinhole shaped like a crescent works as an obscuration and is hereafter called a "mask" in this chapter. The overlap between the pinhole and the optical spot is called an "aperture." The signal can be detected from the aperture area. Since the aperture is formed at the rear of the light spot, the detection method in Figure 9.5(b) is called rear aperture detection (RAD).

The situation is reversed in Figure 9.5(a). The ellipse at the rear of the spot works as an optical mask. The signal is detected from the crescent-shaped aperture. This detection method is called front aperture detection (FAD). The third one, called center aperture detection (CAD), will also be discussed later.

All the detection methods can be realized by using magnetic multilayer films as described in detail in the following section.

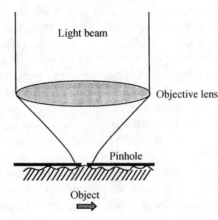

Figure 9.4 Optical system for superresolution with a pinhole smaller than the spot size close to the object.

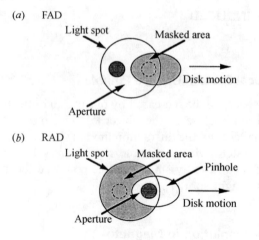

Figure 9.5 Two detection methods in magnetically induced superresolution: (*a*) front aperture detection (FAD); (*b*) rear aperture detection (RAD).

9.4 PRINCIPLE OF MSR

9.4.1 Read-Once Superresolution Disk

Before conceiving the idea of MSR, an optical mask can be created in a magnetic single-layer film only once for readout. When the readout power P_r was increased to 4 mW (which is greater than the 1.5 mW normally used for MO disks) and an external magnetic field was applied, a C/N ratio of 40 dB was obtained for a 0.4 μm mark length, or equivalently for a recording wavelength 0.8 μm using current MO disks [6]. The C/N ratio for the same mark length was less than 20 dB at a readout power 1.5 mW, which was not unreasonable if one considers the optical limit given by Equation (9.2). Therefore, superresolution occurs at $P_r = 4$ mW in the current MO disk.

However, a high C/N ratio was observed only once, not twice. This experimental result can be accounted for as follows (Fig. 9.6). The magnetic film is heated by the dc readout light focused on the light spot area. In an actual optical disk system, the light spot remains fixed while the disk moves to the right. Since the heat is transferred to the right of the disk, an elliptically shaped high temperature region is formed at the rear of the spot (at the right-hand side of the spot). The heated region is fixed with respect to the light spot. Now recall that the coercivity of the magnetic layer decreases with temperature, as typically shown in Figure 9.1. When a magnetic field is applied during readout with a magnitude greater than the coercivity in the heated region, the magnetization is aligned parallel to the applied field, which corresponds to an erasure process. The heated region behaves as an optical mask because the erased area does not contribute to the signal. The remaining crescent-shaped area effectively apertures the light spot and thus increases the resolving power in the same manner as reducing the light spot size by decreasing the light wavelength or by increasing the numerical aperture of an objective lens. Superresolution occurred only once because the recorded mark was erased at the rear of the light spot and remained erased even after the magnetic layer is cooled down.

Destructive superresolution is possible in a single magnetic layer MO disk at high readout powers under an appropriate magnetic field. Thus, the issue to be solved is how to produce a nondestructive superresolution scheme in MO disks.

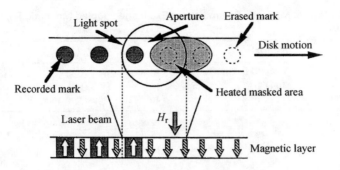

Figure 9.6 Read-once superresolution disk. Upper figure shows the top view of the disk irradiated with dc readout light power. Lower figure shows the cross-sectional view of the magnetic layer in the disk. Upward and downward arrows in the layer symbolize the direction of the magnetization and correspond to data 1 and 0, respectively.

9.4.2 Front Aperture Detection

The problem can be solved by using an exchange-coupled magnetic triple-layer film as shown in Figure 9.7 and Table 9.1. Figure 9.8 shows a typical Faraday hysteresis loop of an exchange-coupled magnetic triple-layer film for FAD at an ambient temperature [7]. Since the switching layer is so strongly coupled to the recording layer at an ambient temperature, the loop can be analyzed by an exchange-coupled magnetic double-layer theory [8]. According to the analysis in Chapter 8, the changes in Faraday rotation depicted in Figure 9.8 are interpreted as the magnetization reversal of each layer which takes place at the external magnetic field H equals

$$H = -(H_{w1} \pm H_{c1}), \quad H_{w1} = \sigma_w/(2h_1 M_{s1}) \tag{9.3}$$

and

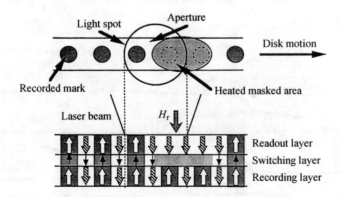

Figure 9.7 Principle of FAD. Upper and lower figures denote top view and cross-sectional view of the MSR disk by FAD, respectively. Magnetic triple layers consist of the readout layer, the switching layer, and the recording layer. The signal is read out from the readout layer through the substrate. Upward and downward arrows in the triple layers symbolize the direction of the magnetization.

TABLE 9.1 Typical Magnetic Parameters of Exchange-coupled Magnetic Triple Layers Used for the MSR Disk by FAD

Layer	Material	Thickness (nm)	T_c (°C)	H_c (kA/m)
Readout	GdFeCo	30	> 300	< 400
Switching	TbFeCoAl	10	≈140	> 800
Recording	TbFeCo	40	≈250	> 800

$$H = -(H_{c2} - H_{w2}), \quad H_{w2} = \sigma_w/(2h_2 M_{s2}) \tag{9.4}$$

where layers 1 and 2 correspond to the readout layer and the recording layer, respectively. σ_w is the interface magnetic wall energy at the boundary between layers 1 and 2. Parameters h, M_s, and H_c are the layer thickness, the magnetization, and the coercivity, respectively. H_{w1} and H_{w2} are bias fields applied on layers 1 and 2, respectively. H_{w1} and H_{w2} are the effective magnetic fields caused by the exchange coupling through the boundary between the layers, which align in parallel the spins of the transition metal ions in the layers. When the condition $H_{w1} > H_{c1}$ is satisfied, as is the case in Figure 9.8, the magnetization in layer 1 is aligned parallel to the magnetization in layer 2 at zero magnetic field. For −1200 kA/m (−15KOe) < H < −600 kA/m (7.5KOe), the magnetic spins in the two layers are antiparallel as indicated in the figure. This hysteresis loop characteristic ensures that after the recorded mark in the readout layer is erased by the applied field in the heated area during readout, the information which is retained in the recording layer is copied onto the readout layer due to the exchange coupling when the temperature of the magnetic layers becomes lower. Thus, the exchange coupling between the readout and the recording layers through the switching layer enables recorded marks in the readout layer to be read out many times.

A "read-many" MSR disk by FAD is realized by adopting exchange-coupled magnetic triple-layer film, as shown in Figure 9.7. The magnetic layers consist of the readout layer, the switching layer, and the recording layer. The typical magnetic proper-

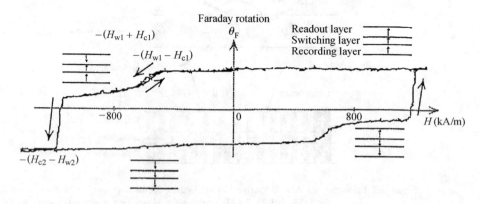

Figure 9.8 Faraday hysteresis loop of a magnetic triple-layer film for FAD. Arrows in the triple layers symbolize the direction of the magnetization. Arrows along the loop indicate the scanning direction of the magnetic field.

ties of each layer are shown in Table 9.1. The exchange coupling between the readout and the recording layers through the switching layer enables marks to be restored in the readout layer after they are erased in the heated region. The exchange coupling force is evaluated by the interface wall energy σ_w. The condition necessary for marks in the recording layer to be copied onto the readout layer at the ambient temperature T_a can be given as

$$H_{wl} > H_{cl} \tag{9.5}$$

The condition given by Equation (9.5) shows that the exchange-coupling force is essential in restoring marks and reading many times.

Multilayers are designed so that σ_w is strong enough at an ambient temperature and is weak at a masking temperature T_m, above which marks in the readout layer are erased by the readout magnetic field H_r. In the masked area the switching field H_s defined by Equation (9.6) must be reduced below H_r as given by Equation (9.7).

$$H_s = H_{cl} + H_{wl} \tag{9.6}$$
$$H_r > H_s (T > T_m) \tag{9.7}$$

The temperature dependence of H_s was measured as shown in Figure 9.9. Since σ_w decreases more rapidly than M_{sl} as the temperature increases, H_{wl} approaches zero at the Curie temperature of the switching layer. The switching layer plays an important role in creating a mask with a clear edge. For $H_r = 24\,\text{kA/m}$ (300 Oe), the masking temperature T_m is determined as 130°C from the condition $H_s = H_r$. The area above the masking temperature works as an optical mask because the information in the readout layer is erased by the magnetic field during the readout process. A signal can be detected out from the crescent-shaped aperture, as shown in Figure 9.7. The mechanism of MSR was verified by experiment and also by a calculation using a thermal-analysis simulation. Figure 9.10 shows the temperature distribution and masked area calculated for various readout powers at a linear velocity of 8 m/s [9]. It is known from Figure 9.10 that the mask is not formed for $P_r = 1.5\,\text{mW}$, while a mask sufficient to achieve super-resolution can be formed within the light spot for $P_r = 2.5\,\text{mW}$. The Curie temperature

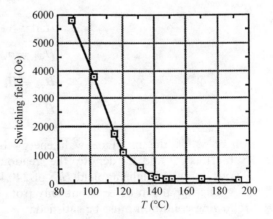

Figure 9.9 Measured temperature dependence of the switching field H_s.

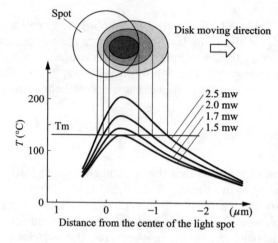

Figure 9.10 Temperature distribution and masked area calculated for various readout powers at a linear velocity of 8 m/s. The masked area is defined as the temperature region above $T_m = 130°C$.

of the recording layer must be high enough so that the condition [Equation (9.8)] is satisfied at temperatures below the maximum temperature T_{max} during readout.

$$H_{c2} - H_{w2} > H_r(T \leq T_{max}) \tag{9.8}$$

$$H_{w2} = \sigma_w/(2M_{s2}h_2) \tag{9.9}$$

Under the condition [Equation (9.8)], the magnetization in the recording layer is not reversed during readout, and as a result, the recorded information is retained in the recording layer.

9.4.3 Rear Aperture Detection

The principle of MSR by RAD is explained using magnetic double layers, as shown in Figure 9.11. In MSR by RAD, the aperture is limited to the heated region. The information in the readout layer is erased by the initializing field before readout, and therefore, the crescent-shaped area in Figure 9.11 is effectively masked. The conditions required for initializing the readout layer while retaining the marks in the recording layer are given as

$$H_{c1} + H_{w1} < H_{ini} \tag{9.10a}$$

$$H_{w1} = \sigma_w/(2M_{s1}h_1) \tag{9.10b}$$

$$H_{c2} - H_{w2} < H_{ini} \tag{9.11a}$$

$$H_{w2} = \sigma_w/(2M_{s2}h_2) \tag{9.11b}$$

where σ_w is the interface wall energy between the readout and recording layer. Subscripts 1 and 2 denote the readout and the recording layer, respectively. Typically, the initializing field H_{ini} of 240 kA/m (3KOe) is used.

The signal can be read out only from the aperture area in Figure 9.11, where the following condition must be satisfied.

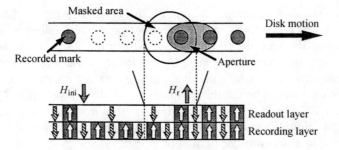

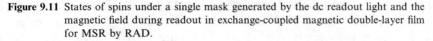

Figure 9.11 States of spins under a single mask generated by the dc readout light and the magnetic field during readout in exchange-coupled magnetic double-layer film for MSR by RAD.

$$H_{c2} - H_{w1} < H_r < H_{c1} + H_{w1} \tag{9.12}$$

The information recorded in the recording layer is imposed onto the readout layer in the aperture area, which means that the spin in the readout layer is reversed to be directed upward in the direction of the readout field only when the spin in the recording layer is directed upward.

The Curie temperature of the recording layer must satisfy the following condition during readout, similar to FAD:

$$H_{c2} - H_{w2} > H_r(T \leq T_{max}) \tag{9.13}$$

Actually, the most promising structure for RAD is believed to be the magnetic quadrilayer film. Table 9.2 shows typical magnetic properties of quadri-layers: the readout layer, the subsidiary layer, the intermediate layer, and the recording layer. The intermediate layer with its easy axis in plane is inserted to reduce σ_w as is the intermediate layer in overwritable triple-layer film. The subsidiary layer has a high coercivity at an ambient temperature and a low Curie temperature, while the readout layer has a low coercivity at an ambient temperature and a high Curie temperature. H_{c1} and H_{w1} in conditions [Equations (9.10a) to (9.12)] should be replaced by values H'_{c1} and H'_{w1}, respectively, which are the values of the readout layer combined with those of the subsidiary layer. H'_{c1} and H'_{w1} are expressed by

$$H'_{c1} = (H_{c1}M_{s1}h_1 + H_{cs}M_{ss}h_s)/M_{s1}h_1 + M_{ss}h_s \tag{9.14}$$

$$H'_{w1} = \sigma'_w/2(M_{s1}h_1 + M_{ss}h_s) \tag{9.15}$$

TABLE 9.2 Typical Magnetic Parameters of Exchange-coupled Magnetic Quadri-layers Used for the MSR Disk by RAD

Layer	Material	Thickness (nm)	T_c (°C)	H_c (kA/m)
Readout	GdFeCo	30	> 300	< 320 (combined)
Subsidiary	TbFeCoAl	10	≈140	
Intermediate	GdFeCo	15	≈250	< 40
Recording	TbFeCo	40	≈250	> 800

where H_{cs}, M_{ss}, and h_s are the coercivity, the magnetization, and the thickness of the subsidiary layer, respectively. σ'_w is the reduced interface wall energy between the readout layer and the recording layer through the subsidiary layer and the intermediate layer. The data in the recording layer are copied onto the readout layer and can be read out at the aperture area where the temperature is raised below the Curie temperature of the subsidiary layer. The combination of the readout layer with a Curie temperature higher than 300°C and the subsidiary layer with a low Curie temperature satisfies two requirements simultaneously: high carrier level and data copy.

The masked areas in the light spot calculated for $P_r < 1.0$ mW and $P_r = 2.0$ mW are shown as the lightly shaded regions in Figure 9.12(a) and Figure 9.12(b), respectively. Actually for a high P_r, another mask is created in the highest temperature region, as shown by the heavily shaded area in Figure 9.12(c) for $P_r = 3.0$ mW. The state in Figure 9.12(c) is called a double mask state. Figure 9.13 shows the states of spins under double masks in a magnetic quadrilayer film for MSR by RAD. In the up-spin mask region, the magnetization in the readout layer is aligned upward in the magnetic field during readout, while it is retained downward in the crescent-shaped down-spin mask region in the readout layer. The spin state in the recording layer is copied onto the readout layer only in the aperture.

It was found from the calculation for various readout powers that although the area of the double masks changes noticeably with an increase in readout power, the area of the aperture changes little. This suggests that a stable minute signal can be obtained for a wide range of readout power.

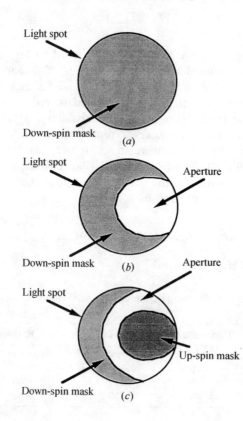

Figure 9.12. Mask structure generated in the light spot for various readout powers. The disk (not shown) moves to the right at a linear velocity of 8 m/s under the light spot with a diameter of the first Airy disk $d = 1.8$ μm. (a) All of the area is masked when $P_r < 1.0$ mW. (b) Down-spin mask is generated in the crescent area when $P_r = 2.0$ mW. (c) In addition to the down-spin mask, up-spin mask is generated in the highest temperature area when $P_r = 3.0$ mW.

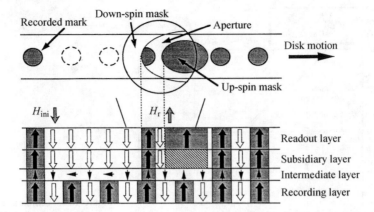

Figure 9.13 The states of spins under double masks in magnetic quadrilayer film for MSR by RAD. Upper and lower figures denote the top view and the cross-sectional view of the MSR disk by RAD, respectively. Magnetic quadrilayers consist of the readout layer, the subsidiary layer, the intermediate layer, and the recording layer. The signal is read out from the readout layer through the substrate. Upward and downward arrows in the quadrilayers symbolize the direction of the magnetization or spin. The magnetization of the readout layer is erased by the initializing field H_{ini} prior to the readout.

In each area in Figure 9.12(c), the conditions to be satisfied are

$$H_{c1}' - H_{w1}' > H_r \quad \text{in the down-spin mask area} \tag{9.16}$$

$$H_{c1}' - H_{w1}' < H_r < H_{c1}' + H_{w1}' \quad \text{in the aperture area} \tag{9.17}$$

$$H_{c1}' + H_{w1}' < H_r \quad \text{in the up-spin mask area} \tag{9.18}$$

The temperature dependence of switching field $H_{c1}' \pm H_{w1}'$ was measured from asymmetrical Kerr hysteresis loops, and is given in Figure 9.14. The temperature range for the down-spin mask, the aperture, and the up-spin mask is indicated in the figure. The range for the aperture was obtained from 80°C to 140°C. Areas in Figure 9.12(b) and 9.12(c) were calculated based on thermal analysis using the above temperature range.

9.5 DISK CHARACTERISTICS

9.5.1 Spatial Frequency Dependence of Carrier and Noise Levels

The wavelength λ of 780 nm and the numerical aperture NA of 0.53 were used for all the experiments in this chapter. The resolving power is experimentally determined by measuring the relative carrier level as a function of the spatial frequency, which corresponds to the theoretical modulation transfer function. Figure 9.15 shows the relative carrier level for the MSR disk by FAD and for conventional detection as a function of the spatial frequency. The spatial frequency where the carrier approaches zero for conventional detection agrees with the theoretical cut-off $2(NA)/\lambda$. The measured cut-off spatial frequency for MSR disks by FAD is more than twice that of

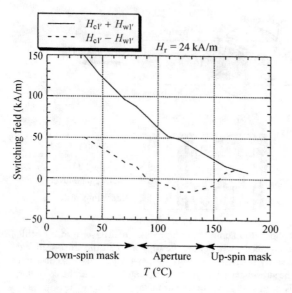

Figure 9.14. Temperature dependence of the switching field $H'_{c1} \pm H'_{w1}$. The temperature range for the down-spin mask, the aperture and the up-spin mask is indicated in the figure when conditions [Equations (9.16) to (9.18)] apply.

conventional detection. Thus, two times higher linear density is expected for MSR disks by FAD.

Figure 9.16 shows the relative carrier level as a function of the spatial frequency for an MSR disk by RAD. The carrier (*a*) for $P_r = 2.0$ mW was obtained by conventional detection without initializing process. The cutoff spatial frequency is expanded by RAD with a single mask (*b*) for $P_r = 2.0$ mW. This is the superresolution caused by the down-spin mask corresponding to Figure 9.12(*b*). The carrier (*c*) corresponds to double masks shown in Figure 9.12(*c*). The cutoff by RAD with double masks (*c*) for $P_r = 3.0$ mW is expanded to more than twice that of conventional detection. Better superresolution with double masks than with a single mask is derived from the narrower aperture

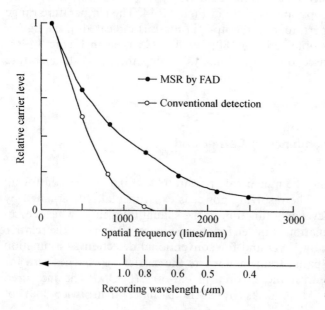

Figure 9.15 Relative carrier level for the MSR disk by FAD and for conventional detection as a function of spatial frequency and as a function of recording wavelength.

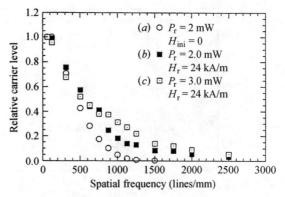

Figure 9.16. Relative carrier level for the MSR disk by RAD as a function of the spatial frequency: (*a*) conventional detection when $P_r = 2.0$ mW for marks recorded without initializing process; (*b*) RAD with a single mask when $P_r = 2.0$ mW; (*c*) RAD with double masks when $P_r = 3.0$ mW.

area with double masks than with a single mask. At the linear velocity of 8 m/s used in Figure 9.16, the aperture spreads over more than half the area of the light spot when $P_r = 2.0$ mW, as shown in Figure 9.12(*b*). The aperture becomes narrower with the appearance of the up-spin mask, as shown in Figure 9.12(*c*). The resolving power is improved for RAD with a single mask by increasing linear velocity, since the heated region is shifted toward the rear side of the light spot.

Figure 9.17 is the C/N values as a function of the mark length for the MSR disks read by FAD and RAD and also for a reference disk read by conventional detection. The C/N by conventional detection becomes considerably lower at a mark length of 0.4 μm, because the mark length is near the theoretical optical limit of 0.37 μm. On the other hand, a high C/N of 47 dB for a mark length of 0.4 μm with MSR disks is obtained. The C/N is still as high as 42 dB for a mark length of 0.3 μm which is much smaller than the optical limit for conventional detection. A slightly higher C/N for RAD than FAD may be ascribed to the narrow aperture with double masks.

Figure 9.18 shows C/N as a function of a mark length for RAD with double masks at $P_r = 3.0$ mW. Here, both laser modulation and magnetic field modulation were used as recording methods. Magnetic field modulation was carried out by using a floating magnetic head which supplied a signal at a frequency associated with the synchronized

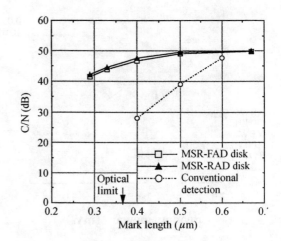

Figure 9.17 Mark length dependence of C/N for MSR disks by FAD and RAD and for conventional detection at a linear velocity of 8 m/s and readout power of 2.5 mW.

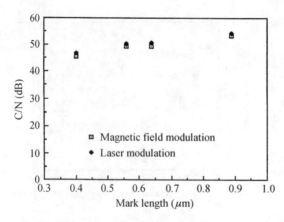

Figure 9.18. Mark length dependence of C/N for the MSR disk by RAD with double masks at a linear velocity of 8 m/s.

light pulse. Although magnetic field modulation provides lower CNR than light modulation, it has an advantage for direct overwriting as well as superresolution.

9.5.2 Read Power Dependence of Carrier

Figure 9.19 shows the carrier and noise levels as a function of the readout power P_r for FAD for a mark length of 0.4 μm at a linear velocity of 8 m/s. The Curie temperature of the switching layer was higher for the FAD disk in Figure 9.19 than that for the disk in Figure 9.9 and 9.10, as shown in Table 9.1. As a result, superresolution takes place at higher readout powers. The steep increase in C/N at $P_r = 2.0$ mW is caused by the generation of the masked area. The P_r is divided into two regions as

$$P_r < 2.0 \text{ mW} \qquad \text{``full moon'' aperture state} = \text{conventional detection} \qquad (9.19)$$

$$P_r > 2.0 \text{ mW} \qquad \text{crescent aperture state} \qquad (9.20)$$

The fact that C/N is fairly constant for $P_r > 2.0$ mW assures that the signal can be read out with a wide margin of P_r.

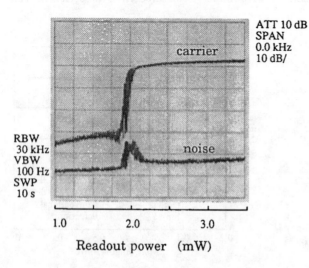
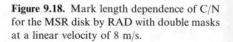

Figure 9.19. Carrier and noise level for a mark length of 0.4 μm in the MSR disk by FAD as a function of the readout power at a linear velocity of 8 m/s under a readout field of 24 kA/m.

Figure 9.20 shows the carrier and noise levels as a function of the readout power for a 0.4 µm mark length at a linear velocity of 8 m/s in a quadrilayer MSR disk by RAD. The steep increase in the carrier level at 1.0 mW denotes that the aperture area appears in the heated region in the light spot at a readout power higher than 1.0 mW. The entire light-spot area is masked when $P_r < 1.0$ mW. C/N in Figure 9.20 steps up at a critical readout power of 2.3 mW. This experimental result suggests that the aperture becomes narrower and the resolving power is increased with readout power above a critical value. The three regions of P_r correspond to Figure 9.12 (a), (b) and (c), respectively, as

$$P_r < 10 \text{ mW} \qquad \text{``new moon'' state} \qquad (9.21)$$
$$1.0 < P_r < 2.3 \text{ mW} \qquad \text{single-mask state} \qquad (9.22)$$
$$P_r > 2.3 \text{ mW} \qquad \text{double-mask state} \qquad (9.23)$$

9.5.3 Readout Waveform of MSR Disks

Figure 9.21(a) and (b) shows readout waveforms of a random pattern for (a) $P_r = 1.5$ mW and (b) 2.5 mW, respectively. Random data were written on a MSR disk by FAD using (1, 7) RLL mark length recording modulation. Marks with a recording wavelength of 0.76 µm are not resolved for (a) $P_r = 1.5$ mW, while they are clearly resolved for (b) $P_r = 2.5$ mW. The experimental observation agrees with the result shown in Figure 9.19, concluding that superresolution is achieved for $P_r = 2.5$ mW, but not for $P_r = 1.5$ mW.

The characteristics of superresolution can be evaluated by readout response to an isolated mark. Figure 9.22 shows waveforms of the MSR disk by FAD for an isolated mark obtained by calculation and by experiment. Response to an isolated mark was measured for repeated 0.4 µm marks with a very long period. The readout signal was calculated as a spatial convolution of the recorded mark with the intensity distribution of the effective aperture, as will be described in Section 9.6. As shown in Figure 9.10, the mask is formed at readout powers above 1.5 mW. Then, a small mask is formed at

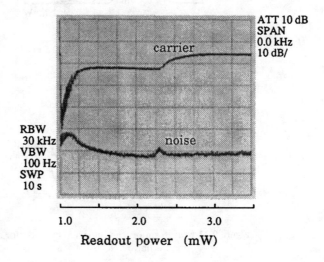

Figure 9.20. Carrier and noise level for a mark length of 0.4 µm in an MSR disk by RAD as a function of the readout power at a linear velocity of 8 m/s under a magnetic field of 24 kA/m during readout.

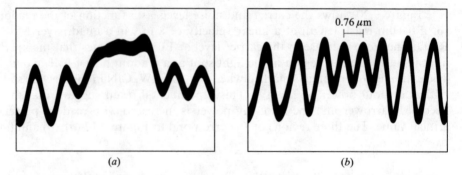

(a)   (b)

Figure 9.21 Readout signal for a random pattern written on the MSR disk by FAD. (a)
With readout power of 1.5 mW. (b) With readout power of 2.5 mW.

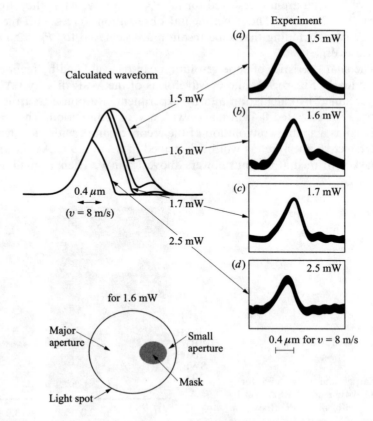

Figure 9.22 Waveform of readout signal by FAD for an isolated mark with a length of 0.4
μm at a linear velocity of 8 m/s.

$P_r = 1.6$ mW, as shown at the lower left hand corner of Figure 9.22. The double peaks appear at $P_r = 1.6$ mW for calculated and experimental waveforms, indicating that a small aperture exists at the rear edge of the light spot besides the major aperture at the front side of the spot. The waveform becomes narrower and more asymmetrical as the masked area grows.

Figure 9.23 shows waveforms of the MSR disk by RAD for an isolated mark with a 1.0 μm mark length obtained by both calculation and experiment for the readout powers corresponding to Figure 9.12. The waveform (a) was obtained at $P_r = 2.0$ mW for a mark recorded without initializing process, which corresponds to conventional detection. In other words, the aperture coincides with the light spot. The calculated amplitude of the waveform was normalized by that for (a). By RAD with a single mask (b) for $P_r = 2.0$ mW, the calculation shows a steep rise and the same fall as (a) in the waveform. The steep rise is caused by fast switching from the down-spin mask area to the aperture area. By RAD with double masks (c) for $P_r = 3.0$ mW, in addition to the steep rise, a steep fall in the waveform is obtained by calculation. The steep fall is also ascribed to the fast switching from the aperture to the up spin mask. The experimental result agrees well with the calculation. The experiment shows that a clear boundary between the aperture and double masks is realized.

9.5.4 Crosstalk

When the track density is high enough so that a part of the light spot overlaps the adjacent tracks, the crosstalk from adjacent tracks is generally high for conventional detection. By RAD, however, the crosstalk is small since the width of the aperture by RAD across the track is smaller than the light spot by conventional detection, as shown in Figure 9.11. The potential for greater track density was evaluated by measuring the crosstalk using two types of RAD disks.

For one type of RAD disk, the magnetic parameters are optimized so as to obtain a small aperture for the single mask state at a high readout power [10]. Crosstalk was measured as a function of the readout power using a 1.6 μm track pitch (1.0 μm land, 0.6 μm groove). The light spot was first scanned on the land where 1.6 μm marks had been recorded and then scanned on the groove, as shown in Figure 9.24. Since hidden marks do not contribute to the crosstalk as long as they do not pass through under the heated aperture area, the crosstalk for the RAD disk with a single mask was expected to be very low. The crosstalk was obtained by subtracting the signal on the land (S_l) from the signal on the groove (S_g). The crosstalk as a function of the readout power for RAD and for conventional detection is shown in Figure 9.25. The crosstalk obtained for RAD at high readout powers is sufficiently low to permit a track pitch of 0.8 μm. The low crosstalk arises from the fact that the width of the effective aperture is much narrower for RAD than that for conventional detection, as shown in Figure 9.24. Thus, a RAD disk with a single mask offers the possibility of not only doubled linear density but also doubled track density.

The other RAD disk was prepared by depositing quadri-layer films which were similar to those in Table 9.2 to get a double mask state [11]. A photopolymerized (2P) glass substrate with wide grooves was examined in addition to conventional substrates. As shown in Figure 9.26, a high C/N ratio of 47 dB was obtained for 0.4 μm mark using 1.0 μm track pitch (0.3 μm land, 0.7 μm wide groove). The obtained C/N ratio ($\sim$ 47dB) is much higher than that ($\sim$ 43dB) using a conventional substrate with a 1.0 μm track pitch (0.6 μm land, 0.4 μm groove), and is comparable with that for 1.6 μm track pitch.

Calculation

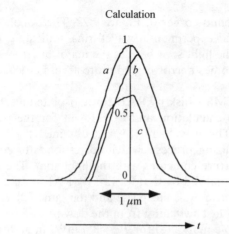

Experiment

(a)

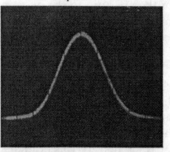

(b)

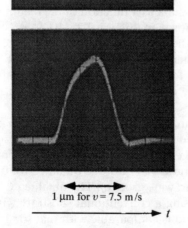

(c)

1 μm for $v = 7.5$ m/s

t

Figure 9.23. Waveform for an isolated mark with a length of 1.0 μm at a linear velocity of 7.5 m/s obtained by calculation and by experiment. (*a*) Conventional detection when $P_r = 2.0$ mW for a mark recorded without initializing process; (*b*) RAD with a single mask when $P_r = 2.0$ mW; (*c*) RAD with double masks when $P_r = 3.0$ mW.

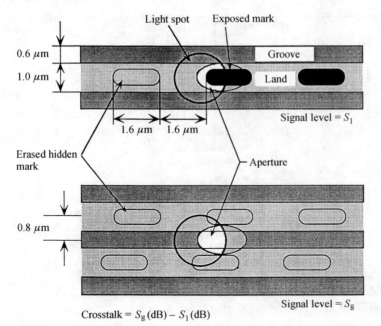

$$\text{Crosstalk} = S_g\,(\text{dB}) - S_1\,(\text{dB})$$

Figure 9.24 Measurement method of crosstalk in the MSR disk by RAD. Marks with a length of 1.6 μm are written on the 1.0 μm wide land. Erased hidden marks are not detected because the magnetization in the readout layer is erased by the initializing field.

Using the wide groove RAD disk, the 1.6 μm marks were written on grooves. The light spot was scanned first on the groove where data had been written, then on an adjacent groove to measure the crosstalk. The crosstalk level as small as −33 dB was obtained for the RAD disk with double masks using 1.0 μm track pitch. Although it is expected that the width of the aperture is wider for the double mask state than that for the single mask state, the experimental result shows that the track density can be much increased by using the RAD disk with double masks compared to the conventional detection.

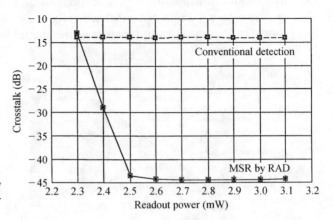

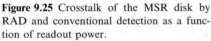

Figure 9.25 Crosstalk of the MSR disk by RAD and conventional detection as a function of readout power.

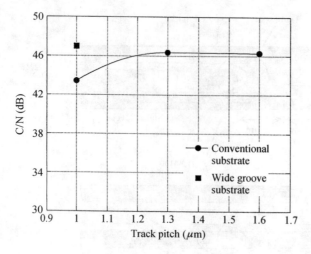

Figure 9.26 The track pitch dependence of the C/N at 0.4 μm mark for the MSR disks by RAD.

9.6 OPTICAL TRANSFER FUNCTION OF SUPERRESOLUTION

9.6.1 Superresolution Optical System

In this section, superresolution is theoretically discussed for various sizes and positions of a simplified pinhole [12]. Figure 9.27 shows the superresolution optical readout system used in the calculation. In an actual optical disk, the collector lens coincides with the objective lens because light is reflected from the disk. Superresolution can be analyzed by the optical diffraction theory with a pinhole close to the optical disk.

9.6.2 Optical Diffraction Theory of Conventional Readout of Optical Disk

A periodic pattern as shown in Figure 9.28 is written in an optical disk. In the figure, u and v indicate the tangential and radial directions of the disk, respectively. The disk moves at a constant velocity in the u direction. Since the periodic marks can be regarded as a grating, the ± 1st order light is diffracted from the disk in addition to the zero order light as shown in Figure 9.29. The modulation transfer function (MTF) is expressed as an area where the first order diffracted light is overlapped with zero order light. MTF is shown in Figure 9.30 as a function of the spatial frequency n. MTF can be expressed by

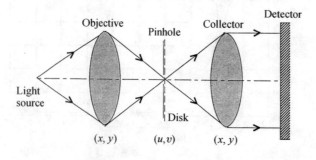

Figure 9.27 Superresolution optical system using a pinhole.

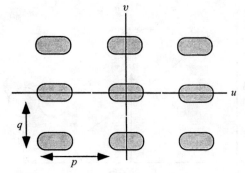

Figure 9.28 Marks periodically written in tangential u direction and in radial v direction.

$$\text{MTF} = \frac{1}{\pi}(2\theta - \sin 2\theta) \tag{9.24}$$

$$\cos\theta = \frac{v\lambda}{2(\text{NA})} \tag{9.25}$$

Diffraction theory of a readout system for an optical disk was analyzed in detail by Hopkins [13]. The coordinates (x, y) and (u, v) in Figure 9.27 are normalized by the radius of the lens and by λ/NA, respectively. The pupil function $P(x, y)$ is the amplitude distribution of light on the objective and is given for uniform incidence by

$$P(x, y) = 1 \quad \text{for} \quad x^2 + y^2 \le 1 \tag{9.26}$$

$$= 0 \quad \text{for} \quad x^2 + y^2 > 1 \tag{9.27}$$

The pupil function $P(x, y)$ is Fourier transformed to the point spread function $h(u, v)$ on the disk plane so that it is given by

$$h(u, v) = \int\int_{-\infty}^{\infty} P(x, y)\exp\{2\pi i(ux + vy)\}dxdy \tag{9.28}$$

Employing the amplitude transmittance functions $t(u - u_s, v - v_s)$ of the disk, the amplitude distribution $a(u, v; u_s, v_s)$ of the light leaving the disk plane can be written by

$$a(u, v; u_s, v_s) = h(u, v)t(u - u_s, v - v_s) \tag{9.29}$$

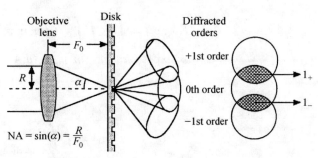

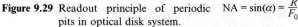

Figure 9.29 Readout principle of periodic pits in optical disk system. $\quad \text{NA} = \sin(\alpha) = \dfrac{R}{F_0}$

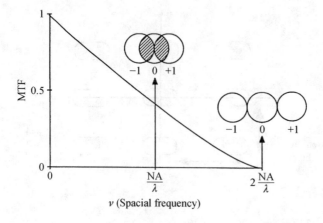

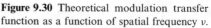

Figure 9.30 Theoretical modulation transfer function as a function of spatial frequency v.

where (u_s, v_s) are the displacements of the disk. In the detection of magneto-optical marks as shown in Figure 9.28, Kerr rotation of the polarization direction of the reflected light is converted into the modulation of light intensity. Since this is a linear process, the magnetic domains have equivalent complex reflective coefficients, which allows us to calculate $t(u - u_s, v - v_s)$ by employing the scalar diffraction model.

The inverse Fourier transform of $a(u, v; u_s, v_s)$ gives the complex amplitude $A(x, y; u_s, v_s)$ diffracted backwards to the point (x, y) on the collector lens as

$$A(x, y; u_s, \ v_s) = \int\!\!\int_{-\infty}^{\infty} a(u, v; \ u, v_s) \exp\{-2\pi i(xu + yv)\} du dv \tag{9.30}$$

$$= \int\!\!\int_{-\infty}^{\infty} P(x - m, y - n) T(m, n) \exp\{-2\pi i(mu_s + nv_s)\} dm dn \tag{9.31}$$

$T(m, n)$ is the Fourier transforms of $t(u - u_s, v - v_s)$ given by

$$t(u, v) = \int\!\!\int_{-\infty}^{\infty} T(m, n) \exp\{2\pi i(um + vn)\} dm dn \tag{9.32}$$

m and n are coordinates of the diffracted light in the collector plane. $T(m, n)$ can be calculated when $t(u - u_s, v - v_s)$ is given for marks shown in Figure 9.28. The total light intensity which is diffracted back to the pupil bounded by the circle $x^2 + y^2 = 1$ and finally fed into the detector can be written as

$$I(u_s, v_s) = \int\!\!\int\!\!\int\!\!\int_{-\infty}^{\infty} C(m, n; m', n') T(m, n) T^*(m', n')$$

$$\times \exp\{-2\pi i[(m - m')u_s + (n - n')v_s]\} dm dn dm' dn', \tag{9.33}$$

where

$$C(m, n; m', n') = \int\!\!\int_{\text{lens aperture}} P(x - m', y - n') dx \tag{9.34}$$

is the partially coherent transfer function (PCTF) which is purely determined by the optical system. Calculated waveforms of readout signal shown in Figure 9.22 and Figure 9.23 were obtained from Equation (33) using calculated $T(m, n)$ and $C(m, n; m', n')$.

The spatial frequency response of the fundamental wave component is discussed assuming the disk has a periodic structure. The optical transfer function (OTF) is defined by $C(m, 0; 0, 0)$. The absolute value of the OTF is the modulation transfer function (MTF), and its phase is the phase transfer function (PTF). Then, the OTF is given by the autocorrelation of the pupil function.

$$\text{OTF} = C(m, 0; 0, 0) = \int\int_{\text{lens aperture}} P(x - m, y)P^*(x, y)dxdy \qquad (9.35)$$

Equation (9.24) is derived from Equation (9.35) as normalized spacial frequency m is related to n by

$$m = \frac{\lambda}{p(\text{NA})} = \frac{v\lambda}{(\text{NA}} \qquad (9.36)$$

9.6.3 Pinhole Model on the Disk Plane for MSR

An aperture of RAD can be approximated by a circular pinhole located at distance s from the center of the spot with a radius w as shown in Figure 9.31 The amplitude distribution $a(u, v; u_s, v_s)$ given by Equation (9.29) is replaced by

$$a(u, v; u_s, v_s) = h(u, v)t_p(u, v)t(u - u_s, v - v_s), \qquad (9.37)$$

for the optical system with the amplitude transmittance function $t_p(u, v)$ of the pinhole. The complex amplitude $A(x, y; u_s, v_s)$ is obtained from Equation (9.30) and (9.37), and is calculated by substituting the "extended pupil function" $E_p(x - m, y - n)$ given by

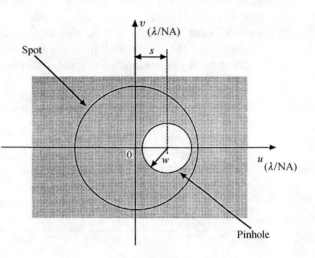

Figure 9.31 Pinhole model on the disk plane for MSR by RAD.

$$E_p(x-m, y-n) = \int\int_{-\infty}^{\infty} P(x-m-m_p, y-n-n_p)T_p(m_p, n_p)dm_p dn_p \qquad (9.38)$$

for the pupil function $P(x, -m, y-n)$ in Equation (9.31), where $T_p(m_p, n_p)$ is the Fourier transform of $t_p(u, v)$ given by

$$t_p(u, v) = \int\int_{-\infty}^{\infty} T_p(m_p, n_p) \exp\{2\pi i(um_p + vn_p)\}dm_p dn_p \qquad (9.39)$$

$T_p(m_p, n_p; w, s)$ of a pinhole shown in Figure 9.31 is expressed by

$$T_p(m_p, n_p; w, s) = \pi w^2 \frac{2J_1\left(2\pi w\sqrt{m_p^2 + n_p^2}\right)}{2\pi w\sqrt{m_p^2 + n_p^2}} \exp(-2\pi i s m_p), \qquad (9.40)$$

where J_1 is a first-order Bessel function. Hence OTF of the superresolution is obtained by

$$\text{OTF} = C(m, 0; 0, 0) = \int\int_{\text{lens aperture}} E_p(x-m, y)E_p^*(x, y)dxdy \qquad (9.41)$$

Two examples for the OTF of superresolution are given. One is the OTF for a pinhole positioned concentrically on the spot. $E_p(x, y; w, s)$ and the OTF are real functions in this case. Figures 9.32 and 9.33 show the calculated $(E_x, y; w, s)$ and OTF, respectively, for various w when $s = 0$. $E_p(x, y; w, s)$ becomes broader than the pupil function $P(x, y)$ as a pinhole size decreases. Figure 9.33 clearly indicates that the spatial frequency response beyond the optical cutoff frequency is obtained in the presence of the pinhole. In this case, the effective spot size is determined by the pinhole size.

The second example is the OTF for a displaced pinhole for actually realized effective aperture in RAD. The displacement gives $T_p(x, y; w, s)$ as the phase factor and therefore $E_p(x, y; w, s)$ consists of real and imaginary parts. The MTF and the PTF, which are the absolute value and the phase of the OTF, respectively, are shown in Figure 9.34 for various s at the value of $w = 0.5$. In this case, the effective spot size is determined by the region in which the spot overlaps the pinhole. Therefore, a higher cutoff frequency is obtained for greater displacement of the pinhole.

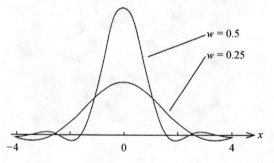

Figure 9.32 Extended pupil function calculated for various w and $s = 0$.

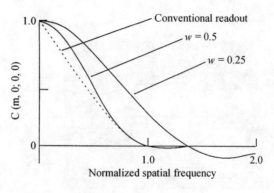

Figure 9.33 Optical transfer function $C(m, 0; 0, 0)$ for various w and $s = 0$. The spatial frequencies are normalized by a conventional optical limit $2\,\mathrm{NA}/\lambda$.

9.6.4 Comparison of Calculated OTF with Measured OTF

The elliptical aperture shape calculated by the thermal analysis can be replaced by a pinhole located at $s = 0.25$ with the radius $w = 0.35$ as shown in Figure 9.35, since the region in which the spot overlaps the aperture should be discussed. Therefore, the OTF of MSR was calculated using the displaced pinhole model. In Fig. 9.36 the MTF and the PTF, which are shown by the solid lines, are compared with the experimental results. The experiments examining readout after recording were performed using a conventional optical pickup and a readout laser power of 2 mW. The $1/e^2$ Gaussian spot radius calculated taking into account the experimental conditions is shown in Figure 9.35.

The carrier levels of the readout signals were measured for various recorded spatial frequencies. Without applying an initializing magnetic field, a conventional readout can be realized by the MSR disk. Figure 9.36(a) shows the calculated MTF of MSR, the measured relative amplitude of readout signals of MSR and the measured relative

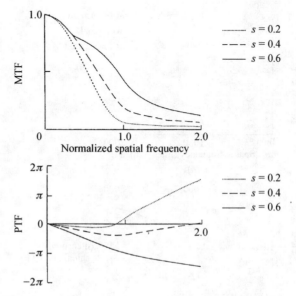

Figure 9.34 The MTF and the PTF calculated for various s at $w = 0.5$.

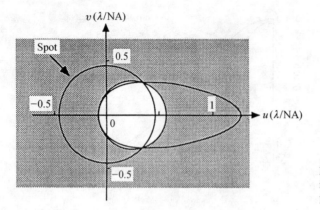

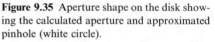

Figure 9.35 Aperture shape on the disk showing the calculated aperture and approximated pinhole (white circle).

amplitude of the conventional readout. The calculated MTF agrees well with the measured relative amplitude of readout signals by MSR.

The phase shifts of the readout signals were measured for various spatial frequencies using the MSR disk. The peak shift in MSR compared to the recording signal was measured by some procedures. Figure 9.36(b) shows the measured phase shifts and the calculated PTF. The measured phase shifts of the readout signals are similar to the calculated PTF. The resultant phase shifts cause the waveform of the readout signal for the isolated mark in MSR to be asymmetric, as shown in Figure 9.23.

9.7 DATA RECORDING AND JITTER ANALYSIS

9.7.1 Data Recording

High-density recording FAD and RAD were investigated [14], [15]. Both (2, 7) code modulation mark position recording and (1, 7) code modulation mark length

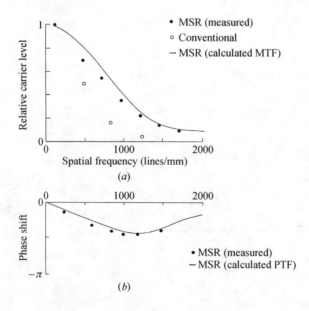

Figure 9.36 Measured relative carrier level and phase shift by MSR for various spatial frequencies: (a) measured relative carrier level and calculated MTF; (b) measured phase shift and calculated PTF.

recording were employed. In (2, 7) code modulation mark position recording, data 1s correspond to the centers of the recorded marks and data 0s correspond to the erased regions. The name (2, 7) indicates the number of 0s allowable between 1s which, in this case, may be as low as 2 and as high as 7. In contrast, the data 1s in (1, 7) code modulation mark length recording correspond to the leading and trailing edges of the recorded marks. Again the name (1, 7) indicates the number of 0s allowable between 1s. Specifications for both modulation methods for the MSR disks and the current magneto-optical disk are listed in Table 9.3. The byte error rate was less than 10^{-4} for each recording on both MSR disks. If the same recording method as that for the current ISO MO disk is chosen, the linear density is doubled. However, by adopting mark length recording (edge detection), more than three times higher linear density on MSR disks can be obtained. Figure 9.37 shows the eye pattern for random data using (1, 7) code modulation mark length recording at 0.3 μm bit length. The eye which is clearly open in the figure assures the data can be read out with a low error rate.

9.7.2 Writing Precompensation and Equalization

A byte error rate less than 10^{-4} was achieved for the MSR disk using the precompensation technique for writing and waveform equalization for readout. However, the thermal interaction in the writing process and the intersymbol interference in the readout process affect the readout signal through the jitter, especially in mark length recording. Thus, writing precompensation is required to minimize the mark edge shift caused by thermal interaction. A writing precompensation technique was introduced by optimizing the laser power and the width of pulse train recording. Random data of the (1, 7) code by mark length recording with a bit length of 0.3 μm are succesfully recorded.

The waveform equalization to minimize the intersymbol interference was also examined. Although the resolving power is much improved in MSR as described in Section 9.5, equalization is still useful to correct the phase distortion of the readout signals caused by the asymmetric response shown in Figures 9.22 and 9.23.

TABLE 9.3 Specifications for Two Types of Recording on the MSR Disks by FAD and RAD As Well As Those for the ISO Standard MO Disk

	ISO standard disk	MSR disks by FAD and RAD	
Modulation code	(2, 7) mark position	(2, 7) mark position	(1, 7) mark length
Disk size (inch)	5.25	5.25	5.25
Rotation rate (rpm)	2400	2400	2400
Clock (ns)	68	33	27
Clock frequency (MHz)	15	30	37
Data transfer rate (Mbps)	7.5	15	25
At the innermost track			
linear velocity (m/s)	7.5	7.5	7.5
window (μm)	0.5	0.25	0.2
bit length (μm)	1.0	0.5	0.3
mark length (μm)	0.76	0.38	0.4

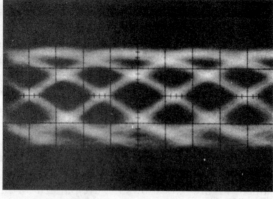

10 ns/div

Figure 9.37 The eye pattern of the readout signals of the MSR disk by RAD at 0.3 μm bit length (0.4 μm minimum mark length) 10 ns/div.

9.7.3 Jitter Measurements

The stability of readout signals is evaluated by measuring jitter. If the effective aperture in MSR fluctuates during readout due to inhomogenity of the material characteristics, the fluctuation should cause edge shift of the readout signal. Thus, the time interval between leading or trailing edges was measured for the MSR disk by RAD with double masks as shown in Figure 9.38. As is realized from the overview in Figure 9.13, the deviation of time interval between leading edges should be related to the fluctuation of the boundary between the down-spin mask and the aperture. Similarly, the deviation of time interval between trailing edges results from the fluctuation of the boundary between the up-spin mask and the aperture. Figure 9.39(a) and (b) shows the distribution of the time intervals before equalization at a mark length of 0.4 μm, or equivalently for 2T marks in (1, 7) mark length recording, where $T = 26$ ns is called the window. The standard deviations of the time interval of the leading edges and of the trailing edges are 1.42 ns and 2.38 ns, respectively, for $T = 26$ ns. These values are as small as those for the current MO disk.

The distribution of edge variation of readout signals was also measured for random data written on the RAD disk by (1, 7) mark length recording with a bit length of 0.3 μm. Standard deviation of 3.55 ns was obtained for $T = 26$ ns using equalization described before.

From a viewpoint of practical use, an MO disk system must have enough margin for allowing variations of parameters such as writing power, readout power, external

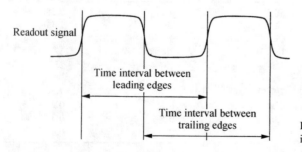

Readout signal

Time interval between leading edges

Time interval between trailing edges

Figure 9.38 Schematics of measured time intervals between leading/trailing edges.

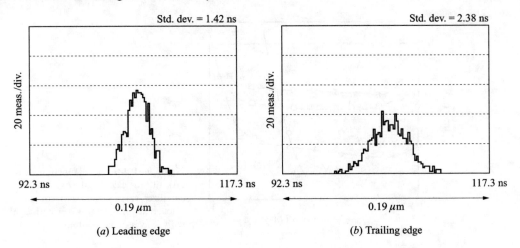

Std. dev. = 1.42 ns

Std. dev. = 2.38 ns

92.3 ns   117.3 ns   92.3 ns   117.3 ns

0.19 μm   0.19 μm

(a) Leading edge   (b) Trailing edge

Figure 9.39 Distributions of the time intervals between leading/trailing edges at a mark length of 0.4 μm.

magnetic fields, defocusing, tangential disk tilt, and radial disk tilt. Here, two examples are discussed: defocusing margin and tangential disk tilt margin. Figure 9.40 shows the calculated and measured jitter as a function of defocusing. The jitter was calculated using Equation (9.33) as a time-varying signal. The calculated jitter indicated by (a) remains small up to a defocus of ±1.5 μm, which is enough for practical use by considering the focusing servo performance. Although the measured jitter has a similar dependence on the defocusing, it contains a large intrinsic jitter caused by imperfections of the recorded mark shape and electric and optical noise. The jitter as a function of the tangential disk tilt is shown in Figure 9.41. In conventional detection, the tangential disk tilt seriously affects the jitter because the side lobe intensity is increased by the tilt. The deterioration of the jitter is especially significant for a high-NA lens or for a short wavelength light source, as shown in (d) for a case λ = 0.4 mm. In case of MSR by RAD with double masks, a wide tangential disk tilt tolerance is expected as shown in

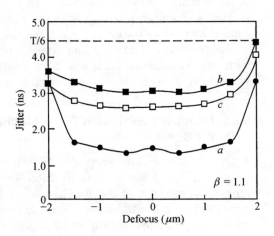

Figure 9.40 Jitter as function of defocusing: (a) calculated, (b) measured without equalizer, and (c) measured with equalizer.

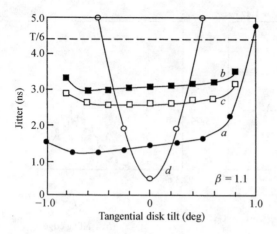

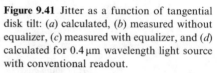

Figure 9.41 Jitter as a function of tangential disk tilt: (*a*) calculated, (*b*) measured without equalizer, (*c*) measured with equalizer, and (*d*) calculated for 0.4 µm wavelength light source with conventional readout.

(*a*) because the side lobe is blocked by double masks. A wide margin for the tangential disk tilt is also confirmed by the experiment, as shown in (*b*) and (*c*).

9.8 OTHER SUPERRESOLUTION DISKS

9.8.1 MSR Disk by FAD for Recording with Magnetic Field Modulation

As described in Section 9.2, recording by magnetic field modulation is a promising method for recording minute marks as well as for direct overwriting. A high magnetic field sensitivity is required for MO disks, because it is difficult to apply so high a magnetic field for writing with a high data transfer rate using a magnetic head. Thus, many studies have been reported on MO disks for which overwriting by magnetic field modulation is possible with a magnetic field less than 8 KA/m (100 Oe). The technique for reducing the switching field was applied to the MSR disk by Ohnuki et al. [16]. Figure 9.42 shows the structure of disk A investigated for MSR by FAD. A magnetic capping layer was inserted between the recording layer and the SiN layer for disk B in order to reduce the switching field. The transition metal rich TbFeCo with low perpendicular magnetic anisotropy and with 5–10 nm thickness was used for the capping layer. Figure 9.43 shows the carrier and the noise levels for disk A and B as a function of the applied magnetic field in magnetic field modulation. Overwriting by field modulation with a field of only 60 Oe is possible for disk B with the capping layer. Superresolution was confirmed by measuring a C/N ratio of 44 dB for a mark length of 0.4 mm for both disks.

9.8.2 MSR Disk with an In-Plane Magnetization Layer (CAD)

A unique MSR disk was reported by Murakami et al. using an in-plane magnetization layer [17]. This scheme is called center aperture detect (CAD). Figure 9.44 shows the cross-sectional view of the double-layered disk structure. GdFeCo and DyFeCo layers were used for the readout layer and the recording layer, respectively. The readout layer has the in-plane magnetization at an ambient temperature, but has the perpendicular

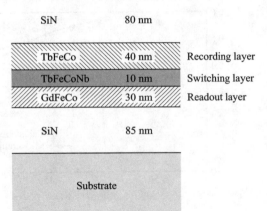

SiN	80 nm	
TbFeCo	40 nm	Recording layer
TbFeCoNb	10 nm	Switching layer
GdFeCo	30 nm	Readout layer
SiN	85 nm	
Substrate		

Figure 9.42 Structure of disk A for MSR by FAD. The capping layer was inserted between the SiN layer and the recording layer.

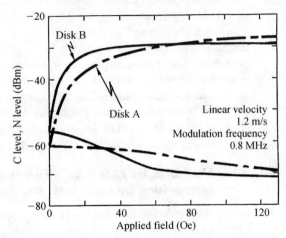

Figure 9.43 The carrier and the noise level for disk A and disk B as a function of the applied magnetic field.

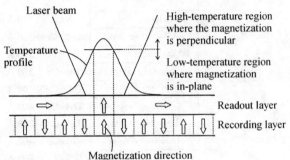

Figure 9.44 Principle of superresolution for the magnetic double-layer disk with an in-plane magnetization layer.

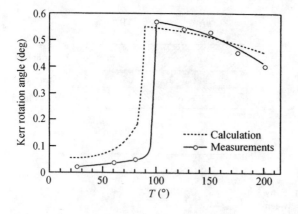

Figure 9.45 Kerr rotation angle of the magnetic double-layer film measured from the readout-layer side as a function of temperature.

magnetization at temperatures above a critical temperature, as shown in Figure 9.45 where the calculated and measured temperature dependences of the Kerr rotation angle are shown. Since a signal is not detected from the low temperature region where the magnetization of the readout layer is in-plane, the region works as a mask. The signal is detected only from the high temperature region where the magnetization is perpendicular. A C/N ratio of 34 dB for 0.4 μm mark was obtained. The C/N ratio seems to be degraded by the imperfect mask behavior which results from the perpendicular component of the magnetization at low temperatures as shown in Figure 9.45. Since the principle of superresolution is essentially based on RAD, the double-layered CAD MSR has an advantage of increasing track density. A low crosstalk of −33 dB was obtained for a 0.8 μm track pitch. Besides, the MSR disk has another advantage that it does not need the initializing magnet. Thus, the double-layered CAD MSR disk will become attractive when the C/N ratio for small marks is improved.

9.8.3 MSR Disk by FAD with a Function of Direct Overwriting by Light Intensity Modulation

Overwritable MSR disk by FAD was proposed by Fujii et al. [18]. Direct overwrite by light intensity modulation is possible using the magnetic septilayer structure shown in Figure 9.46. Figure 9.47 shows the C/N ratio as a function of the laser power for readout of 0.37 μm marks. The readout power dependence is shown by the solid circles,

Substrate	PC	
Dielectric layer	SiNx	500 Å
FAD-readout layer	GdFeCo	300 Å
FAD-switching layer	TbDyFe	100 Å
Memory layer	TbFeCo	300 Å
Intermediate layer	GdFeCo	100 Å
Writing layer	DyFeCo	400 Å
Switching layer	TbFeCo	200 Å
Initializing layer	TbFeCo	400 Å
Dielectric layer	SiNx	800 Å

Figure 9.46 Structure of the magnetic septilayer disk which enables direct overwriting as well as superresolution.

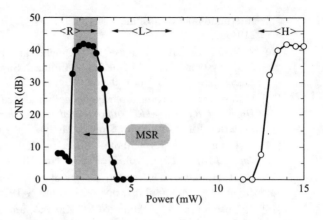

Figure 9.47 C/N ratio for the septilayer disk as a function of the readout power (the solid circles) and as a function of the high power at $P_r = 2.1$ mW (the open circles).

and the overwriting power dependence under a constant readout power of 2.1 mW is shown by the open circles. Regions R, L, and H in the figure correspond to readout by FAD, the low power for erasure, and the high power for overwriting, respectively. Super-resolution is achieved with a C/N ratio of 42 dB for readout of $0.37\,\mu$m marks at readout powers between 1.6 mW and 3.0 mW. MSR on overwritten marks is obtained at high power, more than 13 mW.

REFERENCES

[1] K. Aratani, A. Fukumoto, M.Ohta, M. Kaneko, and K. Watanabe, "Magnetically Induced Super Resolution in Novel Magneto-optical Disk," *Proceedings of SPIE*, vol. 1499, Optical Data Storage Topical Meeting, Colorado Springs 1991, pp. 209–215.

[2] A. Fukumoto, K. Aratani, S. Yoshimura, T. Udagawa, M. Ohta, and M. Kaneko, "Super Resolution in a Magneto-optical Disk with an Active Mask," *Proceedings of SPIE*, vol. 1499, Optical Data Storage Topical Meeting, Colorado Springs 1991, pp. 216–225.

[3] E. Ikeda, T. Tanaka, T. Chiba, and H. Yoshimura, "The Properties of Sony Recordable Mini Disk," Proceedings of the Magneto-Optical Recording International Symposium, Tucson, 1992, *J. Magn. Soc. Japan*, vol. 17, Supplement S1, pp. 335–340, 1993.

[4] B. G. Huth, "Calculations of Stable Domain Radii Produced by Thermomagnetic Writing," *IBM J. Res. Develop.*, vol. 18, pp. 100–109, March 1974.

[5] T. Wilson and C. Sheppard, *Theory and Practice of Scanning Optical Microscopy*, London: Academic Press, 1984, pp. 140–156.

[6] M. Kaneko, K. Aratani, and M. Ohta, "Multi-layered Magneto-optical Disks for Magnetically Induced Superresolution," *Japan J. Appl. Phys.*, vol. 31, Part 1, No. 2B, pp. 568–575, February 1992.

[7] M. Kaneko, K. Aratani, A. Fukumoto, and S. Miyaoka, "MSR-Magneto-optical Disk for Magnetically Induced Super Resolution," to be published in *Proceedings of IEEE*, April 1994.

[8] T. Kobayashi, H. Tsuji, S. Tsunashima, and S. Uchiyama, "Magnetization Process of Exchange-coupled Ferrimagnetic Double-layered Film," *Japan J. Appl. Phys.*, vol. 20, pp. 2089–2095, November 1981.

[9] M. Ohta, A. Fukumoto, K. Aratani, M. Kaneko, and K. Watanabe, "Read Out Mechanism of Magnetically Induced Super Resolution," Proceedings of Magneto-Optical Recordings

International Symposium, Tokyo 1991, *J. Magn. Soc. Japan*, vol. 15, Supplement S1, pp. 319–322, 1991.

[10] S. Yoshimura, A. Fukumoto, M. Kaneko, and H. Owa, "Large-capacity Magneto-optical Disk System Using Magnetically Induced Super Resolution," *IEEE Trans. Consumer Electronics*, vol. 38, pp. 660–664, August 1992.

[11] I. Nakao and M. Kaneko, "Magnetically Induced Superresolution for High Track Density," *Digest of the 3rd MRS International Conference on Advanced Materials*, Symposium V, Materials for Information Storage Media, Tokyo 1993, VAa 1.2

[12] A. Fukumoto and S. Kubota, "Super-resolution of Optical Disk Using a Small Aperture," *Japan J. Appl. Phys.*, vol. 31, Part 1, No. 2B , pp. 529–533, February 1992.

[13] H. H. Hopkins, "Diffraction Theory of Laser Read-out Systems for Optical Video Discs," *J. Opt. Soc. Am.*, vol. 69, pp. 4–24, January 1979.

[14] S. Yoshimura, A. Fukumoto, M. Kaneko, and H. Owa, "High Density Magneto-optical Disk System Using Magnetically Induced Super Resolution," *Japan J. Appl. Phys.*, vol. 31, Part 1, No. 2B, pp. 576–579, February 1992.

[15] A. Fukumoto and S. Yoshimura, "Magnetically Induced Super Resolution for High-density Optical Disk Systems," *Proceedings of SPIE*, vol. 1663, Optical Data Storage Topical Meeting, San Jose, 1992, pp. 216–224.

[16] S. Ohnuki, K. Shimazaki, N. Ohta, O. Inagoya, and A. Sakemoto,"Switching Field Reduction in MSR Type Magneto-optical Disks," Proceedings of Magneto-Optical Recording International Symposium, Tucson, 1992, *J. Magn. Soc. Japan*, vol. 17, Supplement S1, pp. 205–208, 1993.

[17] Y. Murakami, N. Iketani, J. Nakajima, A. Takahashi, K. Ohta, and T. Ishikawa, "Super Resolution Readout of a Magneto-optical Disk with an In-plane Magnetization Layer," Proceedings of Magneto-Optical Recording International Symposium, Tucson, 1992, *J. Magn. Soc. Japan*, vol. 17, Supplement S1, pp. 201–204, 1993.

[18] Y. Fujii, Y. Nakaki, T. Tokunaga, and K. Tsutsumi,"Direct Overwriting and Superresolution Readout by Exchange-coupled Multilayer Film," Proceedings of Magneto-Optical Recording International Symposium, Tucson, 1992, *J. Magn. Soc. Japan*, vol. 17, Supplement S1, pp. 167–170, 1993.

Chapter 10

MAGNETO-OPTICAL RECORDING SYSTEMS

Y. Nakane, H. Yoshimura, S. Igarashi

10.1 INTRODUCTION

Magneto-optical disk technology has been applied not only as an external memory for computers, but also in digital audio and video recorders. The characteristics of MO drive systems are designed for the application requirements such as data transfer rate, unit memory size, and address structure. Depending on the application, MO disks have different structures and specifications. On the other hand, MO disk systems are constructed using many common servo technologies to achieve large memory capacity and to exhibit stable operation over a wide range of environmental conditions.

In this chapter, the current products for computer data application and digital audio applications are introduced. Some future prospects of these systems are also discussed.

10.2 CURRENT PRODUCTS

10.2.1 Outline of the Disk Operation Technology

10.2.1.1 Introduction

The data density of a MO disk is very high: one bit of written data covers an area of only one square micrometer. Therefore, the technologies of accurate positioning of a focused laser beam spot and of high-speed access to required data from the huge memory capacity are very important key technologies for the system—as important as the recording media structure. The disk drive is constructed of many servo systems to achieve good positioning and access as shown in Fig.10.1. How to create an error signal using these servo systems is a key design point for MO disks and the drive systems, especially the optical block of the drive. Figure 10.2 shows a typical example of the optical block construction.

10.2.1.2 Focus Servo System

An objective lens in the optical block has to move quickly in the up and down direction according to movements of the disk plane, since the focus depth of a lens is only about 1 μm. Thus, an auto focusing system is needed as a positioning mechanism for the axial direction.

An astigmatism method is one of the most popular focus error detection methods. The principal of the method is shown in Figure 10.3. A return laser beam reflected from

385

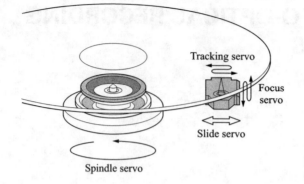

Figure 10.1 The servo systems in the MO drive.

the disk passes though a convergence lens and a cylindrical lens and then impinges on a photo detector that is constructed of four elements. The shape of the beam spot on the detector is a circle in the case of the just focused condition, but changes to an oval in the case of a defocused condition. The focus error signal can be obtained from a simple calculation of the outputs of the four elements of the photo detector

$$\text{Focus error} = (I_a + I_d) - (I_b + I_c) \tag{10.1}$$

where I_a, I_b, I_c, and I_d are the output currents of elements A, B, C, and D, respectively.

10.2.1.3 Tracking Servo System

The track pitch of the optical disk is designed to be almost equal in size to the beam spot diameter. A typical track pitch is 1.6 µm for the first generation of magneto-optical recording systems. The laser beam spot must track at the center of the track within 10%

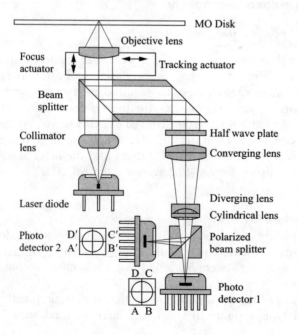

Figure 10.2 The structure of the optical block.

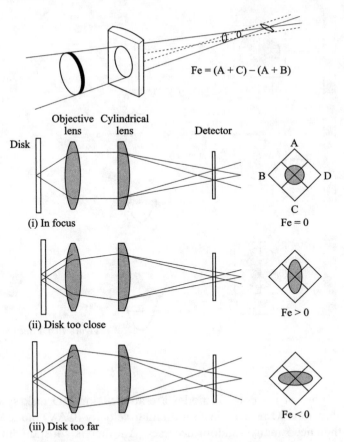

Figure 10.3 Astigmatism focus error detection method.

of the track pitch tolerance. The tracking servo system functions as a beam positioning technology along the radial direction. In the case of the ROM disk such as the Video Disk (DVD) or Compact Disc (CD), the tracking error can be derived from the array of pits. The spiral guide groove is preformed on the substrate surface to obtain the tracking error signal, since MO disks do not have any array of pits in the recordable area.

A push–pull tracking servo method is a popular servo error detection method for MO drive systems, as shown in Figure 10.4. Both right and left side edges of the beam spot cover the guide groove in the case of tracing the track center. The reflected laser beam is partially diffracted by the diffraction effect at the edge of the groove. Then, the intensity profile in the reflected beam spot on the detector changes. The difference between the intensities on the right- and left-half detectors keeps the equilibrium in the case of tracing the track center. However, the intensity of each half spot becomes unbalanced if the beam spot moves off-center of the track. The tracking error signal can be derived from the difference in outputs from the right and left half of the detector.

10.2.1.4 Spindle Servo System

The optical block does not control beam positioning in the parallel direction of the track. The positioning of this direction means a linear velocity control of the disk rotation.

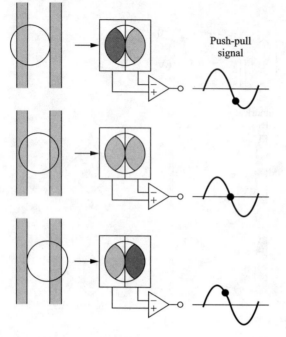

Figure 10.4 Principle of the push–pull servo.

Two types of the control modes are applied for MO disk systems depending on their applications. One is a constant angular velocity (CAV) mode for computer applications that need many random accesses. Another is constant linear velocity (CLV) mode for audio, video applications. A disk rotates at different speeds depending on the track radius of the beam location in the case of CLV mode. An error signal of the spindle servo can be made from the comparison between a standard clock rate and readout data rate using, for example, address marks.

10.2.1.5 Slide Servo system

The optical block has to slide linearly on the slider along the radial direction of the disk because the objective lens in the tracking servo system can move only within 5 mm. A short distance access uses the objective lens action, but a long distance seek also requires the use of the slide servo system. An error signal of the slide servo is generated from the low frequency component of the tracking error signal.

10.2.1.6 Phase Locked Loop (PLL) of the Data Clock

PLL is not a physical action servo but a very important pure electric circuit servo for control of the data clock rate. Since the spindle servo cannot control the high-frequency component of the error in linear velocity, the data clock generator has to control a clock frequency to fit with a readout signal data rate. An error signal of the PLL is generated from the phase difference between the clock pulse rate and the readout data pulse rate.

TABLE 10.1 Servo Specifications

	Focus servo	Tracking servo	Slide servo	Spindle servo
Gain	Reflectivity	Push–pull signal	Crosstrack signal	Header signal
Acceleration	Axial acceleration	Radial acceleration		Radial runout
Run-out	Axial runout	Radial runout		

10.2.1.7 Servo Parameters on the Disk

Quality issues of a disk must be standardized as the interface specification between a drive and a disk. Since the MO disks are removable media, it follows that interchangeability between many drives and disks is a very important characteristic for the MO disk applications. In order to understand the design points of the MO disk, some key servo parameters in the specifications are discussed.

An MO disk drive system requires a high-quality disk even though it has powerful servo systems, because any servo system has marginal utility. There are three kinds of drive/disk interface specifications for the servo systems: (1) gain of the servo error signal, (2) acceleration of the displacement, and (3) runout range of the displacement. These servo specifications of a disk are shown in Table 10.1.

The real displacement of a disk contains a wide frequency range of the spectrum, as shown in Figure 10.5. The specification of acceleration does not mean the limitation of the maximum peak on each spectrum, but the criteria of the maximum peak value on the real disk displacement. The cutoff frequencies of the focus and tracking servo systems are both about 2 kHz. The objective lens cannot follow the disk movement beyond the cutoff frequency. Therefore, the displacement spectrum over the cutoff frequency should be much less than the focus depth ($\sim 0.2\ \mu m$). The upper criteria on the lower component of the spectrum should be 10% down from the specification of the acceleration.

The gain of the tracking servo error signal, called the push–pull signal, is a very important parameter for design of the pregroove conditions. It depends on both groove

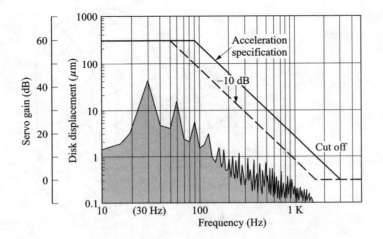

Figure 10.5 Spectrum of the disk displacement.

width and groove depth, as shown in Figure 10.6. On the other hand, other specifications such as a crosstrack signal for traverse count directly depend also on the groove conditions. Therefore, optimization is necessary for groove conditions to fit all the specifications.

10.2.2 Design of Optical and Thermal Properties

10.2.2.1 Introduction

MO disk systems must be capable of stable operation not only in a wide range of environmental temperatures, but also with any combination of disks and drives. The typical operating temperature range under normal conditions is from 0°C to 60°C, and the typical deviation of the drive conditions is about 10% of each designed value. The allowance of the design in the erase/write/read operating conditions is rather limited. The write power margin window in which the drive can write and read exactly is one of the most important design parameters for stable operation under a wide range of conditions.

10.2.2.2 Temperature Dependence of the Write Power Window

A typical example of the dependence of data error rate on the write laser power is shown in Fig.10.7. Almost all MO disk systems have a similar shape of the error rate characteristics. The bottom error rate depends on the actual defect density on the disk, or on the noise level of the readout signal. Since every MO disk drive has an error correction system, the drive can exactly correct the data when the raw error rate is less than some criteria of the error rate. The width of the write power range at the criterion level is called the "write power window." The normalized write power window at the center point of the window is called the "write power margin." Higher data density makes for a narrower write power margin, and higher carrier-to-noise ratio of a disk makes a wider margin. The power margin also depends on the write and read condition

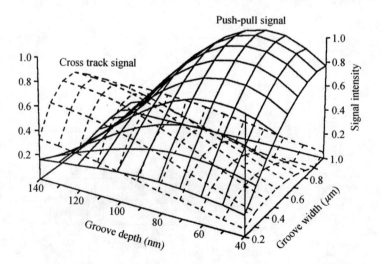

Figure 10.6 The groove condition dependence of servo signal.

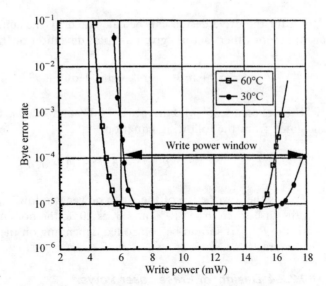

Figure 10.7 Write power margin.

of the drive, such as the write pulse width and the frequency characteristics of the equalizer amplifier used in the system. The narrower the write pulse width is, the better the margin becomes. Therefore, the pulse width and the equalizer parameters must be optimized to obtain the maximum write power margin.

The write power window changes depending on the environmental temperature, as shown in Figure 10.8. The hatched area in the figure is the zone of conditions with readable data, and the dotted line (E) is an upper limit set by the erase laser power. The erase laser beam partially erases the written data on the adjoining track when the laser power exceeds this criteria. The write and erase laser powers must be controlled along the line depending on the temperature of the disk.

10.2.2.3 Design of Write Laser Power

The lower the write power is, the longer the drive life. However, the write power of a drive should be much higher than the lower edge of the power margin. Many degradation mechanisms of the effective laser power must be considered when designing the write conditions. These are shown in Table 10.2. A reasonable value of the total

TABLE 10.2 The Degradation of the Effective Write Power

• Deviation of write sensitivity	$\sigma1$	$\approx \pm 10\%$
• Deviation of the power setting	$\sigma2$	$\approx \pm 10\%$
• Temperature difference between the disk and sensor	$\sigma3 = \Delta T \bullet \partial P_w/\partial T$	$\Delta T \approx 10°C$
• Detracking effect	$\sigma4 = \Delta t_r \bullet \partial P_w/\partial t_r$	$\Delta t_r = 0.1 \ \mu m$
• Defocusing effect	$\sigma5 = \Delta f_o \bullet \partial P_w/\partial f_o$	$\Delta f_o = 1.0 \ \mu m$
• Disk tilt effect	$\sigma6 = T_{ilt} \bullet \partial P_w/\partial T_{ilt}$	$T_{ilt} = 5 \ mrad$
• Magnetic field variation	$\sigma7 = \Delta M_g \bullet \partial P_w/\partial M_g$	
• Track runout effect	$\sigma8 = R_o \bullet \partial P_w/\partial R_o$	
• Contamination of the disk and lens	$\sigma9$	

deviation for the drive design can be calculated by the summation of $\sigma 2$ and the root mean square of other factors, given as total deviation of the drive

$$\sigma t = \sigma 2 + (\sigma 3^2 + (\sigma 4^2 + \sigma 5^2 + \sigma 6^2 + \sigma 7^2 + \sigma 8^2 + \sigma 9^2)^{1/2} \tag{10.2}$$

Typical values on a 5.25" MO drive are $+10\%$ and -20%. The nominal write power P_0 is calculated from the following equation.

$$P_{\min}(1 + \sigma 1 f) \le (1 - \sigma t)P_0 \tag{10.3}$$

Here, $P_{\min}$ is the lower edge of the write power window.

In the case where $\sigma 1$ is 10% and σt is 20%, the nominal write power P_0 becomes 138% of the $P_{\min}$. It should be controlled depending on the temperature, as shown for (P_0) in Figure 10.8.

10.2.2.4 Design of Erase Laser Power

The maximum size of a written dot can be made in the maximum magnetic field with a write laser power 10% higher than P_0. In the erase process, written dots with the maximum size must be erased sufficiently even under the weakest conditions, which corresponds to a 20% decrement in effective power with a minimum magnetic field intensity. The nominal erase power is experimentally determined by taking into account the above conditions.

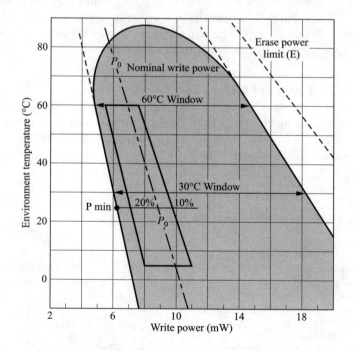

Figure 10.8 The temperature dependence of the write power window.

10.2.2.5 Design of Recording Layer Structure

Many types of disk structure have been studied. A typical example of a MO disk structure is shown in Figure 10.9. The MO layer is sandwiched between two thin dielectric films to protect the MO film from chemical reactions such as oxidation or corrosion. These three layers on the substrate are over-coated by an Al reflective thin film.

10.2.2.6 Design of Optical Properties

The incident laser light is transmitted through the MO layer, when an MO layer is thin enough. Then, the laser beam is reflected from the layers, by multiple reflections from each boundary of the four layers. Therefore, all the optical characteristics of the recording layer strongly depend on not only the characteristics of the materials, but also the thicknesses of these layers. The optical properties are very important parameters for optimizing the layer structure, since the Kerr rotation angle θ_K of the MO layer itself is very small. The optical properties such as Kerr rotation angle θ_K, Kerr ellipticity η_K, and reflectivity r can be simulated by solving Maxwell's equations under the boundary conditions appropriate for a thin multilayered medium. In this calculation, the incident laser light should be handled as a summation of right-handed and left-handed circularly polarized light [1]. Typical refractive indices of the TbFeCo MO layer at the 780 nm wavelength are $3.56 + i4.07$ and $3.64 + i4.13$. Some examples of the simulation results are shown in Figure 10.10. The larger the $r\theta_K$ and the smaller the ellipticity angle the better signal quality becomes. The maximum Kerr signal is obtained when the MO layer thickness is around 20 nm as shown in Figure 10.10.

10.2.2.7 Design of Thermal Properties

The thermal dynamic response of a recording layer is one of the most important properties for the design of the MO layer structure, since the recording mechanism is based on a thermal writing process. The thermal properties depend on not only thermal conductivity, but also on layer thickness.

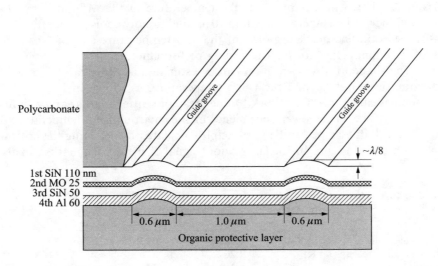

Figure 10.9 The MO disk structure.

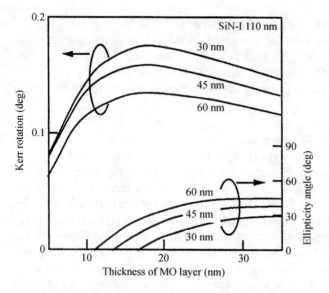

Figure 10.10 The Kerr signal depending on MO layer thickness. $\lambda = 780$ nm. The thickness of the third layer SiN is the variable parameter.

The thermal dynamic response can also be simulated by solving the following three dimensional Fourier heat diffusion equation.

$$q = \lambda \operatorname{grad} T \tag{10.4}$$

In this equation, q is the heat flow per unit time in a unit cell, λ is the thermal conductivity, and T is the temperature at the unit cell. The estimated values of each thermal constant of each layer are shown in Table 10.3. An example of the thermal dynamic response on the recording layer is shown in Figure 10.11, and a temperature profile in the radial direction of the track is shown in Figure 10.12.

Roughly speaking, about 80% of the exposed laser energy is absorbed in the MO layer. As shown in Figure 10.11, the temperature in the MO layer rapidly increases beyond the Curie temperature within 10 ns, and rapidly cools down after the laser beam is turned off. The quick response of the MO temperature and the sharp temperature profile are important for high recording performance.

The shape of a written mark can be estimated as the area within which the temperature increases beyond the Curie temperature, as shown in Figure 10.13. (This is sometimes called the "Curie disk.") The array of written marks can be simulated in the same way. The write power dependence or the environmental temperature dependence of the mark dot shape can be in principle calculated by changing the critical boundary of a contour in Figure 10.13. The readout signal of the written marks can also be found

TABLE 10.3 Thermal constants

	PC	SiN	TbFeCo	Al
Thermal conductivity (J/cms K)	0.002	0.03	0.12	2.38
Specific heat capacity (J/g K)	1.26	0.74	0.39	0.90
Density (g/cm^3)	1.2	2.6	8.0	2.7

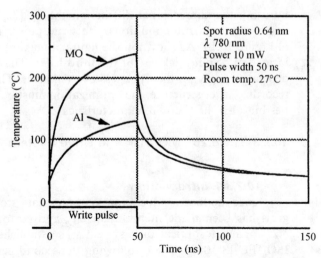

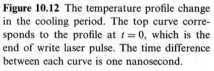

Figure 10.11 The thermal response in the write process.

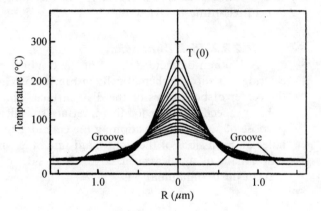

Figure 10.12 The temperature profile change in the cooling period. The top curve corresponds to the profile at $t = 0$, which is the end of write laser pulse. The time difference between each curve is one nanosecond.

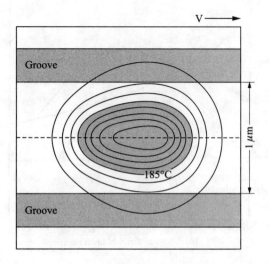

Figure 10.13 The shape of the written dot.

by using two-dimensional diffraction theory [2]. Using the estimated readout signal under various write conditions, the write power margin can be evaluated, as shown in Figure 10.14. As shown in the figure, a maximum peak of the write power margin is located at 55 nm thickness of the third layer. The write characteristics of the MO disk depend strongly on the thickness of each layer. Therefore, in the design process of the recording layer structure, the optimization must be made of not only the optical properties but also the thermal characteristics.

10.2.3 The 5.25″ MO Disk and Drive System

10.2.3.1 Introduction

Since the first products for computer data storage application in 1989, much progress has been made in both capacity and performance. The standardization of the 5.25″ magneto-optical disk system was established in 1991 (International Standard; ISO/IEC IS 1089). Then, following the second generation of the system with 650 MB per side of a 5.25″ MO disk in 1993, the so-called 3X drives (3 times capacity, 1 GB/ side) became products in 1994. In this section, the current technology of magneto-optical recording is reviewed.

10.2.3.2 Disk Dimension

A 130 mm diameter (5.25″) of the double-sided disk is stored in a polycarbonate cartridge, as shown schematically in Fig.10.15. The disk has magnetic clamping hubs in the center of both sides of the disk surface. The dimensions of the cartridge and the hubs are specified as the loading interface specification between disk and drive. For the purpose of accurately positioning the cartridge in the drive, the cartridge has centering holes on both sides of the right-hand side of it, and four points as reference. A shutter slider, made of stainless steel, covers both sides of the window on the cartridge shell to prevent dust contamination.

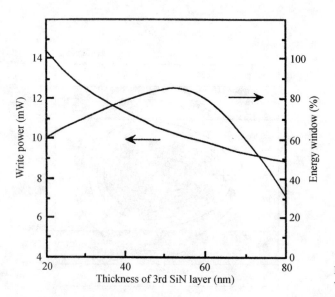

Figure 10.14 The computer simulated energy window.

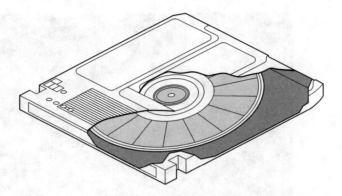

Figure 10.15 A 5.25″ MO disk cartridge.

10.2.3.3 Track Format

In order to take wide interchangeability between several kinds of drives and media, each disk has not only user recordable tracks, but also special tracks at the head and table of the tracks. These formatted zones of the disk extend from the radius 29.00 mm to 61.00 mm and are divided as shown below in Table 10.4.

10.2.3.4 Sector Format

Every track is divided into 17 sectors in the case of the 1024 bytes per sector media, or 31 sectors in the case of the 512 bytes per sector media. The sector consists of an embossed, 52 bytes long, pits data area and a 1308 bytes or 765 bytes long recordable area. The embossed pits data correspond to the sector header. Figure 10.16 shows a microscopic view of the pits observed with a scanning electron microscope. Figure 10.17 shows the data structure of a sector. The sector header consists of a sector mark, three address data blocks and a post amble, as shown below.

- **Sector Mark**   Five bytes of long mark pattern for easy detection of a sector header.
- **VFO**   For the phase lock of the variable frequency oscillator
  VFO1: 192 channel bits = 01001001001——010010
  VFO2: 128 channel bits = 10010010010——010010
  VFO3: 192 channel bits = 01001001001——010010

TABLE 10.4   Track Arrangement of the 5.25″ MO Disk

Zone Name	Radius (mm)	Track Number	Comment
Control track PEP	29.00–29.50		Format and media information
Transition for SFP	29.50–29.52	−312 ~ −301	Format changing zone
Control track SFP	29.52–29.70	−300 ~ −189	Media and system information
Media manufacturer	29.70–30.00	−188 ~ −1	Media performance test area
User zone	30.00–60.00	0 ~ 18,750	User data area
Media manufacturer	60.00–60.15	18,751 ~ 18,845	Media performance test area
Control track SFP	60.15–60.50	18,846 ~ 19,063	Media and system information
Lead out	60.50–61.00	19,064 ~	Used for positioning purpose

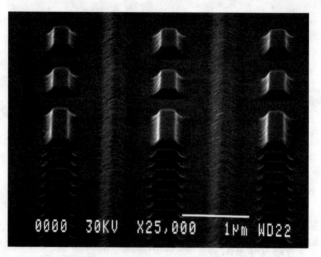

Figure 10.16 A SEM photograph showing the pit features embossed in digital sound and random access disks.

- **Address Mark**   1 byte long for detecting ID field.
  AM: 16 channel bits = 0100 1000 0000 0100

- **ID + CRC**   ID has 2 bytes of a track address and 1 byte of a sector address followed by 2 bytes of check byte named cyclic redundancy check code.

Track address 2 bytes	Sector Address 1 byte	CRC 2 bytes
MSB LSB	ID No sector no.	

- **Post amble**   One byte data for closure of a few uncertain bits of the last CRC byte in the 2, 7 encoding scheme.

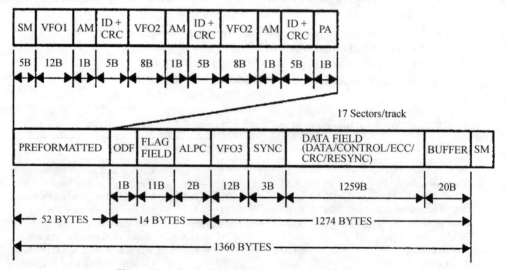

Figure 10.17 Sector format of the 1024 Bytes/sector media.

The recordable area of the sector consists of not only a user data field but also 49 bytes or 44 bytes of additional area explained below.

- **ODF**   One byte long of mirror area with neither grooves nor embossed pit for detection of servo error signal offset.
- **Write flag**   Five bytes long of the reserved flag area to prevent inadvertent over write on the previously written data.
- **ALPC**   Two bytes long of a test area for laser power level calibrations.
- **Gaps**   Three bytes long buffer area for absorbing timing shift when writing the flag.
- **Sync Mark**   Three bytes of synchronization data must be written to give the data separation timing for the succeeding user data field.
- **Buffer**   Reserved space to allow for linear speed tolerances caused by motor speed or eccentricity of the track.

The data field consists of 1024 or 512 bytes of user data, 59 or 40 bytes of resync marks, 4 bytes of CRC data, 160 or 80 bytes of error correction code data (ECC), and 12 bytes of control information data (DMP), as shown in Figure 10.18.

- **Resync Mark**   In order to prevent the loss of the byte synchronization when the VFO must ride through defects within a data field, it resynchronizes VFO and limits the propagation of the errors.

10.2.3.5 Defect Management Strategies
The defect management of an MO system is one of the most important issues for reliable operations, and is a key design feature. The 5.25″ MO system uses more than 30% of the disk as overhead for defect management. The defect management system consists of multi-ID, data error correction, alternative sector, and write protection.

The probability of a defect in a disk decreases linearly on a logarithmic scale against error length. Generally speaking, the probability distribution consists of the random error part and the burst error part, as shown in Figure 10.19. The error detection and correction method used in the system is the Reed–Solomon code, known as long distance code, with a degree of redundancy of 16, as shown in Figure 10.18. Less than 8 bytes of the error in each file (104 bytes + 16 bytes) can be corrected by this method. In order to increase correction capability for the burst error, the 10-way interleave is adopted in the case of 1024 bytes/sector media, and the five-way interleave for 512 bytes/sector media.

The flow chart of the total error management and the file structure of a system are shown in Figure 10.20. At a media production site, all disks are certified under severe conditions. The sector that has two or three ID errors or more than 3 bytes of error in any ECC file is designated as a defective sector, and its address information is registered in a *primary defect list* (PDL). The certified disk looks like a defect-free disk, since the drive system skips the defective sector using the PDL information.

In a write process at the user site, the drive system always checks the ID field. If the drive detects two or three ID errors in a sector, then the drive does not write data in the sector, but in the spare sector and stores this information into a *secondary defect list* (SDL). The tracking servo error is checked during the writing process, if the servo error

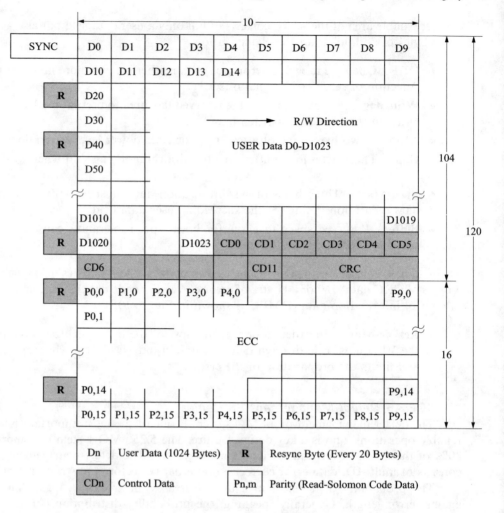

Figure 10.18 The construction of the data field.

signal exceeds some criteria, then the drive stops writing, and rewrites the data into the spare sector.

The drive should verify the written data after the data writing. In this process, the drive checks the ID error and data error. The sector that has two or three ID errors or more than 4 bytes of errors in any sector is considered a defect sector, and its address information is registered into SDL.

10.3 MiniDisc

10.3.1 Introduction and Features of the MiniDisc System

The MiniDisc (MD) system, developed by Sony, offers both digital sound and random access features. In addition to these features, the following three types of MiniDiscs have been developed for various applications:

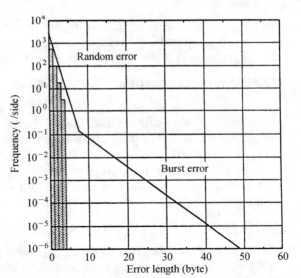

Figure 10.19 Probability of each error length.

1. Playback-only MiniDisc for prerecorded music;
2. Recordable MiniDisc allowing up to 74 minutes of recording time; and
3. Hybrid MiniDisc, a combination with premastered and recordable areas.

The intrinsic recording technology supporting the recordable MiniDisc is the magnetic field direct overwrite method, applied to a consumer product for the first time in the world.

The distinctive features of the MiniDisc are

1. Overwrite function:
2. Maximum 74 min. recording time on a disk only 64 mm in diameter, achieved using data compression and high-density recording;
3. Quick random access supported by address information in the wobbled groove; and
4. Disk protection with the cartridge and shutter.

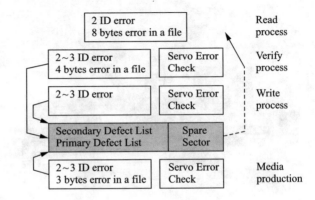

Figure 10.20 Defect management strategies.

Moreover, durability and reliability for the recordable MiniDisc have already been proven with data storage media for computer peripherals, such as the magneto optical disk. Figure 10.21 shows the various MD systems.

10.3.2 System Concept and Specifications

The specifications of the compact disc (CD) were first proposed in 1982, and are described in the so-called "Red Book." Since then, the technological developments for both data and recording applications have been specified in the "Yellow Book" and "Orange Book," respectively. The MiniDisc specifications, which are an extension of these last two books are given in the "Rainbow Book," as shown schematically in Figure 10.22. A block diagram and the main specifications are shown in Figure 10.23 and Table 10.5.

10.3.3 Random Access Functions

Figure 10.24 shows the cross section of a playback-only MiniDisc. Both the lead-in area and lead-out area are on the inner and outer circumferences, respectively.

Recordable MiniDiscs are formed with special pre-grooves that cover the entire disc recording area. The pre-grooves enable tracking and spindle servo control operations during both recording and playback, as illustrated in Figure 10.25. These pre-grooves meander slightly at 13.3 ms intervals to maintain a specified linear velocity and to create addresses which allow very stable high-speed random access.

In addition to the meandering pre-grooves, a UTOC (User Table of Contents) also contributes to user-friendly quick random access. As shown in Figure 10.25, the lead-in area on the inner circumference of the disk followed by the UTOC area, the program area, and finally the lead-out area similar to the playback-only MiniDisc.

Each sector in the TOC (Table of Contents) in the lead-out and the UTOC is specified as in Table 10.6.

10.3.4 Signal Recording Format

The MiniDisc system uses the popular eight-to-fourteen modulation system (EM) in writing data on a disk and the Cross Interleave Reed–Solomon Code (CIRC) for error

Figure 10.21 Various MD systems.

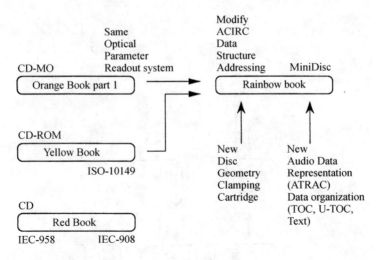

Figure 10.22 Relationships between industrial standards for optical disk products.

correction. Audio data reduced by ATRAC is grouped into blocks for recording in a format very similar to the CD-ROM mode 2 standard, as in Figure 10.26.

The first three sectors of one 36-sector cluster are used as link sectors during recording, with the fourth sector reserved for subdata. In the remaining 32 sectors, the compressed digital data are recorded. When the last sector has been written, error correction data must be written in the first link sector and half of the second sector of the following 36-sector cluster.

TABLE 10.5 MiniDisc Specifications

Major Specifications	
Recording/playback time	74 min (max)
Cartridge size (WHD)	72 × 68 × 5 mm
Disk specifications	
Diameter	64 mm
Thickness	1.2 mm
Diameter (center hole)	11 mm
Diameter (beginning of program)	32 mm
Diameter (beginning of lead-in)	29 mm
Track pitch	1.6 microns
Linear velocity	1.2–14 m/s (CLV)
Signal Format	
Sampling frequency	44.1 kHz
Compression system	ATRAC *1
Modulation system	EFM *2
Error correction system	CIRC *3
Optical Parameters	
Laser wavelength	780 nm
NA	0.45
Recording power	5 mW (max.)
Recording system	Magnetic field modulation

*1 Adaptive transform acoustic coding
*2 Eight to fourteen modulation
*3 Cross interleave Reed–Solomon code

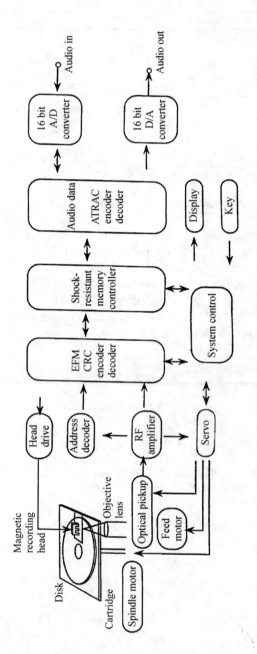

Figure 10.23 Block diagram of MiniDisc system.

TABLE 10.6 Sector Role in TOC/UTOC

TOC	Generic terms for all subdata
	Track number, playing time, etc.
	Recording power and recordable time for recordable MD
Sector 0	Generic terms, start and finish address
Sector 1	Disk title, music title and artist
Sector 2	Recorded date and time for disk and music
Sector 3	Barcord for disk and ISRC for music
Sector 4	Disk title, music title, and artist (ISO-8895-1)

During ATRAC encoding, the audio data are compressed to one-fifth its original volume, and then handled in 424 byte units called "sound groups" with left and right channels allocated 212 bytes each. Eleven of these sound groups are distributed into two sectors. Recorded sound groups in the first sector comprise the left and right channels of five sound groups, plus the left channel of a sixth group, while the right channel of the sixth group and the left and right channels of another five groups are recorded in the second sector. Each of the two sectors can be expressed as $425 \times 5 + 212 \times 1 = 2332$ bytes.

In this manner, 11 sound groups are written per every two sectors in each 32-sector cluster. ATRAC decoding restores the data block to its original volume and time axis, with one sound group becoming equivalent to 512 samples ($512 \times 16 \times 2/8 = 2048$ bytes) for both channels, with a playing time of 11.6 ms.

10.3.5 ATRAC Data Compression

MiniDiscs are recorded using Sony's Adaptive Transform Acoustic Coding (ATRAC) system, shown in Figure 10.27, which was designed specifically for high fidelity audio using digital data compression technology. For each block of time, ATRAC analyzes the music signal and determines the sensitivity of each frequency region. The sensitive regions are recorded accurately with very little quantization noise. The remaining regions are recorded less accurately, but since they are not overly sensitive, the quantization error is hardly noticeable. The result is high-fidelity audio in actual listening, recorded at only one-fifth the bit rate, thus enabling ATRAC to allow MiniDiscs up to 74 min of recording and playback time on a disk only 64 mm in diameter.

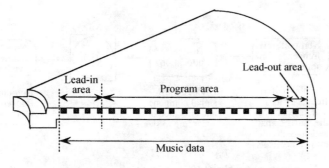

Figure 10.24 Cross section of a playback only MiniDisc.

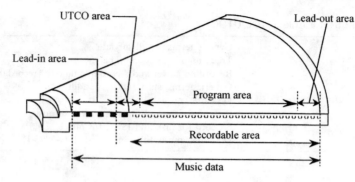

Figure 10.25 Cross section of a recordable MiniDisc.

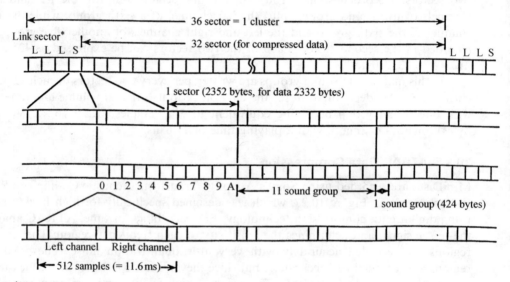

*This becomes a subdata sector in playback-only MiniDiscs

Figure 10.26 MiniDisc data format configuration.

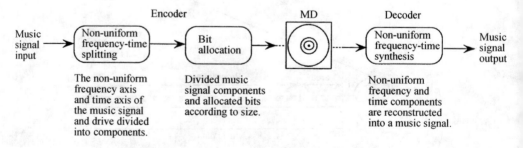

Figure 10.27 ATRAC operation layout.

10.3.6 Construction of Recordable MiniDisc

Magneto-optical technology is central to the functioning of recordable MiniDiscs. Since a magnetic recording head and a laser are used on opposite sides of the disk, the shutter opens on both sides of the disk, as shown in Figure 10.28.

The construction of the recordable MiniDisc is illustrated in Figure 10.29. The wobbled groove is 1.2 μm wide and λ deep. A 1.6 μm track pitch is specified for the recording track in order to coexist with the address information which is formed by meandering at set intervals of every 13.3 ms. These dimensions have been adopted to satisfy the servo characteristics, in consideration of thermal crosstalk form adjacent tracks, and to gain the maximum C/N.

The design concept behind the MO layers has been reported by Y. Tamada et al. [4]. The current 5.25″ and 3.5″ MO disks, employ a four-layer structure, and the MiniDisc has also adopted the same layered structure.

10.3.7 Magnetic Field Modulation Overwrite

The recordable MiniDisc is required to realize the same storage density as that of the compact disc, which is 0.85 μm/pit for the 74-min model.

The magnetic field modulation method has certain advantages for this application in terms of system stability and margin between media and drive, compared with the laser modulation recording method. The edge of the marked pattern is determined by the flux reversal, and its shape is intrinsically independent of the laser power fluctuation. Moreover, the magnetic field modulation method intrinsically possesses the feature of overwrite recording. In the case of the MiniDisc, the maximum required field modulation frequency is 720 kHz at a linear velocity of 1.2 to 1.4 m/s.

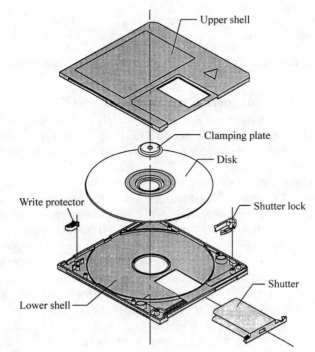

Figure 10.28 Cartridge assemble.

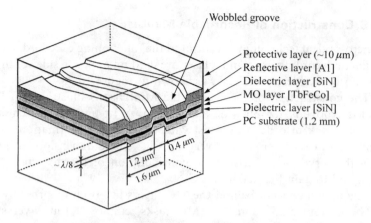

Figure 10.29 Structure of recordable MiniDisc.

10.3.8 Magnetic Head for Overwrite

The recording magnetic field for the recordable MiniDisc is required to be over 8 kA/m (100 Oe), and the magnetic head is allowed to contact the disk. In consideration of portability for the MiniDisc system, a contact type has been designed and achieved with the following conditions:

1. Spacing is 150 μm;
2. The magnetic field is over 8 kA/m (100 Oe) within ±0.5mm from the center of the core.

Figure 10.30 shows the magnetic field distribution of a recording head at a spacing distance of 150 μm.

10.3.9 Recording Characteristics and Film Properties

10.3.9.1 Magnetic Characteristics and C/N

The comparison of Kerr loops near the Curie temperature between the recordable MiniDisc (*a*) and conventional MO (*b*) is given in Figure 10.31. Remarkable differences between (*a*) and (*b*) in squareness, and the required minimum magnetic field saturation H_s should be noted.

The temperature dependences of residual θ_K, H_c, and of H_s (saturation field) are shown in Figures 10.32 and 10.33. The difference in H_s between MD and conventional MO is clearly demonstrated. Note that the magnetization of the MiniDisc is easily reversed by a field of less than 8 kA/m (100 Oe), at temperatures near the Curie temperature.

Figure 10.34 shows the magnetic field dependence of the C/N for the conventional MO and MiniDisc. The C/N of the conventional disk at 8 kA/m (100 Oe) is not high enough to satisfy MiniDisc specifications and gradually increases with H_{ext} up to 16 kA/m, and a C/N of about 49 dB. On the other hand, the C/N of the MiniDisc is much higher even at a field 8 kA/m (100 Oe); this value far exceeds the minimum requirement of the MiniDisc system of 46 dB.

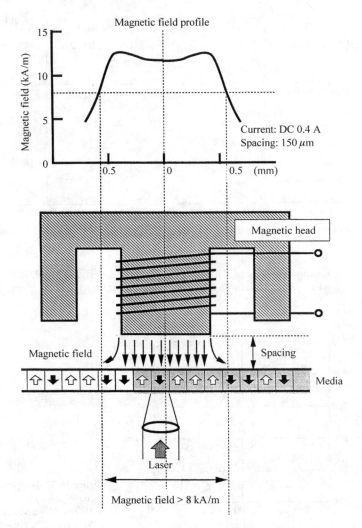

Figure 10.30 Magnetic field profile of a magnetic head.

Figure 10.35 shows the individual trends for the carrier and noise levels. The carrier level of the MiniDisc starts to saturate even at a very low field, and the noise is the dominant factor governing the C/N value in a low field.

10.3.9.2 Power Margin

During actual application, the laser power on a disk may not always be constant, but rather it fluctuates. The fluctuation should be taken into account in an actual drive system recording. For this purpose, the BLER (block error rate) must be less than 3×10^{-2} even when the laser power fluctuates ±20% of its specified values.

Figure 10.36 (*a*) and (*b*) shows the laser power dependence of C/N, and jitter at 8 kA/m (100 Oe) and BLER, respectively. As the C/N remains more than 46 dB and BLER is less than 3×10^{-2} from 3.6 mW to 6.5 mW, this is wide enough for practical

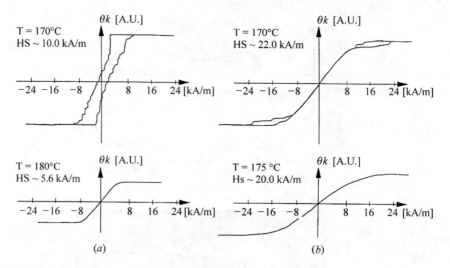

Figure 10.31 Kerr hysteresis loops at 170 and 180°C for (*a*) Recordable MiniDisc (*b*) Conventional MO disk on a glass substrate with the layers glass/SiN(110nm)/TbFeCo(250nm)/SiN(350nm)/Al(550nm).

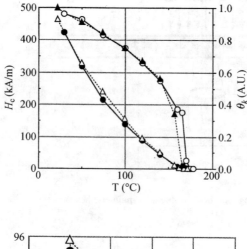

Figure 10.32 Temperature dependence of residual θ_k and H_c.
○ MD θ_k ▲: conventional MO θ_k
● MD H_c △: conventional MO H_c

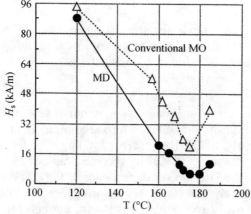

Figure 10.33 Temperature dependence of saturation fields (H_s).

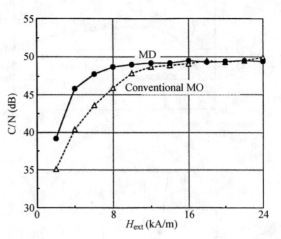

Figure 10.34 Bias field dependence of C/N for MD and conventional MO $v = 1.22\,\text{m/s}$, laser power = $4.55\,\text{mW}$, Mark length = $0.85\,\mu\text{m}$.

applications. High BLER on a low power side is caused by low C/N; on the other hand, BLER on a high power side mainly comes from large jitter, due to heat from the adjacent tracks.

10.3.10 Reliability and Durability

Sufficient reliability has been designed into the MiniDisc as in the case for the conventional MO disk. Figure 10.37 shows no change in BLER when the same area has been repeatedly recorded a million times over. The MiniDisc system allows for the magnetic head to contact the disk. To obtain sufficient durability for this interfacing, the recordable MiniDisc has a lubricating feature on the overcoat layer, which covers the sensitive layers and faces the magnetic head. The magnetic head has been specially designed to reduce the friction. Figure 10.38 shows changes in friction when the head continuously contacts the same track, under various circumstances. This gives evidence that the durability for contact is sufficient for practical applications.

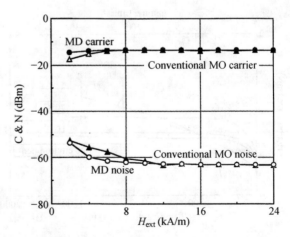

Figure 10.35 Bias field dependence of carrier and noise $v = 1.22\,\text{m/s}$, laser power = $4.55\,\text{mW}$, mark length = $0.85\,\mu\text{m}$.

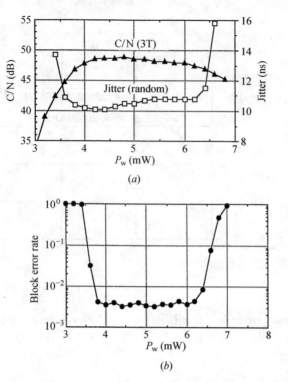

(a)

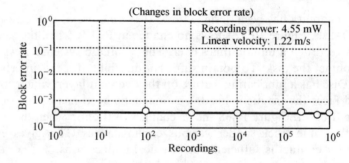

(b)

Figure 10.36 (a) The laser power dependence of C/N and jitter $v = 1.22$ m/s, $H_{ext} = 8$ kA/m, C/N mark length $= 0.85$ μm. (b) The laser power dependence of block error rate $v = 1.22$ m/s, $H_{ext} = 8$ kA/m.

(Changes in block error rate)

Recording power: 4.55 mW
Linear velocity: 1.22 m/s

Figure 10.37 Durability in repeated recordings.

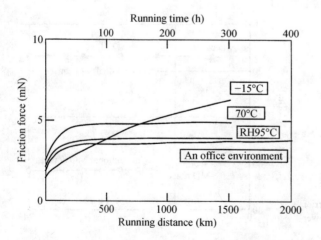

Figure 10.38 Friction force of a magnetic head.

TABLE 10.7 Rewritable MD-Data Specifications

Format	User area (radius)	mm	16–30.5
	Sector size (mode 4)	bytes/sector	2048
	Configuration of track		Spiral
	Track pitch	μm	1.6
	Direction of rotation		CCW (seen from optics side)
Mechanical characteristics	Outer diameter of disk	mm	64
	Cartridge dimension (W/R/H)	mm	72 × 68 × 5
	Substrate thickness	mm	1.2
Read/write conditions	Nominal write magnetic field strength	kA/m	8–24
	Carrier-to-noise ratio	dB	> 46
	Block error rate		$< 3 \times 10^{-3}$
Recording capacity		MB	140
Reliability	Read cycle		$> 10^6$
	Write/read cycle (rewritable)		$> 10^6$

10.3.11 Future Applications

The recordable MiniDisc and MiniDisc system represents the world's first implementation of magnetic field modulation overwrite in a consumer product. This technology will find further use in a data storage model, the MD DATA, which has a storage capacity of 140 MB with the same 64 mm diameter disk. Specifications are shown in Table 10.7. Moreover, this technology has been introduced into the Digital Audio Master Disc for application in professional recording studios. Recording densities for the Master Disc are presented in Table 10.8, comparing these with the MiniDisc. It has been possible to raise the resolution potential by setting the optical head to NA 0.5, and wavelength to 780 nm. As a result, the recording density of the Master Disc is 20% greater than the 74 min version of the MiniDisc, in addition to using 2–7 modulation. Figure 10.39 offers a comparison of recording densities for different magneto-optical disks.

In summary, the technology for magnetic field modulation has been realized with overwrite features for both consumer and professional applications, and for audio entertainment as well as data storage.

TABLE 10.8 Recording Densities for MASTER DISC and MD Format

	MASTER DISC	MD (74 min.)
Disk format		
Modulation system	2–7 RLL	EFM
Track pitch	1.55 μm	1.6 μm
Smallest pit length	0.78 μm	0.847 μm
Optical pickup		
Numerical aperture of lens (NA)	0.50	0.45
Laser wavelength	7.80 nm	780 nm
Comparison of recording densities		

$$\frac{\text{MASTER DISC}}{\text{MD}} = \frac{1/2}{8/17} \times \frac{1/1.55}{1/1.60} \times \frac{1/0.785}{1/0.847} = 1.18$$

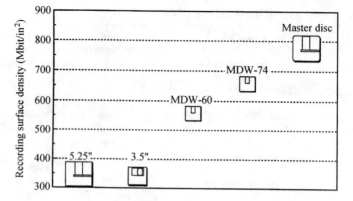

Figure 10.39 Comparison of MO disk recording densities.

10.4 FUTURE PROSPECTS

10.4.1 Overview of Magneto-Optical Disks

As stated in Section 10.3, magneto-optical disks have the added feature of direct over-writing by the magnetic field modulation technique.

The characterization of magneto-optical disks in comparison with other rewritable media is already discussed in Chapter 1, but a brief review is given here.

Figure 10.40 shows how the areal recording density among the major recording media has been changing over time. Although the magneto-optical disk is still superior in areal recording density, its performance in a complete system is generally inferior to

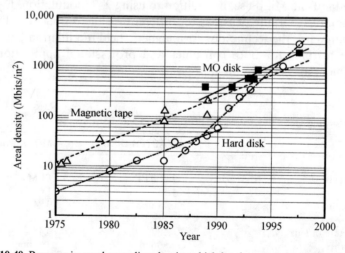

Figure 10.40 Progress in areal recording density which has been commercially achieved for three major data storage media. The magnetic hard disk has experienced a rapid rate of improvement compared with magnetic tape and magneto-optical disk media. One key factor is the "fixed" nature of the hard disk. The other media, in contrast, must support removability and interchangeability.

that of the HDD (hard disk drive). This is mainly because the HDD's read/write heads are much smaller and have simpler structures compared to those in optical disk drives. This also allows the development of HDD multiplatter and high-speed access systems.

As ROM (read only memory) disks, optical disks function as data replication/communication media as well as data storage media (see Fig. 10.41). In the case of CD-ROMs, 640 MByte of data can easily be copied onto a single disk in a few seconds using CD (compact disc) mass production techniques. The demand for such recording media has become increasingly high, particularly in electronic publishing. Therefore, in order to expand the market for magneto-optical disks, it is important to develop a way to use it as removable media while also maintaining compatibility with ROM disks.

The recording and playback of digital audio signals are now realized by the CD, MD (MiniDisc), etc. The next target is to deal with digitally encoded moving pictures. Data compression algorithms for moving pictures have been internationally standardized by MPEG (Moving Picture Image Experts Group) [5], [6]. To retain an image quality comparable to that of NTSC (National Television System Committee) broadcasting, 4 to 6 Mbps transfer rate is required. Figure 10.42 shows the relationship between storage time and areal density for some disk sizes. The user capacity divided by the total capacity, including ID (identification), ECC (error correction code), defined as overhead, is assumed to be 0.7. For a movie of one hour duration on a CD-sized optical disk with a transfer rate of 5 Mbps, a density of more than 1.5 Gbit/in^2 is necessary. This is nearly more than twice the areal density in current CDs.

Before discussing the techniques to make higher density magneto-optical disks, the characteristics of optical- and magnetic-recording is discussed first [7]. Table 10.9

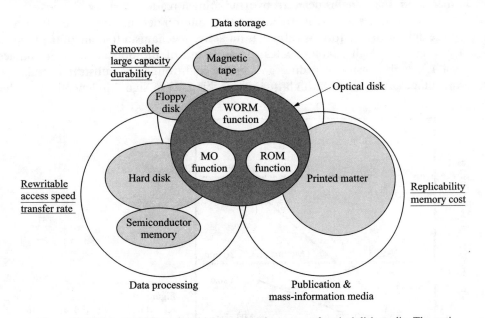

Figure 10.41 Schematic diagram which explains the nature of optical disk media. The optical disk has three major functions. The first is the duplication and distribution of huge amounts of data as typified by CD-ROMs. The second is mass data storage as realized by WORM (write once read many) media. The third is to provide rewritable memory for data processing.

TABLE 10.9 Comparison of the Principal Characteristics Between Magneto-Optical and Magnetic Recording Systems

	Magneto-optical Recording System	Magnetic Recording System
Signal sensing method	Active	passive
	infra-red ~ visible light (convergible)	magnetic field (not convergible)
Resolution	beam spot diameter (~ wave length)	head gap dimension
Recording material	ferri magnetism (RE-TM material)	ferro magnetism
Output signal	Proportional to sub lattice Ms	proportional to total Ms
Curie temperature	~ 200C	over ~ 600°C
Coercive force at RT	no limitation	limited by rec. head field
Tracking signal	pre-groove or pit signal	magnetically recorded mark signal
Dependence of rec.	yes	no
Condition on velocity	(rec, power)	
Depencence of readout	no	yes (inductive head)
Condition of velocity		no (MR head)
Suppression of DC component in read channel	no	yes (inductive head) no (MR head)

summarizes the major characteristics. In the readout of magnetic recording media, the magnetic leakage flux from the recording film is detected. The playback resolution is restricted by the gap size in the magnetic head. In magneto-optical recording, on the other hand, the signal is detected by irradiating a readout beam which is focused down to the diffraction limit. Consequently, the resolution depends mostly on the wavelength of the light source. Moreover, there is an active mechanism to control the focusing and tracking. Although it complicates the structure of the optical head, it enables non-contact, high-density recording and playback through the substrate. It also has the advantage of obtaining a high-quality tracking servo signal independent of the mag-

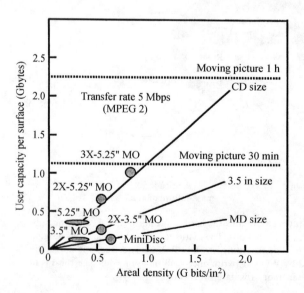

Figure 10.42 Relationship between areal recording density and user data capacity for each disk size. The broken horizontal lines indicate recordable time for a moving picture assuming a coding rate of 5 Mbits/s. Major MO disks commercialized before the end of 1993 are also indicated in this figure.

neto-optical signal. Obtaining a tracking signal of similar quality from a magnetic disk with a track density as high as that of optical disks would be more difficult [8], [9].

Next the recording materials are discussed. The rare-earth-transition metal compounds which are usually used for magneto-optical recording are ferrimagnetic materials and the readout Kerr signal depends on the saturated sublattice magnetization. In magnetic recording, however, since the output signal increases in proportion to the total saturated magnetic moment, ferromagnetic materials must be used. Moreover, the allowed coercive force is restricted by the strength of the magnetic field in the recording head. By contrast, there is no restriction on the coercive force at room temperature for magneto-optical recording materials. Magneto-optical materials consequently have better intrinsic potential for high-density recording.

Magneto-optical recording materials with relatively low Curie temperatures of about 200°C are generally used, so the recording is essentially thermal. Therefore, the recording process is not only dependent on the linear velocity of the media but is also easily affected by changes in the ambient temperature. On the other hand, the Curie temperature of conventional magnetic recording media is usually over 600°C, and therefore, the magnetic properties depend weakly on the ambient temperature within the drive system. Furthermore, the linear velocity dependence of the reading and writing processes is different from that of the magneto-optical one. Since the read channel of (magneto-)optical disk drives can transmit signals from DC to high frequencies, various modulation codes can be adopted and servo signals can be placed in the low frequency band. For high-density magnetic recording systems, the MR (magneto resistive) head [10] has been developed to avoid some of the deficiencies present in inductive heads by using the magnetoresistive effect [11].

10.4.2 Techniques for Higher Density Recording

The mark position recording method has been used in both the 1st and 2nd generations 3.5″/5.25″ MO disk ISO standard disks. The presence and absence of a recorded mark corresponds to binary data "1" and "0," respectively. The data are recovered by detecting the position of the peaks in the playback signal. The mark edge recording method, on the other hand, interprets magnetization reversals as binary data "1." Upon playback the transition points of these reversals are detected as digital signals in the optical head.

The original data are usually encoded first in order to improve the recording density and to recover the clock from the playback signal [12]. For example, the (2, 7) RLL (run length limited) code requires at least two "0"s between consecutive "1"s in the encoded data, and the number of consecutive "0"s is restricted to a maximum of seven. Figure 10.43 schematically compares mark position and mark edge recording. As shown, if the recording density is the same, the minimum mark length is longer for mark edge recording. At the optical resolution limit, the minimum mark length can be shortened further to increase the recording density. However, the mark edge recording is more difficult to control because of thermal diffusion. The length of the magnetic domain is varied through a change in ambient temperature. On the other hand, in mark position recording, the position of the peaks in the playback signal does not change even if the recording power fluctuates to some extent. Therefore, the margin of error is less severe, especially while recording. For this reason, the mark position recording technique was adopted for first- and second-generation magneto-optical disks. Nevertheless, the encoding method will inevitably change to mark edge recording.

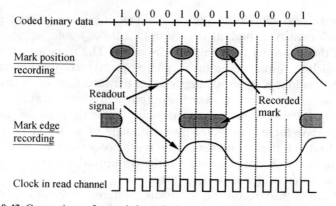

Coded binary data

Mark position recording

Readout signal

Recorded mark

Mark edge recording

Clock in read channel

Figure 10.43 Comparison of recorded mark shapes resulting from the mark position and mark edge recording techniques.

Hence the maximum density achievable will be determined more by the thermal response of the recording film.

Next, light intensity modulation and magnetic field modulation recording methods are discussed. One of the important recording characteristics of the magneto-optical disk is the dependence of the error rate upon recording laser power. This is indicated in Figure 10.44. The region (a) corresponds to an improvement in the S/N of the playback signal as the recording power increases and illustrates how quickly the error rate drops after passing a threshold. The error rate remains constant over a certain range, after which it increases due to overpower effects such as preheating and post-heating of the recorded marks. Therefore the appropriate recording power level is restricted to within a range delimited by "Pa" and "Pb." This extent will become more restricted as the recording density increases. Therefore it is particularly important to maintain a practical recording power range.

Here, the limitation in the maximum recording power for both the light intensity modulation and magnetic field modulation recording methods is discussed. Figure 10.45 shows a schematic comparison of mark shapes recorded under various irradiation power levels. When the recording laser power exceeds a certain limit, the mark size with

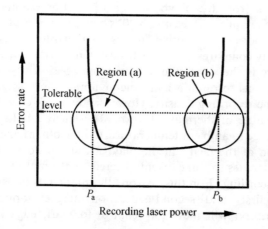

Figure 10.44 Schematic diagram illustrating the dependence of the error rate in the readout signal on the recording laser power.

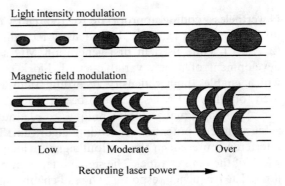

Figure 10.45 The general shape of marks recorded by the light intensity and magnetic field modulation methods. The dependence on recording laser power is also shown.

light intensity modulation becomes too large to detect "0" signals present between the recorded marks, which naturally causes errors. Assuming that the recording beam spot is circular, the accumulation of heat flow causes the recorded mark to elongate along the track and to gradually widen in the lateral direction to become teardrop shaped [13]. Fluctuations in the recording laser power easily varies the mark length and thus the timings of the "1"s and "0"s in the readout signal. The precise control of the edge positions then becomes a key issue, especially for high-density mark edge recording systems. When employing edge detection write compensation [14] must be employed to properly control the recording irradiation pattern to avoid excessive heat diffusion. It is also necessary to use sophisticated read compensation techniques [15].

In magnetic field modulation systems, however, the length of the recorded mark depends merely on the time intervals between the reversals of the recording magnetic field. The width of the mark is affected by fluctuations in the recording laser power, ambient temperature, recording sensitivity, and so forth. Consequently we are convinced that magnetic modulation is preferable for mark edge recording. As shown in Figure 10.45, the upper limit of recording power Pb is restricted by the increase in crosstalk from the adjacent tracks. Hence, the crucial issue for high-density recording is to make recorded marks with suitable widths.

Second, several coding techniques [16] which improve the readout process and also enhance the effective recording density are discussed. According to standard information theory [17], the channel capacity C [bit/s] of bandwidth W [Hz] with white noise can be represented by

$$C = W \log_2(1 + S/N), \quad [\text{bits/s}] \qquad (10.5)$$

where S is the average signal power and N is the noise power in the channel. The read channel bandwidth of optical disk systems is the product of the linear velocity and the cutoff spatial frequency. The cutoff frequency depends on the wavelength of the readout light and the numerical aperture of the objective lens within the readout optics [18]. The channel capacity, namely the maximum data density within the readout signal, approximately increases in proportion to the logarithm of S/N (the signal-to-noise ratio of the readout signal). The "channel coding theorem" guarantees the existence of a coding method that achieves the channel capacity given by the formula. Achieving this density in practice is very difficult because of discrepancies between ideal and real white noises and other disturbances, which degrade the frequency response of the channel.

Nevertheless, coding appropriate for the read/write channel for optical disks has been investigated. For example, high-density recording has been achieved by changing the (2, 7) RLL code used in first-generation MO systems to (1, 7) RLL code [19]. The development of a new variable-length block code, VFM (variable five modulation), which enables higher density recording than EFM (eight to fourteen modulation) used for CDs and MDs, has also been reported [20].

Applying equalization techniques to readout signal detection is also important to achieve the full potential of a coding algorithm. These techniques suppress intersymbol interference present in the readout signal, which basically comes from the finite bandwidth of the read channel. The signal interference between adjacent marks causes signal jitter. The frequency response of a read channel in optical disk systems is represented by optical MTF (modulation transfer function) which decreases monotonically. Cosine filter equalization is widely used to restore the high-frequency portion of the readout signal. However, unlike a conventional transmission channel, the optical transmission channel is greatly distorted by aberrations in the optical pickup. The inclination of the substrate generates an especially serious aberration called "coma" which is described by the third-order coefficient of aberration W_{31} given [21] by

$$W_{31} = \frac{(n^2 - 1)d(\text{NA})^3\theta}{2n^3}, \tag{10.6}$$

where θ is the tilt angle, NA is the numerical aperture of the objective lens, and d is the thickness of the substrate with refractive index n. Although optical resolution is improved with a high NA objective lens, the aberration increases in proportion to the third power of NA. Hence several ideas such as the utilization of a thin substrate and electronic adaptive equalization have been examined to obtain practical readout margins. These ideas will play an important role in those cases where higher density optical recording is to be achieved without improving the channel capacity.

The partial response technique is a high-density coding method, which takes advantage of intersymbol interference. This is a sort of multilevel detection scheme, which superposes the recovered waveforms of adjacent marks by restricting the bandwidth. This technique has been classified according to the rules of waveform superposition. In the case of optical disk systems, the partial response class I technique (denoted by PR (1, 1)) especially fits the read channel's MTF characteristic, and its combination with the maximum likelihood sequence technique [22] has attracted much attention. The required bandwidth can be reduced almost in half with the PR (1, 1) technique, although the number of detection levels changes from two or three and the S/N of the readout signal decreases.

To compensate for the degraded S/N, the readout signal is subjected to a maximum likelihood sequence analysis in which the received bit sequence including noise is decoded to the most probable bit sequence. The method is contained in a comparatively simple algorithm called *Viterbi decoding*. The Viterbi algorithm is a decoding technique for convolutional codes, which is very useful when the noise has no correlation. Since the intersymbol interference in the partial response technique is equivalent to a kind of convolutional encoder, these two make a good combination [12], though, it has had only limited use in fields such as satellite communication. Progress in LSI (large scale integrated) chip technology, however, has realized the Viterbi algorithm in very fast and easy-to-use hardware which permits its application to be aggressively promoted in the field of optical recording as well as magnetic recording.

10.4.3 Shorter Wavelength Light Sources

In the previous subsection, the ways to realize higher density recording within the limit given by the channel capacity were discussed. Here, the magnification of the bandwidth W appearing in Equation (10.5) is discussed. MSR (magnetic super resolution), which is explained in Chapter 9, is an example of a technique to realize high-density recording by expanding the bandwidth of the readout channel. In this subsection, other techniques are considered by reviewing the latest technological trends in shorter wavelength light sources and related optical disk properties.

The semiconductor laser diode first adopted for magneto-optical disk drives and also used for compact discs is composed of GaAlAs and has a wavelength of around 780 nm. The InGaAlP laser diode of III-V semiconductor crystal has also been developed for 670 and 690 nm. The room temperature continuous wave operation of this laser was realized in 1985, and it has already become practical for read only optical disk drives. Currently, higher power lasers are under development [23] for use in magneto-optical disk drives. II–VI semiconductors have also been undergoing research for many years. In 1991, a ZnSe material system lasing in the blue-green at low temperatures was reported [24], and the room temperature continuous wave operation was demonstrated [25]. More recently, a GaN (375 nm) laser diode has been successfully developed. In the near future, anticipated improvement in reliability and output power will allow it to be used as a light source for magneto-optical disk systems.

SHG (second harmonic generation) is an alternative technique to obtain coherent blue-green light sources. For a long time SHG by nonlinear optical materials could not obtain practical conversion efficiency. However, remarkable progress was made in 1985 by positioning the nonlinear optical crystal KTP (KTiOPO$_4$) within the cavity of a Nd-doped YAG (Y$_3$Al$_5$O$_{12}$) laser pumped with laser diode [26]. This is called intra-cavity SHG in which the fundamental wave is amplified within the laser cavity. A stable SHG-green light whose fundamental wave has a narrow spectrum and a single mode was obtained by merely using a relatively unstable laser diode as the pumping light source for a solid-state laser. Figure 10.46 schematically shows an example of the optical configuration [27]. The volume of the total device has been miniaturized to several

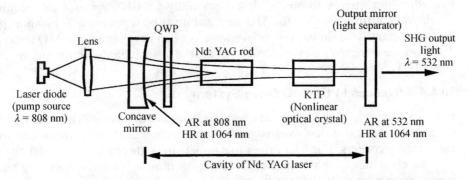

Figure 10.46 Schematic diagram of a compact green laser based on a laser diode-pumped Nd: YAG laser and second harmonic generation. AR and HR stand for "anti-reflective" and "highly reflective" coatings, respectively.

cubic centimeters and has been tested as a light source in optical disk drives for high density recording [28], [29]. In another SHG technique using bulk crystals, highly efficient direct conversion from a semiconductor laser by a monolithic ring resonator with a $KNbO_3$ nonlinear crystal has also been achieved. The application of 20 mW of blue coherent light (429 nm) derived from a 60 mW laser diode fundamental wave (858 nm) to magneto-optical disk drives has been reported [30].

Research in coherent blue-green light sources has entered the development stage for practical use and investigation of magneto-optical recording materials for shorter wavelength light sources is also in progress as discussed in Chapter 6. As Equation (10.5) indicates, the signal-to-noise ratio of MO signals detected by blue-green light sources must be high enough to achieve higher density recording. Noise caused by substrate surface roughness and recording media inhomogeniety tends to increase with the improvement of resolution in readout optics designed for shorter wavelength light sources. Another factor, which reduces S/N is the decreasing sensitivity of the silicon PIN photodetector in the readout optics as the wavelength of the light source shortens toward the blue region. Substrate birefringence, tilt angle, and other optical aberrations, and errors arising in the drive servo system such as defocus and detrack become worse with decreasing wavelength of the readout light. In order to benefit from the expanded bandwidth in the read channel brought about by blue-green light sources, other related problems need to be solved and the S/N of recording material itself needs to be improved.

Thermal diffusion within the MO material plays an important role in the magneto-optical recording process. The thermal diffusion length L can be calculated by the formula

$$L \sim \sqrt{a \cdot t}, \tag{10.7}$$

where t is the duration time of the recording laser beam pulse and a is the thermal diffusivity of the material. For example, if a is 0.4 [cm^2/s] for TbFeCo and $t = 10$ ns, then L becomes 0.6 μm. This size is not negligible compared with the recording beam spot diameter d given [21] by

$$d = 1.22\lambda/(NA) \tag{10.8}$$

Recording onto magneto-optical disks, especially with blue-green light, requires that the thermal diffusion within the MO material must be suppressed as much as possible. This important issue should not be overlooked when developing new MO materials and designing new recording layer structures that also include dielectric and/or reflective layers [31].

10.4.4 Advances in the MO Drive System

First, issues concerning higher data transfer rates are discussed. The data transfer rate of magneto-optical disk drives is generally low compared with audio and magnetic video tape recorders. For MO drives to compete in fields of high-speed data processing such as computer graphics and high definition moving pictures, this rate should be improved substantially. One way would be to modulate the magnetic field at very high speeds, which would require a flying magnetic head [32] instead of a contact magnetic head as found in the MiniDisc system. However, the flying head is more difficult to modulate at high frequencies than the conventional magnetic head such as HDDs because the area over which the magnetic field is applied is very large. Therefore, reducing the magnetic pole area by using a special kind of tracking servo and improving the head efficiency are necessary. For light intensity modulation recording, multibeam recording by laser diode arrays may be effective. A transfer rate of more than 300 Mbit/s by eight multibeam channels have been reported [33]. If an exchange-coupled MO film is incorporated, then direct overwrite by light intensity modulation becomes possible.

Second, the miniaturization of optical heads is a very important technique to improve the performance of optical disk drives. For the readout head in Compact Disc players, miniaturization was accomplished by designing a special objective lens and optical module and by mounting minute optical components and the laser diode chip onto the photodetector [34].

Polarized optical elements, which are required for the detection of magneto-optical signal, may also be miniaturized with the development of optical gratings that can control light polarization [35]. Fundamental research on integrated optics using waveguides is also in progress [36] and, this technology is expected to be available for optical heads in magneto-optical disk drives.

REFERENCES

[1] Sakuya Tamada, Shuich Igarashi, Susumu Sakamoto, Hiroshi Nakayama, Mikio Yoshida, and Yasuaki Nakane, Proceedings of the International Symposium on Optical Memory, 1989. *Japan J. Appl. Phys.*, vol. 28, Supplement 28-3, pp. 67–70, 1989.

[2] H. H. Hopkins, *J. Opt. Soc. Am.*, vol. 69, Nos. 1,4, 1979.

[3] SONY SMO-E502, *Specifications and Operating Instructions*, 1992.

[4] S. Tamada, S. Igarashi, S. Sakamoto, M. Yoshida and Y. Nakane, *Japan J. Appl. Phys.*, vol. 28, Supplement 28-3, p. 67, 1989.

[5] D. J. LeGall, "MPEG: A Video Compression Standard for Multimedia Applications," *Communications of the ACM*, vol. 34, April 1992.

[6] ISO/IEC JTC1/SC29/WG11/602, "Generic Coding of Moving Pictures and Associated Audio," *Committee Draft ISO/IEC* 13818-2, November 1993.

[7] C. D. Mee and E. D. Daniel (ed.), *Magnetic Recoding*, vols. I–III, New York: McGraw-Hill Book Company, 1987.

[8] M. Futamoto, F. Kugiya, M. Suzuki, H. Takano, Y. Matsuda, N. Inaba, Y. Miyamura, K. Akagi, T. Nakano, H. Sawaguti, H. Fukuoka, T. Munemoto, and T. Takagaki, "Demonstration of 2 Gb/in^2 Magnetic Recording at a Track Density of 17kTPI," in *MMM-Intermag Conference*, Paper MA01, June 1991.

[9] K. Watanabe, T. Takeda, K. Okada, and H. Takino, "Demonstration of Track Following Technic Based on Discrete Track Media," in *INTERMAG'93/digests*, FD 10, April 1993.

[10] F. B. Shelledy and J. L. Nix, "Magnetoresistive Heads for Magnetic Tape and Disk Recording," *IEEE Trans. Magn.*, vol. 28, pp. 2283–2288, September 1992.

[11] C. Tang , M. Chen, T. Yogi, and K. Ju, "Gigabit Density Recording Using Dual-element MR/Inductive Head on Thin Film Disks," *IEEE Trans. Mag.*, vol. 26, pp. 1689–1693, September 1990.

[12] P. H. Siegal and J. K. Wolf, "Modulation and Coding for Information Storage," *IEEE Communications Magazine*, vol. 29, pp. 68–86, December 1991.

[13] H. Sukeda, M. Ojima, M. Takahashi, and T. Maeda, "High-density Magneto-optic Disk Using Highly Controlled Pit-edge Recording," *Proceedings of the International Symposium*

on Optical Memory, Tokyo, 1987, *Japan J. Appl. Phys.*, vol. 26 Supplement 26-4, pp. 243–248, 1987.

[14] H. Ide, T. Toda, F. Kirino, T. Maeda, F. Kugiya, S. Mita, and K. Sigematsu, "Precise Mark Shape Control in Mark Length Recording on Magneto-optical Disk," *Japan J. Appl. Phys.*, vol. 32, pp. 5342–5348, November 1993.

[15] T. Maeda, H. Tuchinaga, H. Ide, A. Saito, T. Toda, F. Kugiya, M. Ojima, S. Mita, and K. Shigematsu, "Read Channel and Format for High-density Magneto-optical Disk System," *Japan J. Appl. Phys.*, vol. 32, pp. 5335–5341, November 1993.

[16] A. J. Viterbi and J. K. Ohmura, *Principles of Digital Communication and Coding*, McGraw-Hill, 1979.

[17] R. G. Gallager, *Information Theory and Reliable Communication*, New York: John Wiley & Sons, 1968.

[18] G. Bouwhuis, J. Braat, A. Huijser, J. Pasmann, G. van Rosmalen, and K. Schouhamer Immink, *Principles of Optical Disc Systems*, Bristol and Boston, Adam Hilger Ltd., 1985, Chapter 7, pp. 228–255.

[19] T. Iwanaga and H. Inada, "High-density Recording Using Mark Length Recording Method for Magneto Optical Disk," *Japan J. Appl. Phys.*, vol. 31, pp. 580–583, February 1992.

[20] N. Eguchi and Y. Akiyama, "High Density Optical Disk System Using Variable Five Modulation and Second Harmonic Generation Green Laser," *Japan J. Appl. Phys.*, vol. 32, pp. 5307–5311, November 1993.

[21] G. Bouwhuis, J. Braat, A. Huijser, J. Pasmann, G. van Rosmalen, and K. Schouhamer Immink, *Principles of Optical Disc Systems*, Bristol and Boston, Adam Hilger Ltd., 1985, Chapter 2, pp. 7–81.

[22] M. Tobita, T. Yamagami, and T. Watanabe, "Viterbi Detection of Partial Response on a Magneto-optical Recording Channel," *SPIE, Optical Data Storage*, vol. 1663, pp. 166–173, February 1992.

[23] G. Hatakoshi, K. Nitta, K. Itaya, Y. Nishikawa, M. Ishikawa, and M. Okajima, "High-power InGaAlP Laser Diodes for High-density Optical Recording," *Japan J. Appl. Phys.*, vol. 31, pp. 501–507, February 1992.

[24] M. A. Haase, J. Qiu, J. M. DePuydt, and H. Cheng, "Blue-green Laser Diodes," *Appl. Phys. Lett.*, vol. 59, pp. 1272–1274, September 1991.

[25] N. Nakayama, S. Itoh, T. Ohata, K. Nakano, H. Okuyama, M. Ozawa, A. Ishibashi, M. Ikeda, and Y. Mori, "Room Temperature Continueous Operation of Blue-green Laser Diodes," *Electronics Letters*, vol. 29, pp. 1488–1489, August 1993.

[26] T. Baer and M. S. Keierstead, in *Digest of Conference on Lasers and Electro-Optics*, ThZZ1, 1985.

[27] M. Oka and S. Kubota, "Second-harmonic Generation Green Laser for Higher-density Optical Disks," *Japan J. Appl.*, vol. 31, pp. 513–518, February 1992.

[28] I. Ichimura, Y. Sabi, Y. Takeshita, A. Fukumoto, M. Kaneko, and H. Owa, "High Density Magneto-optical Recording with a Second-harmonic-generation Green Laser," *Japan J. Appl. Phys.*, vol. 32, pp. 5312–5316, November 1993.

[29] M. Takahashi, J. Nakamura, M. Ojima, and K. Tatsuno, "High Density SHG Laser Readout with Pt/Co MO Disk," *SPIE, Optical Data Storage*, vol. 1663, pp. 250–256, February 1992.

[30] W. J. Kozlovsky, A. G. Dewey, A. Juliana, J. E. Hurst, M. R. Latta, D. A. Page, R. N. Payne, and H. Werlich, "Optical Recording in the Blue Using a Frequency-doubled Diode Laser," *SPIE, Optical Data Storage*, vol. 1663, pp. 410–415, February 1992.

[31] S. Tamada, S. Igarashi, S. Sakamoto, H. Nakayama, M. Yoshida, and Y. Nakane, "Design Concept of Magneto-optical Disk," *Japan J. Appl. Phys.*, vol. 28, Supplement 28-3, pp. 67–70, 1989.

[32] T. Kazama, "Flying Magnetic Head for Magneto-optical Recording," *Japan J. Appl. Phys.*, Series 6, *Proceedings of the International Symposium on Optical Memory*, pp. 192–196, 1991.

[33] R. Arai, M. Mizukami, T. Tanabe, K. Kato, T. Yoshizawa, H. Yamazaki, S. Murata, Y. Tanaka, and I. Sato, "Feasibility Study on High Data Transfer Rate of 300 Mbit/s with 8-beam Laser Diode Array," *Japan J. Appl. Phys.*, vol. 32, pp. 5411–5416, November 1993.

[34] R. Katayama, T. Nagano, S. Sugama, and Y. Ono, "Compact Optical Head Integrated with Chip Elements for CD-ROM Drives," *SPIE, Optical Data Storage*, vol. 1663, pp. 46–57, February 1992.

[35] C. W. Haggans, T. Fujita, and R. K. Kostuk, "Integrated Device with Diffractive Polarization Components for a Magneto-optical Disk Head," *SPIE, Optical Data Storage*, vol. 1663, pp. 46–57, February 1992.

[36] H. Nishihara, T. Suhara, and S. Ura, "Integrated-optic Pickups," *SPIE, Optical Data Storage*, vol. 1663, pp. 26–36, February 1992.

Chapter 11

DVD

Takao Suzuki

11.1 CD-REWRITABLE TECHNOLOGY

The audio compact disk read-only memory (CD ROM), which was introduced in 1982, is the most widely known digital optical storage device. Although not usually thought of in such terms, paper is the most common analog optical storage medium, whereas CD ROMs are past masters at distributing encyclopedias or catalogs or other voluminous collections of data having a longish shelf-life. However, unlike paper, they excel at distributing the masses of data intended for computer use or analysis, such as software or raw research data. The CD-ROM drives shipped in 1994 numbered around 17 million, and today they are standard equipment on about half of all new PC systems rolling off the assembly lines. It stores digital bits as pits (or the absence of pits) impressed in its reflective surface along concentric tracks. Transparent plastic protects the surface, which is scanned by the beam of a solid-state laser having a 780 nm wavelength. The audio CD stores 640 to 680 MB of information, or about 74 min of music, assuming standard sampling rate, frequency, and encoding. While magneto-optical recording disk capacity has been continually leaping ahead, the CD-ROM had yet to budge from its original density of 650 MB/disk until just recently. The situation has been changed dramatically. Major electronics and movie companies decided to replace videotapes with compact disks. Their premise is that the quality of digital video on CD would be much better, and better quality would carve out a new market, not only for disks and players, but for higher quality television sets as well. Since the amount of digital data needed to store a 2-h movie is massive, makers of optical disks and drives must increase the CD format's capacity.

In order to achieve high-density CDs, four parameters are reduced: the laser wavelength to 635 nm, adjacent tracks from 1.6 μm to 0.84 μm, and pit-width and pit-length are halved to about 300 nm and 0.83 μm, respectively.

While these physical changes net around a 5.7:1 increase in CD storage, what is required overall is about 10:1. The shortfall is supplied by a videocompression technique spelled out in the MPEG-2 standard. This standard was developed for the transmission of high-definition TV in the current U.S. broadcast-channel bandwidth of 6 MHz. With all these changes, now these high-density disks can carry the information capacity of 3.7 to 5 GB per single side, which corresponds to about 135 min playing time compared with 74 min for a conventional CD.

Apart from the CD-ROM, other types of CD disks have been developed. They are recordable CD (CD-R) and rewritable CD (CD-RW). CD-RW media promise greater compatibility with CD-R and DVD-R and CD-ROM and DVD-ROM drives than does the only other plausible contender, magneto-optical (MO) technology.

Figure 11.1 shows the comparison of the three types of recording disks, CD-ROM, CD-R, and CD-RW. In each case the positions of the recorded pits are detected by sensing laser light reflected back from the disk. In the case of the simple read-only CD, the information is stamped as low-reflectivity pits on a high reflectivity background— and thus reflected light is detected except when a pit passes under the laser beam. CD-R uses dye-polymer recording layers and CD-RW uses phase-change thin films. Figure 1.20 in Chapter 1 shows the cross section of a CD-R medium when a written bit is formed [1]. The disk structure is as follows: on top of a polycarbonate substrate (0), with a spiral and continuous pre-groove, a CD-R dye layer (approximately 150 nm thickness) (1) is spincoated. After evaporation or sputtering of a thick metal reflector (2), for instance, a 70 nm thick Au (or Ag) layer, a 7 μm thick UV-curable lacquer is spincoated and cured.

Typical materials for CD-R are the phthalocyanine dyes that have excellent light stability [2]. Figure 1.19 in Chapter 1 illustrates the formula for such a dye used for CD-R. Here the X groups are in the β position and each n is independently selected from 0, 1, and 2 such that at least one of the X-groups is selected from the formulas given in Figure 1.19. Figure 1.20 shows possible deformation effects compatible with a CD. The corresponding optical path differences are also given. In the first article on CD-R [3], it was reported that a bubble arises at the dye/Au interface, due to the decomposition of the heated dye during writing in the groove. In a following paper [4], a second explanation of the mechanism was proposed: It was assumed that during writing the dye decomposes and diffuses into the substrate. Atomic force microscopy reveals a 70 nm high bump on the stripped substrate. The dye/Au interface remained flat. The real writing mechanism of CD-R is believed to be a combination of both deformations (a

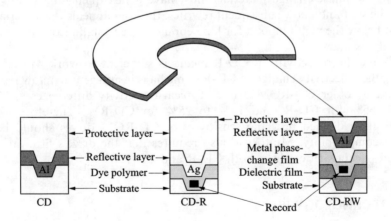

Figure 11.1 Three types of CD media. In a CD-RW disk (right), the active layer is a metallic film that changes its phase (from crystalline to amorphous) when it is locally melted with a laser and then allowed to cool rapidly. Unfortunately, the difference in reflectivity (between recorded 1's and 0's) for CD-RW is much lower than for CD-ROM and CD-R. Therefore, older CD-ROM drives cannot read CD-RW disks unless their design conforms to the new "MultiRead" specification [8].

bump at the interface between dye and polycarbonate substrate, a pit at the dye/Au interface and/or a bubble at the dye/Au interface). They are all related to the softening of polycarbonate substrate at 170°C and with a transition of the dye at 265°C. For higher density of CD-R using shorter wavelengths, the type of organic dye may have to be changed from one wavelength to another to optimize writing condition at each wavelength, since the optical constants of organic dye are a strong function of wavelength.

In summary, the CD-R disk has the following features:

1. It has a high reflectivity ($\geq 70\%$), a high modulation ($\geq 60\%$), low jitter (30 ns for 3T, T: clock time) at 786 nm and thus has compatibility with the current CD-ROM.
2. Written marks are in the groove regions, the reflectivity of which decreases.
3. The information area of a blank disk has a wobbled pregroove, which is for tracking and timing purposes.
4. The media cost in volume can be made very low as compared to other optical media because of spincoat fabrication.

For CD-RW, a thin layer of so-called phase-change alloy such as Ag-In-Sb-Te is usually used [5]. The concept of the phase-change optical storage is not new, but more than 20 years old [6]. Phase-change media have two stable phases. The detection of written marks is based on the reflectivity difference between the amorphous and crystalline phases. The difference must be high enough to give rise to a high contrast, or high signal in reading. Normally, a written mark is amorphous in the matrix of the crystalline phase [7]. To record a data point, the material is melted under a focused laser spot and then allowed to cool rapidly into an amorphous (more opaque) state. For this reason, the phase-change materials must have a fast quenching rate ($\geq 10^{10}$ °/s). To erase the spot and allow subsequent rewrites, the laser anneals the material by heating it to just below the melting point for long enough to recrystallize the material and remove amorphous marks.

While the reflectivity of CD-R media is sufficient to work with all types of CD drives, the reflectivity change of CD-RW media is insufficient to allow recorded disks to be read by older CD-ROM drives. Typical reflectivity differences are 70% for CD-ROM, 65% for CD-R, and 15% to 25% for CD-RW. Therefore, the MultiRead specification defined how the sensitivity of CD-ROM drives should be modified to ensure compatibility. MultiRead also requires that the drive's firmware must be able to read packet-written disks both CD-R and CD-RW.

11.2 DVD TECHNOLOGY [8]

Known as digital video disks or digital versatile disks (or simply DVD, since the full name was not spelled out in the original specification), the new optical media have the same 120 mm diameter as audio CD or CD-ROM, yet they can store about 14 times as much data (in a dual-layer version with the same 1.2 m total thickness). DVD is seen as a potential replacement for current compact disks, CD-ROM, laser disk, and even conventional videotape.

The first generation of DVD drives plays back at a maximum data rate of 11 Mbit/s, roughly corresponding to the data rate of a fast nine times (9X) CD-ROM drive, even though the drive's rotation speed is less than that of a 4X CD-ROM drive. In video-playing applications (using MPEG-2 and Dolby AC-3 coding for the video and audio, respectively), a single-layer DVD (with a capacity of 4.7GB) offers 133 min of playing time, which means that about 92% of all feature-length films can fit on one side of a single disk.

The rewritable DVD, which enables users to store and modify data in addition to playing back prerecorded data, will have a capacity of 2.6 GB for a single-sided disk and double that for a two-sided disk.

The standardized format for rewritable DVD was a compromise between a method endorsed by Matsushita Electric Industrial Co. and Toshiba Corp. and another one backed by Sony Corp. and Philips Electronics NV of the Netherlands.

The adopted format, called the "wobble land groove" recording method, will record signals on both the lands, or areas between grooves, and the grooves formed on the disk. Clock data are formed on the track wobbles at the disk manufacturing stage.

DVD-R, the write-once disk, can be used as a test disk for developed applications. It has a single-sided storage capacity of 3.95 GB. A two-sided DVD-R has double that capacity.

To assure compatibility with other DVD formats, modulation and error correction codes for DVD-RAM and DVD-R are the same as for DVD video and DVD -ROM, which are only for playing back prerecorded data.

A DVD-ROM disk differs substantially from a CD-ROM disk. Though the basic structure is similar, the DVD-ROM has a much higher storage capacity. Characteristics of both technologies are compared in Table 11.1.

The most obvious difference is the much higher areal density for the DVD-ROM. The minimum pit diameter is less than half that of the CD-ROM (0.4 μm versus 0.83 μm), which allows linear bit density to be increased from 43 Kbit/in to 96 Kbit/in. and the track density to be increased from 16,000 tpi to 34,000 tpi. To read the small pits accurately, the focused laser spot must be made smaller.

TABLE 11.1 CD vs. DVD [8]

Feature	CD Format	DVD Format
Disk diameter	120 mm (5″)	120 mm (5″)
Basic Structure	One 1.2 mm substrate	two 0.6 mm substrates
Storage Capacity	680 MB (single-sided, single layer)	DVD-5: 4.7 GB (single sided, two layers) DVD-9: 8.5 GB (single sided, two layers) DVD-18: 17 GB (double sided, four layers)
Minimum pit length	0.83 μm	0.4 μm
Laser wavelength	780 nm	635 to 650 nm
Numerical aperture	0.45	0.6
Areal data density	0.68 Gbit/in^2	3.28 Gbit/in^2
Track density	43,000 bit/in	96,000 bit/in
Data rate (for same rpm)	Variable, 4.8 Mbit/s max.	Variable 11 Mbits/s max.

Multilayer disk construction also complicates the design of DVD drives. One of the biggest challenges is the need for a dual-focus optical system, which can target each reflective layer and preferably switch rapidly between layers (thus preventing the use of mechanical strategies such as rotating lens turrets or pivoting mirrors). A single laser and some sort of dual-focus optical system are being used.

11.3 FUTURE TRENDS

All of the optical technologies including magneto-optical recording, phase-change erasable recording, CDs, and DVDs have the potential to provide removable high-capacity data storage before the end of this century. However, a number of technical hurdles must first be overcome before they can be manufactured and shipped in market. Further, in the move from the laboratory to the production line, some compromises in storage capacities and data rates are likely, since real-world storage systems must withstand a range of environmental, shock, vibration, and media-aging conditions. In general, four key metrics—entry cost, standard capacities, cost per gigabyte, and data rate—indicate how the performance of current magnetic-based devices may be expected to improve. The initial cost of the system and the capacity of the standard media count heavily for day-to-day storage applications, while the cost per gigabyte matters most in archiving applications. Data rate, coupled with media cost, is important in video-server applications.

Though drives and media (along with finalized industry standards) for the recordable and rewritable DVD are attractive, the writable versions are unlikely to have the same capacities as read-only DVD-ROM, because of an absence of reliable and cost-effective short-wavelength (i.e, blue green or blue) laser diodes. Initial DVD-RAMs are expected to have a capacity of around 2.6 GB, though much larger capacities have already been achieved experimentally.

The market demand for rewritable optical storage has until now been largely met by magneto-optical (MO) disks which have been significantly increasing storage capacity. Compatibility issues make it more probable that the DVD-RAM will use phase-change recording (PCR) media. There are still fundamental issues to be solved, however. Cyclability and media sensitivity to short pulse width writing must be improved for DVD applications.

Clearly, if costs can be reduced, there is a potentially huge demand for DVD-RAM drives and media in such applications as computer backup and archiving (to replace tapes, high-density floppy media, and removable hard-drive cartridges). Until recently, MO drives were almost exclusively used in high-density archiving applications. However, MO drive technology is inherently more expensive (with costs of over $1000) even though they offer some performance advantages over PCR drives. Playback of MO disks requires special components that can provide magnetic bias and detect small changes in the polarization of the reflected readout beam. In contrast, without substantial modification, a DVD-ROM drive should be able to read a PCR medium while a DVD-RAM drive should only be slightly more expensive because it will use the same basic components as the read-only version.

Researchers are already improving the characteristics of PCR media making it ready for the potentially huge DVD-RAM market. For example, a reflectivity of 25% to 35% has been achieved. Higher reflectivity will, of course, simplify the design (and thus lower the cost) of DVD drives that must read DVD-RAM disks.

Though DVD-RAM media will initially be quite expensive (as are CD-RW media now), analysts expect costs to fall to below 0.5 cents per megabyte as storage densities increase and increased market volume allows manufacturing economies of scale. Similarly, costs are already plunging for CD-R media, and the cost per megabyte of the higher density DVD-R will be proportionately lower.

As an example of what's ahead, a prototype of a DVD camera has been unveiled. While a storage capacity of 2.6 GB per side for the first DVD-RAM disks is accepted, 8.2 GB on a two-sided disk has been also proposed for professional use of a video camera which records 40 min of 720×512 video, along with audio, on both sides of the disk. Looking further out, a 10.2 GB DVD-RAM phase-change disk with a track pitch of $0.56\,\mu\text{m}$ and a pit pitch of $0.24\,\mu\text{m}$ has already been proposed.

REFERENCES

[1] A. H. M. Holtslag, E. F. McCord, and G. H. W. Buning, *J. Appl. Phys.*, vol. 31, p. 484–493, 1992.

[2] For example, "European Patent Application" (# 0519395A1) (June 16, 1992).

[3] E. Hamada, Y. Shin, and T. Ishiguro, *SPIE Conference Proceedings* (TuC4-1), February 1989.

[4] E. Hamada, Y. Shin, and T. Ishiguro, *SPIE*, vol. 1078, p. 80, 1989.

[5] T. Suzuki, *Ouyou-Butsuri*, vol. 64, no. 3., pp. 208–219, 1996.

[6] S. R. Ovshinsky, *J. Non-Cryst. Solids*, vol. 2, p. 99, 1970.

[7] R. J. von Gutfeld and P. Chaudhari, *J. Appl. Phys.*, vol. 43, p. 4688, 1972

[8] M. Elphick, *Data Storage*, vol. 4, no. 1, pp. 25–32, 1997.

INDEX

ABOUT THE EDITORS

Richard J. Gambino received his M.S. degree in chemistry from Polytechnic Institute of New York in 1976 and his B.S. degree from the University of Connecticut in 1957. He is professor of Materials Science and Engineering and director of the Laboratory for Magneto-Optical Materials at the State University of New York at Stony Brook. His work on magneto-optical storage materials began at IBM Research, where he was a member of the research staff from 1961 until he retired in 1993.

In 1995 Mr. Gambino was awarded the National Medal of Technology by President Clinton for the development of the amorphous magnetic materials used for magneto-optic disk media. He received the Morris N. Liebmann Memorial Award of the IEEE in 1992 and the IBM Corporate Award in 1991 for his work on amorphous magnetic materials. He holds 40 patents on materials and devices. He is a member of the IEEE Magnetics Society, the Materials Research Society, the American Vacuum Society, Sigma Xi, and Tau Beta Pi. Mr. Gambino is an IEEE Fellow.

Takao Suzuki received his B.S. and M.S. from Waseda University, Tokyo, in 1962 and 1964, respectively and the Ph.D. from California Institute of Technology in 1969. He worked at Max Planck Institute in Stuttgart, Germany, as a post-doctoral fellow from 1969 through 1972 and at Tohoku University, Japan, from 1972 to 1988. Dr. Suzuki worked at IBM Almaden Research Center from 1988 through 1995. Since 1995, while on a leave of absence from IBM, he has been a principal professor and the director of Information Storage Materials Research Laboratory at Toyota Technological Institute, Japan, where he has been involved with materials research for high-density data storage applications, especially on magneto-optical and magnetic recording. He is also a visiting professor in the Department of Materials Science and Engineering at Stanford University from 1998 to 2001.

Dr. Suzuki has been active in serving various academic societies, including the IEEE Magnetics Society and the Magnetics Society of Japan. He has also served in organizing various international conferences, including the conference chair of the Magneto-Optical Recording International Symposium (MORIS) in 1997 and the program chair of Magnetism and Magnetic Materials Conference in 1995. Dr. Suzuki received the IBM technical award in 1995. He has published more than 150 scientific papers and three books and holds 13 patents issued in Japan, USA, and Europe. Dr. Suzuki is an IEEE Fellow.